Women in American History

Series Editors

Mari Jo Buhle
Nancy A. Hewitt
Anne Firor Scott

*A list of books in the series appears
at the end of this book.*

Writing Out My Heart

Writing Out My Heart

Selections from the Journal of Frances E. Willard, 1855–96

EDITED BY

Carolyn De Swarte Gifford

University of Illinois Press   Urbana and Chicago

Publication of this book was supported by a grant from the
National Endowment for the Humanities, an independent
federal agency.

Manufactured in the United States of America
C 5 4 3 2 1

This book is printed on acid-free paper.

Library of Congress Cataloging-in-Publication Data

Willard, Frances Elizabeth, 1839-1898.
    Writing out my heart : selections from the journal of Frances E.
Willard, 1855–96 / edited by Carolyn De Swarte Gifford.
       p.   cm. — (Women in American history)
    Includes bibliographical references and index.
    ISBN 0-252-02139-8 (alk. paper)
    1. Willard, Frances Elizabeth, 1839–1898—Diaries. 2. Women
social reformers—United States—Biography.   3. Woman's Christian
Temperance Union. 4. Women—Suffrage—United States. I. Gifford,
Carolyn De Swarte. II. Title. III. Series.
HV5232.W6W55   1995
322.4'4'092—dc20
[B]   94-43878
                                                  CIP

Brief passages from the General Introduction and the introductions to parts
1 and 3 appeared in Carolyn De Swarte Gifford, "'My Own Methodist Hive':
Frances Willard's Faith as Disclosed in Her Journal, 1855–1870," in *Spirituality
and Social Responsibility: Vocational Vision of Women in the United Methodist
Tradition,* ed. Rosemary Skinner Keller (Nashville: Abingdon, 1993). Brief
portions of the General Introduction and the introductions to parts 1–4
appeared in Carolyn De Swarte Gifford, "'Writing Out My Heart': The
Journals of Frances Willard, 1855–1870," *Documentary Editing* (December
1990): 87–91. Brief portions of the Essay on the Source appeared in Carolyn
De Swarte Gifford, "New Light on Frances Willard," *Methodist History* 30, no.
2 (January 1993): 109–12.

In loving memory of
my mother, Bernice Williams De Swarte,
and my father, Walter Bigelow De Swarte,

and

to my sister, Alice De Swarte Smith,
with deep and abiding affection

Contents

PART FIVE

1 January 1893–31 December 1896

Illustrations follow pages 186 and 332.

Preface

A year before I began to transcribe and edit the journal of Frances Willard, I read *Between Women*, a collection of essays by women biographers, novelists, critics, teachers, and artists who wrote about their relationships with the women who are the subjects of their work. I was struck by a question posed in the introduction to the book: "How are we to represent justly and generously the complicated lives of the women we honor?"[1] According to the book's editors, each of the essayists raised this question in one way or another, as she struggled to present her subject.

That question—and, particularly, the three words "justly," "generously," and "honor"—have always been at the back of my mind as I labored to prepare this edition of Willard's journal. If, in its preparation, I could strive to do justice to the woman who was Frances Willard, if I could act generously toward her, and thereby honor her, then I would feel that I had fulfilled my responsibility toward her. The thoughtful question posed in *Between Women* helped me to see *how* I would approach the journal and defined the spirit in which I would relate to Willard.

As I read Willard's journal for the first time, I pondered the issue of privacy, as so many other biographers and editors had done before me. People's journals, diaries, and correspondence are understood as private, personal, even secret documents, not intended for public scrutiny. Would I be unjust to Willard, would I be acting dishonorably toward her if I included in my edition, for instance, the intimate story of her engagement and her difficult decision to end it, which she revealed in her journal? Intertwined with that story was the account of her passionate love for the young woman who would become her sister-in-law.

These stories had never been fully revealed before. Willard chose not to speak of them in her autobiography. Some of her biographers never saw the portions of the journal that told of her engagement and her reasons for ending it; one who read them left these revelations unexplored and unexamined, for whatever reasons. When such significant aspects of Willard's life remained so long undisclosed, could I dare to disclose them? Would I be doing violence and not justice to my subject if I did?

Seeking guidance in answering these weighty ethical questions, I turned to Willard's autobiography. In a section she titled "Companionships," she summarized briefly, yet candidly, the story of her love for her sister-in-law, and pointed to her journal as the source in which to find a fuller account of this troubling friendship. "I met Mary B.," she wrote, "for whom my attachment was so great that when she very properly preferred my brother, although I had devotedly desired their union, the loss of her was nothing less than a bereavement, a piteous sorrow for a year and more, as my journals testify, one of the keenest of my life, to which the death of my only sister Mary put a sudden, and as I have always thought, a well-nigh miraculous end."[2] And, indeed, in her journal, she did tell this story at the same moment she was living through it, including all the agony she experienced in this passionate love.

Right after she described her friendship with Mary B. in her autobiography, Willard mentioned her engagement in a short summary that captured the essence of the event, stripped of the great emotional struggle she lived through in coming to her decision to break off with her fiancé. Again, she referred to her journal as the place to seek an understanding of the emotional toll her engagement took, not only on her but on all those she loved most. She noted: "In 1861–62, for three-quarters of a year I wore a ring and acknowledged an allegiance based on the supposition that an intellectual comradeship was sure to deepen into unity of heart. How grieved I was over the discovery of my mistake the journals of that epoch could reveal."[3] And she did pour onto the pages of her journal the account of how she mistook respect, admiration, and congeniality for love. She detailed her struggle with herself, her fiancé, her family, and friends over whether to marry a man she did not love or end the engagement and risk never meeting a man for whom she could care deeply.

A little farther on in her autobiography, she wrote about her one true love: "Of the real romance of my life, unguessed save by a trio of close friends, these pages may not tell. When I have passed from sight I would be glad to have it known, for I believe it might contribute to a better understanding between good men and women."[4] Her biographers have speculated about the man who might have been Willard's "real romance." I believe that she recorded the details of this relationship—with a young mathematics teacher at Genesee Wesleyan College—in her journal. Its pages tell of the beginning of a mutual love, thwarted by the jealousy of a woman friend of Willard's who could not share her friend with another.

It is now over one hundred years since she wrote most of her journal volumes. Those she mentioned in it have all "passed from sight." While she and they lived, she was concerned not to bring up details of their relationships so that no one might be needlessly hurt or embarrassed. Her wishes in that regard have been honored. Now, I feel, the journal may be published; indeed I have come to believe that Willard would want someone to do so.

She very often used experiences in her life in order to make a point or teach a lesson. For example, in *How to Win: A Book for Girls*,[5] she compared her own growing-up years with those of her young readers who were coming to maturity a generation after her, calling attention to the changes in society's expectations for women and urging girls to choose wisely from the many new opportunities available to them. In the passage from her autobiography quoted above, one can discern her hope that revealing the nature of her particular experience of "real romance" might enhance relationships between the sexes. She clearly intended that events in her life serve a didactic purpose. And while knowing about her life may not fill quite the same sort of didactic purpose for late twentieth-century readers that she imagined it could for those in the late nineteenth century, it still has much to teach us about what it meant to be a woman living in the United States over a century ago.

As I immersed myself in the process of reading and transcribing Willard's journal, another world—that of mid-nineteenth-century, midwestern American Protestantism—took on a shape, a concreteness, and a meaning. The text of Willard's journal vividly evoked that world and its inhabitants, their manners and morality, their expectations and limitations, their openness and expansiveness, as well as their occasional rigidness and narrowness.

Willard's world was not totally unfamiliar to me. Many times, as I sat working on the journal in the Frances E. Willard Memorial Library in the Woman's Christian Temperance Union national headquarters, I found myself remembering my maternal grandmother, born two generations after Willard, who grew up on a farm in southeastern Wisconsin very near to the place where the Willard family farmed. She graduated from Lawrence University, a Methodist school in Ap-

pleton, Wisconsin, where she met and married a classmate who became a Methodist minister. My grandmother's husband was a Garrett
Biblical Institute graduate, as was Willard's brother, Oliver. My grandmother became a widow in her late twenties when her husband succumbed to tuberculosis, the same disease that claimed Willard's father and younger sister. My grandmother remained in the small
Wisconsin town where she was widowed. There she was what was
known as a "pillar of the church," a longtime Methodist Sunday
School superintendent and probably also a WCTU member. She was
certainly strongly antidrinking, antismoking, and, especially, antislang
and antiswearing.

My father's family were also Methodists from southern Wisconsin
who sent their daughters to Lawrence and their sons to another
Methodist school—Northwestern University in Evanston, Illinois. My
father and his two brothers stayed in Evanston after they graduated
from Northwestern, and worked in Chicago as Willard's father had
done when the Willard family moved to Evanston. The Willard family's life revolved around Evanston's Methodist church for many years,
the same one my family attended generations later. And my sister and
I even went to Frances E. Willard elementary school.

As I worked on Willard's journal I began to look forward eagerly
to each day's transcription session, when I would continue my dialogue with Willard. And dialogue it was. While I transcribed the journal text into my laptop computer, I found myself laughing out loud
at Willard's jokes and witticisms or suffering along with her as she
grieved the death of a beloved relative. At some points in her journal, she recorded weeping in sorrow or frustration over a great moral dilemma. At those points, I wept too. Her world became mine for
many hours each day and I often had difficulty dragging myself back
to the late twentieth century.

Finally, the journal was completely transcribed. The time had inevitably come to select portions of it for inclusion in the one-volume
edition I planned. But I was unable to begin selecting. It seemed to
me that I would be abruptly breaking off the dialogue. I would have
to step back from Willard's world and begin to control and manipu-
late it, trimming the massive amount of material to fit a structure and
form that would be more my creation than Willard's. The thought
of doing this worried me. It was something I mulled over for what
seemed a terribly long time, since I thought of almost nothing else.
(In actuality, it was only a few weeks, but they seemed endless.)

As I floundered in indecision, I read an article by Suzanne L. Bunkers about her work with nineteenth-century midwestern women's

diaries.[6] I was merely looking for distraction from my problem and hoping for a few tips on how to present Willard's journal from someone whose subjects were women from the same general region and time period as Willard. What I found instead was a moving and sensitive discussion of the ethical responsibility of the editor/interpreter toward the women whose diaries she interprets and also toward present-day readers. In reading the article, I came to realize that I was procrastinating, trying to avoid the difficult but essential task of interpreting the text. When I began to do that, the dialogue between Willard and me would continue as I chose entries and wrote introductions and annotations. If I could keep the words "justly," "generously," and "honorably" before me as I provided background and context for her own words, then at least the ethos of my interpretation would be appropriate. I had no illusions about "objectivity" as a goal. I had long ago given up the notion that as a historian I must or could be objective. I had a background, a context, just as Willard did. But I thought it should be possible to meet her across generations and present that meeting to readers. That is what I have tried to do in these pages.

When I was almost finished preparing the edition, I read *The Challenge of Feminist Biography*, like *Between Women* a collection of essays, this time by women historians who discussed the process of writing biographies of women and told of the relationship that grew between the biographer and her biographical subject. Each of the essayists treated her subject with the great dignity that she deserved. All of the essays had something uniquely significant to say about the writing of biography. But I was struck, above all, by one sentence in the volume. In the mid-1970s, Jacquelyn Dowd Hall had written a biography of Jessie Daniel Ames, a southern white woman who, during the first third of this century, organized a struggle against lynching. When the biography was published in 1979, Hall moved on to new research, putting her work on Ames behind her, thinking it was finished. "As it happened though," Hall wrote, "I was not through with Jessie Daniel Ames, or rather she was not through with me."[7] Hall's essay in the new volume was a revisiting of and with her subject.

This was what I was beginning to realize about my dialogue with Willard. Even though I was nearly at the end of my work on this volume, I was not through with Willard. But even more compelling was the sense that Willard was not through with me. While the selected edition of her journal was complete, Willard had more to teach me and I had more to ponder about this complex woman whom I had come to know and respect over the last seven years. Our dialogue, which I had come to cherish, would continue.

Notes

1. Carol Ascher, Louise De Salvo, and Sara Ruddick, eds., *Between Women: Biographers, Novelists, Critics, Teachers and Artists Write about Their Work on Women* (Boston, 1984), xx.

2. Frances E. Willard, *Glimpses of Fifty Years: The Autobiography of an American Woman* (Boston, 1889), 640. Hereafter cited as Willard, *Glimpses of Fifty Years*.

3. Ibid., 465.

4. Ibid.

5. Frances E. Willard, *How to Win: A Book for Girls* (New York, 1886), 13–19.

6. Suzanne L. Bunkers, "'Faithful Friend': Nineteenth-Century Midwestern American Women's Unpublished Diaries," *Women's Studies International Forum* 10, no. 1 (1987): 7–17.

7. Jacquelyn Dowd Hall, "Living through Time: Second Thoughts on Jessie Daniel Ames," in Sara Alpern et al., *The Challenge of Feminist Biography: Writing the Lives of Modern American Women* (Urbana, Ill., 1992), 141.

Acknowledgments

Many people and institutions have encouraged and supported the preparation of this volume in a variety of ways, and I am deeply indebted and very grateful to every one of them. Several institutions have funded my work and that of my research assistant. Work on the volume was made possible in part by a grant from the National Endowment for the Humanities (NEH), an independent federal agency. Two NEH staff members, Douglas M. Arnold and Kathy Fuller, helped to guide me through the intricacies of submitting a proposal and made excellent suggestions. The National Historical Publications and Records Commission (NHPRC) has also supported my work: first, by selecting me to attend the yearly Editing Institute that it sponsors and, then, by awarding the Frances E. Willard Journal Project funding for two years. Several NHPRC staff members have given me encouragement and good advice: Roger Bruns, Mary Giunta, Nancy Sahli, Richard N. Sheldon, and Donald Singer. The Women's Studies in Religion Program of Harvard Divinity School and its director, Constance H. Buchanan, provided me with a research fellowship, a feminist environment, and sympathetic colleagues at a crucial stage in my work. The Women's Studies Program at Northwestern University, its director, Arlene Kaplan Daniels, and its former director, Rae Moses, named me a research associate for two years, thus considerably easing my access to the Northwestern Library, a valuable contribution, especially to the annotation process.

The officers and staff of the National Woman's Christian Temperance Union (NWCTU) have been truly gracious and hospitable during the entire time I have worked on the journal. They have been enthusiastic about the Willard Journal Project and have found many ways to help it along. I am especially thankful to Rachel Kelly, president of the NWCTU, both for giving permission to the University of

Illinois Press to publish portions of the journal and for her genuine interest in the project, as well as her encouragement at every stage of the work. Alfred Epstein, NWCTU Librarian, has been a key figure in the preparation of the edition. His knowledge of the WCTU collection is prodigious and he has generously given of his time and expertise in response to many, many requests.

Colleagues in the Association for Documentary Editing have helped me to understand something of the art of documentary editing. In particular, Barbara B. Oberg, editor of the Benjamin Franklin Papers, introduced me to the field of documentary editing and gave me many excellent suggestions, most of which I followed. Members of the Women's Papers Consortium—Mary Lynn McCree Bryan, editor of the Jane Addams Papers; Candace Falk, editor of the Emma Goldman Papers; Esther Katz, editor, and Cathy Moran Hajo, assistant editor, of the Margaret Sanger Papers; Ann D. Gordon and Patricia G. Holland, editors of the Papers of Elizabeth Cady Stanton and Susan B. Anthony—welcomed Frances E. Willard and me into the consortium.

A host of staff members of archives, libraries, and historical societies responded to my queries with dispatch and reams of information. They include: Marguerite Fallucco, Senior Research Associate, American Medical Association Archives, Chicago; Nina D. Myatt, Curator of Antiochiana, Antioch College, Yellow Springs, Ohio; Cecilia Wiltzius, Appleton Public Library, Appleton, Wisconsin; Agnes Masson, Department de Paris, Direction des Services, d'Archives de Paris, France; staff at the Beloit College Alumni Office, Beloit, Wisconsin; Katherine K. Dibble, Research Library Service, Boston Public Library; Katherine Kominis, Rare Book Selector, Boston University Library; Roxane Coombs, Reference Librarian, Cambridge Public Library, Cambridge, Massachusetts; John Forbis, Librarian, Music and Art Department, Carnegie Library, Pittsburgh; John W. Cummins, Professor Emeritus and Director of the Archival Project, Chatham College, Pittsburgh; Erika S. Bruner, Assistant Director, City of Cambridge Historical Commission Library, Cambridge, Massachusetts; staff at the City of Pasadena Department of Information Services Library, Pasadena, California; Helen G. Clear, Historian of the Commission on Archives and History, Western Pennsylvania Conference, United Methodist Church, Pittsburgh; Judith Ellen Johnson, Reference Librarian and Genealogist, Connecticut Historical Society, Hartford; Jacqueline Hoyt, Director, Cordelia A. Greene Library, Castile, New York; Daniel P. Sailor, Historian, Des Plaines Camp Ground, Des Plaines, Illinois; Mark Burnette, Archivist, Janet Messmer, Costume

Curator, and Richard Hartung, former director, Evanston Historical Society, Evanston, Illinois; Katherine E. Art, Archivist and Historian, First United Methodist Church, Evanston; Helen M. Wilson, Library Assistant, Historical Society of Western Pennsylvania, Pittsburgh; Pamela D. Arceneaux, Reference Librarian, Historic New Orleans Collection, New Orleans; Paul Millette, Archivist, Ira J. Taylor Library, Iliff Theological Seminary, Denver; Carol A. Shidler, Kankakee County Historical Society, Kankakee, Illinois; Brenda Fuller, Kentucky Department for Libraries and Archives, Frankfort; Donald J. Winslow, Professor Emeritus and Archivist, Lasell College, Auburndale, Massachusetts; Mary Clough, Town Historian, and Selma M. Cate, Library Director, Lisbon Public Library, Lisbon, N.H.; Ann Dizier, Conservatrice, Mairie de Paris, Direction des Affaires Culturelles, Paris; Lucy Cooke, Library Director, Mount Vernon College Library, Washington, D.C.; Lon Dagley, Nazarene Archives, Kansas City, Missouri; David T. Thackery, Curator of Local and Family History, Newberry Library, Chicago; Irene Wainwright, Reference Librarian, New Orleans Public Library, New Orleans; staff of the Reference Department, New York Public Library, New York City; Charles S. Fineman, Humanities Bibliographer, and staff of the Inter-Library Loan Department, Northwestern University Library, Evanston; Patrick M. Quinn, University Archivist, Northwestern University; Carol Kelm, Executive Director, Oak Park Historical Society, Oak Park, Illinois; Gary J. Arnold, Head, Research Services Department, Ohio Historical Society, Columbus; James G. Ward, Passaic County Historical Society, Paterson, New Jersey; Glenn Colliver, Assistant Archivist, Presbyterian Church (USA) Archives, Philadelphia; Kenneth J. Ross, Reference Librarian, Department of History, Presbyterian Church (USA), Philadelphia; Pamela Scheffel, Librarian, Local History Division, Rochester Public Library, Rochester, New York; Rajeswari Swaminathan, Syracuse Library Archives, Syracuse, New York; staff at Union Theological Seminary Library, New York City; David Himrod, Research and Reference Librarian, United Library, Garrett-Evangelical and Seabury-Western Theological Seminaries, Evanston; and Eliana Paris Holmes, Reference Librarian, United States State Department Library, Washington, D.C.

There have been many scholars who have shared both their own work and their insights with me over the past seven years since I began to plan this edition, and I am delighted to acknowledge them. William Hutchison and members of the American Religious History Colloquium at the Harvard Divinity School read one of the earliest papers I wrote on the journal and offered astute comments. I have had fruitful conversations over the years with Russell E. Richey, Kenneth E. Rowe, and A. Gregory Schneider, historians of Methodism in the United States. Rosemary Skinner Keller and Rosemary Radford Ruether first steered my interest and research toward American women and social reform, a direction I have happily traveled ever since 1979. Annamary Horner DeWitt first brought Willard's journal to my attention and shared her transcriptions of a portion of the journal with me. Others who have contributed by sharing their work, giving me research leads, commenting on sections of my research, or suggesting other people who might be able to answer some of my most difficult questions include: Erin A. Bannon, Ann Braude, Irene Quenzler Brown, Joan Burstyn, Thomas Collins, Delight Wing Dodyk, Ann E. Feldman, Christine Froula, Nancy Hardesty, Wendy Kolmar, Glenn LaFantasie, Mark Lender, Claire Lindenlaub, Larry Lipking, Miriam Littell, Gail Malmgreen, Annelies Moeser, Jeanne Lockridge Mueller, Olwen C. Niessen, Frances Freeman Paden, Dana Robert, Regina Morantz Sanchez, Mary Seghers, Martha Vicinus, and Louise Wade.

I feel that I must single out some people who have helped in somewhat unusual ways: Don Mar Wee, my calm and patient computer consultant; Phyllis Tholin, book dealer extraordinaire, whose knowledge of where to find some of the most obscure women's history sources never ceases to amaze me; Lynn Heft, who helped me launch this project with a wonderful party that included a sheet cake with the words "Onward, Upward, Willard!" emblazoned on it in blue frosting; my colleagues on the editorial staff of the Historical Encyclopedia of Chicago Women: Adele Hast, Jean Hunt, Bea Inglehart, Mary Ann Johnson, Cheryl Johnson-Odim, Peg Strobel, Rima Schultz, and Clarice Stetter, who gave me other women to think about besides Frances Willard; and others who listened to me talk on and on about Willard—relatives, neighbors, friends from the Church in the Chapel congregation, Alice Millar Chapel, Northwestern University, the "high school friends reunion" group—and many more who have put up with Willard and me for a very long time.

Many persons at the University of Illinois Press have given excellent guidance in the preparation of this volume: Carole S. Appel and Karen Hewitt, senior editors; Carol Bolton Betts, copy editor; Theresa L. Sears, managing editor; and Mari Jo Buhle and Ann D. Gordon, who reviewed the manuscript for the Press. I would also like to thank Laura Moss Gottlieb, Madison, Wisconsin, who prepared the index.

Finally, there are some I want to recognize especially—people whose counsel and support have extended throughout this project, from beginning to end. Ann Gordon and Esther Katz have given generously of their time, their advice, and their gift for strategizing to a neophyte in the documentary editing game. They have also shared their humor, which has buoyed me up through this whole process. I have had many intense conversations with Betsy Clark and Amy Slagell; in these exchanges, I believe, we have each come to understand Willard better. My friendship with June Underwood extends back to the summer of 1980 when we were both doing research on the Kansas WCTU and the Kansas Equal Suffrage Association at the Kansas Historical Society in Topeka, driving back and forth from Lawrence in 100 degree weather, talking and laughing nonstop all the way. We have never stopped talking and laughing with each other. Rachel E. Bohlmann applied for the position of research assistant on the Willard project at precisely the right moment and has done her job with resourcefulness, diligence, cheerfulness, and insight. It has been a joy to work with her. My sister-in-law, Mary Gifford, has supported me in many ways since I began reading and transcribing Willard's journal. She has known when to offer dinner and chocolate treats, and those have been essential. My sister, Alice De Swarte Smith, has been my unfailing friend for many years and has been convinced that I could edit Willard's journal even when I have not been so sure about it. Without doubt, my most faithful friend and companion along the way of this project, and beyond, has been my husband, Bill. I do not believe that I could have done it without him. All of the people and institutions I have named above have contributed to this book. (My apologies and thanks to any I have inadvertently omitted from these acknowledgments.) Of course, any mistakes are mine, not theirs. They have made the edition better than it would have been without their help.

Editorial Method

Selection

This selected edition is intended to present the journal of Frances E. Willard to both general and scholarly audiences, calling attention to its existence and giving readers a fair idea of what can be found in it. The edition is an introduction to Willard's life and thought for the general reader, and an inducement to scholars to do further work with the journal itself. Willard's journal consists of over fifty volumes totaling more than eight thousand pages. Since this edition includes less than one-tenth of the total journal material, care has been taken in both the selection process and the introductions to present the main themes that run through the journal. Selections have also been chosen to give readers a clear sense of the chronological unfolding of the events in Willard's life for the periods during which she kept her journal.

The selected edition should give readers insight into Willard's personality: her emotional life, her religious and intellectual development, her relationships with other people, and her self-understanding. Selections from the journal volumes written from 1855 to 1870—Willard's sixteenth through thirty-first years—which comprise well over nine-tenths of the material, will help in understanding how and why Willard became the kind of woman she did. Selections from the two volumes she wrote during the 1890s—in her fifty-fourth and fifty-seventh years—show her as the woman she became, the internationally famous reform leader of a large and powerful women's organization.

The production of such a highly selective edition means that large portions of the journal must be left out. For example, the first five volumes of the journal (1 January 1855–31 December 1857), written during the time Willard lived on the family farm in southeast Wisconsin, contain repetitive descriptions of daily life on the farm, including a record of weather conditions, types of work that the Willard family and farmhands were engaged in over the period, visits to and from neighbors, and so on. There is comparatively little introspection on Willard's part that would help the reader to understand the development of her intellectual and religious life, both key themes in this edition. Thus the edition will contain very little material from the earliest period of Willard's journal keeping, and even that will appear only as brief quotations in the introduction to Part 1.

The twenty volumes of Willard's journal written while she was on a two-and-one-half-year tour of Europe and the Middle East (June 1868–September 1870) make up two-fifths of the total journal, yet the portion of the selected edition allotted to these volumes is less than one-fifth of the total. Large sections of the volumes written on Willard's European tour are devoted to extended accounts of sightseeing trips. Much of this sort of description is excluded from the edition. Only a few representative samples are included in order to trace a phase of Willard's intellectual development.

For many readers, a selected edition of Willard's journal will provide idea enough of its contents. For others, a selected edition may serve to pique their interest, inviting them to read the whole journal themselves.

Transcription

Since this is a selected edition, I have not been as concerned to reproduce an exact facsimile of the journal as I would have been were I producing a complete edition. However, I have kept closely to the appearance of the original journal text in several ways. Willard's spelling, capitalization, abbreviations, and punctuation have been transcribed as they appear in the original with only a few exceptions. Willard often used dashes and other means to signify the beginning of a paragraph. In this edition a new paragraph is indicated by indenting. Words that Willard underlined for emphasis are presented in italic type; words that she double-underlined are presented in underlined italic type. Willard sometimes copied letters from other persons into her entries. In this case, the body of a letter from another person is indented on the left, and paragraphs within the letter are further indented. Willard often included in her entries various sorts of lists, and these have been reformatted slightly for easier reading. Willard's abbreviations are not expanded unless the meaning of the abbreviation is unclear without expansion. It is often difficult to determine whether some of Willard's letters are capitals or lowercase (e.g., her c's, e's, k's, m's, s's, w's, and y's). I have used my best judgment as to whether a letter is meant to be capitalized or not. Willard sometimes misspelled proper names; these misspellings are corrected in the notes.

Cancellations in Willard's original text are silently omitted and interlinear additions are silently lowered or raised into the line where Willard indicates they belong. I have chosen not to retain cancellations in the original text because the meaning of the text is usually not substantially altered when a word or phrase is substituted later. Rather a slightly different shade of meaning is conveyed by the change. Willard made later editorial changes in some of her journal text in order to submit portions of it for publication, either in her autobiography or in articles. Her editorial changes were made in pencil or with a different color of ink from her original entries; such editorial changes have not been retained in this edition. Her marginal notes, which often comment years later on earlier thoughts, feelings, and events, are included in footnotes to the entry in which they occur. Willard's very occasional slips of the pen (e.g., repetition of a word: "that that," or miswordings: "such much" rather than "so much") have been silently corrected. Willard sometimes left out a period at the end of a sentence; in these cases, periods have been silently added. When Willard has included parenthetical material within a sentence and has placed a period or a comma inside the closing parenthesis, that punctuation is silently placed outside the closing parenthesis, in conformance with modern usage. When Willard has left out one of a set of quotation marks, it has been silently added.

Square brackets are used to enclose any editorial interventions in the text, and the interventions appear in roman type. For example, square brackets indicate letters mistakenly left out by Willard (e.g., lea[r]ning) when the meaning is not entirely clear without such intervention. Square brackets are also used to enclose translations of foreign words and phrases in the text. Translations are placed directly after the word or phrase being translated. If the foreign word appears more than once in the text, it is not translated again. If the meaning of a word or phrase is still not clear even with a translation, then that word or phrase is not translated in the text, but is explained in a footnote. Foreign words whose meaning is obvious (e.g., la grande passion) are not translated. Willard's occasional misspellings of foreign words and phrases are retained.

Ellipses are used to show that portions of the text of a particular entry have been omitted (e.g., ellipses at the beginning of an entry signify that a portion of the entry has been omitted before the ellipses). Ellipses do *not* indicate that entire entries have been omitted before or after the entry where the ellipses occur at the beginning or end. Entire entries have been silently omitted rather than cluttering the text with many marks signifying the omissions. Illegible letters within a word or a single illegible word are indicated by three ellipses within square brackets; where more than one word is illegible, that fact is dealt with in a note. A question mark enclosed in square brackets signifies that I am not absolutely certain of the accuracy of transcription of the letter, word, or number that precedes the question mark.

Dates and other numbers are preserved as they appear in the original text, except in the case of the date of an entry, which will appear on a separate line at the beginning of each entry, with day indicated first in arabic numerals only, month written out in full, and year indicated with four arabic numerals (e.g., 28 September 1863).

Because Willard wrote journal entries from a variety of different places, the location where an entry was written is added, underneath the date of the entry. If a series of entries is written at the same location, then the location will appear at the beginning of the first entry written at that location and omitted in succeeding entries in the series. Well-known cities (e.g., New York City, Paris) do not have a state or country after them, but all other locations include the state or country after them the first time that they appear. The state or country is not included in subsequent appearances.

Persons other than Willard occasionally wrote in her journal at her invitation. In the case of entire entries written by others at her request, the author's name appears enclosed in square brackets at the beginning of the entry, opposite the date. Brief comments by others at the margins of Willard's entries appear as footnotes to the entry in which they were written and the author identified.

Annotation

Annotations identify all persons who can be identified, all biblical, literary, and historical allusions that can be established, and all place names, when first mentioned (either in journal entries or in my introductions), unless these are so familiar to the reader as not to need identification (e.g., Abraham Lincoln, Civil War, Chicago). Women's birth surnames are enclosed in parentheses [e.g., Mary (Bannister) Willard], in the notes, the editor's introductions, and editorial interventions in the text, with the exception of women well known by their full names (e.g., Elizabeth Barrett Browning). As many birth and death dates as could be discovered have been given for persons mentioned in the journal who played more than a passing role in the events of Willard's life. However, I have not attempted to determine birth and death dates for persons whose names appear only once in a list or in a brief mention (e.g., Willard's students at her various teaching positions). Biblical, as well as literary and artistic, allusions have been annotated in order to draw attention to Willard's frequent use of such allusions, since it is a style that recurred in her speeches and published writings. While she rightly assumed a knowledge of such allusions among her hearers and readers, one cannot necessarily assume that all late twentieth-century readers possess such knowledge. In the case of a biblical allusion, if Willard has paraphrased it, the actual biblical verse as it appears in the King James Version of the Bible, the version with which Willard was familiar, is supplied in the note. In the case of literary allusions, the city and date of first publication of the work alluded to are given in parentheses if they can be found. If an item cannot be identified a note will so state. Terms that may be unfamiliar to the reader are defined in a note (e.g., class meeting, presiding elder). Annotations also explain portions within the entry that may not be entirely clear to the reader.

Abbreviations Used in
the Introductions and Annotation

BWTA	British Women's Temperance Association
GBI	Garrett Biblical Institute
MEC	Methodist Episcopal Church (the name of the northern United States branch of Methodism in Willard's time; U.S. Methodism split in 1844 over the issue of slavery)
NU	Northwestern University
NWCTU	National Woman's Christian Temperance Union
NWFC	North Western Female College
WCTU	Woman's Christian Temperance Union
WWCTU	World's Woman's Christian Temperance Union

Writing Out My Heart

General Introduction

Over a decade ago, in 1982, forty-nine volumes of Frances Willard's journal were discovered in a cupboard in the Frances E. Willard Memorial Library at the National Woman's Christian Temperance Union (NWCTU) headquarters in Evanston, Illinois. Scholars had long been aware of the journal's existence since Willard included portions of it in her autobiography, as did her earliest biographers in their works. But when it was found, the journal had been missing for nearly fifty years and large portions of it were thought to have been destroyed, along with other personal papers, by Anna Gordon, Willard's longtime companion and secretary.[1] Happily, this was not the case, and the exciting discovery of the journal brought to light a rich, new source from which to reconstruct the life of one of the most famous reformers of the nineteenth century.

For more than eighteen years—from her sixteenth through her thirty-first years and during her fifty-fourth and fifty-seventh years—Willard kept a journal. In it she recorded what she referred to as her "outside" and "inside life":[2] what happened to her and how she understood and interpreted what happened. She wrote in an astonishing variety of forms of expression ranging from conventional piety, sometimes tiresome pedantry, and mannered prose styles reflecting whatever author she might be reading, to writing so unselfconscious, so candid, that it is literally breathtaking.

Willard used whatever she could find for her journal keeping. Often she wrote in pasteboard-cover notebooks intended for school exercises, occasionally taking over her sister's or brother's exercise books after they had abandoned them. Less frequently she received gifts of tiny leather-bound page-a-day diaries for the purpose. Once she even appropriated a ledger in which her brother had kept his farm accounts.[3] In all, she filled nearly eight thousand pages with a poorly formed, almost illegible handwriting, which changed size according to the dimensions of the page on which she was writing. Many times, in the page-a-day diaries, she found it difficult to confine herself to the small space allotted for a particular day. When she came to the end of the page, she wrote around its edges, her words getting smaller, more cramped, and more illegible as she struggled to keep her thoughts within the boundaries dictated by the size of the diary.

She cut out articles and poems she found in current magazines and newspapers and pasted them on the inside front and back covers of her journal volumes, underlining sections that were particularly meaningful to her. She affixed small oval photographs of family members or friends next to entries where she mentioned them, and tucked flowers and leaves into the journal to press them as mementoes of a cherished person, place, or event. Occasionally, she stuffed lists of books to be read or items to be purchased between the pages of her journal, and several times she kept an account of her expenses on the back pages of journal volumes.

From time to time, Willard invited others to write in her journal. Visiting cousins penned thanks for the Willards' hospitality. Roommates and other school friends wrote fondly of good times shared with "Frank" (Willard's nickname throughout her life). Her Aunt Sarah,[4] a longtime teacher, offered counsel as Willard prepared for a teaching career. She and her best friend, Mary Bannister,[5] exchanged journals when Bannister left home to teach in Tennessee. Each filled the other's journal with assurances of her abiding love, her dream of teaching together one day, and her prayer for the other's safekeeping while they were apart. After a month, they mailed back the journals and each spent hours every night for weeks reading the words of encouragement and affection her friend had sent her.

Willard kept a journal for several reasons. When she was nineteen she wrote: "I use [a journal] chiefly to record facts met with in reading, & fancies of my own. I want it for a daguerreotype of my mind— for a measure of my mental attitude in the year 1859."[6] During that year and for several years afterward, Willard copied into her journal portions of the writings of well-known American and European authors whose works she read and admired. She summarized sermons and lectures she attended, commenting on whether she agreed or disagreed with the speakers' conclusions and criticizing their rhetorical skills as well. Timidly at first and then more boldly, she began to form her own opinions about the reigning ideas of recognized cultural authorities, whether arbiters of literary taste, interpreters of theological doctrine, or commentators on the current political and social scene. She would try out an opinion at length in her journal, admitting that she was reluctant to express it aloud to others, but nevertheless insistent that "It is my think, and I've a right to it!"[7] Eventually she became more sure of herself and her views, and was able write them out in essays and submit them to newspapers for publication.

Sometimes she wrote in her journal because she was lonely and needed a confidante. "I only come to you when I have an idle hour, and no friend to talk to,"[8] she confided to her journal in spring 1859. Shy and sensitive, she longed for a friend to whom she could reveal her most daring aspirations and with whom she could share her joys and sorrows. Some months later she wrote: "There are times in my life when I want a friend to talk to. A glorious sunset, . . . a fine picture—a poem—an unkind word—always makes me wish I had some one to speak to, who would answer as—I would be answered. I seem to turn involuntarily to meet an eye, that should gaze kindly & inquiringly—to hear a voice that should love the beauty too, or be sorry for the pain. To speak & not be spoken to, to laugh, and hear no answer, to offer a hand that is not accepted—these seem to me very terrible."[9] She wished for "a young friend of my own age nearly, who shall love me,—understand me,—bear with me!"[10] Until she found such a friend in Mary Bannister, she continued to use her journal as the place to record her loneliness and longing.

Even after she had a trusted friend, there were times when she felt she could not disclose her deepest thoughts and feelings until she had sorted them out for herself. At such times, she turned to her journal as the one place where she could be completely truthful. Even there, she sometimes found it difficult and frightening to reveal herself fully, especially if her beliefs or desires were at odds with the wishes of family members, the advice of friends and teachers, or the expectations of society.

In October 1861, in the midst of deep emotional turmoil over her engagement to a young Methodist minister, she wrote: "Journal! I'm not honest with you! I find it next to impossible to be so. Never, more than twice have I written out *my heart* any where. My brain—my will, judgment, conscience—all these report truthfully and with no need for reservation;—but the *heart* throbs away in darkness,—voiceless & mysterious."[11] For several months after she wrote these words she attempted in her journal to probe the depths of her heart—to give it voice—in order to decide whether or not to break her engagement to a man she admired and respected but did not love. Her mother, father, and brother all urged her to marry, insisting that she was foolish not to do so. She feared the lonely future she saw awaiting her if she remained single. During this worst crisis of her young life, she felt that even God had abandoned her, leaving her entirely alone.[12] Using her journal to sort through the confusion and contradictions that swirled within her, she heeded her heart's desire and weighed it along with the counsel of brain, will, judgment, and conscience. After much agonized deliberation, she ended the engagement, with obvious relief.

The journal volumes of Willard's young womanhood—from the time she was nineteen until she became thirty-one—are full of the outpourings of her heart. In them, she grieved over the deaths of family members and friends and confessed her own fear of dying. She wrote of her growing faith in Christ as revealed in the biblical teachings and of her doubts as to whether she could trust that the Bible contained the truth. She told of her great love for her family and her disappointment that she could not bring herself to express her love for them either in words or affectionate gestures. She described her longing to meet "the one man in all the world" for her, yet wondered if she were destined to remain single. The journal pictures Willard's complicated soul—idealistic, reflective, self-critical, questioning, and passionate. Reading it helps one to understand why the process of writing out her heart was so important in her transition from childhood to adulthood.

Her journal was also the place where she first dared to give substance to her desire for accomplishment and fame. Although revealing her ambitions was not precisely what she had originally meant by the phrase "writing out my heart," dreaming of her future, devising plans to realize her dreams, and encouraging herself to carry out her plans—all of which occur often in her journal—surely may be understood as an expression of her deepest desires, and thus another powerful instance of writing out her heart. During her teens and twenties, she wrote often about her yearning for the chance to experience a wider world, to gain a better education, to travel, to develop her talent for writing. Throughout the 1860s, she continued to record her intent to learn more, do more, and be something more, confident that she was meant for greater achievements.

By the end of the decade, Willard's ambition became focused on what she could do for the cause of woman. From the time she was in her teens, her journal had contained occasional sharp comments on the position of women in American society. In 1860 she recorded her support for women's right to vote.[13] From the mid-1860s on, her journal hinted at, and then more boldly stated, her wish to become actively involved in enlarging women's possibilities. By autumn 1870, she was ready to make a public declaration of her commitment to the women's rights reform.

At the same time, she announced her intention to stop keeping a journal.[14] She understood that she had moved beyond the need to conceal her aspirations between its covers. She realized that it was time to act, to achieve her ambitions. Over the next two decades she did just that, becoming an internationally renowned leader of temperance and women's rights reforms. She still wrote out her heart as she did when she was a young woman. But her writing was no longer tentative, exploratory, confined to the private medium of her journal. It was, instead, a public act—confident, authoritative, and powerful. She poured forth speeches, pamphlets, articles, and books, expressing her views on a wide range of issues. Her statements shaped public opinion and helped mold the belief and thought of a generation of Americans and thousands of others around the world.

Frances Elizabeth Caroline Willard was born 28 September 1839 into a western New York farm family.[15] In 1841 the Willards moved to Oberlin, Ohio, where her father, Josiah Flint Willard,[16] intended to prepare for the ministry at Oberlin College.[17] They moved again in 1846 to southeastern Wisconsin for Josiah Willard's health. Frances Willard spent the years from 1846 to 1858 on the family farm outside Janesville, Wisconsin, reveling in what she later remembered as a carefree country existence. She received much of her three and one-half years of formal education during this time, first in a one-room schoolhouse that her parents and their neighbors established, and then, for one term in 1857, at Milwaukee Female College.[18]

Willard's mother, Mary (Hill) Willard,[19] encouraged her and her younger sister, Mary,[20] to take up journal keeping. Willard began to keep a journal regularly in 1855, documenting her life on the farm and her brief time at school in Milwaukee. In 1858 she and her sister entered North Western Female College (NWFC) in Evanston, Illinois, as boarders.[21] Shortly afterward, her father leased his Wisconsin farm, and the Willard family moved to Evanston permanently. Frances and Mary attended the school as day students and their older brother, Oliver,[22] enrolled at Garrett Biblical Institute (GBI)[23] to become a Methodist minister. Frances Willard continued writing her journal, noting the expanding intellectual opportunities opening before her in her new home. She graduated from NWFC in June

1859, and taught school for almost a decade. She diligently recorded in her journal a series of teaching positions that took her from Illinois to Pittsburgh, Pennsylvania, to Lima, New York. When she traveled in Europe and the Middle East from 1868 to 1870, she carried her journal with her, jotting down her itinerary and commenting at length on her impressions of the tour.

It was shortly after Willard's return from Europe to Evanston in September 1870 that she put aside her journal for more than two decades. During that time, she moved from the relative obscurity of schoolteaching to international fame as a reformer. The first step out of obscurity occurred when she accepted the presidency of the newly founded Evanston College for Ladies in 1871.[24] As president, she became well known in the Chicago area through her fundraising efforts as well as by her direction of the college. Her participation in the National Women's Congress in 1873 introduced her to many eastern women's rights reformers.[25] When the college united with Northwestern University (NU),[26] she became dean of the women's division of the university. She remained dean until spring 1874, when she resigned in a disagreement with NU's administration over the governance of the division. Suddenly faced with the prospect of finding another position, Willard began to investigate possibilities, including the burgeoning temperance movement with which she had sympathized for several years.

During the winter of 1873–74, a Woman's Crusade against liquor dealers had begun in Ohio and spread quickly throughout the northern United States. By summer 1874 a permanent organization, the Woman's Christian Temperance Union (WCTU), was launched.[27] That same summer, Willard visited women temperance leaders in New York City and attended the first Gospel Temperance Camp Meeting in Maine. While in Pittsburgh on her return home, she joined a band of Crusade women as they knelt praying outside a saloon in an attempt to persuade the saloonkeeper to give up his trade. Convinced that her future lay in temperance reform, yet worried that she would not be able to support herself and her mother through this work, Willard received a letter asking her to become president of the Chicago WCTU. With some hesitation, Willard accepted the offer and embarked on her reform vocation. As a delegate from the Chicago WCTU, Willard participated in the first national WCTU convention, which met in Cleveland in November 1874. She was elected corresponding secretary of the NWCTU, with the task of traveling throughout the country, speaking and establishing local unions. She rapidly became a power within the organization and was elected president in 1879, a position she held until her death on 17 February 1898.

Under Willard's direction, the WCTU grew from a small, struggling group focused on the single issue of temperance to the largest women's organization in the country, with a broad program of reform encompassing temperance; woman suffrage; women's economic and religious rights; the reform of the institutions of marriage, home, and family; and the support of measures advocated by the rising labor movement. Willard understood her organization as a powerful vehicle for women's self-development. It became a kind of school to train women for responsible participation in the public life of their country. Throughout the late 1870s and 1880s Willard led a campaign within the WCTU and beyond for "The Ballot for Home Protection": the vote for women so that they could embark on what she termed "political housekeeping." When women could vote, she claimed, they would quickly clean up politics and "make the world home-like," bringing the moral influence of the home into the institutions of government.[28]

Once she had gained the WCTU's endorsement of woman suffrage by the mid-1880s, she began to urge its members to see themselves as a potentially powerful pressure group within national, state, and local party politics, with the ability to bring about changes in laws and government policies even before gaining the vote. Following her lead, WCTU women brought their considerable influence to bear on all levels of government by lobbying, forming coalitions of groups working for the same reform ends, and pursuing more informal avenues of persuasion. Willard and other prominent WCTU leaders politicized the organization and shaped it into a strong force capable of setting reform goals and effecting them. With the founding of the World's Woman's Christian Temperance Union (WWCTU) in 1884, Willard fulfilled her dream of mobilizing women's reform efforts on a global scale and linking American reform women with reformers in other lands.[29] During this period, Willard returned once more to journal keeping, first in 1893 and, again, in 1896. From 1892 until her death, Willard spent half her time in England and half in the United States, strengthening the transatlantic reform connections she created.

During the 1880s and 1890s in her speeches and writings—indeed, in the way she lived her life—Willard continually announced the arrival of "the dawn of woman's day" with the fast-approaching twentieth century. For millions of Americans and thousands more around the world she represented a new kind of womanliness. They viewed her as a strong, independent, intelligent, articulate leader, active in the nation's public life. Yet, at the same time, they saw her as a "womanly woman," one whose gentle, generous spirit and sincere religious-

ness did not threaten those more comfortable with an earlier generation's ideal of womanhood. To a large segment of the American
public, Willard's demeanor was a welcome alternative to what it perceived as the strident, demanding stance of more radical women's
rights leaders. As much as any other woman of her time, she symbol-
ized for her contemporaries the woman of the coming era. By her
impassioned rhetoric, she mobilized WCTU women to work diligently
for reform, convincing them that their efforts were vital to the dawn-
ing of that new day she predicted so enthusiastically.

The first three decades of Frances Willard's life epitomized the lives
of thousands of other young American women during the second
third of the nineteenth century, many of whom would become her
constituency in the WCTU. She and her family participated in the
great migration from the northeast to the old northwest, settling in
Wisconsin when it was still a territory. Although Willard proudly
harked back to her New England ancestry, she loved to think of herself as a daughter of the prairie frontier, infused with the new energy, power, and drive of the west. Nevertheless, although she frequently
invoked her carefree childhood on a farm in later years, she eagerly
moved with her family to Evanston, Illinois, a new Chicago suburb.
She looked forward to participating in its intellectual and cultural life,
which she felt was missing in southeastern Wisconsin.

This shift from a rural to a metropolitan environment was repeated by many families in many parts of the northern United States as
people moved off farms to growing cities like Chicago, which were
beginning to vie with older, eastern cities as centers of economic
growth, political power, and cultural prestige. Willard's father's
change of occupation from farmer to banker in that move was part
of the emergence of a solid upper middle class of white-collar workers and professionals, many of whose wives and daughters would
become WCTU leaders in the last three decades of the nineteenth
century.[30]

The Willard family shared its evangelical Protestant religious beliefs with a majority of nineteenth-century Americans. When the
Willards became active in the Methodist Episcopal Church (MEC)
during the late 1850s, they joined nearly one million other Americans who belonged to what was, by that time, the largest single Protestant denomination in the United States.[31] During the 1830s, 1840s,
and 1850s, the Methodists, along with other Protestant denominations, established hundreds of educational institutions, including
preparatory schools for girls, throughout the settled regions of the

country. At the same time, the increasing national interest in universal education led to the founding of more and more public schools. For the first time in the nation's history, large numbers of girls could acquire an education up to the college level. Frances Willard and thousands of other young women took advantage of this new opportunity, receiving their educations in a combination of public and private, denominational schools. After graduation, they often became teachers in the same or similar institutions, as the establishment of more and more schools required teachers to staff them. During this period, greatly increased numbers of teaching positions offered many more young women than in previous decades the chance to earn a living and to become financially independent.

Willard's similarity of experience with other young women of her generation—young women who shared her regional roots, social class, religious faith, education, and occupational choice—created a strong bond between them, which accounts, at least partially, for her great personal appeal to her followers. They felt, within Willard, a depth of sympathetic understanding, a resonance with their backgrounds, their daily lives, their disappointments, and aspirations. They believed she was one of them; and, indeed, she was. Page after page of her journal documents in abundant detail what it was like to grow up in Protestant America at midcentury, to move from a midwestern farm to a new suburb in a growing metropolitan area, to attend and teach in newly developing educational institutions, to consider a career as an alternative to marriage.

Willard's description of her "outside life" could have been replicated in the journals of many other young girls of her time. She was, as she liked to portray herself, a representative woman. Yet at the same time, she was unique. It was this, as well as her representativeness, that accounted for the allegiance of her supporters and earned for her great respect and admiration, even from those who disagreed with her. Willard's uniqueness can be traced throughout her journal, as she reveals her "inside life." On its pages, one can discover the process by which she grew to adulthood, painstakingly shaping herself into the kind of person she wished to become: a person of character.

For Willard, the term "character" meant, above all, moral strength. But it had other connotations as well: ease in social situations, a thorough education, firm self-reliance, and a strong religious faith. To develop character, she attempted to bring her disparate faculties—intelligence, will, emotions, conscience—under her control and direct them toward living a moral life. As she entered her twenties, she assiduously cultivated traits that she believed were essential to good character. Employing her journal for self-examination and self-assessment, she listed numerous components of good character and put marks beside those that she thought conspicuously lacking in her makeup.

On the front and back pages of her journal volumes she often inscribed short mottoes (her own inventions or quotations from her current heroes) to remind her of her goal and the rigor with which she would pursue it. Written along the margin of an 1861 journal volume, emphasized with underlinings, flourishes, and capital letters, appears this statement: "*My word*—than any other word more *Royal*—CHARACTER."[32] Six years later, she boldly inscribed on the front page of another volume this stern reminder: "We can hardly be too severe in judging ourselves, or too lenient in judging others."[33]

Occasionally, her energy for this moral pursuit waned and in the summer of 1860, when she was twenty, she confided to her journal: "I almost despair, sometimes, of ever coming to be a noble and finished character,—and I would rather be this than any or all things else in the world."[34] But perseverance and steadfastness—along with truthfulness, honor, judgment, calmness, patience, magnanimity, charity, geniality, generosity, and sensitivity to suffering humanity—were virtues that made up what Willard believed to be "a noble and finished character." And so she persisted. Her aim was to make good character habitual, integral to who she was, definitive of her self.

To late twentieth-century readers, Willard's concern with developing character may appear excessive—even obsessive—but it would not have seemed so for her contemporaries. American Victorian society, particularly in its evangelical expression, was relentlessly moralistic and didactic.[35] Several of its most important institutions—home and family, church, school—played strong, intertwining roles in character building, fostering intellectual, moral, and religious growth. For the Methodist world in which Willard lived as she grew to adulthood, a moral life was synonymous with a holy life, one lived in conformity with God's will and with God's aid. All three institutions reinforced the crucial link between morality and faith. The intellectual and moral aspects of one's character were integrally connected as well. An intellectual life without an accompanying moral dimension was impermissible; a moral life without an intellectual aspect to it was an impoverished existence.

As Willard persevered in her efforts to acquire character, her Evanston Methodist environment provided her with a lively and intense community of intellectual, moral, and religious striving, one that comes vividly to life in her journal. The community offered settings intended by the denomination to encourage and support the intellectual, moral, and religious self-examination in which Willard participated. The main settings—Evanston's Methodist church, NU, GBI, and NWFC—formed a cluster within walking distance of each other. When the Willard family was seated in its assigned pew at the Methodist church for Sunday morning worship, it was surrounded by neighbors and friends, many of whom were professors from NU and GBI, with their families and students alongside them. They were joined by rows of young women from NWFC who had walked in procession from their dormitory to the church, led by their teachers. In this company, the Willards knew themselves to be at the center of a powerful community of intellectual, moral, and religious striving that they had purposefully sought.

Many of the same friends, neighbors, and teachers whom Willard greeted at Sunday morning worship she also saw throughout the week in a round of events that had as their primary purpose the strengthening of Christian character: class meetings and reading circles, Sunday School and missionary meetings, and public exercises of the colleges and the biblical institute.[36] At weekly class meeting, Willard joined a small group of young people who examined their religious progress aloud in turn, encouraging one another to grow in faith. They prayed for each other during meetings and agreed to do the same in their daily private devotions. Class meetings were led by persons chosen for their strong faith and sense of moral rectitude, who functioned as both models and counselors of mature Christian life. While not having a specifically religious aim, Reading Circle brought many of the same young people together to discuss topics of mutual interest, often concerned with ways to lead an upright, useful life.

At public exercises of the three educational institutions, students fielded examination questions from their professors and prepared addresses and sermons for delivery before a good part of the Evanston community, gathered in the university chapel or the Methodist church sanctuary (the largest meeting place in the town). It was not unusual for them to speak on such subjects as "Citizenship & Politics," or to debate the question: "Resolved that great minds are developed more by the spirit & character of their possessors than by all other causes."[37] Not coincidentally, all of these activities trained young people to think and speak on their feet. They honed rhetorical skills that they would use throughout their lives, since many of the young men at NU and GBI intended to be ministers or lawyers, and the young women at NWFC expected to lead a variety of women's groups in churches and the wider society. A close reading of Willard's journal allows one to discover where she gained at least some of her ability to speak well in public.[38]

As Willard participated in activities meant to strengthen character, she sought models and mentors who could guide her toward a mature Christian character by example and advice. Besides her parents—her most constant guides—and her class leaders, she identified others in her community from whom she could learn. There were many men and women to choose from in the elite Methodist circle gathered around the newly established educational institutions in Evanston. The entire community felt a lively interest in maintaining the cultural and religious environment that it had created, with its aim of educating the young people of upper-middle-class Methodism, and thus took an active role in their guidance. In addition to the formalized structures of church and school, the community provided more informal occasions, such as "sociables" held in homes, where its older and younger members could mingle with one another. After Willard overcame her shyness in social situations, such events gave her an opportunity to become acquainted with people whom she engaged in lively conversations about literature, art, morality, and religious faith. She borrowed books from older women in the community who sympathized with her hunger for intellectual and moral improvement, and discussed them with the lenders and as well as with friends her own age.

In her turn, Willard became a mentor, first, to her Sunday School students and, then, to her pupils in the public and private elementary and secondary schools where she taught during the 1860s. She took a keen interest in her students' moral and religious progress, as well as their academic achievements. As had been true in her own educational experience, there was no clear line of demarcation between intellectual, moral, and religious learning. A conscientious teacher, she assumed responsibility for developing all three facets of her students' character. During her years as a teacher and college president, Willard polished her definition of mentoring. She referred to it in her autobiography as "Moral Horticulture," meaning the careful nurture of students by teachers, administrators, and the wider community, toward the aim of independence, self-government, and intellectual maturity. In her role as mentor, Willard thought of herself as "an elder sister" to the girls in her charge, encouraging them to develop character, in the way that her mentors had encouraged her.[39]

Willard's friendships played an important part in the growth of her character. She was initially attracted to her first close friend, Mary Bannister, because of Bannister's seriousness of purpose, manifested in her strong desire to be of use in the world, and her sincere endeavor to lead a Christian life. Willard shared these aims and was delighted when Bannister showed a willingness to be her friend. Later that year, away from home, teaching school, Willard listed Bannister immediately after her own family members as one with whom she would correspond regularly: "*Mary*—write always on Sabbath evening—she is my *Friend*—the only one after the *spiritual* intent that I have in the world."[40] Writing to each other on the Sabbath became a highly valued ritual for both young women, who looked upon their friendship as a gift from God.[41] For nearly two years, the young women were partners in their quest of developing character. Together they studied German, talked over the books and articles they were reading, planned Sunday School lessons for their classes, discussed their faith, and supported each other in their struggle to become well-educated, responsible adults and faithful Christians. Willard's friendship with Bannister was, as were all her friendships, a testing ground for the maturing of character. Her journal functioned as a vehicle for reflection and self-examination, as she traced the unfolding of the most significant friendship of her early twenties.

Journal keeping, friendships, a community of intellectual, moral, and religious striving whose members took seriously the task of mentoring—all of these were tools for character building in the evangelical Victorian culture of mid-nineteenth-century America, the environment in which Willard grew to maturity. The explanation of Willard's uniqueness does not lie in the fact that she was so different from other young women of her generation, but, rather, that she succeeded to such a high degree in learning the lessons that her community imparted to her and achieving the goal of good character that it set. She became, for her followers, a model of good character. When Willard had been WCTU president for many years, she summarized, in a deceptively simple statement, what she believed to be most significant in a person's character: "To be genuine—to be what one seems & to seem to be true & kind—this is the core of life."[42] Certainly she understood character to be made up of many more attributes than merely truth and kindness, although these two, she believed, were absolutely essential to character. But what is striking about her statement is her insistence that seeming and being should be brought into congruence in order for a person to be genuine. When such congruity exists, there can be no room for hypocrisy. Being genuine is a simple enough notion to express but supremely difficult to achieve and maintain

throughout one's life. Willard's followers perceived in her a congruence of seeming and being, a genuineness.

Besides being a model of good character, Willard had learned to
be a highly skillful mentor, encouraging, praising, exhorting, and
appealing, always, to the high ideals she believed the members of her
organization shared with her. Furthermore, she was convinced that
they were capable of realizing their ideals and, more important, she
convinced them of it. Implicit in the mentoring relationship that
Willard assumed was trust between those in the relationship. She was
able to elicit both trust and confidence from her followers to a remarkable degree.[43]

Willard's concern with character remained central to her life and
a theme running through her journal. She considered it the core of
personhood and the foundation of reform. Always a mentor-teacher,
she never lost an opportunity to discuss the formation and maintenance of character. As a leading reform figure during the 1880s and
1890s, she had a far wider "classroom" than she had had during her
school-teaching years, reaching many thousands with her speeches
and articles. She also resorted to other, less obvious means to dissem-
inate her message. For instance, her printed New Year's card for 1894,
which she sent to hundreds of friends and colleagues, contained this
statement: "Never forget that the only indestructible material in
Destiny's fierce crucible is character."[44] It is reminiscent of the re-
minders the twenty-one-year-old girl wrote to herself on the margins
of her journal. But that girl had grown up to be a powerful and influential model of character.

The friendship of women is another recurrent theme in Willard's
journal, linking the years of her young womanhood with those of her
late middle age. Close relationships with women remained essential
to her for her entire life, sustaining her physically, emotionally, and,
above all, spiritually.[45] Her most longstanding friendship was that with
her mother.[46] For all but five-and-one-half years of Willard's life, Mary
(Hill) Willard was her daughter's anchor, mooring her to home, family, and the religious faith that the family shared. She kept the household intact and waiting while her daughter taught away from home,
toured Europe, and traveled all over the United States as WCTU
president. Willard understood her mother's continual prayerful intercession for her as vital for her soul's well-being, keeping her linked
to God no matter how negligent she might be of her own spiritual
discipline.

When Mary (Hill) Willard died in August 1892, her daughter was utterly disheartened. In her journal, Frances Willard mourned the loss of her most beloved companion and counselor. Near the first anniversary of her mother's death, Willard relived her last days and pondered how much her mother had meant to her. Worn out and ill herself, Willard, who once feared dying, began to welcome death because she yearned to join her mother. Yet in the midst of her profound grief, she knew she could rely on two friends especially dear to her and her mother: Anna Gordon, her personal secretary, and Isabel (Lady Henry) Somerset,[47] president of the British Women's Temperance Association (BWTA).

Gordon was Willard's faithful companion for twenty-one years, organizing and arranging her increasingly busy schedule, as well as looking after the smooth running of Willard's home base in Evanston. In that time, Willard's mother had come to regard Gordon as a daughter, one who helped to fill the void in her heart left by the death of her daughter Mary many years earlier. Frances Willard thought of Gordon as her other self,[48] the same phrase she had used to refer to her sister. During the 1880s and early 1890s, the three women formed a tight-knit group, surrounded by several NWCTU staff members who also lived in Rest Cottage, the Willard family home in Evanston, which served as the headquarters of the NWCTU during much of Willard's presidency. For many years these women were Willard's immediate family, and its matriarch was her mother—Madam Willard (as she was called by the entire WCTU). It was a household of women friends, bound together not so much by marriage or actual kinship as by deep love and a shared commitment to work for reform. Unfortunately, this home was broken up by the death of Madam Willard. Thus Willard mourned not only the loss of her mother, but of her home as well.

Isabel Somerset offered Frances Willard a new home. The two had met in 1891 when the British temperance leader was in the United States to attend a meeting of the WWCTU, and both Willard and her mother found Somerset delightful. After Madam Willard's death the following year, Somerset invited Willard to come to England as her guest, to recover from her great grief. The two women became intimate friends, their relationship blessed, Willard believed, by her mother and by God. Willard's description of her friendship with Somerset hints at a much stronger and more impassioned attachment than the one between herself and Gordon. For Willard, Gordon was like a younger sister or niece, whose loyalty and service was greatly appreciated but whose mind was not creative or daring enough to engage Willard's for long. Somerset was a partner equal in stature to

Willard and eager, as Willard was, to explore new ideas such as Fabian socialism. She and Willard spent many hours in lively discussion of issues, strategies, and plans for further reform. The two women urged each other on to more and more active involvement in a number of events and movements of vital interest to them both.

During the 1890s, Willard, accompanied by Anna Gordon, spent much of her time in England with Isabel Somerset. She told of their unfolding friendship in her journal, although not with the abundance of detail that she wrote of her first long-term friendship, that with Mary Bannister. She had neither time nor energy for lengthy reflection, nor did she feel a need to document this relationship in the same way as she had her relationship with Bannister. Yet it is apparent, even from her brief notations, that theirs was a tender, loving partnership, fulfilling for both. Unlike several of Willard's earlier friendships—particularly those with Bannister and with Kate Jackson (her companion on her European tour)[49]—which had troubled, stormy periods, the course of her friendship with Somerset was relatively serene. There were only poignant moments of sadness and longing when they were apart. All three friends—Willard, Somerset, and Gordon—hoped that they could make their home together always, but they understood that their commitment to reform must often take precedence over their desire to be together.

Over the period from her twenties to her fifties, Willard redefined her notions of "family" and "home." The terms, as Willard often envisioned them in her adult years, differed from the traditional definitions that she held during her teens and twenties. Then, her ideas more closely conformed to the dominant mid-nineteenth-century ideal of a home containing a family of close kin with husband as its head, surrounded by his wife and their children. This was Willard's youthful experience in her own family, as well as what she observed in neighboring families. She continued to wish for just such a traditional home and family for herself, as her journals attest. Yet, at the same time, she began to imagine and, ultimately, to create for herself, the alternative arrangement described above: a family of women who chose to live with each other, and who might or might not be kin.

During Willard's WCTU presidency, she championed the reform of the traditional family, advocating equality between wife and husband, and insisting the sexual double standard be abolished.[50] But she also modeled an alternative family pattern into which a single woman like herself could comfortably fit.[51] Her organization was quite familiar with Willard's own female-headed family of women. Her mother was revered by the membership as a kind of "honorary moth-er" to them all, making of the organization a large family. Willard understood it so, and characterized herself in relation to its members as their "elderly sister."[52] When the WWCTU was established in the 1880s, the idea of family widened even further to encompass a world-wide "family" of "sisters," linked by their high ideals and allegiance to reform.

Men had a place in this broadened conception of a matriarchal family, but they were not at its center, as they were in the traditional notion of family. There was no "father" in the family she envisioned, as there had been no father in her birth family since the death of Josiah Willard in 1868. Thus the relationships within it would not be governed by female deference to male authority. There were broth-ers, but not with the same potential power as they might hold in a traditional family whose patriarch had died. Willard referred to male reformers and other male leaders with whom she associated as "broth-ers" and regarded herself, in her position as leader of a large and powerful organization, as their "sister" and their equal. Yet, their place was at the periphery of this family of women, and they held little power within it, although they might be extremely powerful outside of it.

Willard's redefinition of "home" and "family" is typical of the way in which she infused traditional institutions and values with new con-tent, transforming them into vehicles for social change. By document-ing her particular experience of such institutions and her reflections upon them, her journal gives specificity to abstract ideas and ideals, and shows the frame of reference out of which her thinking and writing emerged. As one reads Willard's journal one can better com-prehend what she envisioned when she invoked the words "home" and "family," so fraught with particular meanings and so integral to her thought.

During the late 1880s and early 1890s, she was still redefining the terms, pushing them beyond their usual circumscription. Her notion of "family" began to stretch beyond kin, nationality, race, or class to encompass the whole of humanity, with each family member acknowl-edging responsibility for the well-being of the entire family. Her ide-al of "home" was not limited to a certain house, street, town, or coun-try. "Home" was not so much a place as an attitude: one of welcome, care, respectfulness, and affection. When placed in the context of Willard's evolving thought, her references to home and family take on great ethical significance. Her call to "make the world homelike," for example, cannot be reduced to mere sloganizing. Instead, it may be understood as the heading for her broadest reform agenda and her hope for a world transfigured.

As Willard neared the end of her life, weary and ill, her notion of home and family underwent one last transformation. She began to look toward a heavenly home beyond the bounds of time and space, and to long for a reunion there with all of her dear friends who had gone before her into heaven, most of all her beloved birth family. "Home" and "family" once again acquired a deeply personal meaning for her. She yearned to rejoin her mother, father, sister, and brother where she believed they would never again have to part from each other, where they would truly be at home.

Notes

1. Anna Adams Gordon (1853–1931) was born in Boston to Mary Elizabeth (Clarkson) Gordon and James Monroe Gordon. She received her early education in the Newton, Mass., public schools, attended Mount Holyoke Seminary, and also studied at Lasell Female Seminary in Auburndale, Mass. She was raised a Congregationalist but converted to Methodism as an adult. She met Willard in 1877 at a noon meeting Willard led during a revival in Boston organized by the evangelist Dwight L. Moody, for whom Willard was working. Gordon had just returned from a year of music study in Europe and contemplated a musical career, but she chose to become Willard's personal secretary, a position she held for twenty-one years, until Willard's death in 1898. In addition, Gordon undertook organizational work of her own within the Woman's Christian Temperance Union (WCTU), focusing her attention specifically on the Loyal Temperance Legion, the WCTU's juvenile organization. In 1891 she was made superintendent of juvenile work of the World's Woman's Christian Temperance Union (WWCTU). Gordon became vice-president of the WCTU upon Willard's death and continued to be a leader in children's temperance work. In 1914 she became president of the WCTU; during her tenure the Eighteenth Amendment, legalizing prohibition, was passed, in January 1919. With its passage, Gordon placed emphasis on other reforms including child welfare, social purity, and Americanization of the foreign-born. In 1921 she was elected president of the WWCTU, and four years later she resigned her national office to devote her time and energy to the presidency of the WWCTU. She died in 1931 at age seventy-seven.

2. The Journal of Frances E. Willard, 5 June 1860, hereafter cited as *Journal*. All transcriptions in this volume were made from the original journal, not from the microfilm edition. (See "Essay on the Source" at the end of this volume for a discussion of the microfilm edition of Willard's journal.) Occasionally, brief portions of the journal that do not appear in entries selected for this edition are included in the general introduction and section introductions, as is the case with this quotation.

3. Journal for 17 August 1859–2 January 1860.

4. Sarah B. (Hill) Hall (1813–99) was Willard's mother's youngest sister. She made a career teaching at girls' preparatory schools for two decades, first at Riga Academy in Riga, N.Y., for a number of years. She accompanied the Willard family to Oberlin College (see n. 17, below) in 1841 and took courses at Oberlin for several years. She taught at the Methodist-sponsored Female College at Columbia, Tenn., during the early 1850s, and then at Milwaukee Female College in the mid-1850s. She married Ward Hall in 1862 at age forty-nine, and lived in Churchville, N.Y., until her death.

5. Mary (Bannister) Willard (1841–1912) was an Evanston neighbor and a classmate of Willard's younger sister, Mary, at North Western Female College (NWFC) (see n. 21, below). Bannister was born in Fairfield, N.Y., to Lucy (Kimball) Bannister and Rev. Henry Bannister (see Journal, 23 March 1860, n. 1). She graduated from NWFC in 1860, taught school briefly, and then married Oliver A. Willard (see n. 22 below), Frances Willard's brother, in 1862. They had four children, two sons and two daughters. When Oliver Willard died in 1878, she and her sister-in-law Frances Willard took over publishing the Chicago *Post,* a paper her husband had edited and published before his death. Financial problems forced them to sell the newspaper in the same year and Mary Bannister Willard began to edit *Our Union* (later the *Union Signal*), the WCTU's weekly newspaper. In 1886 she moved to Berlin and opened the American Home School for Girls. She continued to live in Europe until failing health caused her to return to the United States a few years before her death. She died at age seventy-one at the New York City home of her daughter, Katherine (Willard) Baldwin (see Journal, 11 April 1896, n. 1).

6. Journal, 2 May 1859.

7. Ibid., 26 May 1859.

8. Ibid., 15 March 1859.

9. Ibid., 8 September 1859.

10. Ibid., 10 June 1859.

11. Ibid., 7 October 1861.

12. Ibid., 15 October 1861.

13. Ibid., 21 February 1860.

14. Ibid., 28 September 1870. This journal entry was taken from Ray Strachey, *Frances Willard: Her Life and Work* (New York, 1913), 153 (hereafter cited as Strachey, *Willard: Life and Work*), because the volume of Willard's journal that contains this entry is missing. (See "Essay on the Source" in this volume.)

15. Several biographies of Willard have been written since her death in 1898. Anna A. Gordon, *The Beautiful Life of Frances E. Willard* (Chicago, 1898), hereafter cited as Gordon, *Beautiful Life,* is a memoir, interesting because it was written within months of Willard's death, by one of her closest companions. It contains several of Willard's speeches and many memorials and tributes to Willard by reform leaders in both the United States and the British Isles. Strachey, *Willard: Life and Work,* was written by the granddaughter of

Hannah (Whitall) Smith (see Journal, 11 January 1893, n. 2), one of Willard's colleagues in the WCTU and the British Women's Temperance Association (BWTA), who interviewed several WCTU and BWTA leaders to hear their personal impressions of Willard. Mary Earhart, *Frances Willard: From Prayers to Politics* (Chicago, 1944), hereafter cited as Earhart, *From Prayers to Politics,* was for over four decades the biography most utilized by historians. It contains more details than any other biography and is a good analysis of Willard as a political figure, but it suffers from inadequate documentation of materials used. Ruth Bordin, *Frances Willard: A Biography* (Chapel Hill, N.C., 1986), hereafter cited as Bordin, *Frances Willard,* takes account of the vast literature of the relatively new discipline of women's history and of the history of alcohol consumption in the United States. It is a competent biography that places Willard in the spectrum of women's rights reformers during the nineteenth century. All four biographies quote from Willard's journal to some extent.

16. Josiah Flint Willard (1805–68) was born in Wheelock, Vt., and grew up in Churchville, N.Y. He married Mary Thompson Hill (see n. 19, below), in 1831. Josiah Willard was a successful farmer in western New York for a decade and then moved to Oberlin, Ohio, in 1841, where he attended Oberlin College to prepare for the ministry. Because of his ill health, the family moved in 1846 to a southeastern Wisconsin farm just outside of Janesville. A civic-minded person, he served a term in the Wisconsin legislature, was for several years a trustee of the state institution for the blind, and was active in the Wisconsin Agricultural Society. Although raised a Congregationalist, he became a Methodist at some time between 1846 and 1855. In 1858 the Willards moved to Evanston, Ill., and Josiah Willard became a banker with the Chicago firm of Preston and Kean. During the 1860s, he served on the board of trustees of Evanston and was elected president in 1867. He retired from banking in 1865 because of ill health, and died of tuberculosis at age sixty-two.

17. Oberlin Collegiate Institute was founded in 1833 by the Congregational Church in order to educate ministers and schoolteachers. It was chartered in 1834 and by 1850 it was known as Oberlin College. Oberlin was the first coeducational school of higher education in the United States. In 1835 it became the first to admit students "without respect to color," and it took a strong antislavery position well before the Civil War. When Josiah Willard attended Oberlin, its president was the antislavery advocate Asa Mahan, a Congregational minister, author, and educator, and Charles Grandison Finney, a famous revival preacher, taught theology there.

18. Milwaukee Normal Institute, a Congregationalist school, was founded in 1848 by Mrs. L. A. Parsons. In 1853 its name was changed to Milwaukee Female College to reflect improvements made in its staff, curriculum, and facilities suggested by the noted educator Catharine Beecher and carried out by Mary Mortimer, a protégé of Beecher's.

19. Mary Thompson (Hill) Willard (1805–92) was born on a farm in North Danville, Vt., and moved to Ogden, N.Y., when she was twelve. She

began to teach school at fifteen and taught for eleven years. She married Josiah F. Willard in 1831. She bore five children, three of whom survived early childhood. While the family lived in Oberlin, Ohio, from 1841 to 1846, she took courses at Oberlin College. After living in Wisconsin from 1846 to 1858 she moved to Evanston, Ill., with her family. Between the 1860s and the 1880s she was active in several women's groups, including the Ladies Educational Association of Evanston (see n. 24, below) and the local WCTU. She died in Evanston at age eighty-seven.

20. Mary Eliza Willard (1843–62) was born in Oberlin, Ohio. She attended the district elementary school outside Janesville, Wis., the Milwaukee Female College for one term in 1857, and graduated from NWFC in 1860. She died of tuberculosis at age nineteen.

21. North Western Female College was founded in Evanston, Ill., in 1855 by William P. Jones, Jr. (1831–86), a Methodist Episcopal Church (MEC) minister and an advocate of women's higher education. He was principal of NWFC from 1855 to 1862, when he was appointed by President Lincoln to be U.S. consul in China. He returned to Evanston in 1868 and was again principal of NWFC until he turned over its control to the Ladies Educational Association of Evanston. The school, a Methodist-sponsored institution, consisted of a preparatory department and college for women and a preparatory school for boys. The college, academically equivalent to a high school, offered two courses of study leading to two different degrees: the scientific course and the classical course.

22. Oliver Atherton Willard (1835–78) was born in Ogden, N.Y. He briefly attended Oberlin College and graduated from Beloit College, Beloit, Wis., in 1859. He graduated from Garrett Biblical Institute (GBI) in Evanston, Ill., in 1861, was ordained a Methodist minister, and began serving a congregation in Edgerton, Wis. In 1862 he married Mary Bannister and left for a new ministry field in the Colorado Territory. He was appointed a minister in Denver and in 1863 became, at age twenty-seven, the youngest presiding elder (see Journal, 17 January 1860, n. 4) in American Methodism up to that time. He resigned from the ministry in 1866 and became an insurance agent for a Wisconsin firm, living in Appleton, Wis. In the late 1860s he and his family moved to Evanston, and he became editor of the *Chicago Evening Mail* (later the *Post and Mail,* still later the *Post*). He died at age forty-two after a sudden, brief illness.

23. Garrett Biblical Institute, a Methodist theological seminary located in Evanston, Ill., was chartered and opened in 1855. It was founded through the generosity of Eliza Garrett, a Chicago woman who bequeathed her large estate for its establishment. By the time Oliver Willard enrolled at GBI in 1859, Bishop Matthew Simpson (see Part 1, Introduction, n. 24) was acting president and there were three faculty members: Daniel P. Kidder, professor of practical theology (see Journal, 6 September 1860, n. 2); Henry Bannister, professor of New Testament exegesis; and Francis D. Hemenway, professor of exegetical theology and biblical literature (see Journal, 15 July 1861, n. 1).

24. The Evanston College for Ladies was chartered in 1869 by the Ladies Educational Association of Evanston, Ill., with the aim of promoting education for girls that was directed and controlled by women. Shortly after, William Jones, principal of the NWFC, agreed to transfer his school to the Evanston College for Ladies, and Northwestern University (NU) (see n. 26, below) changed its policy to admit women. By June 1870, the Evanston College for Ladies, having absorbed the older NWFC, agreed to a union with NU. Students at the Evanston College for Ladies took classes at the university, supplemented by a course of study in fine arts and history taught by the college's all-women faculty. The college provided its students with the supervision and protection commonly thought to be necessary for young women. It also offered a dormitory and a system of self-government that was unusual for the time. In 1873 the Evanston College for Ladies merged its board of trustees and faculty with those of NU and became the Woman's College of Northwestern University.

25. The National Women's Congress was held 15–19 October 1873 in New York City. Sponsored by Sorosis, one of the earliest women's clubs, the congress drew women from all over the United States who read papers on various topics relating to women's status in American society. Many women's rights leaders attended, including Elizabeth Cady Stanton, Mary A. Livermore, Lucy Stone, and Julia Ward Howe. The ideas expressed at the congress were to form the working agenda for the Association for the Advancement of Women.

26. Northwestern University was chartered in January 1851 as an institution of higher education under the patronage and government of the MEC. Classes were first held in November 1855. When the Willards moved to Evanston in 1859, Randolph Sinks Foster was NU's president (see Journal, 23 October 1859, n. 1), and the subjects taught included English, Latin, mathematics, moral philosophy, and natural science. Two of the faculty members in particular—Henry Noyes, mathematics professor (see Journal, 27 November 1859, n. 1), and Daniel Bonbright, Latin professor (see Journal, 26 December 1860, n. 2)—were good friends of the Willard family.

27. See Ruth Bordin, *Woman and Temperance: The Quest for Power and Liberty, 1873–1900* (Philadelphia, 1981), hereafter cited as Bordin, *Woman and Temperance,* and Susan Dye Lee, "Evangelical Domesticity: The Origins of the WCTU under Frances Willard" (Ph.D. diss., Northwestern University, 1980), for accounts of the Ohio Woman's Crusade and histories of the early years of the WCTU.

28. See Elizabeth B. Clark, "The Politics of God and the Woman's Vote: Religion in the Suffrage Movement in America, 1848–1895" (Ph.D. diss., Princeton University, 1989), which contrasts the evangelical feminism represented by the WCTU with the liberal feminism represented by women's rights leaders such as Elizabeth Cady Stanton and Matilda Joslyn Gage. Clark traces the differences in the two feminist positions to their differing ideas of human nature, the stance of the human being in society (evangelical relationalism versus liberal individualism), and the consequent differences

in notions of governance between the two groups (the maternal state versus a less intrusive state that emphasized individual liberties).

29. See Ian Tyrrell, *Woman's World/Woman's Empire: The Woman's Christian Temperance Union in International Perspective, 1880–1930* (Chapel Hill, N.C., 1991), for a fascinating and insightful look at the WWCTU, particularly in regard to the issue of cultural imperialism.

30. Bordin, *Woman and Temperance*, 163–75.

31. Edwin Scott Gaustad, *Historical Atlas of Religion in America* (New York, 1962), 78.

32. Journal, volume covering 2 February 1861–19 June 1861, 4.

33. Ibid., volume covering 1 January 1867–31 December 1867, 2.

34. Ibid., 22 July 1860.

35. See Walter E. Houghton, *The Victorian Frame of Mind* (New Haven, 1957), for the British Victorian worldview as reflected in the most important writers of the period. These writers were also immensely popular in the United States and helped shape American Victorianism. Daniel Walker Howe, "Victorian Culture in America," and David D. Hall, "The Victorian Connection," both in *Victorian America*, ed. Daniel Walker Howe (Philadelphia, 1984), characterize the specifically American manifestation of Victorianism. D. H. Meyer, *The Instructed Conscience: The Shaping of an American National Ethic* (Philadelphia, 1971), describes the ethical values instilled in generations of college students through several of the most influential textbooks for courses in moral philosophy required during senior year. Willard read one of the most popular of these texts, Francis Wayland's *Elements of Moral Science* (Boston, 1834), in November 1859.

36. See A. Gregory Schneider, *The Way of the Cross Leads Home: The Domestication of American Methodism* (Bloomington, Ind., 1993), a provocative study of the social religion of Methodists in the upper South in the first four decades of the nineteenth century. Although Willard's journal depicts the rituals of Methodist social religion in the Midwest rather than the upper South, and two decades later than those analyzed by Schneider, Schneider's analysis is valuable in highlighting the important effects of social religion on Methodist life. Similarly, Russell E. Richey, *Early American Methodism* (Bloomington, Ind., 1991), details how Methodists acted toward each other. Although, like Schneider's volume, it deals with an earlier period than Willard's journal covers, Richey's work helps articulate the meanings underlying behaviors and shows how such meanings may have as much significance as beliefs or doctrines for understanding a people's ethos.

37. Journal, 3 and 5 November 1859.

38. Richard W. Leeman, *"Do Everything" Reform: The Oratory of Frances E. Willard* (New York, 1992), and Amy Rose Slagell, "A Good Woman Speaking Well: The Oratory of Frances E. Willard" (Ph.D. diss., University of Wisconsin–Madison, 1992), the latter hereafter cited as Slagell, "Good Woman Speaking Well," are recent studies of Willard's rhetoric. Leeman's introductory chapters weaving together Willard's life and thought are excellent, particularly on the meaning of Willard's socialism. Slagell's extended introduc-

tion is thoughtful and she has reconstructed the most complete texts possible of fifty-three of Willard's speeches, with headnotes placing each speech in its context. She includes a list of 186 of Willard's speeches, arranged chronologically, with information on where they can be located, the first time that scholars will have this information readily available to them.

39. Willard, *Glimpses of Fifty Years,* 206.

40. Journal, 3 October 1860.

41. Ibid., 26 June and 21 September 1860. Irene Quenzler Brown, "Death, Friendship, and Female Identity during New England's Second Great Awakening," *Journal of Family History* 12, no. 4 (1987): 367–87, looks closely and carefully at the spiritual dimension of nineteenth-century friendships, an aspect of great significance in Willard's friendships.

42. Journal, 27 August 1893.

43. One can get a strong sense of the charismatic quality of Willard's leadership in the section "Character Studies—Tributes," in Gordon, *Beautiful Life,* 334–416.

44. One of Willard's 1894 New Year's cards is in the editor's possession. In Willard's last journal volume, written in 1896, she copied onto the front page a quotation from George John Romanes (1848–94), a British biologist who studied the development of intelligence: "I have come to see that cleverness, success, attainment count for little; that goodness of character is the most important factor in life."

45. William Rounseville Alger, *Friendships of Women* (Boston, 1868), describes the many facets of women's friendships and is a key text for understanding how Willard perceived her friendships with women. Willard mentioned Alger's book when she was traveling in Europe (27 June 1869), perhaps having read it or reviews of it by this time. She returned to reading Alger's book in later life.

46. See Frances E. Willard, *A Great Mother* (Chicago, 1894), Willard's memorial to her mother, written in the year after her mother's death, for a detailed description of Willard's relationship with her mother as Willard herself understood it.

47. Lady Isabella (Isabel) Caroline (Cocks) Somerset (1851–1921) was the eldest child and heir of Charles Somers-Cocks, Viscount Eastnor, later Earl Somers. Her mother was Virginia (Pattle) Cocks (see Journal, 19 September 1896, n. 1). Isabel Cocks married Lord Henry Somerset in 1872 and had a son in 1874. The marriage was extremely unhappy, and she obtained a legal separation in 1878 on the grounds of abuse, also gaining custody of her son. Left alone and socially ostracized because she made public the scandal of an aristocratic family, Isabel Somerset turned to philanthropy among the poor of Ledbury, near her family home, Eastnor Castle, in Herefordshire. Seeing the consequences of drunkenness on the poor of Ledbury, she espoused the temperance cause. Her father died in 1883 and Somerset inherited his estates. In 1890 she was elected president of the BWTA, an organization formed in 1876. In 1891 she went to the United States to attend the WWCTU convention in Boston. On that trip she met Frances Willard and

remained in America until spring 1892, traveling with Willard to observe the WCTU's organizational methods. Until Willard's death in 1898 the two temperance leaders worked together on a variety of reform goals. At Willard's death Somerset took her friend's place as the president of the WWCTU. In 1903 she resigned as president of the BWTA and in 1906 she stepped down from the presidency of the WWCTU. In the mid-1890s she had founded Duxhurst, a farm colony for inebriate women, near Reigate, her home outside London, and she continued to take an active interest in this innovative treatment center until her death in 1921.

48. Journal, 15 August 1893.

49. Katharine (Kate) A. Jackson (ca. 1836–1900) was a longtime friend of Willard's. Their friendship began in 1864 when the two young women taught school together in Evanston, Ill. Jackson was originally from Paterson, N.J., where her father, James Jackson (see Journal, 21 December 1866, n. 1), was a wealthy locomotive manufacturer. Her mother was Caroline Ross (Burnett) Jackson. Kate Jackson graduated from a female seminary in Wilmington, Del., and taught French for a time at Chapel Hill Seminary at Brenham, Tex. In 1868 she and Willard traveled together in Europe for two years. When they returned, Jackson taught French language and literature at the Evanston College for Ladies and, later, at the Woman's College of NU. Except for ten years when she lived with her sister, Caroline (Carrie) (Jackson) Whitely (see Journal, 21 December 1866, n. 4), in Europe, Jackson spent the rest of her life in Evanston where she and her sister lived next door to Willard's home, Rest Cottage.

50. See Willard's speech "A White Life for Two," in Slagell, "Good Woman Speaking Well," 575–88.

51. See Lee Virginia Chambers-Schiller, *Liberty, A Better Husband: Single Women in America: The Generations of 1780–1840* (New Haven, 1984), which presents in rich detail the single life as an attractive alternative to marriage for women in the nineteenth century. See also Carol Lasser, "'Let Us Be Sisters Forever': The Sororal Model of Nineteenth-Century Female Friendship," in *Signs* 14, no. 1 (Autumn 1988): 158–81, which convincingly sets forth a mode of women's friendship—"idealized sisterhood"—helpful in describing and defining Willard's adult relationships with women friends.

52. Journal, 21 October 1893.

PART ONE

14 February 1859–28 March 1861

I see clearly that I shall never be the "grown up person" that I ought to be, until I have "borne and labored and had patience.". . . if every thing is hard for me, and I am alternately the "Hammer" and the "Anvil" (but *always one*)—I think I may grow to be strong and earnest in *practice* as I have always tried to be in *theory*.

—*28 May 1860*

Frances Willard began to keep a journal systematically in 1855 during her sixteenth year, when she was living on the family farm outside Janesville, Wisconsin.[1] She recorded a round of duties dictated by the seasonal nature of agriculture: planting, harvesting, lambing, hog butchering, which involved the entire Willard family and several hired hands. Like all the family members, Willard and her younger sister, Mary, were responsible for tasks each day. They helped fix breakfast, straightened up several rooms, and were called on when needed for many other chores, from chasing after cows in the cornfields to helping hang wallpaper in the parlor. These jobs were not onerous, and Willard spent a good deal of time playing with neighbor children, reading, and writing short essays, poems, and even an adventure novel entitled "Rupert Melville."[2]

The cyclical farm rhythm was punctuated by events such as the Fourth of July celebration, election day, and the annual Rock County Fair held in late September. But by far the most anticipated event Willard noted in her early journal was the opening of the district school that she and her sister attended. Her mother and a neighbor had chosen the site for the schoolhouse on 13 November 1855, and two months later the building was finished. On 21 January 1856 school opened, to Willard's great delight, and she eagerly began her studies. Only a few days before, she had written: "I long for school to begin to relieve the tedious, unendurable monotony, if for nothing else. . . . I might write in advance, what I do, for it is the same unvarieing round—my life, my *young*, life, which should be as glad & free as a playful lamb's, has been for the past year precisely like that of a hermit,—every want provided for, every taste gratified, *at home,* but *at home* ever & only,—it is enough to dry the fountains of hope & ambition,—it is *terrible*—but *School* is going to begin on Monday. . . ."[3] Although this passage was far more histrionic than her journal writing had been up to this point, she was, at sixteen, beginning to be bored with what she considered an uneventful life and looked to school to break the monotony.

After returning from her first day of school she noted: "Have enjoyed it exceedingly—Have tried to learn my lessons well, & do the best I knew how, & feel, tonight, satisfied with the world, myself, & 'the rest of mankind.'"[4] And after the second day: "Enjoyed it as much as ever, ardor not in the least diminished."[5] Her enthusiasm continued to the end of the winter term, even through many days of sub-zero temperatures. She especially enjoyed "spelling down" the school at frequent spelling bees and ruefully noted the words she missed the few times she did not win.

Although Willard had been taught at home, first, by her mother and, then, by a young neighbor, and had attended a small private school in Janesville for a short time, she received almost all of her formal schooling during the four years from 1856 through 1859. She attended the district school for four terms, and, in February 1857, she announced in her journal: "Father is going to send us to Milwaukee to school in the spring. My *great* wish gratified!!"[6] Willard's Aunt Sarah was teaching at the Milwaukee Female College, and Willard and her sister were to board with their aunt while attending school there. After much preparation, including several trips into Janesville for dress fittings, the two girls, accompanied by their father, took the train to Milwaukee. Josiah Willard saw his daughters settled in their boardinghouse and returned to the farm, leaving them away from home without their parents for the first time in their lives.

Immediately the girls were plunged into a busy school schedule, along with evening travel lectures, excursions around Milwaukee after school and on Saturdays, and sermons and Sunday School at either the Congregational or the Presbyterian church on the Sabbath. Three weeks into the term, Willard wrote: "Am getting acquainted quite fast. Like my new life very well. Have not been homesick a moment yet! Good!"[7] During the school term, she went to a concert by Thalberg ("reputed to be the greatest piano performer in the world"),[8] heard the abolitionist Gerrit Smith[9] speak, and saw a circus ("for the first & last time in my life . . . *wonderful*—but, I think, demoralizing—Intoxicating too, but no *good* resulted from it").[10] One memorable Sunday, she visited for the "first time in life" the Catholic cathedral for morning mass ("verdict, mummery"), a Unitarian church in the afternoon ("verdict, beautiful thoughts, no religion"), and heard a woman preach on Spiritualism in the evening ("verdict, Fine thoughts, that's all!").[11]

When the school term finished in mid-July, Willard hated to leave. Not only would she miss her courses and the extracurricular activities she so enjoyed; she would particularly miss the friends she had made. It was the first chance she had to have friends her own age, since her playmates on the farm were all younger. She hoped to convince her father to send her back to school in Milwaukee in the fall. In early August she reported: "Had 'scene' about going to school! Hope to succeed."[12] But a only a week later, she wrote with great disappointment: "Had 'final conference' with Father, in which he said he should *not* send me to Milwaukee.—I am able, I can do, I *will* send *myself!* Note the vow!"[13] Shortly afterward, however, she seemed resigned to her father's decision: "Have 'settled down,' much as usual,

with the memory of my 3 months at M. as a candle lit at night,—&
alas!—*extinguished* again!"[14] Yet she was determined to study on her
own in order to keep up with her Milwaukee classmates.

Once Willard had gotten a taste of the world beyond the farm, rural life was no longer as attractive to her as it had once been. In mid-
October 1857, she copied a long excerpt from a short story in the
current *Harper's* that expressed her feelings about being far removed
from cultured and learned society. In the story, a simple country girl
listens to a sermon given by a well-educated young minister, which
impresses her with its cultivated language. The girl realizes that he
comes from vastly different surroundings than hers and begins to day-
dream about the opportunities those surroundings afford. Willard
underlined a portion of the excerpt in which the girl imagines herself
going forth into that different, wider world, where all her capacities
would be tested, "into the broad plain, where were bugles and trum-
pets calling strong souls onward to victory in the wonderful battle of
life." She wrote below the underlining: "The italics are my own, & show
the portions of the extract most admired, & for which it was made."[15]

As Willard diligently pursued the course of study she had set for
herself, she undoubtedly imagined that she would some day be able
to engage in "the wonderful battle of life," like Elinor Turnbull, the
heroine of the short story. But she knew that she would first have to
find a way to leave the farm for a place perhaps even larger and more
cosmopolitan than Milwaukee. One day toward the end of the year,
she wrote in total exasperation: "There are great cities,—but I'm not
in one!—but I *will* be!"[16] A few days later she decided not to keep a
journal anymore "till I have a more *various* life."[17] And on 31 December she wrote what would be her last journal entry for over a year. In
it she wondered where she would be the following New Year's Eve and
hoped that she would be "greater, wiser, better."[18]

By New Year's Eve 1858 the Willards had moved from their Wisconsin farm to Evanston, Illinois, where Willard was in her final year
at North Western Female College, preparing to graduate in June
1859.[19] In February of that year, she took up journal writing again,
in a style markedly different from her pithy accounts of farm life. Her
entries became lengthy and introspective because she had many
things on her mind. Her upcoming graduation meant choices about
her future, decisions concerning what she should do with her life, and
she wished to unburden herself about these in her journal. She
agreed with Margaret Fuller, whose memoirs she read with great pleasure and a sense of identification, that "the only object in life was to
grow."[20] But she was unsure just how to proceed.

It was at this time that Willard, who had been an avid reader, became a voracious one. Her journal documents literally hundreds of books and magazines—fiction and nonfiction—that she saw as a significant part of her continuing self-education. The act of reading opened a kind of dialogue between herself and the authors whose works she read. These dialogues, recorded in her journal, aided in her self-definition. They show that the works she read provided her with ideas and ideals with which she could agree or disagree, and with heroes and heroines who embodied good character, as well as figures who lacked such virtue. Reading a novel, a poem, a sermon, or a magazine article was often the impetus for several pages of rumination on such topics as the meaning of womanhood and manhood, marriage and singleness, work and vocation, all subjects vital for Willard to explore in order to shape her self and her future.[21]

As Willard understood it, she was presented with two possible courses her future could take: teaching of some sort and marriage. Teaching offered her the possibility of at least a small degree of personal and financial independence, a prospect attractive to her. Marriage would fulfill societal and family expectations for her, but she was ambivalent about it. Although she often daydreamed about her ideal man, the one who would be "more than all the world" to her, she sometimes doubted that she would ever marry. As she began to search for a teaching position, she continued to develop her thoughts about marriage and her fitness for married life.

Teaching was important to Willard not only for the possibility of independence it might bring, but also, indeed primarily, because it was the means by which her character could be tested, strengthened, and matured. She was aware that her life had been relatively easy up to that point, without great sorrow and loss or difficult work, either of which could summon forth the qualities of character she was most anxious to develop in herself. She felt herself poised at the brink of adulthood—of real, earnest living—in which she might carry out the vocation of doing good in the world. This was her task, she believed, as it was the task of all serious Christians. And she intended to become a dedicated Christian. The decision to embark upon a Christian life was a step—perhaps the most crucial one—on the way to adulthood.

Willard had been involved in church life since she was a small child. She had attended daily family prayers and Sunday morning worship, and kept the strict Sabbath upon which her father insisted, so she was well acquainted with that life and its demands. But she differentiated between her childhood faith and the religious commitment she would make as an adult. As a child, she made no conscious choice to be a Christian; she was simply reared in a faithful family. But as she entered adulthood, she was asked by her Methodist community, as it asked all its youth, to make the choice for a Christian life. Through 1858 and 1859 she pondered that choice, resisting pressures made on her during revivals to go forward to the altar and declare herself a Christian.[22]

In the summer of 1859 when Willard was dangerously ill with typhoid fever, she experienced a crisis of faith, which she recreated thirty years later in her autobiography. She presented the crisis as a dramatic choice between skepticism and belief, resolved when she decided to "try to be a Christian girl."[23] Throughout the late summer and fall of 1859, she attempted to carry out her resolve to become a Christian. Her journal documents regular participation in the ongoing religious life of her community, as well as the study of literature on Christian faith and doctrine and discussion with family and friends about their faith. But she was troubled by an inner tension between her intellectual knowledge of Christ and her continuing inability to transform that knowledge into the trusting certainty of Christ's presence that others had described to her. Such certainty seemed to her a prerequisite for becoming a Christian. She was convinced that she must feel Christ in her heart as well as comprehend his Person and meaning with her mind. But she did not know how.

In December 1859 her church held a revival preached mainly by Matthew Simpson,[24] a Methodist bishop whom Willard admired greatly for his personal holiness. As she attended the revival she still struggled over whether she could and would obtain the personal experience of Christ's love, that feeling which she believed would compel her to seek forgiveness for sins and enable her to lead a righteous and holy life. Midway through the revival, Bishop Simpson delivered a sermon that offered Willard a way out of her dilemma. He assured his listeners that if they would just begin to lead holy lives, the powerful feeling of Christ's presence would follow. This simple, straightforward advice had the effect of removing a roadblock on the spiritual path Willard pursued. Though she still did not feel converted, she was certainly able and willing to employ her intellect to discern what was righteous and just, to seek a moral course for her life. Two evenings later, she went forward to the altar and publicly declared her intent to be a Christian. Within a month, she became a probationary member of her church and began to participate fully in its spiritual life.

Entering decisively on the moral and spiritual path she had chosen, Willard was joined by a new friend, Mary Bannister, who became her companion on that path. Their deepening friendship made it easier for Willard to remain firm in her resolve to lead a life of "'endless toil and endeavor,'"[25] knowing that someone she loved was committed to the same struggle to live a Christian life and to make a difference in the world. When the two friends went off to teach in different places, Willard found it difficult to maintain the spiritual discipline she had set for herself, particularly since the families with whom she boarded were not churchgoers. Without either her own family or her new friend, she had many moments of doubt as to her ability to be a conscientious Christian on her own. Her journal became the place where she could deplore the lack of interest in religion she observed in the towns where she taught; and in its pages she upbraided herself for her failure to practice her faith and speak about it to nonbelievers.

Although Willard wrote beautifully in her journal about her intent to develop what she termed "an antisectarian spirit" in her heart, to be manifested in a tolerant, ecumenical stance toward all churches as "branches . . . of the *One* Church,"[26] her broadmindedness did not easily extend to those who belonged to no church. Yet her severity toward people who did not profess a Christian faith was mitigated by her realization that they could be moral without being church members. She slowly learned to temper her censorious judgments with the kindliness, charity, and openness that became the hallmarks of her public life.

As Willard pursued the vocational and religious course she had set for herself, she did so against the backdrop of a series of momentous events in the life of the nation, as it moved toward civil war. The Evanston community was well aware that the unity of the country was endangered. Since most of the community, including the Willards, held antislavery sentiments and were staunch, and in some cases, influential Republicans, they enthusiastically supported Abraham Lincoln's bid for the presidency. They watched with a growing sense of unease the signs of disunion developing over the fall of 1860. Willard's primary concern was for her friend Mary Bannister's safety since she was teaching in Tennessee. Willard was overjoyed at the news that Bannister would be returning to Evanston in early December rather than remaining until the following June with the family whose children she was tutoring. Willard had survived her first attempts to be independent and self-reliant by teaching away from home, in Kankakee, Illinois. Her reward would be her return to the comfort of family, friends, and familiar places for a time to renew her moral energy, before she entered once more into the "wonderful battle of life" she had so longed to experience as a young girl on a Wisconsin farm.

Notes

1. Although Willard mentioned in her autobiography, *Glimpses of Fifty Years,* 49, that she began keeping a journal when she was twelve years old, only one tiny journal volume has been discovered for 1852, when she would have been twelve, and none for 1853 or 1854, when she would have been thirteen and fourteen. (See "Essay on the Source," in this volume.)

2. According to Willard's journal, she began writing "Rupert Melville" on 15 December 1855 and finished the novel on her eighteenth birthday, 28 September 1857.

3. Journal, 15 and 16 January 1856.

4. Ibid., 21 January 1856.

5. Ibid., 22 January 1856.

6. Ibid., 20 February 1857.

7. Ibid., 12 May 1857.

8. Ibid., 28 May 1857. Sigismond (Fortuné François) Thalberg (1812–71) was a Swiss pianist, said to rival Franz Liszt in virtuosity, who performed throughout the world.

9. Ibid., 18 June 1857. Gerrit Smith (1797–1874) was a wealthy New York philanthropist, reformer, and abolitionist who contributed millions of dollars during his lifetime to numerous causes, including support of John Brown (see Journal, 2 December 1859, n. 1). Politically active, he was a founder of the Liberty Party in 1840 and its candidate for U.S. president in 1848 and 1852; ran for governor of New York on an antislavery platform in 1840 and 1858; and served from 1853 to 1854 as an independent congressman. Willard heard him speak on 17 June 1857.

10. Ibid., 15 July 1857.

11. Ibid., 5 July 1857.

12. Ibid., 8 August 1857.

13. Ibid., 15 August 1857.

14. Ibid., 18 August 1857.

15. Ibid., 15 October 1857. Willard copied an excerpt from "The Pride of Moses Grant," an unsigned short story in *Harper's New Monthly Magazine,* October 1857, 621.

16. Journal, 8 December 1857.

17. Ibid., 11 December 1857.

18. Ibid., 31 December 1857.

19. In Willard's autobiography, *Glimpses of Fifty Years,* she explained her father's decision to send his daughters to a Methodist-related school. After hearing the president of NU describe Evanston, Ill., as "the Athens of the West," he determined to move to that town and enroll his daughters in

NWFC (97). Her autobiography also gives a sense of Willard's activities during 1858, when she did not keep a journal (97–123).

20. Journal, 5 February 1860. Margaret (Fuller) Ossoli (1810–50) was a Transcendentalist author, translator, and literary and social critic, and one of the outstanding intellectuals of nineteenth-century America. Willard read the two-volume *Memoirs of Margaret Fuller*, edited by Ralph Waldo Emerson, William Henry Channing, and James Freeman Clarke (Boston, 1852), in May 1859.

21. For discussions of the significance of the act of reading and the reading community in the lives of young women in the nineteenth century, see Barbara Sicherman, "Sense and Sensibility: A Case Study of Women's Reading in Late-Victorian America," in *Reading in America*, ed. Cathy N. Davidson (Baltimore, 1989), and Helen Lefkowitz Horowitz, "'Nous Autres': Reading, Passion, and the Creation of M. Carey Thomas," *Journal of American History* 79, no. 1 (June 1992): 68–95. In order to understand what reading meant to Willard, one must read what she read as well as her comments upon her reading. This is especially so for the many novels she read, since the novel, in the mid-nineteenth century, was one of the most important literary forms for the discussion of ethical issues. Novels also traced the developing traits of an emerging middle class. Thus, Willard and her friends, all members of that class, gained from novel reading some of their ideas of what to think and how to behave appropriately.

22. Willard included in *Glimpses of Fifty Years* a letter she had written to Prof. William B. Jones, the principal of NWFC, explaining why she would not go forward to the altar again during a religious revival until she decided she was ready to do so (112–13). Jones had asked for prayers on behalf of Willard's conversion at a college prayer meeting. Embarrassed by Jones's description of her religious state before her classmates, Willard had gone forward to the altar once, but felt that this was hypocritical, given her present doubts about God's existence.

23. Willard, *Glimpses of Fifty Years*, 622. In her autobiography, Willard recounts in some detail her crisis of faith during her illness (622–24). She did not keep a journal at that time.

24. Matthew Simpson (1811–84), an MEC minister and college administrator, was elected bishop in 1852. While bishop, he served as the acting president of GBI from 1859 to 1863. During this time he was the Willards' neighbor. A powerful speaker and an opponent of slavery, he was active on behalf of the Union at the national level in the Civil War years. During Abraham Lincoln's presidency Simpson was able to persuade him to appoint several prominent Methodists to posts within his administration. Simpson preached Lincoln's funeral sermon in 1865. During the 1870s and early 1880s, Bishop Simpson lectured at Yale Theological Seminary on preaching (1879), made several official visits to Europe as a delegate to various Protestant meetings, gave the opening sermon at the Ecumenical Methodist Conference in London (1881), and wrote several books.

25. Journal, 23 March 1860.

26. Ibid., 20 January 1860.

14 February 1859
Evanston, Illinois

. . . It is evening. I am all alone. I will talk with myself awhile.

Father wishes me to be a musician. I have asked myself, "what is the power, the ability to strike in succession several chords upon the piano, melodeon or organ, worth, if it is merely mechanical? If it is no more than an ingeniously constructed automaton might do?" and I have decided with myself that it is worth comparatively nothing. When I hear *music,* it means something to me. It talks with me and tells me that which I did not know before, and makes me by that much, wiser than I was. It conveys ideas to me. If I were somewhat more spiritual, I know I might translate it into words;—and they would be beautiful ones, and the world would listen to them. I do not despair—the time is coming I hope when I may be able to *talk* the music of a few pieces I have heard.—Of the "Silvery Shower," "Mozarts Requiem," "Dead March in Saul," and one piece I heard Mary Bannister play, not long since. Mary B.'s music suits me better than any I have ever heard. I think it is because she comprehends her pieces herself,—renders the soul of them. I wish she was here tonight and I could hear "The desire of an imaginative thought," (I think it is,) played by her.

Mother has been (again) trying to persuade me to relinquish the idea of taking the "Classical Course,"[1] at the N.W.F.C. I will write some of her arguments, and some of mine. She says "You are over nineteen years of age. The romantic numbers,—sixteen—seventeen—eighteen,—are 'passed with you.' The prestige of youth—fresh, blooming youth will soon be over as far as you are concerned. I desire to see you comfortably and happily 'settled in life,' before many years. You are not strong—you cannot protect and sustain yourself—you cannot battle with this great, cold world alone. Your Aunt Sarah has tried it—you know the result;—she cautions you not to follow her example. Your Aunt Sarah was tall and strong too, and better able to 'tug with fortune,'[2] than you are. God has ordered it so. If you act in opposition to His decree you are out of the right path—you are in danger. At the close of the next term, you will have acquired a good education. Your tastes and habits are studious. You will never cease to progress intellectually. Another year of hard study will *'tell'* upon your appearance and your vitality. Another year of subjection to the routine of college duties and regulations will fade you, too. Graduate next July. Be relieved from college restrictions. Then study at home if you choose;—travel—learn to draw nicely—take music lessons—add the polish of the accomplishments to the solid structure of your education, and it will be better. The *world* will like you better. You must take the world as it is, and *not* as it ought to be,—you must not war with your fate. You are *in* Rome;—you *must* do as Romans do.[3] 'They that are not with us, are against us.'[4] It is for your best interest to please the world. Accomplishments—a song—an opera piece well executed,—an elegant sketch—a French translation—fine manners—entertaining conversation—'*takes*' in the 'world,' and will go farther than Latin and Greek—than an extensive acquaintance with literature—than Logic or Geometry. (I mean with regard to *women*.) So be amiable and accomplished and you will derive more happiness from this life than if you are a 'Blue Stocking'—no matter how 'blue.'"

These are Mother's ideas, in my words. They remind me,—some of them,—of one of Lady Kew's speeches to Ethel, in "The Newcomes."[5] Mother has no selfish interest in the matter, (I will be frank and candid,) and has lived much longer than I, and has had much more experience. Oliver advises me to the same course. Many—almost all—of my friends—no, *acquaintances* (remember the *Essay*,)[6] urge me to abandon my intention. And what have I to say to this?

"My mind to me a kingdom is."[7] I have more pleasure in solitude—in Thinking, Reading, and Writing, than in anything else. I feel that I am "coming up higher," every time that I acquire a new idea. I am thirsty for knowledge. Am I to be chained down to the *world*? To do as the world thinks best, and wisest? Have I not more pleasure in my quiet room—lear[n]ing, ever, something new—than these girls—girls that I might name, who "care for none of these things" and care only for those other,—but I forbear. Do I care what people think so long as I know I am honest and pure and true? Shall I cater to the wishes of those who have no interest in me, and who could follow me to the grave tomorrow without a single sigh? Shall I not rather vindicate myself? be true to my own soul? and follow those pursuits that I find most congenial? Ah! I would;—I wish I might "the Spirit" is all resolute and willing. But is it well to beat thus against the prison-bars? shall I not lacerate my own heart by so doing? Am I a suitable judge? do I know what is best for me?

I am not yet decided. When I played those two measures of "Stradella" over and over—I was strong at heart—I was brave and buoyant. But I'm sick now—I waver—hear let it rest for now. . . .

<hr>

1. The two courses of study offered by NWFC led to two different degrees. The two-year Scientific Course that Willard completed required algebra, geometry, trigo-

nometry, logic, natural philosophy, moral philosophy, mental philosophy, botany, chemistry, astronomy, mineralogy, geology, analogy, Bible, biblical antiquities, rhetoric, and domestic economy. The Classical Course required the same subjects as the Scientific Course, plus an additional year of study in Greek and Latin.

2. Willard paraphrased part of a line from William Shakespeare, *Macbeth,* act 3, scene 1, line 112: "So weary with disasters, tugged with fortune."

3. Willard's mother paraphrased a line from Miguel de Cervantes, *El Ingenioso Hidalgo Don Quixote de la Mancha* [English title: *Don Quixote*] (Madrid, 1605–15), chapter 2: "When thou art at Rome, do as they do at Rome," a phrase that by Willard's time had passed into popular speech.

4. Mark 9:40 and Luke 9:50.

5. Willard was reading William Makepeace Thackeray's novel *The Newcomes: Memoirs of a Most Respectable Family, edited by Arthur Pendennis, Esq.* (London, 1855). In the novel Lady Kew urges her granddaughter, Ethel, to make a socially acceptable but personally unsatisfying marriage.

6. Willard had been reading Ralph Waldo Emerson's essay "Friendship" in *Essays* (Boston, 1841). Emerson defines friendship as a spiritual relationship between two people, not a relationship based merely on proximity. Friendship is that which leads to the transcendent beyond the individual. Willard realized that the relationships she had with most people did not reach this profound level of experience, so she termed them "acquaintances" rather than "friends."

7. Willard quoted the first line of a poem by Sir Edward Dyer set to music by William Byrd and included in his *Psalmes, Sonets and Songs* (London, 1588).

30 April 1859

. . . Read "John Halifax, Gentleman,"[1] last week. It is a splendid story. The character of John Halifax is *noble.* I never saw such a man, doubtless I never shall, but *if I do,* I shall feel like worshipping him. O, John Halifax, John Halifax! if we but had men like thee for fathers and brothers how different would we, girls of America, be!— I'll talk frankly with you, Book, I think I'm never to marry. I think I'm to go through the world "single-handed & alone." I think no man is ever to love me,—ever to tell me that I'm dearer to him than any other woman. I've always thought this. But if God wills it differently, if He were to bless me, *glorify* me with the love of a man like John Halifax, I would make myself worthy of him;—I *could* do it! I am hasty, wilful, proud, but there are three powers before which I should be humbled,—God, The Right, and a man like John Halifax! *He* was truly a

> "Man who bore without abuse
> The grand old name of—gentleman."[2]

Not a polite-man . . . not a man "who can smile & be a villain too,"[3] but a man who scorned a mean action as he scorned the devils in hell;—who feared the wrong, more than the pestilence,—who was kind, & meek, & gentle, & *humble;* who never forgot that he was a *man,* not an angel;—that *it was possible* for him to judge incorrectly. Such a man, though the humblest ditch-digger, though regarded with *contempt* by refined society, (bah!) is one of *God's* gentlemen. . . .

1. Willard referred to a novel, *John Halifax, Gentleman,* by Dinah Maria Mulock Craik (London, 1856). John Halifax is an orphan boy who, by hard work and honesty, becomes financially and socially successful. The story illustrates the idea that a true gentleman's character lies in integrity, not in birth and wealth.

2. Willard paraphrased two lines from Alfred Lord Tennyson, *In Memoriam* (London, 1850), part 3, stanza 6, lines 1–2: "And thus he bore without Abuse / The grand old name of gentleman."

3. Willard paraphrased a line from William Shakespeare, *Hamlet,* act 1, scene 5, line 108: "That one may smile, and smile, and be a villain."

3 May 1859

. . . We have a "celebrity" in Evanston;—viz. Lucy Stone Blackwell,[1] ("Mrs. Stone," as she wishes to be called!) I respect her intellect,—I think she beleives she is in the Right. I can't but admire her utter disregard of custom; no, I don't mean that exactly,—I mean I respect *courage* anywhere, & Lucy Stone must possess it, or she would not dare to conduct as she does! I don't like her views, but I would be generous, tolerant, towards them, even as I would have any peculiar beleif I may have respected, not for itself, but because a *human being* honestly maintains it. We're all finite,—God alone can judge between us;—let us not be bitter against each other's pet theories so long as they do not involve vital principles, (by which I mean, so long as they do not tend to overthrow doctrines to which we must be faithful if we would be finally saved). O yes, let us be generous & kindly to our opponents even. So shall we be nobler, so shall we be ascending the glorious Stairway to the Infinite. . . .

1. Lucy Stone (1818–93), the abolitionist and women's rights leader, kept her birth name after marrying Henry Browne Blackwell in 1855. She and Blackwell publicly protested the marriage laws that placed a wife's property, person, and children under her husband's jurisdiction.

16 May 1859

Myself[1]

What I wish to Have
x indicates that I have accomplished what it is placed against.

1
Morally

A conscience void of offence.—(Entire freedom from "undue" obstinacy or egotism.)

A well-founded expectation of a glorious & beautiful life beyond the grave.—Open heartedness.—Dignified respect towards my superiors.

A generous disposition.—Kindness towards my inferiors. A forgiving disposition.—Genial cordiality towards my equals.

The ability to control, *perfectly*, my temper, so that there shall be no "outward manifestation" of it.

2
Intellectually

An excellent education. Possess a rare cabinet of curiosities.

A gold (hunter-case,) watch, and chain. A diamond ring. Ivory Tablets. A jewelry box. A silver pistol. An elegant pair of skates. A protean pen.[2] Fountain ink-stand. Correct "views" of "Forest Home" from twelve different points. One of Prince's melodeons. A music-box playing *American* tunes. Flute. A beautiful secretary, with "secret drawer" &c. completely furnished with writing requisites. A good library of reference. An "Index Rerum."[3] A large, easy chair. Chair with writing apparatus attached. Autograph book. Correct likenesses of all my valued friends. Nice drawing apparatus. Pleasure boat. Newfoundland dog. Life-preserver. Splendid horse & complete equipment for riding. Large & beautiful Bible. Salary of 600 dollars per. year, with a "reserve" for old age. . . .[4]

3
Physically

A neatly,—"attractively"—dressed hand & foot. Darker *hair* than I at present possess!—Clean teeth.—An erect figure. A better complexion.—A freckle-less face.—The ability to dress with entire comfort and well-bred elegance this mortal frame.

What I wish to be and to do.

1
Morally

"Study to be quiet."

2

Intellectually

I wish to *be* a graduate of the N.W.F. College. x To Study French. Study-Phonography. Study Latin.—Go to Europe for intellectual improvement. The ability to *talk* elegantly, usefully, & entertainingly.— To be able to use a sewing machine handily. Have more taste in dress.— Understand more about housekeeping.—An instructive, moralizing, & inspiriting [?] writer.—Study German. Learn not to mix up what I wish to say; and to be able to carry out any classification I attempt. (Note: as I *haven't* done in this Chart!) Be very intelligent,—especially in Literature, History, Philosophy, and the Natural Sciences.[5]

3

Physically

Learn to play the Flute & Melodeon, (for my own Satisfaction)

Learn to play a few pieces on the Piano, (for my friends' [Satisfaction]). Learn to sketch, (finely). Learn to Sing *alto*. Learn the Deaf & Dumb (Manual) Alphabet. Learn to Swim. Learn to "row" & "manage" a small boat. Learn to use Live arms.—Become a good marksman. Learn to Skate.—Go to Europe.—Collect a fine cabinet of curiosities of all descriptions. Take riding lessons until I can ride "famously."

1. In Willard's journal, this entry appears on two facing pages in the form of a chart. On it she organized her schedule of self-improvement for the years 1859–64.

2. A protean pen was a steel pen whose nib could be changed, depending on the degree of flexibility or stiffness the writer wanted to feel between paper and pen.

3. An Index Rerum was a nineteenth-century reference book with information by subject; it included blank pages for the reader to make notes on the contents of books read.

4. Willard later wrote in pencil in the margin, "$700. at Lima." which was the salary she received for her year as preceptress at Genesee Wesleyan Seminary in Lima, N.Y.

5. Willard wrote "(Middling)" in the margin next to the words "Natural Sciences," to indicate the level of knowledge she thought she had achieved.

29 May 1859

The "Grammar Party"[1] is over. There were 150 guests, & all passed off pleasantly. Misses Gordon, Silvey, Bragdon, Atkins, Stewart, H. Wood, J. Wood, McKee, Stilson, Wilson,[2] & myself, were waiters. My dress was nearly ruined. Mary & I were considered worthy to "hold a candle" to Miss Stowe & Miss Shackeford, Editress & Assistant.[3] My dress was tight, & I was very faint once, in the heated rooms, but I quickly recovered. I never enjoy "mixed society." I was not made, I am not, fitted, for it. I am in this one respect like Charles Lamb.[4] He enjoyed the society of a few persons, his *equals,* & companions with whom he was well acquainted, & in whom he had entire confidence. In such society, he was interesting,—by those few friends, he was much loved. Beyond that circle, he was not himself,—appeared grave & confused,—& was considered uninteresting. This is my position now, as nearly as I know how to state it. I am sorry. It is unfortunate, it will cause me much unhappiness, but,—I cannot help it.

"Somehow," I have an unconquerable aversion to intercourse with my superiors in position, age, or education. This is unpleasant, too. I shall lose many opportunities for improvement by this means. I have had opportunity of becoming acquainted with Mrs. Foster,[5] Mrs. Noyes,[6] &—several others, but the *dread* I have of such relations, I cannot overcome. When speaking with such individuals, I can never divest their characters,—their intellects,—of the accidents of wea[l]th, age & position. Hence, I can never be at ease. And if I can not forget these "surroundings" how much less do their possessers forget them! A sublime *rememberance* of our differences,—of the preponderance in the favor, surrounds them,—unconsciously to themselves, perhaps,—with an atmosphere that is suffocating to me. *I cannot help it.* This is one reason why I like books so well. They do not chill me,—they are content that I should absorb the knowledge-nectar they contain, without reminding me of my inferiority to them. They are great, yet most familiar,—they say to every reader, "I am for you, my greatest pleasure is in having your attention." They are great without arrogance,—wise without hauteur,—familiar without degredation. They are full of power & pathos, yet not conscious of it, "they make no sign."[7]

All this is natural, for each man gives us his *best self* in his books, and our *best* selves are above & beyond our fortunate accidents. To books then let me flee. They never frighten me. They "never molest me, or make me afraid." . . .[8]

The paper was good. The refreshments excellent.

The party is over, & I'm very, *very* glad. . . .

1. At the end of every term at NWFC the students and faculty gave a "Grammar Party" with money collected from the fines levied against those who made mistakes in grammar. The students paid a penny per mistake and the faculty, five cents.

2. Cynthia H. Gordon, Fanny E. Silvey, Mary E. Bragdon (see Journal, 28 August 1866, n. 1), Julia Atkins, Martha Jane Stewart, Harriet Wood, Julia Wood, Ortencia Stilson, and Elizabeth D. Wilson were all students at NWFC in May 1859. Margaret (Maggie) McKee (1839–86) and Willard were the only two young women in the

NWFC graduating class of 1859. McKee and Willard remained friends and Willard visited McKee at her Batavia, Ill., home in late summer 1860.

3. Celia E. Stowe (also spelled Stow) and Amelia J. Shackelford (b. ca. 1843) were students at NWFC. They were editor and assistant editor, respectively, of the student newspaper, *Casket and Budget*. The first issue of the paper was published in December 1858. Shackelford, an Evanston resident for several years, was a friend of Willard's during the 1860s.

4. Charles Lamb (1775–1834), the English essayist and Romantic poet, had a stammer, which made him ill at ease in gatherings where he did not know people well. But, as Willard noted, he was relaxed and a good conversationalist with his friends, among whom were eminent British Romantic authors such as Coleridge.

5. Sarah A. (Miley) Foster (d. 1871) was an Evanston neighbor of the Willards, and the wife of Rev. Randolph Sinks Foster, then president of NU.

6. Harriet (Newell) Noyes (1827–1908) was also an Evanston neighbor of the Willards, and the wife of Henry S. Noyes, NU faculty member.

7. Not identified.

8. Not identified.

4 June 1859

. . . Have been looking over the first few pages of this "instalment" of my Journal, & find that I complain bitterly of school's duties & cares. From this, hereafter,—when I've forgotten,—I may infer that I was so narrow-minded as to hate study. I will defend myself. The case is this:— I truly love Knowledge. I thank God most, that He has made us so that we may make ourselves great & wise & good. That we may change ourselves (in mind,) from helpless babes, to strong, steadfast characters. At school we acquire discipline. We learn how to use the implements with which we are provided, for "working" the mine of Truth. Along with this, rules are, perhaps necessarily, I'm not certain,—imposed upon us. These are unpleasant. And the reason why I'm glad that I'm soon to leave school, is this. I can learn, I truly think,—as well alone now. I shall be free from a restraint that is irksome to me. But then, I love my teachers, the Institution which has been truly to me an "Alma Mater," the fellow-students who have been uniformly kind & loving. I hope I take a correct view of the case. O! the glory of *knowing* always when you are in the right! I shall arrive at it!

23 July 1859

. . . Since [23 June] . . . I have suffered much physically & mentally. I have borne great disappointments (for me,) but, as I have suffered, I have *thought*, & I am the wiser & the better for my trial. I have had the Typhoid fever,[1] & am just recovering. The pen trembles in my hand as I write this, I am not strong. Very much of interest has occurred during these unchronicled days. I have seen Oliver's Diploma, & my own. We are *graduates!*[2] How very little does the word mean, & yet, how much! It means years of patient, silent, brain work, discipline, obedience to the will of others. It means that we have started on the Beautiful Search after Truth & Right & Peace. Only started— only opened the door. Thank God! We may go on forever alone. I was unable to receive my Diploma & Mary took it for me. There was no Valedictory.[3] The Examinations & Commencement Exercises passed off creditably to the Institution, I have been told. . . .

It was the disappointment of my life, that I was unable to bear my examinations, read my essay, & graduate regularly. I have borne it stoically; I have shed no tear, & said little about it,—but I have thought.

His hand has crushed me, & not without reason,—not, I hope, in vain.

I shall be twenty years old in September, & I have as yet, been of no use in the world. I have been a trouble & a burden. When I recover—when I possess once more "a sound mind in a sound body"— for I have been thus blessed—I will earn my own living—"pay my own way"—& try to be of use in the world. It will,—it shall—be better that I have not died. . . .

1. Typhoid fever is an acute infectious disease spread through polluted food or water. The infection lasts three to four weeks, the patient either recovering or dying in the fourth week. The disease was common in the nineteenth century because of contaminated water supplies, and was very often fatal.

2. Oliver Willard graduated from Beloit College, Beloit, Wis., on 13 July 1859, and Frances Willard graduated in absentia from NWFC on 14 July 1859.

3. Willard was to have given the valedictory speech but since she was ill, no one gave her speech, "Horizons," which she had written before her illness. The text of the speech, with explanatory headnotes, appears in Amy Rose Slegall, "Good Woman Speaking Well," 88–94.

28 September 1859

My twentieth Birth Day! Ah well! The "Beautiful Ages" are over. Girlish "fifteen," "sweet" "sixteen," graceful "seventeen," proud "eighteen," dignified elegant "nineteen" have "circled, singing, out of sight,"[1] & bleak & cold and ringing, "twenty" whistles in my ear! I pause before the mirror; a very rare act with me; I pause, though the pin is "all right,"—and the thick short hair smooth. What practical right have I to gaze "yet a little longer"?[2] Surely, I have little reason to look;—small pleasure can come of it! for,—& I say it quietly, & reverently—I settled it long ago with my heart, that God saw it to be right that I should have "no beauty that I should be desired";[3] that no sunny locks & sparkling eyes, & winning looks should ever soften any heart to me. That none should ever gaze upon my poor face,—as I have gazed on some,—till the tears should fill their eyes,—tears of pride & thankfulness that the Great Fashioner had sent upon the world one so beautiful.—No, I am not deceived. I have read the face that has been given me, over & over, & I know it all by heart, & need not that mirror or thoughtless tongues should tell me that I'm plain. When I was younger, I was rebellious & angry that it was so. I longed for beauty as the flowers, for sunlight. Not more for beauty intrinsically, did I pray than for the regard it would awaken. For, talk of Human Nature's dignity as we will, the world's Heart is not easily softened, and happy is it for those who, by the strange alchemy of beauty, can undo its many & mysterious folds. But I was telling why I stood before the glass.—Because I wanted to see what the two decades had done. And truly their work is wonderful! They have changed the little four pound baby with white, blue-veined face and dimly covered crown,—they've changed the "muling, puling" little thing that kept its pa & ma awake "o' nights," & irritated the temper of its four year old brother—to a very different being, who is 5 ft. 2 1/4 in. in height, weighs 95 lbs. and looks—far differently—its hair having increased in quantity, & improved (by *darkening*) in quality; its face exhibiting freckles not a few, & traversed here & there & everywhere by the blue veins afore mentioned—mouth wholly negative & characterless, nose ditto, teeth quite good, eyes serving one lone purpose—that of seeing,—"other, none." As I gaze calmly, I think the expression of my "phiz" when "in repose," rather severe, somewhat determined,—nothing more. Two or three wrinkles are just visible, traversing the forehead "latitudinately."(!) And thou, O soul, lookest out upon the body thou inhabitest, scannest coolly, the work thou hast wrought upon it, & remarkest, as would another! Be not so uncharatable. Love the poor, plain face, for none other will love it so well. Be very good friends, & comfort ye each other. Yes, I have seen twenty years. God forgive me for the little of good, the much of evil that I have done! I have lived twenty years, & no soul is the better or the happier! I have breathed the freshening air of so many beautiful young springs; seen so many summers round into splendor; dreamed through the hazy autumns & the winters severe. Well, the world has been good to me,—I find it pleasant to live. I hope I am thankful for the calm happy life I've enjoyed. Childhood was holy & sweet, but it has passed away; youth is strong & courageous—youth the dewy & balmy! youth the vigorous & tense! your energy inspires me now. If not in my eye, yet is the eagle light gleaming in my heart! If God shall help me—you shall not have been given me in vain! I will strive always to be young in soul. I will be strong & steadfast for I am eternal! The body may tire—the hand droop—but within all, I'll keep the soul alive!—Aught else is but accidental—be it of good or ill. A woman's life is a glorious one lived well—but it is not easy. Then must I struggle the more faithfully. And O, I pray devoutly, "May the twenty years coming whether on earth or beyond it, prove that I have not striven in vain." Repining not, may I accept my destiny. . . .

1. Not identified.
2. Willard may have paraphrased either Isa. 10:25, "For yet a very little while, and the indignation shall cease . . . ," or Heb. 10:37, "For yet a little while, and he that shall come will come, and will not tarry."
3. Willard paraphrased Isa. 53:2b, "and when we shall see him, there is no beauty that we should desire him."

23 October 1859

Just returned from listening to a fine lecture by Dr. Foster,[1] and an excellent sermon by Bishop Simpson. . . .

Ever since I was sick, I have thought much of Religion. I wish that I stood in right relations to God. I wish I could practically apply the intellectual belief I have in Christ. I wish I could trust in him whom I have not seen, as I trust even in my friends on the earth who are tangible to me. I wish when Bp. S. says "Leave it all to Christ," "give him your heart, just as it is, with all its sins upon it," I knew how to give it him. I wish I could *feel* my sinful condition.—I see it, I acknowledge it, intellectually, but I don't *feel* it. O, Christ and Heaven seem to me *afar off,* and my conscience is very quiet, seared by my long neglect of its admonitions. Though not an "outbreaking" sinner, yet I have been a fearful one. My influence has been all wrong, my purposes intensly selfish. I have sinned in the broad light of noon day. How carefully have I been reared—how diligently have I been instructed; how have I been shielded from the evil influences that are in the world! Yet I have disregarded it all. And I sit here, surrounded by mercies and blessings, and love and kindness;—I sit here bathed in the sunshine of this hallowed and beautiful day, and write all this with perfect calmness, nay, almost with serenity! I am indeed, very, very far astray. But I shall not give it up. I intend immediately to be a Christian. For Christ's sake, I ask Thee, O Lord, to spare me until then. Divest me of all false pride, let me *feel* as I *see,* how glorious a thing it is to be at peace with Him by whom I was created, by whom I am preserved. Let me truly repent, and help me to please Thee, and to be useful in the world, I ask it very humbly and sincerely, *only* for Christ's sake.

1. Randolph Sinks Foster (1820–1903), minister, educator, and bishop of the MEC, was president of NU from 1857 to 1860. The rest of his long career was spent in churches in and around New York City, and as professor and, then, president of Drew Theological Seminary, Madison, N.J., from 1870 to 1872. Noted for his preaching, Foster also wrote voluminously. He was elected bishop in 1872.

13 November 1859

Sabbath. This morning, attended Dr. Foster's lecture at the University. The text was Prov. 23.7. (or vice versa, I cant say which,) "As a man thinketh in his heart, so is he."[1] Dr. F. demonstrated with sufficient certainty, that any one may know by his thoughts—by carefully analyzing them, & ascertaining what his habitual trains of thought are,—just what he is himself, & may from them predict what he will be. This he dwelt upon at length, with convincing earnestness. I never before thought much of the subject, but this morning I did. I think it right for me to be candid with myself,—and to write down in my Journal today, what my thoughts habitually are. O Lord,—if Thou wilt hear any prayer of mine,—I ask Thee, very humbly, to help me to be honest with myself, while I write of the things of which I "think in my heart."

All my life, I have thought much of myself. What I was to do & be, to acquire and enjoy, has been my cheif concern. Probably I have thought ten times of myself where I have thought once of any thing else. Indeed, taking a broad,—yet none the less a *truthful* view,—*all* my thoughts since I began thinking have been selfish ones. If I passed through my mind the thoughts of others,—of poets,—historians—men of science—it was that in them or through them, I found enjoyment. I have studied because in most instances, I had a keen relish for the act itself, or because in other instances, I saw that "good would come of it,"—not to my fellows,—to my family—to my friends, but good to *me*—simply that & nothing more. If I have a generous thought—as men would call it—and embody it in a kind action,—as those who observed me would consider it,—it is yet selfish, for I do it, not so much for the good of the recipient as for the reflex, pleasurable influence upon myself. If, when I was younger, I looked into the clear sky of an exhilerating June day, & said "I thank Thee O God that Thou hast made me,"—the act, the words were selfish still. Indeed I find, that all these twenty years, I have unthinkingly been living wholly to myself. My thoughts may be thus classified. They have flowed on in these eight channels. . . .

(1) The Aesthetical—

(2) The Ambitious
(3) The Acquisitive. (This refers purely to knowledge.)
(4) The Love of Truth as Truth. (desiring to know of it)
(5) The living over & over in my mind, past scenes & incidents which had been pleasant to me.
(6) The living over unpleasant scenes & incidents with an accompanying feeling of anger or "displacence."
(7) The wishing many & many times for an intimate & congenial friend.
(8) The occasional wish that I were a Christian simply that at last I might not be eternally lost.

Having written the forgoing, I paused, & pondered seriously. I looked over the list, and I am certain that every thought I ever had in my life may be referred to one of those eight divisions. They are my Thought Channels written out as candidly as I can write them.— I have had longings to know of God, regrets for past misdemeanors, resolutions for amendment—but these may be classed, the first with the 4th division, the second to the 6th, the third to the 6th, also, or as a consequence of it. It is not creditably to you "my heart"!—this inventory I have taken. What is the inference from it, what is the prediction which it involves?

The inference is that mine is an unregenerate, a totally depraved nature. That when I have, in my blindness, dared to think that I had some noble qualities, some generous impulses, some attributes worthy of respect & love, I deceived myself—ah how woefully! The Prophecy = That, if I continue as I am, I shall be useless to the world, hateful in the sight of God, and shall *procure for myself* everlasting misery after this life.

I have, formerly, thought most in the 1, 2, 7, 3, & 5 divisions named. Since my recent illness, it is just to say that I have thought most of God. Underlying all my ideas & wishes, has been the idea that Christ would love & pardon me, if I rightly asked him,—the wish that I were reconciled to God, and doing good in the world. As yet, I have no light, but, I will not, if God will help me, be wearied in striving.

This morning, Mr. Bragdon[2] gave us—or *read to us*—a sermon on evil speaking. I honestly think the spirit manifested by the Rev. gentleman hardly gentle & loving & forgiving, & I also think the sermon to have been ill advised, nevertheless, I will try to profit from it. It brought the subject clearly before me, & vividly reminded me of my numerous violations of the commandment to "bridle the tongue." I *will* strive, earnestly, to say nothing detrimental to the character of any one who is not present to defend himself, unless to protect the innocent from wrong. (*memorandum*. To read the chapter in Wayland's Moral Philosophy,[3] on "Character.")

Joined Mrs. Pearson's[4] Bible Class. She requested us to pray this prayer often, during the week that is coming. "O Lord, show me myself." *Query*—will it not be right to add—"show me as much of my sinful nature as I can *bear* to see"?

Here are two things I will certainly keep in mind, & cause to become habits of thought & action.

1 Speak evil of no one, &c,
2 Think over at night all I have learned or done, during the day.

1. Prov. 23:7.
2. Charles P. Bragdon (1808–61) was Willard's minister at the MEC of Evanston, Ill. He was appointed to Evanston in October 1859 and served there for one year.
3. Willard was reading Francis Wayland, *The Elements of Moral Science* (Boston, 1834). This popular textbook, designed to systematize basic rules of conduct and to suggest the most efficient way of cultivating one's moral character, went through numerous editions between 1835 and 1870.
4. Hannah Stevens (Bailey) Pearsons (1820–1909) was an Evanston neighbor and member of the MEC of Evanston. In 1872 when Willard was dean of women at NU, Pearsons became the president of the Woman's Educational Aid Association of NU.

27 November 1859

. . . Spent all day Friday at Prof. Noyes.[1] Mrs. N. is one of the most intelligent ladies I have ever seen. She is eminently one of the Right Thinking. I derived much profit from her conversation,—particularly on religious subjects. She says, that from her own experience & observation, & from what she knows of the views of eminent Divines, (among whom she mentioned Dr. Arnold, of Rugby,)[2] she thinks any one seeking to gain the Quietness of God, has but to read the Bible thoughtfully, prayerfully, in a teachable Spirit, & to pray to God just so much, & no more, as they can pray with earnest sincerity, at the same time, in their every-day, outside life, doing as well as they can, asking for help always from Him who heareth prayer. She advised me to read the Bible slowly, carefully, thinking always, "How should I understand this if I had never heard it before?"

Beleiving what Mrs. N. has told me to be reasonable, I will try to do these things. . . .

1. Henry Sanborn Noyes (1822–72) was professor of mathematics, Latin, and other subjects at NU. He served as acting president of the university from 1855 to 1856 and from 1860 to 1867.

2. Thomas Arnold (1795–1842), the British minister, educator, and historian, was the headmaster of Rugby, a renowned British boys' school. Willard was reading Arthur Penrhyn Stanley, *Life of Dr. Arnold* (London, 1844).

28 November 1859

. . . Every morning I make these four resolves:—

1. To keep my Temper.
2. To avoid "back-biting."
3. To converse as well as I know how.
4. To "think over" every night, the deeds, thoughts, & acquirements of the day.

I regret to say that every day I *don't* keep, inviolably, any one of these resolutions! . . .

2 December 1859

There stands my text—the engraving at the head of the page.[1] Contemplate it! "Under sentence of death for treason and murder." Would you think it? Does John Brown look like a bad man? This is the day of his execution. Even as I write, at eleven o'clock of this clear-winter day, the brave old man is anticipating the fulfillment of that terrible sentence—"you shall be hanged by the neck until you are dead."

I have been reared a beleiver in Anti Slavery doctrines. At first, I received them on faith—afterwards on evidence. Thomas Jefferson's memorable words: "All men are born free and equal," lie at the foundation of our noble Declaration of Independence, and I receive them in their full and significant meaning. Such beleif is above and beyond parties and politics & statesmen—it is an abstract Idea, and is one of the grandest ever comprehended by a human soul. In the light of it, American slavery—the absolute control of one body & soul over another body & soul—is a living and daily repeated lie; a lie told by the people of the United States to the world. For we said all men were born free & equal, & by our acts we contradict our own assertion. John Brown saw this. He thought it possible that he might wipe this monstrous Falsehood from the land. Acting upon the Bible command, "Do ye unto others as ye would that they should do unto you,"[2] he risked his life to help his fellow men—the slaves of the South, & he has lost it. I do not beleive him to have been insane or fanatical. I beleive him to have been a Christian man of strong, unwavering mind. I beleive that in his sight who is greater than Virginia and her rulers, John Brown's *intention* was righteous—and his death the death of a martyr as much as was that of John Knox or Hugh Latimer.[3] Posterity will view it so. A shame has come upon our Nation today that no repentance shall avail to dissapate. Viewed in the pure Moral Light, beside which all else grows paltry and insignificant, Gov. Wise,[4] "Democracy," "Policy," "Public safety," sink into nothingness, and the great, eternal *Wrong* that has this day been done, rises fearful to contemplate, portentious in character, before the Mind. Men may prate their puerile, shallow theories of safety and pleas of necessity; men may raise their poor, weak hands against immutable Justice today, but the Infinite Jehovah ruleth over Tomorrow. "Judgement is not executed speedily,"[5] but it shall come at last.

Governor, Judge, & Jury are great men today, and think and act as they will, but Tomorrow they pass away;—and yet, the Power that transcends all other powers, continues, sure & steadfast.

Because I love my Country truly, I could weep for her today—for I remember that when John Brown went to the Scaffold God saw him, and angels covered their grieved faces—for, if their were ever tears in Heaven, methinks it was today, when the wrong unspeakable was done, and the consequence terrible was dared.

It is evening. Tidings have come that Brown was executed this morning. For him I can have no regrets. He is happier tonight than all of us who are upon the earth.

But towards those men who have this day brought us into reproach before God and our fellows, I feel mingled anger, pity, and disgust. If I might speak to them of their crime, I would but wish to stand with them out under the stars tonight—and when all was still and tranquil, I would wish to point them up to the watchers in the Heavens, and say "God saw; God will remember"!

1. Willard had pasted into her journal at the beginning of this entry an engraved drawing of John Brown (1800–1859), the radical abolitionist whose single-minded determination to free slaves, by violent means if necessary, led him to attack a federal arsenal at Harper's Ferry, Va. (now W.Va.), on 16 October 1859. He and his small force of African Americans and whites were captured, tried, and sentenced to death. Brown was hanged on 2 December 1859. Northern abolitionists looked upon him as a great hero and he became something of a martyr for the antislavery cause.

2. Matt. 7:12 and Luke 6:31.

3. John Knox (1505–72), the Scottish preacher and leader of the Calvinist Reformation in Scotland, did not die a martyr's death, as Willard suggests, although his career was marked by sharp attacks on the rulers of England and Scotland for their accommodations to Catholicism. Hugh Latimer (1485–1555), an English priest, bishop, and reformer, was burned at the stake in 1555 during the persecutions of Protestants initiated by Mary I of England.

4. Henry Alexander Wise (1806–76) was governor of Virginia from 1856 to 1860 and signed John Brown's death warrant.

5. Willard paraphrased Ezra 7:26, "Let judgment be executed speedily upon him."

12 December 1859

. . . Yesterday Bp. Simpson preached in the evening. He feels what he says. He is, I think, the most holy man I have ever seen. I would give much to have him pray for me to God. Several went forward to the Altar for prayers. I shall go when I feel impressed with a desire, a need, a necessity to go. I shall not go before. I hope I may feel on *The* Subject. But certainly,—I almost fear to say it,—I never felt more fiendish indifference than I did last night. God help me—God forgive me!

14 December 1859

Last night attended church. Bp. Simpson preached. His sermon was—as I think—the most movingly practical of any I have ever heard. A few things that he said, I will write here for the truth and value that is in them. He told us that it was idle in an unconverted person to wait for *feeling* before he attempted to become better. He said you might as well tell a frozen person to feel warm as a frozen heart to melt. First the sinner must commence to do what his reason taught him was best, and in the act of striving for the right, feeling would come. He said these three things were what a seeker after Righteousness should do: 1st. Read the Bible. (The New Testament.) He would not attempt to say how it was, but in reading God's Revelation to man there was great benefit—even when it was read coldly by the unconverted. 2nd. Asking God to show you the true meaning of what you read, and to impress it upon your mind. 3d. Reflecting upon Life, Death and Eternity and our relation to things Past, present, & to come. (He compared the position of the soul—with angels waiting & watching from above, & fiends grasping at it from below, to an incident which I will not stop to relate, but which I shall not forget. The picture is in my memory forever—the eternal human soul in jeopardy!) About going forward to the altar for prayers, I have always had doubts. Friends of mine who are Christians have advised me not to do so, and I have thought it unwise to do so. Bishop Simpson presented the matter in a new light. He said we had sinned publicly. We had not been careful to do evil and say evil in private. But now we think we must repent in secret places. He said, "My dear friends, you have thought it a little thing to sin publicly, and it is just and right that you *publicly* declare by your actions if not by your words that you intend to stop sinning;—that you intend with Christ's help to be reconciled to God."

This seemed to me reasonable. I wished to go—I was very much agitated—I could see my heart beating—and yet I stood there apparently calm and careless & *resisted*. No, I did not go, I did not try for forgiveness as I have often thought I would. I stood in my place very quietly. Fool! Fool! I shall never again think it idle to openly declare oneself on the Lord's side. I think I will go tonight. And yet I may not. I cannot tell. Alas the day has come when I cannot rely on myself—cannot master myself!

Not in particulars perhaps, for that I have fought against—but in generals, I think myself fearfully, wonderfully, shamefully proud. I am unwilling to commit myself sufficiently to acknowledge to my best friends the love I truly have for them. I think as an invariable rule that among my companions—outside the family,—I treat those most haughtily whom I love most sincerely. I despise this trait in myself;—in the very moment in which I find myself conquered by it, I am always wishing I could do otherwise,—I am always

"Sighing, cursing this undying Human Pride." . . .[1]

1. Not identified.

16 December 1859

I have commenced! O Lord! I am trying to redeem the solemn promise I have made to Thee. I have publicly declared my determination to forsake my sins—to seek forgiveness for the past and help for the future; to endeavor with Christ's help,—always with Christ's help,—to live a good, true, valuable life—a life that shall glorify God and be a blessing to my fellow toilers and sufferers on the earth.[1]

I have not yet the change of heart that Christ has promised to those who ask Him rightly, but I expect it.

I feel inclined to do right more than I ever did before;—it is easy for me to be obliging and patient today, and it was never *easy* before. This is not of myself. I know that the *third person of the Trinity*[2] is helping me, even as Christ has said.

I will never stop trying. I have not commenced in my own strength,—I never could have done so—nothing is more distasteful to my *nature* than what I did last night—and yet, I found it easy, for Christ,—the Christ part of God—was helping me! . . .

1. Willard wrote in the margin beside this entry, "The Day that stands Alone." On this day she publicly declared her intent to lead a Christian life.

2. Willard alluded to John 14:26, where Jesus promises to send the Holy Spirit—the third person of the Trinity—to help his followers remember Jesus' teachings.

22 December 1859

. . . Though I have yet no evidences of that change of purpose—that reconciliation to God—that active Peace—which I beleive accompanies conversion, I am not discouraged. I see many reasons to hope that gradually I shall come to be "in the light as He is in the light."[1] I enjoy reading the Bible, and I used to dislike it; I am willing & glad to talk with my friends about the Interest of all our lives, and I used never to mention it; I find it today comparatively easy to be silent when angry—not as easy as it was on one day I have referred to—a day that stands upon my calander alone in its purity,—but yet, not as hard as it is usually. I beleive that if I pray earnestly for Christ's sake & if it be God's will,—for more light; if I read the Bible thoughtfully, & reflect upon what the Past has done, the Present is doing & the Future will do for me, I shall "through the forbearance of God"[2] come to be a child of His. There are several chapters in the book of Romans that help & comfort me, and anything that Christ has said I love to read & think about. O! how kind and loving and gentle was Christ! He never was harsh; he never was severe; he "knew our frame, he remembered that we are dust."[3] He had sympathy and pity and compassion for us always! He never was impatient, He never was tyrannical; He was tempted even as we are tempted, and yet, without sin! How forgiving was his spirit, how tender! What a Heart was that which beat in the bosom of the Christ-God! What a great, yearning, pitiful Heart! What comforting words He left for us, before he went back to His "Father's house"[4] to plead for the children of men as long as one shall remain upon the earth who is unforgiven! What a message is this that has gone out into all the world: "Come unto me, all ye that labor and are heavy laden, and I will give you rest; take my yoke upon you & learn of me, you shall find rest for your soul."[5] I have come to beleive that in one way or another, every human being is "weary, and heavy laden." We try to disguise it, but we are tired and faint in our hearts; we find it not a little thing to live bravely and well; we find that toil is our portion; labor of body or of brain; labor in the heart, aye! in the heart;—how very cheering then are Christ's words. And these, "In the world ye shall have tribulation, but fear not,—I have overcome the world."[6] O, Thou who art so kind, help me to see the glory of Thy character! Help me to serve Thee, and to *strive* always to be like Thee! . . .

1. 1 John 1:7.

2. Rom. 3:25.
3. Ps. 103:14.
4. John 14:2.
5. Willard paraphrased Matt. 11:28–29, "Come unto me, all ye that labor and are heavy laden, and I will give you rest. Take my yoke upon you, and learn of me; for I am meek and lowly in heart: and ye shall find rest unto your souls."
6. John 16:33.

2 January 1860

Resolves for 1860. (If I shall live.)

1. I will try to live a Christian life, God helping me.
2. I will bear with the whims and trying peculiarities of those with whom I am nearly connected, remembering their ceaseless friendliness to me, & not forgetting my own faults and unfortunate idiosyncrasies.
3. I will endeavor to improve myself intellectually and socially. The former by study, writing & thought, and the latter by conversation, and the cultivation of kind & friendly feelings towards all my fellow beings.
4. I will studiously devote one hour every day to Historical Reading—beginning with Gibbon's Decline & Fall of Rome. . . .[1]

1. *History of the Decline and Fall of the Roman Empire* (London, 1776–88) was the best known and most ambitious work of the English historian Edward Gibbon.

17 January 1860

On Sunday went to Love Feast.[1] I have united with the M.E. church on probation,[2] joined the Class at the College,[3] have publicly declared my determination to endeavor in Christ's strength, to live a right life—as *right* as I am able. After a sermon by Rev. Mr. Hitchcock, (Presiding Elder,)[4] I partook of the emblems of our Savior's blood that was shed, & his body which was broken for us. It was very solemn, & I prayed earnestly that I might never falter in the new life I have begun to live. Amid many errors and wanderings & failings, my *purpose* to be a Christian is firm & steadfast. *God hears my prayers.* After Sabbath School went to the Congregational church and listened to a beautiful and thought-provoking sermon by Rev. Prof. Bartlett,[5] a minister whom I like exceedingly to hear. His text was (Rom. 2.4.) "or despisest thou the riches of His goodness & forbearance and long-suffering, not knowing *that the goodness of God leadeth thee to repentance?"* I never was more impressed with this wonderful and glorious truth.

How near God comes to us, and we know it not! How blind we are to His infinite, unceasing, all-encompassing goodness! Filling the whole universe—finding its simile only in light that floats richly & joyfully & abundantly over every thing—God's goodness; God's pity! Themes for an angel to dwell upon, but for mortals to *feel* and *know* every moment of their lives. . . .

1. The Love Feast in the Methodist tradition was a service of thanksgiving and fellowship, where small groups of church members gathered around a table, broke bread, gave thanks, and took offerings for the poor. Love Feasts began among the early Christian churches. German Pietists revived the practice in the late seventeenth century, and John Wesley, Methodism's founder, influenced by Pietism, established the practice among Methodists.

2. Willard joined the Evanston MEC as a probationary member, which meant that for a six-month period she became acquainted with church members and studied the discipline and doctrines of the church, while church members examined her life and habits. At the end of six months, Willard could appear before the congregation to answer questions about her faith and knowledge of her church. If the answers were satisfactory, she could then be admitted to full membership.

3. The class meeting developed in early Methodism in England and America partly to respond to the need for better pastoral care for members. Class meetings occurred once a week for Christian fellowship and nurture; members gave and were given spiritual advice or reproof by the class leader, and misunderstandings between members were corrected. The class meeting ended with prayer and thanksgiving. Willard's class meeting was held at NWFC.

4. Rev. Luke Hitchcock (1813–98), an MEC minister, was a presiding elder of the Rock River Annual Conference of the MEC for seventeen years. The MEC was (and still is) divided into geographical regions called annual conferences, over which bishops presided. Each annual conference was divided into several districts in which presiding elders superintended. The elders' duties were to supervise and care for all the ministers in their district and to act as a sub-bishop in matters of discipline.

5. Samuel Colcord Bartlett (1817–98) was a Congregational minister who served Chicago's New England (Congregational) Church in 1857. In 1858 he became professor of Biblical Literature at Chicago Theological Seminary but continued to preach occasionally in the surrounding area.

20 January 1860

. . . Attended Prayer Meeting[1] last eve. I have united with the Methodist Church because I like its view of the Doctrines taught in the Bible, better than those of any other branch of God's militant church, because I have been reared in it, & for me to attach myself to any other would cause great sorrow & dissatisfaction in quarters where I should most desire to avoid such consequences,—other things being equal. In my life, I have seen a great deal of narrowmindedness & bigotry—down right *bigotry* manifested by church members—those who profess to be followers of Him who said in his great, all-encompassing wisdom & kindness "There is neither male nor female, bond or free, but ye are *one* in <u>*Christ.*</u>"[2] Before I ever declared myself determined to live,—being helped by God—a Christian life, I resolved to educate in myself an antisectarian spirit—to live against it, write against it, talk against it, always. And I honestly believe that I regard all the churches—the branches, rather, of the *One* Church—with feelings of *equal kindness* & fellowship. For myself under existing circumstances I prefer the one to which I belong, but that a person belonged to *that* church & was a true Christian, would be to me no more of a recommendation than that he was a true Christian & belonged to any other. The churches are all good & fighting nobly & zealously to make the world better and happier. O, I earnestly pray that as I grow older the kindly, all-loving, catholic spirit may more deeply seat itself in my heart!

I intend to observe all the customs & usages of the church. I have resolved never to be absent from Sabbath services, Communion, Sunday School, Class Meeting or prayer meeting, save when it is *unavoidable.* I will talk to any one upon the only Great Subject in the world, whenever & wherever, & however, my best, prayer-guided judgement teaches me that it will be appropriate—that it will *not* be so ill-timed that it will so jar upon the individual's prejudices & modes of thinking as to be the means of ill to him rather than of good. . . .

1. In Methodist tradition, prayer meetings were evangelistic services with sermons exhorting sinners to come forward to the altar to repent.
2. Willard paraphrased Gal. 3:28, "There is neither Jew nor Greek, there is neither bond nor free, there is neither male nor female: for ye are all one in Christ Jesus."

26 January 1860

Last night the "Minervae"[1] held its public meeting in church, and I read my "effort." The exercises throughout passed off successfully. . . . Mary Bannister closed the Debate. It was not so much the arguments she brought forward,—though these were well selected, & well arranged,—as it was the pure & charming *style* of her article, the excellence of her reading & the remarkable sweetness of her voice, that captivated those who listened. It was, as I heard a gentleman say, "'the fitness of things' displayed in the style, ideas, and tones of the voice, and, in turn, *their* fitness to the author of them." I never knew Mary to do as well before. She is a girl of rare ability. The refined, delicate, pathetic character that is in her writings I have never seen equalled by any one I have ever known. That she has much talent is true, &, if *she wills* it the world will acknowledge the truth ere long.

I have always loved Mary Bannister. I knew I should—I knew it was my destiny when I saw her first.—I remember where it was,—the slight, silent figure that was strange to me then,—glided past me on the stairs that lead to the basement where the Chapel is, "over at the College."

I only knew her after the formal fashion, for a long time. At last I came to know something of the life that is out of sight—the only Life I care to know about in one whom I call my friend. And for a while, I am sure she cared about me. But I have many unaccountable & unfortunate moods & ways that I have not yet learned to control, and to them, as I beleive, I owe it that Mary cares nothing—save the common friendliness of a common humanity—for me. And I am accounted fickle and cold-hearted, and, as I beleive she called me once, "incapable of loving very much." It is not true, though she has cause to think it. For a year—I think it is,—we have manifested no particular care for each other—she, I am certain, has none. But,—and it proves that I'm not fickle,—I have loved her next to Father-Mother-sister-brother, all the time. Yet I beleive she does not dream that this is so,— I certainly have tried to "hide it in my heart." I care so much for her, that everything she does or says, seems to me good & pleasant. Whoever speaks kindly & appreciatively of her, I count my friend, for that one act, & think of gratefully. Thus I love her silently & quietly, & "make no sign." It is my *nature,* & I meekly bow to it, & am yet strong & brave, I hope, but, of this strange, untold of friendship that I cherish for the dear girl, I think mournfully, sometimes. . . .

Then came my poem which whether good, bad, or indifferent,— I think I read as though I had faith and confidence in. (Beautiful termination to a sentence?) I expected to be very much frightened, but from some cause that I do not yet understand, I was entirely self-possessed. . . .

1. Willard referred to the members of the Minerva Society, NWFC's literary society, named for Minerva, the Roman goddess of wisdom, technical skill, and invention.

21 February 1860

[*Willard copied into this entry a large portion of Henry Ward Beecher's*[1] *address, "Woman's Influence in Politics," reprinted in* The Independent, *16 February 1860. In his address, Beecher argued that, in the United States, men have the right to rise as high as their capacities allow them and participate in any civic function, unhindered by class constraints. If men, so also women ought to have this right. They should not, any longer, be circumscribed by their gender into a particular sphere in a free, democratic society, no matter what custom or tradition has formerly decreed for their sex. Beecher especially argued for women's right to vote, since they are equally as fitted for civic responsibilities as men.*

Willard drew lines at the left and right margins to highlight the following paragraph of Beecher's address:

> "There is not one thing that man ought to do, there is not one thing that ought to be done, which woman ought not to be permitted to do, if she has the capacity for doing it. For wherever there is a gift there is a prophecy pointing to its use, & a silent command of God to use it. The possession of a gift is a charter conveying to the possessor permission to use it. When God gives man the power to speak, the gift itself is evidence of the Divine intention. When God gives man the power to paint, he is called to be an artist; & when God gives woman the power to paint, she too, is called by that same gift, to do the work which it indicates. And Wherever in all equitable & just functions of civil society, woman has power to do as women do it, a thing which man has power to do as men do it, she is as much called to act, & has as much right to act as he has."]

. . . I should not have copied all of this save that it expresses so truthfully, & so much better than I could, my views on the subject of "Women's Rights." Especially is this true of the passages I have marked.—It seems to me (this passage) to include the underlying Philosophy of the "Movement" in which Lucy Stone is a principal actor. . . .

I am thankful to Thee, O God! that I did not live in the world before the 19th. Century! That I have not acted my part and passed out from the scenes of the earth, but that I am in the midst of the Reforms and Inventions and Civilization of the Present Age. . . .

1. Henry Ward Beecher (1813–87), the famous Congregationalist preacher and writer, was perhaps the most influential spokesman for American middle-class Protestantism during the height of his popularity in the 1860s. An enthusiastic, if cautious, liberal, he supported woman suffrage, evolutionary theology, and scientific biblical criticism. Willard's thinking on many subjects and issues was very similar to Beecher's. He clearly was an influence during the formative period of her intellectual and religious thought.

3 March 1860

On Thursday Evening went to Prayer Meeting with Oliver. With how much pleasure I can never tell, I heard him publicly declare his determination to strive after Righteousness;—to endeavor to live a Christian Life;—to live for the *future,* praying God to forgive the past, & to give him strength in the present.

And now I have to write the pleasantest truth to us, that my note book has ever taken to keep for me: Oliver is going to be a Minister of Jesus Christ upon the earth. Laying aside his long-cherished schemes for acquiring wealth and fame and power—as this world-views it,—he has resolved to consecrate his life to the holy and beautiful work of telling to a blind and suffering world the story of One who so loved it that He gave His Son to die for its redemption; of One whose forbearance and pity and love shuts round us like the sunlight,—enfolds us protectingly and mercifully always;—of One who "knoweth our frame—who remembereth that we are dust;"[1] who is "touched with the feeling of our infirmities,"[2] "who was tempted in all points like as we are,"[3] who "was wounded for our transgressions, who was bruised for our iniquities."[4]

And thus my brother,—my *only* brother—for whom we all have hoped so much, to whom we all have looked so anxiously, is acting worthily;—is following the path to which we have hoped he might be lead, and yet from which we feared he might be driven by Pride and Folly and blindness. And he will travel always safely—and we fear for him no more. Striving for God, for Truth, and for Humanity in this troublesome world, he will walk surely on towards Heaven and Peace and Holiness. And O, I thank Thee Lord, that this has come to pass! I thank Thee that Thou hast guided, that Thou has restrained! I thank Thee for the restful heart I have, because my brother has taken for his own the holiest, highest Calling in all the World! Strengthen him, encourage, teach him, and may he never weary,—never faint till the brief battle is fought, and the eternal victory is won! . . .

1. Ps. 103:4.
2. Heb. 4:15a.
3. Willard paraphrased Heb. 4:15b: "was in all points tempted like as we are, yet without sin."
4. Isa. 53:5.

7 March 1860

. . . Last evening Mary [Willard] and I attended [class meeting], and I spoke in a "Class" for the first time in my life. I know I shall have real enjoyment in going once a week, to this meeting. There is little reserve or formality, and the members are several of them valued friends of mine, in whose presence it is not painful to me to tell of that *life* of the *soul* which I would not relate to indifferent persons.

23 March 1860

It is evening. Father and Mother are in the sitting-room, talking with Dr. Bannister.[1] Oliver is out calling. Mary [Willard] is over at the College. I am sitting in our little room, "alone with myself." I am somewhat sad, and though kindly cared for and sincerely loved by those who are nearer to me than all the world beside, a sense of *unbefriendedness* is in my heart. And I am not sentimental or foolish, either,—this I know. . . . O, if I were but "rich toward God," if I but knew that the Infinite Father at whose behest I started into being, would take me to his loving & pitiful heart, I would like to pass out from among the living, while I sleep tonight. I would like that tomorrow when the sun shines down upon the world once more, and the

"endless toil and endeavor"[2]

is resumed, I might lie, white and quiet,—Oh! very, very quiet,— where the troubles of our life could not reach me any more. To what purpose is all this striving,—and self-sustaining and heart ache? And what is it to pass from this life to another? None but a fool can call it cowardice that would impell me to leave a world that has no need for me, and with it leave much that is hard and painful. God forgive me if I have spoken wickedly! I but wrote out the thought of the moment, as it came into my mind.

1. Henry Bannister (1812–83) was an Evanston neighbor of the Willards, the father of Mary Bannister, and professor of theology at GBI. He and his family moved to Evanston in 1856, when he was elected chair of exegetical theology. He remained at the school for the rest of his career.
2. Not identified.

28 March 1860

. . . Spent the evening with Mary Bannister. Dr. Bannister's kindness and Mary's, in helping me to get a situation as a Teacher, I think I appreciate, and I am very sure I shall not forget. These are not things of which it is my nature to speak much, yet I think about them all the same.

As I sat last night, looking into Mary's beautiful, dark eyes, she little dreamed what great love and tenderness for her, was in my heart! She did not know how much I wished to kiss her forehead and tell her that she was dearer to me than any other save Mother-Father-Oliver-Mary. No, she did not think of this, and it is better, doubtless, for, since she is a favorite with so many, it would be a light thing in her estimation, and it is a very sacred thing in mine. It must be piti-ful—Oh! very pitiful—to ask for love and friendliness and trust, as Miss [Eddie][1] has asked Mary, and to find that the asking is, of ne-cessity denied,—and these are not voluntary matters with us.—I'm quite sure I shall never do this—my pride will be my safe-guard,—and yet, when I saw the noble and loving spirit that was in Mary's eyes—(and,—I *will* say it—they were *glorious* last night,) I almost forgot,—I almost laid my hand upon her head and said—what would have been idle words to her. . . .

1. In her early journal volumes Willard sometimes used an easily deciphered code for short sections of entries. In this entry she wrote Eddy's name in code, "20032," misspelling the last name of Elizabeth Jane (Eddy) Somers (1837–1924), who was preceptress of natural science and mathematics at the NWFC during the 1858–59 ac-ademic year. Eddy may have held this position during the 1859–60 academic year as well. In 1863 she married James W. Somers and moved with him to Washington, D.C., where she continued teaching. In 1875 she founded and opened the Mount Vernon Seminary (later Mount Vernon College) in the city, remaining its head until her re-tirement in 1914.

29 March 1860

Had letter from Mary Bannister telling me what I would rather hear than almost anything else in the world. Telling me . . . that she does truly care for me, that I am not, as I thought,—a cipher to her, but that she has love for me;—and so I know that if, last night, I *had* told her what I wished so much to tell, she would not have disregard-ed it, but it would have been pleasant to her, instead. And so I'm not alone any longer, for one I very dearly love, loves me back again. It is beautiful to me to think of this; it is beautiful to remember that *Mary remembers!* . . .

18 April 1860

Went to "Class" last night. Mr. Taplin[1] was the Leader. I like him very much. He seems so manly and Christian in his views and inten-tions. He has a fine mind and will make a noble Minister of Christ some day.

One thing he said, that I will write:—Perfect faith and Complete Consecration are all that is necessary to a Christian Life.

I gave a very sad account of myself—as the truth forced me to do. I'm not good—and I don't act like a Christian,—but what is worst of all is that I know I might do better—I know if I would pray ear-nestly for help, Christ would guide me, for He has often done so. I know if I read the Bible more and pondered oftener on those words—*Life, Death, Eternity,*—I should become imbued with a right spirit, and the only reason I don't do so is—that I *forget*. Paltry as is the excuse, it is true that I have no other. Forgetfulness is a prominent defect of my character at its present stage of culture. I thought last night that I would try harder than ever before to live *Christianly* this next week. There were pure and good desires in my heart, as I beleive—implanted there by One higher than I, and today I have thought much of my resolve, and next Wednesday I will write of my failure or success. . . .

1. Warren Taplin (1834–65) was a GBI student. He graduated from GBI in November 1860 and from NU in June 1861. He taught at the university for two years, then pastored a church in Yorkville, Ill., until his health failed.

20 April 1860

. . . In evening Oliver and I called for Ella,[1] to go to the "Public Debate" of the Minervae. The Chapel was crowded, and the exercises very good indeed. On the rostrum was a table with lamps and boquets, a melodeon, and seats for the Young Ladies of the Society. As they came in one after another and ascended the steps to the platform, I looked at them with pleasure and thankfulness. I regarded them as, in some sort, the product of all the years of suffering & battle that preceded our American Independence—and going farther back, I thought of the position *woman* occupied in the old Bible times, when they were as ignorant as children and no better than slaves; . . . and I thank God for *Christ* to whom we owe all that we are or may ever hope to be. I looked at them as they sat there,—well dressed and lady-like in appearance, and thought of all the culture and endeavor that had brought them up so high. . . .

Many of them wore the Cross;—the symbol of Christ's death and suffering. I wonder if they thought of the meaning and appropriateness of doing so? They did not doubtless, for it is our unfortunate tendency, to look at secondary causes, and it was thought of, if at all, as a becoming ornament,—a "fashionable" one, just now. I would like always to wear a Cross. Women, of all beings, should remember our Savior. I tremble to think how wretched and demoniac would have been my sojourn on the earth if He had never died;—if He had never taught the world that "there is neither bond nor free, Jew nor Greek, male nor female, but ye are all one in Christ." . . .

1. Ellen (Ella) W. Simpson, daughter of Bishop Matthew Simpson and Ellen

Holmes (Verner) Simpson, was born in Ohio ca. 1843. She was a neighbor and friend of Willard's.

24 April 1860

. . . Went to Class Meeting. Enjoyed it very much.

I can write with truth, that this last week I have been more patient and calm and forgiving than is usual with me. And I find that this is because I have prayed more earnestly, read the Bible more thoughtfully, pondered more upon the three Words—Life-Death-Eternity. And as a natural result of this course, my life has had more *Christ* in it. I have felt that I was being made quiet and strong by One who is higher than I. When I have done right deeds, I have felt that it was not of myself—I have felt surrounded and upheld by God to whom I have prayed. This seems to me now the most beautiful passage in the Bible:—(aside from those that speak of Christ)—

"Thou will keep him in *perfect peace* whose mind is stayed on *Thee.*"[1]

1. Isa. 26:3.

12 May 1860

. . . I read *Mary's*[1] Journal—which she let me take today. As I read it, I pictured my friend, as she looked tonight in Singing School.[2] (Several of us noticed how very well she looked.) I thought of the eyes that to me are more beautiful than any others in the world, looking down upon me as I lay there reading what she had written about me, and I was more happy that she loved me than I shall tell her, ever. O God, may I remember that this Friend of mine—this One Friend who *suffices* me entirely, is a direct gift from Thee! If I can *feel* this I shall be a better Christian for it, and this diamond that glistens among the jewels—few as precious—which I wear, shall only shine to lead me on to Thee—to make me what I wish to be more than any thing else, Calm and Patient and Strong! All my ambitions through the years that are gone, when

> "I heard my days before me,
> And the tumult of my life,"[3]

have merged into this one desire. . . .

1. Willard first underlined Mary Bannister's name in this entry. She explained that it indicated their special friendship, since Willard considered Bannister her best friend outside her own family.

2. Singing schools were a common nineteenth-century social and educational event and were usually taught by itinerant teachers who used methods that did not require the students to read music.

3. Willard quoted from Alfred Lord Tennyson, "Locksley Hall," published in *Poems* (London, 1842), line 110.

17 May 1860

Don't feel well. The old, buoyant, health that was so natural to me until a year or two ago, has not come back, and I think sometimes it never will. The "lung difficulty" I had in the winter of 1859 (and upon conval*escing* (?) from which I commenced—by Dr. Todd's advice (!) [1] to keep a "Note Book") took away the vigor from my life. And I think that often when I call myself intellectually indolent it is unjust, for I feel always dreamy and weak. And I am easily tired. I don't know what it is, anymore, to feel strong and *vigorous* (that last word expresses what I feel that I have lost). But I am free from pain most of the time, (except a chronic soreness in my right side that makes it painful to take a long breath). And this dreaminess that never leaves me, but has gone with me day & night for months, enveloping me in an indefinite *unreality,* is not sufficiently tangible to be talked of, so I say very little about it, even to Mother. . . .

1. In February 1859 Willard was reading Rev. John Todd, D.D., *The Student's Manual: Designed by Specific Directions, to Aid in Forming and Strengthening the Intellectual and Moral Character and Habits of the Student* (Northampton Mass., 1835).

19 May 1860

Yesterday the Republican Convention at Chicago, nominated Abraham Lincoln for President of the United States. I wish I had been in the "Wigwam" [1] when this was done. The accounts which Father and Oliver gave us of the excitement; the cheers, the handshakings, the handkerchief-wavings etc. etc., have made me very enthusiastic. They say we must have laughed or cried if we had been there. I would like to test myself—to try my self control in some such way. . . .

1. The Wigwam was a large hall built especially for the Republican National Convention, 16–18 May 1860, by the Chicago Republican Club. It was located at the corner of Lake and Market streets in downtown Chicago, on land owned by the GBI. The Wigwam burned down in the Great Chicago Fire of 1871.

28 May 1860

Father asked our *Other Father* in his prayer this morning, "to make us feel the responsibility that these peaceful, painless hours impose, and to help us to prepare for the storms that will come—we can not tell how soon."

I have thought much of this. Now when there is not a grief at my heart or a shadow on my path I think but little of God—I find it almost impossible to live a Christian Life. Ah, I need discipline;— the cloud and the torture alone can melt my heart and make God more to me than all the Universe beside. I want to be *right* at whatever cost, so I feel certain if I am made "perfect" it will only be "through suffering."[1]

I am twenty years old and I have neither dignity nor womanliness. I am giddy and thoughtless—as much so as I ever was, I verily beleive. There is a *something* that I can hardly define, but which the word "Character" seems to me to express, that I lack, and which I must acquire. I am not reliable; self-contained; There is not that about me—which those of my age ought always to possess,—which causes people to "keep their distance,"—to have a certain respect for me that will not admit of familiarity. Bell Stewart[2] had it, & she was only twenty; Annie Foster[3] had it and she was barely eighteen when I used to see her last summer. . . .

Now, while it is a shame that I'm not—as they are—it is yet, little wonder. I have not been "brought on" as they have. They have been much in Society, have attended school all their lives, and been trained possibly, to dignity etc.—While I knew no more about "Society" than a—goose or a baby, whichever is more elegant!—until I came to Evanston, and know almost nothing now. Never spent four years in school of all these twenty, "long drawn out" and was "trained" to live "out doors" as much as possible;—to ride and walk and garden and go fishing, if paradventure my life might be saved to me, for I was always "slender"—as Mother calls it. I have never been out in the world, have had no care or trouble, no grief worth mentioning, no "lovyer" (as "Bub"[4] says,) nor any "love affair" to sober me, and *so* since I'm not *naturally* a person of "character," why should I be at all, since the artificial method has never been employed in my case? I am determined to be *just* if not *generous* with myself, for who has a better right?

Now I'm sorry that I'm not more like my Ideal Young Lady, and I'm anxious to be more like her if I can. But I must get my discipline in a rougher school than most young ladies do. I see clearly that I shall never be the "grown up person" that I ought to be, until I have "borne and labored and had patience."[5] And if I become a teacher in some school that I don't like, and if I go away alone, and try what "I, myself" can do, and suffer, & am tired and lonely; if I am in a position where I must have all the responsibility—where there is none to help or counsel me, but I must be "sufficient for myself";—if every thing, is hard for me, and I am alternately the "Hammer" and the "Anvil" (but *always one*)—I think I may grow to be strong and earnest in *practice* as I have always tried to be in *theory*. So I hope to get the school Mr. Eberhart[6] wrote to me about, for it will be *hard* and I need hard things if I'm ever to be a "fine character"—and I wish it more than any one thinks I do—except, perhaps, *Mary*.

If there were no such thing as *striving* forces, I could live contentedly here at "Swampscot"[7] all my days. *But,*—and the knotty little word settles the question.

It is quite curious that just as I wrote the last word John[8] came with "the mail" and on opening a letter addressed to myself, & postmarked "Noyesville,"[9] I found the words "You may consider your self engaged to teach our school" etc. So I'm to go on Saturday to begin my hard battle for myself alone! . . .

1. Heb. 2:10.
2. Isabelle Rebecca (Stewart) Ludlam (1838–99) was an Evanston neighbor of the Willards.
3. Florence Ann (Annie) Foster (ca. 1840–68) was the daughter of Randolph Sinks Foster and Sarah A. (Miley) Foster, an Evanston neighbor as well as a good friend of Willard's. Willard corresponded with Foster during the 1860s about Foster's trip to Europe. While Willard was in Europe, Foster died of tuberculosis.
4. "Bub" was Willard's nickname for her brother, Oliver.
5. Not identified.
6. John Frederick Eberhart (1829–1914) was superintendent of the Cook County Schools from 1859 to 1869.
7. "Swampscot" was the Willards' first Evanston home. They lived there from 1858 to 1865.
8. John Carey (b. ca. 1836), an Irish immigrant, was the Willards' hired man.
9. Noyesville was the post office nearest to the school where Willard would be teaching.

5 June 1860
Harlem, Illinois[1]

I could not write last night. I felt too desolate.

After leaving home, *walking* from the Harlem station to my ugly, dismal *red* school-house through a *marsh;*—riding through the flying mud with some kind hearted ladies to my boarding place and meeting the iciest of receptions; taking dinner, walking more than half-a mile back to my *den* (for it is nothing else than the most comfortless house I ever have seen); going through the tiresome routine, teaching a b c's, spelling, and the like; helping sweep the school house (which is dirty beyond description, with broken windows, *baked* floor and cob webs mingled); walking home again, unpacking and arranging my effects, arranging "Order of Exercises" for my school—after all this, I sat down, very tired and full of heartache, and the tears came into my eyes. To comfort myself I read over two or three of *Mary's* letters—*Mary* my darling,—and the tears fell faster then. I looked around my room;—every thing reminded me of my home, and my friends who love me, and reminded me as strongly of the new life to which I have come with all its friendlessness. *Mary's* portfolio and Ella's[2] daguerreotype lay on the marble-topped bureau of this stranger lady who gives me for three dollars per week a comfortable room with "board & lodging." My desk called *"Our* Room"[3] at home to my memory, and my dresses, arranged in "companies" around the closet echoed the memory back again as it was trying to die away.

And then I wrote to *Mary,* and tears fell on the sheet. No, I'm not very strong; not so strong as I thought. Cold words & heartless looks *jar* me very painfully. And was yesterday, and is today—which is *as* yesterday if not more grievous,—a fair sample of the *wretched* life of the next three months?—I can not bear to think of it. It is like a terrible dream.

It is doubly hard for me, because I have been sick and have done very little for a year—and home is so pleasant and they are kind to me, and I have friends.—My *head* aches as badly as my heart tonight. I'm afraid I can not bear it all. The walk to my boarding place tires me very much, and my limbs are so weary that it hurts me to move. I have written to Ella Simpson and to Han Ludlam[4] today, but I have not told them of any of my troubles—I only mentioned them to *Mary,* the comfort *she* will send me, will suffice.

Father walked over to the School House to bring me a bundle and to say "Goodbye" last night, before he went away.[5] I took what he brought and turned away saying in answer to his half-cheery half-sad words, (for I know he was sorry for me), "Keep up a brave heart and don't let it discourage you."—"Goodbye Father,—I'm not afraid." But the tears blinded me so that I could hardly see to go back to my "teacher's desk" again.

And yet, these people don't know. The rough "school directors" don't dream that I'm not *exactly* in ecstacies even though I'm teaching in *their* "deestrict." And they'll not know, either,—never fear.

I turn to God—the Loving Father who presides over our destinies— with new eagerness. I prayed last night as I have not prayed for months, and went to sleep in the coldness and dark and loneliness with a feeling that somehow, the arms "that reach round all the world,"[6] enfolded *me.* If I can learn to look to Him and try always to obey Him, this bitter life will not have been in vain. And I *shall* learn. Just now I took my Bible and it opened to the passage "Like as a Father pitieth his children, so the Lord pitieth them that fear Him,"[7] and the tears sprang into my eyes afresh!—Those who know my nature would understand that I have suffering now, for I almost never cry;—not twice in a year—if so often. Yes, it is hard—as I knew it would be. But I *can* bear it and I will. None save God and *Mary*—and you, Book, shall know that the Inside and the Outside Life are vastly different. That while one is quiet and unaspiring and firm, the other is full of longing and heart-ache and misery. Of this last I shall not write even in my letters home, for it would do me no good and it would worry Mother.

1. Harlem, Ill., was an area west of Chicago, part of which today makes up River Forest and Forest Park, two adjacent, near-western suburbs, about fifteen miles from Evanston.
2. Ellen W. Simpson.
3. The room in Willard's "Swampscot" home that she shared with her sister, Mary.
4. Hannah Watson (Ludlam) Brown (1841–1927) attended NWFC with Willard and was the Willards' neighbor.
5. Josiah Willard accompanied Frances Willard to her teaching position in Harlem to see her safely settled her first time away from her family.
6. Not identified.
7. Ps. 103:13.

6 June 1860

Last evening had a rather pleasant talk with Clara Thatcher[1] ("the daughter of the house"—at which I board,) and was thus saved an evening's unhappiness. I'm not much of a philosopher. Outside circumstances are very much to me, as yet. Looking at "the case" as hopefully as possible, I think that Clara will make my boarding place a pleasant one, for she is frank and seems kind-hearted. But "School Life" is almost unendurable. Here I have twenty-seven scholars. Five "ABCdarians," the rest all under twelve years old except two girls and one boy. The school house leaks, is small, dirty and meanly constructed as a whole. The children are more than half German, the rest Irish and uncultivated (Oh how emphatically so!) Americans. I have a class in Botany, U.S. History, Algebra, Arithmetic, & Grammar.

It is very cold today, and we have no materials for making a fire. "It rains and the wind is never weary."[2] The house leaks and my desk is wet and I'm completely chilled. I can hardly hold the pen to write of this "hard life"—which I knew was coming to me! I must stay here *three hours* longer—and then walk home through mud that will come over my shoe tops. Yes, it is hard.

Evening. (10 o'cl'k.) I'm half ashamed of the dolorous "tone" in which the above is written, and yet, I need not be, for it is all true, and in stating it *here* I made no one unhappy with the consciousness that *I* was miserable. I only wrote it down for the future "Myself."— After all, I've much to be thankful for. "Billy" Thatcher[3] carried me to school and brought me back, and Clara and I had a very pleasant evening together. We have talked of science and art and books (as far as we were able,) and I find her highly intelligent. Her ideas (in general) seem just and broad, & we shall "get on" well together. My summer—that part of it spent at "Shady Dell," (the name of Clara's home)—will be pleasant & profitable. We've already planned to "pursue" together the following "studies":—

Drawing from Copies. (Clara is quite skillful with her pencil.)
Sketching from Nature.
Constellations.
Botany & Herbarium making.
Entomology. Conchology.[4] Aquarium-making. *and* the
Manual Alphabet.

I think there's something else—but here's enough for once.

Clara is a Senior in the Chicago High School,[5] and we have in tastes & education, many things in common. There can be but *one* "*Mary*" in all the world to me, but she will be a second Ella, and that is more than I ever thought to find here in "Proviso."[6] Thank God humbly & loyally for it all!—I'll try to exert a good influence over this new Friend of mine—I think she has not been reared religiously—and so I'll pray to the kind and wise Father over us, with firm, grateful tones as I try to in my morning devotions at school, and then go to sleep peacefully and more happily than I expected two days ago, or shall deserve—ever.

1. Clara Elsie (Thatcher) Thatcher (1844–1927) was the daughter of David Cunningham Thatcher (see Journal, 10 June 1860, n. 1) and Susanna M. Thatcher (1816–1904). She married Solomon Thatcher, Jr., (no relation) in 1864.

2. Willard quoted from Henry Wadsworth Longfellow, "The Rainy Day," stanza 1, line 2, and stanza 2, line 2, published in *Ballads and Other Poems* (Cambridge Mass., 1842).

3. William H. Thatcher (ca. 1838–64), Clara Thatcher's older brother, often drove Willard to her school in a buggy and picked her up at its close on the way to meet his sister's train as she returned from school in Chicago. William Thatcher was killed in the Civil War.

4. Conchology is the study of mollusks and shells.

5. Chicago High School, from which Clara Thatcher graduated in 1861, was established in 1856 and granted its first diplomas in 1859. It offered a two-year Nor-

mal Department in which students took courses in United States and world histories, theory of teaching, and mental philosophy as well as other subjects; an English (or General) Department in which students took a reading course in English literature and sixteen other subjects including science, political economy, and the United States Constitution; and a Classical Department in which students took Greek and Latin along with other subjects. Thatcher's name does not appear on the list of those receiving the Normal School diploma, so she must have graduated from one of the other two courses, for which graduation records are not available.

6. In 1860 Harlem was a small unincorporated town in the northeast corner of Proviso Township.

10 June 1860

. . . Rose at *nine* o'clock this morning, (!) breakfasted, arranged my room, and am wondering at the strange day I shall spend. Mr. Thatcher's[1] family are not religious—there is no church that I can attend,—no outward form of worship in which I can show the gratitude and love to our Father which is in Heaven, that fills my heart on this bright, beautiful morning. How very different is all this, from a Sabbath in Evanston, where the song of praise is even now ascending from devout worshippers, where the prayer, and words of comfort and healing are even now being uttered. Father & Mother, Sister and Brother are listening to them, *Mary* hears them too, and I know that one of them—if not all,—has prayed this morning that I might be shielded and strengthened and comforted by our God who is over all—"blessed forever."—Mother has wondered what I shall do today, and has hoped in her heart that I might be happy and serene,—that I might live and feel like a *Christian* under whatever circumstances I am placed. And she has prayed for me, and so has *Mary*. They are sitting now in church as I sat, last Sabbath Day. I am alone in my pleasant room—made pleasanter by Clara's thoughtful kindness;—the sunshine is creeping into the window as the day wears on, the breeze plays in and out, bird-worship floats from the grove, and I sit here tranquil and peaceful as then.—The younger members of the family have taken their pony and ridden off to "the strawberry patch" to spend the day. The proprietor of the house sits in the Library below, with six or seven friends who have ridden out from the city, and they smoke their cigars and talk of horses and races and "sporting" and the like. The mistress of the establishment is busy superintending the preparation of the "Sunday Dinner" that "the style" here requires. (Mr. T. is a rich man, and "fares sumptuously every day.")[2] Clara is flying about—poor child, she has a kind heart and many right desires,—more than I should have had I fear, with her education.—'Tis a queer Sabbath—I never spent one like it. God help me to remember Thee and Heaven and Holiness while all around is "of the earth, earthly."[3]

Have had no letters from Evanston yet, though they are more than "due." Though sorry and disappointed about it, I am not angry or "jealous" because they have not written. I trust them wholly, and beleive they have thought kindly of me very often during this first week of my troubles, though I have had no message from them to cheer and strengthen me. . . .

1. David Cunningham Thatcher (1810–69), a wealthy Chicago merchant, moved from Massachusetts to Chicago in 1837 and settled in Harlem in 1854. He established an arms and ammunition store at the corner of Lake and Franklin streets in Chicago that prospered, enabling him to purchase 640 acres of land in and around Harlem.

2. Luke 16:19.

3. Not identified.

11 June 1860

. . . When school was out, I walked briskly up to "Harlem Post Office" *certain* that I should get letters from Home and *Mary*. I noticed that as I thought of this I walked faster and faster,—it was almost laughable. At last I reached the Office and the clerk handed me *four letters*—one from *Mary* (how eagerly I glanced them over in search of it!) two directed in Father's rapid, business hand—and one from my "Naturalist Friend" Edwin Clifford![1] I turned around hastily, tore open *Mary's* letter and devoured it as I walked back to my "Seminary" to wait till Clara should come on her way from school. I didn't open Father's & Mother's & Mary's (W.) first because they are my own, and getting a message from them is almost like receiving one from myself (if such a thing can be imagined!) but *Mary* is kin to me in *soul* and I have waited so for the words of comfort and love that I beleived she would send to me that I was almost perfectly happy when I held her letter in my hand. And then to think that I have been troubling myself with the idea that she didn't answer my doleful letter as soon as possible when the dear, kind girl wrote on the very day that she received it. I never did, don't now, and never shall deserve such holy and sweet and comforting words as *Mary* has written me in this letter. O—my Darling—my Darling! Heaven love and guard you, and make me more worthy of my place in your heart!—I almost hate myself for writing such a sad letter to *Mary*—but I could not help it then;—it was a great relief to me,—and yet, it must have given *her* pain since *she loves me*—how beautiful and quieting is this beleif to me, now that I receive it fully! God knows, but I can never tell it all in words.—Had a kind letter from Father, a kindly-comical one from Mary, a few words from *Mother*—who loves me always and beleives in me and prays for me;—and an off-hand, pleasant letter from *Ed.* . . .

I must write *My Friend* (the meaning I attach to those two words expresses what I would say) a cheerful, loving letter tomorrow. I'm ashamed that I complained even to her—I certainly have done so to no one else save *God*—who knew without my telling Him!

1. Edwin A. Clifford (ca. 1846–1904) was a young Evanston neighbor with whom Willard shared an interest in entomology.

12 June 1860

. . . My pupils have not been as studious or as easily governed as usual today, and they have troubled me exceedingly. I've been obliged to "box the ears" of two little reprobates,—apply the ferule to the brown palms of four more, and lay violent hands on another still and coerce him into a measure that did not exactly meet his views. All this I've done and I'm sorry that it became necessary, for I feel kindly towards them all, and would never speak a harsh word only as they force me to do so by the total depravity manifested in their conduct. . . . The children bring me flowers . . . and evince a kind of regard for me in many little actions, that is very pleasant.

Wrote *Mary* today, in the intervals of "Morning Hour," "Noon" and "Recess," while the clamors of troublesome little pupils disturbed and broke up my reverie.

Went to the Post Office after school. Was rewarded by receiving *Mary's* beautiful, comforting Sabbath Evening Letter. . . . After *Mary's* letter I forgot about my troubles at school, and all the care and fatigue of the day faded out from my memory and I thought only of the Three Words—the three blessed Words that formed the key-note to her letter—"*I* love *you*." And who and what am I that this choice gift has been bestowed upon me? God knows about it—not I.

Well, after this, Clara and I rode home together & she brought me from the city a sachel and some clothes and a blank book, and note from Father—whom she called to see today,—and we picked strawberries for tea and I ate oh! so *heartily!* Work gives me an astonishing appetite—I haven't had so good an one in two or three years.—We didn't go sketching tonight on account of the rain.—And here I sit, tired and contented enough—yes, enough. Must write two letters and "make up" bundle for home, arrange "miscellaneous questions" for my school, then to bed and to the sleep that I have earned & am in need of . . .

13 June 1860

. . . My Room at Shady Dell. (Five o'clock P.M.) "O Hum"!—that's what I say when I'm tired! This has been the most fatiguing "school day" I've had. O-o-o-o! I'm *so* tired. I walked home tonight and I don't do so usually—thanks to Clara's kindness. I'm so hoarse with talking all "the whole day long" that my throat aches & aches—when I speak, & a numb sort of pain is in it all the time. Yes, my life is "real and earnest" now,—and valuable too, I beleive,—which is best of all. I'm "not a bit" discouraged or "down hearted" tonight,—only weary, very weary—that is all. . . .

20 June 1860

(At School. 8–9.) Have come to my work this morning with more than usual cheerfulness & alacrity. These are the reasons:—Last night Clara brought me a satchel from Home, which contained, among other things, a letter from *Mary* with her *ambrotype*.[1] In a moment I had forgotten every thing that had annoyed me during the day— forgotten where I was and what I was—and remembered only, as I looked into the dark, earnest eyes that *Mary* truly loved me and cared for me. Then I read her letter—full of kindly, generous words—with the Beautiful Word that I love so well, coming in now and then—O my Darling! She does not know how dearly I love her, and how of- ten—how very often—she is in my thoughts. I fear for her now—fear that the cares and troubles of Examination and Commencement[2] will be more than she can bear—she says she is weary and faint; I am afraid for her and it worries me. She wrote two extracts from her Graduating Essay which is to be a Poem in Blank Verse, subject "Bur- dens." They are beautiful;—full of faith and comfort, for those who toil and struggle and endure.

Then I read a long, kind letter from Father. He requested me not to write letters on the Sabbath. Therefore, though I think it is not wrong to write a friendly, Christianly letter—with words in it that I would talk if it were possible—I will hereafter, out of regard & respect to his wishes, simply, cease to do so. (*Except* I'll write to *Mary* Sabbath Evening. If he could see my letters he would feel that it is right.)

After tea, as I sat writing to *Mary*, Clara read me an extract from her

Journal—just written—beginning: "with God's help I will try to be better." How glad and thankful I was to hear the words! Clara has not been educated to Christianity, and it will be unusually hard for her, but when she laid her head on my shoulder and cried while I read some extracts from my Journal of last winter when I too, was commencing, I saw how sincere she was and I knew God would make her strong and steadfast. And I prayed for her very earnestly and—best of all—she prayed for herself. This morning I have noticed how patient and calm she has been, so I know Christ helps her and I am not afraid. This is all beautiful to me—I'll try to aid her as well as I can by words & deeds—but by deeds most. O, God! teach me and guide me aright.— And take care of her, and let her not be weary or discouraged. . . .

Morning Recess. "So goes the world." After all my fine expectations this has proved, thus far the most disagreeable of my "school days." . . . Hardly a single class had their lesson. O, it is *delicious*—this teaching!

(After School) Heigho! It has been a hard day for "Sissie"—as I sometimes affectionately call myself to myself.—I count no harder one among those of my "Disciplinary Term." Several "thwacking interludes"—four refractory rebels kept after school and their quartette of shrieks was dulcet music to my poor, tired senses. And I didn't like to punish them, foolish little things,—and so I told them—yet I had to do it. . . .

1. Ambrotypes, which first appeared around 1855, were a kind of photograph on glass. Silver produced the light tones, while the dark background behind the silver was allowed to show through to create the dark shades.
2. Public examinations of the NWFC were held on 11 July 1860 and commencement exercises on 13 July 1860.

26 June 1860

After . . . teaching my naughty, unruly "children" (with a few "honorable exceptions" they richly deserve the "uncanny adjectives,") I *walked* home through a "driving shower" of rain,—holding up my dress as well as I could and going very fast,—but I was quite "drenched" and my feet were soaked and blistered—it was "the hardest thing yet." I hope I won't take cold. To crown my discontent Clara didn't come home tonight! I can see now how thankful I ought to be that "life is as well with me as it is."[1] I could not endure it here, if it were not for her,—and yet, I "crune" and lament when she is here—it's like Human nature, and "there's a good deal of Human Nature in folks" (a la *Samuel* Weller.")[2]

There's a Concert in Evanston tonight—"The Cantata of Esther"—
(?) *Mary* has a part in it. Heigho—and I sit here by my window alone,
so lonely! I'm "not a bit of a" Stoic and I thought and hoped I was.
Perhaps I will be some day—who can tell?—Have made a *Resolution,*
(though I'm afraid I cannot keep it!) viz:

> *Preamble.* Whereas: it does no good to any body for me to think
> of home and friends while I can not see them, and whereas they
> are "getting on" pleasantly and "serenely" in my absence need-
> ing none of my love or regret, therefore
>
> *Resolved* that for the remainder of my "Harlem Exile," I attend
> to my "regular business" with all the heartiness and whole-
> souledness of which I am capable, get all the experience, plea-
> sure and profit out of life that I possibly can, forget what is be
> hind, ("Look not mournfully into the Past,—it comes not back
> again.")[3] regret nothing, pine for nothing, think but little of the
> "Home Folk,": and live but one day at a time, and that as brave-
> ly and cheerily as I am able.

Yes?—Don't sneer at yourself "Frances"! Anyhow the above is fair
philosophy and I'll *try* to actualize i[t]—I can do nothing more.
Certain I am that these Reveries that I have every day and evening
are not strengthening but weakening my character. I can spend the
time more wisely and worthily—and I will! There! I had just written
the foregoing, and while waiting for the ink to dry I folded my hands
& shut my eyes and sat here in the Twilight and reveried away about
Mary in the most babyish, imbecile, weak, homesick style possible! I'm
a poor foolish *human* sort of an "affair." . . .

1. Not identified.
2. Sam Weller was the servant of Mr. Pickwick in Charles Dickens, *The Posthumous
Papers of the Pickwick Club* (London, 1836–37).
3. Willard quoted the motto for book 1 of Henry Wadsworth Longfellow, *Hyperion* (New York, 1839).

27 June 1860

. . . So here comes on another day of half-pleasant, half-painful-
ness. I have some zest for it, and when "going on" through the various duties am sometimes amused, sometimes earnest as I think of my
"position." I fear I don't view the matter of Teaching seriously
enough. It is not easy to look at the stolid little faces—of a majority
of my pupils,—with their natural *expressionlessness* aggravated by the

"German element" in their constitution and education, and "imagine" how they're to live on and on as long as God lives;—how I'm to help them on to endless bliss and the wisdom that lays hold on Eternal Life or leave them,—at best,—but as I found them. It is the hardest thing in the world.

And I shall go to school and strike half-a-dozen hard little hands for twice as many grievous "misdemeanors," and they'll think me harsh and stern—if the poor things think at all which I'm inclined to doubt. I don't want to punish them but,—here's the philosophy of it: I have tried to appeal to their consciences,—I can not find that they have any; to their "honors," they have none;—to their pride, it is latent; to their ambition, it is wanting; to their good nature;—it is undeveloped. Nothing remains but appealing to their *nerves*—they understand that! They're "used to it," are governed so at home and know nothing else. When I *strike* and the tingling, painful sensation creeps over their brown little palms, they wake up, and never otherwise. (I refer to my little Germans under seven years old, uncivilized and "unpromising" in the superlative degree.) Those who have been trained at home require but little discipline—they are studious, quiet & obedient, and I have pleasure in them. Amelia, George, Eunice, Mary, Jane, David, and "Tommy Rattle"[1] are my "civilized pupils"—glorious Septemvirate! "But what are these, among the many?"[2] Seven, out of an average of thirty-seven. . . .

1. Willard listed her students' names and ages in the back of her journal for 13 June 1860–4 October 1860. The students she named in this entry were: Amelia A. Ingols, 15 years; George S. Thatcher, 15 years (or possibly George Wilson, 9 years); Mary R. Ingols, 10 years; Jane R. Tierney, 12 years; David Alfred Thatcher, 13 years; Thomas Rattle, 6 years. There is no Eunice listed; it could be Frances E. Wilson, 13 [?] years.
2. Not identified.

5 July 1860

. . . ("Weary Girl's Rest."[1] 5 o'cl'k PM.)

Have had a very pleasant day's teaching. Have had in view the true aim of the Teacher more than usual. For this I am indebted to the Teacher's Assistant.[2] Everything has passed off pleasantly. Scholars seem inclined to learn, & to do right, think many of them have sincere regard for me,—as I certainly have come to have for them. Gave my school a "talk" on Politeness. Shall begin to "keep an account" of who are Ladies & Gentlemen, when I return from E[vanston]; forwarned them of my intention. Talked of Morals & Rightness more than usual. Feel quite *jubilant* tonight, though tired,—of necessity. I feel certain that I am coming to have truer views of a Teacher's duties and responsibilities;—am not so narrow or selfish in my ideas on the subject. . . .

1. "Weary Girl's Rest" was Willard's name for her room at the Thatchers' house. She wrote on 30 June 1860 that she took the name (modified slightly) from a book that she was reading: Elisha Kent Kane, M.D., U.S.N., *Arctic Explorations: The Second Grinnell Expedition in Search of Sir John Franklin, 1853, '54, '55,* vol. 2 (Philadelphia, 1856).

2. Charles Cushman Bragdon (1847–1932), the son of Willard's minister at the Evanston MEC, sent her a copy of the *Teacher's Assistant,* published yearly by the American Sunday School Union (N.Y.) as a guide for teachers of Bible. It was a commentary on the Old Testament that offered both biblical history and statements for spiritual reflection.

9 July 1860

Bright, breezy morning. Rode to the depot with Clara, then came here to my School House and my *work.* After all, though I think and write so much of Home and Friends, how much better and more worthy of me it is, to be going to my *work* this morning with the rest of the busy, striving world, than to be at Home, idling about, reading some, writing a little, walking with "the girls," and devising ways and means of "Killing Time," yawning and fretting at my own idleness. No, I'm very glad I'm here, learning patience and bravery and self-reliance and quietness, (my list of Beatitudes!) and *earning* more than a dollar a day! That last is nothing much, yet a pleasant item, and *something* for me who am usually a burden to others instead of a burden-bearer. So, reasoning thus, I'll go at my tasks cheerfully and with energy. Remembering how much influence I necessarily have with these forty immortal souls under my care, I'll try to teach them well, and Thou O, God, wilt guide and teach me and make me useful to them. . . .

10 July 1860

Only one day more, and then *Home!*

I'm half ashamed to be so anxious, for I have tried to be quite stoical and indifferent, and I find I'm not indifferent at heart, but full of "forward looking."

Never mind,—I've acted practically as though I didn't much care, and it is just the same "to all intents"—no, not to all *intents*—but to all "purposes." And when I go to the cars tomorrow—*only tomorrow*—

night, I shall look calm and careless I think, I shall hide all the eagerness, out of sight of the indifferent people,—so I'll not "worry"
because I'm so happy to go. . . .

16 July 1860

. . . The beautiful Hours of Rest that bring these long days to their
peaceful ending, have come to me again, and I sit here in Clara's
room tired and happy & calm, to write of my *Visit Home.*

On Wednesday after a day's teaching I came here to Shady Dell—
I said "home" almost, it isn't dreary here now—and with gleefulness
indescribable prepared to go to the five o'clock train. Clara was almost ready, and in a little while we started, I saying nothing for very
joy. Rode to the city in silence—thinking—thinking. Father met us—
dear, kind Father whom I hadn't seen for weeks. Reached Evanston
at last and rode to "Swampscot" behind "Jack"[1] as in the olden days.
Mother and Mary and Oliver met us at the door—how eagerly I
looked on their familiar faces! I flew all over the house, was delighted with the garden, asked a thousand foolish questions, & exhibited
few traces of the Quietness I have been trying to gain. In a few minutes I saw *Mary,* darling, coming down through the grove. How I loved
her as I looked into the bright brown eyes of my Only *Friend* that I
have or ask to have. We walked around the garden & talked of common matters but under it all the current of love & trust was as powerful in *her* heart as in mine I know. She went away soon, and my
blessing followed her, and my love and my prayers. . . .

On Thursday *the Marys* graduated. I sat and looked on quietly, but
my heart was full of thoughts and questions as they read their
essays. . . . While they sang the "Parting Song" composed for them by
Miss Clark,[2] I could have cried,—but wouldn't—at the lines:—

> "And so our brows are shadowed, where
> A common light hath shown,
> For we who have together toiled
> Go forth to toil alone"

Well, it is over. . . .

1. Jack was the Willards' horse who had pulled the wagon carrying Willard, her
mother, and her sister from Oberlin, Ohio, to Janesville, Wis., in 1846, and continued to convey the family around Evanston. He was fatally struck by lightning in the
summer of 1868 and Willard recorded his death in her 4 August 1868 journal entry.
2. Luella Clark (1832–1915) was the preceptress of mental science and belles
lettres at the NWFC from 1858 to 1866. From 1866 to 1868 she was the school's
lady principal, and from 1867 to 1868, teacher of German. Clark taught for many

years in New York, Wisconsin, and Ohio, as well as in Illinois, retiring in 1888 to New Hampshire.

29 July 1860

... Clara & I have established a sort of mission Sabbath School in my School House. The first "meeting" was last Sabbath. We had 23 scholars; the same number today. We have divided them into two classes, Clara taking the younger children, I the older ones. Mine is a Bible Class. Mr. Holden[1] a philanthropic gentleman of Chicago, with whom C. is acquainted has furnished 25 S.S. papers, besides Hymn Books & several packages of smaller books which are to be used as prizes. We sing, pray, call the roll, give half to three-quarters of an hour's instruction, sing, & dismiss. We meet at 1/2 past 4 P.M. Today I prayed a prayer of my own—the first time I ever prayed anything save "Our Father" aloud in *public.*

But I'm not fit to pray or teach. I'm not a good Christian. Don't think much of God or Heaven or Eternity;—not half so much as when I came here first. I am alarmed at myself. Today, wholly forgetful of my promise to Father, I wrote a long letter to Kate Kidder[2] besides my ordinary "Eight-page" to *Mary*. I read books too, that I knew were not suitable for the Sabbath. O God forgive me! for I need it & indeed I'm very sorry, & will *try* very hard—if Thou wilt help me—to do right and to be better. ...

1. This was probably Charles N. Holden (1816–87), a Chicago merchant, businessman, and politician. An opponent of slavery and a Republican, he helped Lincoln win the 1860 Republican nomination.
2. Kate M. (Kidder) Strowbridge (ca. 1843–1908) was an Evanston neighbor, the daughter of Dr. Daniel P. Kidder, a GBI professor, and Harriette (Smith) Kidder. In 1866 she married George Egerton Strowbridge, who graduated from GBI in 1866 and became an MEC minister.

2 August 1860

... At noon my "nice little Charlie Hohmann"[1] went to the Office for me. When I saw him coming back I did not dare & would not look in his hand to see if he had *Mary's* Letter—that always comes on Thursday since she went to Appleton[2]—& when he gave it to me and I was *certain* that it had come I did not know what to do—this is not figurative!—I was so glad. Having given "copies"[3] to all "my children" I went into my desk and read the Letter. Kind and loving as are all her words to me, she never wrote anything that exhibited the love, and perfect confidence in me that this one did. It made me feel so unworthy of her; so common-place and paltry that I despised myself. How can she see me so much purer and nobler than I am, or ever shall become? How can she possibly think so well of me? I do not know, but that God put it in her heart. I will try to love Him better & to be more worthy of her Friendship—I *could not* care for her more than I do—(and yet I could care for God as I do not—poor fool that I am!).

O my Child! My Child! I *hope* this of which you speak, need *not* be "trampled on"! I hope such happiness is in store for us all as I think must arise from your being _____ I will not write it; there is little need for I shall understand. A strange and painful dream I had last night about you. I thought it had all "come true" & that beholding your happiness—*you two*—I was wretched myself, to think that never again could I be "*The* Darling" of your heart. Even in my dream I blushed for my selfishness as I am blushing now at the remembrance of it. I will try—oh! I *will* try—not to be so wicked. And you called me your "Evangel"![4] God grant it may be so! . . .

1. Charlie Hohmann, age seven, was a student of Willard's.
2. Mary Bannister traveled to Appleton, Wis., to visit her aunt and uncle, Cynthia Byrd (Foote) Conkey and Theodore Conkey (1819–80). Theodore Conkey was Mary Bannister's father's half-brother and was in the ashery business, in farming, and active in Democratic politics. The Conkeys had moved to Appleton in 1849 or 1850, remaining there the rest of their lives.
3. Copies were examples of penmanship that students were to copy for practice.
4. Mary Bannister called Willard "Evangel" (from the Greek word *euangelos*, meaning "bearer of good news") because she had given Bannister "good news" about Oliver Willard's feelings for her.

21 August 1860
Evanston, Illinois

. . . After Church, when *Mary* grasped my hand I was *glad—too* glad to tell her of it, too glad to mention it in words. I went home with *her* from Sabbath School, spent the Afternoon, staid to tea—all the evening, & persuaded *Mary* to go home with me to spend the night. This was the happiest part of my visit. We talked of Mary's Work that she is trying to perform—of which going South[1] is but a part, contributing to it in a way that no mortal dreams except us two.—I'm sorry for it all; sorry that my reason and the little judgment that I have must in this matter wholly rule my heart, and make me say words & strive to bring about a result the very opposite of what I wish on personal grounds. I was never before in such a position. Yet in it all I do the best I can, and so I will not let it trouble me.

We talked of our two paths in life—how they are constantly diverging—drawn apart by something stronger and more relentless than Fate—the mighty majesty of *will*—her will & mine, which God is helping onward to right resolves & deeds. How strange it is that the very course that makes our hearts ache hardest is the one that will bring calm and peace to them in fullest measure—one that will make us brave and patient and pleasing in the sight of Him who watches—always watches—from the sky. O, the world is hard with it all, and the Life Beyond looks tempting to me—very tempting—as I toil. God gather us—*Mary* and I—to the Restful Country at last, when we have borne enough and longed & prayed & waited as He wills!

How far apart we are soon to be! The head that she laid so trustingly upon my shoulder will ache a thousand times & I shall know it not, the heart that loves me so purely and truly will often know of pain,—the breath that floated to my cheek will come and go faintly and painfully, and *Mary* will have done & suffered much before we walk again together—if indeed the time shall *ever* come. And I called her *Darling* for the first time in my life and she laid *her* hand upon my forehead & *her* lips against my cheek. I did not sleep, she did not, but laid there quietly and made for myself a whole life-time of sweet memories. But the Sunlight came back again at last;—in our world there is an end to everything save striving—& Mary went to her home, & I prepared to come again to my labors. . . .

Here is a list of the Qualities that,—as I think—combine to make a character lovable and agreeable to the world in general;—not, "observe," the qualities that develop *affinities* from which proceed "the love that is more than love,"[2] & which may not be analyzed or understood so mysterious are they. From them is the love that men have for women,—that I have for *Mary*. Well, first,

+1. Patience; (crowning Excellence.)   6. Frankness,
 2. Generosity,   +7. Honor,
 3. Candor,   +8. Judgment,
 4. Approbation,   +9. Calmness,
 5. Forgiveness,   10. Obliging*ness*,
11. Delicacy, (This is a cardinal virtue. Without it, no man shall have Friends. I mean great tenderness of the feelings of others, never reminding them of unpleasant peculiarities, etc.)
+12. *Perfect Truthfulness.*

There are many others,—these seem to me to be the principal ones. Those indicated thus,— + —I feel a particular desire & *need* to cultivate,—while fearfully deficient in them all. . . .

1. In her 8 September 1860 journal entry, Willard noted that Mary Bannister was planning to go to Lynnville, Tenn., to live with the Laird family on their plantation while she tutored their daughters and their neighbors' children.

2. Willard paraphrased Edgar Allan Poe, "Annabel Lee," in *Sartain's Union Magazine of Literature and Art* (Philadelphia, 1849), stanza 2, line 3: "But we loved with a love that was more than love."

5 September 1860

I am changed, since yesterday! I am sadder & older, & full of pain.

Only one morning before this, I packed my little property into trunk, & desk & band box, & bidding goodbye to dear, kind Clara, & the rest, went to my School House to teach for the last time. On the Noon train Oliver came, & brought a note which, I opened hastily, & which, with his explanation conveyed to me the intelligence that *Mary* Bannister, Kate Kidder & Ellie Simpson were to leave Evanston today, the former for Tennessee, where she was to spend *ten months,* the two last for Cincinnati,[1] where they were to attend school.

And so the dream was over. I never loved any one, as I love *Mary,* & this very love is the instrument of most cruel torture to me. "*Mary is* going"! rang in my ears all the day long while I conducted my "exhibition" which was creditable to me, I think—while I said "Goodbye" to my pupils; while I kissed Amelia & offered to write to her, & help her to learn; while I shook hands with my favorite little Charlie & told him "he had always been a good boy"; while Oliver talked nobly & bravely to me of the work we all have to do in the world, & told me that Life was never to be easy for me any more;—"*never* any more" I repeated regretfully & almost with tears in my eyes as I thought of Childhood, & Home, & Mother.

And I went to the city, & took the cars for home with that one thought in my heart, "*Mary's* going! All the love you've hoarded for her has made it only harder for you to lose her now. Learn to make no being save God, essential to your peace. You should have loved *Him* best. He means that you shall;—He is forcing you, scourging you to it."

Came to dear old "Swampscot," kissed my Mother & my Aunt[2] with sorrowful sort of pleasure—if such a thing can be. Went to tea—according to a previous arrangement—with *Mary,* Kate, & Ellie at Han's. Felt too heart-sick to talk. Listened to Mary's playing, eagerly drinking in every sound that she drew from the keys by her delicate, appreciative touch; went home with her at last, when the evening was over, & as I knelt by her bed, to pray, forgot my usual forms of petition in the great trouble of my heart, and only cried out to God in hurried, broken words: "Take care of My Darling! Love her, love her! Shield & guide her & bring her safely back again, O God!"

As she laid last night with her head upon my arm, I came to know how heroic & noble is my Friend! She says it is the hardest thing in all the world for her. To go so far all alone,—untried,—unbefriended, is what no one else would do—no one that I know. And yet she is not going to let any one see it—not her Father even,—but hiding it all away, "taking counsel with her own Heart"[3] she will bear it, silently.

Today she is going—the brightest star in the zenith of my life. I will not complain. She has more to bear than I.

Just now, I can see no hopeful features of the case; I can only feel this aching—aching in my heart; I can only pray this little prayer "God love her very tenderly! keep her, guard her, & bring her back to me"! . . .

1. Kate Kidder and Ellen (nicknamed Ellie as well as Ella) Simpson attended the Cincinnati Wesleyan College, an MEC female seminary, founded in 1842 in Cincinnati, Ohio.

2. Caroline (Willard) Town (1813–81), Josiah Willard's youngest sister and a resident of Churchville, N.Y., was visiting her brother's family.

3. Not identified.

6 September 1860

So I'm to write in *Mary's* "Book";[1]—to finish it, and where her heart was to have been written out so undisguisedly, I am to write out mine! 'Tis a strange world we live in, and strange, sad things happen to us, as we journey through it. I did not think, one week ago, that tonight My Darling would be hundreds of miles away from me with a new life and toil before her. I hoped sweeter, pleasanter things for myself;— but I must not think of that, God rules us kindly & in infinite wisdom:

> "What *Thou* doest, Lord, is *right*,
> And thus beleiving, we rejoice."

She is gone. I said "Goodbye" & pressed my lips to hers for an instant as we parted last night at Dr. Kidder's[2] gate. How well I can remember how she looked;—the closely fitting traveling dress showing her graceful figure . . . the flowers I had just given, in her hand; the chestnut hair parted away from the high, noble forehead; a flush on the cheek, & tears in the beautiful brown eyes that are *so dear* to me. She turned half away as she took my hand, and kissed me silently; I said "Goodbye"—only that, though my heart ached to add "My Darling, God bless you always"—she did not answer, she *could* not I think;—

I turned away abruptly, & walked slowly homeward, never looking back or even raising my head. I wanted to remember her as she stood there in her youth & her prime, with her sweet face half turned away, & her eyes full of tears. God knows when I shall look at her again!—not perhaps until the golden halo encircles her brow, & the harp is in her hand which only those shall win who toil & suffer and have patience; the harp instead of those poor flowers I gave her, & light from the Beautiful Country replacing the tears in her eyes. I thank Thee, O God! that I can not tell when I shall see *Mary* again; but I thank Thee *more* that I beleive when the time—or the *eternity* shall come—I shall feel sure she loves me and is glad to see my face again!

How much I've thought of her today; how often I have murmured to myself "Love her O God and guard her all the while. Be to her instead of parents & Friends—be more to her than we can ever be; cheer her, protect her—comfort her & make her calm."

I went riding tonight. We passed My Darling's *Home*, &, from long habit, I looked up to the window of her room. The blinds were shut closely—there was no sign of life. I never saw them so before, & O *how sadly* I thought "she will not need light there any more;—the bird has flown, the cage is desolate." Near our house I saw the print of her dainty little foot on the road side. Will it ever tread again the pleasant path-way? ever again? I ask the question mournfully, & with forbodings of ill. Perhaps these fears are idle—all may yet be well, but, in any case, I know that

> "My Heart is very desolate
> To think that she is gone." . . .[3]

I'm glad—O *so* glad!—to get *Home*. I can hardly beleive that my school is really out and I am free. Unless *Mary* gets me a place at the South—which I doubt more than I like to acknowledge—I shall stay in Evanston, & take the "accomplishments" of Music, French & Drawing; review my favorite (?) Mathematics, & endeavor to learn more about the practicalities of a woman's life—sewing, cooking, etc. I think this course the wisest & Mother strongly desires it. But if I get a desirable place, it will be better yet to teach. . . .

1. Willard and Bannister exchanged journals, each writing their entries in the other's book. Bannister wrote in Willard's journal from 8 September 1860 to 4 October 1860. Willard wrote in Bannister's from 6 September 1860 to 28 September 1860.

2. Daniel Parish Kidder (1815–91) was professor of practical theology at GBI from 1856 to 1871. He then took a similar position at Drew Theological Seminary in Madison, N.J. Failing health caused him to return to Evanston in 1888, where he died three years later.

3. Not identified.

20 September 1860

. . . I'm wondering at my prayers. As I knelt in Family Devotions this morning I said to our Father who is in Heaven: "Keep me to-day;—I can not keep myself. Make me very patient, obliging & Christianly. Help me to remember that in so far as I do right it is not of myself, but that in Thee I live & move & have my being.[1] Quicken my intellect; may I understand my lessons and acquire them with facility. May I come to like my Music lesson better—make my fingers quick & agile I pray Thee—Thou canst do all things; give me a little strength out of thine infinite power. May I behave well; may I know what to do—the time to do it and *how* to do it. May I know right words to say. When I am confused wilt Thou cause me to become self-possessed. May I converse fluently & interestingly. May my resources be available to me. May I grow to be a fine character some day—wilt Thou help me. May I be willing to leave the matter of going South to be with *Mary,* entirely with Thee & to be submissive to what Thou shalt decide. May this passage remain in my memory always: 'He that is slow to anger is better than the mighty, & he that ruleth his spirit than he that taketh a city.'[2] Help me to be *truthful,*—to say exactly what I mean; to give an uncolored narration of what I see & experience, & not to allow my love of the marvellous to lead me from the simplicity of the Truth. 'For Christ's sake—because He died for us, wilt thou hear & answer my prayer, God over all, blessed forever'"

I wonder if God is pleased with my prayer? I don't beleive He thinks me foolish, for He never lets me know that He does, & if He did, I'm sure He'd tell me,—some how. . . .

1. Acts 17:28.
2. Prov. 16:32.

24 September 1860

. . . Ah! I have my own troubles to think of now! Life is going always to be *hard* for me, as Oliver said that day when we talked together while waiting for the cars at Harlem. I did not think this morning when I practiced "my hour," studied my French lesson with Mattie S,[1] and talked & laughed so carelessly, when I went to the College and recited to Miss Clark, and sauntered home again more light of heart than I had been before since *Mary's* face faded out from my sight, that before night my prospect would be entirely changed;—that "toil, and stern endeavor" would be my portion for the coming year—that I was to leave home and Friends and "go away alone" again, as *My Darling* has done, as I did once before. But so it is. Mr. Woodruff[2] has written that he wishes me to start for Kankakee one week from to-day, and I am going. But stop a moment! Oliver said just now, as he walked back and forth through my little room, "Rely on God, Frank. I don't do so enough myself, but I can tell you, never-the-less. Pray earnestly to Him. Ask him to guide you and help you to decide. Tell Him you wish to do what He indicates as His will. Say all this humbly & sincerely. Then decide whether you'll go or not, &, in any event, what ever may hereafter occur, be perfectly tranquil, knowing that you asked for guidance in your decision, & beleiving that you have received it."—So I'll lock the door now, and here all alone, in this dear room that has sheltered me so long, but will never be permanently mine again, I'll pray to our kind Friend who loves to help us. Ah! as *Mary* says: "What I love slips away from me." I never knew this to fail in my life. Doubtless it is better that this is so. I have a natural *love* for things on the earth, and God looses my clinging fingers from my dear & beautiful toys that *He* may take me by the hand and lead me "up higher." . . .

1. Martha Jane (Stewart) Smith (1841–1920) was an Evanston neighbor and class-mate of Willard's sister Mary at NWFC, graduating in June 1860. She was a sister of Willard's friend Belle Stewart and married Charles B. Smith in 1861.

2. The Willard family first became acquainted with Charles B. Woodruff during the late 1850s when he was principal of the Wisconsin Institute for the Blind in Janes-ville, Wis., a school less than a mile from the Willards' farm. He began the Kankakee Academy, a private school, in 1860, holding classes in the basement of the Kankakee MEC.

28 September 1860

. . . I have lived in His world where He thought fit to place me, twenty-one years, today. In one sense, that is a long while;—most people view it so. Consequently, the secret thought of almost all my friends—if they had *any* thought regarding me—would be: "Quite advanced, Frank, really! Didn't hardly think you was so old. Twenty-one! 'Pon my word! High time to think of 'getting married,' eh?" . . .

I am not *old*. Any other than this seems to me to be a narrow and unworthy view, so when "the girls" elevate their eye-brows and exclaim "What! so old as *that*, Frank!" I will only nod, & smile carelessly, while in my heart I think "It doesn't matter what they say—so they mean it not unkindly"—I haven't done much in these years—not much. Yet

God knows I'll try to make it up if He will spare me,—and somehow I feel that He will. . . .

2 October 1860
Kankakee, Illinois

. . . Well, this morning I went to the "Kankakee Academy"—where I'm "Second Teacher,"[1] & "on the whole" I've had a tolerable day, & am going to try not to cry once while I'm here, for I'm twenty-one I'd have you to understand, Journal—I've no one else to talk to. It's not so very bad—I won't care. . . .

I'm thinking so much of *Mary*—more than I ever thought before, since her Letter of Saturday last. I'm afraid something terrible is going to happen, for I love her *too well*.—I sent her Journal on Saturday & wrote till twelve o'clock on Sabbath night, to her. O my *Friend, my Darling, my Child!* (I can't help it—I *love* to call her so though she *is* so brave & womanly, for the name implies the loving care & tenderness I have for her—& always must have let her be never so strong.)

Nobody ever wrote me such a letter before—nobody ever will again;—I ought to be so thankful all my life for this one, that I should have no room to regret that I shall have no more—unless from *her.* Indeed, I know of no one else who can express what they desire in such delicate, beautiful sentences—such a pure, chaste style. They would some how get in a "coarse" sentence now and then, but *Mary* never approaches to one. How can she care for me so much? Perhaps it is because she has gone so far alone,—and yet it may be more likely, that—as Mrs. Stowe has said[2]—she locates in me her Ideal of what she can love. I'm not what she thinks me—not so good, not so brave,—but God mercifully permits *Mary* to think so well of me that she can love me, and imagine in me what she loves! I thank Him for this every day, with more earnestness & sincerity [than] any one knows—than *she* dreams, even. This letter I'm going to put in my Book—not the Book of her Letters that I read so joyfully in, that I've brought here with me & love next to my Bible—but my Note Book I mean, so "here goes" for some extracts at least, and I'm not foolish or egotistical to make them;

Sat. Morn. 22 September 1860

"*My One Darling!*
Not one word have I heard from you since last Friday and I *know* you wrote to me on Sabbath eve;—and my heart aches—aches—aches this morning with such a heavy pain that the tears keep coming to my eyes.

I received H—'s[3] letter this morning after walking nearly a *mile* to get *yours* which I certainly expected,—but these mails are *so* vexing—O my Darling I can not live without you—without one word from you for a whole week and *we love each other* so earnestly too. Those mails have no more care for our strong & tender love for each other than for any thing or any one else. No one but God cares any thing about our love— no one thinks of it except to say 'What great friends Frank and Mary are'! I'm glad of this—*so* glad that no one understands how it is that we are 'more than all the world' to each other. I always have such a strange feeling about our Friendship—as if it was in some way sacred. And I feel almost as if I was doing something wrong, to be writing to you on a week day. Sabbath evening seems to be the only time right for it. And my love for you is so different from any love I ever knew before. It seems to me that it can not be quite a *human* love. I don't know how it is—but I beleive I love you just as if you were given to me right from God's hands to keep till He called you back again, & I hold you in my heart just as if I must be very careful & tender of you, for fear at any moment you might slip away from me. I take up your letters so gently & lay them down as if they were little, tender children— as if I was afraid of hurting them. I can not explain this at all, but I can not bear to hear any one mention your name, or to see it written in any one's hand-writing. I felt almost angry at H_____ for saying any thing about you. I never like to call you what the rest do, & so I call you 'Darling' and 'Evangeline'[4] till I fear you will weary of these names. I wish that when you are baptized you would be called 'Frances Evangeline'—that would preserve the initials & preserve also the name I love so well & give me the right to call you by it. Won't you?

Sabbath eve.

O Darling, I love you so earnestly, so truly & fervently tonight. It is only a few hours ago that I read the words [you] wrote me one week ago tonight. How I thank you for them! I presume I have told you how, next to my Bible, I value your words to me—no matter when or how written—even your hand-writing has a charm for me. I remember finding in your portfolio some little scraps of paper on which you had written & I laid them carefully back again, because your hands had touched them. I beleive this love of ours is the one that God has given me in place of that other love that brightens some lives. I only tremble for fear you will not always be satisfied with it—for fear that sometime you will, not exactly leave my love for another's, but that another will be first, I, only second. I know that I can be happily content always, if we can always be together—but will you?—I know 'that other kind of love' must come to you sometime, & then like the Lady Ida you will forget— even learn to hate Psyche[5] (not that I would call myself this only to illustrate my meaning . . .). I do not know how many times a day I say to God, 'oh! give us our work together—& let the coming years find us walking nearer to Thee, side by side, hand in hand'—then I say with an earnestness that only God understands, 'for *Christ's sake*'—for I remember one thing this blessed God-man Christ said—'For your Heavenly Father knoweth ye have need of *these things*.'[6] We have need of each other, haven't we Darling—Best of all the world to me? You won't get tired of this, will you? Every night I sleep with my cheek next to your face—& try to imagine that I feel your breath there—as in the last night we were together—you won't forget? . . . Write me long letters, please, & love me & pray for me more earnestly than if I were with you. Goodnight My Darling—my own blessed Darling! Remember always that *I love you* best of all others. Remember that you are *dearer than life* to me, & that if God wills, I will walk by your side through all my life & *belong* wholly to *you. Your own Mary.*"

Nobody shall see these pages but myself—*my Darling*, my Friend, my *dear, dear Mary! God bless you always.*

F.

1. Mr. Woodruff was the head teacher at the academy and Willard was his assistant.
2. Harriet Beecher Stowe (1811–96), the American novelist, used social reform and religious themes combined with everyday scenes to create powerful social critique. Willard avidly read each of Stowe's novels as soon as they came out in serialized form in various magazines, and also read her articles and travel essays.
3. Bannister referred to Hannah Watson Ludlam, with whom she corresponded while she taught in Tennessee.
4. Both Bannister and Willard were fond of Henry Wadsworth Longfellow's poem *Evangeline: A Tale of Acadie* (Boston, 1847), and Bannister suggested that Willard change her second name "Elizabeth" to "Evangeline" at her baptism. "Evangeline" was also a play on "Evangel," which Bannister liked to call Willard.
5. Bannister referred to Alfred Lord Tennyson's poem *The Princess: A Medley* (London, 1847). In it Princess Ida falls in love with a prince, whose identity Lady Psyche has kept from her. Bannister identified Willard as the princess who would one day find her prince, and herself as Lady Psyche, who came between Princess Ida and her prince.
6. Matt. 6:32.

3 October 1860

Evening. Well, I've had another School Day. Like it "real well." Have a cozy little recitation room all to myself, with carpet, stove, seat, curtains, papered, etc. Prof. Woodruff is very obliging and gives me my choice of classes in most instances;—I have no disciplining to do, but stay in my room & hear my classes. The pupils are highly civilized—so different from most of my Harlemites—& seem anxious to learn. I have two or three among them that I like exceedingly already, particularly little Fannie Hosmer. The best thing I have to record for today is that I'm going to Fannie's Grandmamma's to board tomorrow![1] Though they're kind to me here their accommodations are not pleasant and I'm glad I am to go to a cozy room,—carpeted, well furnished generally & best of all, *rocking-chaired*, to room with a young lady whom I'm sure to like—judging from her looks—little Fannie there, Prof. Woodruff also, & a kind, motherly lady to preside over all. I'm very thankful. (Price of it all, two dollars & 1/2 a week,—washing included.)....[2]

1. Fannie Hosmer (b. ca. 1852) lived at her grandmother Susan B. Cooledge's (or Coolidge; although Willard spells it Coolidge, it appears as Cooledge in the 1860 census record) house in Kankakee. Mrs. Cooledge (b. ca. 1810) ran a boardinghouse where Mr. Woodruff, principal of the Kankakee Academy, boarded. Willard moved from a boardinghouse run by a Mrs. McCullough to Susan Cooledge's boardinghouse because it was closer to the academy and her quarters would be more comfortable than those at the McCullough house. There her room had no carpet or stove, and Willard felt it was dismal.

2. This last sentence in the entry was originally written in code.

8 October 1860

[*Willard copied into her journal a long poem, "Two Portraits," by Henry Timrod, which she read in the August 1860 issue of* Harper's Magazine. *The poem contrasted the life of a single woman with that of a woman who marries, contending that a single woman's capacity to love deeply is never fully realized. A married woman, although she may suffer more than one who chooses not to marry, will experience the full potential of her ability to love through her devotion to her husband and children.*]

... There! I won't copy any more. I've enough for my text. The sermon is this:—

I beleive the doctrine of this Poem,—divested of its imagery. I beleive that no woman ever knows the depth & richness of her nature till she has loved a man—some man, good & noble—better than her own life. I beleive that unless she does this, much of the pain and want described in the lines I have copied must be endured by her. And with all that I've admitted, my Journal bears me witness that I say little or nothing about "the gentleman." Once for all, I will give the reason why, &,—till I am older and sadder at least,—I shall not revert to the subject again. In truth, it is not one of which I often think. I have never been "in love." I never shed a tear, or dreamed a dream, or sighed, or had a sleepless hour, for love. I never treasured—any man in my Heart till he became sacred to me—till his words were as oracles—his smiles sunshine, his voice music. I never hung upon any man's words, or took any man's name into my prayer because I loved him, because he was—as *Mary* is—"more than all the world to me."[1]

But I might have done all this, had I so willed it. I was too cautious—loved my own peace too well;—valued myself too highly—remembered too frequently that I was made for something higher and more worthy, than to spend a disconsolate life, wasting the richest gift I could bestow—*my heart*—upon a man who cared nothing for me;—who never thought of me, but in friendly, common fashion. I was too proud for this—I had too keen a sense of *right & justice.*

Looking out from my seclusion, in which I live, & try to become wiser & better and more helpful to the world, everyday—I have seen several men whom I've known that I *could* love. I've seen enough nobility in their natures,—enough culture of intellect, enough purity of mind & heart & life, to inspire that emotion. I have looked after them as they passed me on the street,—as I saw them in church, or met them in society, & said quietly, & with perfect tranquility to myself, "You might love him, but remember, you must not do so,"—& I have gone on my way calmly & in peace. It is not that I am hardhearted or insensible that I do this, for that I'm neither of these, *Mary,* and my great love & tenderness, for her, shall bear me witness;—but because I know perfectly well, that these men care nothing for me, except as an acquaintance, & therefore, determined to be *even with them* in this, I have shut the door upon them, and said "Get hence" & that's the end of it. As I grow older I may not find it easy—I can not tell. But is it not right for me to do this?—I am *sure* it is yet I am not so dull as to forget what happiness would come to me in being loved, & loving. I am not so dull as to forget that the crowning joy of my life would be a strong arm—stronger than mine—to lean upon, a brave heart—braver than mine—to shield myself within. I have not known, as yet, what it is to *lean* on any being save God. All of my Friends are younger than I—both my Friends in the world's acceptation of the term, & in mine, also.—They rely on me more than I rely on them, I am almost sure. I *love* them dearly, & care for them & would keep them from pain & danger, but I do not expect them to shelter me. This arises, in part, no doubt, from my being older than they. I feel, I think, toward *Mary* as her husband—that is to be—will feel. I wish I could stand in her place, & fight her battles for her—"come between her & harm" always, & keep her from trouble. It affords me great delight even to *imagine* myself doing this, though the circumstances have never been such that I could actually perform this part.

I say every night, in my prayer, "O God! sometime, if it pleaseth

Thee, give me the love of a manly heart—of one that I can love *entirely*,—next to Thee. But if this can not be, make it up to me in some way,—Thou knowest what is right. And in it all may I be very quiet and restful, remembering that 'the fashion of this world perisheth,'[2] & ere very long I shall be gone beyond the need of this blessing for which I have asked."

And I *am* quiet. It doesn't trouble me or turn the song of my life into the minor key. For this I thank God, fervently!

Burke[3] says that the traits which men love in a woman are dependence, softness, trust, timidity. I haven't these particularly,—indeed I'm quite deficient in them all, & as I beleive them needful in the way in which the writer I have mentioned indicates, I don't expect to be loved, in all my life, in that way. Yet I shall do very well doubtless, & besides, "the girls" love me quite well, & I have *Mary*. Thus endeth the chapter.

1. Not identified.
2. Willard paraphrased 1 Cor. 7:31, "for the fashion of this world passeth."
3. This possibly refers to Sir John Bernard Burke (1815–92), who authored books on upper-class courtship and marriage, such as *Family Romance: or, Episodes in the Domestic Annals of the Aristocracy* (London, 1853) and *Vicissitudes of Families, and Other Essays* (London, 1859), as well as producing the annual *Peerage and Baronetage*.

11 October 1860

Read the great red book—*Mary's* Journal & mine—all through to day, from first to last. Paused not unfrequently, and imagined my Friend in the various scenes which she describes;—fancied just how the beautiful brown eyes would look,—the position of the slight, graceful figure,—the flush on the fine, intellectual brow. O my Friend, you are all I shall have, in life, except the Four who are my kindred, & you love me well & truly now, but I see *The Fate* slowly looming up, "over the hills & far away";[1]—a few years more, & I shall be still your very good Friend, loved quite well by you,—written to, spoken of sometimes, favored with all kind & gentle offices, but not "My Darling" any more—not chosen out from all the world. You did not beleive me when I wrote you once that in God's providence others nearer to you would take my place;—relations, not formed now, but lying just ahead—would disarrange those between us. You disclaimed this vehemently & with sincerity—but that didn't make it less certain to come to pass. For *your sake* I am glad the change is coming;—for my own,—it will be harder than you will think—than my pride will let you see, (for I *have* pride even with you,)—but God will know that what I shall have to bear, when the time which is coming, has come, is *very hard* for me! He will see the loneliness & pain—He will be sorry & love me better than before, & be to me instead of all the blessings that he gives to other women. This I have written calmly but very sadly; I shall read it over still more sadly when—in a few years hence it shall have "come true" to both of us—you, & me.

It will not be so easy as I thought—this Teaching in Kankakee. My room has no fire—my *human*-surroundings are not congenial. This is a town of money-getters & fashion-worshippers. They care nothing for what I have spent my life to obtain,—would pity me if they knew what I enjoy & strive after. The family where I board is not religious—I believe they "profess" to be Unitarians, but have no practical Christianity. Indeed, Mrs. C[ooledge] said at the tea-table yesterday that "The Bible had a great many good things in it but was an old fashioned book"! The young lady[2] is kind, but cares too much for "the gent'men" (in general,) & kindred subjects to be much to me,—or I to her;—besides, we have no mutual affinities. So I stay in my room constantly—out of school,—reading & writing & thinking my thoughts. I'm going to try to write *in earnest* this winter. Think I have some ability in this direction, & must begin to manifest it soon if ever,—for I'm *twenty-one* you know. . . .

1. Willard quoted from Alfred Lord Tennyson, "The Day Dream," in *Poems* (London, 1842), stanza 4, line 193.
2. Mary Cooledge (or Coolidge) (b. ca. 1839), daughter of Willard's landlady, worked as a domestic while living with her mother.

25 October 1860

. . . Have rec'd . . . one of Mother's comforting epistles, from which I will make an extract:—

> It gives me pleasure to learn that you are neither lonely nor unhappy. Though you have not the exuberant gleefulness of the little girls whom you "watched" that day "with such a thoughtful face," I am thankful that you have calmness, a quiet endurance,—a something that you can almost call *Peace*. Pleasurable excitement you must now seek in the vitalizing influences of the Holy Spirit. Fruition awaits us in the Land of the Blest. The *infinite soul* may not find *contentment* in the *gifts of a finite world*. Some writer has said, "For suffering and enduring there is no remedy but striving and doing."[1] This remedy you have adopted.

I thank God for *My Mother* as for no other gift of His bestowing. My nature is so woven into hers, that I almost think it would be death to me to have the bonds severed & one so much *myself* gone

"Over the River, the peaceful River."[2]

She does not know—they do not know any of *"them"*—The Four—
how much my Mother is to me, for, as I firmly beleive, I cling to her
more than any other of her children,—perhaps because I am to need
her more. I am very proud of her too. Few women that I have ever
seen have as much *mind* as she. She has a fine intellect, and, as she
said to me once in the regretful tones of one who felt that the world
did not know her full capacities, "might have been *a singer* (with the
heart,) under more kindly circumstances."

Mary and I were talking together once, and I said "I could not
imagine what it would be to love *any one* better than *Mother*—to cling
to any one more than to Father & Brother, & her." The tears were
almost in my eyes, I spoke so earnestly. But Mary answered lightly, yet
decidedly that "she *knew* she could love the man whom she should
marry in this way," & then *I* knew that in a few years my Sister will
love some one alien to us, better than her Mother who is bone of her
bone & flesh of her flesh; better than her brother & sister whom that
Mother has carried under her own heart; better than her Father who
has watched over her ever since she was born into the world, & had
many an anxious thought about her even before that time! She is to
love this stranger better than these who are *so near* to her & who have
been faithful to her always, & will be to the end of the world when *he*
may grow careless & indifferent;—& it is right that she should do so
doubtless;—it is an instinct of God's own appointing. But my heart
ached to hear her say it. . . .

1. Willard's mother quoted a favorite motto of Willard's from Thomas Carlyle,
"Essay on Burns" in the *Edinburgh Review* (1828). Carlyle (1795–1881), the Scottish
essayist and historian, was of great influence in forming the Victorian worldview. From
1859 to 1869, Willard read many of Carlyle's works and she had first copied the aphorism into her journal on 6 December 1859.
2. Not identified.

3 November 1860

. . . This dark, gloomy morning can't dishearten me, for I've heard
again from *Mary,*—My Darling Child. I'm going to stop calling each
letter "better than the last"—it is getting to be rather of a state announcement. It shall make its final "appearance" and take a "benefit" in this connection, *therefore* I proceed to say that she has never
written me a letter that showed her love for me so plainly as this one
does. No single act or expression of the regard she has for me, ever

made her so dear & sacred to me as these last words. O my Darling! I did not love you all those months in vain. I did not pray—that you might sometime come to care for me,—for nothing. You are *mine* now, more truly than any one else will ever be, & I am *yours* as I shall never be anothers. And I can say to you what I can say to no other human being, that I love you *as* my Mother—though differently from her. My heart towards her, is like a mountain;—strong & firm. There is no doubt of her, no fear as to how she will regard me, no unrest;— I rely on her implicitly, speak her name calmly, think of her without feverishness or ecstacy, love her thoroughly & *forever,* & am almost infinitely grateful to her for her love & devotion.

My heart toward her is like the Jungfrau or Mont Blanc;—toward you, it is Vesuvius or Etna. You understand the difference? I'm not so certain of you,—there is, to one of my nature a delicious unqui-etude in the thought that you will love me only as I prove myself worthy & deserving—in some degree. I *might* become so base that *you* would scorn me;—I *could not* sink so low that *Mother* would not love & mourn for me. My pulse quickens when your hand rests in mine, but a *kiss* from mother's lips falls on my brow like a benediction & only deepens the quiet of my heart. You understand? There is no competition between my love for you & for the dear ones at Home. They are as different as sunshine & moonlight,—both sweet & sa-cred,—both enduring & changeless,—both the *light* of my life,—both blessings which I did not merit,—sent to me from God. I *hope* we may teach together at "*the* College" next year—I half beleive we shall. What would exactly suit me would be this. To go South in January. To teach there until Spring—in the meantime obtaining a knowledge of Southern customs, life etc., then, *in June* to come Home again with *Mary,* & after two months vacation to begin our work together at the N.W.F.C., *Mary* teaching Latin, I taking Miss C[lark]'s place, & both of us rooming together,—with our homes in the same town, & all we love around us. What is there impossible in this? Won't God let it come to pass? I'm going to pray for it, any how. . . .

4 November 1860

. . . Went to church with little Fannie. It was a union meeting of all the churches here, & was the anniversary of the Kankakee Co. Bible Association. . . .[1]

When they "took up the collection" and I wrote "F. E. Willard, $1.00" I felt new thankfulness that I can earn & use money according to my own judgment. I hereby promise myself that, always, I will give as much as I can afford, of my earnings, to promote the doing of good in the world. . . .

1. The Kankakee County Bible Association, like many local Bible associations, distributed Bibles for missions both at home and abroad and raised the money to purchase Bibles for distribution through collections taken at Kankakee's Protestant churches.

5 November 1860

Went to school with my hair done up "woman fashion." My smart little "Whittemore girl"[1] exclaimed, passing her hand wonderingly over my "coat" sleeve, "Why, this isn't Miss Willard at all"! I had some such thought as this myself, as I looked in the glass this morning, & saw a tall, slim figure, a plain, thoughtful face & the "tally mark" that Father Time has faintly dashed across my brow to show that I've lived in his dominions a score of years. Every particle of the girl—look faded out of my face when the short locks were tucked away out of sight this morning, to be worn no more, forever;—& I have a regretful sort of feeling, now that "the last link,"—as it seems to me—is "broken" & I am detached from the old, beautiful, careless life. Well, let it go. . . .

1. The "Whittemore girl" was probably a student of Willard's, although her name does not appear on the list of Willard's students recorded at the back of her journal for 2 October 1860 to 12 February 1861.

6 November 1860

. . . Tonight sat me down with thimble on finger, needle in hand and cork behind ear, & coolly bored a "ho-al" (as Bub would say.) in each appendage to the organs of hearing wherewith I am blessed. It h-u-r-t of course, but then, I've concluded that I ought to try to look as well as I can, out of respect to humanity, & I know with my hair up I need ear-rings to "preserve the proportions." I used to think it a barbarous thing, & do still, but people in general don't, & I do it to please *them,* hoping that they'll feel duly obliged to me for my philanthropy & disinterestedness!

7 November 1860

Abraham Lincoln is elected President of the United States! Hurrah!! Under the present state of things I'm not allowed to vote for him, yet I am as glad on account of this Republican triumph as any man who has "exercised the elective franchise" upon this occasion. It is amusing to observe the interest that the children take in politics. This morning Prof. W. read the "returns" aloud, & all "my little girls," (some of them but six years old), crowded around & listened eagerly, clapping their hands at the announcement of an unusual majority in any state. It was a curious, suggestive sight:—"picture it, think of it":—A tall gentleman reading in triumphant tones; twenty young men around him, listening eagerly, a group of "small boys" in the rear, several young ladies paying graceful attention, & "the other teacher" looking with expectant eyes toward the newspaper, surrounded by a dozen little girls, & holding by the hand the "Rose Bud"[1] who dances up & down & exclaims "Aint you glad that Lincoln's elected, Miss Willard."—A picture representing this scene would not inaptly indicate the genius of a Republican Government,— an organization in which every member—male or female, large or small,—feels a keen, & personal interest. . . .

1. "Rose Bud" was a favorite student of Willard's at the academy. Nowhere did she note Rose Bud's actual name.

6 December 1860

. . . Sat up till 12 o'clock last night talking school matters with Prof. W. Agreed to come back next term. I tried to think it all over before hand, and the decision was prayer-guided—as far as any one of a person so thoughtless & careless as I am, can be.—It would be a thousand times pleasanter to stay at Home through all these cold winter months, but I doubt whether it would be *better.* "Life is never to be easy with me any more,"[1] and this discipline is as good as any. Though I will own that my talk about "endurance," "effort," & self-abnegation is every day becoming more like poetry & less like reality. I don't try to control my temper as I did at Harlem. I don't try to grow good and noble as I really *did* try when I came here first. True, I have little cause for the exhibition of temper, & do nothing really bad—as the world views it,—but the glorious Christian life, I know little about; I have not *Mary's* pure, calm, righteous life. Finding that loftiness & Spartan-like severity of conduct could not be attained—with my disposition—in my present circumstances,—I accepted my lower destiny, & grasped the straws with far too much content, since I could not have the roses. I'm not noble-natured, I own it humbly & with infinite regretfulness. I assimilate too readily with a life & actions & companions beneath my beautiful ideal. I am hardly true to myself, and do not adhere swervelessly to uprightness & truth. If I had trusted God enough, I might have lived a grand, royal life among these people; might perhaps have brought them up somewhat instead of descending to their level, (as I feel I have done). But I have not done this— I have pinched & dwarfed my nature, & after all 'twas nature! poor starving soul, it must feed upon something;—it is our being's law. I can not tell;—God judge between me & my sins, but I know my heart is heavy, for I do not live out my true, best self, humble & faulty as it is. I do not come up to the measure of nobleness of which even I am capable, in mind & heart & conscience. With mistaken good-nature I affect an interest in what is so small to me that I can hardly realize it. I adjust myself to my surroundings. I find it very hard to think of God & Christ. (I could groan at the pain this admission causes me.) I am not morally strong and upright. I descend to puny thoughts & the grand & lofty flee away. I sing songs instead of solemn, quieting hymns; talk localisms and nonsense instead of morals & religion; play chess instead of reading History or the Bible, use amusing, quaint expressions (which are coined with amazing facility at our boarding-house) instead of well-selected, elegant language; laugh instead of thinking; make efforts at satire instead of trying to control my temper; think more of doing up my hair nicely than of exercising a pure, refining influence. And thus my life goes on—my poor, make-shift sort of a life, & I am more sorry than my nearest friend can be. I must not be unjust with myself—I am not *wicked*—only thoughtless & rather degenerating even from the place to which I have arrived, I fear. And yet I struggle feebly in the toils—I am not unmindful of it all. I am wakeful & watchful & will pray more than I have before, that God will lift me up.

I've written this out for you, *Mary*, Darling! who will read this book within a month I suppose. Your letter came today, & woke these thoughts—they've been "in a drowse" before. You love me so truly, & are so generous & noble with me, always, that I do not fear to tell you. Pity me & be sorry with God & Mother, that I am of such texture as does not grow finer & better & loftier amid adverse circumstances. Love me because I shall be holier for your love—dearer to Christ & angels. Pray for me—that I may have strength from Him who is mighty, perfected in my weakness, & that through Him that overcometh, I too, may finally overcome, for Oh! I *have* desires for Holiness & peace! A great, silent cry goes from my heart tonight, though you would not think it to see me sitting here so quietly, with Mary Coolidge opposite, & the fire & the lamp & the common household-appointments around me, & little Fannie sitting at my feet! To them I am a companion—rather a pleasant one, I think; an enthusiastic chess-player, a light-hearted, thoughtless girl-woman, "teaching school" with no wish or aspiration beyond my daily round. *God knows* how false their views are & so do you. Pray for me—love me, angel of my life—"more to me than all the world."

And yet, the case has lights as well as shadows. I have more charity for the world—more faith in it than I did have, before. I see these people "without God in the world," exhibiting a nice sense of honor—much tenderness of conscience & a cheering love for justice & truth. I see a thousand signs of nobleness & right-heartedness that I would not have dreamed of in a community of non-professors. It enlarges my charity—my faith in mankind as such, my catholicity—my cosmopolitan spirit. And this is a *gain* surely. I shall not cry "surely we are the people"[2] with half the certainty that I once felt, & it is better.—I see men making no profession of Christianity, contributing liberally to the support of the church & all its enterprises; manifesting the deepest respect for its rites & ordinances;—professing the greatest reverence and regard for its institutions. I hear young ladies—not *bred* to orthodoxy or affecting an experimental knowledge of its worth,—murmuring prayers with sincerity & faith. I see the children of careless, worldly women kneel to pray "Our Father"—taught by their mothers. I see lying & dishonesty in general frowned upon, & noble deeds applauded, & all this in Kankakee,—the most irreligious community in which I was ever placed. And I walk their streets quietly, & they think me a hum-drum person doubtless, but in my poor wavering, silent heart there are more dreams & longings than they've ever thought in their philosophy.[3] Prof. W. praised me highly. He said I was an excellent teacher & he was pleased with me. Is it egotism to write this? Have I not earned it hard-ly & honestly by three months toil? So I am coming back—the prospect is but a dreary one. I have postponed happiness until next June—when I shall go to my Home again & my Darling will come to me.

1. Willard quoted her brother, Oliver, who said this during a conversation they had on 5 September 1860.
2. Not identified.
3. Willard quoted from William Shakespeare, *Hamlet,* act 1, scene 5, line 166.

12 December 1860

Letters from Ellie, Maggie McKee, and *My Darling*. Though all of these were good, Ellie's in her best, & kindest style, Maggie's interesting and cordial, *Mary's* was the one that brought a flush to my cheek, and a painful longing to my heart. I thought so sadly of my brave, brown-eyed Darling, and the tears came to my eyes, to think that I see her no more, and that she is away from all of us who love her, in that mad, fanatical Southern Land, where the very name of "Northerner" is hateful. How soon we may be involved in a civil war, Heaven only knows, & I tremble for *Mary* as I read the Daily News,[1] and see where Southern men have offered forty thousand dollars, to procure the assasination of Lincoln & Hamlin![2] It worries me more than I will acknowledge to any one save God. O if she were but safe at Home, once more! I hardly know what I ought to do, or whether I have acted wisely, but to-day I sent her these words, *"Darling!* Please come Home."...

1. Willard was probably referring to the *Kankakee Weekly Gazette*, the only Kankakee paper in 1860. There was no Chicago paper titled the *Daily News* at that time.
2. Hannibal Hamlin (1809–91), a United States senator from Maine and Lincoln's running mate, had just been elected vice-president.

14 December 1860

... Sam Coolidge[1] sent *my Darling's* weekly letter up to me. O! what *happiness* came into my heart, at the announcement, that on account of the Disunion spirit at the South, & of the fears of a Negro Insurrection, *Mary* expects to come Home immediately—and will probably be there when I return! I thanked God more fervently for this, than for any blessing He has sent to me in a long, long time. I could not sleep last night, for the *gladness* that I felt—*my Darling!*

1. Samuel F. Cooledge (or Coolidge, b. ca. 1844) worked as a clerk and lived with his mother, Willard's landlady.

26 December 1860
Evanston, Illinois

... I doubt if there is a person living who has greater cause for thankfulness than I. I'm in my own dear little room once more. The fire burns brightly, the old, familiar furniture is around me, the pictures look down benignly from the wall. My sister sits at my feet, writing in her funny, off-hand Journal. My Cousin "Sac"[1] sits opposite—my brother, in his room across the hall, is writing a sermon;—down-stairs Father & Mother sit cozily around the hearth;—from his chamber the melodious (?) tones of John's fiddle are resounding, (John is our "gentleman in a subordinate capacity"—a la Prof. B.)[2] & with a heart brimming with thankfulness I think of all my blessings, & thank Thee for them, Father of every good & perfect gift. But I have not yet numbered them all, nor could I though I should write till the pen dropped from my weary hand. The *best* I have not told, for only think! In the pretty house on Chicago Avenue[3] that I never pass without looking at so earnestly, the upper window-blind, at the side, is open, again;—the dearest girl in the world has come back,— *Mary* Bannister is not in Tennessee any longer!—My Darling slept on my arm, again, last night;—she murmured loving words in my ear, and I am not lonely any more. Only to think that she *is really* with us all again! It seems too good to be beleived. But there is no doubt in the case. I've seen her;—have looked again into the beautiful brown eyes, & heard the sweet voice say "my Darling," while I laid silently, with my lips against *Mary's* cheek. O God! I thank thee, and it is enough.

Yesterday was Christmas, and we all went up to the pretty church among the trees, & listened thoughtfully while Bishop Simpson talked to us of Bethlehem where our Savior was born, of Jerusalem where He died for us;—of the church on the Mountain-side dedicated to Santa Claus, & of the origin of the beautiful superstitions concerning the best of all Holidays. Bp. S. has seen all of these things, & made the impression of them, very vividly upon our minds. The thought of Christ's wonderful love & pity came into my heart,—the thought of all that women owe to Him for their happiness in *this* life, besides their salvation "in that which is to come." And the beautiful Christmas closed & my Darling came in the evening of the day. That was the *best gift*, but I received also very gratefully a beautiful picture *of Mary from Mary*. . . .

1. Willard's cousin, Sarah (Gilman) Dusinbury, was the daughter of Mariah (Hill) Gilman, Willard's mother's oldest sister. Sarah Gilman took over Willard's teaching position at the Kankakee Academy when Willard decided not to return for a second term. In 1861 Gilman married Harry Dusinbury (b. ca. 1833), a post-office clerk she met while in Kankakee.

2. Daniel Bonbright (1831–1912), whom Willard quoted, was a professor of Latin language and literature at NU and a frequent visitor to the Willards' home. He later became dean of the NU college of liberal arts (1899–1902) and, in 1900, after declining the presidency of the university three times, agreed to become acting president, serving for two years. He was also the university's librarian for many years, and remained on the faculty until his death.

3. Willard referred to the Bannister home, approximately one-half block south of the Willards'.

[*Although Willard had agreed to return to Kankakee Academy to teach during the winter term, she decided over Christmas vacation to remain in Evanston. Her cousin, Sarah Gilman, went to Kankakee to teach in her place.*]

23 January 1861

My Life is beautiful and comparatively rich & cheery now;—I regret that I have not more spirit for Journal-keeping. Pleasant events—the memory of which might be fragrant & beautiful all down the years,—pass by unchronicled, & are forgotten. I say nothing of the delightful afternoons spent in *Mary's* cozy sanctum—of our German recitations to Dr. Bannister—(commenced on Jan. 7. '61., I beleive) of the calls made & received—books read—songs sung & prayers offered;—of the endeavors,—in much weakness & not without frequent failures—to become better and more quiet; of the renewed customs of Home Life—the pleasant days, here with Mother & Mary, enlivened at evening by Father's return from his business in the city—of the friendly letters written and received—of the walks & rides & many other ways in which the monotony is broken and my life made

"A thing of beauty,"

& hence, "a joy forever,"[1] as I suppose.

With all of this, I feel that in the future there is something waiting for me—what, I can not tell, that will break in upon this quietness, & give to me instead, tingling of heart, & tears, & agony. But I will not anticipate—"sufficient unto the day, is the evil thereof."[2]

1. Willard paraphrased John Keats, "A thing of beauty is a joy forever," in *Endymion* (London, 1818), book 1, Proem, line 1.
2. Matt. 6:34b.

28 January 1861

. . . 'Tis a strange world we live in—a wonderful destiny that waits this soul of mine!

I looked out the other evening, from the "Lake [Michigan] window" of our little room,—Mary's & mine.—The moon was looking down serenely & a thousand stars glistened & sparkled through the frosty air. I thought how small I was—how lost, amid the grandeur of the earth & the firmament;—how short-lived I was to be—walking in quiet pathways for a while, then passing into Shadow-Land forever. And yet, the gleam in my eye as I looked into the sky had more *meaning* in it than the light of all the stars, for I am in *His* likeness who hung them in their "serene & silent spaces";[1]—I shall go on to all eternity—knowing & feeling—enduring & enjoying! There is some loftier, better destiny waiting for me than for those shining ones, look they never so quietly upon my feverish Life.

1. Not identified.

17 February 1861

. . . I remember that I used to think myself "smart";—I used to plan great things that I would do and be;—I meant to become famous,— never doubting that I had the power. But it is over. The mist has cleared away, and I dream no longer—though I'm *only* twenty one years old. "Only,"—did I say?

If it be true that we have need to say "God help us! when we think ourselves strong," I beleive that the opposite is equally true,—nay, that we need *Him* most when most distrusting our own capacities. And I have come to this point—that I think myself not good, not gifted in any way. I can not see why I should be loved—why I should hope for myself a beautiful and useful Life, or a glorious Immortality at its close. Never before in all my life have I held myself at so cheap a rate as since I came Home this last time. It's a query with me though, whether *really* I amount to so little. I can't quite give up, and content myself to belong always to what Dr. L[1]—once called (much to my disgust *then*) "the *happy* mediocrity." Is it inevitable that I'm to account myself one of the "Great Commonalty," during my mortal Life? Let us see: Jump into the scales, F.E.W.! In honesty—(as before God, and I say it reverently,) you shall be weighed. *What you beleive of yourself* is vital to you. Let others think as they will, if you "feel the victory in you" (as my Father says), "all things are possible."[2] Deal generously with yourself—let not an overweening modesty (of which, I think, you've never been accused!) cause you to pass lightly over any redeeming traits you may possess. Let us have just weight and measurement, in all regards.

Well then:—

(Beginning with the lowest,—and yet the highest department,— pardon the unexplained paradox) you are not beautiful, pretty, or even good-looking. (There's the bald fact, make what you can of it!) *And yet* (off set no. 1.) you are not disagreeable or unpleasant, either in face or figure. You have no shocking defects in respect of personal appearance. And *that's something*. Your expression is perhaps rather resolute than otherwise, but naturally (and a little *artfully* too,) you tell but little with your face.

In manners you are rather reserved toward those to whom you feel indifferently. You are too much inclined to *moods, and yet* you are,—as a rule,—exceedingly careful not to wound the feelings of others, and mean to be deferential to those who are your superiors, (*self-respectingly* so), kind to your inferiors and cordial with your equals. (off set no. 2.) You are hardly *natural* enough, when in society, and have a certain air of self-consciousness sometimes, that ill becomes you. However, as you think much upon the subject, it is not unlikely that, by & by, your Manners will assume the half-cordial, half-dignified character that accords best with your nature.

You have a good mind, but one not evenly balanced or developed. Your perceptions are rather quick, your memory,—on the whole—unusual. Imagination, good. Reasoning faculties very fair. Judgment in practical matters, not extraordinary; elsewhere, excellent.

Your nature is appreciative. You are not coarse-grained. You *feel* with surprising, and almost painful quickness. An innuendo or double entendra smites you like a blow. . . . "People" call such as you, "sensitive." It is a trait of your Family. It will bring you pain a thousand times when no one dreams of it, and yet, you are better for its existence. It gives delicacy to your character, and the Friends that you may have, will love you better for it, and for its practical effect upon your conduct. Your nature, though not of the characteristically "emotional" cast is not unfeeling. You have not the all-embracing love for man as man that is so noble and admirable, yet the few Friends that you count among the multitude, have more devotion from you than they dream of, doubtless, for your love for them approaches to idolatry. *And yet,* your "affections" are completely under your control, and are never suffered to have "their own wild will,"[3] but fix themselves only upon those objects—among the many that *might* be chosen—when they are manifestly desired. As for your Will, I can not find out whether it is strong or weak. I hardly think it particularly powerful, *and yet* there is something about you for which I hardly know how to account on any other supposition. There is a sort of independence and self-reliance that gives the idea of *will* and yet is not really such. However the facts may be, on this point, I think you would not be accounted a Negative Character.

For the Religious Qualities of your Mind;—you are not particularly conscientious;—rather inclined to scepticism;—sometimes haunted by thoughts of Unbeleif. The aesthetics of Christianity have far too large a share in your creed both theoretic and practical. *Yet* you have right wishes, and great longings after a pure and holy Life.

Dear me! I don't make you out as bad as I feel you to be. Placed in the scale against your beautiful, ideal Character by which you fain would mould yourself, you'd "kick the beam" quickly enough, of course, but somehow, *my consciousness* affirms that the picture I have drawn has not half the *shades* it merits. In a spasmodic way you're generous, yet beneath this, *Selfishness* is deeply rooted in your heart. You're not a bit religious, naturally;—you're some-what original but haven't energy or *persistence* enough ever to excel, I fear, though you have some facility as a writer;—*less* I candidly think, than you had a year or two ago. (That's encouraging?)

Well, on the whole, I don't make you out as poor or common-place as I thought you to be, and perhaps, if you keep your eyes *wide open* to your faults, and God will help you, you may yet come to be rather good than bad. For this, thank God and take courage. And O! forget what you will, Frances, my Best Friend in all the world,—ask the Kind, Infinite Helper, to mould you by His providences—*let them be what they will*—so that every year you may grow "calmer and calmer";—richer in love and peacefulness and faith. Forgetting the poor dreams of less thoughtful years, have this and this only for your *Ambition:*—to be gentle and kindly and forgiving;—full of *charity* which suffereth and hath patience;—pleasing in the sight of God and men. . . .

1. Jacob W. Ludlam (1807–59) was an Evanston neighbor and Willard's doctor who treated her when she was ill with typhoid in July 1859. He died of typhoid that same month.
2. Matt. 19:26; Mark 9:23, 10:27; Luke 18:27.
3. Not identified.

5 March 1861

. . . Last evening I went to the Reading Circle. . . .[1]

Mr. Linn[2] read an Essay on Art, which was followed by a discussion on the same subject. Mr. Taplin is the Talker of the "Circle," and advances his opinions with a beg-your-pardon, yet candid and persistent air that is quite amusing, o'times.

Miss Kellogg[3] read to us in her sweet, womanly voice, from Henry Giles "Illustrations of Genius."[4] I was greatly interested as I sat there behind my mask. Somehow I talk less and less every time—if such a thing can be averred of one who patronizes silence to an extent and with a liberality that is unequalled. I can't help it—I *won't* talk before those people! They listen so coldly to a "poor dear" and then the silence *aches* when one is "done" and no balm of response is dropped into it. At "Apple-time" I sat beside Miss Clark and found I had some ideas to offer, and was not really *collapsed* after all! It was a comforting discovery. . . .

1. The Reading Circle was an informal literary club, made up of NU students and graduates, and teachers and former students from NWFC who met to discuss literary works that the members chose.

2. Alphonso Clark Linn (1836–64) graduated from NU in 1860 and became mathematics and Latin tutor at the school. In 1864 he entered the army as captain of the University Guards (a part of Company F of the 134th Illinois Infantry) and died soon after at camp in Columbus, Kentucky.

3. Charlotte A. Kellogg (b. ca. 1836) was teacher of instrumental and vocal music at NWFC from 1858 until 1862 or 1863.

4. Kellogg read from Henry Giles, *Illustrations of Genius in Some of its Relations to Culture and Society* (Boston, 1854).

22 March 1861

. . . I went [to *Mary's*] again last evening, and we sat in the cozy, quiet room of my Darling, that has such a charm for me. I have a strange regard for it—every article of furniture, the pictures and books and numerous little articles of curious contrivance that find their way into the sanctums of taste and refinement—I know them all "by heart";—they are in my memory, every one. This room so sacred to my Friend, so marked by her long residence in it—so saturated with her spirit and tastes is the place where I spend my calmest, most delightful hours.

I staid in it last night, and until morning lay there quietly, so *satisfied* & *rested* with her head upon my shoulder,—her cheek against mine. I shall never be more happy—I can never ask to be. How I love *Mary!* How she grows dearer when I thought my power of loving had reached its greatest height & profoundest depth! How my heart closes around her and would shield her from all pain & danger if it could! I *know* her better every day;—I see more reason for loving her, admiring & reverencing, every day. No one on earth can tell what she is to me—she is a revelation—a poem—a picture—a shelter—a defence—she is all I need, & if I could have her always I would never shed a regretful tear for any boon of Life that I may miss. What holy, loving, beautiful words she said to me last night in her sweet, thrilling voice!—words too holy for my pen to write. What pathos, and intensity she pressed into the Beautiful Word of ours that she never has *spoken* before. How delicate and tender she is with me—forgiving much—forbearing and beleiving! For *Mary, My Gift* I am more thankful than I shall ever be able to tell to her or God. May blessings crowd upon her footsteps and *quietness* & *peace* be hers. I wish for her a Life overflowing with *Love* usefulness and the blessedness of God! . . .

28 March 1861

. . . I wish I could write out my thoughts—I wish _____

Somehow I think there are possibilities in me that I do not enough regard. I really think I might be and do more [than] I ever have—as yet. I feel it sometimes—this rising up of powers that I don't use as I might—God forgive me if it's wrong or conceited to say so. It seems to me only the "cry of the Human"[1] the blunt declaration of my best self under its manifold disguises, that it *does exist*—that it might do;— that this poor, unworthy life is *not all;*—that I might do something higher and better,—aye! and that I will. . . .

1. Willard referred to the title of a poem by Elizabeth Barrett Browning, "The Cry of the Human," in *Poems,* vol. 2 (London, 1844).

PART TWO

31 March 1861–6 January 1863

Except under rare conditions it is painful to *love a person*.
So many fibers of your being reach out toward *This Other*
& twine about him; (or *her;*—one of mine has been *her*).
The current of your thoughts sets toward him;—your *affinity* is for him. . . . It costs so dear—this *loving*.

—22 March 1862

During the first months of 1861, Willard and Bannister's friendship continued with the same intensity that had characterized it earlier. But by late spring both young women had beaux: Bannister's was Oliver Willard and Frances Willard's was Charles Fowler,[1] a seminary classmate of her brother's. Both young women's relationships with eligible young men were thought eminently suitable and were encouraged by their families, friends, and community. Willard was surprised and delighted to have the attentions of a young man she found handsome and intelligent and was immediately put at ease because he treated her as an intellectual equal. She confided her new feelings to Bannister, who shared in her delight.

Willard eagerly awaited signs that her feelings were reciprocated, and, by early June, Fowler told her that he loved her and wished to marry her. Throughout the summer while Willard taught school again in Harlem, they looked forward to his fall graduation from seminary and his first appointment as a Methodist pastor, when they would become engaged and make wedding plans. At the same time, the courtship of Oliver Willard and Mary Bannister progressed, and they announced their engagement in July 1861. Two months later, Fowler and Willard were engaged.

Willard's journal from summer through early winter 1861 shows her laboring to convince herself that she was happy since she now possessed what she thought every woman ought to desire more than anything else: the prospect of marriage to a man whom she would love above all others and on whom she could depend for support throughout her life in exchange for her undivided devotion. Much within her upbringing and her present experience had led her to expect and hope for such a love, even though she had, from time to time, expressed reservations about whether she was meant to marry. Her parents had urged her to prepare herself for the eventuality of marriage; young women she knew from Wisconsin and Evanston were rapidly marrying; her own brother and her best friend were happily engrossed in their new relationship with each other.

Yet during midsummer Willard hinted in her journal of great unhappiness, and by September she wrote of a "crisis in my Hidden Life."[2] There were actually two crises with which Willard struggled, although they were tangled together in a confusion of emotions that left Willard spiritually exhausted and despairing for nearly a year. The first, and the most difficult crisis to resolve, had to do with Willard's love for her friend Mary Bannister. She knew in her mind that their relationship must change, that she could no longer be "more than all the world" to her friend, since in both young women's understanding of love, that place was reserved for the man one would marry. Yet Willard's heart could not accept what her mind knew. Agonized, she poured out her frustration in entry after entry in her journal.

Willard's troubling crisis of friendship had several aspects: her displacement in Bannister's affections by her brother; her inability to substitute what she, her family, and her friends believed to be an appropriate, "sisterly" liking for a love that was suddenly labeled "abnormal"[3] and deemed impermissible once Bannister was engaged to Willard's brother; and the startling rebelliousness of her heart, which would not accede to the expectations of society and the commands of her own will, as she continued to love her friend passionately. Underneath all these worries lurked her suspicions that she might, indeed, be abnormal, that her love for Bannister was inappropriate and somehow unnatural. Unsuccessful in her efforts to redefine that love, Willard desperately determined to uproot it from her heart, to "strangle" it.[4] Yet her love for her friend proved stubborn and tenacious.

As if this crisis of love were not enough, Willard was forced to deal with another: though she loved Mary Bannister too much, she did not love Charles Fowler at all. Her journal for summer and early fall 1861 alludes to her uneasiness about her relationship with Fowler, but she was not yet ready to face her feelings and write them out candidly. By mid-October she was, and she began to record the mixture of emotions she felt toward him. She admired and respected Fowler, enjoyed his company most of the time, and was highly flattered by his attention to her, particularly since she had believed, for a long while, that no man would ever care for her. But she was not in the least physically attracted to him, although he was to her. As Willard came to the difficult conclusion that she did not love Fowler, she wondered briefly whether she was incapable of recognizing what it meant to love a man since she had had no previous male lover. But she quickly dismissed the possibility because she was confident that she knew what love was. She had for Mary Bannister a "deep, thrilling, all-sacrificing love,"[5] which she did not feel for Fowler. She asked herself desperately why she could not have the love for her fiancé that she had for her friend.

Willard tried to view her dilemma from every possible angle, taking into consideration the consequences for everyone involved. She was concerned about her family's irritation with what they perceived as her unreasonable expectations for marriage, and she was anxious not to hurt and disappoint her fiancé. She worried about the gossip and unpleasantness she might cause by breaking her engagement.

And she was frightened at the prospect of giving up a secure, socially acceptable future for the lonely alternative of a single life. However, she was even more disturbed by the pain a marriage without love based on mutual sexual attraction would cause for both Fowler and herself. She believed that a husband deserved such love from his wife, and that a wife should not have to endure a lifelong relationship with a husband whom she did not love fully.

In mid-October, her conscience demanded that she tell Fowler of her reservations concerning their marriage. Once she had been completely honest with him, she was prepared to do what he wished. After much discussion, he proposed that they continue their engagement. He would refrain from physical demonstrations of affection for her while they waited to see if her friendly feelings toward him might develop into something deeper. He agreed that genuine love, including mutual physical attraction, should be present in a marriage. So they waited. But by January 1862 the relationship was deteriorating, and Fowler asked Willard for a decision concerning their engagement. After much thought and prayer, she sent him a letter ending it. At last, one of Willard's great struggles was over.

The deeper, more painful crisis of her love for Mary Bannister continued to torment her during the spring, as she vacillated between the hope that they could establish a proper, sisterly relationship and the realization that she was still wildly in love with her friend. In May, however, Willard's attention and energy were diverted from her own interior conflict by the serious illness of her sister, Mary. The entire family took turns nursing Mary, whose condition grew steadily worse. On 8 June 1862 she died of tuberculosis. The family was overcome with grief, Willard so much so that for the whole summer she could record almost nothing in her journal.

A brief entry on 3 July noted the marriage of her brother and Mary Bannister and their immediate departure for Denver, where he was to serve a church. A few months later, her mother left Evanston for an extended stay with her family in western New York, and Willard's father arranged to board in downtown Chicago near his office. They felt that they could not bear to stay in the place where their daughter had died. Willard was offered a teaching position at NWFC, and she moved over to the college building. It seemed to her that in a very brief amount of time she had lost everything she cherished: her home, her mother and father (at least for a while), her brother, her best friend, and her beloved sister. She felt utterly desolate.

To compound her misery, she was also in great confusion about her sexual identity, and she no longer knew what to think about marriage as a possibility for her. She was still convinced that the mutual, all-encompassing love of a man and a woman within marriage represented what she termed "the greatest good."[6] In such a union, the husband would be the strong, steady support on which his delicate, fragile wife could lean. This was the view of marriage she thought society and her own family held. This greatest good, however, would not be hers, she suspected, although she continued to hope that it might. Marriage was probably not to be her lot for several compelling and intertwined reasons. First, she believed that she loved women, not men, with the depth of love she felt must be present in the ideal marriage. But she thought that society viewed such relationships between women as abnormal. Passionate attachments between young girls were acceptable, she knew, but they were expected to give way to a mature love between men and women. Her family and friends had made that abundantly clear to her when they saw how she clung to Mary Bannister although they were both engaged to be married.

Were she to deny or subdue her love for women and agree to marry, she felt that she could not conform to the role that she thought a wife must play in the ideal marriage, surrendering the independence and freedom that she valued so highly, and placing her husband's aspirations before her own. In any love relationship, whether with a man or a woman, she would only be satisfied in what she understood then as the male role. She imagined herself as the strong, independent "husband" on whom her "wife" leaned, the one who confidently strode forth into the world, pursuing a career. If marriage, that greatest good, was not to be her lot, Willard was prepared to live a life of "single blessedness."[7] She expected that it would be a difficult and lonely life, but she would rely on herself. At the same time, she would trust in God's love and care for her, and in her certainty that God had work for her to do. Though she could not allow herself to lean on a man, she would confidently depend on God.

As Willard settled into her teaching duties, she began to feel slightly less bereft. She was busy and relatively happy, surrounded by admiring students, and she fell deeply in love with one of them, Ada Brigham,[8] who returned her love. Willard had learned from bitter experience, though, that their love would be short-lived because her student would soon meet that one man whom she would love beyond all others. Willard seemed, then, to be willing to conform, however reluctantly and uncomfortably, to societal conventions regarding love and marriage. But she was still lonely, separated from all those she loved, and preparing to take another teaching position in faraway

Pittsburgh, where she knew nobody. She desperately needed someone to give her affection, treating her tenderly and with intimacy, if just for a little while. Nevertheless, she bravely readied herself to go off to Pennsylvania, with plans in mind for new writing projects. Still ambitious to make something of herself in the world, she wholeheartedly embraced Thomas Carlyle's aphorism that she had first copied in her journal more than three years earlier: "For suffering and enduring there is no remedy but striving and doing."

Notes

1. Charles Henry Fowler (1837–1908), an MEC minister and bishop, was born in Burford, Ontario, Canada, and moved with his family to Illinois in 1841. He was educated at Genesee Wesleyan College in Lima, New York, graduating with honors in 1855. He graduated from GBI in November 1861. A gifted orator and administrator, Fowler spent the early part of his successful ministry career serving a number of Chicago churches during the 1860s and 1870s. After the Chicago fire in 1871 he ably solicited aid to rebuild Methodist schools and churches destroyed by the blaze. He was subsequently elected president of NU, serving from 1872 to 1876, edited *The Christian Advocate* (1876–80), and was Missionary Secretary of the MEC (1880–84). In 1884 he was elected a bishop of the MEC.

2. Journal, 11 September 1861.

3. Ibid., 4 September 1861. Two novels that Willard read, Henry Wadsworth Longfellow's *Kavanagh* (Boston, 1849; read by Willard in June 1859) and Harriet Beecher Stowe's *The Pearl of Orr's Island: A Story of the Coast of Maine* (read by Willard in serialized form in the *Atlantic Monthly* in 1861–62, published in book form in Boston, 1862), contain very moving passages about the passionate friendships of young women. However, the characters in both novels understand that the love of husband and wife will, to a great extent, displace that between young women. Longfellow describes the love between Cecelia Vaughan and Alice Archer very similarly to the way Willard describes her love for Mary Bannister: "They were nearly of the same age, and had been drawn together by that mysterious power which discovers and selects friends for us in our childhood. They sat together in school; they walked together after school; they told each other their manifold secrets; they wrote long and impassioned letters to each other in the evening, in a word, they were in love with each other. It was, so to speak, a rehearsal in girlhood of the great drama of woman's life" (*Kavanagh* [Boston, 1904], 366).

4. Journal, 29 March 1862.

5. Ibid., 15 October 1861.

6. Ibid., 31 March 1862.

7. The phrase "single blessedness," originally found in William Shakespeare, *A Midsummer Night's Dream*, act 1, scene 1, line 78, was used often during the nineteenth century to describe the life of an unmarried woman.

Willard and her friends used it almost jokingly to refer to their unmarried state.

8. Ada Frances Brigham was a student of Willard's at NWFC for part of the fall 1862 term, although she does not appear in NWFC's records. In scrapbook 3, at the Willard Memorial Library, there is an unidentified, undated (probably fall 1871) newspaper clipping (38) noting that Miss Addie (probably a nickname for Ada) Brigham had accepted an engagement as a teacher of vocal and instrumental music at a new seminary in Elgin, Ill., and another clipping (68) mentioning that Miss Brigham, a professor at the Evanston College for Ladies, served as a volunteer assistant at a concert in Highland Park, Ill., probably in 1872. Willard wrote in her journal on 28 March 1896 that she had spent time in Evanston with Kate Jackson and Ada Brigham, so she evidently kept up her friendship with Brigham.

Last evening the Reading Circle *was had* at Dr. Bannister's. . . .

The College Teachers came, and Mr. Fowler. He is one of "the nice Biblicals"[1]—a very fine scholar, thought by some persons the best student and orator in the Institute. He is fine looking, (in an intellectual "point of view,") and gentlemanly. Withal, I like him very much,—better than any other Biblical, "enough sight" or I wouldn't have troubled myself to say all this about him! Having in my dry, statistical fashion gone the young man over, I proceed "in general principles."

The Subject of Conversation was "Influence of Circumstances on Character."

I liked the "treatment" thereof, very much,—it was rather spirited and somewhat generally participated in by "we, us, & Co." I regarded the evening as the pleasantest the Reading Circle has yet afforded me. . . .

1. "Biblicals" was the nickname Evanston residents gave to young men studying at GBI.

. . . In the evening we went to the Sociable—at *Mary's*. It was the pleasantest I have attended this Winter;—certainly the largest and most *spirited*.

Mary moved about among them with her quiet, lady-like air, and I looked at her & thought—they did not know *how dear* she was to me!

I talked with Mr. Fowler awhile, and enjoyed it very much. Somehow I am so frank with him, and I feel that he is with me. I say what I think of first, certain that he will not misconstrue me, or think me foolish. I don't put him off with the set speeches & frivolities that I have for so many people, but talk seriously and *self-ly* with him. We agreed that there are three sets of persons—whom we meet in Society. For the first we "have no message"—we can't *talk with them,* but under stress of circumstance manage to convert ourselves into a higher order of *parrot* and exchange sentences with not a bit more real meaning in them than if we said "Polly wants a cracker." With the second, we talk of books, countries, occurences lear[n]ing & imparting something, but in studied, *stilted* phrase and with nervous tension and courteous aforethought. With the third, we are ourselves, & Life is the theme;—*Life* under its countless manifestations—with its fears & suffering & aspiration;—with its "noble sorrow," and endless longing for something higher & holier than it has reached. . . .

3 April 1861

Just from down stairs, where Oliver has preached to us the sermon he will deliver at Harlem next Sabbath.

I am surprised at him. He is talented—even more than I thought with all my admiration. I have seldom heard a better sermon than this—the *second* he has ever written! It is full of eloquence and power—and brought the painful feeling that answers me for tears, just as Dr. Foster used to, in his best discourses. I know I don't over-rate. My brother will do a great deal of good in the world and our pride will be in him!

And Fowler! I read a sermon of his. The closing passage—where he appeals to them by virtue of his *youth* and sympathy with them, was *splendid*. As I read it aloud, my voice trembled and I could hardly go on. How must it sound as he would say it! The whole sermon, for force, strength and argument is unequalled;—*as good* as Oliver's—I can not say more. How glorious it is to have the gift of eloquence. After this, I shall think with a sort of pity of the gentlemanly, cultivated *Biblicals* I know, who lack this *one thing needful*—with the Religion they are supposed to have—to their success. . . .

9 April 1861

. . . Mr. Fowler was here, today. I have more ideas and hopes "in common" with him, than almost any one I know. What he says & thinks, suits me, always. I looked at him, as he sat talking with us, & thought how splendid he was;—I have never seen a finer head,—a more intellectual, almost spiritual outline to the face. I liked to look at him, when his face was lit up, with his thought, as at a picture,—it pleased my aesthetic sense. Well, that will do for *him*. . . .

13 April 1861

. . . Father brought startling intelligence relating to the Country. "The war has actually begun!" Fort Sumpter is attacked by those villianous Charlestonians;[1]—cannonading has been going on all day. So "brother has risen up against brother" & *Civil War* has commenced in "the Land of the Free & the Home of the Brave." I think I love my country as truly & intensly as the *words* of the maddest politician would indicate that he did, & I know I feel strange & sad to think how they are fighting, "down there" tonight. But *God* works in these things, & if *the Curse* that *Slavery* entails upon us, can be removed, every true, patriotic heart must say "let it be done." Our greatness must remain problematic, while this shadow of a terrible *wrong* is over us. . . .

1. Confederate troops from South Carolina began bombarding the federal garrison at Fort Sumter, located on an island in the Charleston harbor, on 12 April 1861, technically beginning the Civil War. On 14 April the garrison surrendered and was evacuated by steamer.

20 April 1861

. . . *Mary* & I went to the College. . . . As we came back we saw a flag on the cupola of Bishop Simpson's house, & this made me think of war more than ever, though we hear little else now. The city is in a tumult & Evanston partakes in proportion to its diminutive size. Some of the University students have enlisted—a company is to be formed here. . . . It is terrible—I had not realized it. To think that in a month *my own brother* may be gone to the War![1] For the danger is great—an attack on Washington is feared, & troops are being sent to guard our own state, as Cairo is menaced by the traitors.[2]

Why should he not go? Other young men, as dear to their mothers & sisters as *he* is to us, are going. By what right is he exempt? I would not dare ask him to stay if his country needed him—and I greatly fear it will. I know him well;—I can see his eye flash as we talk of the indignities the North has suffered, & I know nothing would hinder him from going. Dearly as I love him—and he *is* my *only* brother,—I would try to be brave about it, and let him go, saying "Good-bye" in a cheerful voice though my heart was almost breaking,—and praying God as I have never yet prayed, to bring him back to us again. . . .

1. Oliver Willard enlisted for one hundred days in a company formed by GBI students, but the company was never called up.

2. Cairo, Illinois, was an important strategic position in the early stages of the Civil War. It was located at the southern tip of the state, where the Ohio River and the Mississippi River joined, and was the southern terminus of the Illinois Central Railroad. Whatever side controlled Cairo could also control navigation of a major waterway and railway access to the northwest. There was strong support for the South in Cairo, and Union troops were quickly dispatched there from Chicago and other parts of Illinois. They arrived to secure the city for the North on 22 April 1861.

27 April 1861

. . . On Wednesday we had the Sociable at Mr. Beveridge's[1] & after it I went walking with Mr. Fowler. It was beautiful moonlight & we went to the Pier.

If he goes to the war & is killed, I shall be glad to remember how nobly & bravely he talked of it;—how firm & fearless he seemed, though counting the cost & looking the fate of "the unattended dying & the uncoffined dead," in the face. He is the Captain of the Company[2] & in more danger than any one else, except my own brother who is—with a student I do not know—in the front rank. . . .

1. John Laurie Beveridge (1824–1910), a lawyer, lived across the street from the Willards on Chicago Avenue. In August 1861 he enlisted in the Union army and attained the rank of brigadier general before the war ended. He was elected lieutenant governor of Illinois in 1872 and became governor in 1873 after his predecessor was elected to the United States Senate.

2. Charles Fowler was elected captain of the volunteer company formed by GBI students.

29 April 1861

I wonder if I ought? It seems rather hypocritical to keep a Journal and not write in it one's *self*, & one's *entire* self as far as it is known.

I have *never* done this—until now. If I told nothing to you, Book, that savored of romance or secret sighing, or a "heart-affair," it was because I had none of these things to tell. I never permitted them in myself. I beleive we may be creatures of *will* in these matters, & I have been one. Beyond the whim of the hour—the fancy of a day, fleeting as the mist at morning, I have had no "experiences." And very heartily I thank God for this. That my Heart has been *free* & *quiet* all these years;—that it is now as fresh and buoyant as ever;—unscarred, unwounded—O! I am glad of this! Human Hearts are sacred things;—they are tender & delicate, too;—easily hurt,—not easily healed.

I am not sentimental;—could never "pine away" on account of "blasted hopes," "unrequited affections," or "broken vows." (I am not sneering now, nor ever shall, I hope, at those who are so constituted that they can not help doing these things.) I have never known any thing of *Love*—(the kind, I mean, they tell about in Stories,) *until* _____

There's a robin singing on a tree-top, yonder. The music is very sweet, jubilant & beautiful.

Some-how there is a song in my heart—just like the Robin's, only more soft & full of melody. It was never there till—O, a very little while ago.

I've heard Father tell how the brooks come down the mountains, in New England;—out of dark, silent places. Among evergreens &

moss & shadow they steal forth, & gurgle with such a pleasant murmur, down the steep hill-sides. . . . Well I keep on hearing such a
musical sound all the time, & I guess that's in my *Heart,* too. It is rather strange, I know, & not like *me,* but I've read of "the Fountain very
far down"[1] in some people's natures—perhaps it has been reached
in mine! When & how did it happen? Only a little while ago,—the
"*how*" of it, is my affair, isn't it?

I think so often, now-a-days of the beautiful, waxen buds of white
roses. Do they *always* change to *roses,* I wonder? It may be foolish, but
I can't help hoping that they do.

There's a golden light falling over the stream, & the buds;—the
song I spoke of, rises through it;—it is not rich & deep like that coming through stained-glass windows, *yet,* but it makes every thing beautiful—more than it used to be. There's a feeling of zestfulness—like
an evening breeze among pines, I think,—very fresh & pleasant,
whatever it resembles. There are blue domes arching over me—&
stars shine down, & *Life* stretches away *so beautiful!* Like a Landscape
where the trees wave & the grass & flowers are out;—there is a river
in it, grand & strong, its current flowing so calmly & with the majesty of power.

I see all these analogies & many more—between me & the beautiful world I live in.

It is no matter about *particulars,* suffice it that I am some way very
different,—that I wonder & laugh & am surprised at myself. That my
boasted pride has fled away from me, & yet I'm not ashamed. That I
am glad & thankful, & *finally* that for the first time in your life, you
"stony-hearted" personage *who have* smiled wisely upon the secrecy
with which the "other girls" invested *their Journals*—*you* must hang
your head, look remarkably foolish and *hide this book* between the
mattress & the feather-bed! O simpleton! I mourn over your aposta-
sy. Aren't you ashamed of your self?

No, not the least! Why should I be? "So goes the world, & so the
world will always go."[2]

1. Not identified.
2. The quote may be a paraphrase of several lines from John Gower, *Confessio
Amantis* (Westminster, 1493), prol. 570–71: "Now here, now there, now to, now fro /
Now up, now down, the world goth so. / And ever hath done and ever shall."

30 April 1861

. . . I had a pleasant talk with Mr. F. Came Home & spent the night
with *Mary;*—a beautiful Night, in which I told her *every thing,* & won-

dered at my *new-self* & loved her for her generous interest in what was *so* interesting to me.

There are many thoughts I might write here. They lie under what I've said all day;—under the smiles & laughter,—under the careless looks & tones. It is very new to me;—I hardly know myself. The proud, don't-care feeling of all my life before, is gone, & I acknowledge myself *conquered.*[1]

It seems strange to give up;—strange to "care" so much for one I don't know very well;—strange to *think* so much in such a new direction! I doubt my own identity once in a while.

It is all right, doubtless—I can but hope it may be *beautiful.* It is easy to wait—I am quiet & *at rest.*

Spent the P.M. with *Mary.* So queerly, too. I'm changed & the consciousness of it is in our faces when we look at each other, as we talk;—I can see it flashing with such a mischievous expression, from *Mary's* bright, dark eyes. She's glad,—for many reasons, but *because she loves me,*—most, I am sure;—my noble-hearted Friend. . . .

1. Charles Fowler wrote in the margin of Willard's journal, beside this sentence: "First mention in this book, Frank. *May God bless you.*"

5 May 1861

An eventful day to me.

Mary & I publicly declared our determination—to endeavor with God's help—to live as *Christians;*—we were baptized, received into the Church, & Communed.

Those were solemn vows we made!—I almost trembled as our voices mingled in the responses to the questions that were asked us. I felt how solemn a thing it was;—how awful the responsibility that would thence-forth rest upon us.

And yet, the ceremony seemed very beautiful to me. We knelt there at the Altar, *we* whose lives & hearts & thoughts have been *one.* It was eminently fitting that we should in this, as in every thing, be together. I think God looked on us kindly, & Christ loved us, with His infinite condescending love, as we promised, publicly, yesterday, to serve & honor Him always. I know that I will try. I prayed so earnestly for help & strength to keep the promises I made, as the hand of our Pastor[1] trembled while it rested on my head, and he baptized me.

And I felt some strength—some quietness. O! so much more than I deserved!

I will write faithfully here, of my failures or successes. Christ pity me, & make me strong.

Father, Mother, & Oliver were there. I knew that they were glad for us, & looked with loving eyes & thought with prayerful hearts. And My Darling was there too, & I was *sure* she prayed, & loved us as we knelt before the altar, all alone.

God help me to feel that I have given myself to Thee!

I know that there is nothing in Life that does not seem trivial to me, compared with God's approval. I know that there is nothing I would not sacrifice for this;—no desire that is not insignificant, compared with this. And yet Life looks rich & beautiful to me—full of joy & blessedness. I think only too much about it, & with all this, I feel that no *purpose* is so deep & all pervading with me, as the purpose to live for God in the world, & no desire is so strong as the desire to have Him smile upon me here, & take me to Himself *at last.* . . .

1. Willard's pastor was Robert Kendall Bibbins (1824–98), who remained at the Evanston MCE for only one year.

18 May 1861

In the Morning *Mary* & I went walking, & afterwards I spent the fore-noon with her. It grows more & more beautiful & sweet to me, to be where *Mary* is! It *contents* me, somehow & gives me quiet & completeness. Her temperament—so different from mine, acts on mine strangely. It refines me, & gives a warmer coloring to my sensibilities. No experience has been so rich & beneficial in its effects on me, as loving so deeply as I do, this gentle, high-souled Friend of mine, with her finely-wrought nature, & proud spirit that bends but cannot be broken;—that can be led, not driven.

She came to see me in the afternoon, & Fowler called.

He is very entertaining. For more than an hour he talked about the photographs of his professors & class-mates at the College (in a book he showed to me.) & I was greatly interested. He talks *so well*—"like a book," literally. There is no hesitation, no repetition, no "hackling" (as my father calls it). Indeed his mind seems to me so well *sorted out.* Like a "store," where the shelves are all in order, & every thing labelled & arranged so that the proprietor knows exactly where to find any thing he wants to use. (Or like a *library* to use *Mary's* choicer illustration.) Somehow "Charles Henry" (as I call him to myself "o'times") understands me perfectly & knows precisely what key to touch in my nature to bring out the sweetest, clearest tone. I talk better with him, than with other persons; my knowledge seems more as though it were held *in solution* in my mind. He seems to apprehend me always,—can take a hint with remarkable quickness, & never misinterprets. He said "ever so" complimentary a thing to me which quite upset me, but,—I must acknowledge—also rather set me up! . . .

[*Willard went back to Harlem, Ill., to teach at the one-room school where she had taught during the summer of 1860. Once again she boarded with the Thatcher family.*]

5 June 1861
Harlem

I haven't written here since Friday—four whole days. In them— how shall I tell it? For one of my positive, "straight-forward" habits, there is no way better than to "begin at the Beginning" & narrate *this* as if it were not the most blessed, beautiful Event of all My Life!

Well? _____ Much to my surprise & delight *Mr. Fowler & Oliver* came, by the Nine o'cl'k Train, on Saturday Evening;—the *former* to preach, the latter to "visit." The Sabbath—*June 2nd* was the dearest, holiest day of all the days I've lived. Charlie, (I like *so well* to think & speak & write of him, by that name!) & I talked, on the piazza at Shady Dell, all the morning. We "exchanged confidences" on a subject I have thought very much about, but, owing its delicacy, have never yet mentioned (otherwise than covertly) in my Journal—it is one nearly concerning My Brother & My *Friend*. I have such hopes that they may love *each other*—it would make me almost perfectly happy—I should want only *one thing* more, (I thought, as we talked about them)—thank God! I know *now* that I have *that other thing!*

He (what need to explain what every woman refers to when she uses that pronoun, *underscored*—she means the One Man of all the world, to her!) told me why he didn't bid me Goodbye, & tell me he was sick, that evening when I saw him last. It was because my hateful conduct at Georgie's,[1] & my blundering remarks when he said something about corresponding with me, had made him think that I did not care for him in any way, & that he was disagreeable to me! I told him how wrong his fancies were, & we talked pleasantly—I remember it—never fear, & there is little need to write it down—the quiet talk we had.

In the afternoon he preached—*very finely*, it is almost superfluous to say. He looked splendidly in the pulpit (or rather the desk of the little school-house where I've spent many days, very long & very lonely). I thought of him as one inspired—his face was radiant with such a lofty, holy expression. After church & after tea, he asked me to go walking, & we went to the Bridge where Clara & I used to draw & read & talk,—just a year ago, it is. We staid there a long time, & coming back,—I don't know how it was—it is all like a beautiful Dream—he

told me that he loved me—that I was "the first & last & only one."—
And with no fear, no shrinking, I told him I had always loved him—
that it seemed so natural to me—as if there was nothing else I could
do, except that.

I shall not write here, what he said,—suffice it, that I *think it over*
& am no more tired or lonely. I never felt so quiet, so *satisfied*—so
perfectly *at rest,* as on that night, before I went to sleep! He kissed
me, in the morning, before he went away. O *Charlie!* in my calm way
of talking, you do not know how deep & fervent is the love I've giv-
en to you! You do not know, that because I am so quiet is a sign that
I love you most, but you shall see—you shall learn about it, some day.

I am happy now The loneliness don't trouble, the school don't
weary, the annoyances have lost their power. Under them all, is the
consciousness that *he does* "care,"—doubting which has made me
more restless than any thing around me.

As I write, one of my scholars hands me two letters—one from
Mary—written on *Sabbath Evening,* & telling of a strange presentiment
that I was very happy—& *the reason why,* (the *true* one as it has proved!).

The other from Oliver, very charming to me, in its *commital non-
commital*-ness! Ah! dear fellow! I can see plainly enough whither all
these things are tending!

This week has been a pleasant one. Under all of its occurrences I
have had *One Thought,* & that the most blessed & comforting. I have
known that *he* was *thinking* too! . . .

1. Willard referred to a Reading Circle meeting held at Georgia A. Bryce's home
on 28 May 1861, which she and Fowler attended. (Bryce [b. 1841] graduated from
NWFC in 1862 and married Rev. D. H. Muller, a GBI graduate, that year.) In her journal entry for 28 May, she described Fowler's abrupt departure from her after the meeting because he felt that she did not wish to correspond with him. He later told Mary
Bannister that he cared for Willard.

9 June 1861

. . . The Occurrence of today, was the receipt of the First Letter,
signed "*Charlie.*" Its delicate, beautiful words—I know them all by
heart. They have made every thing bright & joyful—I regret nothing,—have no trouble—*his words* have drowned everything sad. . . .

15 June 1861

. . . Prof. Hemmenway[1] . . . brought me a letter from Charlie. All
doubt & uncertainty is at an End. He loves me very much, I know, and
my whole life shall prove to him what I say so quietly in words, that *I*

love him as a woman can who has not *loved any one* before,—who gives the hoarded wealth of a heart that loving but few, out of all the world, loves them deeply, truly,—I some times fear—unreasonably.

How beautiful will be the Home-going next week! I think of it so joyfully! *He* says he wishes much to see me. How glad I shall be to look into the fine, spiritual face of the One Man in all the world, to me!

I am not the same since I knew *he cared*. I am cheery and fearless & full of hope. He says the future looks beautiful to him—& promises to be very careful of his health. I wonder if he knew I would rather he would promise that than any thing else?

1. Francis Dana Hemenway (1830–84) was an MEC minister and instructor of English literature and Greek at GBI. He was also a neighbor of Willard's, living just around the corner from her. He later became professor of Hebrew and biblical literature at GBI.

17 July 1861

. . . How *sorry* I am that nearly a month has passed since I filled my old Journal—an unrecorded month, & yet the most beautiful & rich of my whole Life. In it I have felt more deeply, had more calm, *satisfying* enjoyment, thought more, *lived* in all regards more intensely than ever before. But it is gone & I have no Record save that unseen one, written on "the red tablets of the Heart." . . .[1]

1. Willard probably paraphrased "Written not with ink, but in fleshy tables of the heart," from Harriet Beecher Stowe, *The Minister's Wooing* (New York, 1859), chapter 8, a phrase that Stowe quoted in the novel but did not attribute.

25 July 1861

A letter from *Mary*—my *sister* that is to be! How well I love her, & how true & tender, I will try to be toward her! I have not expressed my pride & thankfulness that to *my brother* I have given up this long cherished Friend of mine. How nobly & calmly their lives will chime in with each other—what years of love & beauty I see waiting for them. I stand to *Mary* in a new relation now. I hope I may be worthy of it, and that *as a sister* I may love her and honor her. How thankful I am that she is *happy—rested—& content.*

[*Toward the end of July 1861, Willard decided to give up teaching in Harlem and go home to Evanston because she felt ill and exhausted. Clara Thatcher, who had just graduated from high school, finished out the summer term in Willard's place.*]

31 July 1861
Evanston

. . . I'm not very happy—"for all" I came Home to get some of the comfortable article.

Three things trouble me. I'm not Religious. I'm John the Baptist.[1] (Never mind what I mean by that!) C[harles Fowler] & I have antipodal fashions. There—let it go. . . .

Coming Home I saw Oliver & *Mary* walking together—his tall, fine figure;—her's slight & graceful. I was glad & proud for them, but for an instant a sharp twinge of pain was in my Heart—I but dimly know the reason. Their backs were toward me & they went away in the twilight—for a moment I thought how *new* it was for *Mary* to be going *from* me, & it hurt me a little—I am not to blame—it was involuntary. But I thought how mean & unworthy it was, & shutting the whole matter away from my thoughts went in, & Mother gave me a kind letter from *Charlie* with his picture. *Dear Charlie!* How kind & noble & loving he is toward me! . . .

1. Willard wrote in later, in pencil, "to O.A.W. with M.B.!" after "John the Baptist." According to the New Testament Gospels, John the Baptist prophesied the coming of Jesus Christ and, soon after, ended his own ministry (Matt. 3:2–3, 10–12; Mark 1:2–8; Luke 3:2–20; John 1:6–8, 15–36, 3:30). Willard meant that she, like John the Baptist, had prepared the way for Mary Bannister and Oliver Willard to fall in love by what she had told her brother about Bannister. Furthermore, like John the Baptist, who drops out of the gospel stories after completing his preparatory role, Willard felt that she had been notably set aside in Bannister's affections by her brother.

11 August 1861

. . . My *novel* is in my mind a great deal of the time _____ Oh! _____

I wish I could tell how the old hopes have revived of late—how the old ambitions have crept back into my Heart—how the thrill of *possibility* goes over me. The great *Perhaps* of my Future, haunts me & makes me full of hope. God has given me more power than I have used. If I shall do my *best*—I would not dare write here my dreams of what might come of it! I'm almost twenty-two;—in the prime of youth, and just at the ripeness of my powers. Tomorrow I shall commence;—at five o'clock tomorrow, in the morning. A great joy goes over me as I think _____ of what may be! How proud it would make all who love me;—& *Charlie! he* would be prouder than they all.

I will not think of his going into the Army—of his possible illness "even unto Death." It is too hard—it *hurts* me, too much. *Dear Char-*

lie! I wish I was worthy of all the *"care"* & kindness you have showered upon me. I *will* repay you—cost what it may.

He writes me beautiful letters—so full of love & generosity. They show too, a splendid mind & delicate appreciation of what suits my taste. His sister Jennie[2]—whom I *know* I am to love—wrote me a sweet, cordial letter—it came yesterday. They must not be disappointed in me—*he* nor *they.* I hope & pray *he* may grow strong & well in these weeks that he is gone, & I hope he may be *happy* and renew the sweet faith & hope of his boyish years. *God bless him* and crowd his whole Life full of sunshine—from earth & Heaven! May I help him & may he be happier for having known me, next to my wish for Heaven I reckon that which would make me *as noble to him as he is to me.*

1. Willard had been thinking about writing a novel on American girlhood, which she intended to title *Women's Rights.* She discussed in her journal methods of writing novels, and how she intended to write hers, including what types of characters she would use.

2. Jennie (Fowler) Willing (1834–1916) was Charles Fowler's sister, and a prominent Methodist reformer in her own right. She was married to William C. Willing, an MEC minister, in 1853. They had no children. She received a local preacher's license from the Rock River Annual Conference, which allowed her to preach and conduct revival meetings in churches. She was awarded an honorary A.M. degree in 1872 (or 1873) from the Evanston College for Ladies while Willard was president. In 1874 she was named professor of Belles Lettres (literature as one of the fine arts) at Illinois Wesleyan University in Bloomington. She became involved in temperance work during the Woman's Crusade of 1873–74 and was one of three women who planned a national women's temperance meeting that met in November 1874 in Cleveland, Ohio. Willing was acting chair of the meeting that organized the WCTU, and she became editor of *Our Union,* the monthly newspaper of the WCTU. For several years she was president of the Illinois WCTU. Also interested in mission work, Willing was corresponding secretary of the Woman's Foreign Missionary Society of the MEC during the 1870s and early 1880s, and later became an organizer for the denomination's Woman's Home Missionary Society. In 1895 she was made superintendent of the Evangelistic Training Department of the NWCTU. At the time of her death, Willing was president of the Frances Willard WCTU of New York City.

12 August 1861

. . . Mary B. came to see us this afternoon, & for me, at least, she made the hours of the long, dreary day, more bearable. *I love her*—I would make such sacrifices for her as she does not imagine me capable of—perhaps she will, some day. I often speak harshly and unkindly to her, for it is my temper, though I *try* not to do so, & am pained at myself, more than I pain her. And I know a careless word from her,—any sign of indifference, even the slightest, cuts me to the heart, though I call myself a fool that it *should* hurt me so. My Darling,—Sister & Friend! God forgive me if I have ever done you wrong, as He is my witness I have tried with all my soul to bring you happiness. In little things & great alike, I have been *true to you* in the deepest, sternest sense of the words. There is no action of mine I fear to have you scrutinize, in this regard,—no word that I have spoken that has not been *for* you, no case in which I have not arrayed myself boldly, unflinchingly *on your side* to the full measure of my strength and possibilities. When the Great Book is opened, on the Judgment Day, I shall not fear to meet the Record of my Account with *You,* and I beleive that you will love me, on that day, with a depth and intensity such as even *your* rich, tropical nature, with its boundless capacity for loving, never knew on earth. I don't know why I write this. Perhaps these lines shall yet plead with you for me—I can't tell where or how or when.

The wind howls mournfully, outside. My heart is heavy, "I sigh and moan under the mysterious burden of Life."[1] I hardly know myself, any more. Does Christ pity me, I wonder? As he sees my poor, halting Life—my wavering & doubting of every thing—on Earth and in heaven, *isn't* He whose heart is so great & loving, isn't he sorry that ____ I am myself? And won't He help me—not just now perhaps;— I see I do not ask Him rightly. But *sometime* when I learn the beautiful simplicity they say there is in *faith,* will He not make me infinitely stronger in *His* strength than I ever was in *my own,* even in those glorious, unforgotten days when I was *sure of myself* at least, & revelled in my power & calmness? I do not know. Indeed, I am sure of nothing now, save that with more cause for thanks & joy than I ever had before, I am more sorrowful—more uncertain—more full of pain.

1. Not identified.

13 August 1861

If I wrote my Internal Life out on this paper, the book would be full and I should not have finished. So many thoughts—such hope— such fear, such pain! O God! In all Thy Universe I feel Thou dost no act, nor hast done—save sending Christ—so awful, so majestic, so fraught with possibilities, as sending forth a human soul to think & suffer,—to be saved or lost! I live more *in my self* of late, than I ever did before. The careless, gleeful days are not the best, I think, though in their stead one is in pain & trial often.

Mary B. & I went to Prof. Hemmenway's "Class" last evening. It did me good. The atmosphere seemed purer—the spirit there seemed loftier than any that has met me in a long, long while. But I get less help from Christ, of late, than ever before when I asked sincerely. I am earnest,—I am urgent in my plea. But my *Life* is not what it ought to be. Indeed, I see little or no amendment in it. If, at night, I think I have lived better for one day, examination shows me that it is merely because I have not been *tempted*—have had nothing to resist!—Patience—charity—*truthfulness*—*these* are the *fruits* for which I look in vain. One of my prominent defects of character is a tendency to *refract* the truth, in passing it through the media of (2) conversation & (1) writing. I am given to hyperbole;—exaggeration is quite natural to me. I *hate* this worse than any thing else I find in my heart, unless it be the boundless *selfishness* that every day reveals more clearly. O Lord! Don't take me out of the world into the misty, shadowy land, till I am *better*—till I know Christ "*cares*" for me. Make me suffer—send troubles thick as the locusts of Egypt,[1] if need be, but bring me out *right;* refine me in the fire, but oh! Infinite, Loving Father do not leave me in the dark!

1. Willard referred to Ex. 10:4–6, where Moses, speaking for God, warned Pharaoh that, unless he freed the Israelites, locusts would cover the land, devouring the vegetation and filling the houses of the Egyptians.

25 August 1861

. . . I went home with my Darling last night. O, every day I sink deeper & deeper into the knowledge & love of her! We talked for hours—lying there in the darkness, her head upon my shoulder, my arms about her, my lips very often pressed to her forehead & cheek. I would give much for that talk of ours, written out. I told her of how different I'm getting to be. Of my keener subjective living;—my close self-scrutiny, my onward-looking toward the vast Eternity with the Life it shall bring to us all. She said "It don't do to be too intimate with ourselves." I defended my position by citing Mother (whom *Mary* loves so much) as an example of almost constant introspection. She said: "I imagine your Mother walking out into her own nature as into a beautiful flower garden. Inhaling delicious perfumes, bending over rare blossoms—talking with friends of her childhood or youth, and growing happy in it all. But you dig down below the surface into the soil & the rocks beneath. You analyze too closely—you dig too deep. To me, there is this difference between her case & yours." I told her I thought that she was right. But any way, as I quarried my own soul— as I went further down, I found the roots of *my love for her* at the greatest depth to which I ventured;—the great tree seemed to have sent them to the very limits of my spiritual self. And *Mary* was glad, & told me one thing that I glory to beleive true, & one that will keep me rich in heart, & brave, tender and cheery no matter what befalls. O *Darling—Mary,* soul *welded* to mine though Fate or circumstance may drift you off from me, *God knows* what wild idolatry is in my heart! And *you* must know that to the center of my being *I love you* with a depth & changelessness that I can not tell in words. I have no pride with you. I *glory* in loving you so much! With justice I may quote your words concerning one who is infinitely dear to you,

> "Such worship may be madness
> But it can not be a sin."[1]

In my thoughts I am growing more careful of *Mary* & I beleive I am & shall be still more watchful & tender in my actions. It *hurts* me with a lively pain that would be surprising if anything could be in *our* case, to see *her* suffering;—& that slender frame of hers that is *sacred & royal* in my sight, is thrilled with pain so often, nowadays! *Mary* you make a child of me—you can do with me just what you will. I say it very proudly. *God bless you* & shower His love & His gifts over your path. When this life on earth is over, may we go together—all of us who love each other so dearly—into the Other Life;—"caring" as you hope that we shall *care* eternally, & as I feel we shall, & may we walk hand in hand through the portal & down the grand aisles of *Immortality.* "*God so loved the world.*"[2] Mary says she always thought of those words so much. The earthly love is the effulgence of the heavenly— makes us more like angels—fits us for Heaven in some degree. The care we have on earth we carry with us. Those with whom we suffered & toiled—whom we loved devotedly on earth shall be our nearest friends in Heaven. 'Tis a blessed beleif of yours, & I'll cherish it too. . . .

1. Not identified.
2. John 3:16.

31 August 1861

. . . I wonder I don't say more in my Journal about "the terrible war that is raging in our beloved Land." It is very much in my thoughts—accounts of it are eagerly read & I'm quite intelligent (for a "female"—Augh!!) on it. It troubles me greatly. I have my own theory of it—its causes, the "proper manner" in which to conduct it, & its probable issue. (Whew! Who are you?) I will write it out some time for "my own personal, private" (as Fowler says) amusement. . . .

4 September 1861

. . . In eve. went with "Bro." W. to a stupid war-meeting. Charlie was there, they said. Charlie _____ oh! I can not write it down.

I am *very* unhappy tonight. My heart *aches* with a severe, *neuralgic* pain. *I have not comfort from any Source.* To outward seeming every thing is "well" with me. *Inwardly* all is wrong, unfortunate, terrible. Heaven is all shut out. Just now no Christ pleads for me—no Father above is merciful. Earth is fated to give me pain. I stand in abnormal or else untrue relations. *Mary—Mary—My Child!* You would pity and forgive me more lovingly tonight than any one else on earth—I almost wrote "or any one in heaven." I haven't you. My Brother—whom I love & admire so thoroughly—sits by your side tonight, & you are perfectly and necessarily happy—both of you, & oblivious to every one besides. It is my pride that this is so *at last.* I will try not to be selfish or to long after you. It is not right or natural—so they say—that you & I should love each other as we *do.* (for it is in the *present tense* & in my wretchedness tonight, be it right or wrong, I *will* say I am *glad.*) Ours is such a Love as no two women ever had for each other, before. It is wild & passionate, deep & all-prevading. It is "abnormal." It is *impossible,* let *him* be never so generous (the underscored pronoun having, this time, *two* applications) for this to be other than a painful & almost intolerable subject of thought. We can not be together. Fate & circumstance decree it. O *how hard* it is, *My Darling!* my *cherished,* blessed, idolized *Mary!* It touches me—it lacerates my heart in its *tenderest* spot. (God forgive me—& not *God* only!—that this *is* so, though I have prayed & agonized & taught myself as best I could to have it as you say it is with you—at least *that* way.) It stirs up the very depths of my nature. *You* are wound in with my heart of hearts. Can I help it? Is it wrong? Will God damn me for it? Did he send this *Friendship* which I thought my choicest Blessing only to poison it & turn it to a curse? What can I do? What *must* I do? I get no light—no answer. How I wrong the truth of my heart. (Whether it be a *right* truth or not.) Tonight when we turned listlessly & indifferently from each other! I could have called you every dear, sacred name our language yields;— I could have pressed you to my heart that *used* to be so proud & *calm* but aches & moans so steadily *now;* I could have kissed your lips & forehead a thousand times in one, & looked into your beautiful, forgiving, regretful eyes till the tears stood in my own—& I would not.

It is for *your* sake—for *theirs*—for *justice.* O God! it *hurts* me so! *You* love me & it pains you, I am sure. I *worship you,* & it takes all the joy out of my Life. *You* have God left, & Oliver. I have the keen beleif that

God is angry, that I am *very wicked*—that Charlie & I are estranged. How I wrong *him!* Who would think that I appreciated his nobleness, & generosity;—forgiving, forgetting, suffering. *I would help it, if I could. I will try.* Oh! I feel so wrong—so lonely—*so dark.*

And I haven't *Mary*—who would see how it is, & comfort me & pour balm into my bruises & wounds. What matter if they are self-inflicted;—is the pain any less? I did not want them;—there is a Fate or Demon over me.

I go to sleep—for that I shall do—thank Heaven! by & by—with no prayer—no kiss—no sweet comforting words from the Book of Life,[1] or from the lips of those I love. And yet, my sister will lie beside me, my mother & father & brother not far off. *Mary* in her room up on the street, & *Charlie* too, in his. Christ up in Heaven—angels perhaps around me. Yet the Human Heart has hours in which like our Savior when he went into the wilderness, it is tempted & torn, *all alone;*—shut out from all the universe, like Him in the Garden;[2]— I know—*I am alone,* I am shut in with myself.

1. Willard referred to the book of life mentioned in Rev. 20:12: "[At the Last Judgment] another book was opened, which is the book of life: and the dead were judged out of those things which were written in the books according to their works."

2. Willard referred to two instances in the synoptic Gospels where Jesus was alone, faced with adversity and desolation. The first was when Jesus spent forty days fasting in the desert (Matt. 4:1–11, Mark 1:12–13, Luke 4:1–13), and the second, when he was in the Garden of Gethsemane, praying for God to spare him the coming agony of his crucifixion (Matt 26:36–46, Mark 14:32–42, Luke 22:39–46).

5 September 1861

. . . I have suffered more tonight than ever before in my Life. Why was it sent upon me? What lesson will it teach? What richer will it make my character?—O! I don't know. I wonder why I need to suffer so? . . .

Two days ago, I gave a note to *Mary* telling her we could not go on with our Friendship as we did before. It could only bring pain. It could only make dissatisfaction with C. & O. It made me *wretched* to tell her so. I did it once before but could not brave the suffering it brought. *Mary*—strong as she is gentle;—proud as she is loving,— met me on my own ground & we have acted strangely, since. I thought it due myself to show her what I wrote last night, so that she might remember my love & suffering for her. She was delicate and sorry for me. I told her it seemed wrong to *them*—especially on my part. We were to live apart. To do each other no good—to give no comfort—to take away no pain. *They* say so,—every body does.

No one should compete with them—no one stand near the lofty place they occupy. . . .

Never till tonight has she beleived this. I told her Mother thought so;—the Bible seemed to require it. She said she thought it true. O *Darling!* it *hurt* you to say so! Your eyes looked into mine, so searchingly—so full of pain. I never saw more trouble in that face I *love so much*—I watch so closely. I can not bear to think it over. How we sat there & talked it over,—& I was selfish & forgetful of *her* share in the pain. How I looked around the room where we have sat so often—where we have said loving words & had very loving thoughts of each other, as if I was leaving it for the last time. How I came home in *perfect agony*—*Mary* walking beside me, feeling very badly,—not so terribly as I, for she has *two* sources of comfort—I have none. She went away, leaning on Oliver's arm. *He* could comfort her, & I was glad for my *Darling Child*. With my heart feeling heavier than it ever felt before. . . . I resolved to tell my Mother & ask her advice. *Thank God for Mother!* How she listened & was sorry & comforted me! She told me if we loved each other so much—if parting was to cause such suffering, it was God's witness that we had *the right* to love each other as of yore. She never knew how much we "cared";—there was no need for us to suffer—to turn a thing so sweet & sacred into a blight & canker. *Mother, dear* Mother! You did not know how thirsty I was for the words! I took them as from an Oracle;—beleived them, treasured them—made her repeat them again & again;—"Love each other all you wish to, make yourselves happy in it—say nothing about it—do your duty by the others for whom you care."

I never loved her more—I wanted to stoop down & kiss her forehead as she lay there—but I did not dare—we never do such things.

Mother views it in the light of *our suffering* now, & thinks justice to ourselves permits the course she showed to me. She never dreamed that it would so un-helm me to lose *Mary*—my child.

Somehow all the pain went away;—silence & rest brooded over the great deep of my Heart—so lately covered with foam & tossing wildly to & fro. "There was a great calm"—as when *Our Savior* (think of those two words!) stilled the waters of Gallilee.[1] I felt kind & loving toward all the world—more loving than ever before, toward *Mary*. Nothing troubled me but the remembrance of her trouble—& then I thought "But *she* has O."

Will she do it, I wonder? Will she be to me, & let me be again to her as in the dear old times? *One thing* I will solemnly promise. *If she will* I will try harder than I ever have to *care* all the world for ____. Duty & gratitude shall point me to it. I will be very earnest in it, & sincere.

I shall be less wicked—more gentle & with more faith. *Mary!* is it right & will you do it once more?

This is the briefest, severest, most valuable lesson of all my Life. It shall never need to be taught me again; if you will love me & let me love you, once more! God forgive me for my blindness & impatience and injustice to you ____ & to myself. . . .

1. Matt. 8:26b, Mark 4:39b, Luke 8:24b.

10 September 1861

. . . *Mary* & I understand each other no longer! I am as wretched as ever. I shall write out all the truth, soon. I feel that I can not keep it much longer. I read a note from *M* a little while ago. Why has my heart throbbed like an ulcer, ever since? *Why? I know.* I wonder if she'll stay with me, tonight? I was thoughtful & tender of her when she was in great pain, instead of the perfect happiness that the loving God (to *her,* He is loving) has given. She won't forget—I'm sure she won't. Why do their voices hurt me & bring the tears into my eyes? They are sitting in O's room. Why am I so full of misery? Is it wicked? Is it strange that when she has been *all mine* (in one sense) so long, it hurts me cruelly that I can't see her quietly—that I am so set aside? It is all right,—& inevitable. I would not have it different for all the world. I glory in her happiness. Yet I can't help *feeling.* Is it mean—is [it] wrong—is it a sin against *her* against *him*—my brother? O, God! love me, *forgive* me! Make it endurable—this Lesson I must learn! Make me strong in Thee and in the majesty of my own nature. Love me— help me to stifle my cry!

Evening.

O *Mother!* You will remember me & love me, though every one else forgets & grows weary. I feel so badly tonight that I can't hide it entirely. It makes me sick to laugh—& I can't talk. I'm not cross though—I'm glad of *that.* Never do I feel so much like being gentle & kindly as when I'm *sorry* & have the heart ache. So I'm up here, sitting with my poor, strong-hearted, suffering cousin,[1] while *Mary—My Darling*—sits below with Oliver, Father, *Mother,* & Mary. I started to say I couldn't help showing a little, here at Home, that I felt badly, & Mother called me in her room, & asked me very anxiously & lovingly, what was troubling me? And I told her, how I haven't *Mary*— how I'm troubled, for one sentence in her letter took all the comfort out. I may be wicked & unnatural—I can't help it though, to save my life. And Mother was so sorry, & said it was all natural, but I mustn't let O—notice it, she said. And she told me she would ask *M.* to stay all night, & so she did. *Mother* you don't know how I love you: your eldest daughter has you deeper in her heart than any one in all the world imagines!

I wonder if *Mary* will despise me? I shall tell her *all*, & abide the result. If I should be *great* someday, & do some noble splendid thing so she could admire me as she did O—on Sunday, would it make her "care" enough?—Why do I long for her so much? Why do I cry after her? Why can't I let her go—in some degree—instead of wanting her more now than ever?

God knows.

1. Sarah Gilman was visiting the Willards while she taught at the Kankakee Academy.

11 September 1861

I shall never forget last night. It was a crisis in my Hidden Life. It is safely passed, though as I steered my little craft through the narrow passage out on the sea, it rocked fearfully & there was danger.

It is strange that I should care. I am made up of curious stuff. *She* don't think it mean or bad—we must both know it is abnormal.

When it is far off we talk of Death very quietly and beautifully. When it comes—the agony is mortal! Always, I had foreseen *this*—had talked of it, had worked *for* it while it hurt me sometimes, but with a heroic kind of pain. Now I was face to face with it. Knowing it *right* & best. Yet it *hurt*—oh! it hurt so much that I sobbed—great heavy sobs, & hot tears fell fast—I could not help it. The *shock*—the *newness* agonized me. And I hadn't much—I shall not write here, the reasons why it left me desolate for a while. It was so *human*—and say what they will I glory in my weak, longing heart—for it shows me— there is a bond strong as life between me & my kind. *She* was sorry— she was very good & patient—I love her as much as ever—even more. I *prayed* when I felt so wretched. Prayed out loud, with faith & child-like feelings. God pitied me, I know, & sent quietness to me, after the shock & the tempest. I am calm now, & generous & reasonable. I will never give *My Darling* any pain. If I can calculate upon myself—& I beleive I can—I shall be more kind & gentle with her always, hereafter. I *feel* that I shall. She knows that she has in me a real, devoted Friend. I know she cares for me, a great deal. This shall satisfy *me*. I hope—I think—that the anguish will be breif.

This will do me good. I feel more like loving God & living for Good & for Heaven. Some way I am chastened—I am *sweetened* not soured by the things that hurt me, in my Life. This makes me very thankful.

O *Heart* of mine! There is *good* in store for thee! There are many that shall yet thank God that I was created—I feel sure of this! There are words of love & comfort for me to speak—faint hearts for me to encourage—weak hands to rest trustingly in mine. Is it egotistical to say it? I feel the Fate upon me! How rich my life will be! Rich alike in pain & peace,—sorrow and singing! The light that comes through windows of stained-glass is an emblem of my inner-life;—subdued, mellow, rather sad. The self-contained, calm, kindly look will come into my face, some day. O Lord! Help me to make happiness for others! To lay the rose-leaf on many a Life-Cup![1] To "go about doing good"[2]— only this, I ask of Thee. Let every thing lead me "nearer to Thee." Make my Life a sweet, clear, triumphant Anthem! May it be beautiful & thrilling—what matter if the most of it be written—*in the Minor key!*

Oliver talked a long while with me this morning, about *My Novel*. He has faith in me—I see it, very plainly & it delights me. We talked of *Mary* as a Character. He said she would be rare.... "She is so fine-grained," he said. I nodded—I told him I "laid it to my soul" that I was nice to *Mary*—that my ways & words were all what she would like, if she knew. "It is so queer," he said;—"You act sorry & as if she had been taken away from you. It is amusing, too." I'm getting over my foolishness—*he* knows, he understands me perfectly. I told him it hurt me a little to talk with him just then, of her, but he might remember that I loved her better than any one else, that I was very fond of both of them & very happy for them—that I was honorable to him & to her, that I would be very careful not to hurt her—that I would be more kind than ever though I was not to her what I used to be. He understood—I'm sure he did, just what had happened. He did not say any thing, but smiled pleasantly, in a puzzled sort of way. *Dear Oliver!* He loves me, I am sure; & he has faith & confidence in me. I feel very sure that I shall never hurt him or her by any action—but shall be a very loving Friend & *sister* to them *both*—God bless them! ...

1. Not identified.
2. Acts 10:38.

16 September 1861

... There is a set of thoughts that must necessarily give me pain for a while. It is strange—incomprehensible save to myself & God who made me as he did. My nature is all that makes them sad, and that I can not help. I can only control it, & make it do what I please, & accomplish that where unto I shall send it. In this I succeed admirably. The result I do not fear. O! it is *very strange* that I should care— I mean it would be strange were *I not I*. It would be humorous if in some aspects it were not horrible! Yet as I float down the years, things will grow different with me. A whole decade shall not have passed when it will not matter to me where ____ is if only _____ is *happy*. And with quietness that is full of feeling,—not cold & proud, I shall put into the present tense what now I say in the prophetic *Future:* "It will all be one."[1] Yet I beleive, that with the cast my nature has in some things, I shall always think of _____,—not with pain, but with a certain regret against which my better self will struggle,—when I read these two verses of my favorite Poet:

> "And the stately ships go by
> To the haven under the hill;
> But oh! for the touch of a vanished hand,
> And the sound of *a voice* that is still.
> Break, break, break,
> At the foot of thy crags, oh Sea!
> But the tender grace of a day that is dead
> Will never come back to me."[2]

I would not have *This* different, in any respect, *for all the world*. How true this is, my anxiety that it should be, continued even through years, shall bear me witness. If any one accuses me of meanness, or—of what *she* hinted at That Night, I will not endure it—because I can not. And yet, the pain is not to be denied or escaped from. God has more love & charity for me than any other Being, for He knows me best. And I am *so glad* for *them*, and don't trouble *any one* or act unworthily.

It rains today, and I'm a little *blue* or I would never have mentioned *it* again. Indeed, it is not *safe*—I run the risk of being turned to ridicule—I can readily see how this should be. I'll try to have this the last reference, & here write

F i n i s.

There is One Thing that troubles me terribly. I wonder I haven't written of it—it was because I *hoped* and *prayed* & *struggled* not to have it true. Perhaps I will write it out some day—here in this book where, of late, I tell so many things.

1. Not identified.
2. Willard paraphrased Alfred Lord Tennyson, "Break, Break, Break" (London, 1842), stanzas 3 and 4.

18 September 1861

. . . Oliver and I talked till very late. He had been reading my Journal,—I can not blame him, for I always allowed it, though now I keep it out of sight. But he found it and _____ I do not blame him for one word he said,—yet for that talk & for all connected with it I am *very sorry.* So I didn't get peacefully to sleep, after all. *One week ago last night!!!*

19 September 1861

. . . I shall always be different, since last night. O—will not tolerate my old ways with Mary B. & she don't need or care for them. I don't blame him at all. I do blame her, a little. I was very angry & thought she did me wrong, when he told me their last night's talk together. Once or twice in my life I have been really unjust to her. These times I will remember, to make me charitable toward her. I write here, that I love her *as much as ever.* God knows & I know what that means. It is all wasted though—not needed, not wanted, any more. She told him "It might be egotistical, but she had not for me what I [had] for her, any longer," etc. That is *natural,* Mary B., and I don't complain. Here after she & I are to be exactly as Mary W. and she are to each other. The Past is *dead.* I have loved her as a man would love her—it must not be manifest, ever again. I don't blame O—he is surpassingly magnanimous, to tolerate any thing, as long as he has, in this matter.

I had a mission to Mary Bannister. I made her happier for two years. She had no one then, like me. I have done *very much* for her—she has for me, but most in loving me;—that was all I wanted. Now it is all over. I shall not write of her—I shall not say it hurts me. I make no comments—no regrets. There are feelings in my Heart that I shall never tell. I shall only keep, as a remembrancer of the "Beautiful, cold, dead thing"[1] (as it is to her), but what is something else to me, the underscoring of her name when I write of her here—no where else. As long as she is in my heart what she is now, I shall keep this one sign of what used to be. I don't say how long I think this will be. When I write it, I *shall remember* a whole host of things, sacred to me alone.

I see a Fate relentlessly bringing *our* Friendship, my *Idolatry* to this extremity. For it all, we are better—I am more sad, more kind & womanly.

Every thing has its use; "Everything is beautiful in its season."[2] To

Mary I have accomplished all I can consistent with her highest happiness, & last night, in the quiet moonlight, while no one thought it, her *care*—her old relation to me, as far as *her* will could do it, came to an end. Like a faded leaf—shrivelling more & more, it fell off *at its articulation,* naturally & necessarily & rustled along to the ground. That was the end. If any one should ever read these pages who never knew *Mary* as I have known her, let him beleive the assertion of one prepared to decide in the case:—She acted as a woman must act, she felt as a woman must feel, she was just & honorable as any daughter of Eve could be in the circumstances, & has lost no whit of my respect. I *did not* think so, an hour ago. I *shall* think so, hereafter. She has not been fickle or shallow. She has been generous enough, steadfast enough. "There is a *Divinity* that shapes our ends."[3] My brother has acted nobly & generously too. The whole affair is to the credit of all concerned.

And lastly, not leastly, either, (for the part I played), *I* have been noble & loving, take it all in one view, & here I dismiss the subject. I write the Beautiful name I have whispered *so* tenderly in her ear, but never on earth shall speak to her again:

My Darling!

and here I close the Story. It has been long & bright & beautiful, I shall think of it gratefully, every day of my life. When I am old, I shall muse upon it with a smile on the lips that will be withered then. There will be no harm in this—it will not hurt my pride, it will hurt neither *her* nor *him*. I shall pray for them always—I shall be kind & true.

Good-bye! . . .

There is but one thing in which I think I act very wrong, just now. And that is concerning the most forbearing, generous, forgiving of men. I must write it out here, soon. Practically I am as swervelessly true to him as the needle to the pole & shall be, always. In heart I do him injustice, perhaps, though all I have for *any man* I have for him.

1. Not identified.
2. Willard paraphrased Eccles. 3:11, "He hath made every thing beautiful in his time."
3. Willard quoted from William Shakespeare, *Hamlet,* act 5, scene 2, line 10.

20 September 1861

. . . What have I to say of my Life?

This morning, I arose with the best of intentions. I meant to write on my story until noon. Instead, I talked with Mother, & had a pleasant call from *Charlie*. Dear, noble Friend—nay, *more* than *Friend* to me. How nicely we get on. He comes up to my room, & we talk as unreservedly as it is possible to do. He looked splendidly today. How deeply in my heart that needs so much some one to love & *trust* I thank the merciful Father above for giving <u>*Charlie*</u> to me! And oh! I have no prayer so earnest as this:—that I may love him as he deserves to be loved—for I fear I don't, sometimes, & it is the greatest worryment I have. But I *will* & I *am* true to him & will be forever—of this I am sure. Well, he was very generous & genial & we had nice times together. . . .

22 September 1861

. . . Charlie was here a long time, yesterday. We had the most unreserved talk that I remember. . . . I told him he was "more sinned against than sinning,"[1] confessed to the injustice I had done him in loving *Mary* as I have, & he answered with surpassing generosity: "Remember that I never asked you our comparative positions in your regard. I have wished to do so, but remembered that you would never *marry* Mary B (!) & that eventually if not now, all would be right between us. You know I never asked that you should put aside your love for her, or your relation to her." Well—now I will try to be just & Christian with them all. Charlie is noble & forgiving. I shall make every effort to be to him what I ought. My nature is not like *Mary's*—sometimes I wish it was. I can not make an idol of him—I stand in all my old relations the same—have the same love & tenderness for my old Friends, with the *added* love & admiration, truth & tenderness for *him*. So I said, & he thought that this was right. . . .

1. Willard quoted from William Shakespeare, *King Lear*, act 3, scene 2, line 60.

24 September 1861

. . . She gave me a note this morning.—I shall put the mark under her name, no longer. I should pity myself if I would. I guess I have an *atom* of pride, though it has been trampled & spit upon until now. Mr. Taplin was right, after all. Love goes in equations. Unless there is as much on one side or the other, or something approaching that, it will die out. *I have loved her*—my tenderness and kindness have followed her all these years of our marvellous Friendship. I declare now that I never took any thing from her of what I gave & have so long been giving. She *forces* it back upon me. She walks away out of my

Heart. She looks at my strange, wild love & wonders at it, smiles curiously & says "Well, you know it is her nature." After all the hot words she has written—the protestations, violent as protestations could be—the acts of sacrifice & tenderness which have made her so wondrously near & dear, she writes these words:—

> "I shall always love you truly—rightly—better than any other girl unless perhaps when I know her better & she shall want me (if ever)— Mary Willard. And I will never willingly give you pain but be to you *both* if you will let me, what you have so kindly called me, your sister."

Am I wrong that these words stung me so? Think of it! Mary Willard doesn't want Mary B—has no affinity for her, never gave her much of her heart, never thought much about her, has not given her the deepest, purest, most *unselfish* love,—the tenderest sympathy, the most thoughtful, minute, watchful, wakeful kindness. Has not prayed for her with more feeling than for herself;—has not wept for her— comforted her when she had no one else to ask for comfort—put her arms about her when she had no one else to cling to—kissed her wildly & passionately when no one else cared to do so—worked for her, steadily, quietly, swervelessly, delicately,—and not without effect. Has not kept her dearest secret for months and cheered, encouraged and comforted her. Has not remembered with unerring instinct all that could make happy, & forgotten with persistent will every thing that could annoy her. Has not been true & firm & generous, unfaltering and thoroughly *her own*. Think of the difference. I say—for there is no one else who remembers it much,—that all these things & *more* I have done & felt for Mary B. I had no object in loving her— it gave me no such kind of pleasure as it did her—I could not learn from her what was said & thought concerning me, by one from whom I was in agony to hear—for then there was no such person, & if there had been, he was nothing to Mary . . . , & she could do nothing for me. She loved me—I beleive that—I shall always beleive it;—I wanted nothing more from her. She has done many kind things for me— but it was not in her power to do what I could do, & did do for her, & found *my* highest happiness in doing. Well that is all past. In her new relation to us all, it may be right & necessary—though just now I do not clearly see it—that she should care for Mary Willard as for me. But that she should coolly & openly say so to me, I regard as thoughtless, inconsiderate, ungenerous, unworthy. I may be wrong & selfish. But think over the Past;—I beleive it is my best, most eloquent defender.

I never *asked* her to care for me as much as for O. I never presumed it, or thought of it—*she knows*. I was hurt at the first announcement, strange as it may seem, but after the pain & outburst on that night I was honorable & consistent & did my best to show her how kind & loving I *would* be—told her everything I could think of that he had said—kept the subject of *him* & their mutual "care" before us all that last night I shall ever stay with her (the night we came from the Fair).[1] If she loved me as much as ever, I was perfectly reconciled that I stood infinitely below him in the depths & heights she had reached in her love toward him. Then came the Talk that made me angry—when she told him she cared for me in a calm, sisterly way, that I had proposed some dishonorable thing or other, I hardly know what, that she had told me, to make me feel better what was not the case, &c I saw she wanted nothing of the old Friendship, & gave her back the ring. It is all over. I have had untold pain, but shall live to look her in the face & not love her an atom—but *like* her very much, feel kind & cordial toward her, be glad she is my sister, be true & faithful—nothing more. I too, have done her wrong, many times of late, but it troubles me little now.

She will not be troubled—I am not so *infinitely cheap*. Her note was kind & well enough. Perhaps I write too harshly—perhaps I judge her too severely;—if so, may God forgive me, for I see only the outside, & am sorely puzzled to think otherwise than I do.

I forgive her freely & heartily for any wrong that she has done me. I have very hard work not to love her as before. (I disrespect myself that it is *possible* for me to say this, yet it is true.) I will show her, all my Life that I can be generous & magnanimous,—in *deeds* if I misjudge her in my thoughts. For the memory of the beautiful *Past* I will watch her though from afar, & if ever I can be of service to her she shall not need to ask for me,—I will come "while she is yet speaking."[2]

I didn't mean to refer to these things again, but *have,* & won't promise for the future. Why I have written this out I do not know. It is a more complete revelation of *my Heart* than I ever made in my Journal before. Let it pass. . . .

1. Willard, Fowler, Oliver Willard, and Mary Bannister had been to the Illinois State Fair in Chicago a few days earlier.

2. Willard paraphrased Isa. 65:24, "And it shall come to pass, that before they call, I will answer, and while they are yet speaking, I will hear."

7 October 1861

Let me see—what has happened since I wrote last? I *live* a great deal now-a-days—more & faster than I ever did before.— Journal!

I'm not honest with you! I find it next to impossible to be so. Never, more than twice have I written out *my heart* any where. My brain— my will, my judgement, conscience—all these report truthfully and with no need for reservation;—but the *heart* throbs away in darkness,—voiceless & mysterious. . . . Every one says that I'm "so frank." Ah! they don't know! . . .

15 October 1861

It was a long time in coming;—it was as a cloud but the size of a man's hand—it did not seem much. It has come at last;—the greatest event of my life—one so solemn and full of consequences that I tremble to contemplate it.

I shall write out here all my thoughts, motives, regrets, and then shut it up in its grave—the gusts that will sweep over my life will pile up leaves upon it—the tears of regret and pain will fall on it like rain, it will be lonely & somber away there in my heart. . . .

Breifly, then:—

I thought I loved Charles Fowler six months ago. I admired him, honored him, sympathized with him,—loved him,—yes, I will say I *loved* him. He met all my requirements, he realized my Idea of an upright, noble, educated, gifted man. I liked to be with him, & to talk with him. I was greatly troubled when a *contretemps* occurred that alienated his friendship from me for several days. He came to Harlem— an explanation was made—we were good Friends again.

He told me indirectly that he *cared* for me, more than for any other woman. I was excited—frightened. It seemed so strange that any *man* should say such words—that a man's face, earnest & glowing should be bent down to mine—that his arm should be around me, & his hand clasp mine so tightly. I remember how I looked up at a star just over toward the horizon & said slowly & distinctly, "I love you."

That was a strange, wonderful thing for *me* to do.—I never thought much about love;—my Journals haven't it in them except once or twice I have given my theory.

In what I said to him, I was perfectly sincere, as God is my witness.

But after that—his caresses were irksome, *always;*—they never aroused an emotion in me. His presence gave me no pleasure, except as I felt him to be a companion,—appreciative, refined & noble-hearted. His absence did not trouble me—his return after weeks spent at Home gave me not a thrill of pleasure. I looked at him— admired & liked him—was grateful to him—was that all? Sometimes it troubled me, but I am of a nature that quickly throws off trouble, & I quickly threw this off. I said to myself: "Life has disappointed you. In the man you are to marry you find every ambition gratified,—but you do not feel for him any thing beyond the calm well wishing, the gratitude and friendliness your sister would feel if he had been equally thoughtful & obliging toward her. His kiss wakes no feeling in your heart more than those of your mere acquaintances, *yet* you are capable of more, for a *kiss*—a caress—a loving word from *Mary* will send the blood hurrying along your veins & give you that peculiar sensation, so delicious, so rare, that people call a "thrill." Perhaps you love him—you said you did, & looked up at a bright, truthful star as you said it; looked up toward the Heaven you hope to win, & the God who dwells there. But his first lover's kiss was pressed upon lips as calm & unfeeling as a statue's.

Perhaps you are not meant to have the feelings said to be infallible signs of love, & which *Mary* has for Oliver, & every woman has been known to have for the man she truly loved & for whose sake she would forsake all others. Perhaps this calm confidence & friendliness are all. Yet *he* don't feel merely these—he tells of the "signs infallible" while I think wearily "I have not one."

This haunted me. I talked of it to the Home Folks & to *Mary*. I prayed about it. I asked God earnestly as I ever asked that he would save my soul, that when Charlie was so good, so noble, so every way what I most admired & was suited with, I might *feel* the love for him that I hoped was in my heart. I begged for it—I implored for it. I asked these Friends[1] so near to me, to pray about it too. But nothing came—no light, no answer. Perhaps I hadn't faith—perhaps my life was wrong & God was not pleased enough to answer me. I make no defence—I only state the facts.

Nothing came. He had said if he was appointed to Jefferson Street[2] he should want to be married in three or four months. I could not bear to deceive him. I thought my duty to God, to Charlie to myself was that he should know my doubts & fears about it. I thought that it would be a living *lie* if I should marry him, he thinking that I had deep, thrilling, all-sacrificing love when I had no *sign* that I possessed it. If my Conscience has mislead me, God pity & forgive it. I declare myself *innocent* in His sight. I talked about it. Was scolded, treated with indignation that I should *think* of such a thing. They said it was a foible. I thought it would be a sin.[3] I thought of his Home where he would come, weary & sad after the day was done, & I thought of myself as his *wife*, with no tenderness, no great, comforting *love* & sympathy. I asked Oliver what he would think of a woman who should deceive him, & leave him to think she *loved* him when she had no reason to think she did. "He would spurn her, of course." I asked myself what I would think, if I were a man, & decided, that, pain me as it would, I should bless a woman's truthfulness, who would not tolerate such unequal love;—such devotion on one side, such coolness on the other. I looked Life in the face, & saw & *welcomed* the alternative—a lonely, toilsome life;—no tenderness, no loving hand to smooth the uneven places,—no watchful, thoughtful eye to rest upon me. I thought of the disappointment to my family, the scandal & gossip involved, the putting away from myself of a noble man's devotion;—the banishment from his congenial companionship, ready sympathy, admiration & faith;—from the pleasant, refined society to which he could bring me, from the Home that he will have. I thought how I might comfort my friends—relieve my Father—enter upon a broad field of usefulness,—but I turned from all of these. I thought of his constant disappointment in me. Of the reproachful look in the fine blue eyes, as I turned wearily from his caresses—the tremulous voice in which he'd say "Frank, you're not kind to me." I thought of long years spent in trying to repress the annoyance a sensitive nature must feel in constant familiarity with one it did not *love*. I thought of my loneliness away from Home, with one that did not call the great Love of which I know myself to be capable, into action. I was cool & thoughtful. I gradually became more friendly, less loving in my letters. I changed equally in my actions. I made no professions. Up to now, I had thought *surely* I *did* love him, I could not have been so much deceived. I don't pretend to account for the fact—I can't see why it was, but know that I have been *innocently* brought to where I am.

Charlie has his own solution:—previous injustice[4] retribution etc. & I am not prepared to think it an erroneous one.

I waited till he was appointed to Jefferson Street, so that he might see how unselfish must be my motive—how uncalculating. I asked him weeks ago how much it would hurt him if our relation were to be discontinued. He carried the idea that it would be no permanent injury—only quick, sharp pain for an hour.

Understanding all this, I merely told him yesterday, when we had walked by the beautiful shore & looked out on the calm water of the Lake,[5] I told him in my own little room, with the pleasant sunshine over us, & the peace & quiet all around, that I feared I could not in the sweetest, most gentle & sacred ministrations, equal his expectations. I told him I had no signs of real love for him, but had the love possibly—my family thought so, & I might be deceived. Dear Charlie! Loving, forbearing Friend of mine! It smites me with keen pain to think how much it hurt him. I did not think that it would be so hard. If only just then, when I saw it, real *love* & *tenderness* for him had rushed into my heart so that I might have made him happy & myself full of peace & joy for all my life, how *thankful* I should have been! But no—I sat there calm & *unawakened*—yet with great *regret* to hurt him. We talked a long while, only with variations on this one subject. Then he went away, & I thought him lost to me, yet felt no loss—only pain for him. *Mary* came—I talked of what had happened to these at Home—I could not help it, they had known it from the first. I don't know what she thought—my Friend, who should try to comfort me now. She went up stairs with Oliver—oh! if I could have loved Charlie, as she loves him! What is the matter—what have I done—where lies the sin, oh God! If I could have loved *him* who had changeless, deep, all-encompassing love for me, *as I love Mary* who don't need or want or know what to do with me, I might have made him happy, I might have been happy too. Look at my Journals—at my letters—at my words—in their connection with *her.* Am I cold—is it "my style" to be undemonstrative & careless? Let her answer—let the years of our marvelous Friendship—nay, more than that—*Love* and *devotion* (for so it *was* with her,—her words, written & spoken, prove it abundantly, & so it *is* with me, as I know to my sorrow & pain!). Let those years, I say, plead for me! Let them show that I have a deep, warm, loving Heart. . . .

[Charlie and I] walked & talked along time, out in the moonlight & dew, & I told him I had no design in all this, but to tell him my true state of heart, & if he could accept what I had to give I would do anything he wished, & left it in his hands. He told me how his hopes were crushed—his happiness banished, & I stood there & heard him with infinite *regret for him*—& nothing more. . . .

I came Home. Mother blamed me without limitation & I saw that the whole family was disgusted with my conduct. I felt wronged & hurt but came off & wrote in my Journal.

Since dinner I have told Mother Charlie's *theory* of my want of love toward him. I shall not write it down, because it involves private affairs of his own. She accepts it, & don't blame me now, I guess, but is my own forgiving, cherishing Mother, as before. . . .

Let people say what they please, I shall let them think he broke it off. On me may come the . . . blame[6] of a cast-off sweet-heart. I owe to him this slight return. I shall write him kindly,—the very best I can. I shall copy the letter here, & his reply, if there is one, & there it may end.

O Lord! Thou knowest why I have done this. For his sake, for my sake,—for truth's sake & justice's sake. I could not conscienciously do otherwise. Love—pity—& forgive me. Bless *him* & give him of Thine availing love & comfort. Give to us all, rest & completeness, by & by.

1. Willard here used "Friends" to refer to her immediate family and to Mary Bannister. She did not usually capitalize the word when referring to others.

2. Charles Fowler had just been appointed to serve the Jefferson Street MEC in Chicago, during the Rock River Annual Conference, 2 October 1861. He was minister there until 1863.

3. Willard added three words to the sentence later in different colored ink, so that the sentence would read: "But I thought to disregard it would be a sin."

4. Again, Willard added three words later in different colored ink, so that the phrase would read: "previous injustice on his part."

5. Lake Michigan.

6. Later and in different colored ink, Willard crossed out "blame" and added "humiliation."

16 October 1861

What a strange history I have! How curious & contradictory are its chapters as I write them out! Yet under all them is a unity & truth, I think;—to God I know it looks right and "hangs in an untangled skein."[1]

Mother cried yesterday about my affair as I never heard her cry before. Father had a wretched day;—"he would not have another like it for all Wisconsin"—so he said. Oliver was greatly worried. Mary sympathized with me in what I have done, & didn't mind it much. It seems to me that through it all, she has acted best, most temperately & wise. But Charlie! He was full of misery—so Oliver said. Its effect upon him was entirely different from what I had thought—from what he had given me reason to expect. It was hard—for there was his plan of life disarranged & defeated,—his real, deep love for me, only a pain & a canker to him. I shudder to think of all he has suffered since Monday Afternoon.

Yet I will make it up. I shall have plenteous opportunity.

I never felt so abused & misunderstood as I have in these days. They (at Home) called me imbecile, "mythical" (!) and I was out of all my old, pleasant relations.

After talks & prayers & tears, I have decided, & acted upon my decision. He *knows* how I have felt. I have not deceived him, *I have taken back nothing.* My conscience absolves me. The course he has pursued has been taken knowingly, & in view of the *truth*. The engagement is to stand. Next Fall I am to marry him, certainly, *sooner* if it is needful to his success.

He is never to refer to the painful episode just past. He is never to mention any thing connected with it, to me. He is never to ask if I "care" for him. He is willing to accept the poor, paltry offering of my truth, my honor, my faith. He beleives me deceived and so do they all. He is kind & manly—does not blame me, does not reproach.

He feels quite happy over the arrangement,—my family are satisfied—our pride is not hurt—gossip is prevented—no pain is felt by any one in all the world save one who can manage it more easily than most women;—who deserves it richly no doubt, and will lock it up in her own heart. The *aggregate* happiness of those dearest to me, is very much increased;—no lie is told or acted;—no deception practised. It is all strange, but very *real*. I wonder what he thought? When it was all arranged—when I had told him, as I have repeatedly, & did in the beginning of my revelation, that the fact once told I would do as he pleased—that I did not tell him this because any one else was in my mind whom I might hope to love & be loved by,—when I had said, that if he pleased I would do any thing—he remembering my revelation, when I had said that I thought more happiness would come to more persons if I married him than if I did not (this last in answer to his questioning), he proposed a return to the old relation & life, which I accepted, & I sat upon his knee & received his words of love, his caresses & kind looks with the saddest face I ever wore. Yet it may all be right. I can not tell.

I will be true & faithful with him. I will bear much pain to repay that which I gave him on Monday & since then till this morning, & in return for what I gave my own dear Mother & my Father & my brother, yesterday.

They have all acted rightly & wisely & kindly—as far as intention goes. They have shown their love & interest—I think only kindness as to them. I have not been inconsistent, either. Always, from the first, I have said I would do as Charlie pleased when he knew the facts. This was his due—I promised to marry him, & I will. But I did not think or dream from what was said on Monday that he would ever think of me in the old ways, again. Therefore I wrote as I did.—I feel I am not worthy such a deep, noble heart as Charlie's;—such devotion & forbearance. But my life shall *try* to be very thoughtful, prayerful, gentle;—very regardful of him, very *helpful* too—if it can be so. I don't know that there is any thing more.

I wonder if *Mary* thinks or cares? I wonder if she—even for the memory of a single year ago,—spares a prayer, a sigh or a regret, from all her full, satisfying *Life* for me?

And yet, I do not wonder. I remember how she sent for me last Sabbath afternoon, to come & see her, as she had one of those painful head-aches that come to her, so often. I remember how she sat on my lap, and told me she thought of me & my affairs a great deal, & prayed about them. I remember she said she cared for me, & when I told her of my poor, unfortunate, strange, needless *love* for her, she kissed my forehead—shall I say with sad regretfulness for my queer nature, or with some thanks & love,—in return?

And though in all these long days—almost three of them, now,—she has said nothing, save the remark I have recorded,—though I have seen her, & wished she would speak of it—I can not say I blame her, when I think it over, or beleive she is unmindful. My own actions toward her have not been the kindest, & I have not broached the subject. Yet I told it all out before her in the sitting-room & had nothing more to say. So they thought me heartless about it! (Oliver & she.) *I am not.* My wild, thoughtless attempts at *fun* could have been nothing but mockery—might they not have had that much charity? _____

No! I would not for all the world beleive that *Mary* does not care. Is the Past a cheat and a delusion? _____

Last night, partially wakened by acorns rattling on the roof, I felt such a *consciousness of God*—such an *encompassment* by Him;—such a shutting down about me of His wrath that for an instant, agony, *sickness,* stifling, mocking despair such as fiends may feel, took possession of me. Oh! it was *horrible.* The greatest pain I ever had was *joy* compared with it. Right off, it left me,—wide awake and frightened. Once before, at Harlem, this same Thing has come, just a moment, when I was waking. Is it night-mare,—is it disease, or is it _____?

1. Not identified.

20 October 1861

[*Mary*] came to our gate with me when I left—we walked on to the Lake, & stood watching the moon & the track it made, upon the water. My arm was around her, & her hand on my shoulder. She looked out, on the water;—once or twice, I turned & looked into her face. I know,—it is "my nature." I know—no other woman of whom I ever heard would feel as I do—as I did. I know—it is unfortunate— it is—it would be—a wrong to Charlie if he did not know—if I had not tried to act right. It is curious—it is unparalleled. Oliver told Mother only yesterday morning that because *Mary* made me feel as I do was no proof I had an emotional nature. They are all bent on proving that I have *not,*—& I don't know but they are right. He said he had not much, but *Mary* could make him feel, & he & I were much alike in many things.

Let all this go for what it's worth—count me queer or weak, any who may never know "my nature," I say unblushingly, that as I stood there with *Mary* a great, wild *Love* for her went surging through my heart. A *love* that if I could give the same to C—would make us both happy all our lives. A Love such as I have prayed & begged I *might* have for him. A Love that would have made me face *death* unflinchingly for *her* and I dread death more than all other things. Thus have I loved her *always;*—sometimes I have struggled with it;—sometimes I have thought she wronged me—was careless & unmindful; sometimes my *Pride* has fought it—when it has been said to me: "Poor fool! she don't want you now—she has something better. You are but a worry to her—irksome and irritating. She would prefer to keep you, in a friendly way, rather than have you go to other girls, just for pride's sake. But have not her words shown often enough, that she didn't feel the need of you any longer." . . .

I am cold & unkind to her, sometimes. But I have many things to trouble me, & in many little, unconscious ways, she hurts me—cheifly because I see she does not think, & the least provocation rouses me. Then, when I think her careless, I go with the other girls & try to forget. *I do not have a happy moment with them.* It is *Mary* that I want,—*only Mary.* . . .

23 October 1861

. . . This evening Charlie & I had a frank talk & "we stand upon another footing now"—& a wiser, better one. Before, I had a feeling of something not unlike compulsion—acting for the greatest good of the greatest number, not for my own. I was not happy in the arrangement. Now it is much better. _____ I wish I could write out the talk we had—our clear, calm, logical, unlover-like talk. Never mind—here are the results.

We are engaged. There are to be no demonstrations. There is to be kindness—candor—trust. The consummation is never to be, unless I'm *sure* "I have the genuine";—until I'm *sure* one way or another we are to "stand & wait."[1] He was very noble—as he is always. I was as fair & just as—I knew how to be, the facts existing. I told him if I

had had it, & *had not* now, it was, I thought because of the demonstrations—which are painful to me,—& because he often (unknow-
ingly) hurt my feelings.

The "culture"[2] has always been the great "bone of contention." I
have often wondered what my nature is in this. I have no other experience to compare it with. I know that with *Mary* I greatly like such
things. That is all. It don't seem "nice" to me from C.

Very baldly & clumsily I have set down the "results." I shall feel
better hereafter. There is no deceit—no false pretense;—there never is to be. I shall be thoughtful & act like a Christian—if I can. The
sequel will show. I shall think & wish & pray to *care* under all the other actions & occupations—I shall write here of it—perhaps.

1. Willard quoted part of a line, "They also serve who only stand and wait," from
John Milton's sonnet "On His Blindness" (1652), in *Poems* (London, 1673), line 14.
2. Willard meant physical displays of affection from Fowler, such as kissing, caress-
ing, and the like.

1 November 1861

What a week has this been to me! Full of experiences—new phases of life—and to crown all the *Proud Day* of all my history! Let me
see;—my head throbs & I am tired, but yet, I would recall them all—
the scenes just past—not one of them must be forgotten.

On Monday Charlie came back from the city & he & Oliver had
some of their examinations.[1] Monday evening he called on me, & we
had a pleasant talk—"our affair" was discussed at length. Tuesday, I
went with Mary Bannister to the examinations at the Institute. In the
evening I went with Charlie, & Mary [Willard] went with Kean[2] to Bp.
Simpson's Missionary Address. It was good but inferior to anything
he ever did before. Wednesday went to examinations in Homiletics
& the Will.[3] The *Two* did very finely. In the eve. Dr. Haven (author
of the Mental Philosophy)[4] delivered a very fine Address on *The Ideal*. After we came home, Charlie & I had a long, long talk in Oliver's
room.——It is well that I have carefully reserved for myself the privilege of being (seemingly) inconsistent! For he & I are all right now—
he is *the one* to me & all my doubts & vagaries are trampled on. I have
prayed in this matter—I have consulted—I have gone forward carefully. Charlie has helped me—his patience & manliness, his calmness
& judgment, his faith & forgiveness, have been my salvation. He & I
have talked over the case as calmly & fully as either one has *thought*
it over. On this final (Wednesday) evening he presented me three
cases: going with him,—having nothing of the kind all my life—tak-

ing instead of him the possibility of sometime seeing one who could inspire in me the *phenomena* I lack, & have it at the same time inspired in himself. He asked me to choose. I said: "all my ambitions, admirations, requisitions are met in *you*. You can give me all I want except these signs that women usually have. I have been honest with you concerning the doubts which their absence inspires. I am stronger than most women—I am unlike them in many ways—I do not cling, like them;—I do not reverence like them;—I am not swallowed up in another's love like them;—why should I be? My love is as likely to be calmer, quieter, undemonstrative, as other traits of mine are likely to differ from the majority of women. I have no love of a man to compare with this;—I have imaginings—whims—fancies—that is all. If you can take me without the passionate love—the all-devotedness—the demonstrations that another woman might give, I will go with you, & be true to you, and faithful & helpful—throwing these foolish doubts & whims (founded upon my singular *phenomena*) to the winds." In substance, that is what I said to him. And in his generosity—his far-seeing judgment, he took me *as I am,*—& resting upon his confidence that I am all right—trusting him, admiring him, preferring a life with him to any alternative that appears, I drop the painful subject, once & forever. He told me how much pain I had cost him by the "revelation" I thought it right & necessary to make. He told me that it had worn & tried him more than all his course of study;—that it was the first sorrow that had ever come upon him; that he had thrown himself upon the ground often, in these few days, & prayed to die. And as he spoke, all his goodness & forbearance & nobleness rose before me, & I felt real tenderness for him. And I, who am *so* undemonstrative, laid my hand on his forehead & promised that I would *remember* this to the last day of my life; that I would be very kind & useful to him if I could—that I would try hard to make it up—that I knew God would make me suffer even as *he* had suffered, that it would be right, & my desert! & I would try to bear it uncomplainingly;—that he must not think I was not pained to think I had been to him a curse & not a blessing;—that I hated myself sometimes to think of all the ways in which I had hurt him. __ And he? The kindness and gentleness which has followed me these five months since he told "The Great Secret" contained in "The Three Words" was in his answer. Sometimes he has hurt me very much—but it has been in little things & only for the moment. His purpose toward me has been generosity & nobleness without a parallel. And now, trampling upon "thrills" & "demonstrations" and "feelings"—setting my face *away* from them, *never to look back;*—I cheerfully, tranquilly turn to a Life with Charlie as a noble, worthy, happy thing. I will be prayerful in it all. At first—last Spring—I was not, but I will be now. Loyalty, truth, kindness, magnanimity, shall characterize my intercourse with him. Nay, more than these! Thankfulness, & penitence for the pain I have given. I do not justify my action. The motives have been fully stated here. It is little if I be thought unjust. But I *will* be of value to him— I *will be* a *Blessing,* if God will help me, & I am sure He will. I beleive this is all. _____

On Thursday we all went to the city, & in Clark Street Church[5] they graduated—*Charlie & Oliver.* It was a proud day for us:—more so than for any one else connected with the affair. For, though all did finely, *the Two* stood far above the rest. There could be no question as to *that.* . . .

1. The examinations for the end of the term at GBI were held on 28–30 October 1861. On 28 October 1861, the faculty recommended Oliver Willard and Charles Fowler for graduation.

2. This was probably Samuel A. Kean (ca. 1837–1913). He later became a banker in Chicago and a business partner of Josiah Willard's. He was also an Evanston neighbor of the Willards.

3. Oliver Willard and Charles Fowler were examined in preaching and practical theology (or ethics).

4. Joseph Haven (1816–74), a professor of systematic theology at Chicago Theological Seminary, wrote *Mental Philosophy; Including the Intellect, Sensibilities, and Will* (Boston, 1857).

5. On 31 October 1861, Oliver Willard and Charles Fowler graduated from GBI. Commencement exercises were held at the First MEC, at the southeast corner of Clark and Washington streets in downtown Chicago.

24 November 1861

. . . I've thought so many things. The Old Story—that is all. And yet, it hurts me—always with new pain;—the canker & corroding of the needless love; the love that has had its day of value—has accomplished its Good;—the Love that was to be eternal we said—uninterrupted & beautiful always—& alike every way, only stronger with age. And she so good & pure—so true & womanly. Filling her destiny— meeting the claims *I* ought to meet—God pity me! Changing to suit the newer, higher Gift! Keeping faith & kindliness for the older, lowlier one! *Doing* what I theorized about;—bringing to pass what I idly *said* must be. Fitting gracefully into her relations in life—wearing her happiness quietly & with sweet thankfulness;—Good & "*pure in heart*"[1]—(as it is her great life-aim to be). Disappointing no reasonable claim;—never so glorious in my heart as now.

And I? *Striving*—striving my very best to emulate her,—failing— failing signally, I, who counted myself stronger than she! Praying for the Love that might make Two Lives calm & rich & full of value. Feeling honor & kindliness where I should feel the deeper, sentiments of vital Love & sleepless *care*. Knowing what is best & beautiful—desiring it above all other earthly things,—separated from *feeling*—as if I were indeed a paralized thing.

Tormented with the abnormal love & longing of a woman *for* a woman—one never so sweet & lovable as now. Open to ridicule from this, to censure from the other side. Not very good—not very near to God. Not very earnest in the life of every day.

It is strange & sad. But I do not talk about it. I am not morose or weak. I think & I am *sorry*—I pray—the very best that I know how.

1. Matt. 5:8.

3 December 1861

A pair of warm, heavy stockings "for the soldiers" went out from our house, only two days ago,—sent to be packed, & forwarded to Washington. They will comfort some poor fellow, who will never imagine how the most important event of my history is knitted in some where between the heel & the toe of one of them. For, on Thanksgiving Day, just before the train that brought Charlie to visit us, I was knitting—worrying,—wondering what would be the result of his coming. For though nominally sure and settled in our love & looking toward its consummation, yet he & I were wide apart, and did not understand each other, or regard as certain or permanent our relation to each other.

Looking from the window, on that day,—I saw him coming. How well he looked—how brave & manly! ____ I went on with my knitting, with feigned indifference. I greeted him politely—he returned to me "mine own, with usury."[1] Till dinner-time he sat talking of the War, with Father. He played with my ball of yarn, & I sat there knitting, silently. After dinner, he went out to make some calls;—I worked on, with unwonted industry, thinking, wondering, waiting for The *Talk* that was to be. . . . Charlie did not come in till we were done, when I poured his tea for him, & we sat in the dining-room, alone together—we had not been, before. He looked tired. He did not eat, or talk much. We came up here to "our room" after tea. (Ah! "our" will not have the old, accustomed *antecedent* to it with me, after a little while!)[2]

All the evening nearly, we talked upon indifferent matters. Mary came up & soon we went to Oliver's Room & there *I kept on knitting!* I don't know how to write it. It was so strange a scene. Such doubt;—such trembling of the balance;—such kindness & forebearance from *him*—always from *him.*

We prayed. It seems that I can hear him yet;—the clear, firm voice, so full of confidence in God, in which he said so many times in that prayer for so strange a purpose: "Father! do Thy will—Thy will, not ours."

I prayed more simply & heartily I think than I ever did in all my Life, before. I prayed that we might never look back regretfully upon this last Decision—might always feel assured that it *was right* since His counsel was beleivingly invoked, let the result be what it might.

I shall not write it out,—what need?—but if he lives,—& I,—I am to be his wife. All the waverings & doubts I most thoroughly regret. But let the Past be past, I feel that I love him—yes, *I love him,* & can go joyfully with him, down the Long Path, & even to the brink of the mysterious River. God make me a comfort to Charlie! I know how kind & good he will always be to me. I am content & happy. For the Past I offer no explanation or apology to myself. I acted honestly & conscientiously. I have the satisfaction of knowing that I am not the only one that has had misgiving, concerning the depth of attachment existing in their hearts;—Charlie gave me many instances of a like nature. Knowing *Mary* so well, loving her so much—seeing her ardor & depth & devotion in her love for my brother, I beleive I have taken her for a standard, whereas, I am not such a woman as she is & must not look for such phenomena as she exhibits. . . .

1. Not identified.
2. Willard probably meant that with her marriage to Fowler, "our room," referring to the room she shared with her sister Mary, would be Mary's room only. However, she could also have been implying that she would no longer think of it as "our room"—hers and Fowler's, where they went to speak privately—if she did not continue the engagement.

7 January 1862

[*In the first part of this entry, Willard recounted in great detail a visit to Clara Thatcher and a day spent in downtown Chicago on her way home to Evanston.*]

. . . All this is not much beside the underlying thoughts & feelings—and they concern *Charlie & me.* His Journal showed me—his face & all his ways—that I am a sorrow & a greif, to him. He is not well—he is not happy. How suddenly he left us without saying Good-bye—how frail he looked, walking before us carrying our heavy bundles. Oh dear!—*oh dear!*

Will it never come straight, & clear, & quiet? I'm almost afraid we shall never see light. Conscious of great wrong & wandering, I can not, yet, see where the trouble lies—where the fault & the wrong.

Right out into the darkness I am walking—like one who is blind. And yet, I do not *grope,* but walk forward vacantly—hoping to find light ahead.

Even for months my life has been the most unreal thing I ever knew. It is only a dream;—when things seem strange, perplexing and inexplicable, I murmur to myself "When morning comes I shall see clearly." "Only waiting"—that expresses it. Yet waiting *very sorrowfully.* Very regretfully for *him* for *myself* & for any Friends who are worried and tired. Where will it end? Are not we all tired? Do we not wish & pray and try as we are able? God's hand is surely in it—yet how or where, I can not see. Not much consciousness of Him—not much rest from Him—not much rightness in Life—not much of any thing.

My Father & my Aunt[1] sit here in her room talking cosily. It is quiet outside—dreamily, painfully chaotic, within.

It is better to sleep, I beleive, and to be for a while sinless and *still.*

I do not rightly know how I should pray—my heart is so dark toward Divinity & Humanity alike. In Christ's Great throbbing Heart tonight, I beleive there is *pity* for me—I dare not think there is forgiveness.

1. Sarah B. Hill.

18 January 1862

Charlie came up on the after dinner train, yesterday. He left at four, today.—We have had much frank and searching talk. Oh I can never tell *how sorry* I am for the trouble & darkness into which we have been brought. Many times as we have tried to adjust our relations amicably, & much as we have prayed & waited, Charlie and I get on no better—no more lovingly. It is entirely impossible for me to express my thoughts & feelings on the subject. Ah! I know "the subject" so *well!* Have studied it so long & carefully—gone over all the ground—studied the possibilities, yet in it all, "I find no light."

The case stands thus:—with all my admiration, kindliness & liking—or, perhaps, *love,* for *him,* I have not what I ought to have—what

I *wish* to have;—no real devotion—*no need* for him. *I write it with great sorrow & regret.* I have tried—I have prayed;—but I am not good, nor worthy to be answered, else I should have been, long since. There is only one Theory that at all explains to me the mystery of my feelings toward this man so noble & generous toward me always—whom I have said I loved—said it to him on a June night, & "*meant* it" in my heart. This explanation involves a private matter of Charlie's own,—a part of his history concerning one innocent & trusting—and who has suffered. It is right that we should be in darkness—he thinks the reason valid—on account of one to whom we did, unwittingly, bring greif & disappointment.[1]

There seem many reasons for, perhaps more against, our two lives being joined together. If they ever shall, I shall beleive it *right*. He is free and I am free as if we never had seen each other—we left it so, today, yet wait, before sundering every tie, till there shall be more light. Time will . . . make it all plain & clear before us;—this that seems so dark and doubtful, *now.* I regret nothing in my Life so much as the pain that I have given him—yet do not feel myself wholly responsible for all the misery that has grown from Charles' having known me;—for in *retribution* I beleive, some what of the tears & grief has come. At this, I shall only hint—perhaps it is not true, but only *seems* so to my dim sight.

It is strange how we have talked all these things over, this afternoon in Oliver's old room. Charlie told me all his thoughts & that he is getting to love me less,—it could not be otherwise,—and how he would not think it *Christian* for us to marry, unless each loved the other better than any thing else in the world. And I told him all my thoughts toward him—and we left it where we found it—unsettled, unsatisfactory & miserable. It was never so uncertain as now—never such "a great deep."[2]

Praying, as well as I can,—& that is very blindly, now-a-days, waiting as patiently, trusting as perfectly, & that is not much—I shall live my life till the Problem is solved.

How mournfully I look at Charlie's kind & complimentary dedication of this book to me![3] How little did he think,—or I—that it would be so full of both of us, yet full of such results—such trouble—such darkness! I beleive I've meant kindly & "at *my* best" toward him—that is saying little, God knows, for I have learned, at last, how weak and shabby is "*my best*"!

Oh! if it had been different! If but the Love that I have had in my Heart only to hurt and hunger there, might have been given to one so good, so worthy, so noble toward me!—we can not tell—we must even say that "All is best, as it befell."[4]

And so, I've written through this book;—a period of my life is here, more momentous than any other I have recorded. "The end is not yet"[5]—I await it,—as quietly as I can. . . .

1. It is unclear just what Willard referred to here. Possibly Charles Fowler had disappointed another woman regarding marriage plans, perhaps during his years at Genesee Wesleyan College. It may be that the woman he eventually married in 1863, Esther Ann Warner (a graduate of Genesee Wesleyan), was this woman.

2. This common nineteenth-century phrase was used to convey great sadness and despair. It may have had its origin in Ps. 36:6, "Thy judgements are a great deep."

3. On Willard's twenty-second birthday, 28 September 1861, Fowler had given her the journal volume in which she was writing. At the front of the book he had written:

Frank,
Record here your *inner* life,
as freely as you think it,
as carefully as you speak it,
as genially as you live it,
as candidly as you would meet it.
Charlie
Evanston *September 28*th 1861.

4. Willard paraphrased "All was best as it befell," from Elizabeth Barrett Browning, "Bertha in the Lane" (London, 1844), stanza 23, line 2.

5. Matt. 24:6b.

22 January 1862

. . . a long & very manly, & very *important* letter from Charles.

A long, kind, Fatherly talk from Father—on the subject of "*my Deep*" "that none but God can sound."[1] He was never nicer to me;—how frankly, humorously & then seriously, he advised me. Father is "Our angel." I want to remember him, lying here on the crimson covered lounge in Aunt Sarah's room;—I sitting by the fire—Mary in the back ground writing in her Journal. Father & his eldest daughter talking of her greatest earthly interest:—as he said, "The most important matter that will be ever brought up in *this* house."

1. Not identified.

28 January 1862

. . . *Mary* the old Friend, *Katie*[1] the *New*. In Bible Class—the two profiles: one wonderfully delicate, & spiritual, the other wonderfully bright ardent & ready for *life*—it was like two worlds coming together—the beautiful Ideal & the sparkling, vivid *Real*. I *love* Katie Pettengill. Her ingenuousness—her wholesome vigor, her warm heart—her beautiful face—all these are captivating to me. I love women so curiously—

I am *sorry* that I do. I am so careful of them—feel as if no one had the right to be familiar with them—I'm ashamed to put it down, but here it is,—part of the *Great Deep*—*Me.* Hannah,[2] I admire, reverence & like *exceedingly.* She is an artist—paints landscapes beautifully, is a perfect lady & a well-educated, unbigotted Christian. How queer that she can't *awaken* me, while her sister "sets me wild." They danced a waltz, here in Aunt Sarah's room;—I'll have a story out of it,—it was itself as if a Chapter from a Novel had acted itself before us. See them:

The tall, graceful, dark-eyed, dark-haired girl, (the one I *like*). The short, plump, clear,—beleiving-eyed, bewitching-mouthed girl (the one I love).

Two sisters, with their arms about each other—one in heart, one in life thus far. I never saw two so well-fitted to each other—so harmonious—so loving. O dear, I'm sorry for my *nature,* but it hurts me *greatly* to think that they must ever go apart—to other homes, other loves, other caresses. What did Paul mean by "He that marries doeth well, he that marries not, doeth better"? & the rest of that Chapter?[3]—I suppose it is another of "*the deeps.*"

They say that it is like to change my Life—that Love of mine for *Mary.* Somehow it seems to have got me jostled from my relations— abnormalized me. It is at the bottom,—sometimes I half suspect, of all my greifs with Charlie. Yet I called it God's best Gift—what was the matter? Would it have been to me a "guide & not a chain"?[4] I suppose not,—otherwise all *this* would not have happened me. . . .

I am in a greater Slough of Dispond[5] than ever before in my Life. An alternative must be taken—a decision must be made & I must make it. The Burden falls squarely on my shoulders. . . . My Journal witnesses how C— & I have tried to make our relation to each other beautiful & comforting to both. Oh! my heart aches for the wavering and darkness over us—all growing from the *One Sad Fact*—how arrived at I can not tell—that I do not feel I love him. And he so true & noble—oh! if I could *rest* in him. Let it pass, with its inconsistency, its strangeness and trouble—to him & to me. Now I must face the Dilemma—Judgment goading me in one direction, Advice of Friends urging the same way, *Heart* fearing to take it—trembling & worrying. And yet I honor, admire, *like,* possibly *love* him somewhat—and yet not as ought—not as I *would.* So I fear to go with him, & yet I fear to break it off. He has left the last Decision with me. Yesterday he came up from the city & talked it over with me, in the old, familiar way. When he went, he kissed me & said: "You remember at Harlem, by the tree full of blossoms I kissed you first & you said: 'That must be the last, unless' ____ You know what you meant & I understood by that. Now I say this is the last, unless" ____ & as he turned away, I knew the Decision must come very soon, & that I should never see him again save as a mere family friend, unless ____ it was affirmatively decided. I fear lest I may regret—lest God may not be in the final determination I may make;—I would not be rash in what involves so much. I would be thoughtful, guided by God—all other help has failed me, & it is well that I am left to *Him*. Oh! may *he* show me. If I am deceived, may I see it—as yet, I am in darkness, but even if that should not be cleared away I must decide, for Charlie has left it with me, & we are to write no more except *decisively*. . . .

1. Katie Pettingill was the daughter of a friend of the Willard family.

2. Hannah Maria Pettingill was Katie's sister. Willard met her again in November 1868 in Germany where Pettingill was studying painting. When Willard became president of the Evanston College for Ladies in 1871, she hired Pettingill for a faculty position as an art teacher.

3. Willard paraphrased 1 Cor. 7:38, "So then he that giveth her in marriage doeth well; but he that giveth her not in marriage doeth better." In the second half of the seventh chapter of 1 Corinthians, Paul wrote about the imminent return of Christ and urged people to remain in the state in which they were since time was so short. Addressing himself to marriage, he urged those who could remain sexually pure not to marry and get involved in the distractions of family life. But those who felt they must marry could do so. Yet Paul apparently regarded an unmarried, celibate life as preferable for those awaiting the End Time.

4. Not identified.

5. The "Slough of Dispond" occurs in John Bunyan, *Pilgrim's Progress from This World to That Which Is to Come*, part 1 (London, 1678). In Bunyan's allegory, the pilgrim, Christian, falls into the Slough of Dispond, consisting of all the fears, doubts, and discouraging apprehensions of sinners, just as he sets out on his journey.

31 January 1862

. . . the Problem is solved by the first light & the best light I have. I am alone and free and to go forward by myself & not with Charlie. So end all the inconsistencies of my Life for the months past, & which my Journal faithfully relates. The inconsistences are *consistent* closely viewed, & hinge on the two facts that, having *somehow* come not to love Charlie, and trying *somehow to* love him, I have wavered to & fro, impelled this way by heart, that way by Judgment, until in the longer & less frequent oscillations, the stronger force has conquered & the Decision is made—after prayers & thinking more than I ever before needed to bestow on any Subject, & the following letter has been written & goes to Charlie very soon. . . .

"My dear Friend.

As I sit down to write you, the year that is past rises before me, and I see its events as plainly almost as if themselves and not their memory were present with me. It has been a strange year, and a sad one. I offer no explanation of the change that has come over me,—I have none for my self—The Fact I accept—I have ceased trying to go beyond it.

In making the Decision you have left for me to make in view of the Fact hinted at, beleive that I act, as *thoughtfully, wisely, advisedly* and *prayerfully* as *I* know how. You are too just to expect more. Looking into my heart I see for you respect, honor, admiration, and regard. I do not see *love* such as it is your right to have from me, such as I earnestly *wish,* that I might give you—such as you and I beleive to be the only basis divinely recognized as right, for a union of two lives by Marriage.—It is not that the love of which I beleive myself capable has been given to any other man than your self—I find only a *negation*—a *want.* If I am—if I shall find myself mistaken you can but know that I shall suffer, keenly, bitterly regretting that the knowledge comes *too late.* Let this prove as it may, I know of nothing safer than to be guided by present *consciousness* on this subject. The facts as I *feel* them *now* compel me to say I think the relation between us must be dissolved. If in any thing I am blind and wrong, I am very mindful that retribution awaits me—suffering and tears. Yet in view of all the possibilities at which I have hinted, I am compelled to abide my decision.

In writing to you for the last time, as I suppose, I have to say that your conduct toward me has always and invariably been, manly, high-minded, generous, and noble in the highest degree. You stand at this moment in my esteem as highly as ever.

I have also most *deeply,* most humbly and *sorrowfully* to regret the pain and trouble I have cost you, I have acted as honorably, and Christianly as I knew how in every case where we have been concerned. My conscience does not reproach me. Yet that I should have been so unfortunately connected with your life will always be a greif and a regret to me. Let me ask that you will think as forbearingly & charitably of me as you can. Remember I have my pain too—I shall have care & trouble, and labors abundant. Do not think there is no light in the Path from which I turn away, and no darkness in the one which, nevertheless, I hope to tread with firm footsteps. God will strengthen you in your weakness, He will strengthen me in mine. _____

I think with pain of all those loving, pleasant Friends of yours who will perhaps reproach me for the trouble that I brought to one of whom they were so fond & proud. Let me ask them, through you, to think of me as gently & as forbearingly as they can.

And now Goodbye. May God bless you & guide and love you;—I shall ask Him to, in all my prayers. I hope you will remember me "at my best,"—*my very best.*[1]

Frank Willard."

That is the end, to all human appearance. What I wrote him was done in all candor, and was as complete & designed a revelation of my heart as it was possible to make. I concealed *nothing* so far as I know.—Concerning the publicity of the affair—I shall merely say that for reasons considered by us both as sufficient, & in all kindness and good-feeling the engagement is broken of. I have ceased to wear his ring, & nothing remains but to send my letter & the necessarily accompanying *package,* when Mr. Fowler & I shall be good Friends—nothing more. I shall not do this till after Sunday as I don't wish to incur the possibility of troubling him with the subject so near preaching-time.

I shall not write him & word my Theory—often hinted at, once or twice blindly expressed, perhaps, of the *why* of all our trouble. Let me say I am not thoughtless of the matter—not heartless though sometimes I like to act so—wicked as it may be. As much as I feel anything, I feel that I have done *right*. My Friends think so too, now that it is useless to think otherwise, & we are quiet & I am already something as I was—ever so many years ago.

Perhaps I have no reflection in the matter pleasanter than this:— That it does not hurt Mr. Fowler—that from all that I can learn on which I most fully rely, he does not love me—is not pained and will think that every thing is for the best. Yet, if I were to intrude the Subject upon him tomorrow, (Saturday), he might be disturbed in his attention to his sermon by the changed aspect of his Future—that is all, & that is natural enough. . . .

Oliver has left us and gone up on the street to Mary B—'s;—he will leave,[2] I suppose on the four o'clock train, at any rate, we shall see nothing more of him. His going away and many circumstances of late, have lead me to think of the changed relation in which he stands to the world—& to us at home, among the rest. . . . But to me I know the pain of *loosening our relation* is gone—the vague, unavoidable regret is dying out. I can give him up—have done so. Yet sometimes I think of days bright & beautiful to us as a Family . . . "before any were lost or gained."[3] I know it is all right,—I would not wish it different, yet I am so bound to my one father, one mother, one sister one brother that the letting go of one after another will be severe. He does not know—my brother—how I have said "Goodbye" to him—to the old unreserve, the old close intercourse & intimacy— the old *oneness* that was between us. It does not hurt me any more— thank God!—*no more.* I say this in no mourning, repining spirit, but firmly, bravely too I hope, and make the record but as one of the closely succeeding events of my Life out-of sight. God bless my brother! Continue him in his happiness and may Life always be to him full of promise—of zest and welcomeness. . . .

1. Willard paraphrased James Steerforth, a friend of David Copperfield's in Charles Dickens, *The Personal History of David Copperfield* (London, 1850): "If anything should ever separate us, you must think of me at my best, old boy."

2. Oliver Willard was headed to his first parish, in Edgerton, Wis. At the Annual Session of the Wisconsin Conference of the MEC on 18 September 1861, Willard had been admitted as a minister on trial and assigned to serve his first church.

3. Not identified.

2 February 1862

. . . Of late, my temper grows much worse—I am easily roused & display my worst side without shame. I need work—change—zest. Evanston, for the first time has lost its charm. Not in this year 1862 have I loved it as I did before. And I'm glad—very glad—It is the drying up of the sap—the shriveling of the tissues—the leaf will fall of *naturally* when it must *necessarily*. Thus I adjust myself. . . .

3 February 1862

. . . This War is a horrible thing, but my own life is so near—it lies so close about me, that I concern myself cheifly with it, and don't go so far off as "the Grand Army of the Potomac" for my material. However I will simply remark that we (the Northern Public!!) are deeply and heartily disgusted with the entire management—with Lincoln, McClellan, Seward & Co,[1] & vote them imbecile, idiotic &c. . . . To think of our soldiers dying of exposure—without ever striking a blow for freedom—to think of two millions a day being spent for nothing. Nothing excites my *ire* so deeply as this war.

The soldiers are dying by hundreds, now—father says there are coffins at the Depot—poor fellows being sent home to their friends, *dead*. . . . Oh it's a strange, inexplicable sort of world. May we seek shelter in Christ—Oh! I *want* to *so much*—there is no quiet elsewhere, "though we seek it carefully & with tears." . . .[2]

1. The Army of the Potomac was the Union's main fighting force in the Eastern theater of the Civil War. George Brinton McClellan (1826–85) was the commander of this army from 15 August to 9 November 1862, when Lincoln removed him from his post for his overcautiousness. William Henry Seward (1801–72) was Lincoln's Secretary of State. By "& Co" Willard referred to others in Lincoln's cabinet, his War Office, and his generals.

2. Willard paraphrased Heb. 12:17b, "for he found no place of repentance, though he sought it carefully with tears."

12 February 1862

. . . This *loving* is so *costly*. It drains one of spirit, when unfortunately centered. How much trouble my "peculiar & unfortunate emotional nature" has brought. . . . All the love I have ever had for all other Friends was not so much as I have had for *Mary*—so that has hurt me most. She told Mary yesterday. . . that I acted very coldly & badly toward her. It is true. I am not unkind, not impolite, but distantly courteous. Oh I wish that I could help it. It is the *reaction*. I must not—can not love her, yet it is so *natural* for me, I have to fight against it, & then my pride comes in, & I am reserved—it seems to be my only defence. If we need not be thrown so much together! I never leave her without a *splinter* in my spirit. We were *so much*—we shall be so little to each other, & there is no help & none is wanted, only quiet & absence. I am, in my nature so foolish & I can't help it a bit more than I can the color of my eyes, that I must overcome a positive passion for her, just as a man would who had been displaced in the heart of "a lady fair" by a more lofty worthy, successor, that's all. And yet, we are to be sisters—I must act careless & kind & cordial as Mary does, yet so many things conflict that it is *hard*. Yet I will try. Here is a note I wrote to *her* last night.

"My dear Mary,
Experience has taught me that multiplying words does only harm, in almost every case. But for this consideration, I should, several weeks ago, have talked with you about—I can hardly give a name to it, but it will name itself to you, as I proceed. For your talk with my sister this afternoon caused me to decide to "say a few things"—as Mother would express it—about myself & my conduct toward you. Your relation to me also—growing out of your relation to my brother—demands more than I have, of late, conceded. To come directly to the point,—I acknowledge that I have not acted as I ought toward you, for a long while. I have been cold instead of cordial, formal instead of frank; I might go on indefinitely, with the alliterative antitheses, but these specimens will doubtless answer. *I wish*—I do not think you can, with your lack of such experience as I have had, know *how much* I wish—that I might act toward you as Mary does—as sisterly, as kind. Upon your beleif in my truthfulness I must rely, for proof of what I say. I had thought of explaining to you the feelings that contend in my heart, & the things that hurt, the things that heal, with the pain & trouble that are there. But I have told you enough—it hurts *my* pride, & would not help *yours*, or you. I ask you to forgive me for all my unkindnesses,—I make no defense, though to myself I can furnish many palliations,—necessarily more valid with me than with you. My knowledge, & long acquaintance and former intimacy with you make me certain that you will forgive me without waiting for a defense—when I acknowledge all that it is right or needful that I should.
And I promise to *act better*. Beyond this, in protestation or avowal I

need not go. I am some how weary of superlatives,—they do more harm than good, at the last. It is not impossible that I may fail—I have done so very often. It is a pitiful acknowledgement, yet I make it because it may be needed. I will *try* & I will pray God for help. All this, though not so trivial to me as to you, perhaps, is yet worthy the saying, & having done, I will close, asking you to be patient toward me, & to allow for a peculiar & unfortunate emotional nature in me;—to let the light of your knowledge of me when I was nicer than I now seem to you, fall upon me, through your memory. And I ask you to remember that I have no such glory in my Life as has come to yours, & that there are some experiences & memories that have cause to make me sad; they have not come to you, & I am very thankful, they have not. I do not mean to complain & mourn to you, but am afraid I shall if I go on, so Goodbye, & beleive that I will try to be truly your sister." P.S. "Of course I think there have been instances in which you have not acted very nicely toward me. But I have only to do with my own affair—have only to acknowledge my own deficiences." . . .

I "can't know" why I copied the poor little letter, save that all connected with this experience is something to me—not to be forgotten, not to be passed carelessly—I can not make it so. If to me, as to her, there had come a greater, more satisfying Love, I should not have had the trouble that, as it was, I count inevitable. She had Oliver—I could not, though I earnestly tried, transfer the Great Love I had given her, to Mr. F. Two such luminaries my zenith would not hold,—nor hers. So with her,—most fortunately,—one sunk below the horizon; with me, the one that might have been better & brighter, never rose above it. Hers seems the happier gift,—she gains so much that the loss is not felt;—we do not miss the moon, when the sun shines, though we cling to it so much when in the night, alone and comfortless. But for me, I beleive some good gift is in store, if not happiness, blessedness;— if not Love,—which I covet most,—then something better for my nature—more sure to guide me upward—always upward. I can wait, not joyfully, yet without tears;—not with pleasure, yet with but little pain.

It seems that I shall never have done this subject. It constantly recurs. Hereafter, I will give it its place—it were but mockery, after all, to be silent upon that which is so much mixed with my thoughts, & which has colored my life for years.

13 February 1862

Some few "last words" (?) now, concerning "My Affair." The letter I had written Mr. F. & have copied in my Journal, I was requested, by a note rec'd from Oliver after he left Home, not to send until I should hear from him, further. I did as he wished. Soon after I rec'd the kindest of letters from my brother, placing the case again before me, and stating results of his visit with Mr. F. which he thought might change my views. They were not new to me, however, only new exhibitions of the honor & nobleness with which, as a rule, I have credited him. Some little correspondence—a letter on each side—passed between Mr. F & me, relative to a statement in O's letter which, as irrelevant, I "rule out" of my Record. Then I sent the letter . . . last Monday. Last night, came this, which I copy. It seems to me manly & kind & every way worthy of its Author. (Underscoring, of course his own.) . . .

> "Frank.
>
> Your 'last' is before me. I have read it. I thank you for your appreciation of my action & for the womanly honesty you have exhibited. I have no comments. I think it due you, to say, that you have in *all things done right*. You know my *heart*. I need not repeat a note I once wrote your *Mother*. . . . I shall be a better, wiser man for our acquaintance. The Savior sometimes exhibits his love by contrasts. *All is dark*. I am innocent. I can wait till we get over the river. I beleive you are also *innocent*. *It is* and that *is all. God bless you*. I thank you for the pleasure I have had in loving & in being loved. It is "a great deep," yet it must be best. We have prayed & thought & I have full confidence that it will be *best*— that it *is best*.
>
> I shall think of you 'at your *best*.' I shall remember you kindly all along life's weary, *lonely* journey. You have given me many hours of pleasure, & their memory will be pleasant. I have acted as I best could, toward you & toward your family. They are all very dear to me. I ask that we may remain *friends*. Your Mother's love has done me good. I am for it, always her *debtor*. If it is your pleasure I will return your *things* & get my own, in person. Our kindly feeling will enable us to meet as we would have met before the 2nd of June, 1861, only we will be better acquainted & less shy. I will call on Saturday. Do not suffer yourself to feel lonely & dispirited. *Never* think of me as *blaming you*. We will drop out these 3/4 of a year & call ourselves square with the world & start *again*. The success of which you speak is not certain, but if it were, it *must* be *empty*. I hope you will live long to feel that you have acted *wisely* and according to *duty*. I close with those sad, *moist* words, 'Frank,' *Goodbye!* God bless & protect & love you. Amen! Farewell!!
>
> C.H. Fowler."

Dear me! Truly, "it is a deep." He so noble & generous & so loving toward me, & I wanting to love him, yet finding it impossible. In God's time the strange problem will be worked out. Sometime we shall see the *why* & the *how*. Now, the best, most charatable friend I have could only say, as I do, & as he might,

"'Tis pitiful, 'tis *wondrous* pitiful!"...[1]

1. Willard paraphrased William Shakespeare, *Othello,* act 1, scene 3, line 158: "'Twas pitiful, 'twas wondrous pitiful."

16 February 1862

Yesterday Mr. Fowler came up, and we exchanged letters, pictures, &c; all in the kindest, friendliest manner. He staid to dinner, and almost all the Afternoon. Mother & I talked very frankly with him. I did not quite understand some of his words concerning the breaking off of our engagement. However, let them pass, with all the rest. *It* is over;—we shall be good Friends, I hope,—he will call on us,—and the past will be buried. I do not know as it is of any use to recount our talk—or any thing else about it. Only, it is over, and I beleive that it is *right* and that some day, we shall *both* know *why*....

17 February 1862

... I write a good deal, now, & am making every reasonable effort to get a school. I can not let myself be a dead weight on Father's hands, now that I am so old, & so well able to care for myself. I think much of devising ways to earn my own *clothes* at least—he would not mind my board so much—I could easily defray that expense.

And Mary & I went to *Mary's*. And while I was there, I was only in constant pain. *She* looked so sweet in the red dress that Oliver likes best, & that she wears so much of late. I never saw her when she seemed more dear & beautiful. And the dull, heavy hurt was in me all the time—because—idiotic & unreasonable as it is—she will never be mine to live near;—to see every day;—to say loving words to & to say those sweet, sacred words I prized more than any thing else, to me. O dear! when will the pain die out? It is a cloud over me, all the time. It is to me, what I suppose I was to Mr. F. Can it be, that thus I am to suffer as he did, for the sake of compensation?

23 February 1862

... I am in no "Deep." Free and quiet, yet more thoughtful and busy than I have been, before. And someday, I feel *sure*, great happiness will come to me—& I shall be of use in the world.

In Religion, for a few days I am encouraged. Not because singing
or prayer or eloquent sermons arouse me, do I count myself Christianly.
But when I see that what was irksome becomes pleasant—that what I
did as a duty, & not without "aforethought" I come to do naturally &
unconsciously;—when I see my self forbearing as a matter of course,
and patient and kindly as a spontaneous thing, then I beleive God's
spirit is within me. Only so far as it comes directly down into my Life—
into its smallest action & most trivial word, do I trust to religion as
connected with me. The mere *aesthetics* will not do;—the elevation of
soul at the prospect of an endless & boundless life—the pictures of the
Future world that hang in my Fancy—these I don't count. An unregenerate heart, I beleive capable of every one of these manifestations.
So, when, as latterly, I find my Life quite pure and patient, I look up
so thankfully to God & Christ, & pray for more of that Love in my Heart
which makes the Life right without our watching it—which "makes no
duty seem a load," "no worship prove a task."[1]

1. Not identified.

27 February 1862

. . . *Mary* came Home with me, & we talked till three this morning. She told me so many things—new & surprising to me—painful,
also. She, with her rich Life, is *hurt* so much, in heart. Her illustration—made me shudder;—the illustration of how it is with her heart.
It is terrible—I can almost conceive of it. My troubles are as nothing
to it. Of course, to help her I can only pray and be thoughtful and
loving towards her. Dear *Mary!*—and she hardly hurts me at all, any
more.

I told her of myself—*every thing*. Things I don't write here, or any
where. And she was—as she is always,—just the comfort, just the
counsellor, I needed.

She told me of a Talk she had with Mrs N[oyes]. How I admire &
love that woman. Her views about loving suit me thoroughly. This
sentence sets forth the Idea, with the Logic of it, just to my liking:—
"For a woman to marry a man whom she does not love, is to make
one man as good, in her sight, as another;—hence it is prostitution—
more than that, it is *infernal*."

Amen! And if I go alone and hungry to my grave, & "spinster" is
written on my tomb stone, I will at least, stand before God, in the next
Life, and tell him I am guiltless of the crime attending "a marriage
of convenience."

And yet, I cherish a cheerful faith that "sometime, God's time,"—as *Mary* used to say—I shall love to the limit of my capacity and be equally beloved. If not, I will go forward, stifling my complaints, and, "like Peter of Cells, thinking on the eternal years." . . .[1]

1. Not identified.

1 March 1862

. . . Father said Mr. F— came into the Office today;—asked after our various healths, etc. It seems queer, how strangely he has gone out of my thoughts & knowledge. Except to ask God, every time I pray, to "love & care for him, and make him good & happy" I do not have him in my mind, hardly at all. So curious it is—all our experience with each other. One year ago today, the Biblical Institute opened its Summer Session. I remember how I wondered if Mr. F— would come—& if he would call—& if ___ & all the rest! . . .

3 March 1862

. . . I am going, once more, to make some "rules & regulations" for myself. Often, before, I have done this, & beyond this, done nothing. Yet it is better to try once more, than to give it up entirely. I feel, some how, as though I am more likely to keep these Resolutions than any I have made before;—because they are taken in a better spirit;—indeed, I think a *spirit* not altogether mine. I will *say* that hereafter I mean to set down my intentions for a day or a week, beforehand, & see how I approximate to my idea. I may not follow this up—"& then again," I may. . . .

Thus much having been said "in a prefatory way" . . . I will . . . write out a Code of Laws, By Laws etc. etc. which I promise to have regard for, and to seek to observe & be regulated by, "as far as in me lieth";[1]—praying for help, and for "strength to be perfected in my weakness."[2]

Resolutions.

1. *Concerning Practical Religious* Duties:
   (in the technical sense of the expression).
   (a.) I will read one chapter in the Old Testament & one in the New, every morning, after my toilet is made. On the Sabbath I will read one or more chapters in the German New Testament.
   (b.) I will attend Class Meeting, & our Young Ladies' Prayer Meeting as regularly as possible.

(c.) Every other Sabbath Evening I will go to church with Father. On the evening that I don't go with him, I will attend our Home Prayer Meeting, with Mother, Aunt Sarah, & Mary.

(d.) I will attend church on Sabbath Morning, uniformly. I will try to hear the Sermon, no matter who preaches.

(e.) I will, as far as I am able, & in the strength "that cometh down from above," be a *faithful Sabbath School Teacher.* I will diligently prepare the Lesson, strive to set a good example, be very prayerful for my Pupils, & have their *Spiritual elevation & welfare* greatly at heart.

(f.) I will pray at least twice a day, & remember my Class, my Sunday School scholars, my friends, my country, & all who suffer, everywhere, in my prayers.

(g.) I will try to be reverential and Christianly in my daily life & deportment, & to exercise a good influence upon those around me.

(h.) I will take for my mottoes, these:
    1. In all things, I will try to do *my best.*
    2. I will beleive that whatever is given to me or with-held from me is done in Infinite Kindness, & will "trust God where I can not trace Him,"[3] beleiving, however much events may surprise or puzzle me, that *"It will all come right."*[4]

In all this, I say nothing of the deep Spiritual Life, which can not be brought inside of rules.

2. *Concerning Social Duties.*

(a.) I will endeavor, God helping me, to love Humanity—to pity it—to help it if I can;—to be very *Charitable* toward my fellow-beings, to put the best possible interpretation upon their actions;—to have broad, generous views concerning them;—to have no strong antipathies;—to be interested in *All* & to have a certain kindly solicitude for all.

(b.) I will seek to make others happy, as far as I am able;—I will study opportunities;—will try to be *uniformly* cheerful & cordial to all.

(c.) I will call upon all new families that "move" to the community where I may live—will manifest regard for their happiness & contentment, as I would have manifested for my own family if I were a stranger.

(d.) I will endeavor to discharge my social duties—to bear my part of Social burdens, in all things where it is fitting & possible.

(e.) To those who are in the lowly walks of life I will be kind &

considerate—whether servants in my Fathers house, or persons in the same grade, outside it.

(f.) I will help the needy always, & not be over-careful to ascertain all the antecedents of a beggar, & to prove him "*genuine*" for fear I might be imposed upon by misapplying my charities.

To those at Home

(g.) I will *of course* be as kind & loving as our mutual relations makes natural. In thoughtfulness of the comfort of my parents—etc. etc

3. *Concerning Hand-work.* I *will* understand house-work & sewing. I will demand it of myself to be as "practical" as the young ladies who are my friends:—than which there is nothing more to be desired in this direction.

4. *Concerning Head-work* I will try to improve in scholarship—in *scope.* I will write what I can—I will have all "these things" very close at heart—indeed, I have had, always.

5. *Concerning* the Graces, Accomplishments, "sweet, small courtsies,"[5] & all that gives beauty and symmetry to a woman's character:—I will be very thoughtful, & anxious to improve. I know I have striking deficiences here, & will *try* "make them up."

6. *In General:*

My two most prominent faults are

(a.) Want of *Patience.*

(b.) Want of strict *Truthfulness.*

About these, I will pray most, & labor most.

To be content with Life—to be thankful, cheerful, unrepining—I *wish* for these things, *ardently.* I have them all, in some degree—I will strive to have them more.

"Not to mind"—as it is simply &, as I think, prettily expressed is a rare, beautiful trait. "Not to mind" when people are severe to us;—when they disappoint us;—when they misjudge us! But to fall back serenely on our good intentions—on our Christian character & Life, & contentedly to *wait.* . . .

I know how "most people" would laugh at my writing these things,—especially my Friends, for I am not wonderful for *adhering* to my "Resolutions." However, it concerns me cheifly, & as it pleases me, I suppose it is "right—right—all right." Besides, for several weeks, I have been doing these things, so I have an "impetus" to go on.—I beleive the matter is settled, now.

1. Willard may have paraphrased Rom. 12:18, "as much as lieth in you."
2. Willard paraphrased 2 Cor. 12:9, "for my strength is made perfect in weakness."
3. Not identified.
4. Not identified.
5. Willard quoted a portion of the sentence: "Hail, ye small, sweet courtisies of life!" from Laurence Sterne, *A Sentimental Journey through France and Italy* (London, 1768).

6 March 1862

. . . We live very pleasantly here at Home. Just now, Mother is in bed, having retired early, because she is not very well. Dear Mother! *nearer* to me than any other on earth. In the rocking-chair, by the "coal burner" of the sitting room, Father sits & rests after his day's work in the city. *Father*—how much he is to me! His funny ways, his sterling manliness—his fine face & figure—his sheltering of us—I have them all in memory. Aunt Sarah on the lounge, talking with Father, about "our folks" in "New York State." . . . By the table, Mary is reading the "History of the Reformation."[1] She looks very "calm & sweet," in her blue dress, with the pretty, new contrivance setting off her glossy hair.

From our own quiet fire-side my thoughts go out to the other Homes & hearths in our beautiful village. I feel as if I knew what they are all doing—my friends, in all these houses around us. I see the light lying softly over the faces & forms, the furniture & walls of many pleasant sitting rooms. And there is much kindly talk & loving glances & smiles. I like best to look into the Libraries—those long, quiet rooms, lined with books,—and to see, by the table in the middle of each room, the Christian Scholar whose holy place is the one he studies in. There are voices of children in my ears, & the tinkle of music & the ring of laughter—the Father with slippered feet & gorgeous dressing-gown, the Mother with her loving, trustful face, turned so often toward "*him*";—the innocent children playing in the corner, while "pa & ma" talk by the fire. O! Life is sweet, & full of comfortable things & glorious gifts!

If God wills, I would know more about it, before I die. I would have great value in some one's eyes;—I would bear burdens & say soothing words & offer earnest prayers for love of *some one* who was good & noble. I would not have said so once;—it may be that I should do better not to say so now. These things do not disturb my equanimity—only I think of them—& most of all, at evening.

1. Mary Willard was reading Jean Henri Merle d'Aubigne, *History of the Reformation of the Sixteenth Century* (Paris, 1835–53; translated into English, 1854).

13 March 1862

. . . "How far are our perceptions confined to our outward senses? Can any one tell?—for that our perceptions are not wholly confined to impressions taken in by the outward senses seems the only one thing proved; & are such sensible impressions the only *real* ones?"[1]— This I read aloud, to my Aunt, & closed the book. Then we had a long talk about "these things." And while we talked, I did not feel the blind-ed, groping creature, I usually am. Some how, I compare myself to a telescope when *shut up* & not in use. You look through the lenses— you don't see much—they are not now adjusted for any but short distances. And that is the *"myself"* of every day. Little pains & small joys;—little things to be done & to be borne. You would think that *this* was all. And then, I can not feel myself, always, that there—is any thing beyond. If my small hope is crushed—if this trivial effort is in vain, I am depressed & wearied. And so I walk around among com-mon things and cheap companions contented with them—studious about them. But oh! this is not all! Sometimes the telescope is dust-ed off—extended to its full length & pointed toward the stars! Then, to the Self that was, *this Self* is supernatural! The years eternal rise before me;—I hear

> "A saint's voice in the palm trees singing,
> All is lost, &"[2]

I seem almost to be

> "'Mid the ransomed throng, 'mid the sea of bliss,
> Mid the Holy City's gorgeousness."[3]

Calm & stately rise before me great clouds of color—& forms so gi-gantic that to contemplate them is a strain upon my fancy;—still air is around me—and far off, banners wave & wings move slow & ma-jestic—like those of great birds at sea. And I seem to feel what *living* is!—What I am to be, out in the Illimitable Fields. Then I forget the little cares;—& the things that I had thought would be *so much* to me, die out of my memory. "It is little difference," I think, "if only I am a loving child toward the Infinite Father of us all." "*Us* all"! And *that* recals me! The strange, close tie *He* made, binding me to those whose nature & whose destiny I share! Then I come back to my life here on earth,—& think of *us!*

It is better. These things are too mighty for me. "Learn to be con-tented with Life."[4] The chrysalis state is a normal one,—be patient with it;—*wait for the wings!* they will *surely come.* . . .

I was not well today, & all these things came so clear & grand before me that I hardly knew myself. To me,—instead of the strangeness being that we have poets who say such marvelous things,—the greater marvel is that we are not poets every one of us;—that we do not live higher up—& not so much in the vallies & the shadows. Yet it is all wise & kind I know;—God knew best, how to content us *here*. . . .

1. Willard quoted from Anna Brownell Jameson, *Studies, Stories and Memoirs* (Boston, 1859). The quote comes from Jameson's personal journal (the first part of the book), where the author reflects critically on art, literature, and society.
2. Willard quoted from Elizabeth Barrett Browning, "The Lost Bower" (1844), stanza 74, lines 5–6. She later added the last word of the poem, "won," in pencil.
3. Not identified.
4. Not identified.

22 March 1862

. . . Except under rare conditions it is painful to *love a person*. So many fibers of your being reach out toward *This Other* & twine about him; (or *her;*—one of mine has been *her*). The current of your thoughts sets toward him;—your *affinity* is for him, (& well I know, an *affinity* is the most sensitive, delicate, painful or pleasurable thing that has come to my consciousness). It costs so dear—this *loving*. It is a constant, internal fever I think. It "corresponds" to the heat & parchedness of the body in a "typhoid." Truly, "the greatest joy, the wildest woe is love."[1] I am very thankful that it has not *hurt* me more. It has made me flush & chill;—it has thrilled my heart with delight & caused it to *curdle* with agony;—it has made me weep aloud & tremble like a tree in the blast, *& yet* I have come safely through—& gained quiet from *that*—but it has *cost* me—& I fear that it will not be the last.

1. Not identified.

31 March 1862

. . . Life has its Gifts—& very beautiful, very sweet & dear they are. The cheif one—of the earth—is, in my thinking, Human Love. Every one thinks so, too—I guess, *at heart*. For a woman, I suppose, to love some man—*the* man whom, afterward, she marries, better than anything else except the God who gave him to her, is the greatest good—if he loves her just as well. Very many women, when they miss of this, fold their arms and mourn, grow thin & querulous or else quiet & gentle (in which latter case they usually die). Other women go on bravely, "doing & suffering" & die at a good & lonly old age. I *think* that I have missed this greatest good of a woman's life. I used to think that it would come to me—afterwards, I thought that it *had* come—last of all I found out my mistake. And now I have returned into the beleif that was earliest with me—not as a sickly sentimentalist but with the calm nature of a woman who has much strength to endure. I do not think myself unlovely—it is not that. For, though I am not beautiful, neither am I disagreeable in face or figure & I can imagine how I might be thought quite desirable by somebody! Nevertheless, I think myself emotionally peculiar—& I think my discipline & experience in this regard, most unfortunate. There are very few whom I could love—possibly none. Naturally I *love* women & sometimes I think, can feel no earnest, vigorous love toward *their brethren!* I should care most for refined, gentle-men . . . & these, care most for delicate, beautiful women, so I should not suffice them. But let this go. The point lies beyond these preliminaries. While frankly admitting *the greatest good* & admitting that I do not think it will be mine, is there nothing left of life? Can I not live without life's greatest good? Am I a slave tied down to *that* for happiness? Nay, verily! There are a thousand pleasant, worthy things beside *that,* & I would say the same though a dozen of the choice gifts were classed along with it & *all* denied me! There is good to be done—knowledge to be acquired—Friends to be made & kept—& over all *God's Love* that *never faileth.* Let me own that always I shall feel the lack. I shall be pensive for the loss;—I shall cry sometimes;—at long intervals I shall incline to be rebellious—yet, withal there may be, in my life, more of sun than shade;—more of joy & sorrow. It is not for the Royal Human Soul to be chained down to any one source of joy or of sorrow—so long as that source is not in itself *Infinite.* Born of Eternity it may not be conquered by any thing in Time. "If not happiness, then *blessedness*"[1] may be for us. Blessedness that comes from a life full of good deeds;—full of kindness & sympathy. May such an one be mine, O Lord! & then I will not murmur though shut out from what our weak hearts call

The Best Gift earth has for us! . . .[2]

---

1. From Harriet Beecher Stowe, *The Minister's Wooing* (1859). A phrase quite similar to this also occurs in Thomas Carlyle, "The Everlasting Yea," in *Sartor Resartus* (London, 1834).
2. Not identified.

7 April 1862

. . . This idea of the *Oneness* of *Humanity*—& the "related truths" & practical results thereof—comes to me more & more. All my Inductions lead on to the conclusion that "each life is an inlet from the same ocean"[1]—that we are so alike—the contemplation is almost startling. And oh! I want suffering & all experiences—all sights & "knowledges" to give me more & more of this *nature absolute*. Then I shall have a message that will be welcome to my brothers—& will do them good in the hearing, as me, in the saying. If I live—someday I *think* it will be so.

1. Willard may have been paraphrasing from the beginning of an essay by Ralph Waldo Emerson, "History," in *Essays: First Series* (Boston, 1841): "There is one mind common to all individual men. Every man is an inlet to the same and to all of the same."

20 April 1862

. . . I have taught school[1] one week—with *Mary*. It is the hardest work I have ever done. There are two rooms, 80 pupils, 32 classes, six (apiece) that are "high." I study on my *Mathematics* all the time I can possibly get, out of school hours. I have Algebra & Arith. "over in the back part of the book." It is almost impossible to keep order in the school. Yet we do our very best, & have *hope*, though every night we *ache*. . . .

1. Willard and Bannister taught spring term 1862 at the Benson Avenue School, an Evanston public school.

25 April 1862

. . . My sister is sick with a mild form of fever. She is patient & gentle as is her custom;—Father & Mother are wonderfully *thoughtful* of her—and restless. Mother would give her life for her children, I feel sure. . . .

6 May 1862

. . . My sister has been very dangerously ill. I never saw any one of "us" so sick as she was a week ago yesterday & today. I saw what *agony* might be—as she lay on the bed groaning aloud at every breath. I felt dimly & horribly what it might be to have her die. She thought about it, too,—I will not try to picture what she has suffered or what we have sufferred as her "nearest & dearest." She has found her outside friends wonderfully kind—every body has been here—*Mary* staid from church last Sabbath with me to take care of her. Mother's face has grown thin but she knows no weariness or lagging—I marvel to see her. Father has been tender & anxious as a woman. And today she is sitting up, & in her quiet, uncomplaining way is thankful & still & looks around thoughtfully, over every thing. We thank God from very far down in our hearts. . . .

25 May 1862

. . . It has occurred to me, that a nobler-natured woman than I am, would never have recorded such an experience as mine with *Mary*, much less have let the object of a love so strange & painful as mine for her, be annoyed with the knowledge of how much my nature hurt me. I am *sorry* & humiliated that I have done both these small-souled things. And yet, I make the excuse for myself that we were so intimate—I am so open-hearted & impulsive that it was very natural.

Let me say here, in self defence, that never but once in all the spiritual-tragedy (for just that,—without sentimentality—*it* has been to me) have I let *Mary* know how I felt, except in explanation of my strange, reserved manner toward her, & these occasions have not exceeded twice, or possibly three times. Twice she has seen me in a perfect *tempest* about loving her so much—yet having that love to annihilate. For, plainly stated, that is just what honor as I interpreted it first, & necessity as it forced me afterwards, has compelled. Once, I descended to reproach—I think I had slight grounds, yet deem it now, one of the unworthiest actions of my Life. In all these times, she has been kind & gentle to me—as much as any one could be. For months our manner has been as a rule, polite—to cordiality, with an occasional "burst of confidence." . . . To this rule there have been exceptions—silence—phlegm—once or twice positive rudeness, in which (last) cases hers has taken the form of ingraciousness, mine, that of *brusquire* [brusqueness].

Except the two or three explanations I have made, & the two *tempests* we have been as indifferently friendly & on-good-terms young women as the village contains. While I have written soberly here & talked mournfully with my aunt, & cried at rare intervals, I have, invariably, met her with entire self-possession & quiet, business like tone has pervaded our intercourse—wonderful to behold—*in us.* I would not have Myself, of Future Years, to think that I have been weak in this matter "as men count weakness." Only *in heart* I have been—as my written words will indicate—a very child in resolution, clinging to what is no longer for me—"an infant crying in the night;—an infant crying for the light"[1]—of a Love that is as a lamp blown out.

She came to the door just now—on her way from Sabbath School, & asked after Mary—a great many of the girls—our friends—do this. And I laid down the pen—& left off a line in the middle,—a line of this *expose*—& told her—as I would have told her Mother, only with a shade less deference;—the subtraction of that article being suited to the difference in their ages. Thus much to show that outwardly I am not—*soft.* Inwardly I am not ashamed to be so—we are all *shell-fish* together—so I do not mind.

As for *Mary* I have "no charge to lay at her door." She is very obliging toward me—very full of kind offices. I *know* that I am not unmindful of them. If I had found some richer love than hers was to me one year ago, I should have failed her as she has failed me—as she was *fated* to fail me;—as circumstances & the law of nature in "these things" commanded. . . . She would have done some-what as I have— I think she would have been more heroic than I, & yet, we can't quite tell. I know it is *right* & some way, *best.* I shall have greater trials than this, though as yet, I have had none so great. Slowly—& with frequent, mortifying, & painful—excessively painful—*relapses* (all kept to myself & not betrayed to her except by greater reserve of manner!—) I *am* recovering. And after a while—though the time is more distant than I used to think—I shall be *entirely free.* Our intercourse then will be much pleasanter than now—it will be sincere—straightforward— affectionate—&, in kind, without reserve. *She* is ready for this now— she was ready months since. For me, I am not yet, though I'm *so sorry* that I'm not & can not be. Then, we shall talk over my troubles about her, & she will say that she was sorry, & I shall laugh—yet, I think it will not be a very cheery laugh even *then*—& say it does not matter now. . . .

Well—I rather "wanted to" write this "Statement of Facts," I don't *think* I'll make another in a great while;—& yet, I can not tell, for in this, I shall be a law unto myself—& a very erratic one,—as heretofore. . . .

Have taken some care of Mary, who requires a great deal, she is so nervous & weak. It almost frightens me to see how thin she has grown—to hear her cough & notice the red spots in her cheeks, afternoons. Her only hope seems to be—going to our old Home in Wisconsin. She talks of it—dreams of it—& wants us to talk of it constantly. Poor child—I shall not write out here, my thoughts—they come from a *good ways* down in my heart. Father & Mother have both grown old during this illness of hers. It is a severe calamity—one of our worst—perhaps it may prove *the worst* of all! . . .

1. Willard quoted from Alfred Lord Tennyson, *In Memoriam* (London, 1850), stanza 54, lines 18–19.

31 May 1862

. . . All day Mother & I have taken care of Mary. Dr. Small,[1] (one of the most eminent physicians in the West) told Mother her case was formidable & he could give but little encouragement. We are in great trouble. The tears are in my eyes every few minutes—no one else save my other three could bring them there so often. Mary has a cruel cough—almost constant fever—hot cheeks.—She does not dream of her danger & we fear the effect of hinting at such a thing, so are perfectly cheerful before her. Words are poor things I find.

For nineteen years *she* has been with me all the time—she has not failed me—she knows my most secret thoughts—there is *nothing* I would not freely tell her.

And then—to think! We are grown together so, she & I! How the very thought of—*Separation*—tears me.

I am going up stairs to bed, alone in Aunt Sarah's room. Will *she* sleep with me, ever again? (Mary, I mean.) She lies in Mothers room,—Mother beside her. They are both sleeping;—not quietly, but lightly: the one very weary, the other very weak. I just went in & bathed my sister's hot, thin hands. And I thought of all our plays together & their busy motion so often. And I bit my lip & hid the tears that are falling now. I *wanted* to kiss her goodnight, yet *could* not do it. I have been bred to entire lack of "demonstration" to my four who are nearest, of my love for them. The habit shuts me in like a steel armor. I feel keenly & painfully that it should have been different with me— but now, it is too late.

I shall pray only this, tonight: (Mary told me to, the other day in these words:) how her voice trembled over them! "Frank pray that I may not cough tonight, & that Mother & I may sleep beautiful & that if God is willing, I may get strong again."

This I shall pray with all my earnestness, & this: That in all things I may be sweet & kind to her—that I may anticipate her wishes—& have insight given to me to be *all* to her that it is possible for me to be.

1. Alvin Edmond (also spelled Alvan Edmund) Small (1811–86) was a Chicago homeopathic physician, a well-trained and respected professional.

9 June 1862

Mary is dead. I write the sentence—stop & look at it—do not know what it means. For God is merciful and the awful truth of my desolation does not shut down close around me all the time;—it comes in paroxysms—and goes again.

At the request of Dr. Bannister (who will preach her funeral sermon) I shall write out many of the things that she has said during her sickness—and at her death. Her sweetness—purity—and childlikeness were remarkable features of her character, during her entire illness. She expected to recover, almost down to the last hour, and her most ardent wish was to get well enough to go to "Forest Home"—where she had spent her childhood. The very night she died she told us to talk about going there. She used to say: "I never had such pleasant times as when Frank & I were children and used to play among the trees & in the garden."

The physician considered her *hopefulness* her best symptom, so we did not talk to her of dying—though of Christ and of religion, a great deal.

She used to wander in her sleep—and often thought she was a child again. One night I slept with her—she put her hot hand against my face and said:—"You're with me in the trundle bed, Frank, as you used to be, aren't you?" . . .

She seemed so anxious to do good—so worried for fear she had not. Once she said to Mother:—"I would like to be well—if only for one day, so that I could do some good to some one. I've never done any unless a little in my Sabbath School Class & I'm not quite sure about that. I've tried to learn & to improve & to prepare myself to be useful, & now I'd like to live & do something in the world." . . .

On the last day of her life she was lying with her head in Father's lap, & she asked to have the Bible read. He said: "Where shall I read?" She told him: "Oh! where it makes Christ seem so beautiful." He read a Psalm. She said: "Please read where it says Christ was sorry for sick folks"! Father read about the "Healing of the Daughter of Jairus."[1] She liked it, but said, when he had finished, "Please read where it says that he is *sorry now.*"

After a while she said: "we beleive that God loves us better than Mother,—yet Mother would like to have me get well, and God don't seem to think that it is best—He don't seem to see fit to make me well—yet He knows what is right." . . .

At four o'clock in the morning of the 8th of June;—Sabbath Morning, we became greatly alarmed. For the first time, Father & I decided that she could not get well.

I went for Mrs. Bannister & Mary. Father said to her—for the first time coming directly to the subject of her danger:—"Mary, if God should think it best to take you to Himself, should you be afraid to go?"

She looked quickly at him, with rather a pitiful face;—she seemed to consider a moment, and then said in her low, rather mournful voice: "I thought I should like to get well—for I am young. But if God wants me to go, I shouldn't be much scared—afraid—but I should say 'Take me *God*'"!

They asked her if there was any thing they could do for her? "Pray," she said, *"Pray thankful prayers."*

Father asked her if she saw Christ,—if He was near her."Yes, I see Him," she said, "But he is not very near, I wish He would come nearer."

I asked her if we should pray, she said yes, & I prayed aloud;—that Christ would come close to her—that she might see & feel Him plainly—that, since she had tried to love & obey Him, he would come right to her now in her great need. She clasped her hands together & said so joyfully: "He's come! He's Come! I have Him here in my hands! He died for me—he died for all this Family—Father, Mother, Oliver, Frank" (and Mary Bannister says she added, "My dear sister").

"I'll have Him all to myself," she said, & then seemed to remember, & added "I'll have Him & every body may have Him—there's enough for every body. He is talking to me—He says: 'She tried to be good—but she wandered—but I will save her!'" . . .

I said: "I want to ask you to forgive me for all my unkind actions to you—for every thing bad that I ever did to you."

She said, so earnestly: "Oh I do—you never did any thing bad—you were always good."

Mother asked her if she didn't want to leave a Message for Oliver, "don't you think he'll be with us in heaven?" She said: "Of course;—he's working for God. Tell him to be good, & to make people good."

And to her Sunday School Class: "tell them to be good;—*tell every body to be good,*" she added, with earnestness.

She said to us: looking so sweet & loving toward us: "I wish I was strong enough—I'd like to talk good to you."

Almost at the last she said with a bright smile on her face:—

"Oh! I'm getting more faith!"

Mother said: "My darling—you will meet us, won't you, at the Golden Gate?" "O, yes! & you'll all come; & Father! Christ wants you right off!"

She worked her hands convulsively and said "I've got Christ!—he's right here!"

Then she said to me: "Oh! I'm in great misery!"—"Dear God! take me quick!" She held out her hands & said "Take me quick, God! Take me on *this side*"! turning towards the left.

She lay still—bolstered up by pillows. I asked if she knew me, & she repeated my name. Father asked her often if Christ was still near her—she would nod, but did not speak. She seemed troubled, after a few minutes—father bent over her—& slowly & with difficulty she told him of her dread of being buried alive & he promised her over & over again that she should not be. Then she gave some little direction about preparing her bed, as she said: "For those who lay me out."—showing her perfect consciousness. She never spoke again—but opened her eyes & looked at us—with such *intenseness*—the pupil so dilated,—the iris so blue. I never saw such soul in human eyes, before.

She groaned a little three or four times;—she did not move—her eyes slowly closed—her face grew white. Father said: "Lord Jesus, receive my spirit! Lord! we give her back to Thee—she was a precious treasure—we give her back to Thee."

Mrs. Bannister closed Mary's eyes. Father & Mother went into the sitting room & cried. I leaned on the railing at the foot of the bed and looked at *my sister*—my sister Mary. And I knew that she was dead—knew that she was *alive*. Every thing was far off—I was *benumbed* and am but waking to the tingling agony.

1. Matt. 9:18–26, Mark 5:22–43, Luke 8:41–56.

26 June 1862

My Life is but *too full*—yet seeks no outlet, any more.

I have no tolerance for pen, ink, or paper. I can not think that I shall wish to keep a Journal or record the past for "a long—long while."

3 July 1862

My brother Oliver married to Mary Bannister and started for Denver City, Colorado[1]—to be gone away off there we don't know how long. And so I am the only one left to Father & Mother of their

"Three Children!"

1. Mary Bannister and Oliver Willard were married on 3 July 1862. On the rec-

ommendation of John Evans, a former Evanstonian and the current governor of the Colorado Territory, Oliver Willard was appointed to the new MEC circuit in Denver.

21 August 1862

O dear—I don't know what it is that I would say. I am crowded with feeling—it was never before so plain to me that I am without the power of expression. "Mary didn't get well"—that is the key note to all my thoughts. I was so sure she would—I refused to think it possible that she could die. And now—under the experiences that crowd thicker upon me than ever before,—like a wave the consciousness of what has happened us flows back & forward in my heart, and—put in words it all amounts to this:—"She is dead—dead—Mary, my sister is dead—her hands are on her breast so cold & still—she takes no note of us—of anything;—and she used to be so merry—so full of motion—she was with us always—she never went away."

Oh! this has crushed out all other feelings—except a vague sense of incompleteness—of wanting some one—something—of reaching out toward the Future Life almost with yearning;—

Sometimes I don't look upon her as dead—I ought not to have said so. And Oh! last Sabbath evening when we walked up to church—all that is left of us—Father, Mother & I—so clear & beautiful I saw her—in her *Unconditioned Life*—*somehow, somewhere* so radiant—so painless so secure! Very near to Christ—the glorious, satisfying Christ!—perfectly *complete* in heart & life—thinking of us—knowing that it will not be long till we should come. And I was quite content—to go to church—to pray & trust & work awhile longer & then I beleived I should go too. It is *His will*—He is as well pleased with us that pray as with those who praise;—with us who try— as them, who triumph. This is one stage—it is alloted by Him. The Time will be breif—the Eternity will pay all—will give us what we missed here—will round every thing to symmetry. All this, if we love & trust the Father of our Souls—& do as well as we can what He has given us to do. And Mary is the favored one—Not sleeping in the grave—but conscious as we are—only so *well off*—so glorified—so restful. It may be only a fancy yet I think I shall be with her before many of our little years are past. . . . We can not tell—the grave for our bodies—the Spirit Land for our souls may not be twenty hours ahead of any one of us. O, God! May I lean on Thee! O, Christ! be with me in that *last, severest Hour* to which all other hours are incident! Oh Father of my spirit! Take it to Thyself—any time—any where only love it—take care of it! Let it see Christ &—Mary! . . .

Frances Willard at nineteen, taken in 1858 when she was a boarding student at North Western Female College, Evanston, Illinois. All photos courtesy of the National Woman's Christian Temperance Union, Evanston, Illinois.

Willard's father, Josiah Flint Willard, taken in the mid-1840s.

Clara Thatcher, the daughter of the family with whom Willard boarded when she taught school in Harlem, Illinois, in the summers of 1860 and 1861. Thatcher remained a good friend of Willard's for many years. Photo is undated, but probably taken when Thatcher was sixteen or seventeen.

Photo of Willard pasted into her journal at the entry for 22 October 1860, when she had just turned twenty-one. Next to the photo is an example of Willard's penchant for list making, to set herself tasks to improve her intellectual capacity.

Frances Willard in a photo dated December 1861, pasted into her mother's album. Willard wrote underneath the photo: "Your (grinning) daughter Frank."

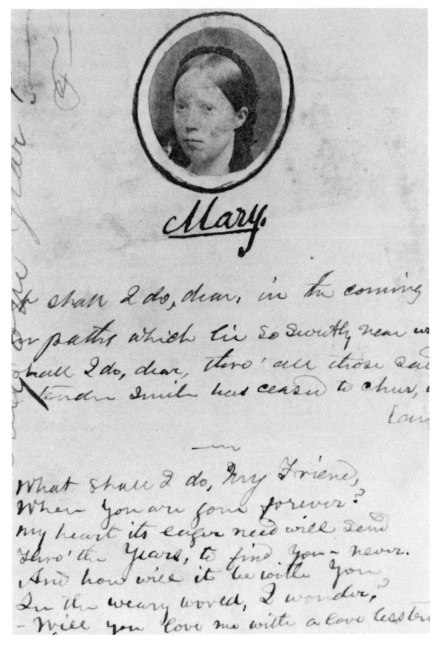

Willard's sister, Mary. Willard noted on the back of the photo, taken in October 1861: "Autumn before she died & when she was 18. F.W."

Mary Bannister, Willard's best friend from 1860 to 1861; photo taken in August 1861, when Bannister was twenty. Willard pasted the oval photo in the front of her journal for 28 September 1861–18 January 1862, above a poem she found that expressed her sense of loss, as her friend became engaged to her brother. She wrote in August 1862: "How different things are now!—She thinks of me pleasantly I hope; I do of her. We are *entirely unnecessary* to each other & have been for a long time. Neither of us are to blame. It was inevitable. Yet, only think!—I wrote those verses (here) one year ago this very month—only one year. Fr._____."

Willard's brother, Oliver, in a photo pasted in Willard's journal in the entry for 4 November 1861. He has written underneath his photo: "Taken in October 1861. The subject of this sketch is an easy-going fellow—noted for no special qualities save those of the *heart*! He starts today . . . to test his capacities in the 'real work.'" Oliver was about to leave for southeastern Wisconsin to serve his first church.

Charles Fowler, photo in Mary (Hill) Willard's album, dated 1860s. Probably taken in fall 1861 when he graduated from Garrett Biblical Institute and was engaged to Frances Willard.

Tintypes of Kate Jackson (l.), in her late twenties, and Frances Willard (r.), age twenty-six or twenty-seven, when Jackson and Willard were preparing to teach together at Genesee Wesleyan Seminary in Lima, New York.

Frances Willard, July 1871, shortly after she became president of the Evanston College for Ladies.

29 August 1862

. . . On Monday I move over to the N.W. Female College. I am "Preceptress of Natural Sciences"[1] there. Very humbly & sincerely I pray to God that I may *be good* over there, & *do good.* I was wild & wicked as a pupil—in the same house may I be consistent & a Christian—as a Teacher. The last days at Home are passing—passing. O Lord! Thou hast good for us some where in store!—Life changes so—Thy heart must ache for us, but that Thou knowest soon we are to enter the Beautiful World. . . .

I want to say that all the old haunting love for my brother's wife is *dead;*—died the moment that Mary's soul went away from the earth. It is inexplicable—but just then God freed me from my long slavery.—I have not always been kind & good to her—& I am *very sorry.* But God's Spirit is in me, I think more than I ever had it before. I *know* I shall always be a good sister to her now—if I am a *child of His.* Dear girl—I want to be a true *sister* to her—she is an angel to my brother—my dear, dear Brother. O, Christ! Help me to act right in my new relation & oh! forgive the Past! I want to live a good Life—to get ready to go to my sister in Heaven. I am afraid that Mary's death will kill Mother.

1. Willard taught natural sciences and mathematics at NWFC for one term, from September 1862 until January 1863. Since her father was boarding in Chicago and her mother was in New York for a long visit to relatives, Willard boarded at the college.

2 September 1862

Sitting in my room at the Female College—a Teacher, regularly installed, in a Ladies' School. The sensation is agreeable. I have a natural love of *Ladies*—as I have proved! To have them around me—pupils, Friends, will be delightful. To think that I am sitting here in the room that was Luella Clark's—as much a Teacher as herself! My dear old books around me—pictures & familiar things. . . .

O! I never knew so many girls that I loved, I think, before. God help me, as a Teacher of most of them to be loving & valuable in precept & example. . . .

14 September 1862

. . . Sitting in my room with the pretty black silk wrapper on that Mother & Miss Burroughs[1] made. . . . I am here—but Mary who was always with me—*where is she?* The question mocks me with its own echo. *Where* is she—who was so merry—who knew the people that I know—who studied the books that I study . . . who read the daily Tribune![2] Who skipped pebbles in the lake—who ran races with me in the garden—who sang "Junita" and "Star Spangled Banner"! O she was so much *alive*—I can not think of her as *disembodied* & living still. Then there is that horrible doctrine held by many who are wise & good—that the soul is unconscious until the Ressurection. That *idea* worries me very much. And then—I am coming right on to the same doom. I who sit here this bright, warm morning with carefully made toilet—attentive eyes—ears open to sound—senses in activity—I with my thousand thoughts—my steady beating heart—shall lie *so still*— so cold—and for *so long*. Poor, butterfly Life!—Long silence & darkness of the shrunken coffin and close-fitting grave! Ugh! It makes me shudder through & through! coming toward me every moment—such a fate as *that!*

But my religion tells me that my Life shall be endless;—one interpretation of my creed tells me my *consciousness* shall be *uninterrupted here & there;* that fruition waits there for me; every unmet capacity shall be filled to overflowing—every thing shall be harmonious— nothing shall disappoint. Destiny so glorious would intoxicate me in *imagination* even, did I feel it would be mine. "Eye hath not seen— ear hath not heard—neither hath it entered into the heart of man to conceive the joys that God hath prepared for those that Love Him."[3] Do *I* love Him? I am not sure. I can not get hold of Him to love Him—not much—not often. Sometimes I am not certain about Christ—not certain that he ever was here on earth—that He *created Himself* in the form of a man—lived here awhile—died for us—ascended into Heaven in bodily form & "ever lives to intercede for us."[4] Sometimes the Bible seems so contradictory & unsatisfactory to me. Sometimes I haven't an atom of faith. Other times it seems natural that we should be immortal—"why shouldn't we"—I say in my thoughts "else than this, Life is a farce—& the world is all gone wrong;"—I see how it will be a little—I beleive. O dear! Why isn't it clear—I wonder? Why isn't *truth* clear? Wishing very much to be religious, I have never had much "witness" of "a change of heart." These things are so vague & shadowy—my present life & its concerns so tangible & real. O! it is a sort of curse to have such a doubting temperament as mine; to feel so *uncertain*. O God! *forgive* me—don't let me be so blind. Or if I must go on so—with not much light or love on earth—not much from Thee—come to me in my last & most terrible *Hour*—that ominous—agonizing Hour whose shadow stretches all along my path;—command as Thou didst to this world in the beginning "*Let there be Light!*"[5] and then—*oh! then*—in that final moment of life on earth may I be able to tell my Friends who have known of my darkness—may I have strength to tell them of *Thy* marvellous light!

Oh! what would my Sunday School Class say to these pages! They think my trust so strong—I seem to them so beleiving. I would not have them know—I would not have any but experienced Christians know how dark things seem to me—most of the time. The undercurrent of my thoughts is always, now, *these things*. Oh! How much we can bear—how we can adjust ourselves. Four months ago today I thought if Mary should die I should be crazed. It made me quiver—right around my heart most, & extending from that all over me. This morning, I think of Mary—*dead*—just as naturally as I used to think of her alive. "Mary—*dead*—yes, dead," I say to myself, and it don't jostle my thoughts out of their channel—it is an interpolation between them;—it don't change the expression of my face—don't make my heart beat differently—yet God knows how well I loved my sister— how deeply I have mourned her. O strange world into which I have come—I might go mad by thinking too much on Thy astonishing— astounding phases.

O, Mary! Where are you? and do *you* know "what Life was for"? O, Christ! Give me *consciousness* of Thee! . . .

1. This was probably Fidelia (listed in census as Fedilia) Burroughs (b. ca. 1846), an Evanston dressmaker.

2. *Chicago Tribune.*

3. Willard paraphrased 1 Cor. 2:9, "But as it is written, eye hath not seen nor ear heard, neither have entered into the heart of man, the things which God hath prepared for them that love Him."

4. Willard paraphrased Heb. 7:25, "Wherefore he is able also to save them to the uttermost that come unto God by him, seeing he ever liveth to make intercession for them."

5. Gen. 1:3.

3 October 1862

. . . My life is peculiar—its phases new—different altogether from anything that I have known before. I love some of my pupils—yes, really *love* them. That is saying a very great deal. Ada Frances Brigham *I love you!* I love to be with you and to have you with me. You make my life much richer than it could be otherwise. I thank God that you love me—as you say you do. My dear, *dear* child—God bless you.

29 October 1862

. . . Ada and I have had fine times up in this cozy room. . . . I undressed and went to bed; took a lunch there—talked with my Darling Friend—for such she is and I do not scruple to state it uncompromisingly. Her love brightens my life—it is to me like wine. Latest and *rarest* of my Friends (with a capital F)! I thank God for the sweet, undisguised girl. Oh *Ada!* How long will "circumstances" let us go on go so sweetly together? Your fresh young cheek against mine;—your eager, loving hand in mine;—your bright, truth-telling face turned toward me? I love Ada with all my heart, I would be useful to her in all possible ways. O, God! put it into my heart—the knowledge of how I can help her most. . . .

18 December 1862

. . . I like to think how sweet it is for women to whom God grants the sweet hallucination of "*la grande passion.*" I know how it might be—to feel one's self *clinging* instead of standing upright or having other's cling to one as my sweet Ada does to me. What it might be to give one's self up so fearlessly—somewhat as we do to God—to feel the supremacy of a loftier—stronger nature. Oh! the sweetness of it— the luxury of it! Philip![1] It might have been, I think. And yet—I do not feel quite sure. I do not feel sure that it is a possibility of my nature ever to give itself up. When I remember a scene in Clara Thatcher's room on Sunday last—Myself, sitting in her rocking chair—a smoking cap on my head—my Garabaldi collar[2] fixed man-fashion—a cigar between my lips—the smoke curling gracefully over my head—and such a *longing* in my heart to be a man—have a man's career and face the world for Ada's—*my wife's*—sake, I think no woman who could ever chafe so—ever long so—ever feel the victory in her so—could ever embroider slippers for Philip, or fasten clinging arms around his neck!—O Frances Willard, I can't tell what you're coming to.[3] It seems sad to think of loving women as their protector—with a love that would sacrifice any thing for them (as I would for Ada) with a love which

> "Strikes the cord of *self* that trembling
> Goes in music out of sight,"[4]

and then when their bloom and beauty is perfected to have them long for something beyond—to have them tire of the apprenticeship I gave them and enter the *masters* throng—seeking Philip—satisfied only with him! You did it Maggie[5]—you did it *Mary*—you will, Emma,[6] with your questioning eyes—and *you Ada*—dearest of them all—your heart will want a stronger one than mine when you're a woman. You'll want a deep voice to mingle with yours in the sweet songs you'll sing;—you'll want a manly head to bend low while you say those dear words "I love you, Darling!" that you are content to give *me* for a while yet;—you'll want to get the slippers & dressing gown ready for *him* when he comes home, tired, at night. For it is *nature,* my little Puss, and nature will not be defrauded even by my great need for you— and my arms are not strong enough to hold you—my voice is not deep enough to charm you—not always, puss, though I think you think so, now. I've never loved a woman who was not intensely feminine—and such women are bound to *find Philip*—& early too, in life. I would like to *be* Philip! O! no longing compares with it, in strength. Some time God will tell me why I wasn't—why I can't love any one *forever*—why under the dearest, wildest love I ever knew, lies the feeling—"Make the most of it—you can have it but a little while"; why I have such a maddening wish to be an orator—why I believe I *could* be one;—why—why;—O, God is disciplining me—he knows I am not meet for angel's company—& shan't be without a world of suffering. I ask Him some how—any how—'to *Educate me for Eternity!*'"

1. "Philip" was the name by which Willard referred to "the one man in all the world for her." Although she did not explain in her journal why she chose that particular name, it was the name of a character, Philip Wakem, whom Willard much admired in George Eliot's novel *The Mill on the Floss* (London, 1860), which she had recently read at the time that she first began to use "Philip" in this manner.

2. Garibaldi shirts, like the red, bloused shirt worn by the Italian republican and patriot Giuseppe Garibaldi (see Journal, 18 October 1869, n. 2), were a popular fashion for American women in the 1860s. The collar was high-necked, with a soft, rounded shape.

3. Willard wrote in 1889 in the margin of this entry, opposite the previous sentence: "The pages, the beginning of which is thus indicated, reveal a state of mind not usual but which came upon me once in a while from my very earliest recollection. As life chastened me more & more, I came to desire not a man's *being* but a man's wide and free *career* & to glory in being a woman & desire to help women to be & do all in their power."

4. Willard paraphrased Alfred Lord Tennyson, *Locksley Hall* (London, 1842), line 34: "Smote the chord of self that, trembling/ passed in music out of sight."

5. Margaret (Maggie) C. Hawley was a student at the NWFC in 1858. She returned home in that year, and Willard corresponded with her from time to time in 1859.

6. Willard referred to Emma B. White, a student of hers at NWFC. White is not listed in the NWFC catalogues as a student, but she was given an honorary Laureate of Science from the Evanston College for Ladies in 1873, when Willard was president of the college. She also served as secretary of the Board of Trustees of the Evanston College for Ladies.

21 December 1862

Four weeks from today—God willing—I shall attend Christ Church in Pittsburgh.[1] The new faces—voices—sounds! I long for them because they *are* new. Mutability is quite my glory—different stages in the onward, endless March. Thank God that sometimes—often, of late, I feel myself *immortal.* I long to get out into Life—to go further away. Every thing beautiful and fine in grain beckons to me to enjoy & to possess. A wild ambition for the refined—the lofty & uncommon grows in me every day. Either *here* or *There* I'm bound to satisfy it— to some extent certainly. To be refined—intellectual—unexceptionable—oh! how I wish for these. I'll try to grow well-bred—self-possessed—easy at all times;—& I shall—I'm sure of it!

1. Willard had been appointed to teach Belles Lettres at the Pittsburgh Female College, a Methodist institution chartered in 1854. Christ MEC was closely affiliated with the college; church and college shared the same city lot.

22 December 1862

Oh my little Ada! My Heart aches for you—and I am tired already with waiting for the gentle, loving touch of the hand—the softly spoken words—the sweet, sweet kisses! I would give or do almost any thing, to have *you* kneeling beside me in your graceful way, and looking in my face—with that word "Darling" on your lips. Do you hunger so for me, I wonder? Do you wish that forever & forever we two— so truly *one* in heart—might be one in Life—in purpose and History? O my Darling—*wife of my Soul*—God guard you tenderly and fill your pure, trusting heart with His grace. In Heaven you will be mine— mine only—I steadfastly beleive. . . .

1 January 1863

"Abraham Lincoln has fulfilled the pledge! The slaves in the disloyal States are free!"[1] So Mr. Jones[2] said, tonight, coming down late, to tea. And, on the instant, all the girls clapped their hands, so heartily that it was fine to see & hear them—& far down in my heart something stirred—some chord was struck that gave out music beautiful & pure. It was something to think about; our girls sitting there—so well-kept as they are—so good-looking, so happy & content—with the thought in their heads that two millions of wretched beings this day became constitutionally free, & the feeling in their hearts of what a gift this freedom is to a human soul. It was a thing that thrilled me—

that I am thankful has transpired in my experience—that I shall think over with frequent pleasure—that some day, I hope I may describe to my little Ada. . . .

And the old year has gone.—The year of my Life that has changed me most—hurt me most—richened me most—taught me most thoroughly that "Life is a solemn mystery—but Christ is true"[3]—a future state certain. In this year my sister has been taken away from me—my Home has gone to strangers, (Forest Home)[4] my present one has been broken up—my brother has married & gone entirely away from us—my engagement with Mr. F. has been broken—my Friendship for *Mary* B—torn to shreds at terrible cost of pain—my Friend Emma has come to me & *Ada* nearest of all—& without fancy, nearer than any other—has been My Gift.

O! I am giddy with thought of all these changes! I can no more take them in than I can the mysteries of my creed. The clear *feeling* of them all, I could not bear. To think of my changed prospects—my new friends & surroundings—soon to be newer still—my *added memories!* All my life before was not to me equal to this year! Last night I thought so plainly of Mary—my sweet lost sister—of how, one year ago today, we fixed to go to Clara's for a week to make "wedding garments" (that I never, as it proved, needed) for me. I saw her—so young & hopeful—so full of merriment. And thinking of how we were always together—how I told her *every*-thing—how near we were—how utterly *unreserved* (more than I ever was or expect to be with any mortal—& I remember *Ada* as I write the words) I got such a longing for her! I thought I could not wait—I wanted that vision which I beleive will rise before me when down here they are saying "There! Close her eyes! She is dead!" That vision of Mary—so bright, so glorious, reaching down for my disfranchised soul & saying "O! Frank—I've been waiting for You!" . . .

O, God! . . . Don't let me be so selfish! Make me more truly truthful! More as I'd like to be—nearer to Christ. I must be good—I will try to be. The day is done. I will make no set of resolves as I used to do, tho' I did think I would. What is the use—& I may go so soon. Only this general one: To try to be *better*—more really a *Christian Lady*—adjusted thus, to Life here, or to go There if God calls me. The New Year is fairly entered. In it I am to hear many recitations (if I live) to make innumerable toilets—to speak thousands of words—smile hundreds of smiles—cry a few times, I don't know what about—suffer pain I can't tell of what kind & wouldn't know for anything—to see many new faces—to travel several hundred miles—to watch the destiny of my poor, glorious native land—to love & be loved—

to read new books & hear new songs sung—to see splendid sun-sets—
to see Boston perhaps & New England mountains—to look in the
faces of my relatives—to feel Ada's kiss again on my lips—to look into
Mother's chastened face—to write letters & receive them—to gather & to smell flowers—to pray many times—to buy new things—to
be of some use to many girls. Am I to do these things? The Future
rises before me—misty—dark—moist—like an advancing wave!
Steadily I march toward it—there is no help—God is in it—God
manages affairs—*God—who is Love!* Oh! If I surely felt this *always* I
might now, be happy with happiness not wholly unlike Mary's—in
Heaven.

Oh! I am tired.

1. On 1 January 1863 President Lincoln issued the Emancipation Proclamation,
which declared that all persons held as slaves within the insurgent states "are and
henceforth shall be, free."

2. William Jones was then the principal of NWFC.

3. Not identified.

4. In her journal entry for 21 August 1862 Willard noted that Forest Home (the
Willards' farm outside of Janesville, Wis.) was sold, she having witnessed the deed that
conveyed it to Mr. Storey, her father's old business partner.

3 January 1863

Here is this morning's Soliloquy:

"Frances Willard why do you plan to go on teaching *ad infinitum*—
now to Pittsburgh it is, thence Cincinnati[1] (in your plans) and thence
some other where? Why do you content yourself with such a hedged
up life—with acquiring money so slowly—with such an obscure life.
There is no need. You have abilities for something beyond this—
don't cheat yourself of your rights. Do you remember your fine plans?
That *Novel* you had on the brain? Those essays—novelettes—what
else? Do you know, that sometimes, as you help arrange the room—
or make your toilette—or take solitary walks, you think out splendid
paragraphs that you never write down—like the idle creature you are.
Do you know that you have a great many kind, fresh, beautiful
thoughts that you never tell; do you know that new & striking comparisons come to you—and queer, pleasantly queer ideas—& you let
them pass in & out of your brain leaving not even a 'sedimentary
deposit' there? Stir yourself—be determined to write—books if you
please, why not? Be intent upon it—your field of usefulness may be
much extended—God thinks it right to have ambitions—you are on
earth now, deal with the earth. 'Feel the victory in you.' (that's your

father's quaint, expressive phrase.) And now, to be pointed & 'make the application.' While you are at Pittsburgh, *write*. It is nonsense to think you can't when you are teaching, do any thing else. You expect to visit Boston in the summer. Take to that city an essay on the writings of William Mountford;[2]—an essay on 'The Tolerant spirit'—a story (novelette) entitled 'Philip: My King' & a chastely-written, brief memoir of your sister Mary. Be sure & do these things. You can— you're in your twenty-fourth year—you're almost in your prime. It is *now or never* with you."

The Soliloquy is over. There *was* a little truth in it, I do contend. Yet, with all my want of—secretiveness which "they say" is my besetting sin, I wouldn't show this last entry "for any thing" to hardly any body. Just think! If I *could* do these things how my limits would scamper further off from me! I could see life—I could feed my aesthetic nature—I could know splendid people—I could have Ada with me!—O—*shall I?*

1. Willard hoped eventually to teach at Cincinnati Wesleyan College.

2. William Mountford (1816–85) was a Unitarian minister who wrote popular theological works and fiction. Willard notes reading his *Euthanasy; or Happy Talk Toward the End of Life* (Boston, 1848) in her 29 December 1862 journal entry.

6 January 1863

. . . My last days are wearing away, of this pleasant, pleasant Life. How many sweet, new memories I have—& *Ada*. I ought not to cling to her. Her Philip is not far before her on the path. . . . Ada will want hers earlier than most women, she has such a loving nature. She will go away from me—it will be best & the inevitable thing. Mary B. went. It was right—I do not quite like the *mode* yet doubtless am to blame for most of it. Let that pass—it is in the past—God forgive me for my sins in it. Why do I love women so? It is a *nuisance* (!) It don't pay—they're sure to go off & leave one lamenting. I'd like a Philip of my own right well, since I can't be any sweet girl's Philip—only as a "temporary" to a "permanent" set of teeth! Every night I ask God for Philip—not weakly & faint-heartedly, but with a heart that can afford to wait—& that cheerily, too.

But tonight—if I had Ada—to say her sweet words & to show so plainly that, just now, I *am* "all in all" to her! . . .

PART THREE

23 January 1863–27 May 1868

My Life here is fairly entered. I will be as good & useful as
I can—as happy, too. I will learn what I can—& in all ways
grow-*up*.

—*23 January 1863*

In February 1863, when Willard had been teaching for a month at Pittsburgh Female College, she pronounced her situation "tolerable" and predicted that "Pittsburgh shall yield me profit,—if not pleasure."[1] Her colleagues on the faculty were friendly, her living quarters pleasant, and her students amiable young girls, if a bit dull. She had a light teaching load and had managed to shift her responsibility for a class in arithmetic, which she simply did not understand, to the preceptress in exchange for a class in elocution, which she loved to teach. In her free time, she read Shakespeare with another teacher, pursued further German study with a native speaker, and continued her habits of wide reading and writing essays on topics she wanted to think through.

She lacked only one thing that would make her stay in Pittsburgh a truly happy one. She had no intimate friend. Far away from her family, still grieving over her sister's death and the loss of her friend Mary Bannister, separated from her new friend Ada Brigham, Willard was terribly lonely. She struggled to come to terms with that loneliness by filling her days with work. For the time being, her correspondence would have to take the place of the intimacy of physical presence, and she anxiously waited each day for letters from her parents, her Evanston friends, and, especially, Ada. Willard's longing for love from one who would satisfy her soul's hunger was, apparently, never fulfilled at Pittsburgh Female College, although she stayed on until the end of her second term, in July 1863, and returned to teach two more terms in 1864.

Willard stopped keeping a detailed daily journal in September 1863. From October to December she took an extended trip to the East, traveling first to New York City, accompanied by a family friend. There she negotiated with Harper and Brothers the publication of *Nineteen Beautiful Years*,[2] a memoir of her sister, Mary, which she had written during the summer. She journeyed on to New England with her father, who joined her for visits to the Boston area and to his ancestral home in Wheelock, Vermont, and then to Philadelphia. After teaching in Pittsburgh until early summer 1864, she returned to Evanston, where she taught school in 1865.

In 1866, when she took up journal keeping once more, her writing style had changed dramatically. Instead of long, reflective entries, she wrote brief ones that she squeezed into page-a-day diaries. At that point she was extremely busy in her position as the corresponding secretary of the American Methodist Ladies' Centenary Association, a group that had decided to celebrate the first hundred years of

Methodism in America by raising funds for a dormitory for GBI. Willard worked closely with several area Methodist leaders and she enjoyed her position very much.

One of Willard's colleagues in her fund-raising work was Melinda Hamline,[3] widow of a prominent Methodist bishop and the president of the centenary fund organization. Hamline was a leading figure in a revival that took place in Evanston during January 1866. Willard and her family, along with many others in the community, participated in a series of prayer meetings led by Phoebe and Walter Palmer,[4] well-known and successful revival leaders, and close friends of Melinda Hamline. Several years earlier, Willard had candidly described herself as "not a bit religious, naturally," and "not particularly conscientious" as far as religious discipline was concerned.[5] Although that self-judgment was somewhat harsh, she was always better able to maintain a vital, active faith when surrounded by others who sought to do the same. With her mother and father, her friends and neighbors all consecrating themselves anew to Christ at the Evanston revival, Willard enthusiastically joined with them. She continued through spring and summer of 1866 to be energized by a renewed faith and a sense of joyousness as she went about her work.[6]

Willard was eager to see her friends filled with the same spiritual energy that invigorated her. Her friend Kate Jackson, with whom Willard had taught for a year in Evanston, troubled her because she had little interest in religion, as Willard noted on several occasions in her journal. Willard was invited to become preceptress at Genesee Wesleyan Seminary, a Methodist-founded preparatory academy in Lima, New York, an excellent position that she intended to take. Jackson wished to accompany her there and teach also, but Willard questioned whether this would be wise. "How," she wondered, "can I risk so much for myself & my pupils, as a constant, intimate, deleterious influence[?]"[7] Jackson was baptized shortly before the two friends left for Lima in September 1866, but Willard never perceived her as someone to whom she could turn for either example or encouragement in strengthening her faith.

Other aspects of Jackson's personality were troubling as well. She could be jealous and extremely possessive, sometimes coming between Willard and her other friends—both male and female. When Willard arrived at the Genesee seminary, she was immediately plunged into her preceptress duties, registering girls, meeting their parents, and comforting those who were homesick. Soon after she had met with the faculty of both boys' and girls' departments, she singled out one of them in whom she was especially interested, Delevan C. Scoville, the boys' mathematics instructor.[8] Like Charles Fowler, Scoville was easy to talk to, and he had a strong religious aspect to his character, which pleased Willard. She viewed him as one who could be a spiritual partner for her as well as a possible beau. As their friendship grew stronger over the school year, Jackson became exceedingly jealous and intervened between them in whatever way she could.

Willard was torn between her two friends. She was immensely touched and flattered by Jackson's love for her, so strong and demanding that she felt she must return it. And Jackson's friendship meant the opportunity Willard had longed for: travel to Europe. The two young women spent many hours in Lima planning a long European tour, Jackson offering to pay Willard's way. From her teens, Willard had dreamed of going abroad to study and absorb the culture of the "old world," to stretch her horizons and complete her education. Yet she was drawn to Scoville, despite Kate's strong and vocal disapproval.

The course of Willard's friendship with Scoville is not detailed in her journal as is her engagement with Fowler, so it is more difficult to understand fully. But through scattered hints, it is possible to piece together at least part of the story, enough to see that, once again, Willard ended a relationship with a young man of whom she was quite fond. She intimated that Jackson was the cause of her breaking off any further contact with Scoville, although her parents were also glad to see the relationship ended, at least partly because they thought that Scoville was not in good health.

The issue of health loomed large in the Willard family from spring 1867 on, because Josiah Willard's tuberculosis had flared up and become acute. His condition deteriorated over the summer and fall, causing Willard and Jackson to postpone the European trip they had intended to begin in July 1867. Although her father had relented in his opposition to her European plans, she knew she could not leave when he was so near death. In September she accompanied him to his childhood home in Churchville, New York, so that he could be cared for by his brother and sister, as well as by Willard and her mother. The journal recounts many touching moments between father and daughter, as he prepared for his imminent death, which occurred in mid-January 1868. Willard and her mother accompanied the body back to Evanston for burial and carried out the funeral arrangements Josiah Willard had specified. After seeing that her mother's financial situation was made as secure as possible, Willard and Jackson departed for Europe at the end of May.

By that time, Willard had finally determined her life's aim. "The Woman Question" claimed more and more of her attention, and in March 1868, she attended a speech on "The American Woman" given by Theodore Tilton, popular women's rights lecturer.[9] Tilton's speech, with which she strongly agreed, had the effect of confirming her purpose to work for women's rights. Her trip to Europe began to take on added significance. Besides absorbing all she could of European culture and history, she would study women's status and situation wherever she traveled. Although she had not decided just what she would do on behalf of women, she had already determined that her work would issue from her Christian commitment. Her faith would inform both her interpretation of the Woman Question and her response to the issues raised by this most crucial question. She would be a Christian first, and only then a women's rights reformer.

Notes

1. Journal, 18 February 1863.
2. Frances E. Willard, *Nineteen Beautiful Years: or Sketches of a Girl's Life* (New York, 1864).
3. Melinda (Johnson) Hamline (1801–81) was the widow of MEC bishop Leonidas L. Hamline (1797–1865) and a leader in the growing Holiness movement among Methodists. Well educated and spiritually sensitive, Hamline held Holiness meetings in her home in Evanston, where she had moved in 1865 after her husband died. Hamline also was elected president of the American Methodist Ladies' Centenary Association in 1865, and in 1868 she was chosen president of the board of managers of the Ladies Educational Association, the group that initiated the Evanston College for Ladies.
4. Phoebe (Worrall) Palmer (1807–74) and Walter Clark Palmer (1804–83) were evangelists, advocates of Holiness, newspaper editors, and lecturers. Raised a Methodist in New York City, Phoebe Worrall exhibited early literary ability through poetry writing. She married Walter Palmer, a homeopathic physician who was also a Methodist, in 1827. In 1832, the Palmers dedicated themselves to spiritual holiness at a revival at New York City's Allen Street MEC. In 1835 Phoebe Palmer and her sister, Sarah (Worrall) Lankford, held a weekly afternoon prayer service for Methodist women, which later became known as the "Tuesday Meeting for the Promotion of Holiness." The members' goal was entire sanctification—God's cleansing of a believer's heart of sin and filling it wholly with God's love—which Palmer claimed to have experienced in 1837. The Tuesday Meeting, now led by Palmer alone, attracted many prominent Methodist figures, including Bishop Leonidas L. Hamline, who became supporters of the Holiness movement. Palmer's published writings widened the influence of Holiness, and, in 1862, when she became editor-in-chief of a popular religious magazine, *Guide to Holiness,* her

ideas reached thousands. Beginning in 1850, the Palmers spent half of each year preaching at Methodist camp meetings and conducting Holiness revivals in the United States and Canada. They traveled to England in 1859, staying for four years of preaching and revivals. In 1863 they returned to the United States, where Phoebe Palmer remained active in Holiness ministry almost to the end of her life.

5. Journal, 17 February 1861.

6. See Willard, *Glimpses of Fifty Years,* 624–27, for her mature assessment of her Holiness revival experience.

7. Journal, 24 May 1866.

8. Delevan Clarence Scoville (b. ca. 1842) taught mathematics in the boys' preparatory department of Genesee Wesleyan College, Lima, N.Y., during the school year 1866–67, the same year Willard was preceptress of the ladies' department. The following school year he taught at Cazenovia Seminary, Cazenovia, N.Y., a Methodist secondary school. Later Scoville became a lawyer and practiced in New York City during the 1880s.

9. Theodore Tilton (1835–1907) was editor-in-chief of the *Independent* when he lectured in Evanston on 9 March 1868. Before the Civil War he had been an ardent abolitionist. At its conclusion Tilton took a radical republican position and also espoused the woman suffrage cause, joining the Equal Rights Association and speaking around the country on behalf of woman suffrage.

23 January 1863
Pittsburgh, Pennsylvania

Here I am. Between the dates of these last entries in my Journal many things have happened to me—& great changes for a life so quiet as mine. I have been quite ill & almost thought I must give up Pittsburgh & my plans. But I was soon well again—examined my classes—said goodbye to dear Emma—to my room & my room-mate—to faithful Belle & kind Miss Clark—& took "Pearsons' Bus"[1]—as I had so often thought "how I'd do"—went to the depot one bright, snowy morning & rolled away in the cars from pleasant Evanston & my friends—from the House in which, once, *we* all lived—past my only sister's grave white & glistening in the snow—& so the Old Life was shut out & the New drew near. . . .

On Tuesday night started with dear Father on the cars for "Pitts." We took a sleeping car & how I thought all night long, nearly, of all that has Past—*that has Past.* . . . All day (Wednesday) we rode—were delayed three hours by an accident & in the evening—oh how dark & muddy it was! We arrived at this *pitchy city.* I like the school—the Teachers—my room-mate, Fannie Fish[2]—my classes & every thing but the dirt & the smoke. They are *truly awful.* Fannie just said to me (we are sitting in the office & it looks bright & cheerful with the grate glowing & the gas-light putting the shadows to route) "Some day we will go up on a hill near here & see the city—it's a terrible sort of a sight—so dark & smoky every thing looks." That's encouraging! . . .

My Life here is fairly entered. I will be as good & useful as I can—as happy, too. I will learn what I can—& in all ways grow-*up*. And then, in *June*—sweetest, *saddest* of months to me—I will see *Ada* if God wills. I will *keep myself for her*—I will *Darling*, to whom this book is going in a day or two—& I ask you to keep *your heart* for *me*—*me only*—until then. Afterward—we can not tell. . . .

1. John Pearsons (1818–1902), husband of Hannah (Bailey) Pearsons, Willard's former Sunday School teacher, ran an omnibus service to and from the Evanston train station. He was also in the lumber and livery businesses and operated an express service to Chicago.
2. Frances A. Fish was a teacher in the Primary Department at the Pittsburgh Female College from 1863 to 1864, having graduated from that institution in 1862 with a Mistress of Liberal Arts degree. Later she taught mathematics at North Western Female College from 1865 through spring 1868.

26 January 1863

. . . I'm glad I came here. I am to like it, I know. By & Bye Im to have sweet friends here—& to be called by beautiful, loving names.

And I am to learn much that is new and good. I am to see a new side of life—indeed I have, already.

I mean to do my best—to be as good a Teacher as my abilities will permit and to win the love & respect of these strangers to myself, if it be possible. I wish to make it a happy thing for some of them that I came here among them—and not a thing unpleasant, for any one.

Today—the first Monday of my new experience—I have got on better than at all, before. My classes have "gone off" creditably and I am not dissatisfied with the results of my day's efforts. Before light, Fannie—nice Fannie Fish, my room-mate—& I rose—dressed & went to devotions in the Chapel before breakfast. . . . Then we went to Breakfast—thence to our room & did our work—thence I went to smart, unexceptionable Miss Scull's[1] room & together we went to Miss Teal's.[2] (The first is "head teacher" among the ladies; the second, teacher of Drawing & Painting.) By much manuvering we managed to arrange for Miss S— to take my Arithmetic—for which I have "no call"—and for me to take her class in Elocution. A weight went off my shoulders, then!—I looked over Geometry, History, etc—went to the Office for Fannie—we went in to public devotions in the Chapel. Prof. Johnson[3] conducted the exercise. . . . Then I heard a class of ten in History, (Wocester's) then a class of ten in Geometry (Loomis)—a class of 29 in Geography (McNally's) of 24 in Grammar, (Penneo's). Then, it was noon. After Dinner two classes in Elocution (with fifty in one of them). (Osgood's & McGuffey's Readers),[4] & a primary class in Geography. Then school duties were over. I have no school-room to preside over—no disciplining except in my own classes;—nothing is expected of me from three PM to nine A.M.—except once in two weeks to walk with the girls & once in six to sit during evening study hours in the school-room for a week. . . .

1. Sarah Amelia Scull (d. 1913) had a Mistress of English Literature degree. She taught modern languages and upper-level English at Pittsburgh Female Seminary from 1860 to 1863, and upper-level English only from 1863 to 1866. Later she was assistant principal at Mount Vernon Seminary, the girls' preparatory school founded by Willard's friend Jenny (Eddy) Somers. Willard saw both Scull and Somers on a trip through Washington, D.C., in April 1896.

2. C. H. Teel taught drawing and painting at the Pittsburgh Female College from 1860 to 1868.

3. Edward Johnson was professor of ancient languages and natural sciences at the Pittsburgh Female College from 1862 to 1864. On a trip to New England in fall 1867, Willard visited Johnson, his wife, Nettie, and their young child, Eddie, in Lynn, Massachusetts, where Johnson was teaching in a public school.

4. The textbooks from which Willard taught included: Elias Loomis, *Elements of Geometry and Conic Sections* (New York, 1843); Francis McNally, *An Improved System of Geography by Francis McNally. Designed for Schools, Academies and Seminaries* (New York, 1855); Lucius Osgood, *Osgood's Progressive First Reader* (Pittsburgh, 1855–88); Alex-

ander Hamilton McGuffey, *McGuffey's Rhetorical Guide; or Fifth Reader of the Eclectic Series: Containing Elegant Extracts in Prose and Poetry, with Copious Rules and Rhetorical Exercises* (Cincinnati, 1844). Penneo's Grammar and Wocester's (probably Worcester's) history are not identified.

31 January 1863

. . . My first week of teaching is over. I am tolerably well suited with it and feel quite to understand myself in my new relations. . . . I have made a bag for my clothes (when they go to the "wash"), have helped do the room-work . . . have written on an Essay for "the Browning"[1]— a Literary Society formed of teachers & young ladies of the college— have read this week's Independent[2]—a splendid paper always—have examined (& like) Quackenbos's Grammar[3]—and now sit here, at three or four o'clock P.M., with nothing much to do, & rather vacant. It's a queer feeling—so far from home as I am—so far from those who love me. . . . I'm going to hear "the Sage of Concord"[4] lecture, on Tuesday eve. That's an advantage I get—with many others—by coming off here. I can see some of the men who have pleased & taught me by the fireside at home. . . .

Think of a man's career! Of his broder sphere than ours. Is it not so? In all this week I have not "stepped my foot" outside this house. Have been *just here.* Yet I've been well & able to go out. What would a healthy man have thought of such confinement? *I'll extend my sphere* some day! I don't complain—I hope I don't. Only, sitting here, I thought about it all.

1. Named after Elizabeth Barrett Browning (1806–61), the English Romantic poet, the Pittsburgh Female College's literary society met in "Browning Hall," a second-floor room of the college building.
2. The New York *Independent* was a popular weekly newspaper published in the 1860s by the Congregational Church, featuring sermons by eminent ministers such as Henry Ward Beecher, essays, and articles of general interest. It ran from 7 December 1848 to 13 October 1928.
3. Willard referred to George Payn Quackenbos, *An English Grammar* (New York, 1862).
4. In 1859 and 1860 Willard avidly read the essays of "the sage of Concord," Ralph Waldo Emerson (1803–82), the transcendentalist philosopher, essayist, and poet.

2 February 1863

. . . Shall I ever—Oh! shall I ever sit down to rest in the Mansions of the Justified? Half-happy no longer, but everything like my Ideal? And where is that Land of Spirits?—am I near it?—can I pass through Death *in calmness*—through His grace who is *love*? For two nights I

have dreamed that I died—for two nights in succession. It don't worry
me—but makes me *think*—indeed, I do that, any way. I sleep heavily
but have troubled dreams—& flashes of heat go over me & my heart
flutters strangely, sometimes. When will my little rôle be acted & I
dismissed by the Manager? O the grave fits closely & I don't want to
be there in unconsciousness—I *hope* the soul don't *sleep*. . . .

15 February 1863

. . . One year ago today Mr. F— & I formally sundered our engagement. I told him not to think there was no darkness in the path I was
going to tread or that I saw no light in the one from which I turned
away. Has there not been darkness, this year? Oh! manly heart that
would have sheltered & strengthened me! If it were to do again I
would act as before, yet why does not God let me love & be loved by
some one who can help me?—I'm not happy. I had much better own
it. I am not well—these people don't care for me nor I for them. Oh
June! June! Thou hast much to restore!

I've joined the church here (Christ church) and today went to class
meeting. Oh—to be good—to be good!

18 February 1863

Another day of my Life has gone away from me. It has not been
happy—none of my days are *that,*—but it has been tolerable—& for
this, I am thankful. Pittsburgh shall yield me profit,—if not pleasure.
I will try to make it pay me for the absence of all that is dear & sweet
to me. No, it can't do that. I hold that one can never be repaid for
the loss of those he loves best;—the loss of them from his home;—
the missing of them every where;—the doing without their loving
words—their kisses & caresses. And yet, other things may some what
atone—& so they shall, to me. I get on bravely. Read a good deal &
learn ever so many new things every day. . . . I compose quite a marvelous amount for me, & this A.M. (before school), copied an article
("Ideals").[1] My "Shakspearian readings" will take me through all the
plays if pursued—as Miss Scull & I mean to pursue it,—until the 25th
of June. Tonight I have negociated with scholarly Professor Johnson
for the loan of Woodbury's Eclectic Reader[2] & I'm going to furbish
my German. Besides, general reading & good talk. . . . In vacation I'll
"do" Pittsburgh & learn what I can. I'll teach these girls as well as
possible. They haven't much love of learning—poor young things. . . .
Have taken quite a walk—across St. Clare Bridge[3]—with little Gerty

Munson.[4] Have had some nice photographs taken and seen fine churches—stores—heaps of people & had the wind blow through my unaired nature a little bit. Withal, have quietly walked into a *baker's* (our "board" isn't the richest. This is *sub rosa.*) & bought some apples, ginger cakes, crullers, dough nuts & an orange. (O earthly tendencies thus candidly revealed!) If I'd only heard from some one dear to me! If it had been the night for "my favorite letter"—as I call *Ada's* to the girls here, though they don't know what I mean. Or if Father's & Mother's had come—or one from Oliver & Mary. How is it, Oliver, that you haven't written to your only sister once since you went away?

I'm sitting "in study" tonight. This is my week for it. It is tiresome & unpleasant. The boarders of the Pitts. Fem. Coll. are before me—cramming their heads with the rudiments of an education;—at least, this is supposed to be their occupation—I'm to aid & abet them at it by keeping them as still & well-behaved as possible. They're a set of girls between fifteen & eighteen years old. They're not at all intelligent or "expanded":—why should they be? A few of them are honest students. They're not kin to me—not near me in heart & will never be I think.

1. A copy of "Ideals" is in scrapbook 1, 73, Frances E. Willard Memorial Library, Evanston, Illinois. The clipping (from an unidentified magazine) was signed and misdated, "Pittsburgh Female College, Feb. 1861."

2. Willard used W. H. Woodbury, *The Eclectic German Reader; Consisting of Choice Selections from the Best German Writers, with Copious References to the Author's Grammatical Works, to Which Is Added a Complete Vocabulary* (New York, 1857), a commonly used text for students of German.

3. The St. Clare Bridge (now the Sixth Street Bridge), which spanned the Allegheny River, was two-and-one-half blocks away from the college.

4. Gertrude A. Munson was a student at the Pittsburgh Female College only for the year 1862–63. She was in the Musical Department, studying both voice and piano.

25 February 1863

I'm perfectly *well* this week, & not blue a bit,—only anxious about Ada, whose usual letter has failed to come. Have had nice letters from Father & Mother who are *going home* this week or next. How *glad* I shall be to have a *Home* to think about, once more! My life has not been so valuable to me in years, if ever, as it is now. Every moment is occupied, either in teaching, composing, copying, reading, German, or conversation with intelligent persons. Prof. Johnson is very useful to me—I learn so much from him. Miss Scull is, also, & our "Shaksperian Readings" are quite interesting. Miss Teel is very kind & teaches me many things. I'm getting out into the world a little,—more than "a little" for me, & find it a place where one must have courage—strength—patience & intelligence. Sometimes my thoughts stray off—to great cities far away—to learned men & women—& I go half wild in my hungering after them. . . .

8 March 1863

. . . What a blessing & a curse in one, is this habit that environs us! This "becoming used" to things! (expressive phrase.) Because it is familiar the thought of Mary's having gone from us, cuts not so painfully. Because it is familiar, the thought of Christ's having died for me wakens less love & wonder in my soul. O pitifulness of this secondary significance! The clear outline of facts is worn off by Thought's frequent handling of them so that the striking becomes stupid & the wonderful, a matter of course. Some times we catch a glimpse of the *real;*—as we see more distinctly, physiologists say, by looking side ways (thus bringing the image on a sensitive, unaccustomed portion of the retina) & then! we are startled as if a new world had opened. Often I've done this—especially last summer—until I was frightened at the "awfulness of Life." . . . I would be very glad to give some hint at my full, intellectual Life. Heart is dormant now,—wakened a little by Ada's letters—when they come,—& jogged somewhat by Emma's. Splendid Emma White! Mother's letters are very sweet & tender—both hers & father's more loving than they've ever written before. Always my heart is *one way* toward *them* of course. And now if I felt Christ nearer to me;—If some one that I dearly loved & who dearly loved me were here; then I should be happy—as we count happiness. . . .

21 March 1863

Yesterday afternoon, Miss Teel took Professor & Mrs. Johnson[1] & me, to see a collection of paintings & engravings collected & owned by Mr. Wolfe,[2] a wealthy merchant of this city. This gentleman is a bachelor—is finely educated, has lived abroad—knows something of the pleasure that one finds in "seeing life." . . . The bell was answered by an old, yellow-faced woman who takes care of the rooms; who on recognizing Miss Teel—who has a standing permit to visit here & bring her friends—she admitted us & motioned us up stairs. The walls of the hall were lined with paintings large & small, in (2) watercolors & (1) oils—but we passed on to the picture-room. The old woman opened it to us, from within. We entered, & I was quite bewildered by the number & variety of pictures around me. From floor to ceiling the walls were full;—there was no vacant space;—even the doors were covered. On the table were books of engravings—Art-magazines, Catalogues of various Galleries & the finest steroscope I've ever seen. The mantle-shelf was covered with statuettes, & a pretty etagere exhibited elegant carvings in wood & bronze.—Easy chairs—tete-tetes,[3] & artist's sketching seats were arranged here & there. A bright fire glowed in the grate. Here we had come from the noise & dirt of the street, on one of Pittsburgh's dreariest days, into this silent, elegant apartment, where beautiful faces looked down at us from the walls—where the aesthetic sense so crossed & outraged only a moment before by the smoke and tumult & dirt of the street, was pleased & enlivened at every turn. The transition, coming so suddenly, made me feel as though some fairy had worked the charm. . . . I like to get out of the common course of things—for I have not yet the rare art of viewing accustomed objects as unique—out "into something rich & strange." I don't like things to feel hard & positive all the time;—the bread & butter side of life it is pleasant to forget once in a while; . . . and to deal with matters that won't satisfy the cravings of physical hunger or thirst, nor abate physical weariness;—that will not even "put money in the purse" but will raise us for the time above the needs they do not attempt to satisfy, into a realm which has analogies to that where "they hunger no more neither thirst."[4] A little ether on a handkercheif lifts "the real Me" beyond the Himalayas and roseate hues gleam on me—a mellow air shuts me in & familiar voices grow distant. I like the sights I see then, the strange, unaccustomed yet spiritual state of mind I'm in. Nitrous oxyd has charms for me, & I can comprehend something of the pleasure that Coleridge & De Quincey[5] found in opium. We were not meant to go so far away, I think, yet in the pleasures of the Imagination when restricted by a cultivated intellect & guided to objects of contemplation by a wakeful conscience there can be no harm. But I'm forgetting about Wolfe's gallery. . . .

I sat down before the splendid stereoscope. It was very large, & by turning a knob,—different views could be brought before the eye. From the time that I looked at the first, I knew but little of what was going on *outside*—for I seemed shut in to a different world. Professor's kind voice, his wife's quickly-uttered criticism or commendation—Miss Teel's pleasantly-given information—all sounded far off and foreign to me & my world, just then. I was looking at actual representations—photographs—of scenes far off;—of which I had visions sometimes;—of which I had read with delight;—which in my prayers I had often asked to see. Paris passed before me first. . . . I seem to myself like a magician as I change the scene;—I'm away over the sea now . . . I . . . think with fast beating heart of those distant, wonderful lands. . . . O wonderful Eastern Land! Cradle of Adam & of Christ! Land of Legend & Song;—of prophecy & revelation;—of fragrant air & sunny sky—may I not see thee before I leave the earth? Why should I not? . . . It was a curious quarter-hour that I spent with the stereoscope. An hour full of dreams—full of vague beleifs that sometime I should go away over the sea—& look on lands "Where the feathery palm-trees rise And the date grows ripe under sunny skies."[6] I got new love of life—new admiration for our world—new thankfulness for personal identity from the paste-boards with light colors & dark shades arranged determinately upon them. It is a great art that our century has brought to light. To the most enlightened of our forefathers—a hundred years back, a sun-picture[7] would have been almost like a miracle, performed. But Mr. Wolfe is exhibiting a sketch-book with drawings by New York artists-friends of his & I must give attention. . . . We left for home when the black shadows were well nigh fallen having to thank Miss Teel for introducing us to a gentleman & his pictures.

1. A. C. W. Johnson was the assistant in the Preparatory Department at the Pittsburgh Female College in 1862–63. In 1863–64 she taught ornamental needlework.

2. C. H. Wolff was an avid art collector who was particularly interested in the work of Pittsburgh and Philadelphia artists, but whose collection was wide ranging and included many works by European artists.

3. Tête-à-têtes are short sofas intended to seat two persons facing each other, hence head to head (tête à tête).

4. Willard paraphrased Rev. 7.16, "They shall hunger no more, neither thirst any more. . . ."

5. Samuel Taylor Coleridge (1772–1834), the English poet, essayist, and critic, and Thomas De Quincey (1785–1859), the essayist, were both addicted to opium. Earlier Willard had read De Quincey's memoir, *Confessions of an English Opium Eater* (London, 1822), describing his experiences with opium, which he used partly for the experiences of alternative consciousness he achieved when taking the drug.

6. Not identified.

7. Willard probably referred to the photographic process developed by William Henry Fox Talbot (1800–77), one of several pioneers of photography. Talbot produced a volume entitled *Sun Pictures in Scotland* to show the results of his photographic method. Willard could easily have read about Talbot and his "sun pictures" in the popular press.

28 March 1863

A letter just received from *My Mother*. It is so much a settled principle of my life—so much a part of myself—that I mention it but seldom—*my love of her.* I do not discourse here of the color of my eyes—the countour of my lips;—I do not often mention my will—temper—capabilites—for I know them all so well it seems not needful. Perhaps I ought to have my Journal for a different purpose, but the facts are that I keep it as a note—or memorandum book. I write in it—not the things that most concern me—that are nearest & dearest, so much as the passing events of the day. Dear *dear* Mother! Her love & mindfulness have never failed me! I am as sure to have them as I am to have the sunshine—air to breathe—& God's mercy exercised toward me.

I am a little homesick for the well-known faces that have looked kindly on me all the days of my life. I was never without sight of them so long as it will be this time. Mother says in her gentle, uncomplaining way: "It seems a long time since we said 'Goodbye' at the Gate. But I long ago decided that whatever is best for my children is for me best, so I am glad that you went away—if you are glad." O I'll be a better child to them than ever I was yet if I should live & they should live until we meet once more! . . .

2 April 1863

Very contented and a little happy, I sit in Fannie's & my new room in the "new house." For the "Pittsburgh Female College" is really a flourishing affair—the number of pupils is so great that two large brick buildings immediately adjoining it have been bought and into one of these,—in a front room—up only one flight of stairs with a nice fire-place, gas, blinds & balcony before the windows—which come down to the floor,—we have this day moved our "bag & baggage." In the heart of a large city—with the noise of boats on the river—which is nearby—& the hum of machinery in my ear—with life & activity on every side of me, I sit tonight in my large, yet cozy room, by the cheerful fire, musing upon a hundred pleasant things—I that shall have no need of ruddy fire-light of couch or easy-chair after a little while, but shall lie in some grave-yard, ("Rose Hill,"[1] I hope), with my hands folded in the endless inactivity—as Mary's are tonight. She loved warmth & light as well as I do—she took in the sense of every thing good & pleasant—yet she came to this. I know this is not the truest way to look at the Thing that comes latest & direst of all. It is but going from what is good to what is glorious, Faith tells me, in her cheery voice. But sitting here so vigorous—so conscious of my hundred & twenty pounds avoirdupois;—of my young, quick-circulating blood, with the Five Gates wide open to take in sight &

sound & odor, flavor & contact what wonder if just now that strange, etherial Life which concerns with—I know not what;—which has no need of powers I have never ceased to use—what wonder if Mary's kind of life seems to me now at an infinite remove from mine? God pardons me I think, for, though He seems so utterly incomprehensible to me I yet beleive that He is good;—I vaguely trust in Him & if I could find Him would pour out hearty thanks for all the blessings of my Life. One among millions of billions that he has created—yet to feel that I am yet remembered—many of my capacities met—my comfort—permitted at least. O God is good—life is bright—I am happy! Do I say this inspired by the mood of the hour? Because I'm "warmed & filled"?—Because things around me are a little novel & I like novelty? Because kind & friendly words have this day been spoken to me? Because Dr. Pershing[2] has just been in, & in his brisk way examined the appointments of our room & told me, with a generous gesture of the hand in wh. he held his pleasantly flavored "Havana" that "He wanted to make me as comfortable & contented as he could for I'd never given him a particle of trouble"? . . . O! I'm afraid these things influence me more than I know, for every kind word and friendly deed moves me much—especially since I've left those who love me best.

Anyhow I'm quite content. So nice a letter I had from Father today! Written hurriedly at his office, yet with quaint old words in it that have been "household words" with us always;—that Mary has said in her merry way—that Father used when we were little children, so *"fatherly"* so friendly & familiar. Telling me of their plans—Mother's & his. How they are to board this summer in the house where we all lived only a while ago. Telling me he can't go to New England this year—& that perhaps I'd better come back here next fall I'm getting on so well; "unless I should get married"—always his first choice for all his children. (A wise one too—I know that well enough . . . .) Telling me how "my old flame" (as he chooses to denominate Rev. C.H.F.) had just called to see him—inquire after me etc & has now gone to see Mother "perhaps," he slyly adds, "to negotiate a new treaty?" No, Father knows that Charlie wouldn't do so—that "old things have past away." He knows that no man has my heart—that no one wants it as we can tell—that Ada has what is tenderest & deepest in me of *that* kind of love. And yet—. . .

A letter from my Darling who loves me as no one ever loved me before who was not of my blood & with a *passion* in exchange for the untiring beat of a Mother's heart, that does not, however burst into *flame* as Ada's does for me. O my little girl. I can not write my love for you—my seeking after you—my needing of you—my waiting for you—my consecration to you—my great hope that we may bless each others lives & be together. God does something strange, inexplicable, yet glorious, I think, when He so adjusts one womans soul to another woman's soul that they have such need of each other as lovers have. He shows that Passion can be something wholly of the spirit—that it may exist beyond our present life. I scorn the name of "Friendship"—sweet & hallowed as it is, for the feeling that we have each toward the other—Ada & I. Whether it live one year or all our lives—whether it smoulder in this long separation or burn clear & strong forever—be these things as they may, we have felt & now feel for each other what Petrarch felt for Laura; Dante did for Beatrice— what Juliet did for Romeo.[3] I know it is wonderful—such we both think it. It is so strange that I have seldom mentioned it to others— except that rare Luella Clark—and speak of her as "a pupil very dear to me." But they little think I never knew another love like this;—so deep and constant they do not dream that she outweighs all other things lovely & desirable to me. So that in books I find my comfort now that I haven't her. So that I turn from all the rest & hibernate my heart till the sweet south wind of her love shall call it into the midst of *happiness*. When shall I have her again? Is there no way?

Since writing the above I've been gazing into the fire a long time— planning for Ada. I beleive I can see "light ahead" for us;—but then, I'm always too hopeful—so "they say." . . .

1. Rose Hill (also spelled Rosehill) was the cemetery just south of Evanston, incorporated in 1859, where Willard's sister, Mary, was buried, as were many other Evanston friends and acquaintances of the Willard family.

2. Israel C. Pershing (1826–98) was an MEC minister and president of the Pittsburgh Female College from 1860 to 1886.

3. Willard listed three famous couples in literature whose love was tender and whose passion for each other was, to a great extent, spiritual. Petrarch (Francesco Petrarca, 1304–74), the Italian poet and scholar, was a major force in the development of the Renaissance. Laura, whom most scholars now believe was fictional, was Petrarch's ideal and his inspiration. Dante (Dante Alighieri, 1265–1321), the Italian poet, held Beatrice (probably Beatrice Portinari, 1266–90) as his spiritual inspiration. In Dante's *Divine Comedy* she symbolizes divine revelation through faith. Romeo and Juliet, in William Shakespeare's play of the same name, are young lovers whose love for each other was doomed by fate to end tragically. Each couple seems to embody a quality of Willard's relationship with Ada.

4 April 1863

. . . Tonight, as I sit alone in my room, with the glowing grate— the wind moaning in a weird way by the window, I have strange, unusual feelings. Eternity seems not far off. A kind of awe is over me. I can't tell why. Nothing unusual has occurred. The premonitions of an unearthly fear are in my heart—stirring faintly, now & then. O what am I—& what is God's purpose with me? I wish that some one dear to me were here. I recognize *Fear* as the strongest feeling of which I am capable in my present state of being.

O, well it is for Mary if on Jesus' breast tonight she feels that perfect love that casteth out the direst of all Demons!

12 April 1863

. . . The days pass tolerably—I don't think that I should say more. *Routine* is hateful to me. I have learned this of late. I sin against what is best in me, when I so surround myself with that which is alien to my nature that I would push Time's chariot forward with double speed if it were in my power. The grave is near enough—the Future awful enough without my wishing that either should be anticipated in my life. The Logic is good—it shall make me say a long *Goodbye* to Pittsburgh on the twenty-sixth of June. . . .

17 April 1863

. . . Another week of school has rolled slowly & heavily from my shoulders as did Christian's Bundle of Sins at the _____ [1] My tasks are irksome—I am sorry. But I have alleviations. Though my *love-heart* gets no food yet it does not need it, really, for away in Michigan there is a sweet-faced, pure-souled girl who is keeping my that-kind-of-heart until I go for it. My *like-heart* is kept alive & in quite flourishing condition by several people, Ella Simpson,[2] for instance, who calls around often to see me with friendly face & confidential chat;—Professor with his thoughtful looks;—Miss Scull the hungry-minded woman,—Mrs. Holmes[3] with her quick words & positive love-you-or-hate-you ways;—Miss Teel who kisses me, says she loves me & is very, very kind; Miss Dole[4] who is cordial beyond beleif & asks me every morning in Chapel "if I adhere to my determination not to come back next year"; Dr. "I.C"[5] who is generous & full of bluff good-nature—besides many of my pupils. (though I know less of them) Then, there are my German Lessons to Mrs. Danse[6]—an educated *Frau;*—my readings—wh. are most valuable & interesting though I say so little of them here;— my writing wh. is educing my powers a little—my walks through these strange streets—looking at these strange faces; patriotic meetings at wh. I hear eloquent addresses & am thrilled through & through by recitals of scenes among our soldiers & made to feel *how dearly* I love my native land;—panoramas illustrative of the war—vespers at the cathedral—"elegant" sermons by Rev. Snively[7] or some other of the best Pitts. divines,—for I go the rounds of the churches;—a tea-party now & then with the best of gustatory comforts;—quiet reveries up here in my large, nice room (the nicest, I guess, that I ever had in my life) & besides all a numerous correspondence—averaging me a letter a day. Add to these the knowledge that many persons love me— that Father & Mother think with solicitude about me—that Ada longs for me more than for any other blessing—that in the prayers of many hearts I am remembered—that Christ died for me & quite likely I shall go to Heaven by & bye, & what need to think myself miserable? No letter from my little Girl tonight—& that has hurt me. . . .

1. Willard referred to John Bunyan's character Christian, in *The Pilgrim's Progress From this World to That Which is to Come* (London, 1678), who, when he approached the Cross of Christ, was freed from his heavy bundle of sins. It fell off his back and rolled away into the Sepulchre (Christ's empty tomb).

2. Ella Simpson was probably visiting relatives of her mother, Ellen Holmes (Verner) Simpson, who was from Pittsburgh.

3. Mary A. Holmes was a teacher in the Primary Department at the college from 1861 to 1863.

4. Martha C. Dole, who had a Master of English Literature, was preceptress in the Preparatory Department of Pittsburgh Female College from 1862 to 1863.

5. Willard referred to Principal Pershing.

6. Mrs. Pauline Danse was the teacher of German at Pittsburgh Female College from 1862 to 1881. She was a native speaker and taught Willard German. During the time Willard was at Pittsburgh Female College, she and Mrs. Danse planned to found a school in Germany, but Josiah Willard would not permit his daughter to go abroad.

7. Willard called Christ MEC a cathedral because of its European-style architecture. It was one of the first large, cathedral-like churches that Methodists built in the United States. William A. Snively (b. ca. 1844–1901) was an MEC minister who was appointed to the Pittsburgh church from 1862 to 1864.

5 May 1863

Evening. Sitting in my room. What is it, I wonder, that I keep wanting to say? It never comes to my lips—nor to the point of my pen. I am almost sure that God does not mean that I shall say it while I live on earth. It stirs in every pulse—it lies back of every true Thought that I have—but it has never yet been said. Some of my best essays are "studies" for it;—sentences that I have hurriedly, earnestly spoken to a friend's soul with which for the hour I was *en rapport* have been as "guesses" about it;—the kindling eye and flushing cheek have told a little of it—but oh! it lives on in my heart unsaid—even in my

prayers unsaid. Music tells me something of the same ever untold
Secret that only my disfranchised soul shall ever declare;—& in
crowds I sometimes see a face that moves me almost to tears—it
comes so strangely near—how or why, I can not tell. I have seen it in
the eyes of animals—so wistful, so hopeless in their liquid depths.
That mournful flower the gentian with its fringed corolla is to me like
the sweeping eye-lash that directs a loving revealing glance and gives
a new hint at *This* which I can feel but can't express. The dripping
of water tries to spell out some simple words of it;—and oh!
a . . . robin's song—or . . . a black-bird's note helps me wonderfully!
Those royal-colored clouds of sunset make it clearer—& a long gaze
up through the depths of the night

> "When the welkin above is all white
> All throbbing & panting with stars,"[1]

makes The Secret clearest of all. The thought of This which I can only
speak *about* has been with me all day like an etherial perfume—has
wrapped itself around me as a cloud of incense might. The usual number of classes has been attended;—the plain, substantial fare of breakfast, dinner & tea, has been relished by the keen appetite which application to my business has given. The Daily papers have been eagerly
read—Hooker's triumphal march—thus far—toward Richmond[2] has
made my heart throb faster than love or pride have caused since the
Garden City[3] was left behind me. Two letters have been received from
two poet-souled women in obscure life and these have transfigured me
for the time. Full of insight they were—insight clearer than mine for
these women "love much" and read the significance of destiny by clear
burning tapers lighted at the altar of consecration to strong, manly
hearts. . . . I've listened to the Bible reading at our quiet, Chapel prayers
& pondered over Job's words: "Why should a man contend against
God?"[4] and my soul has gone out after *Him*—this awful, overwhelming power that holds all things in equilibrium—& I've come back again
with some dim, shuddering consciousness that *He is* and some sweet
faith that "He is a rewarder of all such as diligently seek him."[5] I have
looked at my pliant, active fingers—shut & opened my hand & wondered over this strange, imparted force that is ordained to live awhile
in me;—that joins itself in some weird way to muscle & sinew—tissue
& bone. That filters through my nerves and makes fertile the organic
shape that is called "*Me.*" O this living—*this living!* Were it not for the
constant *habitude* of it we should go mad with marvelling at our daily
acts and thoughts. Not mad in any sense but this: Our Souls would be
so full that they would press upon those strange, pulpy little lobes that

we name "brain" and would derange or paralyze their action. God is wise & good. He don't let us get out of adjustment often, till his purpose with our souls embodied is accomplished—then He says "Off brakes!" the steam rushes on—the boiler explodes. I would so like to talk tonight with some one who would say with quick, emphatic gesture: "I understand! I've felt so too!" "Be Ceasar to thyself."[6] The words are brave, but tonight I am too tired to say them heartily. I'll pray to God—& go to sleep. Ah! "Go to sleep." There is another & one of the profoundest of mysteries.

1. Willard quoted from Henry Wadsworth Longfellow, "Sandalphon," in *The Courtship of Miles Standish* (Boston, 1858), line 44.

2. Beginning on 27 April 1863, General Hooker, commander of the Union Army of the Potomac, moved to enter Virginia in order to take Richmond. The army entered the Virginia wilderness on 29 April and the next day camped at Chancellorsville. Alert to the threat posed by the Union forces in Virginia, General Robert E. Lee quickly gathered his Confederate army outside of Chancellorsville, to block Hooker's further progress. From 1 May through 4 May, Lee's and Hooker's armies fought the Battle of Chancellorsville, with the Confederates finally gaining the advantage. Given the outcome of the battle, Willard's description of Hooker's triumphal march becomes unintentionally ironic.

3. Willard referred to Evanston.

4. Willard referred to the Old Testament Book of Job, especially chapters 21–31, where Job, in his misery, contends against God.

5. Heb. 11:6.

6. Willard quoted from Sir Thomas Browne, *Christian Morals,* part 1, section 2 (Cambridge, 1716).

28 May 1863

Rev. Charlie Fowler is married & he with Mrs. F—[1] give a reception in Chicago this evening. It's a queer-queer world. I can not take it in. Eighteen months ago I used sometimes idly to scrawl these words on odd bits of paper: "Frances E. Fowler." "Frank F.—" &c. And now without any emotion I have heard of the woman who has taken the place I might have had. She is a noble girl—Miss Scull knew her at Lima.[2] Her name is Emma Warner. I always pray for Mr. F—. I promised that I would. Last night I just put in his wife's name too, & prayed very earnestly that they might love each other—that they might be happy and good.

And do I ever get tired of waiting for "Philip"? Or have I forgotten,—& has my need for him ceased? Oh no, I'm quite too human for *that*—but since I came off here I am some way benumbed. Though happy and thoroughly complacent toward my life, I'm some way stupid & hardly can imagine what loving words would be—or how

I should feel to get them again. Even Ada seems far off;—part of another life than this & our past & dead save to memory. I do not wish this, but with my concrete nature it can't be helped. After awhile I shall go away to the strange, unknown kind of Life, & then shall "mind things" even less than I do now.

1. Esther Ann Warner (1837–66) married Charles Fowler on 25 May 1863. Before her marriage she attended Genesee Wesleyan College (where she was a classmate of Fowler's), gaining proficiency in Latin, Greek, Hebrew, French, and German. She graduated in 1859 with an A.B. degree, and received the A.M. in 1862. Between 1859 and 1863 she was preceptress at two seminaries for girls, Springville Seminary and Lawrenceville Academy. In 1865–66 she was recording secretary of the American Methodist Ladies' Centenary Association and worked closely with Willard, the corresponding secretary. Later in this journal entry Willard mistakenly refers to her as Emma Warner.

2. Genesee Wesleyan Seminary was located in Lima, N.Y. It was a Methodist school founded in 1831 in order to educate young men and women at the preparatory level. In 1850 it expanded to offer a college education as well.

8 June 1863

On this same side of the page, in my "red Journal," one year ago tomorrow I wrote these words:—

"Mary is dead."

One year ago this morning, she died. And I haven't words to write, now that this first return of that awful day has come. "Speech is silver,—silence is golden."[1] In silence I will "think my thoughts." A letter, written to Father & Mother the lonely, heart-aching pair,—shall be my Record of this day. . . .

1. Willard quoted from Thomas Carlyle, *Sartor Resartus* (London, 1833–34), book 3, chapter 3.

12 June 1863

Two weeks from today I start for Home! I am very eager for it—more so than I can tell. I think about it all my spare time. Father & Mother—the house & garden—*Mary's grave.* "Thoughts that do lie too deep for tears"[1] go through me as I think of my changed home—of the pleasant face that is shut out of sight. It is idle to write of it. *Death* is *unspeakably* mysterious & awful. The feeling of this grows stronger in my soul. The terrible sentence rings in my ears! "*I am to die! I am to die!*" . . .

If my little Ada might be with me this summer I should be *very glad.*

I mean to try for it. Of late she writes but seldom—though I know she would be prompt if it were in her power. She has explained to me. I know she loves me dearly—is true as ever. And though I seldom mention her name here I think a great deal concerning her— & love her very tenderly. My need of her presence is not so great— I am being Ceasar to myself—& books are being "all in all" to me. But if she were here, my words & ways would show that she has command of me still-sweet girl of seventeen! . . .

1. Willard paraphrased William Wordsworth, "Intimations of Immortality from Recollections of Early Childhood," in *Poems in Two Volumes* (London, 1807), line 204: "Thoughts that do often lie too deep for tears."

16 June 1863

Pittsburgh is in a ferment, 2000 men working on fortifications. Gen. Lee's army said to be approaching.[1] Marshal law to be declared. Trains from the South forbidden to come to the city, &c. Miss Dole is very much alarmed. The girls are distressed—especially those living to the Southward. But I'm not troubled a bit nor any of the Teachers except Miss Dole. Its quite exciting though. The President has ordered out a hundred thousand men—50 thousand of them from Pennsylvania. There are so many false alarms that it don't do to receive all we hear as "gospel" on any subject. . . .

1. As Lee's Confederate Army crossed the Potomac on 16 June and continued its push north into Maryland and Pennsylvania, Pittsburgh was threatened by invasion. As Willard reported, thousands of civilians from Pittsburgh and the surrounding area turned out to construct earthworks on the hills surrounding the city, and citizens formed Home Defense Committees. General Lee's advance was stopped at the Battle of Gettysburg in early July.

25 June 1863

Dr. Pershing just now called me into the music room and complimented me so much that I must write it here—this is my "safety valve." Ahem! he said my success in the [essay] given before the Alumnae was "wonderful"! He said my essay made a very wonderful impression! That he wanted me to come back! Would make it pleasant for me &c. He said if he had only thought of it in time, he would have had *me* make the address to the Graduating class upon the occasion of their receiving their Diplomas instead of the Rev. H. Johnson,[1] Pastor of one of the first Presbyterian churches here . . . *&* further more that he wanted me to write an account of Commencement for "Tom Eddy's paper,"[2] & insisted on my taking a five dollar bill for the same! So now, in great haste & honest joy, I've written this, & will proceed to prepare the article. Praise—when *meant*—is life to me ("in a sense"!) I'm afraid I think too much about it. Any how, I know I'm glad & would like those who love me to know.

1. Herrick Johnson (1832–1913) was the pastor of the Third Presbyterian Church in Pittsburgh from 1862 to 1867 and later became professor of homiletics at McCormick Theological Seminary in Chicago, serving from 1883 to 1908.

2. Thomas Mears Eddy (1823–74) was an MEC minister and editor of the *Northwestern Christian Advocate,* an MEC newpaper, from 1856 to 1868. He was the older brother of Willard's friend Jennie (Eddy) Somers.

1 January 1866
Evanston

At Mrs. Farwell's.[1] Mrs. F., Kate Jackson & I rec'd calls together. The day was spent most pleasantly save that all of us felt the effects of "Watch Night"[2]—Kate & I, at least, having been awake till three o'clock, I suppose. We had thirty-six calls. In the evening the usual Prayer Meeting for those desiring or possessing Holiness[3] was held here. I enjoyed it very much. Thank God! I have begun this Year by consecrating myself to Him whose right it is perfectly to control my heart.

1. Ebenette M. Smith Farwell (1837–1905) was a member of the MEC in Evanston, although she did not move permanently to Evanston until 1876. She was a church leader and, partly because of the business prominence of her husband, Simeon Farwell (he was a partner in the Chicago dry-goods firm John V. Farwell and Co.), she was an Evanston social leader as well. Willard boarded with the Farwells during part of 1865 and 1866.

2. The first watch nights were held in England and were evening prayer vigils. John Wesley, Methodism's founder, heard of the practice and encouraged it, considering such night meetings to be like the ancient Christian practice of vigils. Among Methodists in the United States, the prayer vigil evolved, becoming a New Year's Eve service to welcome in the new year.

3. Willard referred to the Holiness movement in nineteenth-century Protestantism, particularly Methodism, which focused on the believer's experience of a second birth in Christ, called, variously, sanctification, the baptism of the Holy Spirit, or Christian perfection. By receiving sanctification, the believer was relieved of the "sin in believers," thus going beyond the experience of forgiveness for sins to a purification of the heart. Prayer meetings were conducted to encourage believers to experience sanctification and dedicate themselves anew to Christ.

6 January 1866

Felt hardly so well as usual. Kate was here nearly all day. I *wish* I could talk to her so as to lead her into right conceptions of what religion is. Dear Friend!—my truest & best! She does not see her way—she has no feeling—no comfort—nothing but *purpose*. But that is a great deal. If she prays much & reads the Revelation of the Divine Will concerning us, she will be lead. I wish to speak no word that may do her harm. O, Lord, set Thou a watch over my lips![1]—In the eve. worked with Mr. Smart[2] on Centenary documents of the Ladies Assoc.

1. Willard paraphrased Ps. 141:3, "Set a watch, O Lord, before my mouth; keep the door of my lips."
2. James Shirley Smart (1825–92) was an MEC minister, general agent for GBI, and general agent for the American Methodist Ladies' Centenary Association, which raised funds to build a dormitory for GBI. During the fall of 1865, officers had been chosen, and Willard had been elected corresponding secretary then.

12 January 1866

Went to the city. Came home on "Funeral Train"[1]—went to College on an errand then to Dr. Raymond's[2] to Ladies' Prayer Meeting. Mrs. Palmer & Mrs. Hamline conducted the exercises which were to me, very interesting. My dear Mother goes to all the meetings & seems very much interested. She has lead the most unselfish life of any one that I have known, but wishes a more active *faith*. My earnest prayer is that we may all be more & more like Christ—our Divine *Exemplar*— This is what life is for—To *be* & to *do good*. Whatever I forget, may I remember this.

1. The funeral train was the train that the Chicago and North-Western Railroad ran daily from Chicago to Evanston, stopping at Rose Hill Cemetery. Often, one car of the train would be reserved for a coffin and mourners, who would disembark at Rose Hill, where a horse-drawn hearse stood ready to convey the coffin to the gravesite.
2. Miner Raymond (1811–97) was an MEC minister and professor. From 1864 to 1867 he was pastor at the Evanston MEC, and from 1864 to 1897 he was professor of systematic theology at GBI. His home was just a few blocks from the new home Josiah Willard built in 1865.

14 January 1866

In A.M. a Temperance Sermon by Rev J. C. Stoughton.[1] I was interested & profited by it, & resolved to be more active in this matter. In P.M. Sabbath School. My class behaved well & seemed interested. I am much attached to my twelve girls—two of whom were once my *sister's* scholars. Then S.S. Prayer Meeting. Then Dr. & Mrs. Palmer's Meeting at Mrs. Farwell's. This I especially enjoyed. I do not fully comprehend the doctrine of Holiness, but feel no opposition to it

& wish to know & *feel* more of it. In eve. Dr. & Mrs. P conducted the exercises at church. They were very impressive. Think of half the church full rising & going to the altar as a sign they would be *better.* That chant "The Martyrs overcame by the blood of the Lamb."[2] I shall never forget!

1. Jonathan Clapp Stoughton (1820–1900) was a MEC minister and from 1865 to 1867 was the temperance missionary for the Rock River Annual Conference.

2. A line from the hymn "Glory to the Lamb," which was often sung at Methodist camp meetings and revivals.

15 January 1866

. . . I wish I understood not what anybody in particular thinks, but what is the truth about "the full assurance of faith."[1] Is it instantaneous or progressive? Can one be free from inward temptation? This is "a deep" to me. Surely if I pray & am teachable, & bring forth in my daily living "fruits meet for repentance"[2] I shall not be left unenlightened? Dear Susie Lunt[3] brought me home through the storm & I went to bed & to thoughts of God which melted away into a long, peaceful sleep. To please Him—to glorify *Him*—is my ardent desire & prayer.

1. Willard was struggling to understand the debate that raged in Methodist circles, between the Wesleyans, who held to progressive sanctification, and the Palmerites, those who, like Walter and Phoebe Palmer, believed in instantaneous, attainable sanctification. According to John Wesley's view of progressive sanctification, entire sanctification was the moment when the believer gained perfect love, or "fulfillment of faith's desire to love God above all else and all else in God, *so far as conscious will and deliberate action are concerned*" (Albert C. Outler, *John Wesley* [New York: Oxford University Press, 1964], 32). For Wesley, perfection meant that a person was delivered from sinning voluntarily against God; the will was perfected in its intention to love God, though sin remained part of a person's actions. When a person experienced conversion, the process of sanctification began, the process of becoming more and more dead to sin and alive to Christ. Wesley believed, unlike Phoebe Palmer, that although believers hoped for the full appearance of faith (entire sanctification), they almost never attained it in this present life. The Palmers and other Holiness leaders believed that justification by faith absolved believers of their sin, and this was followed by sanctification, a second stage in the conversion process, in which one's sinful nature was transformed. When one would "lay oneself on the altar" (gave oneself unreservedly to Christ), one could lead a completely sinless life.

2. Matt. 3:8.

3. Susan Augusta Lunt was a student at the NWFC during the 1865–66 school year.

18 January 1866

Wrote essay for the Temperance Alliance.[1] Am becoming much interested in the subject of Temperance & hope to be of some little service on the right side "in this connection." In P.M. went to the College to hear Kate examine her class in Ceasar. Was proud of my dear friend's thorough, faithful teaching as evinced by the ready recitations of her pupils. Came home to the P.M. prayer meeting conducted by Dr. & Mrs. Palmer here, daily. It was well attended—the rooms being filled to overflowing. I enjoyed it very much. Dear Dr. Bannister declared himself fully for "the sanctification of believers."[2] Vainly should I attempt to describe this meeting & the one held in the eve. at wh. my dear Mother & Joe Elbert[3]—with very many others—were at the altar.

1. The Evanston Temperance Alliance was formed around 1860 by Evanston residents, who held meetings in their homes. A very early draft of Willard's temperance speech appears in a journal volume for 1864–65, which contained a few brief entries. The text of the speech with accompanying headnotes can be found in Slagell, "A Good Woman Speaking Well," 110–16.

2. Dr. Henry Bannister of GBI was apparently a supporter of the "Palmerites" in the controversy over Holiness doctrine.

3. Josephine (Evans) Elbert (1844–68) was the daughter of John Evans, one of the founders of Evanston and governor of the Colorado Territory from 1862 to 1865, and Hannah P. (Canby) Evans (d. 1850). While living in Denver, "Joe" Evans met Samuel Elbert, the attorney general of Colorado, and married him in 1865. She was probably in Evanston for a visit in winter 1866 because one of her stepmother's sisters lived in Evanston. In a later entry Willard noted that "Joe" Elbert died in childbirth in fall 1868.

24 January 1866

. . . It is very pleasant to me to have Kate here. I feel great tenderness for her. The wonderful love she bears me, has won my heart, at last. I must be *stone* if it would not. Only in books have I seen anything like it—save in one case—M. for my brother. She need not fear that I will be false or unmindful of what I owe her. *I love her* dearly & will do what I can for her happiness. . . .

28 January 1866

. . . In Mrs. Hamline's room, Mother, Mrs. Farwell, Mrs. H. & I had a prayer meeting with Kate & Joe for their conversion. We were there 3 hours, Joe was on her knees most of that time & the two poor children prayed aloud for themselves all the time, nearly. We prayed several times, each of us, & sang hymns, & talked with them. Their cries & entreaties could be heard all over the house, I think, especially Joe's, who, in agony cried out, again & again, after trying to exercise faith: "I would—O, I would—but I dont know how—*I don't know how!*" It was heart rending to see them & we all moaned together. I was half beside my self. My dear Kate kept saying "Thou hast said it— thou art my Saviour—save me! Save me!" I shall never, never forget the inexpressible sadness of the scene. In the eve. we went to church & they went to the altar. Poor children—they seem to "find no light." It must certainly come to them soon. We are all earnestly praying.

7 February 1866

. . . I went to see Nettie Fowler[1] & had a pleasant talk about going to Lima. Through letters written by the Principal of the Wesleyan Seminary there to Mrs. Dr. Raymond,[2] Prof. Kistler[3] & others, I have come to know that there is talk of my being invited to be Preceptress of the Seminary there—& have four hundred young ladies under my care! I should teach but three hours per day—have a nice suite of rooms, & the most pleasantly situated. It looks a great undertaking, but is, perhaps, ordered by Heaven. . . .

1. Esther (Warner) Fowler was nicknamed "Nettie."
2. Elizabeth (Henderson) Raymond (1814–77) was born in Ireland and married Miner Raymond in 1837. The couple had five children. The Raymond family moved to Evanston in 1864 when Dr. Raymond became professor of theology at GBI.
3. Louis Kistler (1835–1904) was born in Strasburg, Germany, and came to the United States around 1896. In 1864 he became professor of Greek language and literature and, later, professor of political science at NU, remaining at the school for fourteen years. In 1878 he began to practice law, and in 1883 he was appointed a justice of the peace.

13 February 1866

All day working at directing envelopes for my lithographed letter & pamphlet[1]—one of each goes to each minister's wife "in all the wide countree."[2] My girls[3] are out in force, to help me. Thirty different persons have helped me more or less & I shall not forget this token of affectionate regard on the part of "our young folks"—most of them my former pupils. Father, Dr. H.[4] Mrs. Farwell & Kate, besides, have helped me today. If, through it all, I kept my faith & love, how happy I should be but I have not the wondrous art!

1. On behalf of the American Methodist Ladies' Centenary Association, Willard sent a form letter to Methodist pastors' wives to enlist their help in gathering funds for the Association. Included with the letter she probably sent a small card, on one side of which was printed a facsimile of the certificate that each person who paid ten dollars or more would receive. The back of the card listed the goals of the association along with the terms on which subscriptions could be purchased.

2. Willard probably paraphrased Samuel Taylor Coleridge, "The Rime of the Ancient Mariner," in *Lyrical Ballads* (London, 1798), line 570: "And now, all in my own countree."

3. Willard referred to the girls in her Sunday School class.

4. Leonidas P. Hamline (1829–97), Melinda Hamline's stepson, was a physician, a Methodist, and an Evanston neighbor of Willard's who occasionally helped out with Centenary Association work.

14 February 1866

. . . This morning when my "right-hand man" Dr. Hamline came to help me awhile before going to the city, he said with his hectoring "uppishness" that I couldn't "finish up" today, & I replied with some asperity that he would see. So Father, Ella Bannister, Sunie [?] Lowell, Allie Beveridge, Belle Pearsons, Fred Raymond & Fred Smart[1] & I proceeded to make a day of it, & write, fold & put up at an unprecedented rate. By dint of constant work of most of us, the directing was all done—& nearly twelve thousand documents were "well nigh" prepared for the Post.

1. The young people Willard listed were Ellen Frances Bannister, Susan Grey Lowell, Alla May Beveridge, Lucy Isabella Pearsons, Frederick Dwight Raymond, and Frederick A. Smart, members of her Sunday School class who volunteered to help her with Centenary Association work.

27 February 1866

In the city at the regular Centenary meeting for the month—I like these "variations" in my life very much. Was never employed so much "to my mind" as now. Its the "top of life" & the perfection of occupation. . . . Went to Nettie Fowler's to dinner & up in the study, she, "Charlie" & I had a cozy 2 hours talk & made the affair (N. & C.) all straight. It seems pleasantly queer for us three to be friends so good—so frank—as we are. I hope it may be so always for I like them both.

14 March 1866

Last night, as I lay in my little bed, alone in the darkness, praying to the Changeless Friend, the Compassionate Redeemer, lovely feelings, new & strong filled my heart. Even on the evening that I have prized most, they were not so intense. I lost all thought but of God my Father & Saviour from sin & its effects. It was wonderful—blissful & strange. To dwell in God! To "perfectly love Him—worthily to magnify His holy name"[1]—to have a conscience void of offence—to exhibit the fruits of the blessed spirit—these are my ardent desires & hopes—& *expectations.*

1. Willard quoted from the Collect (short prayer) used in the Methodist Order of Worship before celebrating Communion.

19 March 1866

So it seems I am to go to Lima next, in my peregrinations about the country! A very pleasant letter came today from Prof. Bennett,[1] with this paragraph: "So we understand that you accept the Preceptresship of the Genesee Wesleyan Seminary at Lima, N.Y. at a salary of $700. per year, to begin your labors Aug. 23, 1866."

I regard this as the will of God concerning me. I did not seek for it—was not anxious in the least, about it, either way. I ardently wish to do good among my pupils that are to be, & by God's grace I may.

1. Charles Wesley Bennett (1828–91), an MEC minister, was principal and professor of mental and moral philosophy at the Genesee Wesleyan Seminary from 1856 to 1858 and from 1864 to 1866. He was also professor of natural science from 1854 to 1862. He left the position to study in Europe before Willard began teaching in New York, but she became acquainted with him in Berlin in fall 1868. In 1871 he was elected professor of history and logic at Syracuse University (where Genesee Wesleyan College had been moved), and he spent the remainder of his career there.

10 April 1866

Letter from Lima, signifying that my dear Kate can go with me in August.[1] This makes the situation most desirable. With *religion & Kate* I can make a success of the new enterprise—do good & please *the Master. . . .*

1. Willard had asked Principal Bennett if Jackson could accompany her to Lima and have a position teaching French at the school. The administrators agreed to her request.

17 April 1866

I shall never, never forget how, yesterday, the clouds dispersed from my mind—the light that never was on sea or shore shown into my dark heart, & Jesus, man's Saviour, was revealed to me as I had not before seen Him *for myself.* So now, to use dear Mother's favorite illustration, "I am like air to sunshine";—that is, I am continually helped to yield my being as the medium through which Christ's strength & righteousness may shine. This is all that I do, or can do, or, thanks be to God!—am *wished* to do. The hand of *faith* grasps the spotless robe of my Redeemer—the eye of faith rests on His matchless face—the heart of faith murmurs "Not as I will, but as *thou wilt* O, Saviour!"[1]

1. Willard paraphrased Jesus' prayer in the Garden of Gethsemane, Matt. 26:39, "O my Father, if it be possible, let this cup pass from me: nevertheless not as I will, but as thou wilt." (This is also found, slightly differently, in Mark 14:36.)

27 April 1866

"Bro. Smart"—genial, whole-souled man came to report & encourage & talk generally. I like him very much & believe he is a good friend of mine. In P.M. he drove Mrs. Haskin's[1] establishment around with herself & Mrs. Hamline inside it, & took me in to go to the University Grove & see the site just selected by the committee—Dr. Eddy, Bp. Kingsley, Grant Goodrich &c. for *Heck Hall*[2]—wh. is soon to be built. It was quite a pleasant thing to make a memory of. . . .

1. Mary Filer (Geer) Haskin (1826–95) was a prominent Evanston citizen, the wife of a Chicago businessman, and treasurer of the American Methodist Ladies' Centenary Association. In 1868 she initiated the organization of the Ladies Educational Association with the goal of establishing a women's college in Evanston. Part of that association subsequently became the Board of Trustees for the Evanston College for Ladies, with Haskin as its first president.
2. Thomas Eddy, MEC Bishop Calvin Kingsley (1812–70), and Grant Goodrich (1811–89) were part of the committee who selected the site for the new GBI dormitory funded by the Centenary Association. Eddy and Goodrich were members of the Board of Trustees of GBI, and Kingsley was a member of the General Centenary Committee for the MEC. In June 1866 a location was selected and in July ground was broken for construction. The building was named for Barbara Ruckle Heck (1734–1804), who initiated one of the earliest Methodist meetings in America.

2 May 1866

Mary B. Willard, Denver City, Col. has a darkeyed, dark haired daughter born Apr. 13, & named *Frances Ella*[1]—for its eldest & next to the eldest Aunt. This is a pleasant piece of news, & her letter, recently written, was kind & sisterly. As I make this entry, imagination fails me while I try to remember & feel that *once* in the center of my heart's heart was this young woman,—the wife of Oliver, the italicized *Mary* of five years ago. Ah life is strange & rich & well worth passing through. To me,—I write the words with reverent, submissive earnestness, I only wish, all to myself, it were richer *by one*. Is that "the cry of the human"?

1. Frances Ella Willard was born 13 April 1866 to Mary Bannister Willard and Oliver Willard. In the Willard family Bible, the name "Kate" appears beside her given name, Frances Ella. Apparently her name was later changed to Katherine, which is the name that appears on her gravestone in Rose Hill Cemetery.

24 May 1866

I say here that Kate J. is one of my "great deeps." So loyal to me—so true & loving hearted, yet so trivial in her talk, so far from being fond of what I like best, intellectually & morally. After the scenes of last winter, wh. I can never forget—after the prayers & tears,—she seems unfeeling in the things that concern eternity;—religious conversation is irksome to her & she does not, apparently try, much, to put her faith in active exercise. The plan is for her to go to Lima with me, but how can I risk so much for myself & my pupils, as a constant, intimate, deleterious influence. O to be in daily converse with a best human Friend whose mind was serene & wise with earthly & heavenly wisdom! Will it ever be? Jesus in Heaven, & this *One* on earth, to guide me! . . .

[*In late spring 1866, Willard's brother, Oliver, returned to Evanston from Denver, Colorado, where he had been an MEC minister since fall 1862. For the first several years of his ministry he was successful and respected, having been appointed presiding elder in 1863, and responsible for overseeing the development of Methodism in eastern Colorado, as well as pastoring the first Methodist congregation in Denver. He was active in the life of the denomination, helping to found the first Methodist secondary school in eastern Colorado and serving on its board of trustees.*

By 1866, however, he had a serious drinking problem and large debts, probably incurred as a partner with John M. Chivington (1821–94), a former MEC pastor, in a freight-hauling venture. Chivington had been assigned to the Colorado Territory in 1860 and resigned his ministry in order to enlist in the Union Army. After the Civil War, Chivington returned to the Colorado Territory and began a freighting business with government contract work in which Oliver Willard became a partner. The route for mule trains owned by Chivington and Willard ran between the Missouri River and the Rocky Mountains. Chivington and Willard's freighting business lasted until 1867.

On 20 June, two weeks after Oliver Willard's arrival in Evanston, the Rocky Mountain Annual Conference met and, at his request, removed him from the active ministry. The Willard family was deeply troubled by Oliver's condition and anxious to help him in any way it could.]

7 June 1866

Oliver suddenly made his appearance this morning, looking care-worn & thin. All day a load has been upon my heart, & a great one upon Mother's, as I know by her words & face,—for his sake. So involved as he is in business—& we knowing so little about him in this respect—it is a great deep. It has come to this:—that we can help him only by way of prayer.—My faith lays hold on Heaven for my brother, with unusual strength. . . .

2 July 1866

. . . Rec'd official announcement from Board of Trustees, *Lima*, of unanimous election as Preceptress. Also news that at Pittsburgh Fem. Coll. Commencement, Grace Greenwood Miss Thickstun & I rec'd "degree" (!) of M.E.L.[1] Dr. Pershing must still be, my very good friend. . . .

1. Grace Greenwood was the pen name of Sara Jane Clarke Lippincott (1823–1904), a novelist, journalist, and lecturer. Miss N. M. Thickstun was preceptress of the Preparatory Department at the Pittsburgh Female College. Along with Willard, they received honorary Mistress of English Literature degrees from the college.

6 July 1866

. . . Our constant thought is *Oliver*—the noble, gifted boy who really is in great jeopardy, in many ways. That wild western country has wreaked its vengeance on him. Since Mary's death—no, without excepting that, our hearts have never had a load like this. Mary is *safe*. . . .

8 July 1866

. . . Went to see Oliver at Dr. B's[1] after S.S. He was lying on the bed in the south room with Shakspeare beside him, & his poor face red & swollen. It was a long, frank talk we had—part of the time both of us walking to & fro. I told him all my secret thoughts & our distress about him & he was more self-accusing & distressed than words can show. Once the tears fell from his eyes, poor boy! . . .

1. Oliver Willard was staying with his in-laws, the Bannisters, while in Evanston.

9 July 1866

. . . Father & Oliver went to the city to fix the conditions of the loan for Kean.[1] I liked to see them walking off side by side as I have seen them often. Poor, noble-hearted, unfortunate Oliver! Who can solve the problem of his tangled life? We can but pray—& this I do, in *faith*. Mother tearfully calls him "our beautiful possibility." Our three hearts, here at home, have but one feeling—one constant anxiety & hope. . . .

1. Oliver and Josiah Willard arranged for a loan with Samuel A. Kean, Josiah Willard's banking partner. Kean remained a friend of Frances Willard throughout her life.

13 July 1866

. . . *Oliver did what will save him* & give us comfort—at last.[1]

1. On 13 July 1866 Oliver Willard signed a temperance pledge.

26 August 1866
Des Plaines, Illinois

A great day, 10,000 persons on the grounds.[1] Dr. Eddy preached a *Holy Ghost* sermon. I greatly enjoy the songs, the prayers, the experiences, the sermons, my heart is full of love for our Holy religion. God has made it the aim of my life *to be & to do good*. I am baffled in my effort to give any conception of what these sweet & sacred things are to me; of what this meeting is from which I go to strangers & to unaccustomed toil. *God help me to be true to Thee!* . . .

1. Willard attended the Des Plaines Camp (Methodist) Meeting (also called the Chicago Camp Meeting), which was located beside the Des Plaines River about sixteen miles northwest of Chicago. Camp meetings were annual revival services held in the open air, often in a wooded setting and near a river, and sometimes lasting for a week or more, where Methodists (and several other Protestant denominations) revitalized their faith by listening to sermons, singing hymns, and joining the altar calls. Walter and Phoebe Palmer, Melinda Hamline, Governor John Evans and Margaret Evans, and other Methodist notables attended the 1866 Des Plaines Camp Meeting.

28 August 1866

How long & pleasantly I shall remember this week of wood's life with so many of my friends, when our time is spent in thinking of the same things that will occupy our minds when we are all together in Heaven! I go around with Mary Bragdon[1] getting autographs & a hundred pleasant words are spoken, & my heart feels how truly I am attached to these nice people whom I have known for years. . . . This A.M. we had a large "experience meeting"[2] that was very pleasant. . . .

The closing exercises were memorable. Shall I ever be there again? It does not matter if God is friendly to me! O, may He be for Jesus' sake! My Darling Kate whom I do truly *love* has made me very happy. She has determined to *be good* & praying for aid—feeling or no feeling. Now she will be strength & not weakness to her well beloved friend!—Went to the city at 10.30, singing all the way in the cars, 4 seats full of us. Sweet sacred thoughts came to me of Heaven & of our singing there. O, Jesus, save us, Thou who lovest us from the foundation of the world![3] Delightful meeting, over.

1. Mary (Bragdon) Shepherd (1843–1918) was the daughter of the late Rev. Charles P. Bragdon and Sarah (Cushman) Bragdon. She was an Evanston neighbor of Willard's and graduated from NWFC in 1861 in the Scientific Course. She married William T. Shepherd in 1867.

2. An experience meeting was a time during which people testified to each other about their spiritual life.

3. Willard paraphrased a portion of John 17:24b, "that they may behold my glory which thou hast given me: for thou lovest me before the foundation of the world."

30 August 1866
Evanston

Last evening, sitting beside Kate, as usual, in the car, I glanced over the Evening Journal & saw the death of Mrs. Charles H. Fowler.[1] It shocked me greatly, & the more because she died in child-birth, poor young thing,—so frail & small. I thought of Charlie & the past—the long, long past, stretching behind us. May God comfort him & lead him to a more consecrated life! Nettie is in Heaven. Ah well! We are to go so soon—so very soon—it does not matter. Let me live for *eternity* & God. "All other life is mad, & vain."

1. Willard read the announcement of Nettie Fowler's death on 29 August 1866 in that day's issue of the *Chicago Evening Journal.*

31 August 1866

All day with Father's kind & efficent help, I "sorted out the Centenary."—Made Annual Report etc. & Mr. Requa[1] & I carried over the numerous documents to Katie[2] who succeeds me. The year has been to me pleasant & valuable. I have learned much about business—about our church—have had correspondence with its dignitaries—etc. I am deeply grateful for this calm year in which God has comforted me in many ways & lead me nearer *Him.* Charles Fowler's wife—is to be buried this rainy, dark afternoon. How life unwinds!—

Dear Nettie Fowler! I loved her living,—I think sadly of her sad death. God keep us all!

1. James Requa (1829–1905) was a senior at GBI who became an MEC minister, serving in the Wisconsin Annual Conference and then in the East Genesee (N.Y.) Annual Conference.
2. Kate Kidder served as the manager for the American Methodist Ladies' Centenary Association at the Evanston MEC in 1865–66. She took over Willard's job of corresponding secretary of the association when Willard left to become preceptress at Genesee Wesleyan Seminary.

1 September 1866

Nice Mrs. Haskin—my very good friend—had a party last night, partly for Kate & my sake. It was quite large   all the young folks were there. . . . I thought how nice it was to be of such society—where thoughts of Jesus are never amiss.—Am not well. Am very busy getting ready to go. One week from now shall be far off from Mother. . . .

2 September 1866

Walked over to Church with "our folks" for the last time. Bent my head in silent prayer as usual on taking my seat between Father & Mother in the familiar pew, & prayed that I might be good;—given up to God & things eternal. O may I *"grow in grace"*[1] & be helped in the guidance of my new pupils. . . . Then, Class Meeting. Then our lunch, up here, *we three,* alone.—Father sits here reading the "Centenary Pictorial"[2]—Mother listening to him. So passes my last Sabbath at home. In eve my dear Kate 2 joined the church 1 & was baptized. The ceremony was most impressive. So ends my last Sabbath.

1. Willard paraphrased 2 Peter 3:18a, "But grow in grace, and in the knowledge of our Lord and Savior Jesus Christ."
2. This book (New York, 1866) marked American Methodism's centennial.

4 September 1866

My last home day. In A.M. The whole family laid under contribution to pack my trunks. Took pictures, books, vases, brackets &c.—to father's scandalization! In P.M. at 3 o cl'k K & I went out & in about 3 hours made 25 goodbye calls. . . . I could write a whole day of all our experiences & fancies during these calls. Of the last sight of the lake & of a 100 pleasant faces. Came home tired—K. here to tea. At 7.30 in came 35 of our best friends & the delightfulest *surprise party* in the world went forward until 11 o clock. The generous Taylors[1] & Mrs. Bragdon[2] did it all! 4 Charades were acted—Lima—Baggage—Surprise & Farewell—the last the best I ever saw. . . . We sang "When shall we meet again" & Dr. Raymond (whom I love), prayed, simply & beautifully alluding to K & me.

1. Edward S. Taylor (1836–1905) and Julia B. Taylor (ca. 1847–90) boarded with the Willards at their home until they bought a house in Evanston. In 1871 they built a house just down the street from the Willards. Edward Taylor was a prominent lawyer and Republican politician.
2. Sarah (Cushman) Bragdon (1816–1900) was the widow of Charles P. Bragdon, Willard's former minister, and a close neighbor. She was a good friend of the Willards for all the years she lived in Evanston.

5 September 1866
en route to Churchville, New York

Wednesday A.M. My last home morning.—Leave at 10.30 A.M. Last breakfast & morning prayers. Father read the 7th Chapter of Hebrews. Father is now locking the trunks. . . . Ever so many at Depot to see us off. Came to city, with a party at Kinsley's[1] to dinner. . . . Went up in Art Gallery. . . . Went to a hair-dresser & got me a water fall.[2] Then Father, Kate & I walked over to the "Michigan Southern" Depot.[3] Took sleeping car—sat up till 8 o cl'k. Went by the sand hills & sloughs & Calumet ("head of the lake")[4] where we came in wagons from Ohio, 20 years ago. Father talked of it reminded me of many incidents. Said "How the centuries play with these sands" as we passed the curious hills.

1. Kinsley's Restaurant was founded by Herbert M. Kinsley in 1865. It was located on the first floor of Crosby's Opera House on Washington Street, west of State Street in downtown Chicago.
2. A waterfall was a type of chignon, popular in the 1860s, in which the hair cascaded from a knot on top of the head to the nape of the neck. This was arranged with a woman's own hair, or with false hair, as a separate hair piece.
3. The Michigan Southern Depot was in downtown Chicago, located on Van Buren Street, between Clark and Sherman streets.
4. In 1866, Calumet, south of Chicago, was a subdivision of Hyde Park.

9 September 1866
Churchville

. . . Father, Uncle[1] & I went up to "the Farm"—the Willard homestead—2 miles from the village, "Up North." Passed the house—2 doors from here—where I was born—passed the "Hall" place where

Caroline Elizabeth[2] my sister (between Oliver & I) was born—passed the "Lane place"[3] where Mother's first baby[4] was born—the "stone church"[5] where she & father went all through their first 30 years of life—the school-house where they were educated—to father's old home a large stone farmhouse where Mother's first married days were spent. Ah my thoughts,—my thoughts! Father was full of incidents— He—Uncle & I sat in the old kitchen two or 3 hours talking. . . . I think of *history*—here—where all my relatives on both sides, have spent their lives. . . .

1. Zophar Willard (1809–90) was Frances Willard's father's younger brother. He lived in Churchville, N.Y., and was a merchant as well as a prominent community leader. During his long life in Churchville, he held the offices of town supervisor, town clerk, justice of the peace, postmaster, and school trustee.
2. Caroline Elizabeth Willard (1837–38) was the third child born to Mary (Hill) Willard and Josiah Atherton Willard. She lived only fourteen months.
3. The "Lane place" was Willard's parents' house when they lived in Churchville.
4. Willard's parents' first child, an unnamed daughter, died at birth, 16 December 1832, when they were living in Ogden, N.Y.
5. The stone church to which Willard referred was her parents' church in Ogden, N.Y., a Union church (Congregational and Baptist) built in 1832.

10 September 1866

. . . In the P.M. visited the old historic cemetery "up north" & saw the graves of my two little sisters, of my grandparents on both sides . . . & many others—pastors & people who were friends of my nearest friends. . . . O my *thoughts*—this little book wont let me put them down. I see *crushed lives* around me;—I see unfulfilled possibilities—unfed capacities—& think of the eternal years that surely, all things will restore, with thankful heart. . . . A great deal of reminiscence is going forward for our benefit in this calm household. I like very much to hear about my relatives who have always lived here together,—Father, only, having (fortunately!) strayed away. I look across the yard to the house where I was born—& think of several lives,— & mine. On no account would I live here, or hereabouts. . . .

15 September 1866
Lima, New York

. . . Took the cars from the pleasant Churchville depot for Rochester—walked across from the city terminus of the road to Depot of Genesee Valley R.R.—took cars for Avon—thence by stage (my first stage ride) 7 miles to Lima—the driver blowing his horn as we entered the town in good old fashioned style. Father & I kept a "bright look out,"—saw a fine brick hotel & bank—churches of brick, with towers & steeples—fine residences here & there, & crowning a high, handsome, tree-covered hill in the midst of all, the Seminary & College buildings. Drove through pleasant streets to Rev. A. D. Wilbor's— agent & Treasurer of the Seminary. Were warmly welcomed by Mrs. Wilbor.[1] Had a nice dinner & walked over to the Seminary. . . . Conducted to my rooms—sitting room & bedroom & closet up one flight of stairs, on the front of the building—nicely furnished—Brussels carpet—nice "couch"—pretty bedroom (matched) furniture—a fire ready in my stove—houseplants on *my* window &c &c. . . .

1. Albert Dutton Wilbor (1821–1903), an MEC minister, was treasurer of Genesee Wesleyan Seminary from 1865 to 1875. Mary Ann (Sleeper) Wilbor (1824–1915) was his wife.

18 September 1866

Am sitting here, Tuesday A.M. by *my* front window, very quiet & pleased in my mind. Father went away yesterday, just after breakfast. He stood on the steps before the great front door, held out his hand with his face turned half away & said "Well, *Goodbye;*—take care of yourself & don't get sick." I shall not comment upon my many thoughts & emotions as he walked off with carpet bag in hand—looking gentlemanly & slight & fragile—too much so for my peace. . . . So the bug-bear "Lima" is nothing dreadful, after all!—Have had my first Preceptress-y duties—to welcome a lot of new comers. . . . I am getting acquainted fast, & am not a bit blue. . . . Long & tedious Faculty Meeting in Ladies Parlor, this P.M. Decision that my beloved Kate shall come & take 2 classes thus giving me but one, beside the Compositions—viz. Rhetoric. I am "perfectly delighted"—have written to Kate—the dear, the faithful & the true. . . .

20 September 1866

Today began my "onerous tasks." At 9 A.M. prayers in the Chapel— conducted by the Principal.[1] Afterward I went to my recitation room & spent the forenoon in registering young ladies who brought "scrips" of admission from Mr. Wilbor the Treasurer—after having pd their tuition. I then took name—age—address of Guardian—studies for the term—& number of room in Sem. or if an "out boarder," place of residence. A large no. registered in this way—most of them interesting & attractive. . . .

1. Spencer R. Fuller (1829–70) was an MEC minister and principal of Genesee Wesleyan Seminary from 1866 to 1868.

21 September 1866

. . . Have had several home-sick girls to look after. Poor things! I like my girls & pray that I may do them *good* in all true & pleasant senses, while I am with them. Have been registering, all day. Have rec'd numerous calls on business from numerous strange-faced, pleas-ant-mannered young ladies—a few anxious fathers & Profs. . . . Have given my girls a brief "Chapel Talk" & taken their P.O. addresses. . . . Verdict: that I shall greatly like Lima, when "seasoned."

24 September 1866

. . . Have met my classes for the first time, i.e. Kate's & mine—for she takes 2 of the 3 when she comes. Like my pupils—enjoy my airy recitation room—& think, as I wrote Mother today, *dear, thoughtful Mother,*—I have found my vocation at last—I was meant for a "Pre-ceptress"! . . .

28 September 1866

My birthday. Not a romantic one, either, not to be desired in any way. I don't wait for & rejoice in it as I used to do in the romantic ages of 16-17-18 & 19. But I am thankful still—more thankful than in days of auld lang syne. This has been my *best year*—what a pleas-ant record is this, to make. God will take care of me.—I enjoy life; I am very glad I came to Lima. . . . Had frank talk with Prof. Scoville—cream of the faculty, in my opinion. He's 23 years old—has the true, poetic nature—the rare insight that so attract me & that I meet so very seldom. Had dull Faculty Meeting. I have my own thoughts about our Principal. . . .

3 October 1866

. . . After tea Prof. S[coville] came in at my request, to talk of busi-ness. Had my 3*d* true *conversation* since I've been here, (wh. means my 3*d* with him—since he alone furnishes this rare comfort to my spirit). It was a queer interview. He is one of the 3 or 4 men I have met in my life to whom I could say anything, nearly, & with whom I am never quite *done.* Just think—to "close the meeting," he asked me to pray for him! & so I did, & he—with deepest sincerity. I lent him my Bible & so ended our unique performance, (3 hours long,) by Kate's watch (who was in the bed room—cold & mad & in the dark!)

6 October 1866

Girls—girls—girls—! Question upon question!—Dear me it is no small undertaking to be "Eldest Sister" to the whole hundred & eighty of 'em! But it's pleasant—truly so,—& I don't at all complain. Katharine is an unfailing comfort & assistance. Tried to write on a talk to them but could get no time nor much inspiration. This time I'll extemporize, I guess.—Last eve went up to the room of the L.L.S.[1]— was introduced—the whole society rising at my entrance &c. They treat me beautifully & I think I reciprocate! . . .

1. The Ladies' Literary Society was a club to which the girls of the preparatory branch of Genesee Wesleyan Seminary belonged. It met for various academic exercises, such as debate, lectures, and literature and poetry reading. Willard, as preceptress, was the faculty member responsible for the L.L.S.

12 October 1866

Gave up school—went to bed—*cried* for the first time in 18 months,— because I was "dazed." The sensation is peculiar & very sad. I wish I had time & space to describe it. Now & then for ten years I have been so. It is painless—but makes one almost tired of life. The best description I can give is—I am out of adjustment with everything. An impalpable veil seems to separate me from the beautiful outer world. I know not whence it comes or why. It is occult. At the first opportunity I shall consult a physician who knows. . . . O dear—to be myself!

15 October 1866

Have had letter from Nina Lunt,[1] dated Geneva, Switzerland. What would I give to have her opportunity of life!—for my pet delight is traveling. If a man I should have liked Bayard Taylor's[2] portion, under the sun. I indulge myself with the confident expectation of a European tour.—Kate & I have exchanged solemn promises to live together all our days—married or single, no matter which. This covenant to be dated yesterday. . . .

1. Cornelia Gray Lunt (1843–1934) was the daughter of Orrington Lunt (1815– 97) and Cornelia (Gray) Lunt (1820–1910), two founding members of the Evanston community, although they did not actually move from Chicago, where they had set-

tled in 1843, to Evanston until 1874. Because of her family's wealth, Lunt was able to spend time in Europe, attending school and traveling. She lived in Evanston her entire life and became a cultural leader in the community. Her home was a center of Evanston social life.

2. James Bayard Taylor (1825–78) was an American author and traveler, known for his lively travel narratives.

18 October 1866

Kate & I are getting more & more of the "divine thirst" for knowledge. Kate amuses me. For lo! these many years she has seemed to care not much for these things but now her appetite is ravenous & we "talk learning" all the time. Ah! it saves many idle words. She told me yesterday many new things about her home & history. We are as *near* each other as two hearts well could be in friendship. . . .

20 October 1866

In the A.M. corrected the Essays of the Senior Class. There is in this Institution the least talent for writing, that I have ever, anywhere seen. Their dreary inanities about Hope—Summer & Home are mournful to contemplate. . . .

22 October 1866

. . . Kate says she "never saw the like" of Lima for "meetings." Even Evanston cannot equal it. On Sunday church twice, S[unday] S[chool] & Prayer Meeting. On Monday eve. Ladies Prayer Meeting—Tuesday Class Meeting—Wednesday Prof. Scovilles Bible Class—Thurs. Prayer Meeting of College Church—Friday nothing Saturday Students Prayer Meeting. I doubt if it is not too much—leaving no time for private meditation—our days are so full of occupation. Called on my girls—several of them to talk about *the best things*. O that I may be good to-day!

20 November 1866

. . . While having Rhetoric my eyes gradually closed, & after Business Hour I came down & gave up. Have lain here all day. (This is written days after ward!) Last night I believe I sneezed 40 times at least. I kept it up all night. So I have taken on a cargo termed, hereabouts, "a heavy cold." It is like the affliction of so many others in school. It is particularly unfortunate for me to be sick now, the end of the term being near, & I in much demand. Allie Hubbard[1] put me in a sweat & gave me bone set tea,[2] Ugh! I was too nervous for description. So this day is about lost I suppose.

1. Alice Hubbard, from Geneseo, N.Y., was a student at Genesee Wesleyan Seminary during the 1866–67 school year.
2. Boneset tea was made from the dried leaves of the boneset plant and commonly used in the nineteenth century as an antidote for colds, fever, stomach aches, and general body pain.

25 November 1866

Staid home from Church as I am too apt to do. . . . Alas that I who had such faith & earnestness am a sort of religious paralytic so soon! . . . I have in me no love—for sacred things. I hope that all will be well—that half I have believed of the requirements of Christian life may prove me true. I am somewhat afloat, & without the affinities of one year since. Were it not better that I had died, then? We can not tell. Life is *"a great deep,"*—especially to me now who live on cheaply & carelessly from day to day. Ah if some one wise & kind, firm & assured, would teach me & confirm me in all right ways!

5 December 1866

Just after breakfast went out for a walk with Prof. Scoville—the "dear boy" (as I call him to Kate) & we had talk about school. This young man (aged 24 years) embodies my idea of the heroic—the "what we read of" better than—perhaps—any other man I have known—& that is saying much. He is deeply *in earnest*—he is chivalrous—religious—talented, sufficit. . . .

13 December 1866

This morning Prof. Fuller & I had a direct encounter with Squire Hale—in his little office.[1] I told him that I was never talked to by any one as by him last eve. in reference to two of my pupils etc. He said: "Did I insult you, Madam?" "No," I replied, "I should then have left the room." Prof. F. laid down the law to him plainly—that the *Faculty* controlled this Institution, etc. Hence forth no doubt there is the old & deadly feud between brain & precedent—between stomach & head. . . .

1. Principal Fuller and Willard had a confrontation with David Hale, the steward of the seminary, concerning the issue of whose duty it was to lock and unlock the

dormitory door every evening and morning. Willard refused to do it, arguing that her job was not that of janitor, and Fuller supported her stand. Hale maintained that the preceptresses had always performed the task and insisted that Willard do so.

20 December 1866

Very busy getting ready to go. Numerous good bye & other calls from pupils &c.—the term is over. In all respects successful & pleasant to remember, except, alas, the *best respects*. In these I have every thing, almost, to regret. I hope it may be different next term—but dare not surely say—to think that I should write it—I who one year ago was vastly different in thought & purpose. . . .

21 December 1866
Paterson, New Jersey

Reached Paterson late in the P.M. Mr. J.[1] was there—delighted to welcome his favorite daughter Kate. We drove to their house on Ellison St.[2]—where K. hasn't been in years owing to "family jars" (a step-mother in the case).[3] The home is all she could desire. Her father is rich—& the appointments of the house, in all respects, show the fact. Her sister Carrie is lovely & pretty, I mean—ladylike & so on. Her brothers—might be nice.[4] Her step-mother—is a lady. . . .

1. James Jackson (ca. 1805–69) was a Paterson, N.J., businessman who emigrated from Ireland in the late 1820s. After working as a merchant during the 1820s and 1830s, he became an entrepreneur and financier by the early 1840s, investing in a machine shop around 1842 and producing locomotives by 1848. In 1851 his shop was incorporated as the New Jersey Locomotive and Machine Company, with Jackson as its president. In 1865 he sold his stock in the locomotive company and bought a large interest in the Passaic County Bank, becoming its president. In 1832 he married Caroline Ross Burnett (ca. 1809–53) and they had five children who lived to maturity.

2. The Jackson house was at 77 Ellison Street, Paterson, N.J.

3. After his first wife's death in 1853, James Jackson married Margaret Clark Imlay from Pennsylvania in 1856.

4. Caroline (Carrie) (Jackson) Whitely (ca. 1849–1920) was Kate Jackson's younger sister. In 1870 she married Robert J. Whitely, a physician, and had two children. After her husband's death in 1879, Caroline Whitely moved to Evanston, Ill., to be near her sister Kate. John Ross Jackson (b. ca. 1846), Kate's younger brother, who was known as Ross, became a journalist in San Francisco. James Jackson, Jr., (1841–1903) succeeded his father as president of the Passaic County Bank.

[*During fall 1866 Willard and her friend Kate Jackson dreamed of traveling to Europe together. At Christmas vacation Jackson asked her father if he would pay for them both to make a European trip, starting in July 1867 after the school term was over. Mr. Jackson enthusiastically agreed. Willard wrote her parents to tell them of her opportunity, hoping that they would be as pleased as she at the prospect. However, they were not. Her father, worried about the impropriety and possible danger of two young women traveling alone, did not want Willard to go at all. Her mother could not believe that Mr. Jackson actually proposed to give her daughter the money for a trip. He must mean, her mother wrote, that he would lend her the money. Jackson asked her father to let her know by mail precisely what he intended.*]

11 February 1867
Lima, New York

I will say just here, though thereby I make an anachronism (?) that Mr. Jackson turned out to be all right. Willing for Kate to take me & as explicit as possible about *non-refundum*. I shall be grateful to him throughout my mortal life & shall dedicate my book of travels (that I'm to write!) to Kate. If Father can only be convinced that for me to go, in a Christian family, is nothing dreadful, I shall consider myself the most fortunate person whom I have met.

14 February 1867

The day passed off as usual. My Composition classes are improving greatly. I have all the young ladies in school in this department. This, with a weekly class in Rhetoric is my work as *teacher*. I believe I am doing the girls good—teaching them decency in letter writing—etc. I have them keep everything they do in a book. I make them write on the board—drill them on the mechanical part &c. It is sometimes quite like drudgery. Kate has a hard time with her three classes. . . .

[Kate Jackson]   22 February 1867

. . . Frank didn't finish telling the occurrences of the day so I will. War to the knife is declared between the Hales & Frank. She & Sister Hale[1] had a re-hearing. Mrs Hale told Mr F. at the breakfast table that some young ladies had been out the night before until 2 o'clock & that Frank had better resign if she could not attend to her duties & much more which I have not space to mention. Frank investigated the matter & found the young ladies were all in before the bell rang. So Frank went to Sister Hale to contradict the report & came up from the "bout" much worn out with her exertions. Miss Waite[2] has had a disagreement also, so we all are of one mind on the subject. Frank & I rejoice that we shall not be here next year. The *"Key"* was at the bottom of all.

1. Diantha Hale was the wife of David Hale, the seminary steward.
2. Emma L. Waite from Alexander, N.Y., was the assistant preceptress at the seminary. Waite had begun teaching English at the seminary in 1864 and from 1868 to 1871 was preceptress.

20 March 1867

Kate is a thousand miles away. The true reason is—as I will write for future years—that she & I are such close friends she cannot bear to have me think of any body else as I inevitably think of D[elevan] C. S[coville]. Of course I shouldn't like it, either, if her John[1] should come from Texas & she should have exclusive interviews with him. But still I think my darling friend ought to count it enough that I love her as dearly as I ever did in all our four years friendship. She will, I hope. . . .

1. John Norton was Jackson's fiancé, who was living in Hebron, Conn. Jackson had apparently met him when she was teaching in Texas in the early 1860s. He later fought with the Confederate Army and was a prisoner of war for some time.

[*For over a week, Jackson's poor health was worrisome to Willard. She was in considerable pain and was suffering from insomnia, but she managed to travel with Willard to Churchville, N.Y., to stay with Willard's aunt, Caroline Town, over spring break.*]

7 April 1867
Churchville

A very long & solemncholy day. Kate sick all the time. Dr. Craig[1] came to see her twice. He thinks she should go to some first class physician & be doctored or she wont be able to go to Europe. He praises me for talking English without mincing to him about her case. I tell her I shall name her "Prolapsus"[2] if she goes on at this rate! She is in almost constant pain. . . .

1. James W. Craig (1825–91) was a physician in Churchville, N.Y.
2. Kate Jackson may have had a prolapsed uterus, meaning that the uterus had slipped downward, due to lack of tone of the muscles of the pelvic floor.

8 April 1867
Rochester, New York

Two or three newsy letters from father & Mother. Affairs at home
look dubious. Father has been quite sick—his lungs troubling him
again. Oliver's business is any thing but encouraging. He, poor boy,
has gone again to the far west to look after the mule-trains of the firm
Chivington & Willard. This A.M. K. & I sallied out into the cold
world. . . . Came to the city. Hired a hack for Mrs. Dr. Dolley's,[1] 30,
E. Avenue & here we are domesticated—Kate to be doctored & I to
spend vacation! Years ago Aunt Abigail[2] had Dr.[3] & Mrs. Dr. Dolly
when she was ill of dropsey, so we have knowledge of & confidence
in, them. They live in a handsome house—have the nicest of books
very many that are in Oliver's fine library—& Kate will be well cared
for. . . .

1. Sarah Read (Adamson) Dolley (1829–1909) was a physician in Rochester, N.Y.
One of the first women in the United States to receive a medical degree, she graduated from the Central Medical College in Rochester in 1851. In 1869 she and her
family traveled in Europe for a time with Willard and Jackson, before she took post-
graduate training in Paris during the winter of 1869–70. In 1875 she took more training in the Hôpital des Enfants Malades in Paris and later attended clinics in Prague
and Vienna. She was a professor of obstetrics at the Woman's Medical College of
Pennsylvania in Philadelphia in 1873–74. Returning to Rochester, she resumed her
practice, largely with women and children. In her long life of medical practice and
leadership within the Rochester community and among women doctors, she remained a close friend of Willard's.
2. Abigail (Hill) Willard (1811–57) was Mary (Hill) Willard's younger sister, who
married Zophar Willard, Josiah Willard's younger brother. She lived in Churchville,
N.Y., until her death.
3. Lester Clinton Dolley (1825–72), husband of Sarah (Adamson) Dolley, was a
Rochester physician. Sarah (Adamson) Dolley and Lester Clinton Dolley practiced
together until Lester Dolley's death in 1872.

18 April 1867
Lima, New York

. . . From my dear brother Oliver came a nice long letter—the first
in years. It was all that I could ask for in its manly, tender tone. Poor
boy! He is in great financial trouble—but brave & true & freed from
his great danger wh. we so bewailed. He said: "I should say unquali-
fiedly *go to Europe in July* did I not fear you would return a *fatherless
child*." Oliver knows I will not take that risk—but I so strongly hope
my father may be well again when the warm weather comes. He has
a buoyant constitution—like grandmother—like me. He is better
even now, they write me, & I will be hopeful as I can. . . .

27 April 1867

Dressmakers again. The "European Question" we regard as settled—if Father's health improves as it promises to do, so are getting our dresses under way. A handsome black silk & black alpaca suit now on hand. Took the little stand into the bedroom & wrote all day on the "address" for the Ladies' Literary & on "A voice from the audience" intended by *me* for the *Independent*—whether or not Theodore Tilton will coincide is yet a problem![1] I am thinking nowadays as not before what I may do for women—on a broader scale than heretofore. Is this presumption?

1. Her essay "A Voice from the Audience" was not accepted for publication by the *Independent*.

5 May 1867

Last night was dreadful beyond compare. Kate & I went early to bed on account of her want of health. At midnight or thereabouts we heard groanings—shrieks—cat-howlings—running to & fro—slamming doors & such like dulcet sounds in the hall outside our door & in some girl's room on the opposite side. I have not been in years before so thoroughly frightened. Kate trembled from head to foot. We stood inside our door & listened! Pretty soon Katie (the chambermaid) came to call me—said Miss Swartz[1] had Hysteria.—I put on my wrapper—undid my "crimping pins" & went to the rescue. Dr. Ellis[2] came—Dora[3] was up—we flew around—got hot water—ginger tea &c. She acted very wild but finally quieted down— In AM Lilla & Dell[4] got us a cute little breakfast up here.

1. Izora Swartz, from South Bristol, N.Y., was a student at the Genesee Wesleyan Seminary.
2. Dr. Ellis was a physician in Lima, N.Y., and a friend of the seminary.
3. Dorcas Mead (Hale) Wilbor (1842–1915) was the Hales' daughter, married to the Wilbors' son, Carleton. She taught piano and guitar at the seminary from 1866 to 1868.
4. Lilla S. Munson and Della A. Smith were students at the Genesee Wesleyan Seminary. Munson was from Chapinsville, N.Y., and was listed in the seminary catalogue as Class of 1868 (although she apparently did not graduate that year), and Smith, from Oswego, N.Y., was in the Preparatory Department.

20 May 1867

For the first time in my life I *fasted* as a means of grace. [Delevan Scoville] told me of what service it had often been to him—referred me to the Apostles & the Christian Fathers—to Luther[1] & to Christ himself! I had never thought of it before. Long ago, I remember, when we lived in Oberlin & I was 5 or 6 yrs. old I went without my breakfast (except a dough nut!) because Father advised me to, since it was "Fast Day."—This A.M. the breakfast gong rec'd no attention from me. A little after it, up came Prof. S.—the thoughtful friend that he is!—& talked & prayed with me.—All day I have thought much of my Saviour & prayed that in all things I might do his will. In Lima I have not had a better day. Ah how I hope I may be *steadfast*—I whom am so unsteady. The Bible has new meaning for me—I have certainly begun a better life. After this I shall believe in returning to the Lord in the use of the old & consecrated means—Penitence—*fasting*—& prayer.—Twenty-four hours though (at this time) is all that I believe I could at present bear without being sick & unfitted for my duties.

1. Although the Protestant Reformation leader Martin Luther did not believe fasting was a means of grace (only baptism and Holy Communion were means of grace for Luther), he encouraged its use, in moderation, as a way of controlling the sinful self, and as an appropriate preparation for Holy Communion.

28 May 1867

If I were here in 1867–8—I would endeavor in spite of old fogyism (which flourishes here like a mushroom after a shower) to have Deo Lewis' Gymnastics[1] introduced; to have Mrs. Dr. Dolly lecture the girls on Health; to have a regular play ground set apart for the girls, up on this sacred sward; to have the Ingelow's[2] Room furnished handsomely; to have some room where the girls could sit on rainy days & do all sorts of things undoable under the present order of things. . . .

1. Dioclesian Lewis (1823–86) was a homeopathic physician who advocated physical exercise, especially for women, as a good way to prevent illness. He taught his system of "free gymnastics" and also undertook lecture tours to promote his health ideas, which included temperance. One of his temperance lectures sparked the Ohio Woman's Crusade of 1873–74.
2. The girls' literary society and the room in which it met were named for Jean Ingelow (1820–97), an English poet, novelist, and children's writer popular in the 1860s. When Willard was in London in the summer of 1868 she asked Ingelow to write a letter to the Ingelow Literary Society, and she agreed to do so.

29 May 1867

The Girls' Reading Room I decidedly enjoy. They have all our best magazines—several Dailies—most of the Ch[urch] papers & a few miscellaneous. The room is on my hall—is light & pleasant. I have helped them all I could in this & in every enterprise—I have failed them in nothing save a saintly example & fervently uttered precepts & prayers! Ah, when this is said—all is said.

At Ch[apel] Roll read them my talk on Woman's Lesser Duties[1]— written for Pitts. Fem. Coll. . . .

1. Willard first gave her speech "Woman's Lesser Duties" on 24 April 1963 for the Browning Society at the Pittsburgh Female Seminary. The subject of the speech was home support for the Union troops. She encouraged the young women of the seminary to write to soldiers they knew, letting them know how much people appreciated the sacrifices the young men made on behalf of the Union cause. "Woman's Lesser Duties" is reprinted with headnotes in Slagell, "A Good Woman Speaking Well," 95–109.

26 June 1867

Yesterday came a letter from Mrs T[aylor] in Evanston, detailing Father's symptoms as Mother, (I suppose to save me pain & worry) has refrained from doing. According to the statements made, he is more ill than he has ever been before—though an invalid, always. If my Father's health is in the danger here represented, I shall not go to Europe—I shall go west at the close of this Term. Poor Mr. Jackson! I am so sorry that we keep him in such indecision. Today I wrote my parents that I had concluded to postpone my trip on acct. of Father's health & that I would be at home by the middle of July. "To bear is to conquer our fate."[1]

1. Willard quoted from Thomas Campbell, "Lines Written on Visiting a Scene in Argyleshire," stanza 4, line 9, in an issue of the *Morning Chronicle* (London, 1800).

5 July 1867

Letter from Father saying he believes I shall yet see the disastrous consequences that must have attended my going to Europe &c. He thinks it equivalent to ruin. I do not, & stay solely because of his ill health.—Rehearsed Seniors in College Chapel.[1] Think they will do pretty well. D[elevan] came by appointment of his own. Had long note from him. He says he will come back if I will, or if I will come the year after next, he will stay. . . .

1. As preceptress, Willard was responsible for preparing the graduation ceremonies for the seminary, which took place 11 July 1867. She was busy helping the seniors finish up their essays and coaching them for the public presentation of their work.

10 July 1867

Rose betimes—went to College Chapel & helped put up wreaths—busts—pictures &c. Rehearsed Class Song. . . . Then spent the A.M. hearing them read—in Sem[inary] Chapel—saying last words of exhortation in reference to the P.M. Dressed hastily but nicely—went to [. . .]ceum room—we formed a procession—went upon the stage in nice order—Faculty & class of Twelve. . . . All went off finely—save that the girls greatly vexed & disappointed me by their low reading. Mary Trowbridge[1] (in the name of the Class) presented me with a beautiful ring with the Class (& my favorite motto) "Ohne Hast Ohne Rast"[2] upon it. I responded as I best could under the surprising circumstances. Libbie[3] dear, came in with a note from D. Kate interfered—I yielded. We had a scene—I cried as I haven't since Mary's death. Kate took pity—& we are reconciled.

1. Mary E. Trowbridge, from Lima, N.Y., graduated in 1867 from the seminary.
2. "Ohne Hast Ohne Rast" ["Without haste, without rest"] was one of approximately four hundred epigrams compiled by the German Romantic writers Johann Wolfgang Goethe and Friedrich von Schiller in *Xenien* (Weimar, 1796).
3. Elizabeth E. Chapin of South Livonia, N.Y., was a student at Genesee Wesleyan Seminary.

11 July 1867

Slept long & heavily after last night's tragic performance. Went to the Commencement of Genesee College—walking in the long procession with Prof. Harter[1] while the Band played a lively march. Church crowded. Exercises good. . . . Kate—wonderful to tell!—had a 3 hour long session with D[elevan Scoville]—upstairs in my recitation room! Developments remarkable—interview altogether unique. In P.M. saw the new Preceptress—Mrs. Scylla.[2] Like her tolerably—told her all I could about matters & things. A surprise got up for me in the Chapel. A crowd collected—prayer made—elegant speech by Ray Brodie[3] & an eighty dollar dressing case presented to me! I was overcome by the goodness of "my girls." . . .

1. Henry L. Harter was the principal of the Commercial Department at the Genesee Wesleyan College from 1865 to 1869.
2. Mrs. W. C. Scylla was preceptress of the seminary during the 1867–68 school year.
3. Rachel Brodie, from Franklinville, N.Y., was a student at the seminary.

12 July 1867

Confusion extensively prevailing. Girls coming in troops with tears in their kind eyes, to say Goodbye. . . . Can hardly realize that my year at Lima is done—*forever.* Ah! if we were not immortal, it has been a good—& an entirely successful year. . . . In eve. saw D. in the Reading Room. A most undesirable & unsatisfactory interview. I could have cried my eyes out—done any thing desparate—but I chose to go to bed & to sleep. I drew a parallel that made K. more kind.

15 July 1867

This morning he went away—the only man I ever really loved—let me write the curious fact out in good English words. Goodbye was said hurriedly & constrainedly—Kate & I standing together at our door. I went into the room—helped Kate make the bed—had silent bitter thoughts of my exceptional fate. A quick rap at the door—*his* rap—I went into the hall—he took my hand—he smoothed my hair—he murmured a few hasty, earnest, goodbye words & was gone. But the day was brighter because he came back to see me—he whom, likely, I shall not see again. I gave him this goodbye note:

"Delevan—Today you go your way—I mine—into the wide, wide world. Very likely we shall meet no more. I cannot bear that we should carry from each other any save the kindest, gentlest thoughts. Forgive any cold looks or words. It was not I.—Let the past have had its error—there has been true & tender feeling, & for its sacred sake I write these lines—almost with tears Goodbye, dear friend. God bless you with success & sympathy & take you to Himself at last in peace, for Jesus' sake." . . .

23 July 1867
Evanston

. . . Uncle[1] walked in from the P.O. & handed me—what I wanted above all things—*Delevan's letter.* Ah! what pleasure had I in reading it—the sad, sweet letter—full of mystery (as he is, always) but full of kindest, tenderest thought! I can not write it down. . . .

1. Willard's Uncle Zophar was visiting the Willards in order to help care for his brother, Josiah.

24 July 1867

I am deeply sorry that Kate feels so unpleasant about my writing to Delevan—whom she acknowledges to be "the most magnanimous of men." She and I are so tried & true to each other—can not that suffice. Today I wrote him all my heart. . . .

Took a long ride with Father . . . talked over poor Oliver's sad, disastrous career—so fatal to the hopes of Father's old age.

28 July 1867

My early morning thought was to spend this day aright. But—sad & strange the words!—I have no spiritual affinities—any more. I had a restless life;—"to speak is to begin to err"[1] & I speak much. Father's reading of the 118 ps[alm] I much enjoyed, also his fervent, simple prayer. He is ready for death—to the tender mercies of his Creator he may peacefully commit his soul. Yet I have great hope that he may live—though he is not so well as he was a few days since, & every body seems to think he is not to recover. . . .

1. Not identified.

2 August 1867

His letter—13 closely written pages came today. So gentle & so tender—so mysterious—as he is, always. He is in the big woods now— went after writing. Goes to Cazenovia[1] next Fall to the Latin Dep't— Asks me if I will accept the Preceptress' place. Ah me! I write not here the thoughts that make my heart a painful place—& tired. . . .

1. Cazenovia Seminary in Syracuse, N.Y., was founded by the MEC and opened in 1824, offering courses of education for women and men. Scoville was to teach in the Latin Department during the 1867–68 school year.

[Kate Jackson][1]   6 August 1867

"*John*" [Norton] has come North so I heard this morning & Frank & I are wondering—what will come of it. Ah! me, I don't want to leave Frank. I *cannot*. She who has grown to be "bone of my bone."[2] Somehow it seems to me that life would be *gloomy* without her even tho' I were married to the man I loved. I love her very, very much, dear, dear Frank more than any one in the world & I think I could never love any one else so well. I am so sorry I haven't been nice to her this year, my darling Friend! The tears spring to my eyes as I recall the past & wish I had been better to her. Why did I talk to her so that memorable night? My love for her is as strong & constant as ever, my esteem has suffered no abatement, then why did I cause her those tears? Dear Frank who is as the "apple of my eye." Forgive me Darling, & beleive me always,

In *devoted love*
Your Kate

1. Willard wrote at the top of the entry: "Great event to Kate & me—whereat Kate cries—dearest of women—& I laugh sorrowfully."

2. Jackson paraphrased Gen. 2:23, where Adam says of Eve: "This is now bone of my bones, and flesh of my flesh. . . ."

16 August 1867

This A.M. my dear Mother worried me by almost crying at her lot—some thing she never did before. We have had a long nice talk. She is the noblest of women I think.

29 August 1867

. . . Yesterday Mother & I talked together of Father & were more than ever discouraged. He has daily fever & nightly sweats—is greatly emaciated—has almost no appetite & coughs & raises a good deal. Dr. Wolfe's book[1] perfectly describes his case & labels it "consumption." But yet we can not tell & must hope. Went to see nice Mrs. Huse in her homelike handsome house & she gave me an electric shock treatment[2] for my dazedness. . . .

1. Willard may have been referring to Dr. Julius Wolff, M.D., of Göttingen, *The Use of Auscultation and Percussion in the Diagnosis of the Organs of Respiration and Circulation with Directions for the Employment of Inspection, Succussion, Palpitation, and mensuration of the Thorax* (London, 1837). Although it is unlikely that the Willards would have owned a copy of the book, they may have borrowed it in order to understand Josiah Willard's illness.

2. Mary (Knight) Huse (1819–78), an Evanston neighbor and fellow Methodist, gave Willard a treatment for her spells of "dazedness" consisting of mild, electric stimulation, probably by application to the skin for brief periods of time.

[*According to her father's wish, Willard accompanied him in early September to his sister Caroline Town's home in Churchville, N.Y., in order to convalesce. Kate Jackson traveled with them, stayed a few days in Churchville, and went on to her home in Paterson, N.J. Mary (Hill) Willard remained in Evanston to recover from her exhausting summer caring for her husband during his illness, but planned to join him in late September.*]

15 September 1867
Churchville

. . . Father is not as well as he has been. Slowly but surely, I greatly fear, he is declining. We talked of it—remotely this A.M. when alone together. Speaking of that wondrous verse "And you are Christ's & Christ is God's"[1] he said "What stupendous meaning there is in that! When one is near the borders of '*that Plain which breaks off suddenly*'[2] these things grow clearer." I never in my life before heard him say any thing so ominous of his apprehensions in this respect. All of us talking in low voices of the gravest possibility. . . .

1. 1 Cor. 3:23.
2. Not identified.

17 September 1867

. . . On the 1.40 train came Dr. Dolley—to my delight. One of the great objects in coming East was to have an examination by a trustworthy physician. Up to this time Father would on no acct. have a physician—above all an examination. But the Dr came out in a friendly way & finally got him to permit an examination! More than I had dared hope. Going to the depot with the Dr. he delighted me beyond words by saying Father was not dangerously ill & that his lungs are not ulcerated at all nor [. . .]ized. He says he has the promise of years of life. We are all delighted at the Dr's. account of Father & the poor dear man is so pleased & relieved by the result of the examination— so nerved up & talkative with his poor, tired face. I was never more solidly thankful at the result of any of my exploits than this. Tonight (Tuesday) I go to bed with a lighter heart than I have had in a long time.

[*By late September, Willard's mother arrived in Churchville and Aunt Caroline's home became crowded. Willard felt that it would be easier on everyone there if she left and began to look for a teaching position. She rejoined Jackson at her aunt's house in New Jersey and began interviewing with a school in New York City. She wrote to New England schools about a job, although she did not expect to find one since fall term had already started. Jackson was being pressured by her father to marry her longtime, long-suffering fiancé, John Norton, and Mr. Jackson encouraged his daughter and Willard to visit with Norton at his parents' home in Connecticut.*]

9 October 1867
Springfield, New Jersey[1]

Mr. Jackson came—obedient to Kate's letter. Gave her a rod of bills with his cordial permission for us both to take a jaunt to New En-

gland—stopping at "John's" & going thence to Boston. I feel a duty
to Kate in this matter. She would not go but for me—so she frequently
announces—& perhaps she does her own best interest harm by such
a course. While the matter of a situation is pending it is well for me
to "see her through" this affair & "lay the ghost" that for 8 years has
hovered near her or else see it transformed into her "Philip" henceforth & forever. Mr. J. brought us his "European satchel." He & I
talked over John [Norton]—he would be vastly pleased & would give
Kate a "cool $50,000."

1. Springfield, N.J., was where Kate Jackson's late mother's sister, Jane (Burnett)
Ball (b. ca. 1821), lived, and where Jackson stayed whenever she visited her family,
since she did not get along with her stepmother.

3 November 1867

. . . Kate says she shall not marry Mr. N. Her love has all died out
& tho' she honors him beyond words—believes he has just the qualities that would render her life happy with him—she can not deny
her heart. It is not for me to upbraid her—whose past has a passage
so similarly sad. But yet, somehow, I can not help the earnest wish
that she would risk her fate to hands so firm, so loving & so true.

11 November 1867

. . . In evening Louise[1] bro't me . . . a letter from Mother—the most
ominous yet rec'd—from wh. I make these extracts; "Your Father is slowly
but surely declining. This is *Dr. Dolley's* opinion now. His suffering from
fever is much less for wh. he is most thankful. He is in a light sweat most
of the time. He suffers most from weakness & prostration." . . .

1. Louisa Jackson (b. ca. 1833) was Kate Jackson's older sister who lived with their
Aunt Jane in Springfield, N.J.

12 November 1867

Today I have written Father two sheets full of my heart toward him.
If he were at home I should go to him immediately. As it is I see they
do not think it best—& it is not for they have enough on their hands
without me. It is far better for him to have Uncle W. & Aunt T.[1] than
to be at home with Mother & me. But my heart is very tender toward
my Father in his crisis-days & how gladly would I aid him. He has the
Heavenly comfort though, thank God!—& needs not my poor words.

1. Willard's Uncle Zophar and his sister, Caroline (Willard) Town, lived together after their spouses died. Willard's father and mother were staying at their house during Josiah Willard's last illness. Willard was worried that it would be too much for her uncle and aunt to have her staying there as well, no matter how much she might wish to be with her father at that time.

18 November 1867

. . . Rec'd letters from Mother to the effect that Father is failing fast—& has no other expectation than to die. Telegraphed him immediately these words: "I greatly desire to come to you—what shall I do?"

19 November 1867

No reply yet to my telegram & am greatly disturbed. . . . Kate regards my telegram as ill-advised & treats me crossly. Ah me! The only wrong was that I went from him at all!—In P.M. this reply from Father: "*Come at once*"! I am truly glad & in haste to go to him. . . .

22 November 1867
Churchville

Went up to Dr. Dolly's where we were warmly greeted by our nice friends. Dr. D. prepared me to find a gt change in Father & said he did not expect him to recover. Quite different from his judgment 2 months ago! He said Father was taking arsenic as a last resort but evidently expected or hoped for nothing more than to make him as comfortable as possible. Mrs. D. & Kate went to depot with me & I came off sad enough, on the P.M. train. Reached the familiar village— so prominent in the past life of all my family. Saw dear Mother's beloved face at the window watching for me. In a moment more had pressed my lips to my poor father's—so pale & cold. Ah! How sadly he has changed. It seems to me he could not be more emaciated, or look more like death if actually he had entered upon the only rest, alas that he will ever know! He has changed, every way. He in whose eyes I never saw a tear except when Mary died, weeps like a child & trembles in his voice with every slight emotion. My poor father! What a wreck he has become in body! A living skeleton he is—without exaggeration. But his mind is clear as ever. "When I do talk, you see I talk straight," he said to me. One of his first remarks was this: "Frances, you know I told you when I went to bed I should go *quick* then!"—I want to put down his sayings—all I can. . . . I am doing all

I can to comfort my poor Father & relieve my tired Mother. Father
has to be constantly watched & taken care of very carefully. Poor Aunt
Caroline has the habit of sitting up till midnight, Mother till six in
the AM! The household has but one idea—the favorite brother—the
husband—the Father—in his last illness. Surely that is thought
enough for one family of relatives! Father's talk to me after I came
today was heart breaking. He had me get out of Mother's trunk a plan
of our lots at Rose Hill that he had feebly sketched in pencil: "Here"
said he "is our Mary's grave marked—here is the place for yours—
here for your Mothers—here is your father's grave—*soon to be dug!*"
(His poor voice broke at the words!) "Here, I marked this 'for Oliver's family'—I thought that would make him feel good. Here will be
a monument—I tho't I'd indicate it in case any of you should ever
feel able to put one up. Here is a tree—& here—& here. I drew this
with as much pleasure as I ever planned a garden plot. How God can
change our minds! I never used to think about that place we owned
at Rose Hill but now as you & your Mother sat here talking I thought
soon we shall all be there in what I love to call '*Our Family* Home'—
Our Blessed Family Home. You will stand side by side upon that sacred
spot—around my grave."—It seems that Father has even chosen his
bearers—requested that Dr. Raymond shall preach his funeral sermon—& arranged about his clothes for that *last time.* His will Uncle
Zophar has made & our property is secured to my dear Mother as
well as it can be in view of Father's heavy obligations on Oliver's
account. . . . "Frances I want to state one thought to you. . . . For my
part I swing out on God's almighty arm—& when God takes me—
let me go!" (This said with tears.) "I have committed my case to my
creator & am perfectly content. If it had pleased him to grant me a
longer respite I should have thanked him for it—but since it does
not please Him I thank Him just the same. I have often thought lately
how much richer I really am than any emperor. An emperor has this
world to back him to be sure but think of me! I have God & his universe pledged to back me, on account of the childlike faith which I,
a poor, trembling, dying man repose in my Redeemer. This is a high
truth! A terribly inspiring thought! People who are well don't know
any thing about my feelings in these crisis-hours. Ah! Ive rested my
case with the eternal God!" . . .

24 November 1867

. . . Oh, how thankful I am that "Europe" was put aside—that Auburndale[1] was given up & that I am here—where I belong—beside my

Father's bed of pain. Though now he doesn't suffer much. He says he has had a gt release from it for the last few days. Opiates soothe him & it seems almost a pity that he did not take them earlier.

1. Willard had been offered a teaching position at the Lasell Female Seminary, a nondenominational private school in Auburndale, Mass.

27 November 1867

For two nights I have sat up with Father till midnight. This is the saddest of pleasures. He is constantly under the influence of opiates & wanders all the time—talking most strangely & pitifully. I am very nervous & my dear Kate is going to sleep here in a quiet bed-room & console me when I do go to bed. . . . Yesterday I read the paper to him . . . & he listened with interest. Sometimes he makes a funny remark & we all laugh—his old way is so natural to him, still. But he looks death-like—takes no solid food—don't sit up at all—&, I fear, grows further from us, every day. Just now . . . he woke from a little nap to cough. I held the spittoon & put my hand on his hot forehead. He said "O Frances! I hope when your time comes, if it be the will of Heaven it may be much more speedy—much more agreeable to you". . . .

29 November 1867

Midnight—Friday night. I am taking my watch from ten o'clock till one o'clock. In all my life I never knew more solemn hours than these. I sit by the fire—or bring Father water, milk or porridge as he desires.—attend to his cough—reply to his feverish, wandering queries—write a letter now & then & so pass through the hours. . . . How glad I am that Kate is in the other room to take me in her arms, when I go back to bed—so nervous & so tired.—Here at midnight Father has dictated a touching post script to a long letter written to Oliver yesterday, in wh. he refers to that letter of last evening—the most son-ly letter ever rec'd from his generous-hearted only son.

10 December 1867

In the A.M. Mr. Simkins[1] called to see if Father felt able to partake of the sacrament. Being rather better than for a few days past he concluded to do so. At two o'clock Mr. S. came & Mr. R. (Uncle's minister, from the Congregational Ch.)[2] The little table that holds the numerous bottles of medicine was covered with a white cloth &

the Communion Service placed upon it & covered with another white cloth. Ourselves & the two ministers were all who participated in the exercise. Mr. S. read the service in a clear, pleasant voice & I never enjoyed it more. It was very affecting when he presented the emblems to Father—"the last time"—all must have thought. At the close we all sang that wonderful Hymn "There is a fountain filled with blood" & I was much affected at the thought that it was Father's favorite Hymn—that he taught it to me—that he & Mary & I used often & often to sing it together in the dear dead days, & that we had as a family often surrounded the Lord's Table while the congregation united in singing it. Tears were in my eyes but I sang bravely on, to the end. The scene I shall *never, never* forget. . . .

1. James Nelson Simkins (d. 1901) was the MEC minister in Churchville, N.Y., from 1867 to 1868.
2. Charles A. Ruddock (d. 1912) was the minister at the Union Congregational Church in Churchville from 1867 to 1869.

12 December 1867

. . . One o'cl'k at night. Sitting here watching Father, in quietness. He is more comfortable than since I have come, he has been at all, I think. No one can tell the nervous misery with wh. I watched with him until now, for I tho't every time, he might die while I was here alone with him—& not without reason, either, he looked & seemed so very bad. But now I have the opinion of two excellent physicians that there is no immediate danger, & I take care of him as I would of any other sick person who required constant & most careful attention. . . . I can not help thinking he may yet regain comparatively comfortable health—though it would really seem almost a miracle. . . .

18 December 1867

. . . He said to me today, after a long silence: "Frances, I have been trying to think of something to give to you, but I have so little that I tho't I'd name the subject to you & let you choose for yourself." I named his spy glass, his Bible given him by Aunt Abigail[1] & his commentaries of Scott & Clark[2] as things appropriate for any one & he proceeded to give them all to me! . . . When I told him today . . . that I had written my last words to Delevan he said "I am rejoiced to hear it—I have prayed about it a great deal. I want you to be married to a strong, healthy[3] kind man who can take good care of you & make you happy." I told him I fully expected to be! & hoped to marry a minis-

ter—He said he should like that. I believe he thinks more of me than
he ever expresses, after all.—This is the last sentence of my brief note
to D: "So ends our intercourse—but thought goes on—& kind well-
wishing, & sincerest friendship, just the same. Adieu!" . . .

1. Abigail (Hill) Willard had given Josiah Willard a Bible shortly before she died
in 1857 and had requested that Bibles be given also to Oliver, Frances, and Mary
Willard.

2. Willard referred to Thomas Scott, *The Holy Bible Containing the Old and New Tes-
taments, According to the Authorized Version; With Explanatory Notes, Practical Observations,
and Copious Marginal References,* 6 vols. (Boston, 1830), and Adam Clarke, *The Holy Bible
Containing the Old and New Testaments: The Text Printed from the Most Correct Copies of the
Present Authorized Translation, Including the Marginal Readings and Parallel Texts with a
Commentary and Critical Notes,* 6 vols. (Boston, 1830). Scott was an Anglican scholar and
Clarke was a Methodist scholar. Methodism for much of the nineteenth century looked
to Clarke's work as the authoritative commentary on the Bible.

3. During January and February 1867, Delevan Scoville suffered from a diseased
leg, so much so that he could barely walk and was in constant pain. He probably had
phlegmasia alba dolens, commonly called "white leg," in which a limb, usually a leg,
becomes enlarged, hard, white, and painful. "White leg" is caused by imflammation
in, and blocking of, the veins of the leg and often occurs in the wake of typhoid fever or pneumonia. Willard's parents were concerned that Scoville was not healthy and,
therefore, could not take care of a wife in the way they hoped their daughter's husband would take care of her.

21 December 1867

This A.M. Uncle brought in a package from the P.O. I picked it up
carelessly—carried it to my room—hid it in my shawl—came back—
wiped the dishes—did up my "chores" & retired to privacy to open
the little carefully fastened bundle containing what I peremtorily
asked of him—"Every written word you have of mine—this last note
that I shall ever send and all. You will not ask my reasons because I
do not offer them but will believe what I aver that they seem to me
vital & just."—There they were—"every written word"—even messages but one line long—even the "permit" I gave Kate, playfully, to enter
his Astronomy Class;—all labelled & dated & arranged chronologically. On the envelope of my last were [. . .]ly these words: "Please
send every word of mine." He is evidently vexed—or hurt, which, I
shall never know. In the package were two unimportant notes Kate
sent him. These he sent back—I know not why. Perhaps he thinks she
is—as she is—at the bottom of this new manifestation. I sent by P.M.
mail his letters with this scribbled in pencil explanation: "Miss Jackson's thanks for the gratuity of her notes.—Those I rec'd before leav-

ing will be returned as soon as access can be had to the desk in wh. they are locked;—it may be in weeks—it may not be in years."—As I burned my own [?] letters here in my Aunt's parlor stove Father & Mother expressed their pleasure in the result.

31 December 1867

It is the exact moment of midnight. The two hands of the watch—Father's faithful old silver watch, carried by him for thirty years or more—lie one precisely above the other—showing the solemn, ominous moment—the dividing line between the dead year & the year that is even as I write on, actually born. . . .

I am sitting with Father—who is much worse tonight than we have ever seen him;—who lies here, the wan, shrunken face ghastly by this lovely lamp—breathing not unlike Mary did the last few days she lived;—wandering in talk of business—of plans—of people, the faintest of voices bringing to my ear his incoherent words—for he is sleeping, most of the time.—So this always emphatic, reflective Hour is rendered doubly so by the remembrance of the past eventful year—the thrice solemn present—the strange & threatening future. "It is a time for memory & for tears;"[1]—for tender penitence & sincere pledges—for that casting of care upon the Infinite, Mysterious God. But what spell is on me, sitting here alone—thinking these shadowy thoughts—for, with what regret do I acknowledge that they have not the sharp, earnest force they bore in earlier—less experienced years. Faith, I fear, was never fainter in my restless spirit than tonight! Alas, what other confession could be so sad as this? What other could at all compare with it? Between the "watch night" spent by Kate, Nettie Farwell & me together at the dear old church in Evanston, when prayer was earnest, love ardent & faith luminous, & this silent, uncertain night, there is a great gulf fixed. Feebly I grope after "the safer, surer way" of Whittier's song,[2] yet lean toward the humanly-divine love of "the eternal goodness" in which the poet shields his own weary & no doubt sometimes foreboding soul.—Just now I sang to Father . . . his favorite tune, "Just as I am, without one plea," & wondered that the sweet words awoke so little feeling or reflection in my heart. Where will this end? O God! be merciful! Be lenient toward me! Lead me to Thyself—thine own true *self*—at any cost.

1. Not identified.
2. Willard paraphrased a phrase, "the sure and safer way," from John Greenleaf Whittier, "The Eternal Goodness" (1865), stanza 21, line 4.

6 January 1868

. . . Have spent a most pleasant & most profitable day—helping take care of Father & revising & copying an article for Gilbert Haven's paper.[1] Truly, if one has congenial occupation, any place, any circumstances are material for happiness & gratitude. I have deliberately taken the resolve, within two days (for the first time in my life) that I will eschew the weak & futile endeavor to learn sewing or housework—& will faithfully try to make the most of my abilities as a teacher, writer, & person who truly loves ideas. Life is short—one can't do every thing—nor, indeed, much. If I shall ever marry—which, may God grant! I will make an arrangement with my husband, that I will be responsible for all the wifely duties of a house-keeping sort, & if I have them done, in a good style, how I have them done, is my affair. I shall employ, & pay, a first-rate *proxy!* I'll do my kind of work, & earn money to pay my proxy in my homelike home. . . .

1. Willard referred to *Zion's Herald,* the weekly newspaper for the MEC of the New England area. Gilbert Haven (1821–80) was its editor from 1867 to 1872.

8 January 1868

. . . How far from *my choice* are my present surroundings—circumstances—occupations. Yet I know I am doing my duty—& what better, more valuable report could I make, any where? Some day my time will come to languish—be blighted in body & soul—be changed in countenance & mysteriously withdrawn to unknown worlds. May I then possess my soul in all of patience & of gentleness that I can muster—& may faithful hands for love's or kinship's sake perform the constant, wearing labors for me which, sooner or later, we shall all require. How mournful—how unspeakably pitiful the thought! . . .

9 January 1868

Last night I sat up again from midnight till nearly morning. Slept not at all hardly, all night. For the first time in my life, I said in my heart, during the "mournful, midnight hours"[1] that, in my sober judgment, life did not pay. I could heartily reiterate the sentiment so incomprehensible to me when my sister Mary uttered it with hopeless face, in the last days of her life: "If God would like it just as well I wish I were quietly back in the *painlessness of nonenity*"—only, in my less gentle nature I put no "if" in with the wish. How rebellious I am against the inevitable. How this watching sets my nerves on edge—

& I *can't* help it! I am not strong. And then—but I will not outpour upon this treacherous page the thoughts so wretchedly familiar—the specters of my whole life. To what purpose would it be?—Alas how have I wandered from all sweet, heavenly-thoughts—all harmonies of every sort!

1. Willard quoted from Henry Wadsworth Longfellow, *Kavanagh* (Boston, 1849), bk. 1, motto. The phrase originally came from Johann Wolfgang von Goethe, *Wilhelm Meisters Lehrjahre* [Wilhelm Meister's Travels] (Berlin, 1821–29), bk. 2, ch. 13.

17 January 1868

All day . . . he seemed more nervous even than usual—not inclined to sleep as he has been most of the time for a month, but constantly wanting something & very nervous-looking about the eyes. . . . At night . . . Father was having a very bad time & Kate & I in gt haste threw on our clothes & rushed across the street. We found him in a convulsion—entirely unconscious—jaws set—Uncle W. holding his head—Aunt Town bathing his face with ether, camphor and ammonia. We all supposed him dying. But after a while he rallied & went immediately to sleep. . . .

21 January 1868

Father has been about the same for two or three days.—Very weak—restless—blunted in perception—but in memory of events unconnected with his illness, correct. Today, for the first time in all his illness he requested to be left alone. Said he was very nervous & wished to be alone—some of us watching what was necessary, in the next room. In a lucid interval while I was out, this A.M. he talked most Christianly & rationally about the future. . . .

24 January 1868

Father seeming very restless—can not bear Mother out of the room a moment. His eyes look strangely wild. He said to me: "Frances, you have never looked into my face when you have seen so much prostration as you see to-day." He again asked to be left alone & we watched him through the crack of the door. . . . Night came on—an awful night, outdoors, with the wind shrieking & the heavens full of flying clouds. At last he slept, & I went across the st. to stay with poor, distracted Kate. At nine o'clock Mr. Bowen[1] came for me—saying Father had another spasm. I went home—& from that time (with brief intervals) witnessed the most heart-rending scene of my whole life—till half-past-four, when his tired, worn spirit went back to God. Ah! what are words for such a scene as that! My imagination has burnt into it images most agonizing—which can never be effaced. So this dreary winter day—Jan. 24th, I am *Fatherless*—my Mother is a *widow;*—the fire that for five months, nearly, has burned in Aunt Town's parlor is succeeded by most piercing cold;—a long, white figure makes the room holy;—the sick, nervous, fevered face of yesterday is white & placid—the cough is silent—the troubled heart is still.— One whole night I have spent awake & up—& *such* a waking! Today we are unnatural in every feeling—the house seems strange—& still.

1. This was either G. W. Bowen or G. S. Bowen, both Churchville neighbors. Several of the men of Churchville took turns with the Willard family in "watching," sitting with Josiah Willard throughout the night to care for him.

4 February 1868
Evanston

. . . (I am by no means well, but, since it is for the first time possible, I will write up this sad & dreary record as well as I can.)—On Saturday, Jan. 25, my uncle went early to the city—as no time must be lost in making preparations for our departure for home—in accordance with the plan made long since by Father. At breakfast, Uncle's voice choked when he said "Though Thou hast smitten us, O Lord, we yet would kiss the rod,"[1] & his voice was even more plaintive than usual in the inflection of his (always) closing sentence, "in the Redeemer's name." Not a word was spoken until the meal was almost over. At nine o'clock the bell tolled—as Father had often imagined—for *him*. Mournfully its muffled tones struck off the sixty-two years of his life on earth—with no [?] jubilant suggestion of the hours he has now spent in Heaven. I spent the forenoon writing a sketch of his life for the minister here & in Evanston—giving very many of his interesting talks in these last months about religious things. Mr. Simkins called for my notes. Dear "Aunt Mari"[2]—Mother's eldest sister—called. Also many other people that I did not see. At night, I slept with Mother. . . . On Sunday at 2 o clock P.M. we had funeral services at my Aunt's. . . .[3] Up early—trunks all packed—baskets of luncheon kindly provided & we ready to undertake our most solemn & sorrowful journey. Mr. Simkins came in & prayed with us. The Four—Father, his only brother, & his two sisters, were together one last moment before the coffin lid was closed. A memorable moment, surely! Faithful indeed had those three living ones been to the speechless one lying so motionless before them. . . . His coffin is placed in the box—hurried goodbyes are said to our dear kind friends;—Uncle, Mother & I take our places in the sleigh awaiting us & the slow procession moves toward the depot. By special arrangement with the Sup't, the express train is to stop for us. The depot is full of our friends. . . . At last the tardy train rushes up to the platform—stops a moment—the conductor alert. Four men carefully place the sacred burden that goes with us, in a freight car. . . . Arrived at the [Chicago] depot we found—first, & foremost! & most desired—*Oliver*—beside him Dr. Bannister—Mr. Langworthy[4] & Mr. Woodson[5] (our Evanston undertaker) who, with Mr. Langworthy & Dr. B., Father had desired should conduct the funeral arrangements. The night was bitter cold . . . finally, at one o'clock at night, reached Evanston. Found sleighs & people waiting us.—Houses lighted— where our special friends lived. At Dr. B's, Mrs. & Ella up & with warm fires & luncheon ready. At our own home—wh. had been opened— aired—warmed & *provisioned* were Mrs. Bragdon (*of course*) Mrs. Pearsons—& Mrs. Raymond. Father's remains were laid in the parlor of his own house. On Thursday at 1:30 P.M. after prayer here by Dr. Raymond they were borne to the hearse by the friends he had chosen. . . . & we walked once more in sad procession up the same aisle through wh. we followed our Mary. I had my Uncle's arm & we went behind Mother & Oliver. . . . A sermon by Dr. Raymond (Father's choice). . . . It was so intensely cold that it was thought best to go to Rose Hill on the Funeral Train & a gt many of our friends accompanied us. Dr. Bannister read the Burial Service & Father lay beside the dear girl among whose last words were these, addressed to him: "*Christ wants you right off.*" So once more we came to the house that he built—that he loved & longed for—that he enjoyed but one brief year before he went to Heavenly Mansions—mystical & far away to us— but very real & rapturous let us all believe to him—& Mary. . . .

Next day, Mother Oliver & I, with Uncle & Mr. Randall[6] in the Surrogate's Court, Chicago, to "prove the will." A place new & strange to me—who watched intently the whole proceeding. . . . Friday Oliver went to the city & got things for our housekeeping & Kate & I were busy as bees all day helping fix the house. We are to live in the two north rooms—having two beds in the dining room (that was) & are making the sitting room just as pretty as possible. The arrangement is temporary as in May the house will be rented. Mr. Huse[7] (to whom Father wrote a private letter, on the Thursday after he had that face-spasm) is our guardian & protector. He was, perhaps, Father's most valued friend in Evanston. . . . We three women sleep here alone—having made the house as secure as possible by six bolts & fastenings extra. . . . Every body is thoughtful of us in our trouble & loneliness. Mr. Huse calls almost every day. He tells Mother everything she is to do. He said to me: "Come to me for any thing that I can do, just as you would go to your Uncle Willard." . . . People come to see us every day & this with household duties & sending off papers, writing letters, &c., keeps me busy. We are a very cosy, quiet, but how changed!—family. Ah Life! What a new riddle is it, at every turn—at every new unfolding! And of Heavenly help or guidance, I have so little, now! But every day we have our family prayers & blessing at the table in which I bear my part with some little feeling of comfort & of trust. Alas that I am so wrong in my soul—so warped, as I suppose, from what might have been! . . .

1. Not identified.
2. Mariah (Hill) Gilman (1802–76) was Mary (Hill) Willard's older sister, who lived in the Churchville area.
3. Josiah Willard's Churchville funeral service was held at Caroline (Willard) Town's house.
4. A. C. Langworthy (1814–91) was an Evanston resident who had been the local agent (business manager) for GBI from 1861 to 1865.
5. William T. Woodson (ca. 1825–77) was a longtime Evanston resident and one of the first undertakers in the city.
6. Mr. Randall was a Churchville, N.Y., resident who traveled to Evanston at Zophar Willard's request, in order to witness Josiah Willard's will.
7. Obadiah Huse (1810–86) was an MEC minister who was the local agent (business manager) for GBI from 1856 to 1859. In 1862 he retired from the ministry but remained in Evanston; during the 1870s Huse served as president of the village board of trustees and township assessor.

21 February 1868

. . . At night Mr. Huse—our kindest of friends—brought us what we of all things most desired—a formal release of our home stead, from Preston & Kean.[1] Isn't that cause for thanksgiving to God's Providence & man's forbearance? Mother's now secure in a comfortable maintenance.

1. Preston, Willard, and Kean was the name of the Chicago banking firm in which Josiah Willard was a partner. After his resignation in 1865 due to illness, it became Scripps, Preston, and Kean. The firm held the mortgage on the Willard home in Evanston as part of the terms of a loan made in 1866 to help Oliver Willard out of his financial difficulties. It forfeited the rest of the loan at Josiah Willard's death, thereby securing the house for Mary (Hill) Willard.

9 March 1868

The long desired letter came straight from Kate's Father—informing us of his . . . unchanged willingness & expectation that we should go to Europe. So there is no longer a "peradventure" in the case &, unless Heaven interposes, we shall go in May. This puts a new & settled look on life, once more. I was getting restless under the long suspense of occupation. Now, all our thoughts are turned toward all the sorts of preparation that must be made.

Mr. Eggleston[1] came in response, to my note. . . . Promised to do all he could to secure correspondence for me. In eve nice Fannie Fish[2] came & we three went with her to Tilton's lecture on "The American Woman."[3] I never heard anything better—or that so much inspired me. Theodore Tilton is the bright, fearless apostle of woman in the 19th century & doesn't utter a word to which my heart fails to respond. Charlie Fowler wrote to me last year, at Lima: "Have you not some brave possibility of work for woman's suffrage, with your pen? It is to be *the question* of your prime & mine." Perhaps I have,— I feel so now more than before. We shall see.

1. Edward Eggleston (1837–1902) was an MEC minister, author, and journalist who moved to Evanston, Ill., in 1866 for health reasons, and to become the associate editor of the *Little Corporal*, a children's magazine, which he edited for a year. He then edited the *National Sunday School Teacher* from 1867 to 1870. During this time he published several articles that Willard sent him from Europe. In 1870 he became the editor of the *Independent* for a brief time. He is best known for his novel *The Hoosier Schoolmaster* (New York, 1871).
2. Fannie Fish, Willard's roommate at Pittsburgh Female Seminary, moved to Evanston and taught mathematics at the NWFC from ca. 1865 to 1868.
3. Tilton gave his speech "The American Woman" on 9 March 1868 at the MEC in Evanston, strongly arguing for woman suffrage.

10 March 1868

This (Tuesday) A.M Mrs. Huse came in to see what we thought. Like all reflecting & liberal minded women she believes we ought to have the ballot. . . . All the educated men I know—with one exception & that is D. C. S.—believe it, too. Well—let us work & pray for it then & the theory so nobly set before us last evening will become the every day fact ten years hence. . . .

20 March 1868

I believe in the *Woman Question* more & more. I'm going to give my little help to it in all possible ways. Kate is *strong* for it—I am amused to hear her talk. She lies on the lounge now, reading John Stuart Mill's speech in Parliament on the subject[1] & "interlarding" with original observations. Oliver was talking of it last night & said in his easy going way: "I'm sure I've no objection to women's voting only so it don't interfere with the *insurance business!*" . . .[2]

1. John Stuart Mill (1806–73), the English philosopher, economist, and woman suffragist, was elected to Parliament for Westminster in 1865. On 20 May 1867 he delivered a speech on woman suffrage that was published that same year as a pamphlet with the title "Speech of John Stuart Mill, M.P. on the Admission of Women to the Electoral Franchise."
2. Oliver Willard worked for the Globe Mutual Life Insurance Company of New York City as the state agent for Wisconsin, living in Appleton, Wis., during the late 1860s.

21 March 1868

. . . Some how since I heard Tilton lecture, my purpose is confirmed—my object in life clearer than ever before. What I can do in large & little ways, by influence, by pen, by observation, for *woman*, in all Christian ways, that I will do. And may God help me! . . .

[*All during spring 1868 Willard and Jackson prepared for their much–postponed European trip by studying guide books and art histories, practicing French, and readying their wardrobes. In early April they escorted Willard's mother to Appleton, Wisconsin, for a long stay with Oliver and his family, and returned to Evanston to prepare the Willards' house for the family who would be renting it for several months. On 6 May, they departed for the east, visiting friends and sightseeing in Washington, D.C., before going to Jackson's aunt's home in New Jersey to make final arrangements to sail on the steamer* City of Paris *for Europe on 23 May.*]

27[?] May 1868
On the Atlantic Ocean,
bound for Europe

. . . Sat. A.M. [23 May 1868] Hurrying off . . . for N.Y.—all the *Jacksons proper.* Dreadful misadventures over our baggage. . . . Hurried to the steamer. . . . We walked off from the safe & solid soil—*up* the long plank upon the undulating deck. A heavy rain duly began to fall. Every place was full—decks—gangways—cabins—saloons. . . . Mr. Jackson called Kate aside—& handed her a bag of gold coin—explaining in a low tone the mysteries of "sovereigns" & "napoleons." . . .

We elbowed our way to the dining room & found seats—& I wrote a note to Mother. . . . A bell rang vociferously, when we had been sitting thus, about a half hour. Hurriedly saying goodbye they left us. . . . The sailors voices in the distance somewhere "sang out" vigorously—& then slowly & heavily the great pulse of the engine commenced beating—the people on shore waved their handkerchiefs—kissed their hands & hurrahed;—we climbed upon the sofas in the dining saloon—put our heads out at the open window and caught the last glimpses of our friends on shore—then, in a somber, drizzling shower, steamed down the bay. So the long dream was coming true—& yet, somehow, "it was not like"—how could it be? O, glorious "ideal," what can ever come nigh unto thee? Kate & I looked into each other's faces. "I could cry this minute—but I won't," she said. And then we talked of the kind, shrewd, grave face of her generous Father & my noble benefactor—of his anxious, pathetic look after us as we started off all alone for strange, unfriendly shores. . . . After a tolerable dinner, we went below—the steamer now lying still,—waiting the tide—& set our house in order for the voyage. Changed our dresses & were innocently & unapprehensively putting the last touches upon our ship-toilettes when lo! a pain—that was not all a pain, but part a prophecy of dreadful things to come, seized each of us about the region of the diaphram! 5 minutes thereafter I had "tumbled up" tumultuously into Berth No. 1. (at the top) & was vomiting, "reaching" (as our stewardess calls it) & groaning with all the more vehemence because so suddenly & totally surprised. For I had calculated with certainty upon the very opposite of this result. Kate lay in her berth below me groaning & heaving dutifully—but then *she* had expected it! Well. For the next 2 or 3 days I thought & did unutterable things. Every body was dreadfully sick. Sunday was a perfect blank of a day. In it I had just this one thought: "Let me lie still—let me keep my stomach in equipoise." . . . Kate has lain here in her berth the veriest martyr—since the day we left. Her double chin has dropped off—her cleanliness is forgotten & she is indeed a deplorable looking object. She has taken every meal duly in bed & deposited it shortly thereafter in the slop-basin. One day she was a while on deck—a strict & the only exception to the rule. I have been twice to dinner, 1 to tea, otherwise taken everything here—& everything means almost nothing for I've but dabbled among the dishes & eaten no more than the veriest invalid on shore. I've been parts of two days on deck. . . . I've been from stem to stern of the boat. Have read guide books. . . . Of what sea-sickness is I have no space here to write. Language might be exhausted but that subject *never*. And every horrid-damp-rolling & pitching night, crawling miserably into my comfortless berth I have in a few quiet moments prayed for my dear Mother,—my brother, his wife & children, for all I love & all who love me, & that I may in peace & safety come to shore.

PART FOUR

9 October 1868 – 28 September 1870

How life unfolds—and from the dog's eared spelling book through the medley of a "regular education" as laid down in the "Catalogues," and the solemn & trivial experiences of ordinary life, the soul goes marching on till rich, historic cities are the chapters in a text-book made up of the choicest civilizations and most interesting countries of the globe.

—5 July 1869

Willard's European tour was the culmination of years of hoping and planning. From the time when she began to keep a journal, she had longed to experience firsthand the great cities, the ancient cultures, the magnificent works of art she had read about in articles and books on travel, heard about in lectures, and viewed through the stereoscope. Rather than being merely the completion of her education, the trip was the gateway leading, in Willard's expectation, toward a life filled with such experiences, which she intended to share with others through teaching and writing. "How I enjoy *learning*—more even than *knowing*," she wrote in the midst of her travels.[1]

In her enthusiasm, she filled more than twenty journal volumes—her "European Notebooks"—with the most minute details of visits to museums, galleries, churches, synagogues, monuments, cemeteries, bazaars and shops, and sites of natural beauty. She wrote page after page recounting conversations with traveling mates, observations on customs, and her opinions on everything from *table d'hôte*[2] to the Italian lottery. She also documented what she called the "shady side" of travel: the continual battle against fleas and others of the "entomologic legions,"[3] the necessity of frequent tips to everyone from chamber maid to museum guide, and the annoyances of traveling "in parties" with others who did not have the same goals as she, and who simply refused to spend the hours she wished to devote to each and every site. She endured the petty annoyances and true discomforts of travel and accommodated to them with her usual optimism and humor. It may be in the "European Notebooks" more than any other part of the journal that the reader can get a sense of Willard's style of humor, which on occasion poked gentle fun at others (in the relative privacy of her journal), but also—and often—at herself.

Willard's near-compulsion to log her trip exhaustively and in sometimes overwhelming detail came in part from her need to gather raw material for the many articles that she sent back home to newspapers and magazines, earning a little money for the "extras" not covered by her travel allowance from her friend and benefactor, Kate Jackson. Her journal entries also would become the basis of lectures and talks she intended to give when she returned to the United States. But perhaps, it was, more than anything else, her acute sense of the great gaps in her knowledge that led her to write so extensively of what she saw. After one of the many days she spent at the Louvre,[4] she wrote, "I never feel the hungering & thirsting for various knowledge so keenly as in these great museums where I pass by so much with unseeing, because uninstructed eyes."[5]

Willard and Jackson, along with most of the American tourists they met, relied heavily on guidebooks for instructions as to which sites to visit, where to find them, and how to interpret what they saw. The guidebooks and Willard's own inclinations led her to explore several particular histories and cultures: the course of the Reformation and the rise of Protestantism; the somewhat erratic and abortive development of democracy in continental Europe; the golden age of Greece and Rome as evidenced in antiquities collections and the ruins of the classical period; the art of the Italian Renaissance; and Europe's scenic beauty mediated by British and German Romanticism. Willard diligently pursued each site, guidebook in hand, and wrote it up in the evenings. Midway through a tour of Reformation sites in Germany, she joyously exclaimed in her journal: "What days are these in which I trace back history to its sources & follow poetry into its chosen haunts."[6] As she crossed the border between Switzerland and Italy, she wrote: "People talk about 'Red Letter Days.' Well, this is *the* 'Red Letter Day' of my life as an intellectual being. . . . The traveler's lessons & delights come to a climax & that climax but one word can symbolize—*Italia*."[7] She eagerly launched into each day's itinerary, tiring out Jackson, who much preferred to alternate sightseeing with shopping expeditions, which, in turn, bored and exasperated Willard. But they kept at it for nearly two and one-half years, during which Willard absorbed as much as she could, realizing that her European tour was a unique opportunity.

The trip was not one endless round of sightseeing, however. Willard and Jackson stayed for two months in Rome, three months in Berlin, and six months in Paris. In each city they arranged to take language lessons, and in Paris they enrolled for a course of study at the Collège de France,[8] where Willard took classes in the literatures of modern France and the early Christian period, a political science course on the rise of modern Europe, and a political philosophy course, among others. She took copious notes on the lectures, translating them in her head from French into English, a feat that attests to a familiarity with the language that she had acquired in a relatively brief time. She and Jackson were fortunate to find lodgings in a private home as boarders with Madame Perrot,[9] a new widow who needed to earn money in order to maintain the living standard to which she and her children had been accustomed. She provided the two American women entrée to her upper-middle-class Parisian Protestant community, including Willard and Jackson in family parties, social evenings with her friends, and Sunday worship at several Protestant churches. She also arranged for and accompanied them on visits to cathedrals, schools, charitable institutions, concerts, and art shows, and was available to discuss the mores and manners of the French, the current political climate, and many other topics of interest to Willard.

During her stay in Paris, Willard began in earnest her investigation of women's situation. She questioned Madame Perrot and her friends about the institution of marriage and the fate of the single woman. She visited a school for upper-class girls and a Protestant deaconess institution that included a refuge for young prostitutes and a school for children of the poor, in order to understand French notions of women's education and opportunities. Anna Blackwell,[10] an American women's rights supporter living in Paris, arranged for her to meet with a French women's rights leader, Julie Victoire Daubié, author of a book on poor women's status.[11] They had a lively conversation about women's rights in which Daubié eagerly requested news of "the movement" in America and acknowledged the debt the French women's rights movement owed to its American counterpart. She sent Willard on her way with addresses and letters of introduction to other Parisians who shared her point of view and with copies of a new journal, *Le Droit des femmes* [Women's Right].[12]

Daubié identified what she believed to be the most urgent problem facing French women's rights leaders: the seduction of young working women by rich men who offered them more money than they could earn at any job available to them. Only a week after her visit with Daubié, Willard went with friends to the Jardin Mabille,[13] where she observed young prostitutes, as Daubié had described them, dancing with their wealthy escorts. Her respectable, bourgeois sensibilities were revolted at the licentiousness of the scene (which she nevertheless detailed minutely in her journal). The shocking spectacle heightened her determination to work for women's uplift.

For the first time, at least as evidenced in her journal, Willard began seriously to analyze women's situation from an economic standpoint. Prior to this in her theorizing she had considered only women's educational and political disabilities as evidence of women's second-class status. Both her discussions with Madame Perrot about the economic basis of many French women's marriages and Mademoiselle Daubié's identification of poor women's inadequate means to earn a living as a key issue led Willard to add women's economic disabilities to her analysis.

It is difficult to separate Willard's deep concern for women's limited employment opportunities from the outraged morality with which she responded to the scene in the Jardin Mabille. While Willard liked to consider herself, by this time, a woman of wide experience, she was not. Until her European trip she had remained almost exclusively within the rather narrow social world defined by American middle-class Protestantism. Although she had lived in different geographic settings in the United States, she had not lived in varied social locations. Her experience was limited to a particular level of society with its specific moral perspective.

Her upbringing had given her a definite sense of the difference between public and private space and of what was acceptable behavior in each. It had taught her to shun almost any public display of affection beyond a sober handshake. It warned her to look upon dancing as an activity likely to lead to wanton behavior and, thus, to be avoided. She was quite unprepared to deal with standards of behavior different from her own. Her six-month stay in Paris was the first extended encounter with a more casual and permissive attitude toward many aspects of social life. She found the experience unsettling as she tried to confront what she considered the moral laxity of French society in nearly everything to do with social relations, from allowing—even flaunting—a double standard of sexual behavior for men and women, to encouraging all manner of Sunday recreation— even horseracing.

Willard also confronted different religious and political perspectives during her stay in Europe. She attempted to understand and judge them in comparisons throughout her European notebooks between "the old world" and "the new world." She usually found the new—virtuous, democratic, Protestant America—to be far superior to the old—decadent, monarchical, Catholic France and Italy. Her attitude of cultural superiority was especially evident early in her European journey when she dismissed the Christmas Day worship service at the Roman Catholic church of St. Sulpice as "the most mummified of mummery,"[14] a phrase reminiscent of her assessment after her very first visit to a Catholic church many years earlier in Milwaukee. And yet there were moments in which she found herself filled with a sense of awe as she listened to the soaring music of a choir or glimpsed the lofty architecture of grand cathedrals. Her aesthetic sense was profoundly touched by Roman Catholic worship. She struggled to imagine an ecumenical Christianity that could combine the rich ceremony of Catholicism with what she considered the purer, simpler truths of Protestantism, with its focus on Jesus as the central figure. She hoped such ecumenism could eliminate what she saw as the ridiculous superstitions and inordinate papal power that had accrued to Catholicism over the centuries.

A staunch advocate of American democracy, Willard rejoiced in signs that the Italian democratic movement was alive. She hailed the election of a few liberal representatives to the French Chamber of Deputies in May 1869. At the same time, she became increasingly aware of the great poverty in which many Europeans lived. As she traveled from southern Switzerland into Italy she began to note in her journal the miserable conditions in which the poor just barely managed to survive. She was especially moved after she had been in Rome for several months and had observed daily the ill-clad and omnipresent beggars who shivered in the cold and the young children who slept in doorways at night.

The stark evidence of terrible poverty continued to trouble her as she and Jackson made their way through Egypt, Palestine, and Syria. She found equally troubling the oppression and degradation of women.[15] She believed that it was the future task of the United States—as a young, vigorous, moral nation—to eliminate the great gap between the few rich and the vast numbers of poor, and to elevate women to their rightful place alongside men. In her opinion, one could not look to the old, exhausted civilizations of Europe and the Middle East for solutions to the problems of poverty and women's oppression.

As Willard entered Jerusalem and prepared to visit biblical sites, her stance changed. She was no longer primarily a tourist intent on viewing historical, cultural, and aesthetic wonders. She was, instead, a pilgrim reverently reliving what she considered to be the formative event of her spiritual history: the life, death, and resurrection of Christ. Not even the relentless souvenir hawkers, the tawdry decorations adorning the shrines, or the contested holy sites, each claiming to be the legitimate one, could dampen her sense of renewed faith and reconsecration to living the life Christ intended for her. Her pilgrimage to what was, for her, a true holy land was the high point of her travels, worth any amount of inconvenience or hardship.

Willard's two-and-one-half-year sojourn in Europe was all she had expected and more. She was pleased with what she had learned and satisfied that she had not missed seeing anything worth seeing. Her trunk was filled with the photographs of beautiful scenery, incomparable art treasures, and grand buildings she had purchased along the way to use in her teaching. Her European notebooks were overflowing with the written record of her trip, and her mind was crammed with enough memories to last her the rest of her life. Her travels had been a success. Yet the account of her uneven friendship with Kate Jackson runs through the journals like an undercurrent, breaking through to the surface from time to time in tales of stormy quarrels followed by cold silences.

Relatively early in the trip, Jackson became intensely jealous of Julie Briggs,[16] a young American woman boarding at the same place Jackson and Willard stayed in Berlin. Willard had very quickly made friends with Briggs, delighting in their common love of music (which Jackson did not share). Just nineteen years old, Briggs was the kind of woman to whom Willard had been drawn before; her description of Julie was reminiscent of that of Mary Bannister and Ada Brigham. Julie Briggs seemed to be everything that Kate Jackson was not.

Predictably, Jackson was driven wild by Willard's attention to Briggs, and the two old friends quarreled violently, Willard threatening to return to America if Jackson would not allow her friendship with Julie Briggs. The drama surrounding the three was considerably heightened by their imminent departure from Berlin. In a final, furtive meeting, Willard bid Briggs goodbye and then watched from a window as Briggs, her husband, and children drove off. She and Jackson left shortly after. Although they effected a reconciliation of sorts, Jackson continued to remind Willard of her unfaithfulness, much as a wronged wife or husband might. And Willard, from her side, was contrite and remorseful. It was a strained, uncomfortable relationship, yet one that Willard needed to repair since she was so beholden to Jackson for making her European travel possible. The two of them stuck it out together for the entire trip, and they remained friends for the rest of Willard's life—but never really close friends. Willard's longing for an "inner heart comrade"[17] would have to await her meeting with Anna Gordon and, much later, Isabel Somerset.

Notes

1. Journal, 8 October 1868.

2. Willard thought that she and Jackson could save time and money by choosing not to have *table d'hôte*, a complete meal offered at a fixed price and at a stated time, but most of the hotels where they stayed insisted on it. The two young women often complained about *table d'hôte* to each other.

3. Journal, 12–13 August 1869.

4. When Willard and Jackson visited the Louvre, it was already a not-to-be-missed site for American tourists, who hungered to see the great art collections of Europe.

5. Journal, 5 May 1869.

6. Ibid., 21 July 1869.

7. Ibid., 2 September 1869.

8. The Collège de France was founded in the sixteenth century by Fran-

cis I at the suggestion of Guillaume Bude, a Renaissance humanist scholar, as an alternative to the scholastic education provided by the much older Sorbonne. It originally offered Greek, Latin, and Hebrew, and added mathematics, medicine, philosophy, botany, Arabic, and Syriac over the years. By the mid-nineteenth century, the college offered lectures without charge, on a variety of subjects, including literature, science, history, law, and Oriental languages.

9. Eglantine (Farjon) Perrot (b. ca. 1838) lived at 90 rue des Feuillantines, very close to the Collège de France. When Willard and Jackson arranged to board with her, she had been widowed only three weeks earlier. When Willard returned to France in October 1896, she learned that Madame Perrot had died some time earlier.

10. Anna Blackwell (1816–1900) was living in Paris while Willard was there, working as a European correspondent for American newspapers. Later on, during the 1870s, her articles from Europe were much in demand, especially by the editor Horace Greeley for his paper, the *New York Tribune*. She was also well-known among American literati for her poetry. Anna Blackwell was the sister of Elizabeth and Emily Blackwell, pioneering women doctors.

11. Julie Victoire Daubié (1824–74) was a feminist and educational pioneer who challenged France's exclusion of women from higher education by taking, and passing, the *baccalauréat*, the principal qualifying examination for university admission. In 1871 she passed the *licence*, which was the advanced examination. A strong voice for women's emancipation, especially through education, she described her experience of self-education in *Du Progrès dans l'instruction primaire: justice et liberté* [On Progress in Primary Instruction: Justice and Freedom] (Paris, 1862). She also wrote *La Femme pauvre au XIX siècle* [The Poor Woman in the Nineteenth Century] (Paris, 1866), *French Morality under the Regulation System* (London, 1870), and *L'Emancipation de la femme* [The Emancipation of Woman] (Paris, 1871).

12. *Le Droit des femmes*, copies of which Daubié shared with Willard, was a women's rights paper and a journal of political opinion. It had just begun its short publication life when Willard read it. It ran for only a year, from 1869 to 1870, under that title. Then its name was changed to *L'Avenir des femmes* [The Future of Women], the title under which it ran from 1871 to 1879; it became once again *Le Droit des femmes*, published from 1879 to 1891.

13. The Jardin Mabille was a public garden in Paris located on the rue de Rivoli. It was notorious in the mid-nineteenth century for its bold dancing and as a place of assignation for women of the *demimonde* (high-class prostitutes) and their wealthy lovers.

14. Journal, 25 December 1868.

15. Willard's first paid public lecture, "The New Chivalry," given at Centenary MEC in Chicago on 21 March 1871, contained many details on the status of women in France, Italy, and the Middle East, taken almost verbatim from Willard's journal volumes for 1868–70. The speech, along with headnotes, can be found in Slagell, "A Good Woman Speaking Well," 124–41.

16. Julia Valentine (Dobbs) Briggs (b. ca. 1849–1933) married Charles Augustus Briggs, a theologian and biblical scholar (see Journal, 18 October 1868, n. 1), on 19 October 1865. She and her husband lived in Germany from ca. 1866 to 1869, while he studied at the University of Berlin. After returning to the United States in 1869, she lived most of her life in New York City, where her husband was on the faculty of Union Theological Seminary.

17. Journal, 7 October 1893.

[On 3 June 1868 Willard and Jackson landed at Cork and spent over a week touring Ireland, moved on to Scotland for two weeks, and then stayed nearly a month in England. They crossed the English Channel in late July and quickly traveled through Switzerland and Germany to Denmark, Sweden, Finland, and into Russia, stopping briefly in St. Petersburg, Moscow, and Nijni Novgorod. They went on through Poland to Berlin, where they settled in for a three-month stay of study and sightseeing.]

9 October 1868
Berlin

Went for a ride with Mrs. Briggs through a delightful part of the Theirgarten. . . .[1] Mrs. B. & I are getting to be great friends—she is very agreeable, obliging, affectionate & bright. I happened to say that I had no strong dislikes (was not "a good hater") but felt pleasantly toward every body I had ever known, upon the whole & always found more to like than to condemn in people—& upon study of them like them more & more. This is a thing of temperament purely, I believe. She seemed quite astonished at the idea.

Read several of my letters to Kate & she liked them. Somehow, they do sound better than I thought they could. But how I wish I had the power & patience to write vastly better than I do!

A letter from Mother—my joy & song—full of good news & pleasant items. It seems my 2 articles (for the Independent & Methodist)[2] are very well spoken of. Wrote article on *Stockholm*—read an hour at German with Mrs. Briggs. Kate & I are greatly stirred up & distressed about our ignorance & K. is reading very industriously while I poor thing must write "for considerations" various & weighty. . . .

1. The Thiergarten was a public park just outside of the Brandenburg Gate in Berlin.
2. *The Methodist* was published in New York City from 1860 to 1882. Some of Willard's published travel letters can be found in *Temperance and Prohibition Papers*, microfilm ed., WCTU series, scrapbook 2, roll 30. *The Methodist* published at least nine of Willard's travel letters describing the earliest part of her European tour (Ireland, Scotland, England, and Russia) under the heading "Foreign Travel."

18 October 1868

. . . Went to Ch. with Kate & Julie & heard Julie's husband[1] preach. . . . In the P.M. went to see my dear new friend a while, she having declined an invitation to dinner that she might give her nice nurse, Lena, a birth-day holiday. Saw her dress sweet little Gracie &

quiet the baby[2] & thought—my thoughts. In eve went to sing hymns with her. She plays & sings with great good taste & appreciation. We had a lovely home-like evening—reminding me of dear, dead days— when Mary sang with me & Father listened, pleased to hear his daughters voices.

1. Charles Augustus Briggs (1841–1913) was a Presbyterian theologian and biblical scholar who studied at the University of Berlin from 1866 to 1869. He was professor of Hebrew and cognate languages and professor of theology at Union Theological Seminary in New York City from 1875 to 1913. In 1892 Briggs, a proponent of higher biblical criticism, was tried for heresy by the presbytery of New York after he publicly questioned biblical authority in his inaugural address upon receiving the Edward Robinson Chair of Biblical Studies in 1891. Although Briggs was acquitted of the heresy charge, the Presbyterian General Assembly suspended him as a minister in 1893. His case caused Union Theological Seminary to sever its Presbyterian ties and become nondenominational. In 1900 Briggs became an Episcopal priest.

2. Emily Grace Briggs (1867–1944), the first child of Julie and Charles Briggs, was born in Berlin. The baby Willard referred to was a son whom Willard never named. He may have died very young because no records of him exist.

19 October 1868

Julie, *I love*. She has so much delicacy of soul—so much sweetness—such gentleness & purity of character. Few that I have ever met—& I have had a wide experience of "human nature"—have ever so much attracted me. And she is very fond of me—the sweet, shy creature—only nineteen—celebrating the third anniversary of her marriage this very day with a kind husband & two lovely children at her side. She is very lovely to me. . . . Dear Kate—the tried & true— looks on with ready sympathy—exhortation & reproof as each is merited. . . .

21 October 1868

. . . I went over to Julie & she translated Dr. S's "[. . .] History"[1] for me in part & I thought sweetest things of her but somehow found her just a trifle different—more reserved & not so fond of me as she seemed awhile ago. At which I should not be surprised of course— the only marvel being that she should have liked me at all. Ah! we think we know a person & straightway find we don't. But Julie can never seem less lovely though she is certainly less ardent & spontaneously "nice" to me. She "thinks better of it"—as the saying is;— repents her care for me & it hurts me, though it ought not. I can not penetrate the womanly "forbidden ground" on which she stands &

whence says sweet words & sends kind looks & soft caresses to me as before—only she *sends* & does not *bring* them. It is a new study & of a fine & sensitive nature & one that has become *dear to me*—for always, though I go from her & see her no more, Julie will have a sweet & sacred place in my heart.

1. Not identified.

30 October 1868

. . . In eve studied French & later Julie came in with her box of laces to show Kate & I retired early, feeling ill, & Julie came & put her head upon my breast & filled my heart with her sweet words. She told Kate today she had never loved any one so dearly as she did me (any lady, of course). It was a lovely thing to know she had thought & said. Kate—the dear & true feels sad over our friendship—naturally I suppose—& I am so sorry & depressed about it.

2 November 1868

. . . Kate & I are a long way apart. I never knew so wide a distance in all our ups & downs before. To think that I should bring grief upon one who loads me with benefits wh. are only the out-growth of her love. Why need it be? Ought I to have restrained what I was only half-aware of until tight in its grasp? I know I am deeply wrong, but Kate herself is so unapproachable—so stony—so pitiless in her displeasure. Dear to me as ever,—she is all, these days. Sweet words & sweet caresses I could give her now, as ever, but she spurns them with violence—will share them with no other, & this is doubtless natural, only she is so hard withal. This A.M. we went with Julie & Mrs. G.[1] to the Egyptian Antiquities of the Museum[2] & to study Kaulbach's frescoes.[3] Kate would not walk with me or hardly speak. I know I have been sometimes unmindful of her & bitterly do I regret & with shame so I confess it, but she punishes me with unsparing severity. In P.M. I was with Julie for two hours. Told her much of my life—told her what Kate is doing for me. She heard it all with her unfailing sweetness & so winning gentleness. In eve we all went to hear Niemann & [. . .] Lucca in "Stern von Turin."[4] How sweet & ♪ & unforgettable was the little verse several times repeated, wh. I will get Julie to write down for me. When we came home Kate tore from my finger the opal ring given me four years ago & bearing the inscription: "Plus chere que la vie [dearer than life]." O it was a bitter thing to bear, but I said nothing. She was desperate or she never would have done so. Another wretched night.

1. Willard referred to a Mrs. Gorran (also spelled Gorren), an American who was boarding along with Willard and Jackson at Mrs. Fletcher's boardinghouse.

2. Berlin's Kunst Austellung [art museum] was opened to the public in 1830 by Frederick William II.

3. Wilhelm von Kaulbach (1805–74) was a painter, illustrator, and muralist associated with the German Romantic movement. His murals decorated the Berlin art museum.

4. Willard attended the opera, where she heard a modern work, *Der Stern von Turin* (first performed on 14 December 1864), with music by Richard Wuĕrst and libretto by Ernst Wichert. Willard heard the German tenor Albert Niemann (1831–1917) and the Austrian soprano Pauline Lucca (1841–1908) sing.

4 November 1868

This A.M. is more approachable but says the foundations of our friendship are jostled irremediably. How sad I am I can not write. How much I have to grieve over! . . . I have no heart to write or to do anything. Have . . . just shown Miss P[ettingill][1] to the Kunst Austellung where she will spend the morning with delight. Kate & Julie have gone out to buy dresses. How Julie's face smote me as I looked an instant, in her pensive eyes before they left the house.—I know not what to do.

Ah! It is all right & I have my ring again! Peace-maker Julie initiated the reconciliation. My pride came to the rescue & I told Kate that if she was going to throw me off—as she said—because I had seen in Julie what I could but admire & love I would no longer be dependent on her as I have been but would immediately go home— as I would have done, grinding though it must have been. My tears of grief and penitence brought her to her own kind self again & all is right—We went in & told Julie. I can never forget that pale, calm, lovely face as she kissed us both & said "she was so glad." Life seems like itself again. . . .

1. Hannah Pettingill was studying in Dusseldorf, Germany, with the American landscape artist Henry Lewis (1819–1904). Lewis was also the American consul in the city.

8 November 1868

One of Berlin's dreariest dawnings—with snow flakes falling before our "Drei Treffen"[1] windows & melting ere they reach the ground. I shall not go to church—spent most of the morning with Julie—which I ought not to have done, but her room was so enticingly near & I knew the days when I could ever see her were so soon to be ended, that perhaps I was not altogether without excuse. I saw

a new side of her character—saw her roused thoroughly, & heard her
say the time had been when she would have given me up to outward
appearance at least—that last Sunday she would so have done, but
"not now for any power on earth." Ah me! It is a strange episode in
our two lives. And sad it is that at such cost of pain we love each other. "Was kann ich thun [What can I do]?" I am not false to Kate. I
love her as well as ever—but I love Julie too, & Kate can not permit
a second in our friendship. I must read Alger's "Friendships of Wom-
en." The more I see of life the more find that women-loves are not
the rare, unheard of things I used to think. . . .

    1. "Drei Treffen" was apparently the name of the boardinghouse where Willard
and Jackson were staying in Berlin.

11 November 1868

    These are among the utterances that made last night memorable
& unutterably sad:
    "I could have borne it better if it were almost any body else—but
Mrs. Briggs has her husband & her children, she is consoled by other ties;—she has not staked her all upon one head—& I haven't any
friends hardly."—"Ah Frank, you are a dangerous—a costly friend.
You are capable of giving frightful grief."—"It almost crazes me to
have you with her."—"You are breaking my heart—mine that has
cherished you so dearly & so long."—Let me remember those words
& the storm of tears with which my tried & true friend uttered
them.—What will become of me I wonder who have cost her so much
pain? What is "the right" of the case? Julie loves me & her pained face
smites me sorely. I love her & would fain make her as happy as is in
my poor power. But I will be true to the older love—since I *must
choose*. I was never more unhappy;—never in a harder straight. . . .
Dear Kate is happier today—vastly so, though she will hardly acknowledge it. I know it consoles her that I stay beside her always—& that
thought deeply consoles me. But a grave & gentle face haunts me—
& a sweet & loving presence from which I shall soon be forever withdrawn gives me a pained heart. So there is trouble enough for us
three who have been so friendly & so kind. I sit here & in her little
parlor in the next room hear Julie playing & singing—dear, gentle
child—*our song*, copied for me by her—which was heard in the opera the last evening we shall ever spend together there.—Went into
her room a minute. She wrote on the margin of her husband's
evening paper: "no kiss for me today?"—Well, a few words & a loving goodnight are comforting indeed. We had them—spite of all.

Dear Kate is happier tonight I know, for my day of entire & glad devotion to her alone.—How vastly silly & profoundly absurd this whole affair would seem to a cool looker-on! And yet to us, it is all very real & very sad.

14 November 1868

Will put in here . . . some of Julie's lovely words to me last evening—the sweetest evening we ever spent together:—"My love for you grows stronger with the light of every morning & the darkness of every night. I have had an experience with a school friend who loved me & every day I sent her sweet flowers—but on whose shoulder I could not bear even to lay my hand. To kiss her was terrible—but to kiss *you!*—I could live at your lips. My love for you consumes me." Ah! Julie Briggs! I will remember those words when you and I are wide apart & thought alone is left me—thought, & the little cross you hung about my neck with the six words upon it! . . .[1]

1. The six words to which Willard referred were "Ich Habe für dich ewig Liebe" [I have eternal love for you].

15 November 1868

. . . In the evening Kate & I have a brief, painful, severe talk & I go for two hours with Julie—*the very last*. She is writing as I enter her tasteful parlor, noting in her little Diary—begun at my suggestion & full of sweetest words about me—her talk with Kate & how Kate told her I should certainly forget her after awhile. Julie adds: "May God forgive her if she does this—*I never could*." She comes over to me on the sofa—dressed in the pretty garments worn on the anniversary of her wedding day, & quite a favorite with me, as she knows. She lays her head upon my shoulder—puts her lips against my cheek & whispers in her gentle voice "Will you forget me, Frank?" I tell her of "my nature"—my inevitable nature—born with me as was the color of my hair. Of how fondly I cherish every love that I win from life, but that I have had many that I never yet left one of them but they have been taken away—as she will be tomorrow—leaving tenderest memories & sweetest possibilities of happiness instead of the realization that comes to other lives. And she—the lovely, fine-souled woman, with her clear, truthful eyes, understands & believes in me. Such an evening as it is! . . . A quiet ten minutes succeeds—*our last*. I hold her tight in my arms—press her dear head upon my shoulder—tell her what I would do, if I could—have her always as now—then a kiss that utters what words cannot, of how dear she is to me—then my own room—Kate's sad reproachful face—long thoughts—then sleep & dreams.

16 November 1868

. . . All the morning Julie making preparations to go at noon—& I, reading Prussian history, & between paragraphs listening to her quick step in the next room—& at last to her tender plaintive singing of our song—*for me,* as I well know. A little while before she goes she calls me to the little vacant room that was her parlor. This is the end. She tells me to take the little song—she has left it for me on the piano. One kiss—one clinging grasp of her kind hand & I go away from what I would give more than I can tell to keep within my sight—to shelter in my arms.—A little later she & her husband come in for the usual goodbyes—then I look from my window—see them enter the carriage—see Julie's pale face at its window—stand & watch their swift passage from my sight as, again & again I have seen depart forever my dearest & my best.—I sit down & go on with my reading. I have perfect self-command—but O, such a pained heart. Dear Kate talks with me—tells me she has gone herself from me to come back no more. That she will not after what has passed. So I have the double grief—the estranged old friend, the vanished new! Ah me—it is well that God has made me brave! . . .

24 November 1868
Dresden

. . . Early in A.M. wrote a long letter to my Mother—sending her Julie's photograph. I have few mementoes of the unspoken past.

Then pioleted by Mr. McGee[1] we visited the picture gallery.[2] Kate & I walked along to that end room in which the Madonna de Sansisto[3] holds court alone. I never had such feelings upon approaching what I had long dreamed about & wished to see. We were really foolish about it, both of us, & I blushed at my timidity. I would not look at the picture for some time after the first side glance on entering to make sure that it was there. Finally I looked up at the cherubs—& then at the perfect beauty of St. Barbara—& then at the wishful, super human face of the Madonna & the mystic, masterful, divine face of her son. We sat there long, in silent study. Many persons came & went while we looked at Raphael's finest revelation—but they were all silent—the place had an air of sacredness—& the manner of its visitors said what words cannot of its impressiveness. We saw a score of pictures familiar by name & engraving & photograph for years. . . .

1. Willard and Jackson became acquainted with Mr. McGee while traveling in Russia in August 1868 and arranged to meet him again in Dresden.
2. The Gemäldegalerie Alte Meister [Old Masters Gallery] was founded in 1722 by Augustus II and in 1855 the collection was moved to its modern location, the Semper Gallery, part of the Zwinger complex, in Dresden. The gallery held a priceless collection of artwork, of which the *Madonna de Sansisto* [The Sistine Madonna] (ca. 1512–16) by Raphael (Raffaello Sanzio, 1463–1520), master painter of the Italian high Renaissance, was considered the greatest treasure.
3. Willard had grown up hearing and reading about the *Sistine Madonna* and had long looked forward to seeing it for herself. She wrote at the top of this entry "*Red Letter Day*" because, for her, being able at last to study the painting was one of the highlights of her European tour.

2 December 1868

. . . Kate finally got up to the point of fulminating a letter to Mr. Norton—which will be final beyond a doubt. It ought to be, one would think! She makes his coming North a necessity, & justly, I think. Dear Kate! I fear her love for me may be a sad thing for her, some day! She says she thinks of & cares for no one else in the comparison—she is so intense in her nature that she can take but few into her heart. She invests me with every quality she loves—*creates* in me, by her imagination, a lovely nature & then delights herself with believing it is real. Ah! if I could thus innocently cheat some other person as I have my dear & generous friend! How earnestly I pray that never may I bring her any more grief! . . .

10 December 1868

. . . Goodbye visit to the Gallery. How it has pleased & taught me! I have had few more delightful friends. Going through all the rooms where hung our favorites we said adieu to each with deeper regret than the word often cost even when uttered to a valued acquaintance. Corregio's[1] Madonna of St. Sebastian has grown upon me wonderfully. Its depth—variety & mellowness have taken a strong hold of my imagination. Of what use to enumerate the favorites—they are everybody's—they have been the solace of thousands & will be when we have passed to still more lofty, lovely scenes. Not least among the pleasures of such a collection is the thought of all the great & generous souls who have delighted in what so charms ourselves. . . .

1. Correggio (Antonio Allegri, 1494–1534), painter of the *Madonna of Saint Sebastian* (1520–26), was an important Italian Renaissance painter whose later works influenced many Baroque and Rococo artists.

25 December 1868
Paris

Christmas Day. Such a funny, French breakfast to open proceedings! We answered the announcement "le déjeuner apres mes demoiselles" [luncheon, later, Misses] by presenting two very hungry individuals at the neatly set out table in the pretty salle a manger [dining room] where Madame & her three bright children[1] were already seated. They had each a bowl with weak tea and bread crumbed into it—nothing more. Fortunately, Kate had suggested eggs when we engaged to come (evidently to Madame's surprise!) so we found before our plates an egg apiece, poached. In the middle of the table butter & at one side a tray with snowy napkin and tiny loaf of bread. We began operations with some trepidation as to results. Soon, in a moment of cessation, my plate was snatched from me & a *bowl* was placed before me—half filled with coffee & quite filled with milk. This I was expected to drink & so close the proceedings. The bread was almost gone & our appetites had only been well sharpened by the few mouthfuls we had disposed of. I called for my plate again to the evident horror of the family & we commenced a vigorous onslaught on what bread remained. Hastily leaving the room Madame ordered the "Bonne" [housemaid] to run for another loaf at the same time producing a "confiture" [jam] from the side board. She & her children had finished eight minutes after sitting down, & it was painful to see them waiting & watching for the end—long delayed—of our repast! And yet, we are not persons of surprising appetite—only human, & unaccustomed to live on air. I could hardly help laughing—it was all so absurd.

Afterward gallant young Henri escorted us to St. Sulpice[2] where for three hours we saw the most mummified of mummery—enough to sicken one's soul. Hundreds of kneeling Catholics received the wafer—scores of priests stretched out their impotent hands in blessing;—brilliant chasubles (reminding me of Murillo's "St. Roderique")[3] decorated the high altar, upon the shoulders of tonsured prelates;—fine music swelled from the organ & the throats of well-trained choir-boys; "blessed bread" was brought in surrounded by burning tapers;—six (civil) worthies marched before it up the long aisle, preceded by the tall & formidable beadle in small clothes[4] & cocked hat; a long procession of cowled monks filed in & out again; the blessed bread was passed around in baskets to all the congregation;—bells rung; genuflexions were gone through with;—four collections were taken up, (one preceded by the explanation: "Pour les pauvres s'il vous plait" [For the poor, please] being the only part of the performance with which we had a particle of sympathy)—& paying six sous for the chairs we had occupied we left the place—thinking with untold gratitude of Him whose natal day is kept most truly in the quiet of our simple service in the home—churches—& of Luthur who gave us freedom from the thralldom of Rome.—A good dinner—with wine. Afterward, pleasant talk & privacy on our part in our nice room to which already we are attached. What do I not owe of love & thanks to my dearest Friend Kate Jackson—who is making life so rich—so valuable—so many sided! Never will I cause her grief again. I have restored the Past, as I believed I could. She has my warm & changeless love, & what can be done by me to make life bright to her, shall not be lacking. I pray very sincerely & earnestly that I may never again fail her;—that on my heart she may ever confidently rest—that we may always love each other as now & live in the same harmony, cheerfulness & peace.

In evening we sat for hours with Madame Perrot & had pleasant conversation & reading. She is very intelligent & unlike dear "Madame" in Dresden,[5] never gets "out of subjects." Talked of politics—the Emperor—of religion (she is a Protestant). . . . Dear Kate slept well, for once & we hope in this so quiet place she may regain her old habits—for weeks, now, broken.

1. Eglantine Perrot's three children were Henri, eleven years old; Mathilde, about nine years old; and Sophie, seven years old. Willard kept in touch with Sophie, her favorite, and visited her briefly when she was in Paris in 1896.

2. St. Sulpice, a grandly decorated seventeenth-century Italian-style church, is on the Left Bank, very near to where Willard was boarding.

3. Willard had seen *The Martyr St. Rodriguez,* by the Baroque master Bartolomé Esteban Murillo (ca. 1618–82), the most popular religious painter in seventeenth-century Spain, in the Dresden Old Masters Gallery a month earlier. In the painting the saint is wearing an intricately decorated chasuble, a garment worn over the alb and stole by the celebrant of the Mass.

4. A beadle was a minor official in Roman Catholic churches who kept order during worship services and walked ahead of dignitaries in processions. In France at the time Willard was there, a beadle wore "small clothes," close-fitting knee britches more commonly worn in the eighteenth century.

5. Willard referred to Madame Marchand, with whom she and Jackson boarded for several weeks in Dresden.

26 December 1868

. . . My pleasant writing table (that was the architect's)[1] is in fine order, & my chief care & stopping place. I am going to do great execution this winter I fondly hope, at French, writing & reading. We mean, at least, to try.

Spent the morning with Madame, who gave me a grammar lesson—phrase-lesson—had me write sentences & we read a chapter of a French story—Kate listening & participating when profitable to her. Madame Perrot says in two months I will speak well, & that I have already a good pronounciation—for which I am indebted to Kate's faithfulness as a "maitresse" [teacher].

After dinner we went out with Madame to the Sorbonne (quite near) where we are to attend lectures[2]—also to the College de France to get a programme of the lectures there—M. Laboulaye being the one we shall be most interested to hear.[3] It seems curious enough that we are to be in some sense students of the *Sorbonne*—of which we have heard all our days, & than which nothing ever seemed less likely to befall.

In the "Students Quarter"[4] we saw a couple of tall, well-dressed, well-looking young men who had between them one of the *demi-monde*[5]—a woman of no beauty and very little neatness, who, holding an arm apiece of the young men, walked with them in the middle of the street bareheaded. Afterward we met them in the same attitude, on the Boulevard St. Michel[6] & one of the men kissed the woman as they walked along the crowded trottoir [sidewalk]. It was the most disgusting—shameless sight I ever saw, but common, Madame told us, in the Students Quarter—the "Latin Quarter" of which we have so often heard.

Kate & I took an omnibus for the Place Vendome[7] & found it quite a complicated performance. Went to the bank to register our names & get letters. . . . Took a return omnibus at the Madeline after dark—came from Pantheon[8] here much later, without fear. Madame says it is nonsense—the impression that ladies can not go out unattended in Paris. Certainly to have a "natural protector" of the masculine gender is always pleasant but when not practicable—let well-behaved ladies go by themselves without fear. . . .

1. Willard referred to Madame Perrot's late husband, Louis Alfred Perrot (1827–68), a minor city official who was assigned to oversee the architecture of a district of Paris. At the time, Paris maintained laws governing the city's appearance, and Perrot was a city planner who enforced and interpreted these laws to Parisians who wanted to modify the exterior of their property.
2. Founded in the thirteenth century as a theological college for poor students,

the Sorbonne grew into a major European center of learning and now makes up the core of the University of Paris. In the 1860s the Sorbonne included three faculties, those of theology, sciences, and letters. The lectures were public.

3. Édouard René Lefebvre de Laboulaye (1811–83) was a lawyer, liberal politician, and senator, and wrote on legal and political subjects. He lectured at the Collège de France from 1849 to 1882.

4. The Student Quarter, also known as the Latin Quarter, was the area around the Sorbonne and the Collège de France.

5. Alexandre Dumas coined the term *demi-monde* (literally, "half-world") to describe that class of women in nineteenth-century France who were kept by wealthier students or other wealthy men, but who were not, strictly speaking, prostitutes. The women lived in social limbo, caught in the sexual double standard of the day, neither completely outcast nor respectable.

6. The Boulevard St.-Michel passes by many important Left Bank sites, including the Sorbonne.

7. The Place Vendôme, on the Right Bank, has at its center a column built by Napoleon to commemorate his victories during his 1805 campaign.

8. The Madeleine, located near the Place Vendôme, is a church built in the style of a Greek temple. The Panthéon, the largest Italian-style church in Paris and the burial site of many of France's great national figures, is located near the Collège de France.

28 December 1868

. . . We were obliged to "déranger" [interrupt] Madame's dinner in order to hear M. Edouard Laboulaye at the College of France, and because "Tout le mond" [everyone] goes to his semi-weekly lectures we left the house an hour before hand & reaching the College—not far off—found about thirty ladies sitting before the doors of his room with work, newspapers & notebooks in hand, many of them having an air "tres instruit" [very well educated]. Half an hour previous to the lecture a uniformed attendant threw open the doors & we ladies pressed in at one end of the large hall while simultaneously in rushed a throng of students and other gentlemen at the other, & stood up with hats on engaged in conversation animated till the lecturer appeared upon the platform, took his seat before a table, pronounced the word "Messieurs" and launched into his subject, being repeatedly interrupted by the applause that signalized his first appearance. Hardly a word of his rapid utterances could I understand & K. was almost equally in the dark as to his meaning—well as she usually understands. But I employed the hour most profitably in looking at the great and gentle author. . . .

1 January 1869

Here I write my first New Year date, with the least realization of the year *as* "new" that has ever been mine on "an occasion like the present." Absolutely I had not a single thought, last evening, of the usual kind. Not because I am growing careless of events, oblivious of times & seasons, but because everything around me is so new, so strange, that my faculties are busied in perceptions rather than retrospects. After all, perhaps it is as well. . . .

What a year it has been! What gains—what *losses* has it witnessed! In it how many Friends have I left—how many, won! The world looks widely different—from what it did this day one year—when by my Father's bedside I wrote the opening lines of this various little book and sadly wondered what the Future held for me. . . . Quiet has been *Father's sleep*—sheltered my Mother's peaceful, sun set days—but mine, more full, more rich, more varied than all my life before. With One faithful, loving well-beloved Friend beside me always, I have encountered many dangers and much hardship but in all have been preserved, and gained a rich reward for every effort to know more about the world in which the loving God has placed me. . . .

23 January 1869

. . . After our readings "haut voix" [aloud] with Madame we took a voiture [carriage], and went with her to her physician—Dr. Laboulebene,[1] who prescribed for my catarrh and eyes and for Kate's sleeplessness and head-inflammation. . . . He ordered for me sulphurous waters from Haute Pyrnees, bottled at Labassere.[2] I inhale it three times each day, with much temporary pain. What would I not give to be rid of the two sole physical disabilities that have been assigned (or acquired) as part of the "weight" which I carry in life? They are not heavy burdens, but have cost me much discomfort and more mental than physical pain. What would it be to have a sound mind in a body equally sound? Ah well! Life treats us fairly. The more I see of it the stronger my conviction of this contested idea. What one loses in one way is atoned for in another and in the great see-saw game we play, the ups & downs are equal to a nicety. Some cases puzzle one, under this law, but the next life explains all and infinite justice and mercy will surely find their vindication here and there. . . .

1. Madame Perrot's doctor was probably the Parisian physician Jean Joseph Alexandre Laboulbène (b. 1825).
2. Dr. Laboulbène suggested that Willard drink mountain water bottled in the village of Labassère, in the Hautes-Pyrénées, the mid-region of the Pyrénées Mountains in southern France.

24 January 1869

. . . One year ago today my Father died. How changed is life since then for Mother and for me!

In the twilight we sang the hymns that Father liked the best, and which I often sang in the midnight hours to him, those "last times"— so sad, so brightened in their clouds by his victorious faith. No other hymns will ever be to me like those on which his fainting spirit, sorely tried, was often borne aloft, toward the calm regions where it has now enjoyed Our Saviour's presence for one whole year;—has learned so much—& delighted itself in the company of those it loved most dearly when in this world. . . .

6 February 1869

Rejuvinated—recreated by eight hours of continuous repose.

I have a mind to indicate here what has much occupied my mind of late—but what I am not brave enough ever to execute, perhaps, though, were I, I believe my usefulness would exceed the measure it will reach in any other line of life.

Briefly: To study as far as possible by reading, learning of languages and personal observation, the aspects of the "Woman Question" in France—Germany & England, & when I return to America after two or three years absence, studying the same subject carefully in relation to my own land, to *talk in public* of the matter, and cast myself with what weight or weakness I possess against the only foe of what I conceive to be the justice of the subject—unenlightened public opinion. Sometimes I feel "the victory within me"—often, I do not. Always, I have dimly felt it to be "my vocation," but a constitutional dread of criticism & love (too strong) of approbation have held me back.

With "encouragement" I believe myself capable of rendering services of some value in the word—& idea—battle that will only deepen with years and must at last have a result that will delight all who have hastened it. . . .

10 February 1869

. . . To "see Paris" is no small undertaking & we have resolved to begin today. After so many quiet, almost monotonous weeks of study, it is a little hard to take up again the occupation which, while so instructive and gratifying to one's curiosity, is at the same time so fatiguing. However, we marched off, cheerfully, under our huge umbrella to the Gallery of the Luxembourg and spent the morning very agreeably among the pictured thoughts of Horace Vernet, Eugene Delacroix, Couture, Ary Scheffer & Rosa Bonheur. . . .[1]

1. The Luxembourg Museum was located in the Luxembourg Palace, on the Left Bank, next to the Sorbonne. Its collection held the best works of recent French painters. Willard saw works by Émile Jean Horace Vernet (1789–1863), painter of military subjects; Ferdinand Victor Eugène Delacroix (1798–1863), Romantic painter; Thomas Couture (1815–79), painter of historical subjects and portraits; Ary Scheffer (1795–1858), Romantic painter: and Rosa Bonheur (1822–99), painter and sculptor, well known for her accurate portrayal of animals.

11 February 1869

Went . . . to . . . Notre Dame. . . .[1] The dim light—the gaunt, silent figures of the priests—the splendor of the architecture—carried me back through centuries—to the time when there was no church but this, & millions rested quietly in its bosom and believed their future *safe*. In that quiet, charmed hour, I could somewhat understand how, in our day, an ardent, questioning nature, weary of endless search and queries unreplied to, flings itself desperately into the arms of the venerable Catholic church—shuts its eyes to all that is absurd & wrong within its borders,—and seeks with honest heart to find in the mystery of its history—the pomp of its pageants—the quiet of its cloisters—something like *repose*. Architecture, most impressive & satisfying of arts—next to music—lends its aid to this illusion. Matchless harmonies of the great masters and pictures revealed to the sublimest artists all combine to one result—and that there is nothing noble—attractive—fascinating even in the church that was once alone in the world as the exponent of God's will & Christ's redemption one should be slow to say—one feels so strongly in an hour like this I spent in Notre Dame, that, with conditions of life somewhat different, he might be left to worship the form instead of the substance—the device of genius rather than the "unseen spirit" that ever inspires, and alone inspires, true worship. I must return to Notre Dame—it is a place where one thinks no ordinary thoughts. . . .

1. The Cathedral of Notre Dame, built during the twelfth and thirteenth centuries, is located on the Île de la Cité in the Seine. Just a few years before Willard's visit, a massive restoration project on the cathedral had been completed.

17 February 1869

. . . Listening to these lectures at the College de France, I often ask myself, if they were in English, would they be interesting? If one of our celebrated professors were to talk to us of Longfellow, Whittier & Holmes,[1] & were to read their poems, so familiar to us, would we think the hour very profitably spent? I think not. There is but little substance in the lectures of MM. Guizot, Chasle, Havet—indeed in any that we hear except M. Francke[2]—& I understand them, now, well enough to judge. Think of M. Guizot saying today "He had proposed to himself in this hour to treat of *all the critiques of French poesy in this age*"! How much "depth of color" would they several get, I wonder, at his hands? But the French sit here & "bravo" between the verses that he reads or weep at the pathetic passages, with enthusiasm ever fresh.

Am reading Miss Gates "Revolutions."[3] A curious paper. Brave to the last degree—rather able—not sufficiently tempered with judgment I think—but on the right track & likely to secure the future blessings which our thankless sex will take someday quite as a matter of course, without enough inquiring who won them, & at what cost.

1. The works of Henry Wadsworth Longfellow (1807–82), the popular American poet and a Harvard professor, served to develop American audiences for poetry. The poems of John Greenleaf Whittier (1807–92), the American Quaker poet and editor, gained attention before the Civil War for their antislavery and social reform themes. After the war Whittier wrote of religion, nature, and New England life. Oliver Wendell Holmes, Sr. (1809–94), the American physician, Harvard professor, and man of letters, wrote works of fiction, essays, drama, and verse.

2. Maurice Guillaume Guizot (1813–92) was a French literature scholar. In 1866 he obtained a position as substitute chair of French literature at the Collège de France and was teaching modern French poetry when Willard attended his lectures in 1869. Philarète Euphemon Châsles (1798–1873) also studied literature and, in 1841, was named to the chair of northern European literature at the Collège de France. Auguste Eugène Ernest Havet (1813–99) was a Latin scholar who, in 1854, was appointed to the chair of Latin oratory at the Collège de France. Adolphe Franck (1809–93) was a philosopher who was named substitute chair of Greek and Latin philosophy at the Collège de France in 1849. In 1854 he was appointed to the chair of natural law at the college.

3. Adelia Gates (1825–1912) was an American student at the Collège de France. She had attended Antioch College in Yellow Springs, Ohio, during the 1850s, and later in life became a noted watercolor artist, painting flowers. She traveled extensively in Africa, Iceland, and other parts of the world in order to view and depict various plants. Gates gave Willard copies of the *Revolution*, an American women's rights periodical, begun in 1868 by the women's rights leaders Susan B. Anthony (1820–1906) and Elizabeth Cady Stanton (1815–1902), who were its publishers and editors. It ran until 1870.

22 February 1869

. . . Funeral opposite of a "liberal thinker"—no ceremonies—priest or prayer. It seems two "ecrivains" [writers] with their wives—all rather young and all extremely heterodox . . . have been writing & talking in public about America & our reforms to the horror especially of French women. Today one of the young wives was carried to her grave. Standing at our window looking [. . .] into those of the "Cinquieme étage" [fifth floor] where this curious quartette had lived & where one of its members has gone out for ever,—Madame & her sister Matilde[1] indulged in a tirade against the idea of women "meddling" [. . .] in what did not concern them & at its climax exclaimed "those people over there even dare to propose that women *vote!!*" Kate laughed immoderately & said [?] "Didn't you know that Miss Willard & I cherish the hope of going to the polls some day & dropping our opinions on white paper into the ballot box?" There was a look of horror on the expressive French faces & that shrug that utters a whole quarto volume was pushed toward the ceiling. For myself, I would not have declared my sentiments to persons so utterly unfitted by education & prejudice to understand them & knowing well that it would do no good whatever to "define myself." While at heart I am thoroughly a believer in the idea that woman's influence clearly pronounced will do for our politics what it has already done for our literature, besides exercising the needed influence on her personal character & the practical possibilities of her life, I would state that belief with moderation, explanation, & to those persons & in those places where it would be likely to avail somewhat [. . .] the noble but misunderstood & too [. . .]ized cause. Therefore I was [. . .] with my upright, downright friend unreasonably, perhaps, but inevitably.[2]

1. Matilde Farjon was Eglantine Perrot's unmarried sister.
2. Water damage in Willard's journal for 4 June 1868 to 23 February 1869 has made several words in this entry illegible.

3 March 1869

. . . This Ecole [des Beaux-Arts] [School of Fine Arts][1]—in all its appointments—with its courts within courts—its enclosed gardens— its rare morsels of ancient architecture lining the modern walls—its plaster casts—its frescoed corridors in imitation of Raphael's *loggie* [galleries] at the Vatican—is a noble symbol of the love & reverence cherished in these old & wealthy countries for Art. Nature is here subdued—the work that in America keeps so many hands busy was long ago accomplished;—to subdue man in the mass is the trade of kings; as an individual, the work of priests, little attended to;—& thus it happens that abundant facilities are afforded for the elegant refinements with which we in America can well dispense for a while until the statue into which Deity himself has "breathed the breath of life" stands on its rightful pedestal, & smiling landscapes dotted with sweet Christian homes furnish "originals" from which artists born & reared beneath their sacred roofs shall copy with a truer inspiration than a merely secular genius can ever attain.

I like to linger in your galleries—to tread the downy carpets of your palaces—to study your museums—to watch the brilliant pageant of your streets—to press close against the solemn tomb the past has reared—but you on this historic side the sea have not our riches— and we are weak as well as wicked when we envy you! . . .

1. The École des Beaux-Arts was founded in 1671. The building Willard toured had been completed in 1862 and, as she noted, contained galleries around a small court that were painted in imitation of Raphael's loggias at the Vatican.

4 March 1869

Today General Grant takes the helm from the trembling, unfaithful hand of Andrew Johnson[1] & Heaven guard the dear old ship of state & send her safely on her way—blessing & blest! . . .

In P.M. we went for the first time to the Louvre Picture Gallery! Eagerness cools with experience & age. What is under one's hand he is not in so much haste to examine—thus it fell out. Words can not utter it. The magnificence—the prodigality of wealth & taste—and on all sides looking down upon us, pictures familiar by engravings readings & thoughts as the faces of old friends. I never spent two hours more delightfully. . . .

In such a Gallery—what a hunger for more knowledge—keener insight—truer sympathy one feels. It is oppresive to pain, sometimes, as yesterday. "I have nothing to draw with, & the well is deep"[2]—this expressive verse was often in my mind. . . .

1. Ulysses Simpson Grant (1822–85) was inaugurated president on 4 March 1869.
2. John 4:11.

5 March 1869

. . . At last my Mother's letter—twenty three days *en route*. Oliver & Mary are coming to live in "our house" & Mother with them. On the whole it will be pleasanter for her—at least I earnestly hope so— though the new little baby[1] will, I fear, sometimes disturb her "calm repose." Ah! If I had that brilliantest of bubb[l]es set on firm foundations: "A Home of my own" how happy it would be for my dearest friend My Mother! The day is long delayed—quite likely, it will never come, alas! If Mary had but lived she would surely have been able to give to Mother what is pleasantest at her age: *a daughter's home*—a daughter's children. Mother whose deserts are superior in my eyes to those of any other woman—surely for her sake this natural wish may yet come true! . . .

1. Mary and Oliver Willard had a son, Josiah Francis Willard (1869–1907), born on 23 January 1869 in Appleton, Wis. He became a writer who used the pseudonym Josiah Flynt (his paternal grandfather's first and middle name).

11 March 1869

. . . We went to the "*Vente*" [Sale] of the Protestant Churches of Paris, with which Madame Perrot & Mademoiselle Aline[1] are prominently connected. It was very similar to ours at home;—tables with every sort of fancy device, well dressed ladies attending thereon; petty lotteries under the guidance of young gentlemen & ladies; a little table where children preside; and in the distance a restaurant where very delectable & very *dear* refreshments are dispensed by active matrons of Martha-like propensities. . . .[2] We wandered about, looking for something to buy. . . . Several . . . Catholic friends of Madame patronized her table liberally. How galling it is to be unable to do what one greatly desires, in the line of charity! I wished liberally to patronize Madame's department, but alas! Every penny that belongs to me comes from my published letters, & that is very little. But for Kate's generosity I could not make out my ward-robe respectably. But I hope soon for larger receipts—if Mr. Eggleston does not weary of befriending me. . . . To be poor with means of honorably & agreeably putting money in one's purse (such as I had at Lima) is no misfortune. To be poor & almost without resource, is *biting* like corrosive sublimate. By my writing I am conscious of being able to earn enough for a comfortable maint[en]ance—aside from what Kate under took when she placed me under her wing & flew across the ocean with me. But what with studying French—seeing Paris—attending to private home correspondence & keeping up my journal I have little time to spare. I am going to tell Madame P. (who is my very good friend I know) the actual state of the case. It will explain many curious things in Kate's behavior & in mine, in relation to finances. . . .

1. Aline Farjon was another of Eglantine Perrot's unmarried sisters. She was younger than Eglantine Perrot.

2. Willard referred to Luke 10:38–42, the story of two sisters who were Jesus' friends. When he visited their home, Mary sat and listened to his teaching while Martha busied herself with household duties. When Martha complained to Jesus that Mary did not help her, Jesus indicated that Mary had chosen to do the "one thing needful."

13 March 1869

. . . Lecture by M. Guizot on Women Poets of France. He read extracts from a book of verses recently published by a young lady of eighteen "whom the French Academy will soon honor & reward" which displayed great merit. He contrasted her treatment of the same subjects handled by Victor Hugo[1] (a choice compliment that!) & her poems well sustained the trial. I liked M. Guizot's protest against the opinion that he displayed gallantry in his manner of dealing with the works of women. He said he felt a contempt for the critic who did not deal with women as with men when they entered the same field. The age, he said, tends toward seeking points of similarity rather than points of difference between nations, & religions. Let us apply this improved philosophy to our studies of the achievements of men & women. Let us consider not wherein they are unlike, but wherein similar. Byron in Don Juan[2] expresses the opinion of woman that the average public has long held. Its idea is (M. Guizot quoted the lines) "For me, love is every thing—deceived in that—I am undone." But Juvenal[3] was more enlightened than the English poet of an era so much later. In on[e] of his finest satires he makes the heroine say to the hero: "I like better our latin word for *man* that equally includes your sex & mine. For you should remember that in all that is highest, best & most lasting in my nature, I am as much a man as you!"

(I render these quotations in the "freest" manner possible—translating & from memory.)

So I find it every where. The men best educated—most gifted—liberated most from prejudice & the unillumined past, think of woman as a human soul placed by a kind Creator on the earth to do & be all that she can—unfettered by any law or custom so long as her freedom touches on the just rights of no other human soul. May I live to see the day when this choice leaven shall "raise" the lump of public opinion nearer hope & Heaven! And may I be brave enough to speak in a womanly voice my honest word in this behalf! . . .

1. Victor Marie Hugo (1802–85), the influential French poet, novelist, dramatist, and leader of the Romantic movement in France, believed that a poet should act as prophet and leader of the people, which led him to an active political career as well as his literary one.

2. Byron's *Don Juan* was first published in London in 1824.

3. Decimus Junius Juvenalis (ca. 60–ca. 140), the Roman satirist, authored sixteen satires, one of which, the famous sixth, is actually directed against women. None of his satires contains the anecdote Willard described, so she may have misunderstood the lecturer.

16 March 1869

. . . Having been often recommended to do so by Miss Gates, we went this afternoon to what is called "La Petite Sorbonne" (Salle Gerson)[1] & heard first—a lecture on Byron's "Giaour"[2] with translations of the poem into French, & afterward another on the Life of Goethe—the topic for the hour being his Strasborgh experiences. The elegant young man who in a very "engaging" manner talked to us of the great Poet who thought all things were permitted him, looked upon the affair with *Frederica*[3] as a very trivial matter, evidently, & smiled at the severity of German critics in relation to it. A Parisian mockery of tone was in his voice as he said that it was a lucrative enterprise in the vicinity of the young girl's former home, to cultivate flowers to sell to the English travelers who visited the place on a pilgrimage of love & pity. For my part I am tired of this trivial manner of judging things so significant & doubly thankful to be a native of the land where vice is at least obliged to conceal its odious deformities from the stern rebuke of a Christian public sentiment. Madame P. can not repress a smile when we maintain that there are any men in America who were virtuous before marriage. "That it is so I hope," she says, "but that idea to a Parisian is laughable. Even in Switzerland where home-influence is so much stronger than here, every young man has learned the ways of the world, thoroughly, before settling down soberly to his life as Head of the Family."

I say, if religion can impart no more resisting power than that, it is a weak affair. If a mother can not better train & influence her son, she had better pray to "mis au monde" [bring into the world] only daughters;—if such false views of right & wrong are the inevitable result of such aggregations of humanity as this in which I am now "making observations"—it were fortunate if an earth-quake should rend asunder this same Paris and put a "gracious interval" between its thousand severed portions. . . .

1. Willard referred to a specific building, La Petite Sorbonne, and La Salle Gerson, a classroom in the Sorbonne's complex where she attended the lecture. The room was named in honor of Jean de Gerson (1363–1429), a theologian and mystic who was a leader in the Roman Catholic conciliar movement for church reform.

2. Willard referred to George Gordon Byron's poem, *The Giaour* [Infidel]: *a Fragment of a Turkish Tale* (London, 1813).

3. Fredericke Brion von Sessenheim (1752–1813) was the woman to whom Goethe wrote love poems but abandoned soon after he fell in love with her. She was the daughter of a pastor and his wife whom Goethe visited when he traveled to Strasbourg, Germany, in 1770–71.

20 March 1869

. . . Kate deals with me severely for not writing more & better letters home for publication—the more, as this is my sole income. Somehow the zest is gone from composition. When I was twenty, it was my highest pleasure—now, it is a sort of task. Reading the crispy journals & books of the French has wearied me to the last degree with my own prolix, vapid style. It seems impossible for me to learn the meaning of the word *condense*. Perhaps my life long habit of detailing events in my diary has been a harm instead of the benefit I have believed it. . . .

24 March 1869

. . . Madame recounted the result of her interview with Dr. Laboulebene. He thinks in K's case[1] an examination necessary. Spoke very slightingly of the remedies suggested by Mrs. Dolley. Said "it was absolutely impossible for a woman to penetrate far into the mysteries of medicine. That as mid-wives they answered very well but should attempt nothing further—indeed in France it was not permitted, happily." That M. L. is a fine physician there can be no doubt, but we are so indignant at his narrow-mindedness that K. is determined to wait until Mrs. D. arrives & submit her case, anew, to her kind & skillful hands.[2] A hundred years from now what will be thought of the man's sense who pronounces such a verdict as this, upon women-physicians? There is *one land*—just one—where *pure prejudice* is gradually getting its deserts—*universal execration*. Prejudice—pre-judging—verdict without a hearing of the case—this is the hideous monster which all liberal souls were sent on earth to fight.—Happy is everyone, who in sincerity & love for what is good & kind breaks the most lances in this warfare! . . .

1. Kate Jackson suffered from headaches that kept her from sleeping, and she also experienced severe leg pains.

2. Willard and Jackson expected the Dolleys to arrive in Paris in late spring and to travel with them throughout the summer. They actually arrived on 22 May 1869.

22 April 1869

. . . *The Maison Impériale de St. Denis*—was founded by the first Napoleon under the superintendence of Madame Caupan,[1] & its object is to educate—gratuitously if need be—the daughters, sisters & nieces of French officers who have rec'd the Cross of the Legion of Honor. . . . A lady . . . took us in charge, & with us, two French officers who wished to visit their daughters & thus we made the tour of the huge *Maison.* Carrying a portentous bundle of keys & walking rapidly with "genteel" swing, this "Dame de Premier Ordre" [Lady of the First Order]—such is her classification among the "Lady inspectresses" & "Lady dignitaries"—explained most courteously the various Dep'tments & seemed pleased that we Americans were enough interested to visit the establishment where first as pupil & afterward as officer she has spent—what I judge to be—her forty years. Upon the left wing of her pretty, butterfly over-garment she wore the Cross of the Legion of Honor. The sight scandalized our conservative & elegant Madame Perrot but delighted Kate & me. (If they will have such play-things for men, why not for women equally deserving? I honor the Empress[2] more for giving Rosa Bonheur this decoration when she was Regent & the Emperor in Italy, than for any other act. Madame P. says the "chevaliers" were disgusted & she herself thinks it was "entirely uncalled for." Ah my beloved, timorous sex! Progress has more to contend with from your gentle hands than from the Lords of creation whom generations of freedom have taught to rise above the dictum: "Things have been so & so they must remain.") . . .

A large garden . . . is the play-ground of the pupils. The[y] are obliged to take two or three turns thus, for their health, after which they disperse over the broad grass-plot, playing, picking daises or talking together—only never more than four must be in company & they must go with their own class! A shady Park extends still farther from the Maison—but there they go only at intervals & as a reward of merit. I innocently asked if the young ladies ever left the grounds? "Why would you have them do so? Mademoiselle," demanded the Dame, in astonishment. Poor thing! Their honor would be imperilled in her estimation. She has always lived here—she regards this place as perfect in all its way—& she has never seen America! . . .

I was so preposterous as to ask if there was such an organization as a "Literary Society." The lady was painfully mystified as to my meaning. She will perhaps ponder on it as a fresh illustration of American lawless-ness. "We permit no societies whatever," she replied. . . . We traversed the great shady court—received a shower of complimentary last sentences from the lady who . . . asked us to call upon the High Dignitary, the Lady Superintendent in her Cabinet—(which we declined) and bowing halfway to the ground, turned the key upon us, whose loud *click* was to me a lively indication of St. Denis' character, malgre [in spite of] its many admirable features.—What wonder that from the ranks of too great innocence & cultivated weakness that go out hence at eighteen, the "demi-monde" is so often recruited— the elegant demi-monde, to be sure! All their lives they look upon the other sex with fear that attracts rather than repells;—as a mystery they fain would solve. Young & romantic they leave this isolation full of dreams & resolutions, often to marry men whom they have never met before & who have inspired no sentiment of love in their untutored hearts. Having no "dot" [dowry]—the most of them—they are not likely to be allied to men as well-educated as themselves, money being given in exchange for their accomplishments. Under the cloak of marriage a French woman ranges society at will. Young, ardent, weak, these new-made wives meet in the intoxicating surroundings of the ball or theatre-box, a man whose refinement & good looks attracts them irresistably—& after pledging love & honor where they could not give them, they wrest from fate the satisfaction of their dreams at the price of their virtue. Poor, untried hearts! One weeps, but can not wonder & should not too severly blame. For society— for a government that fosters all this, no matter how unwittingly, let indignation be reserved & let that word that has all promise in it ring out here as over the hopeful sea: Reform—reform! The other class, who do not marry, accustomed to be taken care of without labor, to mingle with companions who are rich—for many are at St. Denis & enter the rude life of the self-supporting, inadequately-paid work-woman—find it hard & distasteful & accept the offers always awaiting a young, pretty & accomplished woman, to live in luxury at a price—paid all too soon, alas, by a grown-up child, whose heart impels her & whose imagination whispers of a bright future in which all may be retreived.

St. Denis gave me more vivid ideas of the difference between this land of art & culture & our land of *civilization* than I ever had before. . . .

1. The Maison Impériale de St. Denis was founded by Napoleon I in 1807 as a school for daughters of legionnaires. The school was headed by Jeanne Louise Henriette Genêt Campan (1752–1822), a lady-in-waiting to Marie-Antoinette. In 1815 the institution moved to the location Willard visited, the Abbey of St. Denis.
2. The empress of France who conferred the Cross of the Legion of Honor on

Rosa Bonheur was Eugénie, Comtesse de Teba (1826–1920), wife of Napoleon III, who reigned from 1853 to 1870.

23 April 1869

. . . Letter from Mother that did my heart good. . . . She tells me of her hopes & wishes & "sets me thinking," painfully. What has the future for me? I still ask, as doubtfully at twenty-nine as I did at nineteen. When I go home I must take fate in hand! It has played long enough with me! Mother says she can not cheerfully offer me a victim to my ideas (& hers!) of the Woman Question as today presented. My own timidity is so great that I shrink from what I believe my true occupation. Am I fitted for marriage? I am not rich & shall doubtless never be;—I have not the graceful habitudes of dexterity with the needle, the broom & cake-spoon. And yet I am a *woman* & nature never denies herself.—Well—we shall see. . . .

29 April 1869

. . . We visited the Church of St. Thomas d'Aquin and its "chapel of ease" St. Clotilde—both religious rendezvous of the aristocratic Faubourg St. Germain. . . .[1] It pleases every sense of beauty & of fitness—this gorgeous church—these clustering pillars & glowing canvasses; these kind-faced priests walking to & fro among the white ranks of the devotees;—this sweetly-echoing music—these solemn vows that reach into eternity. And yet—our ways—"the good old ways"—are best. "The inward & spiritual *life*" how vastly higher is it than "the outward & visible *sign*." The childhood of a religion requires material helps—its vigorous manhood asks but the unseen Spirit—yet in so doing asks what is highest, choicest, strongest in the universe. And yet, there is the question of consecrating to the Deity who gave them, the inspirations of genius as expressed in the Fine Arts—of making His Temple the Temple of *Beauty* as well as of worship & love. Perhaps we Protestants lean too far toward one extreme;—the Catholics, certainly, have gone too far in the opposite direction. My thought is this: let Architecture with its solemn & infinite suggestions of its lofty columns & twilight arches consecrate its best results to the church of the living God. Let music whose echo might be choirs of angels bear the soul upward in its reachings forth toward Him. Let Poesy celebrate the triumphs of the Gospel of Peace; let Sculpture, even, carve for us in stone & marble white as their earthly record, the forms of Prophet & Apostle; but let not that other art—high & inspiring as it is—whose results Coleridge defined as "intermediate between a *thought* and a *thing*"[2]—let not its glowing poems invade the sanctuary. They do not enough abstract the soul from the world of warmth & color where the demand of doubting Thomas seems so natural & necessary—to touch—to *know*. Faith flies aloft on snowy pinions—along a track ungilded. Let the soul's hope freely follow her. Let the ineffable face of Jesus look on us from Heaven only—and forbid the too daring hand to disclose the form & features of *The Father*—no matter how lofty the imagination to which they are revealed. And on the day when trusting youth takes on its soul the vows to which we have just listened in the beautiful church of St. Clotilde, let no thought of the white robes they wear distract that inward contemplation of Him who alone imparts whiteness of soul. Let the *heart* talk with itself & with its Lord while the outward appearance is as usual;—this surely is most in harmony with the Spirit of Christ's religion.

1. St. Thomas d'Aquin, a Jesuit-style church begun in 1682, and Ste. Clothilde, a Gothic revival church begun in 1846 and completed in 1856, are both located in the Faubourg St. Germain, a district of Paris noted for its aristocratic residences and fine hotels.
2. Not identified.

6 May 1869

. . . Kate and I visited the . . . Musée des Chinois—Galerie Assyrienne & Galerie Egyptienne—at the exhaustless Louvre. . . .

New thoughts come to me in these strange surroundings;—ardent desires to push with my puny arm the chariot that, moving slowly across the earth from East to West, is bearing *humanity* from the pitiless ages whose relics are here, toward that warm, sun-lit, tolerant Future—"When all men's weal shall be each man's care."[1] It smites me with a new heart-ache the thought of those mysterious ages when from the grip of the *stronger* there was no appeal; when thousands lived the life of brutes & died the death of martyrs that an accursed ruler might wreak his blind, benighted will. Ah humanity—tearful & bleeding the day of thy redemption draweth nigh! On the sweet Western breezes does not a thrilling prophesy half-understood— come to you, dark-faced people of Ethiopia telling of better days & milder fortunes, or to you, almond-eyed children of the East, whispering of help that hastens toward you from younger, & more hopeful regions? God likes America! I write the words with grateful tears.

May we be *good*—may we be tender-hearted;—may the sweet words of Jesus be our battle-cry in the new—the holy—the bloodless war.

1. Not identified.

7 May 1869

. . . With Miss Gates I visited Mademoiselle Daubié 70, Avenue Champs Elysee—the author of "La Pauvre Femme de Dix-Neuvieme Siecle"—to whom we had a note of introduction from Miss Anna Blackwell. She is a thorough French woman; tall—dark—talkative—neatly but plainly attired—kind and frank. She was "receiving" in her parlor, but as we wished to have a somewhat extended conversation with her she excused herself, climed with us to her pretty, orderly bedroom;—showed us how she was revising the book she had written ten years since & which is soon to appear in extended form;—wrote notes of introduction for us—gave us addresses—copies of the new journal "Les Droits Des Femmes"—showered upon us questions about "the movement" in America & said "You know it is from you that we first got the idea that woman might dare to be & to do more than she has as yet." She said I must visit the professional Schools—the libraries for books upon the subject—& that she should be glad to see us any time in the morning when she was alone. If all ladies would be as kind to one another as she to us what strength they would find in union! She said the greatest evil here was the seduction of young girls—who worked for their living—by rich men. Wages were so low that the poor things often sold their honor to eke out the pittance they could *honorably* earn. . . .

Called on Miss Putnam,[1] the young lady who is studying medicine in the regular College of Paris. She is the daughter of E. P. Putnam—of Magazine fame.[2] Up six flights of stairs in a fine "hotel meublée [furnished lodgings] in a menage [household] of her own—with an intelligent French woman for company. She is small, younger by several years than I am, brown, soft, & womanly in appearance;—sensible but rather hesitating & not at all brilliant in conversation;—steady & quietly determined. The two ladies were seated opposite a little study table bearing a shaded lamp & a book each. Miss P. had some medical work—her friend "L'Ouveriere" of Jules Simon.[3] A large case of books occupied one end of the room. There are four others—one of which, her pretty sleeping-chamber, Miss Putnam showed us. We had a good long talk about the professional schools—about French politics—about our travels. Miss P. gave us lemonade & cakes—saying she thought she would treat us to an American refreshment. I do not altogether understand this young lady (being, unlike my friend Prof. Scoville, un-clairvoyant in respect to character) & I see some "symptoms" that I do not altogether admire, but she is kind & straightforward—which is *two-thirds* in the summing up, upon the credit side.

1. Mary Corinna (Putnam) Jacobi (1842–1906) was an American physician, a graduate of Female (later Woman's) Medical College of Pennsylvania, who was in Paris from 1866 to 1871 to receive advanced medical training. She married Dr. Abraham Jacobi in 1873 and by the mid-1870s was the leading woman physician in the United States. As well as being a practicing physician, she was a medical educator and a prolific writer on medical subjects.

2. George Palmer Putnam (1814–72) was an American publisher and editor who founded *Putnam's Monthly Magazine* in 1853. In 1866 he established the publishing firm of G. P. Putnam and Sons in New York City.

3. Jules Simon (1814–96) wrote *L'Ouvrière* [The Woman Worker] (Paris, 1861), a study of the horrible working and living conditions of women industrial workers in France in the late 1850s. A prominent French philosopher and republican politician, Simon was also a writer on philosophical and political subjects and edited the work of several French philosophers.

10 May 1869

. . . Went to the bank & Kate drew the last of our Letter of Credit. This year abroad has cost about twenty-one hundred dollars apiece. Where should I ever have found or how have earned as much? Figures make it stand out conspicuous—the generosity beyond the seas, the love this side, that has taken me under its wing. May I be really grateful & may I *act* so—& may these undeserved, unpurchased opportunities be turned to good account for sake of others—since I can never pay my benefactors. . . .

14 May 1869

Spent the afternoon in the department of the Louvre devoted to La Sculpture de la Renaissance—in La Petite Salle Italienne—& in the Salle des chef d'euvres Francais. Among the Italian pictures we took solid comfort—resting our eyes among the colors of Giorgione—Titian—Da Vinci & Raphael. . . .[1]

After the Museum was closed we walked in the shady Tuileries Garden[2]—noted its groves, its statues, its fountains & parterres [flower beds]—its crowds of elegant loungers—& listened to the military music of the emperor's finest band.

It is a full life—an artistic—a manifold that the Parisiens lead—

but it is too public—too charged with impressions & empty of reflections for an Anglo Saxon nature to long enjoy.

I like their gardens—I wish our cities had lungs as large & as free in their play—but I am thankful that our climate drives us to the hearth of home—the one true altar on which the fire of love & of fidelity burns brightly in my native land—thank Heaven! . . .

1. At the Louvre Willard saw the works of the Italian Renaissance painters Giorgione (Giorgio Barbarelli, ca. 1477–1510), Titian (Tiziano Vecellio, ca. 1488–1576), and Leonardo da Vinci (1452–1519).

2. When Willard was in Paris, the Jardin des Tuileries—the large public garden next to the Louvre—was part of the Palais des Tuileries, a royal palace that was destroyed by arson in 1871.

22 May 1869

. . . We visited . . . *Le Jardin Mabille!* Here I am tempted to make a long & a very *black* mark & leave the rest to the imagination. What we saw between the hours of ten & twelve o'clock in this beautiful, fairy like spot exceeds all I had ever imagined of the permitted public indecency of Paris.

Never mind—I permitted my eyes to look upon the gilded abomination & I will honestly write it down. . . .

Hundreds of well-dressed gentlemen, scores of ladies—really such—and crowds of gaily-toiletted, painted, flashing-eyed, bold-faced women who are *lost* in the direst of all senses promenade the wide paths of the garden;—honestly earned poplins & merinoes brushing against brocades & velvets which were given in exchange for honor & for purity;—glances of curiosity from innocent & inexperienced eyes quenched in the bold return-gaze of an abandoned creature whose beautiful lips her husband & her children might this night have pressed in a happy Christian home—*if*—if the "Evangile" [Gospel] of which she speaks so lightly had but taken deeper root in France!

Music begins—a waltz. The circular dancing-ground is cleared. Three or four groups of dancers in different parts of the ground, take their positions. They are all abandoned women but their partners, all young men, well dressed & with the latest Paris style of hat upon their heads, are, in many instances, members of "good society"! The women, or girls, rather, for none of them are over twenty-two and one hardly fourteen, are all in long dresses & jaunty round hats (this last style confined at Paris to the *demi-monde* & foreign ladies). As they whirl in the mazes of the waltz they lift their ample ruffled skirts far above their knees and with the utmost effort at obscenity "strike out" right & left their tiny, high-heeled boots—with smiles upon their faces and hands clasped around the necks of their impudent-looking partners. I turn away with a blush & a sigh—having seen, for the first time in my life, a dance which has not even the poor merit of skill (as has that of the ballet on the stage) but caters to one taste only & that the most depraved of all. . . . Two young, well dressed women form the center of attraction in the cleared space just large enough for their manoevres. They clasp their pale-faced partners with both hands around the neck, raise their garments to a fearful heigth and whirl around the circle—most of the time with their heads thrown back—eyes closed—smiles on their lips and often borne by their partners, their own feet do not touch the ground. At first I can not look at it—a deathly sickness comes over me—I wish to cry—I talk, without thinking where I am about the awfulness of such scenes permitted, nay, authorized, in the capital of the civilized world. . . . When the horrid whirl is ended, the two young "stars" raise their clothing, pretending to pin some under-garment that is disarranged & gentlemen (?) standing by eagerly offer their assistance, which is readily accepted, while others peer under the lifted skirts & one young man playfully puts his hand before the eyes of a youth who accompanies him. Other men lay their hands upon the bosoms of the two dancers & laugh & talk familiarly with them while they respond readily & seem pleased by the "attention"! Soon they resume the dance—with new partners & a new "step" but the old horrors, lifting their feet higher than their heads at every turn—indeed enacting obscenities that I will not write down—& after what I *have* written they must evidently be hideous beyond discription. Strange indeed it is to watch the crowd around them;—abandoned women in large numbers—men in groups, most of them young—& hanging on the arms of husbands & of brothers, English & American ladies by scores—some with eye-glass in hand intent upon the scene—others turning away with sad faces—& French ladies, also, one of whom is with a gentleman who murmurs—"*Helas! C'est bien triste*" [Oh, how very sad]. . . . About midnight, magnificent fire-works were crackling in the air & we departed.

What an evening had we spent—the like of which I never dreamed before & never wish to experience again. I query whether the insight into Parisian peculiarities is worth the losing from my sensibility, even for an hour, that innocent ignorance, that painful shudder at sights impure—for, I confess, that after looking for sometime, the first horror was gone, and my repugnance was intellectual rather than emotional. What then would become of a *young-man* without the safe-guard of religion, in such surroundings! He would be lost in an evening to the rectitude of his early sentiments. I brought from this gilded pit, a renewed resolution to *help women* if I can—to labor for their *financial independence* among other things—which will surely put them on a vantage ground against temptation—and to give them other ambitions—a true aim in life. One woman can not do much, but what one can do let me essay.

23 May 1869

One year ago today we set out from America, alone. Now we are surrounded by friends—assured—well—safe—& looking forward to another year even more full of lessons & of happiness. . . .

Kate & I can not dissipate—were not made for it! I was ill all night, & we did not rise til ten o'clock.

It is election-day in Paris! The walls are covered with "un dernier mot" [one last word], & reiterated "confessions of faith" from men anxious to be sacrificed for their country. Rochefort's sanguinary red placard, Mancel's, in yellow, Thiers & Olliviers brief announcements[1] & the white official bulletin, are pasted indiscriminately along the walls among a dozen other candidates' declarations of loyalty & principles. . . .

1. Victor Henri Rochefort (1830–1913), a political writer and republican, opposed the rule of Napoleon III. Louis Adolphe Thiers (1797–1877) was a statesman and historian, running for reelection to parliament, where he led the anti-imperial movement. Olivier Emile Ollivier (1825–1913) was a republican member of parliament running for reelection. J. A. Mancel also ran for parliament in the spring 1869 election.

[*Willard and Jackson spent the summer of 1869 with their friends, the Dolleys of Rochester, New York, touring Belgium, Holland, and along the Rhine River. They went mountain climbing in Switzerland and from there Willard and Jackson headed south through Italy, reaching Rome in mid-October to stay for three months.*]

30 June 1869
En route through Belgium

. . . We are, on this trip, trying the merits of the second class hotels. Last summer we sounded the depths of expense & the hights of elegance at those of *premier ordre* [first class] & the contrast will give us a greater variety of experience & a less depletion of purse. Our companions are especially desirous of the latter result & doubtless the arrangement is thoroughly sensible. Yet I confess to qualms, as the perspiring porter loaded our trunks & sacs de nuit [night cases] upon a huge dutch wheelbarrow, attached himself thereto & toiled along the street while, from the narrow "Rue du Petit Boucher" [Little Butcher Street] we emerged, following on foot to the Station. It was discreditable no doubt—the repugnance of a penniless person like me, but it seemed not to assort well with our past as it existes & our future as it looms before us. I believe much in the influence of surroundings & somehow feel myself another being in the society of elegant furniture—cultivated persons and a generous style of living.

1 August 1869
Lucerne, Switzerland

Today, in a long letter to my Mother I tried to "give an inkling" of the revelation afforded by my climb to Rigi Kulm.[1] Too weary & conscious of bones & muscles that never before asserted their individuality to repeat the effort I refer myself to said letter with the remark that, in physical pain never exceeded in my history, faint & sick beyond endurance almost, I made the tour of beautiful Lake Zug & my kind friends rested several hours at Goldau[2] while by Kate's & Mrs. *Dr.* Dolley's active aid I was restored sufficiently to mount a horse & keep the ladies of our party company in the long climb, while the Doctor & active little Sumner[3] made the ascent on foot. That day scenery took hold of me as I never dreamed it could before, and the emotions of grandeur & sublimity made an impression for which I am happy to believe I shall be different & better always. . . . We had a distant view of a storm among the Alps which was almost like a revelation of another world & those majestic peaks under any light or shade are wonderful to gaze upon. . . .

Four hundred scenery-hunting tourists slept on the summit in the great damp hotel where the chill air searched our bones though 2) in the valley 1) we had left below us a genuine July afternoon. At four o'clock an Alpine horn announced the sun-rise & before its earliest note was breathed we were upon our feet after a night of indifferent repose. Standing on Rigi's topmost peak we learned the wondrous landscapes with our eyes while our lips repeated the names of "Bernese Oberland," "Eiger," "Wetterhorn" & "Jungfrau"[4]—this last with greatest pleasure for more of poetry hangs round this snowy head than any other reared from Swiss vallies toward the stainless sky. . . .

This was my first experience of mountain climbing; my first view of scenes invested by a thousand imaginings with the charm that renders dearer what is lovely and majestic in itself. To some, perhaps to *most* natures, the first experience of what they had long anticipated with pleasure far exceeds what any repetition can afford. Perhaps this magical land—superior in its attractions to any other I have seen,—may falsify this observation and experience;—so I hope. . . .

1. Willard had reached the Rigi Kulm [the summit of Rigi], an Alpine peak located beside Lake Lucerne.

2. Lake Zug is northeast of Lucerne and just north of Rigi. Goldau is a village in the east side of Rigi, a favorite starting point for ascents to the Rigi Kulm.

3. Charles Sumner Dolley (1856–?) was the son of Sarah (Adamson) Dolley and Lester Clinton Dolley. He became a doctor and marine biologist and by the 1930s was living in the Bahamas.

4. The three peaks Willard mentions, the Eiger, the Wetterhorn, and the Jungfrau, are part of the Bernese Alps (the Bernese Oberland).

7 August 1869
Interlaken

. . . [Interlaken] has been called "an English boarding-house with a road running through it" & this is a vivid & an almost exhaustive definition. . . . Two thousand travelers, changing every day, make of the one long shady street a promenade more cosmopolitan than the Parisian Boulevards—& here, walking along this morning I met handsome Charlie Haskin one of my former pupils, with Dr. Jewell of Evanston, whose praises are in Mother's frequent letters. . . . Dr. Jewell & his boys, (Charlie Haskin, Fred Huse, Philo Beveridge & Jerome Collins)[1] came to see us at our hotel & we had a lively hour's talk about home & our travels & our proposed trip to the East. Somehow I felt lonesome after they had gone. The thought of home came to me with new force—the wish that my higher course of study in these historic lands were ended & I were soon to see my Mother's flower-encircled cottage & to be folded in her faithful arms. How earnestly I prayed that night—I, whose life assorts so poorly with my prayers—that Mother might be safely kept—that I might go safely home to her!—But it all comes back again—the zest for travel—the pleasure in what I learn—the eagerness to gather pictures & fancies for less varied & propitious years. I can *do* so much more when I go home. I shall have a hold on life & fitness for it so much more assured. Perhaps—who knows?—there may be noble, wide-reaching work for me in the steady, mature years that stretch before me—the years of intelligent labor for which we are so long in getting ready—some of us, at least. . . .

1. James Stewart Jewell (1837–87) was an Evanston doctor accompanying several young men from Evanston on a European tour. Willard was acquainted with all of them: Charles G. Haskin (b. 1851), Frederick Josiah Huse (1847–93), Philo Johnson Beveridge (b. 1851), and Jerome W. Collins (1850–69).

12–13 August 1869
Freiburg

. . . We think this picturesque town anchored to the neighboring hills by famous bridges of wire,—one of them boasting the distinction of being the longest in the world, should be re-christened *Fleaburg* if last night's sufferings of ours are a fair sample of the reception given to travelers by its entomologic legions! We were driven from bed to floor;—rallied with our one weapon,—a bottle of ammonia—found it vain & came off wounded & worsted at last! The minor torment of our lives are the *bills* presented by others than the hotel-proprietor and the accounts liquidated in the "solemn midnight hours" when business ought to be laid aside & repose to assert its gentle sway.

"Any how" mutters Kate as she "scratches a match" & "looks" [for] her pitiless tormentors, "when we go home to America there'll be no more of this—so take your fill ye vampires!
You won't have me long!" . . .

25 August 1869
Chamouni, Italy

. . . Coming along the sandy path which ten minutes earlier had lain beside a precipice, my mule stopped—went upon his knees & lurched over for a "roll." Sophie[1] had had troubles with hers & the Guide having taken its bridle, I was left leader of the procession. I knew the position was a dangerous one. If the mule turned & he was in the act of doing so—I should fall under him & perhaps be severely injured. Never before in my life had I experienced any kind of accident worthy the name. Even in my reckless childhood I had never fallen been run away with, thrown from horses or even fallen from my "Eagle's Nest" in the old oak.[2] My first "casualty" was reserved for a famous locality—the vale of Chamouni—foot of the Mer de Glace![3] It is strange how many thots flew threw my brain in that instant of deliberation—for there was a conscious pause in all the hurry of the scene. Briefly—I jumped. And such a jump! I shot clean out of the saddle—over the "horn"—over the mule's head—& landed on my head in a bed of sand not a hand's breadth from a huge granite boulder which had I hit would have opened other worlds to my unready spirit. I made no sound & had no impulse to relieve my mind in that way. But a brace of shrieks rang in my ears—from Kate & Sophie & the latter's querulous voice said: "Are you dead or are you alive—tell us for mercy's sake!" I laughed inwardly in spite of the chaos from which I was emerging. For in that brief flight through the air what thoughts overwhelmed me—& when that pulverized sensation came as my head struck how instinctively I watched with keen, mental vision to see if there was a rift any where in this frail "house I live in" through which strange, phantom light shown in! I seemed to grasp with ready thumb & finger every joint in my frame & instantly to certify them all as sound. I then sprang up & thinking with wild joy "not this time then!" yet without special gratitude or a climbing of my dizzied thought up to the Cause of things & the Preserver, shouted "O—I'm not hurt—not hurt at all" & felt about for my inseparable eyeglass! Sumner came up & smoothed me off a little & condoled with me; Mr. H.[4] seated me upon a stone & wrapped my cloak around me. Just then I saw the boulder which my head had just escaped. I had trembled before with the shock to my nerves. But now, their kindness, & above all the thought of what I had perhaps *just missed*—I so wayward & so unsteady—came rushing in upon me & I covered my face & cried.

All of which analysis is written because the experience was altogether new—& when safely over—interesting to contemplate!

That night, how long I prayed—& resolved to be a better woman than before—& how kind was every one—& how tender was Kate—though she said nothing.

1. Sophia Strong, from Rochester, N.Y., was a friend of the Dolleys and was traveling through Europe with them.

2. The "Eagle's Nest" was Willard's private place for writing during her childhood in Wisconsin. It was located in a black oak tree at the gate of Forest Home. She hung a sign on it reading "The Eagle's Nest, Beware!" to discourage her brother and sister from climbing up to it.

3. The Mer de Glace [Sea of Ice] is part of the Glacier des Bois [Glacier of the Woods], near Mont Blanc. It was the main point of interest for tourists visiting Chamouni.

4. J. W. Hurn was a photographer from Philadelphia who joined Willard's traveling party briefly for the trip to Chamouni.

4 September 1869
Milan

A notable day for in it I am wrought upon by the

Duomo of Milan.[1]

A person largely gifted with "the critical faculty" might smile at the assertion—in view of my large patronage of the adjective family—that I am not "wrought upon," easily. But his sneer doesn't at all alter the fact. I would give much to be more impressionable—but nature says to us "thus far—no farther" in these things.

Europe has yielded me some hours of exaltation—of noble aspiration & tender reverie. At Melrose Abbey, Yorkminster, the English Lakes;—in the Copenhagen Museum of Thorwaldsen—at Frederick's Sans Souci—in Père la Chaise & at the Invalides;—climbing the Rigi—sailing on the Bay of Uri—under the shadow of Mt. Blanc—at Cologne—along the Rhine—& here.[2] Perhaps nowhere *more* than here—as from the bustling street of this city of unwonted activities I walked into the quiet through which the choir-boys voice stole;—into the shadowed air that incense had perfumed;—under the far up arches that dead generations had lifted to their serene places—among the giant pillars & the solemn aisles. I thought of the young fancies that I had so cherished, about these dreamy far-off lands—& above all this land of Italy. Often in my varied wanderings they have been disappointed—but not this morning. All I wished for is around me—and I walk about in grateful, silent mood, knowing that not many times shall I have better thoughts. Away up in an arch of the nave hangs *One* upon the cross. . . . What has it not wrought in the earth—overturning & recreating—that death of the despised Nazerene on Calvary? Renan[3] may turn the Gospels to a legend & Rationalism may dissipate them in thin air with its sneer at the illogicalness of the miracles but when all is done, Christianity may point to this marble mountain with its thousands of glittering statues and demand an explanation of that most transcendant miracle—Christ's church—the visible, of which this radiant cathedral may serve as symbol, the invisible shrined in a million hearts;—the militant, of which all who follow the Master's steps in doing good are members, & the triumphant who died in one sweet faith. We may wander in head—we are truer than we thought, in heart. The brain questions,—the sympathies make soft replies;—the great needy world will never turn away from Jesus Christ.

The believing generations that reared these mighty walls are linked to our faithless age by the sound of the mason's hammer still hewing stone for the same temple—whose ceaseless time-keeping makes no discord in the solemn chorus that strikes the ear. Even so, hand in hand, the past & present lead each other toward the light that shines alone from Heaven.

I wanted somebody to talk to. Sister Dolley is a companion not uncongenial & we exchanged ideas a little. She avowed "a bending tendency" never felt before, in presence of all this majesty of proportion & variety of impression & suggestion. Kate & "Murray"[4] were already making the circuit—"doing" the place for she avowed we had "no time to lose."

But I thought I *had* time. So I wandered off & listened to the music—& felt rather than thought a thousand things not translatable perhaps—at least not by my powers over the word-interpreters of mind. . . .

1. The Duomo in Milan, one of the largest churches in Europe, is an impressive example of Italian Gothic architecture.

2. As Willard noted, these were some of the most significant sights she had seen thus far on her European tour. Melrose Abbey is the site of the ruins of a Cistercian abbey in southeast Scotland. Yorkminster is the cathedral at York in northern England. The English lake district was a favorite of sightseers because of its associations with several English Romantic poets. The Bertel Thorvaldsen Museum in Copenhagen was endowed by the neoclassical sculptor Bertel Thorvaldsen (1768 or 1770–1844) to house his collection of classical art. Willard saw several of his sculptures in cities she visited. Frederick the Great of Prussia (1712–86) built "San Souci," a French-style rococo palace, in Potsdam. Père Lachaise is a cemetery on the northeast side of Paris. The Hôtel des Invalides is a large Paris hospital founded by Louis XIV for the care of wounded and aged veterans. The Bay of Uri is on the east end of the Vierwald-statter See, a lake beside the Rigi.

3. Joseph Ernest Renan (1823–92) was a French philosopher, historian, and orientalist whose study of Jesus, *La Vie de Jesus* [The Life of Jesus] (1863), which rejected the claim of Christ's divinity and portrayed him as merely a man, was considered scandalous by most Christians in Europe and the United States.

4. John Murray (1778–1843) of London published travel guides popular in the nineteenth century. The guides covered most countries and went through many editions. Willard and Jackson studied Murray's guidebooks for nearly every country they visited.

22 September 1869
Bologna

Well, I have spent 22 days in Italy and my pen has worked its industrious way through all the close-lined pages of one stout little book and emerged into this larger place still to go scribbling on & on & endlessly. If I remember rightly it was in high heroics that I set forth those *naive* "first impressions" which are so delightful to the traveler but which soon cloy upon the ear of the unmoved listener. Now I have come to "sober, second thought";—the rainbow side has passed from view by a turn of the kaleidoscope, & the "neutral tints" & shadowy backgrounds;—the browns & greys have worked themselves into the picture. This must needs be in all experiences of life;—I am only thankful that it is not my nature to anticipate the "shady side" while it is my fortunate capability to look upon it undespondingly when it presents itself.

Not that Italy has disappointed me. It has been as different as the Ideal & the Real must ever be—& then its people seem less promising perhaps;—its streets more motley with the poor, the halt the maimed & the mendicant;—its houses a dirtier yellow & their arcades more odorous & somber;—its hotels less immaculate, more strongly saturated with stable-extracts & supporting more six-legged inhabitants to the square inch than is quite pleasant to experience & to remember.

But then, "all, this is nothing here nor there" in comparison with the treasures of art & the miracles of learning that one finds stored away in every nook & corner of this curious land, and if we most appreciate what we have taken the most pains for, as some wiseacre has said, then the pictures we have rode after, the libraries we have steamed after, the landmarks of history & poetry that we have sought in weary, beggar-chased & flea-infested pi[l]grimage have thrice repaid us in all our pains. . . .

A particularly "wet" & gloomy morning did not enhance the brilliance of these "first impressions" but we had, luckily, the most delightful of all refuges from the dolorous "out-doors" aspect—namely, the

Picture Gallery[1]

which seemed to me one of the pleasantest I had ever visited. . . . Well, in this palace of delights we spent most of the day—(untroubled by any impatient "fling" at our silliness in so doing) and as I look back upon those rooms tapestried so royally, I really believe my eyes have learned what the ingenious French chemists have thus tried to learn in vain—how to render colors by the photograph,—so clear & rich stand out the pictures that I copied there! What is the use of talking about art, when one is low down in the abc class as I? But what a keen delight it is & cause for liveliest gratitude than we who do not altogether understand, can *feel;*—that beauty has a sweet, exalting mission to us from her lofty seat and that she beckons kindly to us & bids us be of hope—if only we are humble, willing learners, at her feet. . . .

We presented ourselves at the door of the great old university for which we felt an especial affection because of the enlightened tolerance which centuries ago permitted what Harvard & Yale would scorn today—the admission as students & to professorial chairs of intellectual beings whose only fault was that they were women! The porter who was sunning himself at the entrance door as porters do, hardly knowing what disposition to make of a trio of ladies who seemed to have a resolute purpose but lacked the language to express it, handed our case over to a learned looking gentleman who emerged from some dry-as-dust corner of this learned edifice &, addressing us in tolerable French demanded our errand? We were a little nonplussed, not having any very definite one—beyond the wish to get as far as possible upon the track of the Bolognese Hypatias[2] of a more enlightened day, but, not quite liking to avow this foolish fancy, we stammered something about "visiting the collections of the university" & as Murray had mentioned a mermaid's skeleton we finally asked for that! Hiding an unmistakable smile behind a scholarly white hand, the gentleman pointed out a nondescript fossil in a case before us and said that was the mermaid & that many had been found in the vicinity, with a variety of marine animals but that the collections were closed at present—on account of the vacations. There was nothing for us to do but take our leave—& yet, those learned ladies & their professorial chairs! I bravely broached the subject—saying that we felt particularly interested to come here because of Mademoiselle Novella d'Andrea, teacher of law, whose beauty was so great that she lectured from behind a curtain not to distract the minds of her pupils;—of Laura Bassi, professor of mathematics & natural philosophy; of Madonna Manzolina, professor of anatomy & Matilda Gambroni, the predecessor of Cardinal Mezzofanti in the chair of Greek & Oriental languages.[3] The gentleman seemed to appreciate our interest and to regret that he could reward our diligence no farther than to assure us that, to the best of his knowledge & belief those ladies had once lectured in this very building & that yonder, among the busts & monuments of the long, dim hall where we were now standing was a medallion representing Professor Matilda Gambroni of the languages. Saying which he politely took his leave & we, after a careful inspection of the delicate outlined face of this exceedingly "strong minded" lady, went our way from the somber old edifice, full of respect for its prophetic enlightenment and newly aroused upon the question that is now coming fairly upon the stage for final settlement:—Is there sex in mind?—for, when all is said the clamor & the prejudice amounts to nothing more than this ignoble query. . . .

1. The Picture Gallery of Bologna was formed as a part of the Accademia Clementina di Belli Arti in 1796 by Napoleon. One of its most notable paintings was Raphael's *St. Cecelia,* which Willard wished to see.
2. Hypatia (ca. 370–415) was a neoplatonist philosopher from Alexandria, noted for her work in mathematics and astronomy. Willard considered the learned wom-

en who taught at the University of Bologna to be Hypatia's successors since they were women who defied tradition and became scholars.

3. Novella d'Andrea (fourteenth century) was learned in canon law and lectured at the University of Bologna in place of her father, Joannes Andreae, a distinguished canon lawyer, whenever he was unable to do so. Laura Maria Catherine Bassi (1711–78) received a doctorate in philosophy from the University of Bologna in 1733. She occasionally lectured at the university in physics, mathematics, and logic. Anna Morandi Manzolini (1716–ca. 1774) was an anatomist. Clotilde Tambroni (1758–1817), whose name Willard misunderstood as Gambroni, was a professor of Greek at the University of Bologna. Giuseppe Mezzofanti (1774–1849) was professor of Hebrew and Greek at the University of Bologna from 1803 to 1808 and, again, from 1814 to 1831. In 1838 he became a cardinal.

28 September 1869
Genoa

(Upon which memorable day I enter my *third decade*[1] become sensitive about my birth day—don't tell any body but Kate—who gives me a pretty filagree "sett" by way of condolence—& yet at heart dont feel as solemn & dont regard the catastrophy as great as I did that of ten years ago, when, a sentimental ignoramus at Forest Home I wrote pathetically in the journal I was then keeping as assiduously as now that "the romantic ages had circled singing out of sight & cold, bleak & relentless, 'twenty' fell upon my ear"!²) . . . "If I know my own heart" (as good people say in Class Meeting) I was never braver for the future nor half so well prepared in resolution and in intellect to do some service to my fellow-women.

When I go home—& sweet is the sound of those words to me who came so eagerly & have learned with so much zest—when I go home I mean to turn the splendid opportunities with which dear Kate's generosity has endowed me to practical account—& I dimly know in what direction it will be. . . .

1. Willard was entering her fourth decade, not her third, since 28 September 1869 was her thirtieth birthday.
2. Not identified.

3 October 1869
Florence

. . . Bright & lovely dawned the Sabbath morning & after a leisurely breakfast, during which we took a pleasant retrospect of our five weeks journeying through Italy, & congratulated ourselves on the fortnight of delightful life at Florence upon which we had now entered, we took a carriage & drove to our bankers, confident that we should there find all that we missed from happiness—letters from Home. Yes, there were several. One from Mrs. Dolley, post-marked "Rome," & that we read first, as our plans depended somewhat upon hers, on account of Sophie's being with us. It was a kindly, cheerful letter, & I read it to Kate as we drove along. . . . I opened a letter that I had received from Ross, & this was the first sentence that it contained—& this I read in the bright Florence street: "My dear friend Frank: It is my sad duty to make you the medium for the communication of most heart-rending tidings:—*Our Father is no more.*" What language can convey the faintest idea of that sudden, cruel, relentless thrust of fate! How black became the smiling heavens how leaden were our hearts. *Kate's Father,* loved & honored by her as few fathers are;—so noble, so good & generous, always in perfect health & with a rare promise of long life in his manly face & well-knit form;—my benefactor, the friend who more than any or all others had given into my helpless hands the means of intellectual growth— the power so long & ardently desired, of learning in the world's great school what I should some day use for good in my own home;—my beneficent genius who freely held his hand out to me full of rare & noble gifts, comprehending perfectly the situation though his own busy commercial life had taught him little about demands so different, held to be so visionary by most men whose unaided talent & industry has wrought out wealth. And I could never thank him, now;—could never, in the many ways that I had planned, testify to him my life-long gratitude. These thoughts rushed to my heart and forced sudden & bitter tears upon my cheeks. We drove hurriedly to our hotel, grasping each other's hands & crying like two children. My poor friend, his beloved daughter Kate, how pitiful had grown her cheerful face! "My Father *dead*—my dear, kind Father," she murmured in a voice mournful & grievous to hear, & I tried to comfort her, while the firm bond of our long friendship grew closer & more tender than before. It is a mercy that when such calamities overtake us, a thousand considerations oblige us to give attention to practical affairs. To-day there were numerous letters to be written—telegrams to be sent—plans to be devised for the future—whether we should go immediately home—as Ross suggested—or to proceed to Rome & there await our baggage forwarded from Strasbourg. For some time we had no other thought than to return directly, leaving for Paris the next day, but we were strongly advised by the English physician whom we called to see Sophie who was taken suddenly ill, to await our trunks at their destination, if we would ever see them again, & he has lived long in Italy & knows the uncertainty of its freight department.

9 October 1869

We have now spent a week in Florence, hard at work—the laboriousness of the seeing in painful contrast with the beauty—calm & changeless, of the sights that have awaited us for centuries. But when one's heart is a whole ocean's breadth away, even the great Magicians like Angelo, & Raphael & Giotto[1] weave their spells in vain. The eye mirrors their marvellous visions as faithfully as ever, & the steady brain perceives them, while ready memory performs her pleasing task & treasures for the future the truthful copies that someday will afford so much delight. But all the while a protest from the heart rings in our ears:—"Who spread this wondrous city out beneath your eyes;—who leads you through its gleaming galleries, its sculptured squares, its cool & shady gardens?" . . .

Who thus played the Royal Prince, the loving fairy, the generous friend? Ah, who but he whose grey & honored head lies low this sunny day—whose kind eyes mirror no more the pleasant earth & sky—whose heart that loved us is cold & still! How often in these long and busy days that might have been the most delightful of all that we have spent abroad, has the vision of one kind, grave face in its frame of frost-tinged hair shut out the sweetest picture—the sublimest statue—the most wondrous architecture that human brain & hand have evoked from the rich realm of the Ideal! How often, looking at each other, we have exchanged the unspoken thought—"this seems a mockery since *he* is dead" & then we would remember his counsels & his character & say "But I am sure that he would wish us to do just as we are doing—to improve, even now, the rare privilege he gave us"—& so we have comforted one another with these words. What a week it has been—so long, so full, so rich, so sad! . . .

But what I marvel at is that so firmly & with such self-control my dear friend has taken up the duty of the hour—has anticipated the quiet years when all we saw & learned in these hurried, painful days should yield its lesson.

At night has come the storm of grief—of memory & of tears.

1. Michelangelo Buonarroti (1475–1564) began his artistic career as an apprentice in Florence, and Willard viewed some of his most outstanding early works there. Giotto di Bondone (ca. 1266/67?–1337) was born near Florence and apprenticed there. Several premier examples of Giotto's work, particularly frescoes, are in Florentine chapels. Willard noted in her journal her trips to see the works of both artists.

18 October 1869
Rome

. . . Really, it is very pleasant we find to be in Rome out of season. We are regarded as a savory morsel by custodians of galleries, churches & museums & feel a certain agreeable proprietorship, not less flattering because so transient, in the pictures that are uncovered for our especial benefit while the solemn doors that turn upon their hinges for us alone, have a certain tone of welcome as we think in their unaccustomed creak. At the great & handsome hotel which we inhabit as pensionnaires, we have every thing our own way & are treated with a consideration almost oppressive in our character of Drops before the more plentiful shower. For us the waiters don their long-tailed coats, the porter cleaves to his post with his official cap, the great bell in the court rings its pompous twice repeated summons to the elaborate table d'hote which with all its mystery & importance was concocted in the unknown recesses where two French cooks have their labratory for us alone. Indeed, I am quite sure that never before did I adequately realize my individual importance & if things hold so for any length of time, I shall acquire those loftinesses of demeanor & those fastidious tastes & tendencies so little becoming in a simple American whose chief occupation heretofore has been the inclining of the human twig in the way the tree should grow.

Today, Kate's trunk came—several weeks earlier than we had been told to look for it. Should she now be sent for to go home, there need be no delay & for this reason we shall be the more diligent in seeing the things we should so deeply regret not to have even a casual idea of, were we required to go within a few days.

We spent the evening in the salon with Madame S.[1] the lady-proprietor of our "establishment." She is a "Roman matron" of the modern times, & not unworthy of the character. Handsome, tall, dark, of elegant manners & much intelligence, she is an interesting study. She speaks no English, but French with perfect fluency having been educated by the sisters of the Sacred Heart—of whose order she was once almost a member, having passed a year in the novitiate "after a great disappointment in life which came to her very early." Outwardly she is a Catholic, but at heart a sort of "libre-penseur" [free-thinker] & a Garabaldian.[2] She bemoans the backward state of Italy among the nations, & especially the condition of our own sex. We three "women alone" are a perpetual admiration to her. She says there is not in all Italy a lady of the age of any one of us & unmarried who would dare travel as we have done for the last few weeks. "You Americans are as far ahead of us," she said, "as we are in advance of the Turkish women." . . .

1. Madame Amalia [?] Sopranzi (b. ca. 1835) was the proprietor of the "Pensione du Globe," the boardinghouse where Willard and Jackson stayed for two and one-half months in winter 1869/70. Madame Sopranzi was recommended in Murray's guidebook for Italy as an excellent Italian teacher and Willard and Jackson took lessons from her during their stay. Willard quickly learned that Madame Sopranzi was not a republican free-thinker as she had thought, but a devout and rather superstitious Catholic. However, her two sisters were supporters of Garibaldi, as her father had been.

2. Giuseppe Garibaldi (1807–82), the Italian patriot and military leader of the Risorgimento, the Italian independence movement, was extremely popular with many Italians, as well as many Americans, for his republican views.

13 November 1869

. . . I ought to have rec'd my Mother's letter this afternoon. . . . A nameless anxiety oppresses me;—I seem to hear her gentle voice in tones of pain and to see upon the face of all faces dearest to me, the marks of illness & distress. I do not at all believe in premonitions—having never indeed been subject to them—but this vision troubles me. Kate says it is because of the calamity which we heard at Florence. Let us hope so, & may Heaven grant what I desire more than all things else on earth;—that a few months hence, these self-enforced lessons in which Mother has delighted even as I have, may be ended & I may safely reach her quiet fire-side and clasp again the hand most faithful to me that the whole world contains. But I have lived a life so purely intellectual—so selfish & unconsecrated—since I came abroad, that I dare hope for so much happiness only because dear *Mother* is so good and prays so constantly for me.

3 December 1869

. . . Went to the bank & read the home papers awhile with as much relish as, if I were at home, I should peruse a letter from a friend. Find that things are bravely marching on in the fearless young land— that the President & his cabinet are behaving like honest men & that the noble "isms" of the day are taking greater hold than ever upon the public heart. Most of all I am interested in the "Woman Question" & jealous for its honor & safe-conduct to a just & reasonable issue. I wonder if I shall be so fortunate, on my return baptized into the spirit of *untrammeled life for all,* by the floods of wrong-government that flow in these stereotyped lands, & thrilled by the helpless voice that cries from palace & from ruin, "When shall the heavy hand be lifted, & all rational beings left to grow, as trees do, under the equal sky,"—I wonder if so much happiness is in reserve for me, as to give some honest help in the generous, new crusade? To write or utter some earnest words for evolution, not revolution;—for *womanly* liberty, not the wild license of that nondescript being who is in politics what "Mrs. Jellaby"[1] was in religion. . . .

1. Mrs. Jellaby is a character in Charles Dickens's novel *Bleak House* (London, 1852–53) whose unthinking enthusiasm for philanthropic causes makes her an ineffective busybody.

7 December 1869

The day before the Council[1] & the bells have rung long & loudly;—the roar of carriage wheels has risen to a tempest;—the streets are thronged and the half-filled tables in our salle-a-manger well surrounded by hu[n]gry travelers. . . . Americans & English are not, however, largely represented—the convocation not having interested them particularly, it would appear. . . .

We joined the throng that was passing to the Church of the Holy Apostles (James & Philip)[2] where Pope[3] & Cardinals were to assist at the closing of the "Neuvaine" that precedes the Fete of the Immaculate Conception[4] & Opening of the Council. I have described the pomp & ceremony that we witnessed here & sent it to the N.Y. Independent so will forbear the repetition. It must have been one of the Pope's proudest & happiest moments when he was greeted by ringing bells, clanging martial music, & that more grateful sound of thrilling voices shouting "Viva Il Papa [Long live the Pope]!" while men waved their hats in real enthusiasm & women's handkerchiefs fluttered thickly as wings of flying doves. I could but think if only the Church of Our Lord had remained one & had continued *pure,* if the successor of St. Peter had arrogated to himself no undue power, what a divine significance might have been in the scene I witnessed! Will it ever be, I wonder? Is a sight so blessed in reservation for the happier eyes of unborn generations? Shall she go forth one day in her beautiful garments, the spotless Bride of Christ, whose glorious espousals a united world shall recognize? May it be so! Never until today did I dream of the power & sweetness that is in the dim conception even, of such a possibility.

1. The Vatican Council (now known as Vatican I) was the twentieth ecumenical council of the Roman Catholic Church. It was convened by Pope Pius IX (see note 3, below), opened 8 December 1869, and was suspended indefinitely on 20 October

1870 when Piedmontese troops occupied Rome. The council focused its attention on two issues: the interrelation of faith and reason in light of contemporary ideas such as rationalism, liberalism, and materialism, and the authority of the pope. The council declared the pope infallible when teaching definitive doctrine on faith and morals.

2. The Church of the Holy Apostles, dedicated to Philip and James, two martyred apostles of the early church, was founded in the sixth century and rebuilt in the fifteenth century.

3. Giovanni Maria Mastai-Ferretti (1792–1878) became Pope Pius IX in 1846 and served until 1878, the longest pontificate of any pope. During his reign, state and church were finally separated in Catholic countries, the authority of the Roman Catholic Church was centralized in Rome, and the Church was placed in opposition to liberalizing politics and intellectual life.

4. The pope closed the "Neuvaine" [nine days] of preparation for the Feast of the Immaculate Conception celebrated on 8 December. He set the opening of the Vatican Council on the day of the Feast of the Immaculate Conception.

8 December 1869

Opening of the "Ecumenical Council."

I doubt if Rome, old as she is & varied as her experience has been, was ever earlier astir than on the morning of this day. . . . Crowds had already assembled at St. Peter's[1] before the bells struck off the cheerless hour of five and when our comfortable carriage load, invigorated by the breakfast that awaited our appearance at seven o'clock, set out for the scene of action, the tide of emigration in the same direction was frightful to behold. . . .

Alas for human foresight! Had we not planned to be among the earliest to take possession of the great Basilica & behold the streets many squares distant from St. Peter's, lined on each side by empty carriages which have already deposited their too-enterprising burdens though it is but seven and the Ceremony will not take place till nine. Arrived at the great square we became fully convinced, perhaps for the first time, that "early birds" alone can hope for toothsome morsels! The place is red with Cardinals carriages & black with commonplace humanity all of whom are engaged in a break-neck race for the wide, inviting, blocked-up doors of the Cathedral. We file in between gigantic guards with old-fashioned muffs upon their heads, carrying the burden of our wilted hopes. What . . . a sea of human faces . . . waves of human forms—what a deep ground-swell of human voices! . . .

At last the boom of minute guns announces the long-looked for moment;—the peal of bells joins its rich alto to this solemn bass and the clear, seraphic voices of the Pope's choir completes the chorus. Every soldier stands with lifted bayonet; the crowd exists but for the sake of its eyes & its opera-glasses & standing on tip-toe on my marble balustrade I—one among its forty thousand integers—behold the passage of the august procession. Behold it, yes, but at a distance of one of the aisles & half the nave of the hugest existing church; over the heads of the greatest crowd ever gathered within doors and on the darkest morning that ever rained down shadows. As a veritable chronicler I can pretend to nothing more than having literally looked upon the heads of the Catholic Church—which I would respectfully report as for the most part grey where not bald, tonsured or concealed by skull-caps! The procession was half an hour in passing. . . .

The venerable gentlemen moved very slowly as became their dignity & the majesty of the duties, to which they were going & last of all came the good Pope who left his *sedia gestatoria*[2] at the door & walked to the Council Hall with his brethren—to the scandalization of the commonalty who had comforted one another with these words: "At least we shall get a good view of His Holiness borne in his chair of state."

What was done at the High Altar & in the Council Hall deponent saith not. We all crowded as close as possible to the great open door of the latter when the members had taken their seats & were rewarded by a glimpse of white-robed Bishops sitting in wide semi-circles as the saints are represented in the heavenly visions of Fra Angelico[3] & above them royal personages—the Empress of Austria & the Queen of Hungary[4] and the like—looking very black and unseemly in such a shining company. Four times we charged upon the phalanx that had crowded around the open door aforesaid but were driven back in confusion & disgust. . . .

A droll sight was St. Peter's statue (him of the kissed-off-toe) in golden tiara & glistening metallic robes—his stern bronze face & imperial gesture in grotesque contrast with his old lady's costume and the spirit of that religion of which he professes to be the earthly chief. They were gathered around it as usual—the rich & poor, mean & great, lavishing kisses on the historic toe. This one spectacle would cure me of all Catholic "leanings"—if I had any. Rome is the place where an independent & thoughtful mind first learns how dear to it is the purified, simple faith that brave Luthur & gentle Philip Melancthon[5] won for us from the grim grip of Roman pontiffs. Any Protestant who goes over to the Catholic Church here is not worthy the faith of his fathers & will be true to none except in a formal or esthetic sense. . . . [We] drove home . . . fatigued beyond measure and thankful beyond words that Ecumenical Councils happen not more frequently than once in three hundred years. . . .

1. The ecumenical council was held in Saint Peter's Basilica, the seat of papal authority.

2. The *sedia gestatoria* is a portable throne on which the pope is carried in procession, held high enough so that he can be seen by the huge crowds in Saint Peter's.

3. Fra Angelico (originally Guido di Pietro, ca. 1400–1455) was a Dominican monk and a great artist instrumental in developing the early Renaissance Florentine style.

4. Elizabeth (1837–98), Empress Consort of Austria and Queen of Hungary, was one of the royalty in attendance at the council.

5. Philip Melanchthon (1497–1560) was a humanist educator and a leader of the German Reformation.

16 December 1869

I wonder often, & puzzle myself sadly to understand the change in my heart of hearts since we have come to Rome. Always, before, there was in me an under current of cheerfulness, of bravery of faith in God & man that no grief of my life sufficed to more than check for a short time.

> "But now I know, where'ere I go
> That there hath passed away
> A glory from the earth."[1]

The world seems so sadly out of joint;—"the cry of the human" sounds so wailingly in my ears instead of that wonderful anthem that so charmed them when my hopeful heart delighted to believe that

> "Earth, with her thousand voices praises God,"[2]

And all this comes from no private grief for there is no "worm i' the bud"[3]—& what the years have given & taken I receive in gratitude & patience & grow humbler & softer-hearted as I trust under the sunbeam & the chastening rod. Perhaps what I experience is the deep & awful shadow that the eternal city casts from a past so full of sin, a present that has little to encourage the philanthropist, & a future murky with forebodings. Perhaps the "Niobe of Nations"[4] has a spell to make all eyes grow moist with her own immortal grief. I cannot tell— but life has little charm for me & only by crowding its hours with intellectual occupation can I cheat myself into the guise of happiness. . . .

1. Willard quoted from William Wordsworth, "Ode: Intimations of Immortality From Recollections of Early Childhood," stanza 2, lines 8 and 9, in *Poems in Two Volumes* (London, 1807).

2. Willard quoted from Samuel Taylor Coleridge, "Hymn Before Sun-Rise, in the Vale of Chamouni," first published in *The Morning Post and Gazeteer* (London, 1802), line 85.

3. Willard quoted from William Shakespeare, *Twelfth Night,* act 2, scene 4, line 112.

4. Willard quoted from George Gordon Byron, *Childe Harold's Pilgrimage* (London, 1818), canto 4, stanza 79, line 1.

25 December 1869

. . . We rose at a quarter before six o'clock A.M;—donned the prescribed "black silk with veil," took opera glass, prayer book & copy of "Lives of Italian Poets"[1] to read in case the waiting hours pass heavily, and after a gas-light breakfast sally out into the oozy Roman streets. . . . Off we go to St. Peter's. . . .

The tramp of troops sounds through the nave—Roman Zouaves, French soldiers and the "Pope's own" file in;—music mellows the scene—from far off approach the seven symbolic tapers & the crucifix, the tiara on a cushion—the two great fans & behind all under the Latin canopy, Pius the Ninth, clothed in pure white vestments of satin trimmed with gold & flinging from his aged fingers the usual benediction. . . .

He kneels before the high altar, the vice-gerent of Him who went into a mountain apart to pray; he swings the glittering censer & the cloud of incense curls up into that wondrous dome above our lowly heads—that dome which, to my thought lacks but Correggio's "Assumption"[2] to be a heavenly revelation such as can not be excelled by man (only let "assumption" there refer to Christ, rather than Mary). He intones prayers in a clear, firm voice, marvelous in a man almost eighty years of age. The choir responds (for the people I suppose) in voice almost celestial from its high place—both pope & choir uttering the words of the Evangel grown dear to Catholic & Protestant alike because they speak of Jesus in the touching hours of infancy—because they implore his consolations & his pardon as Mediator & Judge. . . .

We went to vespers at

Santa Maria Maggiore[3]

and the rich, rosy effect of the illumination upon the tapestry-hung columns;—the sweet-voiced choir and stately chant of priests splendidly attired, gave superlative delights to eye & ear. In a costly casket of gold which stood among the glimmering tapers of the altar, were five of Jesus' *manger-boards* exposed to the believer's gaze. Over the heads of the priests, in the tribune were mosaics of great age, representing the coronation of the Virgin & displaying that purity & elevation of expression so characteristic of sacred art in earlier ages. It was pleasant thus to link today with that yesterday far off, & to know that the praises of "the Hebrew Mother's Child" were chanted then as now—nay with sincerer fervor. . . .

What a Christmas it has been to be sure! How full of impressions—how lavish of magnificence. The brain—the eye—the ear—to them this has been a feast indeed. But after all, I have a *heart* also, some where about me, & that pleads in its still small voice—"Let me pass my next Christmas in a little Gothic cottage near Lake Michigan & let me hear some of those simple old hymns, we used to sing when we were *Five* & a plain sermon in the ugly wooden church near by."

Be patient, long-suffering victim of my adventurous years. Next Christmas you shall have your programme carried out or you shall listen to lovelier voices than those of the Pope's choir in a temple compared with which St. Peter's is a gilded toy—even the Heavenly Home to which, in His pity & love may Christ our Saviour admit "even me."

1. Willard was reading Henry Stebbing, *Lives of the Italian Poets* (London, 1831–32).
2. Correggio's *Assumption of the Virgin* (1526–30) is a fresco in the dome of the cathedral at Parma.
3. The Basilica of Santa Maria Maggiore, established in 352, is the principal church in Rome dedicated to the Virgin Mary.

4 January 1870

. . . *Edmonia Lewis*[1]

the "colored lady" from Boston has a pretty little studio very pleasantly located on our street, & her works as well as her manners are very pleasing. I took especial pleasure in my visit, because, it is particularly agreeable to see one who, like her, occupies an exceptional & not a desirable position in the world's estimate, gifted with the power to create beauty & harmony for itself—blessed with that sweetest of all solaces—an engrossing & congenial occupation. She is young, cheerful & strong, unusually good-looking for her race, though she has its salient characteristics of physiognomy & voice.

She has a full-size statue of Hagar[2] in the moment of her despair—her most ambitious work, & one full of promise for her maturer fame. A pretty group called "Hiawatha's Wedding"—one of her earlier works;—a fine, idealized bust of the poet Longfellow for which he gave her sittings when in Rome, last winter; several excellent busts of Americans & a medallion of the Abbé Listz,[3] a friend of hers, whom she told me she often hears play, at his villa near Rome.

A privilege this of her genius to which many a wealthy traveler vainly aspires. . . . We said goodbye, with a cordial hand-shaking & the heartiest good wishes for her future. I took "solid comfort" in the contemplation of this girl, so free, so worthily at work, so thoroughly appreciated for what she has done & will do. An anomaly it is indeed, to find at Rome—the most conservative, most middle-age city of Europe,—the daughter of a proscribed race leading a true & perfectly untrammelled life—uninterfered with, because outside all the interlacing lines of Papal government—time-honored custom—& going her way quietly free as air—just as one day all men & women are to be—a day which, may Heaven hasten!—Heaven & the prayers & generous labors of all thoughtful souls. . . .

1. Edmonia Lewis (ca. 1845–post 1909?) was an American sculptor of African and American Indian descent. She attended Oberlin College for a time and then studied with a sculptor in Boston. In order to continue her career as a sculptor, in 1865 she moved to Rome, where she was encouraged and supported in her work by members of the American colony there, principally the actress Charlotte Cushman and the sculptors Harriet Hosmer, Anne Whitney, and Hiram Powers. (Willard also visited the studios of Hosmer and Powers.) Lewis's subjects included several Indian groupings inspired by Longfellow's *Hiawatha* and a sculpture of two slaves receiving news of emancipation. After completing these representational works, Lewis moved toward the neoclassical style popular at the time in Rome, and her piece *Hagar*, which Willard saw in her studio, was in that style. She was drawn to the subject because she felt great sympathy for all women who have struggled and suffered. She continued working in Rome for the rest of her life, periodically visiting the United States. Her sculptures were very popular at the Centennial Exposition in Philadelphia in 1876.
2. "Hagar in the Wilderness" was a biblical subject (Gen. 21.1–21). Hagar was the slave woman of Sarah, the wife of Abraham, who had borne a son, Ishmael, to Abraham. Sarah had a son, Isaac, and became jealous of Hagar and Ishmael and fearful that Ishmael would be Abraham's heir along with Isaac. She prevailed upon Abraham to send Hagar and Ishmael into the wilderness where they wandered, suffering from great thirst, until God intervened, providing water from a well and promising that Ishmael would be, like Isaac, the father of a nation.
3. Franz Liszt (1811–86), the famed piano virtuoso and composer, took minor orders in the Roman Catholic Church in 1865 from Cardinal Hohenlohe at the Vatican and was thereafter known as "Abbé" Liszt.

6 January 1870

. . . *Ara Coeli*

the strange old church built on the site where stood the temple of Capitoline Jove[1] is the last in which a Catholic pageant at Rome is beheld by our observant eyes. Elsewhere I have spoken of "Il Santo Bambino [The Holy Child]"—an image carved in wood & covered with the costliest jewels, to which great healing powers are ascribed & which "receives more fees than any physician in Rome." Today this doll is taken from the arms of its Mother, where since Christmas it has lain in state, in a carefully arranged representation of the Nativity & worship by the wise men, given annually in this church, & with music by a military band is borne by a bishop, accompanied by a procession of monks all around the church, exhibited to kneeling thousands on the lofty church steps & then placed on the high altar where the priests incense it, the monks sing to it & all kneel down to kiss its toe!

I'm glad this was the last Catholic ceremony I saw in the chief city of "the Church." Apologists would say "it was but another manifestation of that versatility of the Mother Church which adapts itself to all classes, giving milk to babes & meat to strong men;—that the peasants—of whom the congregation was chiefly composed find in this ceremony an expression of faith & that we must give people what they can understand & can enjoy." . . .

But what a cowardly view is this to suit a religion to a people! Rather, bravely & kindly suit the people to the religion as we do in America! If they are so low—so ignorant that they can be taught only through the eye, place under them the lever of the common school—the free press—the simple, truth-telling pulpit! Don't come down into the dirt & wallow with them but take them by the hand & lift them to a higher level. It is all nonsense, though, to claim that this eye & ear pleasing religion is the only one by which the lower classes can be won. Look at our own dear church—the Methodist, for instance—see its simple, gospel precepts sink into untaught hearts & renovate them till they become temples of the Holy Ghost. Put Christ's Evangel straight against man's heart & it will thrill & purify it;—transmute its dross to gold—heal its foul wounds & fill it with the sweet perfume of faith & love. Out upon these empty & degrading shows—winked at by the learned—held up before the weak-eyed multitude instead of Our Saviour's naked cross! For me—I love my country & would suffer, I once thought, all that my nature is capable of enduring, in her behalf. At Rome I have learned that there is one thing for which I could be brave enough to die—& that is my religion! If any body wants to "confirm the feeble knees" set them walking toward Rome & stand a steady head above them that it may contemplate these religious farces of which I have made record!

Truth—*truth* has come to be a word at which my heart throbs quicker & my eyes fill with hopeful tears. Crushed—trampled—spit upon—forever crucified by her foes & betrayed in the house of her

friends, she yet shall rise—triumphant & serene to heal the bleeding wounds of poor humanity—to wipe away the immortal tears that
deluge our fair world. Thank Heaven!
        "The Eternal Years of God—are hers"![2]

1. Santa Maria di Ara Coeli, a sixth-century church, stands on the site of the Temple of Jupiter Capitolinus.
2. Willard may have paraphrased "Since heav'n's eternal year is thine," a line from
John Dryden, "To the Pious Memory of the Accomplish'd Young Lady, Mrs. Anne
Killigrew," part 1, line 15, a poem included in Anne Killigrew, *Poems* (London, 1686).

                                                                7 January 1870

    . . . In afternoon, the incessant souvenir-gathering, so tiresome, &
yet so agreeable when one thinks of all the pleasure thus stored up
for friends at home. Kate excused me from a corset-hunting enterprise in which her heart was much enlisted, & I passed a most pleasant hour at "Hooker's,"[1] reading the home-newspapers. I should think
the grand Republic "moving on" worthily, & President Grant one of
the most honest & trust-worthy of Chief Magistrates. With what pleasure I contrasted his first "message"—recently delivered[2]—with the
"Pope's Bull" for instance! "Let us so discharge our duties that when
we return to our places in private life it may be with the approbation
of an enlightened & free constituency—& of our consciences." I was
glad to see that the coolie-labor scheme is to be nipped in the bud
by Congress; that Utah is likely to be "dealt with" according to her
deserts; that the black man is quietly taking his new & rightful place
& that Wyoming Territory has in its Constitution—already approved
by its Governor—placed woman on the same basis as man before the
law—in duties & in privileges. This will bring the great question directly before Congress—which must approve the Constitutions of
territories before they can be valid, & I am confident that this step
will form a new era in the progress of a reform to which I am more
than ever a friend since I know more of life & of the world. Let the
gentlest creature God has made—the kindest, the most pitiful, take
her place in the scale of intelligent being, in a manner perfectly
untrammelled. Let every weight be taken off—imposed in the long,
dark conflict of might with right & muscle against moral power. Then
we shall see to what level the world will sink or rise;—we shall know
the full value of each integer in the problem of life; we shall have
called all the forces Heaven has given us, into the field, & who knows
if at last the angel of love shall not win & the demon of hate cringe
to his sulphrous lair. . . .

1. Willard went to Packenham and Hooker, a banking firm in Rome that served many American and English-speaking visitors. In addition to financial services, the firm also provided information to travelers and shipped parcels to England and America.

2. President Grant gave his State of the Union Address on 6 December 1869.

[*Leaving Rome in late January, Willard and Jackson met Dr. Bannister as they had arranged and made their way to Cairo where the two women took a tour up the Nile. They planned to rejoin Dr. Bannister and the group of ministers with whom he traveled in Jerusalem by mid-March.*]

7 February 1870
On the Nile River

. . . Steamer "Behera" borrowed of the Pacha[1] for a three weeks trip by "Cook's tourists"[2] & "us Americans."

One week of my restless, varying life has now been passed upon the quiet river that was once the god & is ever the good genius of the Egyptians.

Let me try to give a true sketch of an experience entirely unique.

We thought to make the trip by "dahabeah"[3] would take too long;— we found that to charter a small steamer would be difficult. Cook & his tourists came along—wished "us Americans"—sixteen in number to join them in engaging a large steamer;—in an evil hour we yielded & behold us "in for it" & afloat upon the Nile, a most uncongenial crowd of forty-seven persons, in a big, bloated, blustering steamer, all to be dined & wined, walked on shore & mounted on donkey-back by wholesale;—marshalled by a dragoman[4] in green clothes, an interpreter who speaks nine languages & important Thomas Cook, "tourist-manager" whenever an Arab village, a venerable temple or a tomb old when Joseph was Governor of Egypt, is to be "done."

Ah me! In my most romantic days I had fed my fancies upon the dreamy story of Eliot Warburton's voyage up the Nile[5]—had leaned upon his Persian carpets, sipping the little cup of mocha that his paragon "Mahoumed" placed before me & even indulged a fragrant whiff of his chibouque [Turkish pipe] as the silent boat sailed along beside a landscape plumed with palm-trees where beyond a belt of emerald stretched the desert's golden sands beneath a sky that distilled poetry & with a breeze fanning my cheek, more magical than it had ever felt before. How well told is that story—& why so charming & so impregnated with the rarest spirit of the East? Because a poet guides the pen—because eyes with a brain behind them mirrored these fair shores.

Frances Willard, taken when she was forty, in 1879, the year she became president of the Woman's Christian Temperance Union.

Mary (Bannister) Willard, probably taken in the late 1880s or early 1890s, when she was in her late forties or early fifties.

Willard with Anna Gordon, her personal secretary and companion. Willard has inscribed the photo "from your affectionate Aunt." Probably taken in the mid-1880s.

Anna Gordon   Your affectionate
                   Aunt Frances

Anna Gordon and Frances Willard, taken in 1883 in San Francisco, while on their speaking and organizing tour of the western states.

(l. to r.) Willard's mother, Mary (Hill) Willard; Frances Willard; and Anna Gordon; dated 1885, when "Madam" Willard was eighty, Frances Willard was forty-six, and Anna Gordon was thirty-two. Willard and Gordon wear white ribbons, emblems of the WCTU and its supporters.

A back view of Rest Cottage, probably taken in the late 1880s. The seated figure at the far left is probably Ruby Gilbert, one of the staff of the *Union Signal,* the WCTU weekly newspaper; the white-aproned figures at the left and right doors are servants; the figure on the tricycle is Anna Gordon; Willard and her mother stand on the second-floor balcony. The figures barely visible in the middle by the shuttered first-floor windows are unidentified.

Willard's "den"; Willard is seated at her desk. Probably taken in the late 1880s (from Willard, *Glimpses of Fifty Years,* opposite p. 544).

Willard and Isabel (Lady Henry) Somerset, dated 1892, shortly after they met.

At the apartment Isabel Somerset rented in downtown Chicago, at 229 La Salle Street, from January to March 1892: (l. to r.) Kate Lundeen (?); Anna Gordon; Lizzie, one of Somerset's servants; Isabel Somerset; and Frances Willard.

Isabel Somerset, probably taken at her London townhouse in the mid-1890s, when she was in her early forties.

Willard, taken in the mid-1890s, showing signs of aging and illness on her face.

Willard with her two stenographers, learning to ride a bicycle in fall 1893 at the Priory.

Charlotte Maxwell, a Boston gymnastics instructor, brought to England by Somerset in 1895 to set up a gymnasium at the Priory, where Willard, Gordon, and Somerset exercised.

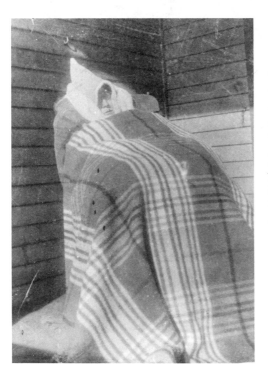

Willard taking the air on the porch at Dr. Cordelia Greene's Castile, New York, sanatorium during the winter of 1896/97. Anna Gordon wrote in Willard's 1896 journal that Willard and two friends were "bundled up like mummies and sit there breathing deeply for an hour" each morning.

Well, a sorry day it was in which Warburton taught me what the East might be to a pale-faced traveler from chilly shores & stormy skies.

The Real is a dragon under whose scaly feet the airy form of the Ideal is trampled almost always in my life's cheerful history.

We came to feel the subtle spirit of the East; instead, we felt—Egyptian fleas. We came to float musingly along the mystic waters of the world's most curious river;—we go snuffing, snorting, shaking over its tolerant breast—eyes full of smoke, ears full of discord, nose full of smells from kitchen & from coal bin. I had thought much & innocently about the pile of Persian carpets—instead, we had a coffin-like stateroom, the floor flooded with water & one small window of a single pane through which to filter in our "glimpses of the Nile." I had imagined "ambrosial nights" with lotus-dreams and wakings to a repose sweeter than slumber even;—instead, I balance myself through the weary, watchful hours on a board not wider than the palms of my two hands and fight the fleas & listen to the hideous scraping of the coal-heaver's shovel until the tears fill my eyes so tired & aching & in the morning I rise feverish and sick to be summoned to the breakfast table in the second-class cabin where Manager Cook has located "us Americans," & where we are crowded together so closely that elbows are pinioned & good-nature taxed to its utmost to keep us from "boiling over." Here we are served to the most execrable coffee I ever drank—to eggs like "loppered milk" & bread of the consistency of gutta-percha[6] & here we munch in silence our miserable fare or mutter our disgust for parties in general & "Cook's party" in particular—count how many days more must be endured and get a glimpse through a dirty window of the dirty saloon at the distant mud banks & the stalking figures of the servile race whose misery has succeeded the splendor of their ancestors. Breakfast over we go on deck but find all the eligible positions secured by the "original party" (*Cooks*)—the wind high & the attractions of the shore not such as to repay us for sitting bolt upright on our camp stools & getting into a chill. So we go down stairs—seek out No. 15 (unquestionably the meanest state-room on the steamer—a pleasant thought to Kate who pays five hundred dollars for these three weeks Nile travel); enter one at a time for the passage between our berths is but little over twelve inches wide—stretch ourselves out, take a book apiece & try to forget our discontent by reading. Sometimes Kate varies this programme by crying out right & expressing her misery in the strongest terms I ever heard her use—declaring that to come *as* she came was "the mistake of a life-time"—that she feels like one boxed up in a huge iron cylinder that rolls on & on & can't be escaped from come life or death. . . .

I never so envied men their blunt nerves—boundless capacity of sleep & of digestion—& freedom from impedimenta as when contemplating these hearty Englishmen, encased in muscles deduced from rare roast beef, as they hop, skip & jump—every where & any where—even poking their blunt noses into our state room where we are both standing on our beds in our night-gowns, & grinning broadly at us as they drawl out their endless "I beg youah paw-don"!

Well, have I scolded enough? Have I fully relieved my mind? Have I honestly depicted the actual feelings of a middle-aged American woman, not of vixenish temper nor very hard to please, during the first days of that voyage to which she had long & expectantly looked forward upon the King of Rivers? . . .

So let us dismiss the dream, as we have silently, sadly taken leave of many an other sweeter even than this, &, turning the clear, intellectual gaze that never fails the honest learner, upon the state of the case as it exists, let us get *instruction* since we can not have poetry from . . . our long, laborious trip upon the Nile. . . .

1. Ismail Pasha (1830–95), the ruler of Egypt from 1863 to 1879, attempted to modernize and westernize the country.
2. Thomas Cook (1808–92) was an English businessman who founded the worldwide travel agency Thomas Cook and Son. Willard and Jackson joined a Cook's tour of the Nile.
3. A dahabeah is an Egyptian sailboat suitable for Nile travel that can accommodate up to twenty-four persons.
4. A dragoman is an interpreter and professional guide for travelers in the Middle East.
5. Eliot Bartholomew George Warburton (1810–52) was a famed Middle Eastern traveler whose book *The Crescent and the Cross* (London, 1844) describes his travels, including a trip up the Nile.
6. Loppered milk is spoiled and curdled. Gutta-percha is a tough substance resembling rubber and made from gum trees of southeast Asia.

9 February 1870

. . . I rode on to *Memnon's statue* alone—thinking of a picture of this very landscape by a great German artist that I had seen in the Leipsic Gallery[1]—& whose wondrous lights & shadows, whose ghostly forms of stone had, as much as any one influence to which I had willingly submitted, formed my ardent wish to see the East. And here I was—riding alone & free over the Plain of Thebes—& yonder sat the vocal statue "on his eternal throne" just as he has been sitting four thousand years. I galloped my lively donkey around the solemn Pharaoh & his mate—though I had eyes for him alone. I measured with long glances his awful hight. . . . I picked up some square chips of the rich brown Nile mud left the last time the river shrunk away from Memnon's feet & [?] the dozen Arabs who had crowded about me gathered leaves & blades of grass from the pedestal's base. Two really pretty girls of twelve smoothed my hand with their hard, slim fingers & looked me over curiously my broad-brimmed hat with the white scarf hanging from it, my eye glass & blue traveling dress being as strange to them as their ochre stained fingers, grease plastered hair & rings in the upper & lower part of each ear were to myself. Another girl passed by as I sat there in reverie, with a clay tray upon her head containing cakes of straw & manure mingled—the only fuel of these poor people & the generator of the fleas which swarm in their miserable villages. This sight brought me back through two thirds of the world's life time & set me thinking about the present of the Egyptian race—a subject the most painful I have ever contemplated. Especially does the awful degredation & oppression (which is i[t]s cause), of women here distress me. When will man learn that if he uses his more muscular arm to hold down to the earth the woman God gave to be with him he is putting the knife to his own breast— signing the death warrant of his own elevation? That two & two make four is not more capable of demonstration than that in every age & country, woman has been the stone around man's neck to sink him to the lowest depths or the winged angel to help him to the purest heights that he has ever gained. And away there toward the sun-set— beyond the mystic Nile, the yellow sands the waste of blue waves in the land where man has grown free enough, wise enough, generous enough to let woman be just what she can become without any of his short-sighted restrictions—his proud but ignorant "thus far—no farther"! I turned toward that hopeful point of the compass & rode onward full of thoughts—& hopes—& purposes.

1. Amenhotep III (ca. 1417–1379 B.C.), who reigned over Egypt at the height of its prosperity and power, had a funerary temple built for him at Thebes. The statue of Memnon to which Willard referred was one of two huge statues known as the Colossi of Memnon that stand near the ruins of the funerary temple. The painting she recalled seeing in the Leipzig Gallery was *Statues of Memnon* by Johannes Jacob Frey (1813–65), a Swiss landscape painter.

6 March 1870
On the Mediterranean Sea, en route to Palestine

Night of March 6th closed my eyes upon Egypt—& in a comfortable cabin of the Russian steam ship "Grand Duke Constantine,"—

after a tranquil passage opened them at 6 am upon a low, sandy coast
& a hilltop crowned by a white walled town while sun-light from behind the clouds spread broad blades of light over the distant landscape—lovelier to me than even light of home. Between me & the
shore shimmered the sea even in the unwonted calm bearing out by
its motion the reputation of the Port—or want of Port at Jaffa—Yonder the Great Apostle had his vision[1] which gave to me, "even me" a
Gentile maiden a right to look upon the country of God's chosen
people with a sense of home stirring my heart & such thoughts of
Him "in whom there is neither Jew nor Greek, bond or free" as filled
my eyes brimful of tears & silenced my voice which in earlier, less
tender years nothing ever could unsteady or place beyond my own
control.

1. The Apostle Peter was living in Joppa (Jaffa) in Palestine when he had a vision
of a great sheet descending from heaven in which were all kinds of animals (Acts 10:5,
6, 9–16). God commanded Peter to kill and eat but Peter replied that he had never
eaten anything common or unclean. God replied that what he had cleansed Peter
must not call common. This vision was interpreted by Christians to mean that followers of Jesus did not have to observe Jewish laws of ritual cleanliness and purity and,
more broadly, that God's people now included both Jews and Gentiles.

12 March 1870
Bethlehem

. . . Visited the churches—Catholic, Greek . . . & Armenian that
occupy the choir of St. Helena's Basilica;[1]—descended the rocky stair
way & bent to read these words inscribed on a star of some bright
metal inlaid in the floor of a grotto where lamps in a half circle are
always burning:

"Hic de Virgine Maria *Jesus Christus natus est*
[Here Jesus Christ was born of the Virgin Mary]."

Near by another row of burning lamps surrounds the cradle where
they laid him & bouquets of flowers stand on an altar on the spot
where "they say" the wise men had their station.

Spite of all this "stretching of points" . . . I felt something of the
spell which must hang about a spot consecrated since the second
century by the tradition & pious reverence of the Christian Church.
He may here have been given to the needy world—the Son of Man—
the Word made flesh;—near here must certainly have occurred the
most joyful event in human history—& why not precisely here? I tried
to get a dim apprehension of the significence of this shadowy grotto

on the Bethlehem hillside & I hope I am better for the honest faith I exercised. . . .

1. The basilica in Bethlehem is located over the grotto where, tradition holds, the Christ child was born; the basilica is thought to have been built by Helena (ca. 248–ca. 328), the mother of Constantine the Great.

13 March 1870
Jerusalem

Sabbath Day. We were early up & off before breakfast to witness the ceremonies at the Church of the Holy Sepulchre.[1] To one who in Russia, has witnessed the Greek mode of worship, there was little of novelty. The same dirty, long haired, ill-smelling crowd of feverishly eager worshippers. The same priests with locks like a woman's hanging down their backs & gorgeous robes of purple, green & gold. The same sing-song ritual though without the splendid harmony of the bass voices at St. Isak's.[2] The Patriarch of Jerusalem[3] is a fine looking old man whose golden robes, huge tiara glittering with gems & heavy jeweled crosier make an appearance not less imposing tha[n] that of Pius IX on a fête day. He blessed the people repeatedly with the peculiar gesture of his church & presented to many of them the consecrated bread (the wine not being offered). . . . Then a procession was formed each priest carrying a candle & a little picture of some scripture scene which the people kissed as they passed by. The crowd, determined to get near to the Patriarch crowded so mercilessly that we were really afraid of being crushed. I thought Kate would faint away & Mrs. P.[4] said I was "white as a sheet." There may have been no danger but there certainly was extreme personal discomfort & if Kate had not caught a huge beadle by the arm & won upon his sympathy so that he wielded his big silver baton in our behalf & set the size of his vast shoulders against the brutal crowd I don't know but something serious might have befallen us. As it was, a few moments brought us to purer air & relieved us from the embrace of as filthy, odorous & uncombed a multitude as I ever saw gathered (even at the opening of Rome's great "Ecumenical,"). I received full upon nose & spectacles a gust of rose-scented holy water—walked once around the Holy Sepulchre in the priestly procession & then gladly left the church—a Turkish guard making way for us by pounding the pilgrims, men & women indiscriminately until they made way for us. . . . The finest—indeed the only fine—architectural effect which Jerusalem has yielded to my eyes, aside from its impressive walls & noble gates—is the dome above the Sepulchre. It is lofty, airy, quite simple in design, & far up its towering sides hang numerous lamps, which, when illumined must heighten the effect. . . .

A Sabbath in Jerusalem! An afternoon upon the Mount of Olives![5] To a devout soul this were worth a pilgrimage longer than any other that the earth's wide belt makes possible. And yet—& yet—we were so cold—the wind blew so searchingly;—curious Arabs pursued us so relentlessly—the intellectual part of studying the landscape & the practical part of keeping on the backs of slippery donkeys distracted our attention so that the spiritual part—those shy, sweet feelings of the heart—those tender, child like aspirations; those deep & solemn contemplations more suited to the spot than to any other in all the earth had little time to occupy us. But I had some quiet moments of a priceless worth. Gleams & glimpses of what all this meant flashed through my soul. The gentle, helpless face of Mary—my sister Mary, shrined for ever in the center of my love looked out upon me from her dying pillow & that failing voice uttered again the words "O, *Christ has come to me*—he holds me by the hand—he says 'she tried to be good—but she wandered—but I'll forgive her—& I'll save her'!"

That same Christ to whom we trusted Mary, walked upon this mountain;—& here spent the night of His infinite agony & purchased her sweet soul's redemption on the bitter cross within sight of where I stand!

Pale & wasted & framed in hair made grey by suffering more than age, another face looks on me, & my honored Father's voice rings in my ears: "Christ lived—& died—& rose again! Upon this faith I walk right out over the awful gulf of death—& I am not afraid!" Ah how these tender memories—so sad—so sacred—so inspiring— bring home to me the reality of that religion which was born into the world in yonder grey & mournful city & hence has swept its way to the remotest corner of our world. . . .

O, I must go again & yet again to Olivet;—no experience of all my life has seemed so sweet & so significant as this. . . .

I dutifully wrote several little letters to dear friends who will especially prize a communication from Jerusalem & as the pleasant twilight fell I read aloud for Kate & for myself such chapters as relate to Jesus' teachings from Mount Olivet;—the Parables of the Virgins & of the Talents;[6]—the mysterious prophecies concerning the destruction of the Temple;[7] the touching verses beginning "O Jerusalem— Jerusalem!"[8] & the narrative of the Last Supper ending with "When they had sung a hymn they went out into the Mount of Olives";[9] & the account of the Ascension when "He lead them out as far as Bethany & lifted up His hands & blessed them, & it came to pass that while He blessed them he was parted from them & carried up into Heaven."[10]

I can never tell what force—freshness & added pathos I found in all these wonderful words after the experience of this marvelous week & this chief Sabbath of my life. Why the Bible is going to be a new book to me after this!—God grant it may be "new" in a deep *spiritual* sense—that it may take hold upon my care*less* life—may make me what all teaching & the most golden opportunities must fail unless they do—a better human creature—nearer to what God meant when He created me;—more as Christ taught us we must be to serve Him on earth & live with Him in Heaven.

1. The Church of the Holy Sepulchre was built by Constantine the Great (ca. 280–337) in 335, over the places where Jesus was believed to have died and to have been buried. The church was destroyed and rebuilt numerous times through the centuries, and the structure that Willard saw was a Romanesque-style church built by Crusaders in 1149.

2. Willard had visited St. Isaac's cathedral in St. Petersburg on 25 August 1868.

3. Kyrillos II (born Cōnstantinos Krātikos) (1792–1877) was the Eastern Orthodox Patriarch of Jerusalem from 1845 to 1872.

4. Eliza Ann (Shearer) Paine (b. ca. 1830–1901) was from Cambridge, Mass., and was traveling in the Middle East with her husband. Willard had met the Paines on her Nile trip several weeks earlier.

5. The Mount of Olives (also called Mount Olivet) is a hill outside Jerusalem where Jesus spent the hours before his arrest and crucifixion in the garden of Gethsemane (Matt. 26:36; Mark 14:32; Luke 22:39).

6. The Parable of the Virgins (Matt. 25:1–13) and the Parable of the Talents (Matt. 25:14–30) are part of the discourse Jesus gave on the Mount of Olives.

7. Jesus predicted the destruction of the temple in Jerusalem in Matt. 24:1–2 and his disciples came to him on the Mount of Olives, asking him what he meant by the prophecy.

8. Matt. 23:37 and Luke 13:34.

9. Matt. 26:17–30 and Mark 14: 12–26.

10. Luke 24:50–51.

16 March 1870

Bp K,[1] Dr. Bannister, (Dr. March & company)[2] reported themselves as comfortably encamped beyond the Jaffa gate & we lost no time in getting our luggage into the prescribed compass ("nos effets [our luggage]") & walking behind the same as piled up on the broad back of one of El Harney's[3] servants through the dark & winding streets. With the least possible ceremony we introduced ourselves in camp, where three large tents—besides the "kitchen" were in order—the star spangled banner floating from that occupied by the wide-awake Presbyterian Quartette Drs. March & Goodwin, Messrs. Coan & Haydon.[4] We found our quarters quite comfortable—one large tent adorned within after the manner of a patch-work quilt of the "basket pattern";—red, white, blue & green calico in circles triangles & at the top branching out into a flaming star. Pieces of carpet cover the ground—four iron bed-steads stand thickly around (Mr.[5] & Mrs. Paine are our companions) a table occupies the center with a decent red "spread" thereon, two tin wash bowls & pitchers & one brass candle stick suitably equipped for evening. We hunt up the gimlets we have provided (at my friend Warburton's suggestion) bore into the tent pole regardless of any sensitiveness on El Harney's part & hereon hung riding whips waterproofs, carriage-top hats & so on. Things begin "to look like living." I get our books & finding in my Bible the discription of the temple built by Solomon, read it, placing myself in fancy where I stood last evening, & imagining its glories replacing the swelling dome of the caliph's mosque & listening with ear intent to that stately prayer of the wise king with its impressive iteration of "hear us O Lord in Heaven thy dwelling place & when Thou shalt hear forgive."[6] Ah but it is a new book altogether this Bible I have read so long & left so long unread! What would I not give now to have it all "at my tongue's end." I . . . made out from the various guide books a list of such places as I yet must see or must revisit in this city which has a charm for me—although it is the darkest, dreariest & most comfortless I ever saw—that no other ever could attain. . . .

1. Willard referred to MEC Bishop Calvin Kingsley (1812–70), who traveled with her in Palestine. She had previously met him in 1866 when he came to look at the site of Heck Hall, the dormitory at GBI for which funds were raised by the Methodist Ladies' Centenary Association. Bishop Kingsley was returning from a trip to visit Methodist missions in China and India and was fulfilling his longtime desire to visit the Holy Land.

2. Daniel March (1816–1909) was a Congregational minister with a Doctor of Divinity degree, serving a parish in Philadelphia, Pa., in 1870. Willard and Jackson joined his party to tour Palestine.

3. El Hani was the group's dragoman.

4. Edwin Payson Goodwin (1832–1901), a Congregational minister with a Doctor of Divinity degree, served a parish in Chicago in 1870. Mr. Coan may have been George Whitefield Coan (ca. 1817–79), a Presbyterian missionary to Oroomiah, Persia. Hiram Collins Haydn (1831–1913) was a Congregational minister, serving a parish in Painesville, Ohio, in 1870.

5. John Shearer Paine (1823–1903) was a furniture manufacturer from Cambridge, Mass. He and his wife traveled with Willard and Jackson from Egypt through Palestine and on to Constantinople, then by boat on the Danube to Vienna. Willard remained friends with the Paines, visiting them in 1874 on her way home to Evanston after attending temperance conferences on the East Coast.

6. 1 Kings 6 contains a description of the temple that King Solomon of Israel built in 957 B.C. Between 685 and 691, the Dome of the Rock was built as a shrine for Muslim pilgrims. It occupied the site where Solomon's Temple and its successors

stood. Willard paraphrased 1 Kings 8:30b, from Solomon's prayer of dedication of the temple he built: "and hear thou in heaven thy dwelling place: and when thou hearest, forgive."

21 March 1870
Nablus, Palestine

Rose earlier than usual—say before six A.M.—breakfasted in the big cistern . . . under leaden skies decked ourselves out until we looked like Esquimaux [Eskimos] in our gutta percha suits & with our big hats fastened on our backs & said Goodbye to Bethel[1] without much regret, finding & leaving it a dreary sort of place.

Picked our way painfully over & among rocks thick as if they had rained down from long past ages;—emerged into pleasenter landscapes where fig & olive trees were combatting successfully with the unfriendliest soil in which trees ever grew;—followed the bed of a dry torrent through a region set down by Murray as "thievish," whereupon our columns "closed up" & our brave gentlemen reassured us by computing that their revolvers were equal to one hundred shots in three consecutive minutes whereupon we felt & voted ourselves to be "a host." Dr. Goodwin of the eagle eye—a man that I like & admire—who reminds me strongly of my brother Oliver—called our attention to "a party of tourists" that he descried in a neighboring lane, but it turned out that the "black coats of Europeans" which he wished us to observe were the long & curling coats of a party of black goats—wending their way to pasture. . . .

And so we came to Shiloh . . . where the ark of the Lord first was established in the promised land,[2] when Jehovah was pleased to speak openly with men. As we flung ourselves from the saddle—scrambled to the slight eminence on which a ruined church & an olive tree mark the old site (unless indeed the ruined mosque & oak tree or another tree near by come more closely to the requirements of the spot) I tried to realize even dimly that here Eli died;[3]—here Samuel's pious Mother consecrated him when but a little boy,[4] to God; & to recall the prophecy of Jeremiah that the place should be destroyed.[5] Utter has that ruin been & in all my wanderings I have not found a spot more dreary—more forsaken than this stony hillside where the wind whistles through the isolated trees. . . . As we ride along through vallies grown more fertile—after leaving this spot—the gentlemen alighting from their horses to gather flowers in the wheat fields through which we pass, where constantly we come upon new & beautiful varieties—the shepherds in their long, striped robes call to us from the hill tops where their tall forms stand out against the sky, cursing us for a pack of Christian dogs.

We lunch coldly & windily upon a stony hillside turning our backs upon old Boreas[6] who scatters rudely the salt & pepper designed to help down our hard boiled eggs; & we use English walnuts instead of butter, on our hard bread—seasoning with rasp berry jam & washing down with lemonade.

Briskly we start on again after a brief halt—cross more fertile vallies—come to a Syrian "high road" which almost equals an Indian bridle path;—wind through pretty dells where olives & figs are growing in fields of tender wheat which "should be heading out"—so Mr. Floyd[7] says—but for the unexampled drouth which has sent the whole population of the country to church & mosque & synagogue praying for rain. I have now happily learned to "read Murray" . . . on horseback, & while my steady great white horse picks his slow way over the stones I trace our route with satisfaction.

At last we come to fertile vallies—"Ephraim's portion"[8]—answering fully the description of its attractions, given in the Bible, & far off Gerizim & Ebal[9] loom & we came out into a pretty, green plain, & stopped at

Jacob's Well.[10]

Here the company made a general rally;—some jumping down to the edge of the well—instituting measurements note-book in hand; others gathered the delicate leaves & grapes at the well's mouth & others still assembled to listen to Mr. Haydon's reading of the beautiful chapter that discribes how once where [we] are sitting Christ sat down to rest; how the Samaritan woman came to draw water and He declared himself to her as "that living water of which if a man drink he shall never thirst again."[11] We looked up at Gerizim to whose temple long since gone to ruin the woman pointed in her argument & over the pleasant fields on which Christ looked when he said "behold the fields are white & ready for the harvest."[12] I have hardly seen a landscape more suggestive of sweet & hopeful thought & certainly, go where we may we can never be so certain that we have found Our Saviour's earthly footsteps—that we are actually in the same place where he actually was, as here. True, the well's mouth is several feet below us,—the crusader's church now ruined, having made this its central point & placed an arch above it on top of which we sit, but He was here—within a few feet of this very spot if not actually in it, whose steps have a charm for us no others can acquire. Only those who have been so fortunate as to prove it can know what life what vividness must ever invest that beautiful fourth chapter of John when it has been read beside this well, with Gerizim on the right hand, Ebal on the left—Joseph's tomb[13] a little distance off & the fields stretching away on every side.

Horseback riding is fatiguing work sometimes;—living in tents is not the method of existence one would choose—but a single experience like that I have discribed repays the thoughtful traveler for more of hardship than he would have believed himself capable of enduring, before the spell of such a land as this was laid upon him. . . .

1. Bethel was the site of a sanctuary to God established by the Israelites before the first temple was built in Jerusalem. Abraham built an altar to God at Bethel (Gen. 12:8) and Jacob set up a pillar there marking the spot of his dream in which God promised Jacob the land on which he lay and that his descendants would multiply through the earth (Gen. 28:10–22).

2. The Israelites established their first permanent place of worship at Shiloh in the promised land of Canaan (Josh. 18:1). The Ark of the Covenant, a special chest containing the stone tablets that Moses received from God on Mount Sinai (Exod. 25:10–22), was placed inside the Tabernacle (tent sanctuary).

3. Eli was a judge of Israel and a priest at Shiloh who taught Samuel (1 Sam. 1:9; 1 Sam. 4:18).

4. Samuel's mother, Hannah, the wife of Elkanah, consecrated her son to service in the temple at Shiloh (1 Sam. 1:21–28).

5. The prophet Jeremiah prophesied that the temple in Jerusalem would be destroyed as Shiloh had been (Jer. 26:6).

6. Boreas was the god of the north wind in Greek mythology.

7. Rolla Floyd was working as El Hani's assistant while he learned the dragoman's trade. He was from Maine and had been a ship's carpenter before moving to Palestine.

8. Ephraim was the second son of Joseph and Asenath, and the ancestor of the Israelite tribe of the same name. When the Israelites divided Canaan after returning from Egypt, Ephraim received a portion of fertile, well-irrigated hill country that included the cities of Shiloh and Shechem.

9. Gerizim and Ebal were two mountains in north-central Palestine important in the Bible for their strategic location (they formed a pass between Shechem and Samaria) and for their sanctuaries.

10. John 4:6, 12, mentions that the well at the foot of Mount Gerizim that Jesus used was known as Jacob's well.

11. John 4:7–30.

12. Willard paraphrased John 4:35b, "for they are white already to harvest."

13. Joseph, the son of Jacob who was sold into slavery in Egypt by his half-brothers, lived to become a leader of his people. When the Israelites left Egypt and returned to Canaan they brought Joseph's remains and buried them at Shechem, a city between Mount Gerizim and Mount Ebal (Josh. 24:32).

28 March 1870
Camped by the Sea of Tiberias,
Palestine

Evening—Kate & I sitting on a ruined wall beside the

Sea of Tiberias[1]

with the waves rippling at our feet. . . . Bells of goats who are feed-
ing back of the camp & twilight twitter of unseen birds make up a
chorus sweet enough to hear. I get out Murray & hunt the references
& Kate reads . . . passages. . . . Beautiful words—& sweet privilege granted me to hear them beside this Sea of Galilee on which my Saviour
walked—whose storms He stilled—whose shores His sacred feet once
trod.[2] But if speech is silver—silence is golden—even when the choicest words the air has ever borne are those we miss. So here we sit long
& silently as the shadows fall;—as the clouds gather & the gentle haze
wraps the blue hills & creeps along the quiet waters that He made
sacred whose touch transformed the humblest object "into some
thing rare & strange"[3] & holy.

We drank the cool, sweet waters, bathed our tired faces in them,
filled our little tin can to carry far away to our homes & ran home to
our tent under the drip of a long-threatened shower. At dinner we
had Sea of Galilee fish & good talk from Drs. March & Goodwin about
the wonderful & lovely scenes by which we are surrounded. On the
dinner table, tasteful Mr. Hutchison[4] of the large blue eyes & poetic
ideas had placed a fine bouquet of oleanders worthy of the richest
hot-house but nurtured beside the waters of Tiberias & in the air of
the Galiliean hills.

> "The patter, patter, patter
> of the rain drops over head"[5]

was our lullaby this evening, as so often since we set forth on this
unique pilgrimage. But sleepers seasoned by 8 or nine hours horse
back riding "up & down stairs" (as Ella Simpson says) are not easily
disturbed &, for myself, wrapped in German vest, heavy cloak & worsted hood besides my night dress, & with El Hani's allotment of two
blankets, a "spread" & Kate's great purple carriage blanket, I sleep
"like a trooper" & dream like another Joseph.[6] A halo of yellow flea-
powder surrounds my pillow—a camphor bottle is beneath it & my
face is varnished with cold cream—all as a guard against intruders
& with an eye to repairing the ravages made in my complexion already tattered & torn. Our getting to bed is a theme worthy of what
Ross Jackson would call "a first-class humorist." The putting up of the
curtain just after dinner by Mr. Paine—Kate making a beeline for the
bed from the tedious sitting at table d'hote where our poor bones
are perched upon camp stools one mortal hour & a half—the distance between courses each being long enough for a smart Yankee
to "bolt" a dinner in;—the taking off of garments, I dare not say how
far from clean & piling them on a stool under our rubber capotes

[hooded cloaks] to "keep out the damp";—the tucking up of beds;— rolling of false waterfalls in pocket-handkerchiefs & packing them away in the tremendous periphery of *those hats;* the "flopping" of under garments, diligently gone through with by my friend careful Martha[7]—each article being turned wrongside out & shaken with such snap as sounds from straining sails in a high breeze. At this juncture nice brother Paine is wont to begin reading his chapter & attending to his family worship on the other side the curtain—about three feet distant. As he always chooses a "portion in season"—relating to scenes passed through that day, I have double pleasure in giving diligent heed & I heartily echo his simple prayers for guidance & thanks givings that no harm has come to us in our long & often dangerous day's travel. Gradually things "quiet down." The candles are extinguished. We hear for awhile Biblical discussions from the tent full of ministers a dozen feet off;—the bells of the mules tinkle soothingly;—the jackals cry out peevishly in the distance—& in these strange surroundings—usually on a stony hill beside an Arab grave-yard, there come to me dreams of those I love who are far away. . . .

1. The Sea of Tiberias (called the Sea of Galilee in the New Testament) was the site of much of Jesus' ministry.

2. The accounts of Jesus walking on water are in Matt. 14:22–33; Mark 6:45–52; and John 6:15–21. The accounts of Jesus calming the storm are in Matt. 8:23–27; Mark 4:35–41; and Luke 8:22–25. The account of Jesus on the shore is in John 21:1–14.

3. Willard referred to the story in John 2:1–12 where Jesus turned water into wine at the wedding in Cana, a village in Galilee.

4. Not identified.

5. Willard quoted from the refrain of a song she had learned to sing several years earlier, one adapted from a poem, "Rain on the Roof," by Coates-Kinney in *Keeuka and other Poems* (Cincinnati, 1855).

6. Willard referred to Joseph, the patriarch, who foretold the future through dreams (Gen. 37:5–11).

7. Willard referred to Jackson as "careful Martha" (alluding to the New Testament figure of Martha, Jesus' friend, who kept house for her sister and brother), as she described Jackson checking their underwear for scorpions and insects that might have crawled into them.

8 April 1870
Beirut, Syria

. . . I sat in the coupé [small carriage] between the "Drs."[1] who put on their skullcaps, muffled themselves in their shawls & slept comfortably the first part of the route. I had Kate's great blanket & was "nice & warm" but the experience on which I was entering was too novel to permit me to sleep. . . . The sun rose in splendor over the far off plain. I must confess to having seen but few sun-[rises] in my life to which the morning nap—half-dream, half-reverie, is dear— but certainly I never saw a sun-rise so beautiful as this. It was full of mystery & suggestion, too—coming fresh from India's mountains & Persia's unimaginable vallies—from the cradle & the Eden of our Race. I leaned from the window & looked long at its many-hued splendor—then watched it touching with wonderful art the snowy mountains of the Anti lebanon toward which we were journeying & finally tinging Hermon's solemn peak with heavenly gold. I want to treasure up that scene—one of the rarest that life can ever reveal to my eyes. . . . Hours wear on & the gentlemen grow talkative while I am, what I long ago learned to be, happily for my improvement—an excellent listener. They share with me their sandwiches & the genuine American cake the delectable art of making which Mrs. Jessup[2] has not lost in her long expatriation. They are a pair of gentlemen worth knowing—both of them, but particularly the missionary. Men of fine education—much thought & experience of life—appreciation of nature & of pathos—broad views & real Christianity. They say a great deal that is worth remembering. . . . Dr. J. talks about the mission in which centers his noble enthusiasm—tells me about its great success & his anticipations for the future & finally falls to sketching, humorously, some incidents & personages connected with it. . . . Dr. J. suggests to me the propriety of remaining in Beirut in connection with the ladies' school, left in an unpleasant position by the sudden withdrawal of Miss Carruth of Boston. . . .[3] But I told him of my Mother & confessed I didn't "feel a call." . . .

The morning wore on—the clouds thickened & the cold increased. A gloomy prospect for Baalbec. We reached Staura[4] before noon. It was snowing fast. I lunched hastily, put on my rubber coat, tied its Capuchin [hood] over my head;—mounted my horse, which was in readiness as our diligence[5] drove up;—drank the strong tea that Dr. Jessup ordered, &, unmindful of his & Dr. Robinson's friendly misgivings, galloped off through the storm with Mr. Pettibone. . . .[6]

We rode off in silence. I could not see a step before me for the snow was blinding. Mr. Pettibone was a notable rider—famous among his friends for his fine horsemanship. Baalbec was eighteen or twenty miles away & must be reached in four hours if we would have any daylight remaining to see it by. I was determined my timidity as an equestrienne should not prevent the success of his expedition—or my own. So, taking the stout olive branch he cut for me—which belied its peaceful reputation in this instance, I belabored my amiable little horse into a splendid gallop which was maintained almost throughout the entire distance, though I confess to such inward quakings as I never felt before & as my too reckless disposition seldom takes time for. . . . But I said nothing to good Mr. Pettibone, who galloped behind me, watching my saddle-girths and encouraging me with compliments upon my horsemanship. "Not one lady in a hundred could ride so long & so rapidly," he said—little knowing that I expected every minute to vault over my horse's head—especially when he stumbled which was at intervals of alarming frequency. I was often unseated & only saved from a fall by clinging for dear life to the saddle-pommel. And all the while—shall I not gratefully acknowledge it—I prayed, "only for Mother's sake" that I might get safely through. For two hours or more it was a desperate ride—the most adventurous of all my varying vicissitudes—but at last the snow-clouds rolled away—the Lebanon & Ante Lebanon stretched grandly on either side of us & the valley of Buka'a—the largest that I saw in Syria (?) lay quietly around. . . .

At last, a little after four o'clock . . . Baalbek reared its noble ruins before us. Of their appearance in this beautiful & distant solitude;—of the gleam of their columns; the exquisite workmanship of their ornamentation;—the speculations of historians & antiquarians concer[n]ing their origin let others tell. I tried to study my guide book before going; to examine as carefully as my limited time would permit by sun, moon & lantern light when there, & for the rest, I have an excellent series of photographs illustrative of the theme. Suffice it that I came—I saw—I conquered—& that the spoils were worthy of the fight. . . .

We wandered among the Temples—of the Sun, of Jupiter & of the Circle (at least the Guide Books call it "circular"!)[7] & staid for an hour's delighted contemplation of that of Jupiter—"the finest in all Syria"—the bijou [jewel] of all ancient architecture on which I have as yet feasted my eyes. . . . And after two hours of pleasant sunshine on the wondrous subject of Baalbec we went home to our dinner, unmistakably fatigued with the day's enterprises.

It was surprising but "table d'hôte" had pursued us into this wilderness! An excellent soup, beef, vegatables, fowl, salad & a dessert of tea & fruits was set before us. . . . We had good talk, nice brother Pettibone & I, over our excellent repast. We theorized about Baalbec;—we talked of mutual acquaintances; he told me of a sister he had in Chicago;—he recounted to me incidents of his missionary life & even told me how the fleas—annoyingly manifest in our present quarters—had tormented him when on his missionary campaigns in Turkey & how he tried to evade them. We talked of our war in America & he told me that he came home & acted as Chaplain for a long time, at the South. We talked of politics & developed our entire accord as good Republicans. And I made so bold as to ask the nice man if he hadn't a brandy flask with him, as I had forgotten mine & greatly needed its restorative aid. Whereupon he put me to the blush by saying that when a very little boy his Mother made him promise never to use liquor in any form & that in none had it ever passed his lips! But Antonio[8] came to the rescue, & after a comforting potion I set out, under the stars, with my good friend & a little Arabe guide—"faint, yet pursuing." We explored the vast crypt of the artificial platform on which the Temples stand & fall;—Mr. P. climbing precariously to the investigation of the side chambers, whose entrances are high up & choked with rubbish, while I stood in the silence & the darkness below, looking away off to the round entrance where fell the moon-light, (happily?) thinking thoughts which I can not pen. Then we emerged from the underworld & while Mr. P. went off on another little expedition, I sat down (in the tourist's attitude as shown in pictures of classic remains) upon a fallen capital & gazed upon the ruin & listened to the silence of Baalbec. It was no fancy—they had surely passed this way—the mysterious footsteps of the world's ancestors. They dreamed not of decay, the men who thus could build, & yet the hands that sculptured yonder lofty columns on which the moonlight falls with touch so gentle, have passed into a thousand forms since then;—have flown in birds, blossomed in flowers & floated as impalpable dust upon the wings of zephyrs that expired a thousand years ago. But here stands their work—though marred—still glorious,—the carving on this frieze as sharply cut as when the artist's chisel had but left it;—& away there in the ambient heavens gleam the unchanging stars;—Orion & the Pleiades, with all their radiant train. O human race, so mighty in achievement, so swift in passage through this beautiful world, what brain that thinks, what heart that feels can contemplate you without pity & grief, among the ruins of the temples ye have builded to that "Unknown God" who only can suffice you! It seemed as if those lofty columns had an intelligence, & as if humbly yet sublimely they called on the Mighty Builder who outlasts all His works to be mindful of & merciful toward man who so long ago had reared them in sad aspiring toward his unseen Father. . . .

I slept on a small section of the stone divan that surrounded my great room in the Arab house aforesaid—having first carefully examined its numerous windows; warmed myself beside its glowing brasier & accepted the aid of the dolorous young Arab in my preparations to retire. The two or three quilts & brick-bat pillow between me & the stones did not sufficiently disguise them;—&, any way, I could not have slept for all night long the Bishop's face[9]—so kind, so full of life, was right before my eyes. It was a horrid night, & welcome was the morning. We breakfasted by candle light & set out while it was yet too dark for the driver to guide the horse. Forlorn was that ride of twenty miles, back to the diligence station, which we reached nearly an hour before it arrived at eleven. I fairly cried—that is, the tears forced themselves from my eyes, with pain & with fatigue. But I took good care not to permit my kind companion to see my distress! "What a good man he is," I thought—"how kind he is to his daughters, I am sure." (& I never knew till a fortnight later at Constantinople that good Mr. Pettibone was "an old bachelor"!)—Delighted indeed was I to see Kate & the Paines & Chevalier W.[10] & his friends. Dear Kate "hadn't half slept," she said "for worrying about me." In a sort of dream I took my seat in the friendly old diligence which was to bear me back to civilization & at evening all my woes were o'er & we were done with all that is good, bad & indifferent;—richly rewarding & unspeakably fatiguing in *An Oriental Tour.* . . .

1. Willard referred to Dr. Henry Harris Jessup (1832–1910), a Presbyterian missionary to Beirut, Syria, from 1860 until his death, and Dr. Charles Seymour Robinson (1829–99), a Presbyterian minister and pastor of the American chapel in Paris in 1870, who was visiting in Syria.

2. Harriet Elizabeth Dodge (ca. 1828–82) of Hartford, Conn., married Henry Harris Jessup in October 1868 and sailed with him for Syria later that month.

3. The Beirut Female Seminary was founded in 1861 to teach Syrian girls English and French as well as Protestant Christianity. One of the school's founders and supporters was Henry Harris Jessup. In 1868 Nellie A. Carruth sailed to Syria with Jessup and his wife to teach at the school, but she returned to the United States in 1870.

4. Willard traveled west from Damascus through the Beka'a valley to view the ruins at Ba'albek, called Heliopolis by the Romans. They built Greek-style temples to Jupiter and Bacchus at Heliopolis in the second and third centuries. Staura was a small village on the way to Ba'albek where tourists met guides to take them on to Ba'albek on horseback.

5. A diligence was a compact, rapid stagecoach.

6. Ira Fayette Pettibone (1824–97) was a Congregational minister and the secretary and financial agent of the Western Turkey Mission for the American Board of Commissioners of Foreign Missions (ABCFM). He lived in Constantinople.

7. Besides the temples to Jupiter and Bacchus there was a third temple, circular in form, built outside the acropolis on which the other two stood. It is not known to whom the circular temple was dedicated.

8. Antonio was the native guide who traveled with Willard and Pettibone from Staura to Ba'albek and back.

9. Willard heard on her trip to Ba'albek that Bishop Kingsley had suffered a heart attack and died just two days earlier, on 6 April. When she returned to Beirut, she

and the Paines and Mr. Wilson went on 10 April to Bishop Kingsley's grave to place flowers on it, and arranged to have a rose bush planted nearby to commemorate the Methodist leader.

10. Willard referred to Rev. John A. Wilson (1839–1934), a Presbyterian minister, whom she called "chevalier" because of his gallantry toward Jackson and her on their Palestine trip.

[*Willard and Jackson sailed from Beirut in mid-April bound for Athens and Constantinople, making brief stops in Cyprus, Smyrna, and Ephesus. From Constantinople they crossed the Bosporus to Eastern Europe and proceeded along the Danube River to Vienna, staying there a few days. From Vienna they went to Paris, where they remained for a month. In mid-June they crossed the channel to England and traveled directly to London to meet Jackson's sister Carrie and her new husband. They spent a month in London, returned to Paris for five weeks, and set sail for the United States on 27 August 1870, arriving in New York City on 5 September.*]

12 May 1870
Munich

Another day's whirl of "sight/seeing." For once & at last I cease my Oliver Twist cry of "more"[1]—& substitute "Enough"! I am desperately sick of sight-seeing "as a pursuit" & so anxious to reach Paris & take "a long breath" that I can hardly restrain my impatience. . . .

1. Willard referred to chapter 2 in Charles Dickens's *Oliver Twist* (London, 1838), where the title character wants more gruel.

24 May 1870
Paris

. . . Somehow I am strangely fond of idleness since our travels are over. A certain lassitude has taken possession of me & my time passes uncoined. Happily I have a worthier report to give of its use in the past. But now I'm tired—every way. . . .

25 May 1870

. . . Was "shampooed" coiff*ed* & set in order. Looked "like a new person." Would give "those *eye-teeth*" of mine to be rich enough to take a hair-dresser by subscription!—Went a-shopping—that is a-sorrowing. Came home heartsick, head-achy & limb-weary. Ah these "cloe"![1]

Letter from Mother, who in her farsighted love keeps the house for "us three" & has gone East to our relatives to stay until we come. *Quelle bonheur* [What good fortune] to have a *home*. How in a hurry I feel—& shall return with even more delight than I came away! . . .

1. Willard used a colloquial expression for clothes.

28 September 1870
Evanston

This is my thirty-first birthday. I have not lived so long for nothing. Many a "school" has done its work upon me and been "graduated" from. Among others that sentimental friend, my Journal, has this day been shaken hands with in a long adieu, and I here record my purpose to write no more wishy-washy pages of personal reminiscence.

Vale [Farewell]!   (Exit.)

PART FIVE

1 January 1893–31 December 1896

"It is not now as it hath been of old." My sense of boundless power to do has suffered loss. . . . My tongue burns—
my sleep grows lighter—I feel my heart & all the left side
rattles a bit (like an old farm wagon), the scaffolding will
come down before long. . . .

—*1 March 1896*

Willard remained true to the intention she recorded on her thirty-first birthday, that she would write "no more wishy-washy pages of personal reminiscence,"[1] and lightly dismissed her journal, the companion and confidante of her young womanhood. While she continued to write voluminously, producing hundreds of articles for newspapers and journals, issuing pamphlets and books with astonishing speed, and churning out mountains of correspondence, she did not systematically keep a journal for the next twenty-two years. Instead her private voice became a public one.

Quite suddenly, however, and in the same bantering tone with which she ended her journal keeping in 1870, she announced on New Year's Day 1893 that she would begin writing a journal once more. "Somehow," she wrote "I am minded to take up scribbling anew." But her tone quickly changed in the next sentence, as she revealed why she did so: "Perhaps it is because I am so utterly taken out of all the dear Past, because this is the first New Year on which no Mother called out her cheery greeting or wrote it to her absent child."[2] Though she couched her reasons in somewhat tentative language, she knew in her heart exactly why she needed to return to her journal. At two similarly traumatic moments in her life—the deaths of her sister and father—her journal became a significant place for grieving. Once again, she was grief stricken. There was no one left of her immediate family—her brother Oliver having died suddenly in 1878—with whom to recall "all of the dear Past" so important to her sense of herself. And her most constant friend, her greatest source of strength and support, was gone.

In her journal, Willard was able to express her bereavement in a way that would not have been appropriate for her public memorializing of her mother. During the same time that she grieved in her journal, she worked on her book *A Great Mother*,[3] in which she celebrated Mary (Hill) Willard's life and conveyed what her mother had meant to her and to the organization she led. But she could not reveal there the extent of her feelings of loss and desolation. Only in her journal could she write out her heart, and, by doing so, assuage her sorrow, at least to some small extent.

As one reads journal entries for 1893 and 1896, one can begin to comprehend just how wrenching it was for Willard to be separated from her mother. Her cries of despair often intrude abruptly into remarks on completely different subjects, and, in brief moments of relative quiet, her thoughts seem to turn almost inevitably toward reuniting with her mother.[4] Her greatest hope and deepest yearning from 1893 until her death in 1898 was to rejoin her mother and the rest of her family in heaven. Yet her faith in the promise of a heavenly future life beyond death and the grave faltered just as it had when her sister and her father died.[5] She lacked both the confident assurance of a heavenly home that Christians often claimed and the certainty of her mother's presence there. In her doubt, she wished for some kind of communication indicating that her mother was safely "home." During a time of great change in Willard's personal life, when she experienced a deep sense of uprootedness, she longed for tangible links to the one who had always been her emotional and spiritual anchor. When they were not forthcoming, her distress was enormous.

The immensity of the changes Willard endured in her mid-fifties and their adverse affect on her should not be minimized. Not only was her mother dead; two other beloved members of her Rest Cottage household had also died in the year before her mother's death.[6] Rest Cottage itself had been closed up for a time and then rented out to strangers. And Willard was living in England, trying to adjust to completely new surroundings. Even though she often expressed her gratitude for the sumptuous hospitality Isabel Somerset provided, she still missed the fellowship of the simple home worship of Rest Cottage, with her mother in the center of the family circle. She also longed for her home church with its Sunday services and social life so familiar to her, because she could not find the spiritual solace she sought in either Anglican worship or English Methodism. Just as she had felt keenly the loss of home, family, and church community after her sister's death in 1862 when the family was scattered and their house temporarily closed, Willard once again endured the same sense of loss. Her "old life" was "now in shreds!" she wrote in December 1893.[7]

Her deteriorating health heightened her impression of a life "in shreds." She was disconcerted by her flagging energy and was fully aware that she ought not to be as worn out as she was. She was, after all, only fifty-four and could have anticipated many more vigorous, productive years. She attributed her sense of malaise to grief over her mother's death. However, the loss of her mother was not the only cause of her debilitation. Over the course of 1892 and 1893 she developed symptoms of pernicious anemia,[8] the ultimate cause of her early death, and the same disease that had plagued her mother during the last few years of her life. Besides the lassitude Willard felt, she ran a low-grade fever. She reported sores on her tongue that were painful and, even worse, made it almost impossible for her to eat. This resulted in a general weakening of her system, making her much more susceptible to all kinds of minor illnesses, which hung on far longer than they should have. Because her body battled anemia, it could no longer fight off colds, flu, and fatigue the way it had always done before.

Somerset was highly alarmed at her friend's condition and called in several physicians to consult and suggest treatment. They warned Willard that she could not keep up the usual hectic schedule she had followed since she had begun WCTU work almost two decades earlier. In fact, by June 1893, she was being strongly advised to refrain from any public appearances for a year. To one whose leadership depended so heavily on her speechmaking ability and her personal relationship with her constituency, such advice was not welcome. Nevertheless, she did agree to cut back on her public life. But she insisted on dictating her usual volume of letters and articles, and still held interviews and conferred with an endless stream of reform leaders who visited her and Somerset. Willard was certainly neither a willing nor a totally obedient patient. Her pattern was to keep going until her energy simply gave out, rest for a few days, and then start in again.

In order to build up her strength, Willard embarked on an exercise and diet regime in addition to limiting her public activity. Her companion Anna Gordon and Somerset encouraged her to take long walks and often accompanied her around the grounds of Somerset's estate. Doctors prescribed a vacation for both Willard and Somerset to get away from all the demands upon them, so in summer 1893 Somerset arranged for six weeks in the Swiss Alps. But at the end of their stay, Willard had lost weight, not gained it as she had hoped to do, and was feeling little better generally.

When Willard returned to England after the vacation was over, Somerset's personal physician reiterated the need for a diet and exercise program. As part of her attempt to follow this advice, she took up bicycle riding in fall 1893 and recorded her progress in her journal. Never one to miss a chance to turn her experience into a didactic opportunity, she quickly published a slim volume, *A Wheel within a Wheel: How I Learned to Ride the Bicycle*, in which she announced: "She who succeeds in gaining mastery of the bicycle will gain the mastery of life."[9]

Willard had lived from her earliest years by such mottoes, expressive of her buoyant and triumphant optimism. For her WCTU followers and many others throughout the world, she embodied energy, vigor, enthusiasm. But now her body was becoming unable to keep pace with her mind and heart, and she could no longer will it into eager service to enact the plans for reform that constantly churned in her brain. Many times in her journal she lamented the disjunction she sensed between her body and her spirit. She feared, with good reason, that her WCTU "white ribboners"[10] back in America would not really grasp the seriousness of her illness and the absolute necessity that she remain quiet.

Willard fought hard to regain her health and it was a great disappointment when physicians vetoed her return to the United States for the NWCTU annual convention in fall 1893. She had thought it essential that she preside over what threatened to become a stormy session with strong opposition mounting against the WCTU's involvement in the Woman's Temperance Building Association. The association had just completed a multistory building in downtown Chicago that would house the headquarters of the NWCTU. The construction of the Woman's Temple, as the headquarters building was called, had run into severe financial difficulties, made worse by the nationwide economic depression. At the same time, there were serious controversies between NWCTU officers, and the WCTU itself was suffering from financial problems.[11]

Willard believed that she must be at the October annual convention in order to be the unifying force that pulled the organization together and set it back on course. But she could not rally enough to convince either her doctors or her friends that she was able to go. Instead Anna Gordon and Isabel Somerset went to the United States to take charge of the NWCTU convention, while Willard waited anxiously for news of the meeting by telegraph. Such a passive role must have been extremely frustrating for one whose finest moments had come when she was guiding her large organization through its annual meeting with consummate skill and tact.

Willard kept no journal during 1894–95. When she took up her journal again in January 1896, she was in the midst of a three-and-one-half-month tour through the southern United States, and probably appeared to the public to be her healthy self again. She often addressed several audiences a day, caucused with southern WCTU leaders, dictated to the stenographer who accompanied her, and even managed to fit a few sight-seeing tours into her crowded schedule. But her journal records that Anna Gordon often had to fill in for her because she was too tired or ill to speak. Once again her tongue was sore, and now her stomach began to bother her.

In March she met with NWCTU officers to plan for the November annual convention, then traveled east to Washington and New

York City, and from there sailed for England in mid-April. Willard's public schedule was greatly curtailed during May and June, although she managed to speak to a few temperance meetings and the annual convention of the British woman's suffrage society. During the summer, both Willard and Somerset spent several weeks at the seaside, hoping the sun, sea air, and exercise would rejuvenate them enough so that they could address the plight of Armenian refugees fleeing from Turkish attacks. Both women had been greatly moved by accounts of the Armenian situation from missionaries and reporters who visited them over the summer with news of Turkish massacres. The Armenian tragedy assumed the dimensions of a sacred cause to Willard and Somerset, who viewed the Armenians as a martyr people struggling against a savage infidel force.

By mid-September the two women were in Marseilles arranging to house and feed several hundred Armenian refugees and provide for their safe passage to England and the United States. Willard barraged American leaders with telegrams and letters requesting money and pushed the government to let the refugees enter the United States. She begged her WCTU constituency to act as sponsors for Armenian families, guaranteeing homes and jobs for them when they arrived. But amidst this flurry of activity, Willard was ill and forced to carry out much of her work from bed in her hotel room. On her fifty-seventh birthday, surrounded by presents and good wishes, she recorded her own wish to die there in Marseilles so that she would not have to endure seasickness through another English Channel crossing or face life with its "contradictions . . . bereavements & *hurts* . . . ever any more!"[12]

This was not the only time Willard had wished to die and recorded that wish in the privacy of her journal. At other times during 1896 when she felt particularly low, death seemed a welcome relief from the strain of her demanding life. There were moments when Somerset felt the same, beset as she was by devastating migraine headaches that occurred almost every other week. Together the two friends looked to "the Life to come" and saw every task completed, every duty done, as a step toward that promised heavenly life.[13]

The volumes of Willard's journal written in her fifties afford a unique perspective from which to understand the effect of serious illness on a powerful leader. They reveal the strains faced by a public figure who found it increasingly difficult to maintain the image of energetic optimism so carefully cultivated over her reform career. The journal was an outlet for her despair. Just as she confided to it her deepest expressions of grief over the loss of her mother, so she wrote there about her sense of depletion and her occasional long-ing for death. Because the journal contains these aspects of her self that she did not show to her public, it provides a sad counterpoint to her usually enthusiastic, joyful spirit.

Willard rested during the last half of October so that she could return to the United States to preside over the mid-November WCTU convention in St. Louis. Anna Gordon, who was, at the time, keeping Willard's journal for her, reported that the convention went off without a hitch, and Willard's speech was all the more powerful for having been extemporaneous, since she had been too ill to prepare it beforehand.[14] With the meeting over and postconvention business settled, Willard and Gordon headed for Dr. Cordelia Greene's sanatorium in Castile, N.Y.,[15] where Willard hoped to be restored to health. She submitted herself to Greene's regime of combined exercise, rest, diet, and treatments. She began to seem her old self once more, determined to prevail over her illness. One can easily imagine that, as she performed her daily exercises, Carlyle's aphorism "For suffering and enduring there is no remedy but striving and doing!" was running through her head. To her it was wise advice that had served her well in the past. As a young woman, sayings such as this had helped to shape her character, giving it the quality of perseverance that enabled her to overcome whatever obstacles she encountered. The question she faced in late middle age was whether her indomitable spirit could triumph over what was, perhaps, the most formidable obstacle she had ever had to overcome: her worn-out body. In the hardest battle of her life, she was prepared, as usual, to try her best.

Notes

1. Journal, 28 September 1870.

2. Ibid., 1 January 1893.

3. Frances E. Willard and Minerva Brace Norton, *A Great Mother: Sketches of Madam Willard* (Chicago, 1894).

4. Undoubtedly Willard's brief entries, which were fitted into a very tiny journal volume, heighten the impression of abruptness, since she had little room to write about any subject. Nevertheless, the effect of abruptness is quite noticeable, since she switches from one thought to another with no bridging sentences.

5. Journal, 14 September 1862, 31 December 1867, 9 January 1868.

6. The two members of the Rest Cottage household who had died in the year before Willard's mother's death were Julia A. Ames (1861–91) and Mary

Allen West (1837–92). The "inner circle" of WCTU officers and staff that lived in Rest Cottage with Willard, her mother, and Gordon called Ames "Yolande" after the heroine of a novel by William Blake, *Yolande: The Story of a Daughter* (London, 1883). Ames began working with the WCTU in 1885, becoming the Chicago superintendent of press work, which meant that she was the WCTU's Chicago press agent. In 1886 she was named national press superintendent, and then assistant editor of the *Union Signal.* Ames became an intimate in the Rest Cottage family circle. She was stricken with a form of typhoid-pneumonia shortly after the NWCTU convention in November 1891 and was dead by 13 December. Her loss was deeply felt by the entire "inner circle," especially by Willard and her mother, who were very fond of Ames. Mary Allen West was a journalist, educator, and reform activist. In 1882 she became the president of the Illinois WCTU and, in 1885, took over the editing of the *Union Signal* when Mary (Bannister) Willard, the former editor, moved to Germany. West remained *Union Signal* editor until her death. She also served as secretary of the Woman's Temperance Publishing Association and was president of the Illinois Woman's Press Association for several terms beginning in 1888. In 1892 she was sent as a WCTU missionary to the Hawaiian Islands and Japan and carried out a successful lecture tour until she became ill and died shortly after.

7. Journal, 12 December 1893.

8. Pernicious anemia is a disease caused by a deficiency of vitamin B12 needed for the normal production of red blood cells, through insufficient diet and an inability of the digestive tract to absorb vitamin B12 necessary for the digestion process. It is an unusual condition that has a tendency to run in families, to start in middle age, to affect slightly more women more than men, and to be more common among people of northern European descent. The symptoms are usually tiredness, a sore mouth and smoothness and redness of the tongue, low appetite, weight loss, headaches, and jaundice. Nowadays, it is treated by adopting a short, intensive course of vitamin B12 injections daily, and then cutting back injections to once a month, indefinitely. However in Willard's time, proper treatment methods were unknown, and the disease was inevitably considered fatal (thus the term pernicious). It was only in 1926 with the discovery of raw liver treatments and, then, in 1948, with the synthesis of vitamin B12 that pernicious anemia became treatable and curable.

9. Frances E. Willard, *How I Learned to Ride the Bicycle* (Sunnyvale, Cal., 1991), 33. This is a reprint edition of Frances E. Willard, *A Wheel within a Wheel: How I Learned to Ride the Bicycle* (New York and London, 1895).

10. WCTU members were nicknamed "white ribboners" because they wore white grosgrain ribbons on their dresses to signify their membership in the WCTU and their support of the temperance cause.

11. See Bordin, *Woman and Temperance,* 140–55, for a clear, concise assessment of the WCTU's financial problems.

12. Journal, 28 September 1896.

13. Ibid., 5 May 1896.

14. See Slagell, "A Good Woman Speaking Well," 648–64, for the text of Willard's 1896 presidential address, with headnotes.

15. Cordelia Agnes Greene (1831–1905) was an American physician who ran a sanatorium in Castile, N.Y., where she treated women for a variety of ailments and illnesses. Greene graduated from Western Reserve University in 1855, and then attended the Woman's Medical College of Pennsylvania. She graduated from the Cleveland Medical College (which later became part of Western Reserve University) in 1856. Cordelia Greene was the daughter of Dr. Jabez Greene, who had established a "water cure" sanatorium in 1849 in New York, and she worked with her father in his sanatorium until he died in the early 1860s. She then founded her own sanatorium in Castile in 1865. Greene combined her academic medical knowledge with a great variety of techniques of healing popular during the nineteenth century, to restore her patients' bodily health. She also emphasized the importance of "soul health," through prayer, work on controlling negative emotions, and deep breathing to decrease stress. She believed in a wholistic concept of health in which body, mind, and soul must be in balance.

It is now over 20 years since I left off doing what my Mother early taught me to do—viz. keeping a journal. But somehow, on this Sunday morning in the writing room of my beloved "Cossie's"[2] suburban home, I am minded to take up scribbling anew. Perhaps it is because I am so utterly taken out of all the dear Past—because this is the first New Year on which no Mother called out her cheery greeting or wrote it to her absent child. . . .

Two *special* desires and purposes I here register with prayers for strength to come a little nearer than before to keeping them:

Give me more Purity, more truthfulness, more charity (Love) more
    Reverence more spirituality
Mottoes for the year:
    Forget thyself,
    Believe the others are trying to do right.
    Bible verse for the year
    Have Faith in God.[3]

Breakfast at 10—prayers, with my little Testament carried in all journeys . . . Fan Barnes'[4] Scripture Calendar. We sang "There's a wideness in God's mercy" "There are Bands of Ribbon white" and "We all belong."[5] We knelt in prayers of penitence and hope. We asked that *Blessed Mother*[6] might be our Guardian Angel. We read in the Testament Matthew xi. We have greater cares than ever because of contradictions in the English work & loss and changes in the personnel of the American. . . .

I thought of dear, dismantled Rest Cottage—so bright one year ago and sacred by my blessed Mother's sunny, God-believing presence. Dearest Anna and I condoled with one another because since New Year's Day last year we have each lost the one bound to us by ties of blood, of birth and nurture,[7] whom of all our kindred we had all our lives loved best.—How we sail on and away!

But perhaps *nearer* at each heart throb—so we hope, so we believe, so I prayed, when I pressed my last kiss on Mother's forehead as all that was mortal of her lay in the casket in the South window at Rest Cottage, and said "Goodbye, Mother, until we meet in Heaven."

We must hold to God, to Immortality, to Duty, to Rewards and Punishment—the necessary outcome of our conduct—and to Christ our Elder Brother, Exemplar and Redeemer.

I think today how the old landmarks are being left behind as I put out to sea and if I live, they will be more and more. But if I can by God's grace still be "True to the kindred points of Heaven & Home"[8] (the Home where all but I, "Last of the Household" are now gathered), they shall be with me more & more and sailing on over life's relentless billows shall not mean separation from them.

1. Willard was living at the Priory, Isabel Somerset's residence in Reigate, Surrey.

2. Willard's nickname for Somerset was "Earl Cosmos," which she often shortened to "Cossie" (sometimes spelled "Cozzie"). "Earl" came from Somerset's father's title, the Earl of Somers. Since Somerset inherited her father's estates, she was, in a sense, an earl. "Cosmos" signified Willard's estimate of her friend's capabilities. Somerset deserved to be "Earl of the Cosmos," and if such a title had existed and were ever to be given to her, Somerset, with her many and varied talents, was eminently worthy of the position, in her friend's opinion.

3. Mark 11:22.

4. Frances Julia (Allis) Barnes (1846–1920) was the superintendent of the World's Young Woman's Christian Temperance Union (Y's) and a close friend of Willard's and Gordon's. As superintendent, she produced both practical and artistic materials for the Y's, an example of which was the scripture calendar that Willard mentioned, a devotional aid with short biblical texts for each day.

5. All three hymns Willard mentioned were included in *The White Ribbon Hymnal or Echoes of the Crusade,* compiled by Anna A. Gordon (Chicago, 1892), and were WCTU favorites, often sung at its conventions.

6. Willard referred to her own mother and not the Virgin Mary.

7. Gordon's father, James M. Gordon (b. ca. 1815), had died on 23 February 1892 and Willard's mother had died on 7 August 1892.

8. Willard quoted from William Wordsworth, "To a Skylark," in *The Poetical Works of William Wordsworth* (London, 1827), stanza 2, line 6.

2 January 1893

Lady Henry up & away early. Cold—for England. Sat in writing room all day & dictated numberless articles paragraphs letters &c to Miss Murrell[1] who came from London. My greatest wish *now*—when nearly all are so abundantly supplied—is a *1st class* stenographer always within ear shot. Blessed little brave hearted Cossie—so good, so tugged and toiling—so intricately involved with many groups of humans all of them an embodied w a n t. How will it end? *Well* I believe.

1. Grace Murrell was Willard's chief stenographer while she was in England during 1893.

3 January 1893

My Mother's Birth Day.
She would have been *88.*
A busy day—regular snow storm & no tricycle[1] outside. Troubled

about the sweetest woman alive until her dear telegram restored me—at noon: "Well—love—Cos" and items showing how that great, radiant, faithful heart is "toiling away" at the Exeter Hall meeting. . . .[2] And all the while, the undertone of my life is: Mother, Blessed Mother where art *thou*?[3]

1. The tricycle was the adult woman's method of bicycling until the two-wheel bicycle was invented in the late 1880s. The tricycle had two large wheels on either side of a chair, with pedals close to a smaller front wheel. By sitting between the main wheels, the pedals out in front of her, a woman could bicycle without entangling her skirts. Willard had taken up this form of exercise in Evanston in the mid-1880s.

2. Somerset was in London making preparations for the huge welcome meeting for Willard from the many temperance, Liberal, and women's groups in England. The meeting was to be held on 9 January 1893 in Exeter Hall, London, a popular place for large reform gatherings since the 1850s.

3. Willard often used "thee" and "thou" in her speech and writing to her mother and to very close friends such as Isabel Somerset and Hannah (Whitall) Smith (see Journal, 11 January 1893, n. 2). It was a style of address she probably borrowed from Smith, a Quaker, who used the objective case of pronouns, as most Quakers did, in normal speech. The use of the case by Willard and her intimates signified the great love between them.

7 January 1893
London

Came up from Reigate and set at work here.[1] The drawing room is in white—all revamped. I was writing away when, at 3:30 (after an interview with *The Chronicle*[2]) in softly came Cozzie, so sweet & strong, so brave yet tender. How my life is enriched by hers and greatened— how I *wonder* that so good and rare a gift has come to me—after I entered 50 and the "region of calms."[3] Blessed Mother! your prescience was infallible—you knew that I was to be sheltered and comforted—companioned and consoled by one whom God had given me. O thou who art my holiest blessing & most steadfast, where art thou?—If I could only *know*—if I could only hear from thee! . . .

1. Willard was staying at Somerset's London house, 57 Gordon Square.
2. Willard referred to the *Daily Chronicle*, a liberal London newspaper.
3. Not identified.

9 January 1893

This is a day of great preoccupations for us all. The bell rings every few minutes; telegrams, messengers, letters, are in floods. Lady Henry has not one minutes peace. I did not feel anxious about my part for I knew that Canon Farrer, Stead, Mark Guy Pearse, Mrs

Chaunt, Madam Antoinette Stirling the famous contralto. . . .[1] would so take the time that I could go scot free.—It was the most representative welcome of which I ever heard.[2] Forty six separate reform & philanthropic guilds were on the platform by their representatives; numerous letters from famous names; testimonials; baskets of fruit & flowers; an overflow meeting & my beautiful Isabel generalissimo of it all.

Mother, blessed *Mother,* didst *thou* know?

1. Frederick William Farrar (1831–1903), an Anglican priest, was a leader of the United Kingdom Alliance, an English temperance society dedicated to securing prohibition by legal measures. He did not attend the meeting at Exeter Hall, but the letter that he sent was read aloud. William Thomas Stead (1849–1912) was the liberal editor and founder of the monthly *Review of Reviews.* Mark Guy Pearse (1842–1930) was a popular British Wesleyan preacher and writer, as well as a temperance worker with the Blue Ribbon Movement. Laura Ormiston (Dibbin) Chant (1848–23), British reformer, lecturer, and writer, was a member of the BWTA, the Women's Liberal Federation, the National Society for Promoting Woman Suffrage, and the Church of England Temperance Society. At the Exeter Hall meeting she represented woman suffrage and peace movements. Antoinette Sterling (1850–1904), an American living in England, was a famous contralto and a WCTU member. She sang "Oh Rest in the Lord" at the meeting.
2. Besides the notables Willard mentioned, many others greeted Willard on behalf of their reform organizations and political groups, and many greetings were read from those who could not attend.

[*At the 9 January Exeter Hall meeting Willard introduced her "Do Everything" policy to the BWTA. Although she received a warm official welcome, many of the organization's more conservative members and a majority of its Executive Committee fiercely resisted Willard's and Somerset's attempt to broaden the scope of the BWTA's goals from its single focus on temperance to a wide range of reforms including woman suffrage. The WCTU's aims and methods might work in the United States, the conservative opposition felt, but they were not suited to the English temperance movement. Leaders opposed to the direction in which the BWTA was moving planned to unseat Somerset as president and set the organization back on its original course of advocating total abstinence by moral suasion. Somerset and Willard spent late winter and spring 1893 traveling through England and Scotland, speaking to the BWTA membership and gathering support for Somerset's program.*]

11 January 1893

All day Isabel in bed. I was with her as much as possible but had to keep up my dictation. She took a chill passing from the Upper Hall to speak to the Overflow Meeting.[1] She is the dearest patient ever seen—To every inquiry she answers *"Better."* I tell her that word would form her fitting epitaph. Hannah Smith[2] was here and they talked of the difficulties among the British women and we are formulating a policy and arranging plans to hold the unity of the B.W.T.A.[3] if possible. What a criss cross is this world! . . .

1. The welcome meeting at Exeter Hall on 9 January was so well attended that those who could not squeeze into the main hall overflowed into a smaller hall, located beneath it. The "small" hall held fifteen hundred people, so the attendance must have been near five thousand.

2. Hannah (Whitall) Smith (1832–1911) was raised a Quaker, but became very much involved in and influenced by the Methodist Holiness movement and began preaching and holding revivals with her husband, Robert Pearsall Smith, in the late 1860s. Their fame as evangelical revivalists spread quickly, and they were invited to England where they carried on a revival tour from 1873 to 1875. Hannah (Whitall) Smith published her best-selling book, *The Christian's Secret of a Happy Life* (New York: Willard Tract Repository, 1875), in the mid-1870s, establishing her as an evangelical leader. She then turned to social reform work, joining the WCTU in the 1870s and becoming a close friend of Willard's. She was also a strong woman suffragist. In 1883 she was appointed the first superintendent of the NWCTU's Evangelism Department, but she resigned in 1886 when she moved to England permanently. She joined the BWTA and held executive roles in the organization from 1888 to 1906. Working with the BWTA, she became a good friend of Isabel Somerset's, and it was she who introduced Somerset to Willard in 1891 when Somerset and Smith traveled to the United States to attend the first meeting of the WWCTU.

3. The BWTA was a national federation of British women's temperance societies founded in 1876. The BWTA was nonsectarian and nonpolitical as far as party politics were concerned, and any women's temperance organization could become a member by adopting the pledge of total abstinence and paying annual dues. Its headquarters was at Memorial Hall, London. The BWTA worked to promote temperance through public lectures and education, as well as through petitioning the British Parliament.

16 January 1893

. . . In eve. Isabel & I drove to the East End & spoke to four thousand people in Charrington's famous Hall.[1] Testimonial address presented, bouquets refreshments, reception—and all. Very hearty audience of "working class."

1. In 1886 Frederick Nicholas Charrington (1850–1936), heir to the Charrington and Head brewery empire, opened a great assembly hall that he had had built in London's East End. His aim in building the hall was to help the poor of the East End and to support temperance. The meeting Somerset and Willard attended there was another welcome celebration for Willard, hosted by the East London WCTU, and was similar in style to the earlier meeting at Exeter Hall.

18 January 1893
Leeds[1]

. . . Cossie torn asunder by calls, claims of temperance & every thing else—so tired she laid her head on my shoulder in the cars & cried. The meanness of Mrs. A.[2] is without parallel—she declares she "will harrass I[sabel] S[omerset] until she quits the B.W.T.A." . . .

1. On 18 January there was a temperance "Mass Meeting" held in the Leeds Coliseum, sponsored by the Leeds WCTU, where both Somerset and Willard spoke.

2. Mrs. Atherton, a member of the BWTA national executive committee, was unhappy with Somerset's methods and leadership of the association. She and other conservative members of the executive committee aimed to oust Somerset as president of the BWTA, but they failed and, later in 1893, withdrew from the BWTA to form the Women's Total Abstinence Union.

23 January 1893
Manchester

We went to Manchester and held the most "monster" temperance meetings,[1] the best planned and carried out that I have ever seen— They took the form of a welcome and Canon Wilberforce, Sir Wilfrid Lawson, John G. Woolley,[2] and "we two" "occupied the time." We held five meetings at the largest of wh. over five thousand were present and two, three thousand, four right along. "His Worship the Mayor"[3] (not an abstainer!) presided in the City Hall. Our dear white ribbon hymns were wonderfully well sung. "We belong" was especially good & the welcome song to Lady H. & me. Beautiful testimonials were given me and the whole five thousand rose, waving hats, & hkfs as I concluded. I had never seen the like.

1. On 23 and 24 January huge temperance meetings sponsored by many different British temperance societies were held in Manchester to welcome and honor Willard and Somerset. Temperance leaders described these meetings as the greatest temperance rallies held in England for thirty years. Manchester, where the United Kingdom Alliance was founded in 1853, was a strong center of temperance activity and support.

2. Canon Basil Orme Wilberforce (1841–1916) was an Anglican priest and a member of both the Church of England Temperance Society and the United Kingdom Alliance. Wilberforce chaired the 23 January meeting where he, Willard, and Somerset spoke. Sir Wilfrid Lawson (1829–1906), Liberal member of Parliament from 1886 to 1900, was president of the United Kingdom Alliance from 1879 until his death. He chaired the 24 January meeting where he, Willard, and Somerset spoke. John Granville Woolley (1830–1922) was an American prohibition lecturer and gospel preacher. At Somerset's invitation, he toured Great Britain speaking on temperance and preaching during 1892–93. He spoke at both the 23 and 24 January meetings in Manchester.

3. Not identified.

15 February 1893
Reigate

There is a *great life*—
Mother is there—
but it is—*where?*
We shall soon know—to God we are already in our graves physically
& spiritually in immortality!

18 February 1893

. . . Miserable cablegrams from the Temple[1] showing the stirring
up of strife. Why is there such a "rising" all "on a sudden?" Is it she
who said "I'm like a cat—when struck I strike back?"[2]

1. The Temple office building was the WCTU's ambitious project to build a modern structure to house its national offices, the Woman's Temperance Publishing Association (see Journal, 20 October 1893, n. 5), and large halls for its evangelical work
and temperance meetings. In 1887 Matilda Carse (see Journal, 25 February 1893, n.
2) incorporated the Woman's Temperance Building Association, and, in 1890, construction began on what was to be a twelve-story, red granite and terra-cotta building
on the corner of La Salle and Monroe streets in downtown Chicago. In February and
on into spring 1893, NWCTU officers who opposed the Temple project began a vigorous campaign to halt the plans and to weaken Willard's and Carse's power as WCTU
leaders.
2. It is not clear to whom Willard referred here, but she probably meant one of
two NWCTU officers: Caroline Buell or Esther Pugh (see Journal, 25 February 1893,
n. 1). They led the faction that opposed Willard, Carse, and the Temple project. At
the WCTU annual convention in October 1893, both Buell and Pugh were ousted
from their national offices, as the faction loyal to Willard retained control of the
WCTU. In February 1893, however, Willard's supporters and her own position were
threatened by these two officers.

25 February 1893

Cables that the Gen. Officers (C. & E.)[1] intend to make a break &
show their ill will to Mrs Carse[2] & Temple. A calamity indeed if true!
To do this when the poor worn [?] woman has gone away and I am
absent is not the highest style of conduct. Of course it is difficult to
judge at this distance. There is such a crisis here that I can't leave.
Alas for poor humans!

1. Willard referred to Buell and Pugh. Caroline (Brown) Buell (1843–1927), the
NWCTU corresponding secretary, had held that office since 1880 and had held a
NWCTU office since 1878. After her expulsion from office in October 1893, she did
not hold a national position in the WCTU until 1898 when she became superinten-

dent of the Department of Christian Citizenship. In 1903 she resigned her national offices and held state office in Connecticut until 1926. Esther Pugh (1834–1908), the NWCTU treasurer, had also held office since 1878. After the October 1893 convention at which she lost her position, she resigned from WCTU work.

2. Matilda (Bradley) Carse (1835–1917) was president of the powerful Chicago Central WCTU, a position she held from 1878 to her death. An entrepreneurial businesswoman, she founded and presided over the Woman's Temperance Publishing Association in 1880, operating a woman-run publishing business until 1903. She was also president of the Woman's Temperance Building Association. By February 1893 Carse had become a focus of dissension because NWCTU officers were divided over whether to continue supporting her. Several officers were concerned about the Temple's financial problems and disagreed with Carse over methods of managing the project.

27 February 1893

. . . House of Commons & wonderful advance for the Government in presentation of Direct Veto Bill.[1] Heard Gladstone, Harcourt Lawson "of ours" Caine, Asquith, Goschen[2] et als. Women speak just as well. Lawson spoke best of all. (Gladstone very briefly any way) Was recepted at John Wesley's Old Church[3]—City Road Chapel—memorable occasion—heart was full & eyes & tongue.

1. The English concept of direct veto or liquor veto was similar to what Americans referred to as local option. It enabled local communities, by a two-thirds majority, to deny the licensing of drinking establishments and to refuse to renew all existing licenses in shops already established (following a three-year grace period). It also allowed communities, by a bare majority vote, to force drinking establishments to close on Sundays. Temperance reformers were working to push the Direct Veto Bill through Parliament.

2. On 27 February 1893 Sir William Harcourt (1827–1904), Liberal cabinet member (Chancellor of the Exchequer), introduced the "Liquor Traffic (Local Control) Bill" in Parliament. Willard and Somerset observed the floor debate from the women's balcony and heard speeches by Harcourt; William Ewart Gladstone (1809–98), Liberal Prime Minister; Sir Wilfrid Lawson, Liberal Member of Parliament; William Sproston Caine (1842–1903), Liberal Member of Parliament; Herbert Henry Asquith (1852–1928), Liberal cabinet member (Home Secretary); and George Joachim Goschen (1831–1907), Conservative Member of Parliament.

3. On 27 February 1893 Willard visited John Wesley's Chapel, where the English Methodists presented her with a box that had been Susannah Wesley's (mother of John Wesley, Methodism's founder); it held small items belonging to Susannah Wesley and other famous English Methodist women.

28 February 1893

I said Goodbye to the dear & faithful friend & helper of sixteen solaced & solacing years. In presence of the crisis at home and here and for sake of the Children's Fountain[1] that she had been urging me to let her go home for so long, she leaves on steamer Germanic White Star Line for America. . . . I held her in my arms & grieved to lose her! But she will return . . . in a few weeks and I must not be anxious. This is God's world all through.

1. Anna Gordon left for the United States to find out just how bad the Temple controversy had become. She was also bringing the Children's Fountain (sometimes called the Willard Fountain) to the United States to be part of the WCTU's exhibit at the World's Columbian Exposition held in Chicago in 1893. The bronze sculpture, created by the British sculptor George E. Wade, was a gift from the Loyal Temperance Legion, the WCTU's children's organization headed by Gordon. The sculpture featured a child offering a cup of water.

28 March 1893
London

. . . At night great Direct Veto Bill "Demonstration" in St. Jamcs' Hall.[1] Isabel got it up but couldn't be there.[2] Packed hall—overflow into Prince's Hall. Sir Wilfrid presided—Price-Hughes[3] and I spoke—with others. The two meetings were addressed by us all. Great enthusiasm.

1. On 28 March 1893 there was a great "Women's Demonstration" at St. James Hall in Picadilly Square on behalf of the Direct Veto bill being debated in Parliament.
2. Somerset's brother-in-law had died several days earlier so she was in mourning and staying with her sister.
3. Hugh Price Hughes (1847–1902) was a British Methodist minister, an advocate for total abstinence, and a powerful evangelist who believed in social reform effected through political means. In 1887, he established the West London Mission, which held popular services on Sundays in St. James Hall, site of the Direct Veto demonstration.

7 April 1893

Isabel & I went to London after a grand morning's work. Met Sidney Webb the "scientific socialist"[1] & his wife Beatrice Potter[2]— brought up under influence & presence of Herbert Spencer[3]—a most unique pair! *She* says "She never met any man however low but she felt his mental superiority"!! H[annah] W[hitall] S[mith] called out "And I never met one however high but I felt mine"! I *guess Herbert* subjects women-souls along side of him! Sidney is charming—broad, generous & without "kinks." I got a grand interview from them. . . .[4]

1. Sidney James Webb (1859–1947) was one of the founding leaders of the Fabian Society, a group of British reformers dedicated to the establishment of a socialist form of government through evolutionary means. When Willard met Webb he was embarking on a long career as an author of works on socialist theory, an

active participant in government, and one of the founders of the London School of Economics.

2. Martha Beatrice (Potter) Webb (1858–1943) was, like her husband, a leader of the Fabian Society and an influential economic and social reformer. She authored several works on aspects of socialist reform and coauthored others with her husband. Both husband and wife strongly influenced British radical thought and institutions during the first half of the twentieth century.

3. Herbert Spencer (1820–1903), one of the most eminent social philosophers of the Victorian Era, advocated a scientific, naturalist view of the world over super-naturalism. He was the prophet of Victorian progressive optimism and a supporter of extreme liberal, *laissez-faire* attitudes, coining the phrase "the survival of the fittest." Spencer was a great friend of Richard Potter, a wealthy industrialist, and was particularly fond of his daughter, Beatrice, spending much time with her throughout her childhood, forming her intellect.

4. Willard wrote up her interview with the Webbs; her article appeared in the *British Weekly* on 29 June 1893 and excerpts were published in the *Review of Reviews*. The article also appeared in the October 1893 issue of *Our Day*, an American reform journal. Willard, Isabel Somerset, and Hannah (Whitall) Smith questioned the Webbs on land reform, socialism, woman suffrage, and the drink question.

18 April 1893

Not well—red blotches on tongue—inflamed throat—cough—no appetite whatever. It is "pernicious anemia" I suppose—what my blessed Mother had off & on 2 or 3 years before her final flight. . . .

[*By 18 April Willard had been bothered by "blotches" on her tongue for well over a week. This particular symptom of pernicious anemia was to recur many times over the next several years, causing increasing debilitation because the condition often made eating nearly impossible for her. During 1893 she continually battled ill health as she strained to keep up her busy schedule. On 20 April she turned over the task of daily journal-keeping to Anna Gordon. Willard did not entirely curtail her activities, however. The annual meeting of the BWTA Council was held in early May; Somerset was reelected president and her policies were affirmed by a majority of delegates. Willard attended the sessions but did not give any speeches. In early June she spoke at a meeting of the Women's Liberal Federation and at sessions of the WWCTU. By mid-June both Willard and Somerset were completely worn out and Willard was alarmingly ill.*]

[Anna Gordon]   17 May 1893
                                                          Reigate

. . . Quiet day with stenographers and letters. Frances seems possessed to dictate from morning until night and nobody can do anything with her. She never will do differently until she goes off to some retreat where letters do not follow her—would the "two leaders" could flee away.

[Anna Gordon]   22 May 1893

. . . Many letters from home telling of the World's Congress of Women—of the great Exposition[1] etc. How strange that we are not there when we have so long looked forward to the occasion. . . .

1. The Congress of Representative Women met from 15 May until 21 May 1893 as a part of Chicago's World's Columbian Exposition (World's Fair), held to celebrate the four hundredth anniversary of Columbus's landing in America. The congress gathered women from all over the world to engage in dialogue, exchange reports from women's organizations in various countries, and celebrate women's work and accomplishments. Willard, as a member of the Board of Lady Managers for the World's Fair, was involved in the initial planning of the Congress.

[Anna Gordon]   2 June 1893
                                                         London

. . . This afternoon came the World's Meeting in Prince's Hall. . . .[1] At night a most wonderful Purity Meeting in St James Hall.[2] Lady H. surpassed herself & Andrew Bushnell[3] Mrs Butler[4] & Frances did *grandly.*

1. On 2 June 1893, the British section of the WWCTU held its annual convention at Prince's Hall in Piccadilly Square, London, with Somerset presiding.
2. The social purity meeting held on the evening of 2 June 1893 in St. James Hall in Piccadilly Square was a public meeting of the WWCTU. Its purpose was to hear reports from WWCTU missionaries on the regulation of vice (i.e., prostitution) in India by the British Army, and also to hear Josephine Butler (see footnote below) speak on the issue. Social purity became an important issue for British and American women's rights reformers in the 1880s and 1890s, as they sought to abolish the sexual double standard by holding men equally as responsible as women in acts of prostitution, and to protect young girls from sexual abuse and enforced prostitution by raising the age-of-consent laws.
3. Elizabeth (Wheeler) Andrew (1845–1917) and Dr. Katharine C. Bushnell (1855–1946) were WWCTU around-the-world missionaries, and, on behalf of Josephine Butler, superintendent of the WWCTU's Social Purity Department, investigated the British colonial government's regulation of prostitution in India. Andrew and Bushnell gave their reports at the WWCTU meeting at St. James Hall that Willard mentioned. A debate over social purity was beginning in the WWCTU by this time. On one side were Bushnell, Andrew, and Butler, whose ultimate aim was the elimination of prostitution and who, therefore, opposed all legislation that merely regulated it. They were also concerned about the poor treatment of Indian women by the British colonial power. On the other side was Somerset (and, tacitly, Willard), who

eventually came to believe that some government intervention was necessary to protect British women from venereal disease brought back from India by returning British soldiers.

4. Josephine Elizabeth (Grey) Butler (1828–1906) was a British women's rights leader whose campaign for social purity began in the 1870s and highlighted the necessity of changing male behavior, thereby eliminating the double standard. From 1891 to 1897 she was the superintendent of the Social Purity Department of the WWCTU.

[Anna Gordon]   9 June 1893
                                                      Reigate

We are getting anxious about F. because the fever although slight does not disappear and in her depleted condition we cannot bear to have any thing the matter. Lady Henry has been at home all day today. If F is not better in the aft she is going to send for an old family physician whom she has great confidence in and let him consult with Dr Hewetson.[1] Frank's heart is broken because she cannot go to the Hyde Park Demonstration in favor of Direct Veto[2] tomorrow—Tis hard to be sick in bed.

1. Dr. Hewitson was a local physician in Reigate.
2. On 10 June 1893 a huge demonstration in support of the Direct Veto (Local Option) bill took place in Hyde Park, London. Police reported that it was the largest demonstration that had ever been held there, and Somerset's coach was so surrounded by supporters that it took her hours to travel a fairly short distance from the BWTA headquarters to the park. Somerset presided over the demonstration and speakers included Sir Wilfrid Lawson, Mark Guy Pearse, and James Hayes Raper (1820–97), a leader of the United Kingdom Alliance and noted temperance speaker.

[Anna Gordon]   11 June 1893

Dr. Holman[1] came at noon with Dr. Hewetson. . . . He says F. has no organic disease but simply *must* rest if she ever expects to be well enough to do any efficient work hereafter. Urges her to give up entirely except a few hours pleasant literary work each day. Says she cannot go to meetings as a looker on. Her temperature is normal today and we are immensely relieved. Poor darling she has paid dearly for her week in London!

1. Sir Constantine Holman (1829–1910) was Somerset's family physician.

[*On 18 June Willard resumed journal keeping but stayed relatively quiet, obeying her doctor's orders. By 5 July she and Somerset were off for a vacation in the Swiss Alps in order to regain their health.*]

4 July 1893

Republic's Day! And for the first time I have small sense of elation; for the first time I am ashamed of my country because of Chicago. Think of it! The Columbian Exposition Managers—from every state— after getting millions from Congress on condition of not opening the Fair on Sunday have set at work [?] & *opened* it—the money being spent! And besides this, in violation of Hyde Park law that says no liquor & Illinois law that says none to be sold on Fair or Exposition grounds[1] "the management" (mis) has farmed out the right to sell. Temperance people have buried themselves under speculation and blinded themselves with marvels. . . .

1. Hyde Park, the Chicago neighborhood where the exposition was located, had forbidden the sale of liquor by local ordinance, and the State of Illinois passed a law that no alcohol would be sold on the grounds of the exposition.

16 July 1893
Engelberg, Switzerland

A heavenly day after 1 week of rain. We walked four miles up the valley & back—were gone 4 hours & took our lunch at the waterfall. "Earth with her thousand voices praises God"—this was the burden of our thoughts & talk. . . . A heavenly gospel of out doors seems to have come to me among these hills—I believe I shall never sit over my work so constantly again.

21 July 1893
Andermatt, Switzerland

. . . Had vision in the night of a novel I might write in which a woman becomes Pres't of the United States after a complete Revolution which she leads! . . .

24 July 1893

We read socialistic books of Bax & Schäffle,[1]—I like many of their ideas but detest the point-no-point of the former against Immortality. It is but a recoil from the two intense individualism of the past. The religion of Humanity will wreak itself in the next century & well it may—Christ is its Founder, Prophet and Exemplar. But as the German poet Hoffmann[2] said in his last hours "We must think of *God* also" aye & of the Endless Life! Isabel & I are Christian socialists—not pagan. . . .

1. Ernest Belfort Bax (1854–1926) was a lawyer, an author, and a founder of English socialism. Albert Eberhard Friedrich Shäffle (1831–1903) was an economist and sociologist and served briefly as Austrian minister of commerce and agriculture in 1871. Bax wrote several books, including *Religion of Socialism* (London, 1887), *Ethics of Socialism* (London, 1889), *Outlooks from the New Standpoint* (London, 1891), and *The Problem of Reality* (London, 1892), any of which Willard could have read. Books by Schäffle on socialism include: *Kapitalismus und Socialismus* (Tubingen, 1870), English edition, *Socialism: Its Nature, Its Dangers, and Its Remedies Considered* (London, 1874); *Quintessenz des Socialismus* (Gotha, 1874), English edition, *The Quintessence of Socialism* (London, 1889;) and *Aussichtslosigkeit der Socialdemokratie* (Tubingen, 1885), English edition, *The Impossibility of Social Democracy* (London, 1892); and *The Theory and Policy of Labour Protection*, ed. A. C. Morant (London, 1893). Willard might have read any or all of these.

2. Ernst Theodor Wilhelm Hoffmann (1776–1822) was a German Romantic author, composer, and painter, as well as a lawyer. On 30 August 1859, Willard had written an extended description of Hoffmann's creative but profligate life and, especially, his death, which she had read about in Longfellow's *Hyperion*. Willard had been particularly impressed by Hoffmann's exclamation on his deathbed: "We must then, think of God, also!," still remembering his deathbed utterance over thirty years later.

26 July 1893

. . . Turmoil & tumult about the Autumn Conventions of World & Nat WCTU Oct 16–21.[1] Shall I be able to go home? Will Isabel? It now looks as if I shall & yet Dr B W Richardson[2] forbade any public work for 1 year. The whole subject is open at both ends—waiting developments. Isabel's opponents are briskly on the war path here as mine are yonder—but leaders must always expect this. . . .

1. The WWCTU biennial meeting was held 16–17 October 1893 in the Memorial Art Palace in Chicago, in conjunction with the Columbian Exposition. The NWCTU annual convention followed, on 18–21 October 1893, in the same building.

2. Sir Benjamin Ward Richardson (1828–96) was a well-known and prominent London physician. He was also a temperance advocate who published on the subject of alcohol consumption and health. A letter from Richardson and Dr. Constantine Holman stating that they believed Willard needed a complete year of rest to recover from her malaise was published in the 5 October 1893 *Union Signal*.

28 July 1893

Rainy—busy all day with letters—books & papers. So glad we have nice rooms & fire. C. got off the First Annual Leaflet of BWTA which will be lots of help to her women. Indeed we have done a good bit of work since we came here and planned & talked not a little about the future of the societies whose interests are so near & whose members so dear to us. Heaven help us to be true & loyal to each & all.

1 August 1893

Nannie[1] came back—dear little one. . . . She is to be with me now right on. She found me in bed . . . and cossetted by Cossie "as one whom his mother comforteth."[2] We meant to read so much especially in German works on socialism. Made a beginning up on these hills of God and thought much & talked. We have joined the Fabian Soc.[3] & so far as we understand ourselves we are New Testament Socialists. . . .[4]

1. "Nannie" and also "Nan" were Willard's nicknames for Anna Gordon. Gordon had left Willard and Somerset on 22 June to vacation in Paris and in Spain, where her sister, Alice (Gordon) Gulick, lived.

2. Isa. 66:13.

3. The Fabian Society was a socialist organization founded in London in 1883 by Sidney Webb, George Bernard Shaw, and Annie Besant, among others. Sidney and Beatrice (Potter) Webb became the leaders of the society, whose goal was to establish a democratic socialist state in Great Britain. The Fabians advocated a moderate form of socialism that did not include revolution as a method but, instead, favored an evolutionary approach. Willard joined the society while in Switzerland in August 1893, and, according to Sidney Webb's memorial tribute to her (in Gordon, *The Beautiful Life of Frances Willard* [Chicago, 1898], 407–8), contributed annually to the society until she died.

4. Neither Willard nor Somerset could agree with socialist thinkers who rejected immortality and a Christian framework for their social and economic theories. Many Christians found a New Testament basis for their socialism in Acts 4:32–37, where the sharing of goods in common and their distribution according to need is described.

5 August 1893

Mother's last day was 1 yr ago. She said faintly to Nan "*So long*"— slept much—breathed faintly mouth wide open—eyes so changed, a green color. Watched me as I sat smoothing hand or limbs—her tongue too dry to speak until by happy tho't Nan moistened it & then said "*Berlin*—Mary—Mamie[1]—awful sorry" / sorry not to see them they were so soon to come & did 10 days later. She nodded when I helped out her wish by saying the messages I knew she wanted given. She kissed me on the cheek as I knelt beside her & I kissed her on the brow. We knew it was our leave taking! . . .

1. As Willard indicated, Mary (Bannister) Willard and her daughter, also Mary Bannister Willard (1875 or 1876–1931), known as Mamie, visited in Evanston later in August 1892. However, Willard's mother had already died by the time they arrived.

6 August 1893

Mother—Gone.

One year ago she went away—12 minutes after midnight & the date Aug. 7. *She* went away who for 53 years had been & who must be always nearest of souls to me. She went away who at nearly 88 had no sense in any wise abated & was full of love, wisdom & hope.—Today I live & see & know it all & think hers the most blessed life—the best—that ever came to my ken. And I feel that she is surely with God and those she loved best—only if I could but *know!* "In whatever land thou art"[1] "the Lord bless thee & keep thee"[2] thou great & blessed one!

1. Not identified.
2. Num. 6:24.

14 August 1893
Villars sur Ollon

Sitting on Cossie's balcony to get a sun bath. Goggles on over eye glasses; lips [. . .] to cold sores; general feeling of lassitude. In night was low in my mind about immortality & had a talk with dear comforting C. who came & warmed me up. Who should despair with 2 such blessed & lovely friends as she & my Little Nan? Somehow I seem to myself like a dog that has lost his bone—*work* was my bone & a meaty one I found it.—My Two say I must not go home to the Convention that I have gained so little—Exposition, silver crisis[1] &c absorb everything & Convention will not be crucial this year—I lost all I had gained by insisting on going last year &c—&c.

1. During the severe economic depression that hit the United States in early 1893, when the U.S. gold reserve had fallen below what was considered a safe minimum of one hundred million dollars, some politicians, economists, and others advocated the free and unlimited coinage of silver, which would have infused the economy with "cheap money" based on the silver dollar, worth only sixty-five cents in gold. This would have taken the pressure off debtors but caused inflation and, possibly, economic paralysis. The gold standard versus the silver standard was debated throughout 1893. In October 1893, President Cleveland pushed the repeal of the Sherman Silver Purchase Act through Congress, thus limiting silver coinage and reestablishing the gold reserve.

15 August 1893

Cossie was not well. . . . We rose late & sat about & sunned ourselves & didn't go down stairs. We read no end & wrote important letters & the dear patient one had her fearful headache. She says it never came till as a sequel of her griefs with Lord Henry[1] but for 8 years there after she had it about once in 10 days—that she has given a ball

& left it every few minutes to vomit—for this is a feature right along. Dear Isabel! She has suffered *much* but now she says she is content & I am & we are so glad & grateful while my beloved little Nannie— for nearly 17 years[2] my other-self loves us both & is such a comfort.

1. Willard meant by Somerset's "griefs" her separation from her husband because of his homosexual behavior, and the subsequent court hearing where Somerset presented evidence of her husband's unfitness to care for their son. Somerset was awarded custody of her son in 1878 but was ostracized by society for making the scandal public. For years after the breakup of her marriage, she suffered from migraine headaches.
2. Anna Gordon's association with Willard began in fall 1877, which would have made it almost sixteen years, not seventeen as Willard wrote.

17 August 1893

. . . Not very lively but resumed dictation to dear little Edith[1] after a six weeks interval. Endless letters always rise up between me & what I call "doing something." But one should remember that relationships official & long continued, to great movements must involve tens of thousands of letters per year & that thus one is actually at work vitally for "the Cause" however little he may realize that fact. Read no end in the endless newspapers. The International Socialistic Congress in Zurich holds my thought. . . .[2]

1. Edith Goode was Somerset's stenographer.
2. The congress met in Zurich 6–12 August 1893 and discussed such issues as legislation for the eight-hour work day, arbitration, religion, war and peace, the protection of working women and children, political action of Socialists, and international trades organizations.

18 August 1893

All day nearly among the pine woods with their healing balm. . . . Bluest of skies—Mt. Blanc in sight that "Kingly spirit throned among the hills."[1] Some little spring of life in me & I lay on the ground & dictated to Edith while dear attendant Nannie, faithful tender & true spread the cloaks for me & took my head in her lap. Heaven bless my younger sister who reminded Blessed Mother of "our Mary." She goes soon to America to look after interests mutually dear—how I *hope* to follow! Nan read Epictetus[2] aloud at recess time under the trees. What great & noble philosophy—how full of love & faith toward God. Nan read from Mary Wilkins[3] the gifted New England girl. A rich full day.

1. Willard quoted from Samuel Taylor Coleridge, "Hymn Before Sunrise, in the Vale of Chamouni," first published in the *Morning Post and Gazeteer* (London, 1802).

2. Epictetus (b. 50 A.D.) was a Greek Stoic philosopher, primarily interested in ethics, who taught that there is only one thing truly one's own: the will. Human beings are not responsible for the ideas that present themselves to their consciousness, but are wholly responsible for the way in which they use ideas. The human being's will comes from God, who directs the universe, and the human being can learn to conform the will to God's will, which is also the will of nature. Epictetus advocated a serene approach to life, free of unfulfilled desires, and calm in the face of death. The religious tone of Epictetus's teachings appealed to many Christians.

3. Mary Eleanor (Wilkins) Freeman (1852–1930) was an American author known for her realistic portrayals of New England life.

22 August 1893

Another of those colds. I remember when I had so much vigor that they were thrown off readily but now on the least provocation they "settle."

Nan had a lovely note from Isabel about our trio dwelling together as I hope we may ever do. It seems so good to have it so & illustrative of sense and good will among women. Poor, beautiful Cossie made a sorry marriage—great in the world's eyes but piteous in heart. At 40 she found a woman she could love & trust after a life of loneliness. She was for me a blessed consummation but my Little Nan the true & tried, faithful, loving & beloved, nestles always in my heart & always will just the same. She has shown a heroic spirit & so has Isabel—Cossie came—very worn & melted by the heat—& Nannie went with her brave, sweet face & our kerchiefs waving until we could see each other no more.[1]—I shall be glad when we all get to Heaven! Poor Cossie sick all night & I feverish—a sorry pair we started up the hill on our 3 1/2 hour ride, Cossie in such pain that only her patience kept her still which patience is wonderful in all physical distress & in all exigencies save when she gives way just a minute because her dear head has ached so much.—She crawled into bed with a distracting head ache as soon as we arrived. I sat at my writing table & nagged on—corrected 30 pp Eng. Ed. Glimpses[2] & finally gave in to a drooling right eye & nostril & went to bed. Feverish at night—I wonder why for nothing is the matter. But somehow I lack resistance. Sir B W Richardson's letter came last night—he will not relent & let me go to our Conventions—he says as a faithful physician he can not. This is a good deal of a blow—but I may yet "pick up amazin'" who knows? I shall go right on—do all I can to help make the Conventions what they ought to be and wait developments. . . .

1. Somerset had been visiting her mother (see Journal, 19 September 1896, n. 1) at her chateau in Savoie, Switzerland. Gordon left for England, where she took a steamer to the United States in order to prepare for the WWCTU and NWCTU conventions in October.

2. The English edition of Willard's autobiography was entitled *My Happy Half-Century: The Autobiography of an American Woman* (London, 1894).

27 August 1893

We walked 3 hours wh is more than I have done since we first went to Andematt. I can but think 6 months utter absence from care would build me up—but it seems not possible even for Isabel's all-surrounding efforts to *quite* bring this to pass.—I was weighed at Chesiere[1] boulanger's [bakery] & came to 117 pounds—2 less at when I first reached Switzerland & this after nearly 2 months of the most rest I have known since I grew up. . . . Exquisite scenery—arches green & landscape "climbing to heaven" all the day & way long. . . . Somehow all objective observances are less & less to me since Mother went away & since experiences of the last three years (that shall be nameless) have shown me how profession mocks performance. Doctrines mean less & duties more with every added year. To be genuine—to be what one seems & to seem to be true & kind—this is the core of life.

1. Chesières is a resort town in southwest Switzerland.

5 September 1893
Reigate

Pegging away at speech as usual[1]—poor work—disjointed stuff but best I can all things considered. I fear our women at home do not appreciate that though I "can't stand the racket" of Convention drum & trombones or public speaking fifes I can toot my little flute & fiddle here alone in this dear quiet den to a congenial stenographer like Edith Goode or Grace Murrell. . . .

1. Willard was at work on her annual address for the NWCTU convention.

9 September 1893

. . . My poor scalded tongue is better thanks to the wash prescribed by good little Dr Hewitson. What a surcease! The last of her 50 years of mindfulness was my Mother's coming to me with a wash basin when she was hardly able to walk—a few days before she went to her last bed—& saying as I wrote on with mouth full of Dr Mettie's wash "spit that out Frank—you are holding it too long!" Where art thou, loving one?

19 September 1893

Went to Dr Holman with Isabel—He gave me solemn lectures on my food & exercise—If I had my way would drop everything & put myself for 6 months in charge of a trained nursewoman who was also an athelete & would teach me swimming the bicycle & trapeze! We always reach for the impossible! . . .

22 September 1893

For days I have ground away on my speech. How sick of it I am! Have no *pith* to put into it—not ill—not in pain but—"worthless" & e'en a most 54! However at that age I ought to be in full tilt & should have been—except that Mother died. So soon I shall & Isabel & Nan & all the rest—& great peace will be upon us here—& as I strongly feel—uplift to other planets & their work & worth.

25 September 1893

One of the greyest of England's autumn days—after almost 6 months of sunshine. I have never enjoyed such an amount of celestial weather in a given time. Unlike Mother & like father I am dependent on sunshine for exhileration—the whole tone of my spirit is different under blue skies & golden beams. I would I were as equable as Mother but no other ever has been that I know of! Isabel comes pretty near it—she is wonderfully even in her cheerfulness. . . . My speech is practically done—& ever so poor. In the Temple difficulty I tell the origin of the great enterprise and that we always clearly stated that we would take no financial legal responsibility as a National WCTU for any affiliated enterprise.

[*Although Willard continued to hope that she would feel well enough to return to the United States and preside over the WCTU annual convention in Chicago, she gave up the idea by late August. Instead Somerset was to read Willard's annual address and preside over the WWCTU convention, and Anna Gordon would accompany her. Willard stayed behind in England at Hannah (Whitall) Smith's home, Haslemere, cared for by Bess Gordon, one of Anna Gordon's sisters.*]

7 October 1893

. . . Going to the steamer I said "You go for God & Home & Every Land"[1] Her dark eyes twinkled & she said "For Conk[2] & G. & H. &c." I said "Did I make thee go—was I not anxious to go myself?" She said "Certainly you were—I go first for the ransom of your presence (if you went, sick or well they would not let you come back); & I go for the Cause & to meet my boy." . . .[3] tender words were between Cossie & me as we sped in the special to Southampton. . . . [4] C. threw her arms around me—we went—Bess[5] & I down the ship's side. . . . We staid in the rain . . . till the great ship slowly rounded out to sea. And I had tears—& life seemed so changeful & pathetic—& I wished we were all of us "in the ether"—which we are already if we did but know it. I thought of little Nan & her heroic spirit & behaviour & thanked God who had given me two such inner heart comrades.

1. "For God and Home and Every Land" was the motto of the WWCTU, modeled after the NWCTU motto: "For God and Home and Native Land."
2. "Conk" was Somerset's nickname for Willard. The journal gives no clue as to the derivation of "Conk."
3. Somerset's son, Henry Somers Augustus Somerset (1874–1945), had been on an extended expedition to the interior of Canada. She was to meet him in New York City at the close of his travels.
4. Southampton was the main port city in the south of England from which transatlantic steamers embarked.
5. Elizabeth Putnam Gordon (1851–1933) was Anna Gordon's older sister. In 1893 she was the corresponding secretary and general organizer of the Massachusetts WCTU and was later made Evangelist for the NWCTU.

16 October 1893
Haslemere

. . . Mrs. Bramwell Booth & Mrs. Walker came[1]—leaders in Salvation Army; met them at station & had helpful talk of vegetarianism—"Dr. Page's Natural Remedy" has helped her greatly[2]—nuts & fruit are her chief portion & her childrens; she has six & they are never ill; Bramwell B. ditto.[3] I mean to take some of her suggestions. She entered into a gentle "labor" ("had a concern") for me religiously. But I told her "I had suffered much of many physicians"[4] & had come into the "region of calms." It seemed to me she regarded us white ribbon women as secular which thing I resented. She spoke of building on hay, wood & stubble—I told her that was much better than nothing—that we claimed every realm—science, invention, reform, philanthropy—*all* for Christ & as radiations from His Cross which is the central figure of civilization. She evidently thought me a "poor dear" &

I *knew she* was a dear. I got a little constrained & was sorry afterward & said so. Cable from Cosie—all going well—cable from world's convention—Colossians second-fifth. I sent Proverbs 25–25 & "Love never faileth."[5] I rejoice & am glad about the convention & know it will go well.

1. Florence (Soper) Booth (ca. 1862–1957) was the Salvation Army's chief organizer of social service programs in England. Mrs. de Noe Walker was also a Salvation Army leader.
2. Dr. Page's Natural Remedy was probably a vegetable-based home-care medicine made in England.
3. William Bramwell Booth (1856–1929), son of William Booth, founder of the Salvation Army, was the army's chief organizer and an able speaker for the cause of social perfection through Christianity. He became the second general of the Salvation Army in 1912, upon his father's death.
4. Mark 5:26.
5. WWCTU leaders at the biennial convention in Chicago sent Willard a cable reading "Col. 2:5," which was: "For though I be absent in the flesh yet I am with you in the spirit, joying and beholding your order, and the stedfastness of your faith in Christ." Willard sent a cable in return reading "Prov. 25:25," which was: "As cold waters to a thirsty soul, so is good news from a far country," and a paraphrase of 1 Cor. 13:8, "Charity never faileth."

19 October 1893

. . . Had boofulum[1] cable from convention "Illimitable love & loyalty." I dont know why I should be so blessed—with such a heredity, ancestry, parentage, kinship, home, ability, opportunity, vocation, comradeship, success, Love of God & love of Humanity—Expectations well & sweetly growing, of Immortal Life. Why should two such rare women as Lady Henry & Anna Gordon be supremely devoted to poor old "sissy" whose "dress ached"[2] even when she was little but whose hurt heart has been healed by help from Heaven & Humanity. . . .

1. Somerset and Willard used baby-talk on occasion in private communication. "Boofulum" meant "beautiful."
2. Willard referred to a story she recounted early in her autobiography (*Glimpses of Fifty Years,* 5). Once, when she was very tired as a little girl, she put her arms around her mother's neck, saying, "Mama, sissy's dress aches."

20 October 1893

Another telegram—this time from "national" WCTU—dear old thing! "Love illimitable & loyalty—abiding faithfulness Read 2 John 2 1st Thess. I,2,3."[1] This is the fifth cablegram—all lovely & of good report[2] but no news. Hannah says in view of this *she* is going to send one "Fewer texts—more information.". . . I *do* wish I knew outcome of world's & fate of Mrs. R.[3] in stockholders meeting but "never a word." I told Cossie & Nan that they would "miss my guess" if there wasn't a falling away from me this year & if the opposition to the Temple & Carsie[4] didn't take definite form in the retention of "certain" whom leaders have proposed to "oust" for "the good of the order."

Almost while I wrote, came another cable "Temple victorious" which means much in view of this years unequalled complications at the temple, in publishing house Dept[5] & in 2 General Officers rooms & with Mrs. FHR &c. I feel grieved over it all & do not pretend to understand it. . . .

1. 2 John 2 reads: "For the truth's sake, which dwelleth in us, and shall be with us forever." In the first three chapters of 1 Thessalonians, Paul praises the Christians in Thessalonica for their steadfastness to the faith, reminisces about his former visit with them, laments his absence from them, and tells them his decision to send Timothy in his place. NWCTU leaders who sent the cable saw a parallel between Paul's situation and Willard's since both had loyal and hardworking followers in a distant land and both regretted not being with them but sent a colleague instead.

2. Willard paraphrased a portion of Phil. 4:8, "whatsoever things are lovely, whatsoever things are of good report. . . ."

3. Frances (Fanny) H. Rastall (1844–1920), president of the Kansas WCTU from 1884 to 1891, was the business manager of the Woman's Temperance Publishing Association from 1890 to 1892, when Carse fired her for improper business practices. (The *Union Signal* reported on 2 February 1893 that Rastall had "retired" as the association's business manager.) She, along with Esther Pugh and Caroline Buell, had been using the *Union Signal* to promote their private business schemes in real estate, insurance, and a baking company.

4. Carsie was Willard's nickname for Matilda Carse.

5. The Woman's Temperance Publishing Association was a stock company of women only, begun by Matilda Carse in 1880 to publish temperance literature first for the NWCTU and, then, for the WWCTU also. It published the *Union Signal* and, by 1890, produced over 125 million pages of literature annually. The troubles in the association to which Willard referred had to do with the unethical practices of Rastall, Buell, and Pugh and also with the association's serious financial difficulties due to the nationwide economic depression.

21 October 1893

Cable "Reelected—only 10 votes adverse—Hail beloved chieftain"

How my heart bubbles up in gratitude to God and my comrades! Four hundred votes & more & only 10 who were against their absent "elderly sister!" I can well imagine that these were against the WTPA the Temple &c and the only wonder is that there were not more—I predicted 30 to 50. Late cables say "Board of Directors satisfactory"[1] so it looks as if the deadlock is broken & cable says Woodbridge is Cor. Sec. Stevens Rec Sec Hoffman ass't—later Pugh who was treasurer resigns & Helen Barker (one of Board of Managers World's Fair) takes her place—a strong team that! Never have we had the like.

1. At the 1893 convention there were several changes in the officers of the NWCTU, who also made up the Board of Directors. Mary Ann (Brayton) Woodbridge (1830–94), was elected corresponding secretary; she had been the WCTU's recording secretary since 1878 and was also president of the Ohio WCTU. Lillian Marion Norton (Ames) Stevens (1844–1914), president of the Maine WCTU, was elected recording secretary. Clara (Cleghorn) Hoffman (1831–1908), president of the Missouri WCTU, was elected assistant recording secretary. Although Esther Pugh was reelected treasurer, she resigned, and Helen (Morton) Barker (1834–1910), president of the South Dakota WCTU and member of the Board of Lady Managers of the World's Columbian Exposition, was elected in her place.

27 October 1893

My beloved brother Oliver would, had he lived been 59 today. It passes the wit of man to believe that Mother's boy would have entered his *60th Year* this day! I can but feel that he and Mother must be talking over all the dear ones and good & sorrowful times past. He was the most gifted child she had; his native wit and love of letters were always uppermost; but for tobacco and alcohol he would have become the chief pulpit orator of our church; when he was 27 Mrs Gov. Evans of Denver Col.[1] said she had heard the best speakers in England & America & her pastor Oliver Willard was equal to any one of them. My heart recalls how he always stood by Mother in the hard work & difficult days of our pioneer life when father was so far from well; how nice he was to Mary & me; how in later years he was one of the most brilliant collegians minister editor he grew to be "tugged with fortune & weary with disaster"[2] and went away at 42.

1. Margaret (Gray) Evans (1830–1906) was the wife of John Evans, governor of the Colorado Territory from 1862 to 1865, who had used his influence to have Oliver Willard assigned to the Colorado Territory in 1862. While he served the MEC there, the Evanses were his parishioners in Denver.
2. Willard once again paraphrased William Shakespeare, *Macbeth*, act 3, scene 1, line 112: "So weary with disasters, tugged with fortune."

28 October 1893

Two years ago today our beautiful Isabel came to Rest Cottage. Nan & I met her at the train; Mother was at the door as we came up the vine-wreathed steps; the American & English flags were festooned over the pretty portico; the dinner was daintiness itself; the den was brilliant and cozy with electric lights and wood fire in the grate; Yolande was with us and Mother in her favorite rocking chair was center of the group. Dear Hannah Smith lead in the evening prayer when I had read a chapter & we had all sung "Blest be the tie."[1] What a happy, hallowed, sorrowful two years they have been; what failure & what triumph in God they have recorded for us each & all!

1. "Blessed be the tie that binds" is the title and first line of a well-known hymn, a favorite still among many Protestant denominations, especially Methodists.

2[?] October 1893

I have felt the loss of church & social religious meetings & our warm hearted temperance gatherings, more than I can say. How true it is that heart warms heart in holy talk along the heavenly way! But I am thankful to have known so much of "the assembly of the faithful" all along the journey now full spent.

1 November 1893
Reigate

Cossie Comes Home.

I am more than ashamed of my anxieties for this morning at 8 behold a telegram from the bravest of the Braves, off Queenstown "1.15 AM Nov. 1 safe—well—love—E[arl] C[osmos]." So she has come safely & on time—the woman with the head of a statesman & heart of a child. How great a thing she has done in these 24 days neither she nor we can realize. She is the first reformer to preside over the great rally of clans in the country of the Crusade, though herself the leader in a land three thousand miles away.—She has come; I heard the clatter of hoofs within 5 minutes of the time we looked for her— 10:15 P.M. We had set a light in every window from top to bottom; put a wreath of Chinese lanterns around the portico & were all gathered in the hall. She came in, that dark-bright face, so arch, so sweet. . . . We talked till 2—it was bad but I *had* to know of the Convention— so many questions! All seems to have gone for the best & harmony is restored at headquarters. She says nothing can exceed the love & loyalty of the women for their old friend. . . . She went to dear Rest Cottage; she went to Mother's grave. . . . The Fair is a miracle. . . . She says that by scores & companies people have come out to Rest Cottage from Chicago all summer. . . .

6 November 1893

Somehow, though I do not go to church I think I never had a more God-smitten consciousness than now. I cannot see the sun shine but it is to me God's spirit's emblem; all the laws of nature so far as I have learned them, are to me living lines leading to our Heavenly Father. Nothing is temporary or profane. Thought is all—matter is thought that has cooled; we are in eternity as much as we ever shall be; the Kingdom of Heaven is within us; the veil grows thin; Mother seems my guardian angel; I have no such horror of the world to come as in my cruder years but the universe seems Home and the throbbing heavens full of happy beings & all of us, the two footed, & the four footed on our way to something better—growing on & up toward God.

10 November 1893

News to stir the blood—Colorado enfranchised its women—four thousand majority![1]

This has been a great day with the "bike." Grace Murrell coached me & I went 12 times from cottage to Priory with her "moral support" only! She says in a week at this rate I shall be master of the steed of steel. I find I like as I always claimed—purposeful exercise but not aimless traipsing. . . .

1. Colorado voted to enfranchise women on 7 November 1893 in the general fall elections.

12 November 1893

. . . We had a charming talk of God, Nature and Humanity, with quips and turns, pleasantries and pathos.

Evolution came in of course & Isabel told of the Evangelical Alliance[1] in England a generation ago, who thought that if Archbishop Usher's chronology[2] were overthrown the Bible must go with it & I remembered how when I came home from Prof. Jones' class in Geology one day, and told of Hugh Miller's theories[3] my good father said "I didn't put you in school to learn a lot of infidel notions; the world was made in 6 days and man has been in it 6000 years & whoever teaches to the contrary let him be anathema maranatha."[4] Dear father! His Puritan back bone & loyalty were noble qualities but had he lived & studied on into the realm of "Higher Criticism,"[5] the geological revulsion would have seemed but a trifle. Yet his daughter has lived on & finds *Truth* in the Bible which is a higher thing than *fact* and reverences God in the Word as much as ever he did the Word of God. . . .

1. A forerunner of the twentieth-century ecumenical movement among churches, the Evangelical Alliance was formed in London in 1846 as an interdenominational and international movement of church leaders to promote Christian unity and religious liberty. It agreed on a nine-point doctrinal basis emphasizing the authority of the Scriptures and the individual interpretation of them. The impetus for founding the Alliance came from Anglican and other British religious leaders' reaction against the Oxford Movement, a High Church or Anglo-Catholic renewal movement in the Church of England that emphasized apostolic succession and priestly authority, and sacraments as the source of grace. It was looked upon by the Evangelical Alliance as a move toward "popery."

2. James Ussher (1581–1656) was an Anglican Archbishop of Armagh who devised a chronology of biblical events. From his calculations the Creation occurred in 4004 B.C. When Darwin's theory of evolution suggested a much older time frame for world history, Christians who subscribed to Ussher's Bible-based timetable felt that if the chronology were found to be fallacious, the Bible would be also, and, thus, its authority would be endangered.

3. Hugh Miller, an English geologist whose writings Willard studied while at NWFC, wrote *The Testimony of the Rocks: Geology in its Bearings on the Two Theologies, Natural and Revealed* (New York, 1857). Miller attempted to reconcile Christianity with evolution, subscribing to the theory that, while the world was created in six days, as the Bible said, Scripture did not specify how long each day was. Therefore, on the basis of geological evidence which showed the earth to be millions of years old, each "day" of creation was millions of years long.

4. From 1 Cor 16:22, "If any man love not the Lord Jesus Christ, let him be Anathema. Maranatha." "Anathema" is Aramaic, meaning "accursed, morally unworthy." "Maranatha," in Aramaic, means "Our Lord, Come!" "Anathema" was the phrase with which the early church excommunicated members. By Willard's time, the word meant something odious or intensely disliked.

5. Higher criticism was a discipline within biblical studies developed in the eighteenth, nineteenth, and early twentieth centuries. It was concerned with the literary and historical study of the Bible, attempting to determine authorship, date, place of origin of the text, audience, circumstances of composition, purpose of the author, and the historical credibility of the biblical texts, as well as the intended meaning of the author. (Lower criticism was concerned with textual criticism: reconstructing the original biblical texts by using original languages.) Higher criticism of the Bible was threatening to those who believed in the divine origin and infallibility of the Scriptures.

18 November 1893

Working away with my "bike." It's a regular study in mental philosophy, Christian science mind-cure[1] and balance all in one. When I think Im all right, or better still think nothing about it, I go nicely; when I waver in my mind wobble goes the machine. When I put before me a picture of my Mother, that great balanced character, &

figure her holding a pair of balances in hand I go like a bird; when I think of the words "Reel to & fro & stagger like a drunken man"—over I go! There's more taught by the bike than meets the eye & ear.

1. Willard referred to the teachings of Mary Baker Eddy (1821–1910), the founder of the Church of Christ, Scientist. She taught, through her book *Science and Health*, that Mind or God is the only reality, and sin, evil, sickness, and death are not real, but only errors that can be overcome by right belief, that is, by Christian Science. The phrase "mind over matter" is a simplified statement of her teaching, which Willard probably had in mind as she struggled to master bicycle riding.

29 November 1893
London

Rose at 7—breakfast 8. Sat in my pretty, quiet den & read my mail—now grown so large—from all parts of Christendom. All th[r]ough my public life this mail has come between me & the speeches, articles, stories! poems! that I have "felt it in my bones" I could write. I have grieved over it too—but doubtless it was best. A reformer must keep in touch with his cohorts & temperance, labor & the woman question—to have helped them onward but a little is greater than to have written what would probably have made haste to die. A shout in the hall at 9 AM—Bess has heard from London by telephone that *Nannie's ship* is sighted off the Scilly islands. So we pack up & go to London & Bess to Southampton. How good is God!—And some day *Mother* will sight my ship bound [?] for the land of Immortality!

31 December 1893
Reigate

. . . I am writing all this as a sort of making up the log, at 10 P.M on the last night of the Year. It is a curious sight—dear Hannah standing on one side of me, by the glowing fire place & Isabel on the other, like a pair of guardian angels and hurrying me to bed—while I, thinking of Mother & Nan & Yolande, am inclined to scratch away with what they call "the tireless little hand."

Well, God have mercy on us all & bring us through the rapids to the sheltered harbor & give us "with the dawn" those presences so loved & lost so long—and best of all for me, my Mother's great, brave, tender presence once more. On this new year night I ask the forgiveness of all the world & grant to it the same with a kiss of sorrowful & hopeful peace. *The End.*

[*No journal volumes have been found for 1894 or 1895 and Willard probably did not keep a journal then. During those years she divided her time*

between the United States and England, spending six months in one coun-
try and six in the other. Exhaustion and illness continued to plague her,
yet she insisted upon trying to keep up her hectic schedule, however with
increasing difficulty. Although she rallied sufficiently to preside over two
rather stormy WCTU annual conventions—Cleveland in 1894 and Bal-
timore in 1895—and to participate in the 1894 and 1895 sessions of the
BWTA Council, she spent weeks at a time in relative seclusion, resting from
the demands of her public life. Although she was worn out physically, her
mind remained active and her heart courageous. During 1894 and 1895
she took some of her most radical positions, undoubtedly leaving most of
her constituency behind. In her 1894 annual address she announced that
she had come to the conclusion that poverty caused intemperance as well
as the reverse—at that time still a somewhat startling declaration. By the
1895 convention she was urging WCTU members to create a Department
of Politics with the aim of bringing about a grassroots coalition between
the rising Populist movement and the Prohibition Party as she looked ahead
to the 1896 presidential election. As her 1896 journal opened, Willard was
beginning a speaking tour through the South, strengthening old ties with
loyal WCTU leaders who had worked with her since her first Southern tour
in 1881, recruiting new members, and encouraging the formation of more
local unions.]

2 January 1896
Asheville, North Carolina

I took a novel resolution who am given to self-reproach.
This year instead of thinking myself the "worst of people" I shall recur as the pivot of my thinking to those words divine: The Kingdom
of Heaven *is within you.*"[1]

Cozzie, who is the descendant of gay cavaliers has a frequent,
laughing speech "I'm a good little thing"! & she really believes it! She
was never taught the Puritan theology that shadowed my ancestral
tree. But after all who knows but her philosophy is best? Any how I'm
going to try it & to lift my heart to God for faith to make it true. *Se-*
lah [So be it].

1. Luke 17:21.

11 January 1896

One day is like another—same routine. New York papers and *let-*
ters make the only stir. Those from Cossie are my solace. She is so dear
and mindful. All her goodness to us is not "of record" and cannot

be—she forbids it. But the heart remembers and is loyal. Nan is out on errands—she is so capable and true. Maxie[1] said in a letter today that she thought her to be the most unselfish person she had ever known. Nan's character is formed on the New Testament & Epictetus—her favorite books. Lovely days—sweet skies—time flies and one doesn't mind for if it is not "eternity cut off at both ends," then nothing makes much difference and if it is then the years of God are ours!

1. Charlotte E. Maxwell (ca. 1856–1936) was an instructor of gymnastics who owned and operated St. Botolph Gymnasium in Boston, Mass. Willard and Somerset had engaged Maxwell in 1895 to set up a gym in the Priory at Reigate and instruct them in a Swedish gymnastics system. Maxwell also was a specialist in medical massage and gave Willard massage treatments. She spent several months of 1895 and 1896 in England with Willard and Somerset, working with them on a health regime.

12 January 1896

Cossie wrote from her Christmas visit to the St Alban's:[1] "Here we are and how my heart yearns for *thee*. The great Atlantic roars between us but my hands are held out, and I sometimes feel I must go after thee. . . . And now my own one I must end. Before this reaches thee the year will have gone—the year that brought us so much joy, such a heart-break at parting and leaves us so longing and loving? How the coming year will end we know not, only I know it will leave us loving still—whether Here or Beyond!—Do not make our separation an hour longer than it must be for I love thee." . . .

1. Isabel Somerset's only child, Henry (Somy) Somers Somerset, married Katharine Vere de Vere Beauclerk, daughter of the Duke and Duchess of St. Albans, on 23 January 1896. Isabel Somerset spent Christmas 1895 with the Duke and Duchess, Somy's future in-laws.

13 January 1896

Sending off . . . an introduction to Edward Bliss' book on Aremenia.[1] Nothing in all my life—not even our Civil War has outraged my spirit like the fate of that *martyr nation*. And God sees it all! He must know ways out of the wilderness that we little ones do not see—compensations hidden from us. In that one can find solace but not elsewhere. . . .

1. Willard wrote a short introduction to Rev. Edwin Munsell Bliss's book *Turkey and the Armenian Atrocities* (London, 1896), urging American Christians to respond to the plight of Armenian Christians who were being persecuted by the Turkish sultan Abdul-Hamid II. Alarmed by rising Armenian nationalism, the sultan ordered his troops to carry out large-scale massacres in 1895 and 1896. Bliss's book detailed the

history of the Ottoman Empire in what is now Turkey, described the various ethnic groups living in the region, traced the Christian presence there, and explained the present situation of the Armenians, giving restrained accounts of the massacres. By the beginning of 1896 both Willard and Somerset were vitally involved in the Western response to the Armenian situation. Willard was vice president of the Armenian Relief Committee in the United States and Somerset was secretary of the Armenian Women's Committee in England.

16 January 1896
Greensboro

Dearie Cartland[1]—a capable & sweet-hearted Quaker, Pres't of N. C & an "Eastern Shore" native came to talk the state over. I feel so *comforted* when a state or territory has such a leader—wise, gentle, ingenious, ingenuous. Things are moving steadily in the Old North state. We had a Conference of white ribboners and a public meeting[2] and tied on no end of ribbons. In the evening I met the colored people[3] who packed the court house and addressed them securing large additions. As is my habit I said no word to show I knew they were another race. It has been my life long custom to speak to all classes in terms of *Humanity*. It helps their self respect for Old Father Man is a great relative!

1. Mary E. (Cox) Cartland (d. 1918) was the president of the North Carolina WCTU in 1896.

2. On 16 January 1896 Willard spoke to a large meeting at the North Carolina Normal College of both WCTU members and interested people presided over by Cartland. As was usual at such meetings, Willard issued an invitation for listeners to come forward to the platform to greet her and "take the white ribbon," that is, pin on a small white ribbon as a sign that the wearer would take the WCTU pledge not to use alcohol. The wearing of the white ribbon was not totally limited to WCTU members; women and men who supported temperance might wear one.

3. In conformance with prevailing southern customs, Willard held segregated meetings on her 1896 southern tour, speaking to African Americans often at educational institutions, sometimes in churches, and, in this instance, in a courthouse.

18 January 1896
En route to
Spartansburg, South Carolina

We came on our winding way South—dictated to Mamie[1] a lot. She improves in rapidity and accuracy—Our correspondence is a picture of the world of reform—I wish I had time to characterize it. Our letters written and rec'd and the *N.Y. World* daily read will make any one a Cosmopolitan!

Wrote and sent off petition to Senate & House at Washington for help to Armenians—moral & material support—on behalf of Nat. WCTU.[2]

1. Mamie Powderly, one of Willard's stenographers, accompanied her on the 1896 southern tour.

2. The petition Willard wrote is in scrapbook 75, roll 44, WCTU Series III, microfilm edition. In addition to two stories about the petition in the *Union Signal* (23 and 30 January 1896), there are also in scrapbook 75 several newspaper clippings about the WCTU petition to Congress. One notes that Willard had asked every state WCTU to duplicate the petition and submit it to their state legislatures.

23 January 1896
En route from Augusta, Georgia, to Charleston, South Carolina

A pastor here told an evangelist now at work to "make the dry bones live"[1] that "in his meetings he must not put women of the WCTU forward or show them favor." The churches that oppose these women are dead and have at least enough honesty to say so. Of male members they get practically none that are new. The women are their sole dependence & they are determined to keep the women reminded that "being first in the transgression" they are "under subjection."[2] The last struggle of the "medicine man" in theology and the tribal "chief" in politics is going on while we are hardly aware—then comes the *people's* reign! . . .

1. Ez. 37:3–6.
2. 1 Tim. 2:13–14; 1 Tim. 2:11.

28 January 1896
St. Augustine, Florida

Kate Jackson, who was here all last winter, sent us advices by [. . .]. We have profitted & here we are in a sunny, large room, Mamie—next door with her type-writer, and Nan & I "hard at it" when not out of doors. It is *heavenly-balm.* If only Cozzie were here! How she would delight in it & how she deserves it & how she never has it—"a bit of peace." I wrote her long & long—thought of her *much* as I did my constitutional on the piazza. She is so dear—she is so far! . . .

1 February 1896

I fear Cozzie is overdoing to such degree as may go far to break her down. Her secretary dear "Pooley"[1] writes a bit anxiously—says she has rheumatism & headaches are worse than ever—which one hardly sees to be possible for when in them she often wishes she might die. How much pain of head & heart that rich soul has endured! How chastened her dear face! Where will it all end? When I read her tender, lovely, longing letters I often feel that I did wrong to leave her with the heavy burdens she is staggering under. If any thing should happen to harm her, I should have endless regrets!

1. Mary Allard (Ward) Poole, Somerset's secretary, was also superintendent of the Press and Literature Department of the BWTA and assistant recording secretary of the organization.

2 February 1896

Often this is the program—as last night: I get cold in the back—ask for "my Blaikie" (shetland wool shawl given by Mrs. Prof. Blaikie Prest Scotch white ribboners)[1] It is just "handy by" & Nan tucks it "well in"—I say "O that one could turn off his *think* as he does his electric light!" She gets me pencil & paper (if I haven't put them under my little "dream pillow"—Hannah Smith's gift). If matters go from bad to worse she makes malted milk (no alcohol) over alcohol lamp—& then we quiet down—but this occurs hardly more than once a week upon an average—Nan says "only twice in two months." . . .

1. Margaret Catherine (Biggar) Blaikie (1823–1915) was the first president of the Scottish Christian Union (the Scottish branch of the BWTA), serving from 1877 to 1906.

3 February 1896

. . . Mrs. Gen. Buford[1] wants to give me a "Society" reception. I have never done the likes o' this but "guess" I will for once to help make the cause known to uninitiates. . . .

1. Mary (or Nancy) Anne Greenwood (Pierce) Buford, widow of a Civil War general, Napoleon Bonaparte Buford, was vacationing in St. Augustine, Fla., and gave a reception for Willard at the Alcazar Hotel, which Willard described in the *Union Signal* as a "hotel-palace"—one of the large, fancy hotels being built at the end of the nineteenth century for wealthy Florida vacationers.

6 February 1896

I am much interested in watching the development of good "movements" that have come up since the Women's Crusade of 1873–'74. The Christian Endeavor, the Women's Federation of Clubs,

National & International Council[1] etc. They are all helping the one cause—the evolution of man toward God. But I should be glad if somebody who has a gift that way would analyze their methods and pick out all that our WCTU has set going—for I fancy that when eliminated there wouldn't be a vast amount of *new lines* & ways of working, visible. . . .

1. The United Society of Christian Endeavor was founded in 1881 for the purpose of encouraging young people to become useful, active Christians. The organization grew rapidly in the United States in the last two decades of the nineteenth century, and, in 1895, a World's Christian Endeavor Union was organized. The General Federation of Women's Clubs was formed in 1890 and grew to rival the size of the WCTU over the last decade of the nineteenth century, combining an interest in culture and reform. Both the International Council of Women and the National Council of Women of the United States were organized and founded in March 1888 in Washington, D.C. Elizabeth Cady Stanton and Susan B. Anthony of the National Woman Suffrage Association issued a call to an international meeting of women's groups interested in woman suffrage, inviting a large number of women's organizations throughout the United States and abroad. The meeting was the first attempt to bring women from all over the world together to discuss mutual concerns about women's status and their rights. Those who attended hoped the meeting would not be a one-time event. They provided that the National Council meet every three years and the International Council, every five years. Willard was elected first president of the National Council of Women, serving from 1888 to 1891.

11 February 1896
Jacksonville

. . . Mrs Thurman & Preston of our colored work came for a re-hearing—discontent &c[1]—I said they'd better stay but whatever happened—we should go on with our work for their race just the same. O the "scenes & unseens"! Wrote H. M. Barker gave Lucy T. 50 dols.

1. Lucinda (Lucy) (Smith) Thurman (1849–1918) had been active in the WCTU since its beginning and was chosen the WCTU's Superintendent of Temperance Work Among Colored People at the 1893 annual convention. She lectured and organized extensively among whites and African Americans in both south and north throughout her WCTU work. Frances E. L. Preston (ca. 1840–1929) became a member of the WCTU lecture bureau in 1891 and, like Thurman, traveled extensively encouraging African-American support for temperance aims. It is not clear what Willard meant by "discontent &c" but the fact that she gave Thurman fifty dollars and wrote to Helen Barker, the NWCTU treasurer, may indicate that Thurman and Preston were inadequately funded to carry on the work of their department. In the *Union Signal*, 26 March 1896, Willard wrote: "Both [Thurman and Preston] are devoted and loyal to the white ribbon, and I wish we could keep them moving the year round," perhaps hinting that further funds were necessary to keep the work moving. Thurman and Preston may also have been upset because of Willard's equivocal statements against lynching in 1893, which had drawn strong criticism by Ida Belle Wells, antilynching leader.

16 February 1896
Tampa

So tired I staid quiet. . . . My tongue feels very miserable & is "angry looking" as mother was wont to say of her—which she had, from her illness in '88 to her departure in '92—the result no doubt of the failure of the mucus membrane—never normally strong. I have the same symptoms I have had four years or so—& I begin to feel them in stomach as well as mouth. I tell Nan that gives me not a moment's anxiety—"to depart is for better" be it soon or late. The universe & not the little planet earth is *Home.*

23 February 1896
Montgomery, Alabama

If I wrote all the tribulations in this book there would be no room for other matters. Just now they may be hinted at by the words F. Murphy,[1] Lucy Thurman, Mother Stewart, Dearie Thompson[2] Fessie,[3] Susan B. & San Francisco[4]—Anthony Comestock & Mary Burt[5]—Carsie & Louise Rounds,[6] Temple & opposition, &c &c &c—and new crops grow like weeds in a fence corner. But these things must be—& we must just "Gang ahead & never mind"[7]—keep the peace the best we can and keep the tenor of our way because we will—and pray "Give me love for all & all love for me." . . .

1. Francis Murphy (1836–1907), a reformed drinker turned temperance evangelist, favored moral suasion, not political action, as the means to address drunkenness. He had apparently offended the WCTU and other Prohibitionists by insisting upon moral suasion as the best means of reform during a series of men's temperance meetings he conducted in Chicago at Willard Hall. (By 5 March he had come out for the Prohibition party in a letter to the WCTU published in the *Union Signal.*)

2. Eliza (Daniel) Stewart (1816–1908), called "Mother Stewart" by WCTU members, was a longtime temperance reformer and a leader of the Ohio Woman's Crusade of 1873–74. Eliza Jane (Trimble) Thompson (1816–1905), called "Mother Thompson" by WCTU members, was also a leader of the Ohio Woman's Crusade. There had been a rivalry between the two women and their supporters over which was the real "Mother of the Crusade" since 1894, when the twentieth anniversary of the crusade and the founding of the WCTU were celebrated. The matter had been considered settled at the 1894 annual WCTU convention when Hillsboro, Ohio, was named "cradle of the Crusade" and Mother Thompson, as leader of the Hillsboro band of praying women, was named "Crusade Mother." However, bickering had flared up again in early 1896, prompting an editorial in the 5 March *Union Signal* reminding WCTU members of the decision made in 1894 on the matter.

3. Susan (Snowden) Fessenden (1840–1932), former Franchise Superintendent of the NWCTU, was president of the Massachusetts WCTU in 1896. She probably had become involved in a controversy begun by the Boston WCTU over the inroads that

the Boston Union feared Roman Catholicism was making in the WCTU. In December 1895, the Boston WCTU had protested the appearance of fraternal delegates who were Roman Catholic priests on the platform at the 1895 Baltimore annual WCTU convention. They further protested the pronouncing of a benediction at a convention session by a Roman Catholic priest. Willard replied to the protest, reminding them that one of the WCTU's principles was nonsectarianism in religion, and that many Roman Catholic priests and parishioners were for the temperance cause, as witnessed by the forming of the Catholic Total Abstinence Association with local associations in many towns. But in late January, the controversy still went on, as evidenced by a statement printed in the 23 January *Union Signal* from the Boston WCTU objecting to the way their earlier protest had been presented.

4. Susan B. Anthony, president of the National American Woman Suffrage Association, was worried that the 1896 NWCTU convention, scheduled to be held in San Francisco in the fall, would jeopardize California's vote on woman suffrage in the November 1896 election, since it might frighten off the "wet" vote counted on by California suffragists. She had asked Willard to try to change the convention site.

5. Anthony Comstock (1844–1915) was an antivice reformer who led a forty-year crusade against obscene literature. Mary (Towne) Burt (1842–98) was the president of the New York WCTU from 1882 until her death. What tribulation they were causing Willard at this time is not clear.

6. Louise (Jones) Rounds (1839–1918) was president of the powerful Illinois WCTU from 1886 to 1901. In her October 1895 presidential address to the Illinois WCTU, Rounds had stated that in her opinion the WCTU should focus on only two aims, total abstinence for the individual and prohibition for the state, pulling back from involvement in "every scheme which has no legitimate claim on us." Although Rounds did not mention the Temple project directly, she was probably implying that the troubled project, which Carse directed, was at the top of her list of "schemes" that should be dropped by the WCTU.

7. Not identified.

25 February 1896
Mobile

I woke thinking: Is it possible that after all, I am to be living on the planet Earth not only when the sources of the Nile, the heart of Africa and the secrets of the poles are hunted out, but when electricity is harnessed, printing is done by steam, the flying machine is invented (as a sequel to the bicycle where we well nigh take our leave of Earth) and that by phonograph or telephone or cathode ray or spectroscope we are to hear the sounds & see the sights that "make the Life Immortal sure?"[1]

Thought much of Cozzie and that we should be together in the Better Life and counted up the days since I left & till I go—if God will. . . .

1. Not identified.

29 February 1896

New Orleans

A young Creole—Miss Points—of the Picayune[1] a "rising journalist" came for an interview—also the *Times Democrat*[2] man—and got them! The daily papers had columns of biography, interview and incident. Mrs. Judge Merrick—wife of the former Chief Justice[3]— had, it seems, written to each leading editor before we arrived & here was the result. I notice that *nothing happens*—I wish White ribbon women were keener-minded than they are. But then—women have *brooded* so long! Passivity has been their greatest grace. . . .

1. Willard probably referred to Marie Louise Points (d. 1931), a longtime reporter for the *Daily Picayune*, which ran a long, unsigned report on Willard's speech in New Orleans on 1 March 1896.
2. "The *Times Democrat* man" is unidentified, but that newspaper did carry two articles on Willard's speech of 1 March.
3. Caroline Elizabeth (Thomas) Merrick (1825–1908), the president of the Louisiana WCTU, was also the leading woman suffragist in the state. Her husband was Judge Edwin T. Merrick (1809–97), former chief justice of the Louisiana Supreme Court. Caroline Merrick was responsible for publicity about the New Orleans segment of Willard's southern tour. Willard had always stressed the importance of advance publicity, believing thoroughly in the saying "nothing just happens." The excellent press coverage of her New Orleans stay was an example of the truth of the saying.

1 March 1896

"It is not now as it hath been of old."[1] My sense of boundless power to do has suffered loss and though I swing along like a pendulum & am not down hearted or ill I have a sense of loss. My tongue burns—my sleep grows lighter—I feel my heart & all the left side rattles a bit (like an old farm wagon), the scaffolding will come down before long—ah what will the temple be—"not made with hands"[2]— shall it be "*eternal—in the heavens*"? Nothing less is in my hope & purpose th[r]ough Him "who hath brought life & immortality to light."[3] And Cossie—dearest & most adequate companion of them all who are cherished in my heart's heart—will *she* be with me—shall we still be "two cherries on one stem"?[4] I pray for it! . . .

1. Willard paraphrased William Wordsworth, "Ode: Intimations of Immortality from Recollections of Early Childhood," published in *Poems in Two Volumes* (London, 1807), stanza 1, line 6: "It is not now as it hath been of yore."
2. Mark 14:58.
3. 2 Tim. 1:10.
4. Willard paraphrased William Shakespeare, *A Midsummer Night's Dream*, act 3, scene 2, line 211: "Two lovely berries moulded on one stem."

2 March 1896
Jackson, Mississippi

. . . Flowers, festoons of violets &c—brought to us on the train from local unions—stalwart men with white ribbons on left lapel of coat—big, generous-hearted *pastors* too—now & then—carriages at station & committee—of men & women—white ribbons all about—Gov's wife[1] on committee—kindest words in press—all so different from reception in 1881 when Judge Watson[2] bro't Nan & me at his own expense & "there was a pig in the parlor of the best hotel" & "none so poor to do us"—any attention whatsoever. But temperance has *marched*—this whisky scourged town is under local option law. . . . The Legislature adjourns to attend my meeting! Who says there is not *hope?*. . . Wonderful to tell the Presbyterian ch opens for the meeting & the dignified old pastor sits on the pulpit steps—as lots of legislators do for the place is packed & crowds standing—every door & window open—sun so bright—air so balmy—spirit so cheery. . . . The Governors wife (McLaurin) took the ribbon from me the Ex Govs wife (Stone)[3] wears it on all her dresses—the Gov came to introduce me but was just too late—I had urged no waiting for I'm "not much used to Governors"—so I told those about me on the platform *but this one* really meant to be there & *was.*—One poor dear whisky member of the Legislature said "She's an abolitionist[4]—I object to the adjournment" & he was so hissed & frowned down & voted out of sight [?] that he apologized next day! "The world do move."

About 1854[5] my dear father came to Jackson & other Southern towns to get away from our Wisconsin winter because he had hemmorhage of the lungs. . . . He little dreamed that 40 years later the Legislature would adjourn to hear his red headed "little Frances" speak!

1. Laura (Ranch) McLaurin (b. ca. 1853) was the wife of Anselm Joseph McLaurin (1848–1910), who served as governor of Mississippi from 1896 to 1900.

2. William Clark Watson (1808–90), a Mississippi circuit court judge, was an early supporter of prohibition in the state.

3. Mary G. (Coman) Stone (b. ca. 1835) was the wife of John M. Stone (1830–1900), who served as governor from 1890 to 1896.

4. Willard elaborated on this incident in "Field Notes" in the *Union Signal,* 9 March 1896, writing that the legislator said: "This woman is a Northern abolitionist; I am opposed to this resolution, I move to lay it on the table," indicating that at least in some quarters sentiment against northern speakers still existed in 1896.

5. Willard was mistaken about the year her father went south for his health. According to her journal for 1857, her father spent two months in the south from just after Christmas 1856 until 15 February 1857, and a part of that time in Jackson.

15 March 1896
Dallas

. . . I was offered $400 for two lectures by La. Chautauqua[1] but gave it out that I could not afford to make money—no reformer can.

And all the time crises crowd upon each other. There is no end of contradiction over the California Con. Susan B. Anthony will not hear to our having it there this year even after the voting on suffrage amendment. On the contrary we think the liquor people will vote against it any way & nobody can win the decent element like the WCTU & we believe our soc. has made more converts to woman's cause than any other but Susan is "set" & I think for good feeling's sake we would better change. But several Gen. officers do not agree & we must call a meeting. So we are closing up to get back Mar. 23. . . . Then there are the national "wars & rumors of wars"[2]—England—Aramen [Armenia]—Cuba. But these will all blow over.— And all of them do not set a sharp tooth in my heart like the fear that Cossie is not well—which letters are beginning to reveal—& that a great crisis is upon her in my absence and growing out of the combined hate of her husband & his family, the liquor power & the enemies of purity.[3] It has given me many wakeful hours. In Dallas today immense meeting[4] & overflow—hundreds standing & no end of ribbons given out. . . .

1. The Louisiana Chautauqua was one of many centers of the Chautauqua movement, an adult-education system that developed over the last three decades of the nineteenth century. The national movement produced a correspondence course for adults, and the local centers, as well as the original Chautauqua Assembly in western New York, offered a place for summer vacations combined with lectures, sermons, concerts, and other events. Willard was a favorite speaker at the New York Chautauqua throughout the 1880s and 1890s and had a summer cottage there.

2. Matt. 24:6; Mark 13:7. The "wars and rumors of wars" to which Willard referred were the events leading toward the Boer War and the Spanish-American War and the continuing Armenian repression.

3. Willard often worried that she was not with her friend Isabel Somerset in order to lend her support to the British temperance leader as she faced various difficulties not only from those opposed to the reforms she advocated but also from the Beauforts, her former husband's family. When her son had been married earlier in the year, none of the Beaufort family attended the wedding because the bride's parents did not invite the groom's father, Lord Henry Somerset. Isabel Somerset continued to receive occasional slights from some of the aristocracy by whom she was seen as a traitor to her class and position for making a public matter of her legal separation from her husband, and such slights still wounded her.

Like any temperance reformer, Somerset was the target of the liquor industry's harassment, but the harassment may also have been coming from others, including some of those in her own organization, because among the vast properties she owned and from which she received a small part of her income were public houses that served liquor. Although Somerset had tried to sell off such properties, she apparently could not do so because of complicated restrictions on the selling of properties from her estate. Her implication, even against her own wishes, in the liquor trade was fair game for attacks against her BWTA leadership position.

By 1895 there were serious differences between the English social purity leader Josephine Butler, and Somerset and Willard, which continued on into 1896 and 1897. Butler felt that the WWCTU, although it had entered the social purity crusade later than Butler, was trying to take over the leadership of the social purity reform and claim it for itself. Butler also thought that Willard, and more particularly Somerset, were not social purity "abolitionists," as Butler described herself and British Social Purity reformers. "Abolitionists" aimed at the complete outlawing of prostitution, while she feared that Somerset would support halfway measures designed to contain and regulate prostitution. (Butler's fears would prove correct when, in 1897, Somerset supported the Contagious Diseases Act, which regulated prostitution in British-controlled India.)

4. Willard reported in the *Union Signal* that she had "one of the most overflowing audiences of the whole [southern] trip" in Dallas, with many new members joining ("Field Notes" 9, 23 April 1896).

21 March 1896
St. Louis

. . . To train & St Louis—where we founded our society *five times* & it lived at last under the leadership of Mrs. Lide Ingalls[1] who is a live woman. . . . We had our meeting in the M E Ch—a 2500 people one— & I shook hands with all after speaking & gave no end of ribbons. Dear Clara Hoffman introduced me in her hearty brave way—a reform in the vile dairies within St Louis limits has been started by our WCTU[2]— indeed they are the best municipal reformers that I know.

1. Eliza ("Lide") (Buckley) Ingalls (1848–1918) was the president of the St. Louis WCTU from 1891 to 1918 and served as superintendent of the Antinarcotics Department of the NWCTU for twenty years.

2. An editorial in the 16 April *Union Signal* describes an investigation of several St. Louis dairies by the St. Louis WCTU, led by Ingalls, in March 1896, after a tip from newspaper reporters. The milk cows were found to be diseased and treated with great cruelty and the conditions filthy and unsanitary. The unhealthy milk the dairies produced was sold cheaply to unsuspecting poor families. Ingalls gave an interview to the press, calling upon the "city fathers" to do something about dairy conditions, since they refused to let women help run the city government.

22 March 1896

All day at Sissy Ingalls home where, in 1892, Cossie, Nan & I came to participate in the Gt Labor Convention with its 1000 delegates from nearly every State & Territory[1]—at which I was made Vice Pres't (with Ben Terrell of Texas)[2] and C. & I sat up all night with the Com on Resolutions to get prohibition & suffrage in (Ignatius Donolley . . . being Chairman)[3] they voted suffrage *in* & put it *out* the minute we had gone—7 in the AM. . . .

1. The St. Louis Industrial Conference held 22 February 1892 was an effort by reform groups of many types, including labor organizations, farmers' alliances, the Prohibition party, and the WCTU, to create a third political party to address the growing nationwide discontent with the worsening economic situation. Besides economic concerns, each group pushed its own pet reforms, Willard and other WCTU delegates insisting on including woman suffrage and prohibition as planks in the platform of the new party.

2. Benjamin F. Terrell was president of the Confederation of Industrial Organizations and, as temporary chairman of the conference, had urged at the beginning of the meeting that the delegates confine their discussion to economic reform, leaving moral reforms until later on, a move that displeased Willard.

3. Ignatius Donnelly (1831–1901) was a Minnesota politician, at first active in the Republican party but by the 1890s interested in political reform via a third party. He was one of Willard's allies at the St. Louis conference and had been present earlier, in January 1892, at a private meeting held in Chicago to which Willard invited those reformers she felt would support not only economic reforms but woman suffrage and prohibition. She hoped that those at the meeting in Chicago could form a united front to push for their agenda at St. Louis.

24 March 1896
Chicago

Dressed to go to the Temple & put in the day with the General Officers. Gripe & nausea "took me" & I went to bed. It has always been my salvation that I couldn't stand physical pain & so took it reclining.—Mamie [Powderly] went to tell my comrades they must come to Hattie's home[1] & returning she brought Cossie's dear cable "*Longing—blessings—love—well.*" God be thanked! I shall go to her soon.— We wrestled with the California problem & decided not to go for Susan B. Anthonys sake—& because "the white ribbon means peace." We think we can do more good in Kansas where a crisis is on.[2] etc. etc. . . .

1. Willard stayed with her cousin Harriet (Brace) Lemon (1852–1922), who lived in downtown Chicago, convenient to the Woman's Temple building.

2. In Kansas a struggle was beginning during spring 1896, one of many during the 1890s over enforcement of prohibition in the state. This time it was over passage of a proposed U.S. law prohibiting the issuance of federal permits to sell liquor in prohibition states like Kansas, introduced into Congress by the Kansas Populist senator William Peffer. The Kansas WCTU was in the process of a petition effort in support of the proposed law.

25 March 1896

All day planning & meeting people at our "House Beautiful."[1]

The different parts of the Country & their needs passed in review—the program of the next Convention—the tour of Agnes Slack[2]—the prime importance of dear Lady Henry's coming over if she can—the attitude of the prohibition party & that it must hold to the ballot for woman—the enmity of Helen Gougar[3] toward the WCTU—the financial plans of Mrs Ba[r]ker—these and a score of subjects equally important were considered by our General Officers at length. Mrs. Barker and Katie Stevenson[4] are very nice comrades to have and easy to get along with. I thought of Esther & Callie[5] & all the years we sat together in these Councils & all the pleasant converse that we had and never so far as I can recall, an unkind word. We only differed temperamentally & such differences seem to be without remedy—save as Emerson intimates they demand "a gracious interval" of elbow room! I feel the utmost good will toward them both and have a notion that they do toward me. In other worlds where temperament is not so much the climate of character we shall know each other better & that will not make us love each other less.— Lunched with the dear editors & had nice confidential talks with each & all—as with Dearie Grow & Sadie Johnson & Ruby Gilbert[6] "of ours." And so my "temple days" are over.

1. Willard referred to the WCTU's Woman's Temple in downtown Chicago.

2. Agnes Slack-Saunders (1865–1946) was the corresponding secretary of both the BWTA and the WWCTU and a tireless organizer of WCTUs in many parts of the world. After a long temperance career, Slack married fairly late in her life. In 1896 Willard asked Slack to speak at a series of state WCTU conventions in her place since she was too ill to return to the United States. Slack carried out an extensive speaking tour in the United States and Canada under the auspices of the NWCTU and WWCTU.

3. Helen Mar (Jackson) Gougar (1843–1907) was a leader in the fight for both woman suffrage and prohibition in Indiana during the early 1880s. She was an excellent speaker and by the mid-1880s spoke widely throughout the country for the vote for women. In the late 1880s she joined the Prohibition party and quickly became one of the party's leaders. By 1896 Gougar was a key figure in the wing of the party that favored a "broad-gauge approach," championing a variety of reforms rather than prohibition alone. This should have made her an ally of Willard's, but there had been rivalry between the two women since the 1892 St. Louis conference. Gougar was jealous of Willard's popularity and power in the Prohibition party and had worked to undermine her. Willard, for her part, disliked Gougar and did not trust her. Thus Willard was not inclined to support the "broad-gauge" Prohibitionists at the party's upcoming convention.

4. Katharine Adelia (Lent) Stevenson (1853–1919) became corresponding secretary of the NWCTU in 1895. She had previously been active in the Massachusetts WCTU and, by 1894, became the editor of books and leaflets for the Woman's Tem-

perance Publishing Association as well as associate editor of the *Union Signal.* She went on to become president of the Massachusetts WCTU in 1898 and held the position for twenty years. Stevenson served as superintendent of Temperance and Missions of the WWCTU and in this capacity made an around-the-world tour in 1908.

5. Willard referred to Esther Pugh and Caroline Buell.

6. Caroline F. Grow (ca. 1837–1928) was the business manager of the Woman's Temperance Publishing Association (WTPA). Ruby I. Gilbert (ca. 1850–1945) was the WTPA's cashier and bookkeeper. Sara (Sadie) G. Johnson was the financial secretary for the Woman's Temple from 1892 to 1899.

2 April 1896
Churchville

Thursday was invested with my few remaining kin in Churchville. Day so cold I hardly dared venture three miles "up North" to see my Mother's youngest sister—Aunt Sarah Hill Hall—in her 83*d* year. But I did it—with 3 hot water bags—fur cloak, shawls &c. Anna I did not dare to risk so she staid with Cousin Mary Gilman Ross.[1] I was glad I went for the dear one is steadily failing & I shall hardly see her again. She was sitting up in her pretty parlor but O how thin the hands I once so much admired. We talked over all the long past. She said "I had been her providence for many years, as I was poor Uncle John's,"[2] & that was a solace. I told her neither she nor her husband should ever want. As I left her fine, reverend head was lifted & her eyes turned toward me with tenderness. I thought it meant farewell.

1. Mary (Gilman) Ross was Willard's first cousin, the daughter of Willard's mother's sister Mariah. Ross, several years older than Willard, had been a favorite cousin of hers from the time she was little.

2. John Hill (d. 1893) was Willard's mother's brother to whom Willard contributed financial support from the early 1880s until his death. Willard also helped her Aunt Sarah financially during her aunt's later years.

8 April 1896
Martinsburg, West Virginia

. . . Got Washington train & made a bee line to West Va. I was so busy writing for the U[nion] S[ignal] that I never noticed until—perhaps attraction?—caused me to look up & there was my country's capital a few hundred feet away! I thought of the speeches I had made under the dome for prohibition & woman's ballot[1]—of the inauguration of [. . .]sar Garfield[2] that I heard from the portico—of J. Ellen Foster[3] who was with me then & said as she looked down on the House "Frank, you & I ought to be there." . . .

1. Willard addressed the House Judiciary Committee on 1 February 1878 and the Senate Committee on Woman Suffrage on 2 April 1888.

2. James Abram Garfield (1831–81), twentieth president of the United States, was inaugurated on 4 March 1881.

3. Judith Ellen (Horton) Foster (1840–1910) was a lawyer, Republican politician, and temperance leader, and, for many years, one of Willard's chief lieutenants in the WCTU. Foster's connection with the WCTU began in 1874 when she was a delegate from Iowa to the founding convention in Cleveland, Ohio. By 1880 she was the organization's legal advisor and its national superintendent of legislation. Her latter position meant nationwide public speaking tours on behalf of both prohibition and woman suffrage. Although a firm friend of Willard's since the beginning of the WCTU, she disagreed with Willard's decision to lend the organization's support to the Prohibition party during the 1884 campaign. She wanted the WCTU to remain officially nonpartisan, allowing individual WCTU members to work at the state and local level with whatever party was most committed to prohibition and woman suffrage. This serious disagreement over both principles and tactics continued for several years. Finally, in 1889, Foster and the Iowa WCTU delegation withdrew from the WCTU and by 1890 had formed the Non-Partisan WCTU, a small organization with little power. Meanwhile, Foster had organized the Woman's National Republican Association and remained head of that organization until her death.

11 April 1896
Washington, D.C.

. . . We rolled on to Washington & to 2019 O St the home where my brother Oliver's daughter Kate & her young husband W W. Baldwin (3d Assistant Secretary of State)[1] have settled for a season. We went up into what K. says she shall call "Aunt Frank's Room" & "Mamies Room" & Babie's Room"[2] as they respectively arrive! The latter is expected in August. Mother's picture was on the table—Isabels on the mirror—Tootsie's[3] was there abouts—Olivers on Kate's door in her dainty parlor & *all* "our folks" of both sides—even "our Mary's" who left us 34 years ago! It was lovely to be with my dear ones who are so nice & loveable & who are in the flush of their early prime. K. & Mrs. Cleveland[4] are much together and every opportunity is open to them. . . .

1. Katherine (Kate) (Willard) Baldwin (1866–1932) was Willard's niece. She and her husband, William Woodward Baldwin (1862–1954), were living in Washington, D.C., during William Baldwin's term as third assistant Secretary of State in President Grover Cleveland's second administration. Kate Baldwin was musical director of the NWCTU in 1896.

2. The Baldwins were expecting a baby in August, as Willard indicated, but in the meantime were using the baby's room for guests: first Willard and, then, Kate's sister Mamie.

3. Tootsie was Willard's Persian cat, given to her by Isabel Somerset on Christmas 1892.

4. Frances (Folsom) Cleveland (1864–1947), wife of Grover Cleveland, was a good friend of Kate Baldwin's. The two young women had attended school together at Wells College, Aurora, N.Y., in the mid-1880s.

16 April 1896
New York City

Dictated & wrought & Nan & Madam & "Mrs Will" D.[1] worked over a hat & our "fit-out" for the ship. They are most helpful. I have declared off from the slaughter houses called "Stearns" & "Aikens"[2]— caravansary of women & "store clothes" & hats big as a bee hive & covered with flowers & weeds & rags. I went today, as I trust for the last time. Ten minutes in one of those hot, breathless, gabbling, moving-panorama places almost gives me paralysis. And my friends promise to fetch the "rags" home to me. . . .

1. Ellen Louise (Curtis) Demorest ("Madam") (1824–98) was a successful businesswoman and fashion arbiter from the 1860s through the 1880s. In 1860 Demorest had conceived the idea of making dress patterns from thin tissue paper for home dressmaking; she and her husband, William Demorest (1822–95), launched what became a huge business mass-producing patterns, creating a quarterly fashion magazine, *Mme Demorest's Mirror of Fashions* (begun in 1860), and opening a private dressmaking and millinery establishment on Broadway aimed toward New York City's wealthy. The Demorests developed their fashion industry over the next two decades, branching out in many different directions, but always related to fashion. Ellen Demorest and her husband increasingly devoted their efforts toward reforms at the same time they built up their business, and she was particularly interested in widening the possibilities of employment for women and encouraging them to work beyond the home. Both Demorests supported temperance reform. Ellen Demorest and her daughter-in-law, Alice (Gilbert) Demorest ("Mrs. Will D") (1863–1939), in whose home Willard and Gordon were staying, assisted Willard in choosing suitable new clothes, a task Willard had always disliked.

2. Aitken, Son & Company on Broadway and Stern Brothers on West Twenty-third Street were both upscale New York City department stores during the 1890s.

17 April 1896

Mrs Will Demorest came to the rescue & she & Nan & Mad. D. have bro't me hats & things—furbished up my dresses into more attractiveness & made me most grateful. For these things tell immensely in one whose principles antagonize the majority. Such an one owes it to the public (& more still to the reform) to be, in appearance & manner as presentable as possible & as to conciliate opponents & disarm them by all honest & genuine manifestations of good will.

22 April 1896
On board ship,
bound for England

Up early, packing last things and sending no end of goodbye notes & suggestions about the work, & telegrams far & wide. . . . Today twenty or more of "our folk" assembled with flowers & books & notes & dear farewells. I looked at them on shore when they had been driven off & each was an expert Christian worker. . . . And so we sailed away for England and our dear comrades & the loveliest one that lives.

1 May 1896
Reigate

Getting settled. Maxie here with Nan & me. Much of the time I am with Cozzie but have a "Den" at the Priory & Cottage both. Dear Cozzie seems less strong. Something pains her in the left side—sometimes keeping her awake. She is most sweet, tender & pathetic. Her cares are endless. She has become much more devout—has a chapel & holds prayers every morning—it is a most sweet & tender service—has a little oratory next her room—kneels & prays there most devoutly. The influence of dear Canon Wilberforce is marked. His poet-theology has been best suited to this great heart—she has, in her troubles & sorrows, her triumphs & joys come back to her early faith. I am glad for her but could by no means accept either that or the social requirements of such an entourage as has supervened—& must no doubt, when one's only child marries the daughter of a duke & is on the road to be one himself with the "off chance" that his Mother might be the one! It is a different world! Dear, brave Cozzie! May my motto be to add to her happiness all that I can while I am with her, rather than to add in anywise to her worries & cares. . . .

5 May 1896

Cossie said when I asked if under all, the dominant, recurrent, vital thought was not *the Life to come:* "Assuredly—I think of nothing else save on the surface. When I have performed some task I say to myself '*That* is done—that is past—that which is to come has come the nearer because this is past.'" We seem "to hear, through our life's deep dream" the solemn surges "of that great ocean we shall sail so soon."—Is it years with me & failing health with her or a presentiment with both? God knows & all is well.

31 May 1896

. . . How I miss the old home church! Here it is high or—empty. But I *had* it when most formative in mind & I am docile toward the eternal verities and loyal to my early faith.

4 June 1896
London

Dear Cossie bears up admirably under her duties of presiding. How she has grown since '94 when I sat beside her & prompted at her request. And now she steps out strong and firm in her parliamentary knowledge and leads her host. They love her leading better every year—she has them in the hollows of her hand for love. All but seven votes were hers—and those were the little Balgarnie faction,[1] not inimical to Isabel personally. She is a wonderful woman—the great woman of her century. In saying this I have regard to a great social position & a great fortune as well as great abilities all placed at the service of a great Cause. Gifts of oratory, writing and organization are *all* hers. And she is so cheery in contradiction—so patient in pain.

1. Florence Balgarnie (1856–1928), an English temperance advocate and woman suffragist, was the political superintendent for the BWTA from 1893 to 1896 and also a paid member of the staff of the *Woman's Signal*, the newspaper of the BWTA. In 1895, Balgarnie and other members of the London Anti-Lynching Committee (of which Balgarnie was the honorary secretary) led an attack on Willard and the WCTU over what she and her supporters felt, with some justification, was the WCTU's equivocal attitude toward lynching. Isabel Somerset and the BWTA Executive Committee were drawn into the controversy, which went on until June 1896, when Balgarnie was not retained as either a BWTA superintendent or a member of the executive committee. The matter was laid to rest, in the BWTA at least, with a decisive vote for Isabel Somerset to continue as president, as Willard indicated.

6 June 1896
Reigate

For about the third time in my life I lay in a hammock—in our sweet garden. . . . Some how we are all so tired & done out we like to sit about and are not ready to resume routine. These great meetings take the soul out—as Isabel says they "drive nails in our coffins." I have little vigor or verve. Inertia has me tight & my poor tongue is *so* raw. I must bicycle more & behave better to the Big Outdoors.

10 June 1896
London

. . . Went with Nan to Crystal Palace[1] to see horseless carriages—
too much kerosene stench & too everlasting a-shaking up! But it will
evolute. . . . Remembered being here in 1868 and felt how lessened is
my enthusiasm. C. says "Not a bit! The trouble is you've seen every
thing almost—but if you were in Japan & India how you would rise
in your stirrups!"—Well,—perhaps.

1. The Crystal Palace was a huge glass-and-iron exhibition hall that had been built
in London's Hyde Park for the Great Exhibition of 1851. Moved to Sydenham two
years later, it was the site of many later international fairs, exhibitions, and sports
events, until it burned down in 1936.

26 June 1896

Went with Hannah [Whitall Smith] to Annual Mtg of Nat Suffrage
Soc.[1] Not a corporal's guard! They don't know how to plan a meeting. Mrs Haweis there, Miss Cons, Mrs. Scatcherd, Walter & Chas.
McLaren, Nora Phillips, Alice Stone Blackwell[2] &c. I spoke 15 m. &
came away. There seems a lull just now—in Ch. & State. Men looking more narrowly into the problem of "Woman's Rise!"

1. Willard must have attended a planning meeting for the National Union of
Women's Suffrage Societies' annual general meeting held 2 July 1896. She had been
elected a vice president of the Central-National Society for Women's Suffrage, a British
suffrage organization, in 1893, and also worked with the Women's Liberal Federation on woman suffrage.
2. The planning meeting included Mary Eliza (Joy) Haweis (1852–98), author
of books on the condition of women in England; Emma Cons (1838–1912), vice
president of the London Society for Women's Suffrage and member of the executive committee of the Women's Liberal Federation; Alice (Cliff) Scatcherd, honorary treasurer of the Women's Franchise League and author of *Legal Conditions of
Women in the Three Kingdoms of Great Britain and Ireland* (London, 1888); Walter Stowe
Bright McLaren (1853–1912), Liberal Member of Parliament and supporter in Parliament of the vote for women; Charles Benjamin Bright McLaren (1850–1934), Liberal Member of Parliament, and, like his brother Walter, a staunch supporter of
woman suffrage, first in the House of Commons and then in the House of Lords; Nora
Phillips, member of the National Executive Committee of the National BWTA; and
Alice Stone Blackwell (1857–1950), an American woman suffragist visiting in England.

27 June 1896
Reigate

Same routine—not well—handicapped by appetiteless condition—
symptoms almost identical with Mother's in her later years but Cozzie

laughs her lovely, musical laugh when I say so & Nan will none of it. Anyhow, I am "low in my mind." ...

28 June 1896

... Spoke in the Wesleyan Ch[apel] Red Hill. ...[1] I should have loved best of all to be a Gospel Preacher.

1. Red Hill was a market town about two miles from Reigate.

6 July 1896

... The Princess Mary Duchess of Teck[1] drives with four horses, postillions &c from the White Lodge[2] to Priory & Duxhurst today to open the Farm Colony[3] wh Cozzies genius & money have set going— backed by the white ribbon women—And Princess Mary is ... Victoria's cousin.

Later. Well, there were 30 to lunch—Duchesses and Countesses & Dean's wives & barons & baronets &c. And Lady Battersea[4] presented me to Princess May & I made a curtsey & said no word—& she nodded & said no word & we all went out to lunch according to precedence—which bro't the untitled well at the end! ... We drove to Duxhurst & there the Princess laid the corner stones & rec'd purses—Cossie read her an address. It was another out-raying of the white ribbon movement though no body said so & there was wine at the lunch—the Princess would not have come otherwise!—But Cossie & Sir Wilfrid & Lady Lawson—the Dean of Hereford, Mrs Wilberforce & daughter, Eva McLaren[5] & I abstained. The Princess was two hours late & threw every thing into *pi.* ...[6]

1. Princess Mary of Teck (also called Princess May, 1867–1953) was a member of the royal house of Würtemberg, and a member of the British royal family as Queen Victoria's cousin. Princess Mary married George, Duke of York (1865–1936), in 1893. He became Prince of Wales in 1901 and in 1910 became King George V of Great Britain. Princess Mary thus became the British queen.
2. White Lodge was the residence on the grounds of the Priory where Somerset's mother (see Journal, 19 September 1896, n. 1) stayed when she visited her daughter.
3. The Farm Colony at Duxhurst was a pet project of Somerset's, who established it on behalf of the BWTA. It was, at the time, an innovative way of treating women alcoholics by placing them in small group homes on a farm close to the Priory, Reigate, with a young woman superintendent trained both in medical techniques and as a Christian (though nonsectarian) worker attached to each group home. Police magistrates sent women to Duxhurst as an alternative to the usual prison sentence. Later in her life, after she retired from her duties as BWTA and WWCTU president,

Somerset devoted most of her time to working at Duxhurst, counseling with the women placed there.

4. Constance (de Rothschild) Flower, Baroness Battersea (1843–1931), was a wealthy philanthropist, involved in many British social reform movements, including social purity and temperance. As the wife of Cyril Flower, a leading Liberal politician, she participated in many Liberal political campaigns along with her social reform work. She also took an interest in the situation of her Jewish coreligionists, working to establish rescue-and-training homes for Jewish prostitutes and seeing that Yiddish-speaking immigrant-aid workers were available to meet Jewish immigrants at London's docks.

5. Mary (Pocklington-Senhouse) Lawson (1839–1910); Rev. James Wentworth Leigh (1838–1923), Anglican Dean of Hereford; Charlotte (Langford) Wilberforce (d. 1909); and Eva (Muller) McLaren (d. 1921), vice president of the BWTA and also active in the women's suffrage campaign in England, were all temperance reformers. Willard must have mistakenly identified one of the women present as Mrs. Wilberforce's daughter, since Wilberforce's only child, a daughter, died within a month of her birth.

6. To "throw into pi" was a slang phrase meaning to throw into disorder.

8 July 1896
Littlehampton-on-Sea

. . . Nan & I with Morell[1] wended to Littlehampton hoping sea air & bicycling might help my poor tongue now for two months so troublesome & irritated that each meal is a misery & I eat almost nothing.

Nan & Murell went into the sea—I rode on bike 5 miles with Murrell & took goat milk in a fragrant garden.

1. Willard meant Grace Murrell, her stenographer.

10 July 1896

Cossie & I rode five miles on our bikes (Her first outing) under Grace Murrell's sheltering wing. She sits like a Major General (C. I mean) she is fearless, rapid and so full of happiness. Her bright ringing laugh is music to my ear. We lunched in a lovely little garden not unlike that at the cottage only more old-fashioned. I said "Many a time I have thought if I were sure of conscious life forever, as happy, in its totality, as it has been for well nigh 57 years, I would be glad & grateful to go on. Would thee?"

Tears filled the sweet brown eyes. She said, after a serious, silent moment, "Except for my life with thee I would rather the painless grave with what unbelievers call 'its dreamless sleep' than the life that I have led—with tongues of scorpions stinging me."[1]—How heartbreaking & how can I leave her—so "tugged with—fortune & wearied with disaster" & her health not so good as of old. Does this chronic hurt of the tongue point me to new departures? Surely I can not speak at this rate. I missed two engagements this week & must make no more.

1. Rev. 9:5.

20 July 1896
Reigate

Mrs Bowen of Turkey[1] . . . came to see us & we had talk of Armenia. She sees little help save in emigration. That possibility is to me like a fire in the bones. O that I were ten years younger! "The spirit how willing—the flesh—how weak."[2]

Dear H B Blackwell & Alice[3] came to tea—all went to Priory & all about. Armenia our chief theme—they have helped it wonderfully, Alice by translating poems & the Woman's Journal has not spared its cry.[4]

1. Willard probably met with Flora Pierpont (Stearns) Bowen (1849–1927), wife of Marcellus Bowen, Presbyterian missionary of the American Board of Commissioners of Foreign Missions in Turkey for nearly twenty years.
2. Matt. 26:41.
3. Henry Browne Blackwell (1825–1909) was an abolitionist, woman suffragist, and joint editor with his wife, Lucy Stone, of the *Woman's Journal*, a weekly newspaper devoted to women's rights reform, until Stone's death in 1893. He then edited the paper with their daughter, Alice Stone Blackwell. She was an ardent supporter of the Armenian cause, having heard first-hand accounts of Turkish atrocities against the Armenians from a young Armenian theological student who was a close friend.
4. Alice Stone Blackwell had translated a group of sixty poems from Armenian into English and they were published in spring 1896. The *Woman's Journal* ran many articles on the plight of the Armenians during 1895–96.

5 August 1896

Miss Melliger[1] of Armenia came to see us—straight from that heroine Miss Shattuck.[2] Her accounts of the cruelty show the Turks to be the Apaches of the East. It seems to me I can not endure to have my tongue idle & raw at this crisis! If I were 30 I would lead a Crusade that would free & *carry away* that people. But I must sit by & wait & try to see what rest, massage & the bicycle can do! Poor Prometheus of a human soul chained to the Caucasus of 130 pounds of weary flesh!

1. Ida Mellinger (1866–99) was a missionary with the American Board of Commissioners of Foreign Missions serving in Oorfa (Urfa), Turkey, from 1890 to 1896, and in Smyrna, Turkey, from 1897 to 1898.

2. Corinna Shattuck (1848–1910) was also a missionary with the American Board of Commissioners of Foreign Missions, serving from 1873 in various mission stations in Turkey. By 1892 she was serving at Oorfa with Ida Mellinger. Oorfa was the site of several Turkish and Kurdish attacks on Armenians, one particularly horrible one at the end of December 1895, in which Shattuck managed to hide over one hundred Armenian men so that they survived the raid, in which five thousand men were killed. She then began to provide for the many orphans left after the attacks.

6 August 1896

Anniversary days—*four years* since she went away! I feel that I am following on just the same lines—so gradual & painless & all dread of going—so *inherent* in me—is gone. I am so glad that Nan will be well provided for after her life of loving toil. It may be months—it may be years—it *has begun to be.*

10 August 1896
Sheringham

Came to Sheringham near Cromer—famous resort on Norfolk coast. Air divine—straight from North Pole. Felt better from first. Cozzie has taken a cottage—Nan & I, Murrell & Mamie,[1] the helpers Franklin, Lizzie, Robbie, [. . .], Edward & Boots[2]—horses, dogs & all. Here we hope to store oxygen & ozone for the Armenians & Nat[ional] Con[vention] et als.

1. Mamie Powderly, Willard's chief stenographer in the United States, traveled with her to England.
2. Willard, Gordon, and Somerset were accompanied to the seaside by several of Somerset's servants.

14 August 1896

We were out 8 hours & bicycled 12 miles—the longest yet—Cossie, Nan, Murrell, Mamie & I. It seemed so lovely & strange to get "near to natures heart"[1]—lying flat on one's face beside a hedge or on a st[. . .] of oats! I thought a dear, warm, clean grave under the sunshine, better than cremation—a cedar coffin mind you and laid in my own Mother's grave. . . .

1. Not identified.

[*Willard and Somerset remained at the seaside until the beginning of September. After several days in London and at Reigate, where Willard issued*

*a Call to the WCTU for aid to the Armenian refugees, they left for a bicycle
tour of northern France. Making their way to Paris, they stopped briefly
before heading south to Marseilles to assess the situation of the hundreds
of refugees arriving there and to do what they could to help them.*]

19 September 1896
Marseilles

Poor little Coz! After an all day work, getting a refuge open for the
Armenians—which she did!—she dreamed that her mother[1] bro't to
her the Sultan's head—not "on a charger" but in a bandbox (quite
in keeping with the Countess Somers' ruling passion)! I said "How
did you feel?" "O enchanted!" answered Coz with all the cuteness of
which she is chock full. She says she has written Canon Wilberforce
that he must "construct a little hell for the Sultan" though the Canon declares that there is no such place.—The Refuge is a large un-
used ward in a hospital—with outdoor corridor & arches [?]—a
roomy place. The municipality gives it rent-free. . . . One hundred &
fifty are in the refuge tonight & 300 will be very soon. We went with
young Crawford[2] & got bread, onions, olives &c for them & Coz & I
gave it out to the women & children. A deputation of Armenians
came to see us—they have raised 2 thousand francs. . . .

1. Virginia (Pattle) Somers, Countess (b. ca. 1826–1910), was Isabel Somerset's
mother. The daughter of James Pattle of the Bengal Civil Service and Miss de l'Etang,
she married Charles Somers-Cocks (see Journal, 14 October 1896, n. 2) in 1850.
2. Mr. Crawford may possibly have been Francis Crawford (1854–1909?), a newspaper correspondent who studied several Middle Eastern languages.

20 September 1896

A gospel day even tho' we did not go to church. Armenian priest,
Ch of England pastor—Armenian merchants—journalists—called—
all in the interest of our brothers & sisters the refugees. Coz went over
to the refuge to see them fed—I wrote letters & cables & articles to
help them. Rec'd 800 francs from our Nat WCTU—which has paid
out so much for the dear Armenians—for I have issued urgent &
repeated appeals. . . .

21 September 1896

Out all the morning with Coz. getting potatoes, beans, oil, olives,
salt &c. for our "Poor Dears!" 150 more expected today—we are

going to the ship—have got passes. We carried the food to them (by proxy)—they rose as we entered & made their pretty salute, dear, silent, patient things. Lady H. handed out a chemise apiece(!) to each woman & special articles for *the* P.M—I gave chocolate to all the children. . . . I wish I were less unworthy to minister to these dear ones. God have pity upon us all!

22 September 1896

. . . Money comes in well—we shall soon have enough to transport the refugees. I suggested to Coz to cable Jno D Rockefeller (to whom I became persona non grata when I joined the Prohibition party!)[1] & he has cabled a thousand dollars.

Saw poor dear Armenian Priest making his little chapel & putting up his picture of the Cross—the magnet of Humanity!

1. John Davison Rockefeller (1839–1937), the millionaire industrialist and philanthropist, founded the Standard Oil Company, the first large American "trust." During the 1890s Rockefeller devoted a good deal of his time and energy to his philanthropic activities, enabling the founding of the University of Chicago through his financial gifts and setting up the Rockefeller Foundation and several other philanthropic institutions. Willard may have become *persona non grata* to him because he was a Republican supporter while she supported the Prohibition party, and, perhaps, also because of her increasing support of the American labor movement.

24 September 1896

Wrote, dictated, assorted numerous cables, letters &c. Went to Mr Thomas, American consul,[1] with Coz & nice Mr. Crawford, to make sure about emigration of the poor dear refugees. We think it can be compassed. Rec'd by cable this A.M. (first thing in bed) "Draw on us for one thousand dollars Chi. Herald,[2] N.Y." Wasn't that good? We think we can help them all off in a few days. They are now altogether comfortable—food cooked by Armenians & to their liking, savory & oniony & taken squatting! Miss Frazer is doing well—getting all their names, histories etc. She was in Van all last winter through the massacres with Dr. Kimball[3] & solaces them more than any one. Took our first bicycle ride since leaving England! 2 hours of forgetfulness of all that *weighs—oxygenation* is a form of religion.

1. Claude M. Thomas (1863–1936), a Kentuckian, was appointed the United States consul in Marseilles by President Cleveland and served in the post from 1893 to 1897.

2. Willard referred to the *Chicago Herald and Examiner.*

3. Katherine B. Fraser (1867–98?), a missionary sent to Turkey by the American

Board of Commissioners of Foreign Missionaries, and Dr. Grace Niebuhr Kimball (1855–1942), a medical missionary sent by the ABCFM, were both serving in Van, a Turkish city with a large Armenian population. From October 1895 on there were terrible massacres at Van, and Kimball, aided by Frazer, organized relief efforts to feed and shelter several thousand starving and frozen Armenians, who were entering the city from the surrounding countryside. Frazer accompanied a group of Armenian refugees to Marseilles and was helping Somerset and Willard get the refugees fed and adequately housed temporarily while they waited to see if they would be received by either England or the United States.

26 September 1896

. . . I am sending discriptive letters to many papers in America & England. About $7000 have already been sent us—$2160 from America (by cable). I believe that for emigration there will be lots of money. Do not let us feed them until the Turk cuts their throats—but let us put those throats beyond his scimitar.

27 September 1896

We went to Armenian Ch services in the impromptu Chapel at the refuge. It was memorable & [. . .] pathos too deep for tears. In his gold-embroidered robes here stood the gentle old priest at the altar above which was a large painting of the Ascension of Christ—a scene full of inspiration for these dear people who believe that a hundred thousand of their country folk who have been slaughtered have made a similar ascent. But how full of humanity's death-wail were the deep voices of the men as they sang the Gregorian chants! The most grief-stricken notes I ever heard came from their sorrowful breasts. The women joined in softly—the host was lifted—all knelt and I felt a fixed determination to try to bring these people out from under the heel of the barbarous Turk on whom it is useless to waste language. God help us to take them to America tens of thousands of them & there find homes for them in Christian families.

We gave out clothes—150 new refugees today.

28 September 1896

Am through with 57 years! . . .

Was feverish all night. . . . I thought "How well to slip away *here*— & not have the sea to come[1] nor the contradictions smiting bereavements & *hurts* of life [. . .] ever any more!" And I who so feared death once would have *voted* to slip away then & there only I had not the power. I planned to have Nan telegraphed & that I'd make another will & leave my little all to her to do with as she would for I know how devotedly she would carry out Mother's wishes & mine as to our relatives & the National WCTU.—And today I am 57! . . . Coz. gives me a splendid new bicycle "the Rover" (the 3d she has given) & a lovely bouquet—Nan sends me a silver glove buttoner—Mamie & Edith a silver pencil—& so on. I am thinking of those early birthdays on the farm when my blessed Mother had so little to do with & yet would make a cake & *lend* me to wear the gold pencil she wore when a teacher, & would give *me* a cherished shell to hear the sea-music & gather flowers & set me in the best chair—she meanwhile busy with her household cares, cooking sweeping &c. We had a rag doll "Anna" that Mother made & dressed & father painted—it was big as a baby. Mother was very choice of it, but on Mary's & my *birth day* we could play with it *all day*. Father made no acct of our birth days—he was a regular Cromwellian & hated "days"[2] but he made us toys & was very proud of his "two forest nymphs" but Mother was more tender to Oliver than he—somehow they were early alienated to some degree. I think my brother's taking up tobacco at 14 was a thing my father never got over.—He always said "You must have habits & stick to them or you're nobody." (He *meant good* habits.)

1. Willard was apprehensive about the sea voyage back to the United States in early November for the annual WCTU convention because she suffered from seasickness.

2. During the nineteenth century, the term "Cromwellian," referring to the regime of the Calvinist Oliver Cromwell (1599–1658), Lord Protector of the Republican Commonwealth of England, Ireland, and Scotland from 1653 to 1658, implied sober, strict Puritan attitudes and behavior. Neither birthdays nor Christmas were celebrated in any lavish way in Willard's family during her youth.

1 October 1896

Lying on lounge all day in our drafty salon. Don't dare let dear Nan know I am not well. Tongue in a Vesuvian eruption & a cold to boot! Clinique thermometer showed slightly abnormal temperature. Alas I fear I am not what I was! . . .

Dear Cossie's vigor & elasticity are quite my admiration: She goes into this work "up to her eyes." She & Miss Frazer are at the refuge all day—Murrell & I are getting off letters & paragraphs to bring subscriptions & prepare the way for the poor dears & Carrie[1] keeps the accounts to perfection acknowledges all sums rec'd &c. Every thing moves on like clockwork & Col Stitt[2] is a balance wheel among the refugees.

1. Carrie was Somerset's personal maid.
2. Col. Samuel S. Stitt was a Salvation Army officer and the head of the Army's Social Department, sent from London by General William Booth, head of the Salvation Army, to aid with the Armenian refugee work in Marseilles.

2 October 1896

In bed all day but writing & at work. Dear Nan keeps me informed of every thing. Mrs Barker[1] sent severe letter about "bringing in paupers" & "the harm it will do WCTU." I felt she did not adequately measure the argument & wrote her mildly. . . .

1. Willard referred to the NWCTU treasurer, Helen Barker.

11 October 1896
London

Working for the Armenians—letters to papers that have opened their columns for subscriptions urging them to keep it up—acknowledgements of help rec'd—cables—telegrams—letters to be read at public meetings—interviews &c—all meaning food covering shelter & eventually homes I hope—for the word I would speak is

Emigration

"The Powers" do not act—now let the *Power* bestir itself & the people are that power _____ Selah.

12 October 1896

I am impressed that so far as I am a "Case" it is just like my Mother's. This *tongue* does not let up—it is angry & a little swollen & smarts when I eat & takes away every atom of appetite. Last night I vomitted at 2 A.M. & my food was thoroughly undigested. Today Dr Dowson[1] a noted London lady Dr. came with stethescope & sounded my heart & declared it weak when four yrs ago Sir Andrew Clarke[2] declared it "beautiful." Her daughter who is giving me massage declares my pulse was down to 52 beats wh. I can't credit for here I am busy & equipoised as ever. Isabel is on the warpath that I must not take a sea voyage—because I have been so ill these last times & Nan & I are "struck of a heap." Coz. has cabled Dr Green to come over! The dear—I think she is too anxious. Perhaps the sudden death of the Archbishop of Canterbury[3] (yesterday) has had some thing to do.

1. Not identified.

2. Sir Andrew Clarke (1826–93) was a noted British surgeon, whose practice was in London.

3. Edward White Benson (1829–96), the Archbishop of Canterbury from 1883 to 1896, had died on 11 October, as Willard indicated.

[*Once again Willard turned journal keeping over to Anna Gordon, who wrote all the entries from 14 October to 29 December. Although Willard was under doctor's orders to rest, she kept close watch on the progress of efforts to have Armenian refugees admitted to the United States and began to work on her address for the WCTU annual convention. On 31 October, Willard, Anna Gordon, and a nurse, whom Somerset had hired to care for Willard during her inevitable seasickness, sailed for the United States. The nurse quickly succumbed to seasickness herself, but Willard had a relatively easy crossing, arriving in New York City on 7 November, proceeding to preconvention meetings in St. Louis on 9 November.*]

[Anna Gordon]   14 October 1896
                                                                        Reigate

Yesterday dear F. yielded to the loving anxieties of those who could see how worn out she was and concluding that discretion was the better part of valor[1] agreed to go to bed and be nursed and coddled and fed and rested in the hope she would get strong enough to take the voyage. Lady Henry has spared no expense to surround her with everything beautiful as to bedroom and attendance. She is in the handsome "Dome room" with its exquisite hangings of yellow satin and is in the bed where Earl Somers was born.[2] Dr. Dowson's daughter, a bright smart girl comes down every day to give her a magnetic massage treatment,[3] a trained nurse has come from London, and a "reader" has been sent for, while every body in the house from Lady Henry down to the scullery maid and not least of all Maggie[4] would consider it a boon to do something for her comfort.

1. Gordon paraphrased a line from William Shakespeare, *Henry IV*, Part 1, act 5, scene 4, line 120: "The better part of valor is discretion."

2. Charles Somers Somers-Cocks, Earl Somers, Viscount Eastnor of Eastnor Castle, and Lord Somers, Baron of Evesham (1819–83), was Isabel Somerset's father. From 1841 to 1847 he represented Reigate in the House of Commons for the Conservative party. In 1850, he married Virginia Pattle, and in 1852 he succeeded to the earldom on his father's death. From 1853 to 1857 Somers was Lord-in-Waiting to Queen Victoria and oversaw the affairs of his vast estates and business enterprises.

3. Practitioners of magnetic massage combined a knowledge of the body's muscle, bone, and tissue structure with the techniques of massage, claiming to heal by influencing the temperature, energy, or electrical flow in a patient. They stroked, kneaded, or otherwise manipulated specific regions of a patient's body in order to

cure various diseases. Some also claimed to impart their own vital forces into a patient to aid in the healing process. Dr. Dowson's daughter, who gave the magnetic
massage treatments, is not identified.

4. Maggie was Isabel Somerset's border collie.

[Anna Gordon]   24 October 1896

. . . It is heartbreaking that they must part. It puts a shadow over
everything but F. says she *must* go. Let us hope the separation need
not be long. F. needs a good long rest & I wish she could go somewhere with Lady H. where they could neither of them hear of "causes" of any kind. Then they would build up and feel better.

[Anna Gordon]   11 November 1896
                                                     St. Louis

Reporters began to come before we were out of bed and one of
them was evidently provoked and said miserable things about F. being ill and general officers meeting[1] around her bedside etc etc. We
were all indignant F. held two sessions with Gen. Officers and was
lively as a cricket. The women are pouring in and familiar faces are
all about.

1. The WCTU Annual Convention was to begin on 13 November and meet
through 18 November. Willard held two days of preconvention meetings with the
NWCTU Executive Committee made up of the NWCTU officers, Anna Gordon as
Willard's private secretary, the WCTU state presidents, and the General Secretary of
the Young Woman's Christian Temperance Union.

[Anna Gordon]   12 November 1896

Executive Committee all day White ribboners as thick apple blossoms in Springtime. . . .

Have helped the Ex. Com. choose seats and we had the usual scrab-
ble. The Hall[1] seats 5000 people and the outside rooms are most
convenient

1. The annual convention was held in the Music Hall of the St. Louis Exposition
Building.

[Anna Gordon]   13 November 1896

Beautiful bright day. By some mistake the hall was not warmed at
opening but otherwise all went off without break. The President's

Address was fine despite its not being written and given without notes was all the more eloquent in its delivery. The audience was most responsive & dear F covered herself with glory as she always does.

[Anna Gordon]   14 November 1896

Another lovely day. Everything is going on beautifully. We got through the entire program yesterday & today. The women are most gentle and considerate and F. seems jollier and more wide awake than usual in presiding. We sleep well and enjoy our food. Heaven be thanked. Exectutive Meeting was held all the evening and I saw a little of the Y Meeting.[1]

1. The evening of Saturday, 14 November, was "Y night" at the annual convention; Fan Barnes and the "Ys" (Young Woman's Christian Temperance Union) were in charge of the program, which included singing, short speeches by the young women, and a stereopticon presentation called "Studies in Reform." The executive committee met several times before, during, and after the annual conference.

[Anna Gordon]   15 November 1896

We did not or at least I did not go to the Annual Sermon by Miss Greenwood[1] which they say was very fine. F presided and Agnes Slack[2] who arrived last eve. led the devotional exercises. The After Meeting for the Armenians lasted three hours. Rebecca Krikorian[3] made an impassioned plea for the salvation of the Turk closing with the words *"And thus we shall have had our revenge."* Lots of speakers.

1. Elizabeth W. Greenwood (1849–1924), WCTU and WWCTU superintendent of the Evangelism Department, gave the annual sermon at the Union MEC. The sermon subject was "Christian History: this age is that of reaction from doubt" and the biblical texts from which she preached were Esther 1:13 and 2 Chron. 32:8.
2. During the same church service where Greenwood preached, Agnes Slack read the "Crusade Psalm" (Psalm 146) and led the congregation in prayer.
3. Rebecca K. Krikorian (d. 1948), an Armenian Protestant from Aintab, Turkey, was in England and then in the United States during 1895 to raise money for a hall for the Protestant mission in Aintab where she was one of the workers. When the Armenian massacres started in 1895 she began to raise funds for relief work, continuing to lecture in England and the United States under the sponsorship of Somerset and Willard. She spoke to the WCTU convention at the "Armenian Meeting" the afternoon of Sunday, 15 November.

[Anna Gordon]   16 November 1896

Weather continues fine and warmer. The bright skies are so blessedly good to see. F. says she feels better each day of the Convention and the love of the women buoys her up. She is quietly glad and takes things easily. Enjoys her meals and sleeps better than at many previous conventions. We feel that the back bone of the Convention is broken now.

[Anna Gordon]   17 November 1896

Today has been a memorable one. Election of officers resulted in the entire staff being retained, and dear F. was elected by 351 out of 356. The Convention is bright and interesting. Press reports most kind. The "Presidents Night"[1] was a great success but we went to bed instead of to meeting and had a nine hours sleep. . . .

1. On "Presidents Night" all state WCTU presidents whose states had gained five hundred members in the preceding year addressed the WCTU convention.

[Anna Gordon]   18 November 1896

The last day of the Convention is over. The Booth Tuckers[1] have been with us and from 3–4 we shook hands with a thousand people I should think—Tonight the "Demonstration"[2] came off with Grand March—Department Parade and State Songs.

We are glad for all the good, regretful for mistakes, hopeful for the future, rejoicing that the meetings are over.

1. Emma (Moss) Booth-Tucker (1860–1903), Consul in America of the Salvation Army, and her husband, Frederick St. George de Lautour Booth-Tucker (1853–1929), Commander of the Salvation Army in America, attended the WCTU annual convention as representatives of their organization. On Wednesday, 18 November, the NWCTU officers gave a reception for the Booth-Tuckers at which Consul Emma Booth-Tucker spoke.
2. The "Demonstration" (also called "Pageant") was the closing ceremony of the convention during which the NWCTU officers marched in with the WCTU banner and the United States flag, followed by the state delegations, each with their own banners and emblems, and, after them, the department superintendents. Agnes Slack spoke briefly, state WCTU songs were sung, and Willard said a few closing words and gave the Aaronic benediction (Num. 6:22–27).

[Anna Gordon]   20 November 1896
                                                                 En route to
                                                          Castile, New York

F in meeting with General Officers all the morning. I busy with packing and going to dentist settling bills etc. In the afternoon they all went to a meeting called as an aftermath of the Convention to get new members. At 8 25 we left St Louis by the "Big Four"[1] route for Buffalo and Castile. . . .

1. The "Big Four" route was the result of a merger in 1880 between four separate railway lines into the Cleveland, Cincinnati, Chicago, and St. Louis Railway in 1880.

[Anna Gordon]   23 November 1896
                                            Castile, New York

. . . Dr. Greene has been here for a serious talk with F as to what she might come to if she did not rest. Frances told her she could not be easily scared and Dr. G. exclaimed with mingled fun and impatience "*Well I wish you could.*" She is a dear.

[Anna Gordon]   27 November 1896

Frances is beginning to fall into line and although we get a number of hours to work we put in several on building up the casement of F's soul.

Miss Daily's[1] house is very comfortable and is prettily furnished. We have a bedroom on the first floor and another above it which F. uses for a sitting room. We could not have been more satisfactorily settled with no other boarders and near enough to the Sanitarium for Dr. G. to run in often.

We are called at 6:30 A.M. when F. has a glass of water with hypophosphites[2] and at 7.30 we have breakfast. Coffee is awfully rationed here and F. does not have it or tea. Immediately after breakfast F. and Alice[3] & Bess go out on the piazza and are bundled up like mummies and sit there breathing deeply for an hour.

Then follow a set of exercises with arms & leg works and after that F dictates and reads until 11 30 At that time she has another glass of water and lies down for an hour. Dinner at 12 30 and after dinner another hour on the porch. At four oclock we go to the Sanitarium for electricity, cupping or baths[4]—F's diet is carefully watched but her tongue hurts her again although not as painfully as sometimes.

We get lots of letters altogether too many. And its hard to keep up with them—in fact I can't, for F. is full of plans for the future and there is so much to do that grew out of Convention.

1. Willard referred to either Jennie Dailey (1844–1924) or Mary Dailey (1840–1921), sisters who lived together in Castile, N.Y., and took patients of Dr. Cordelia Greene's as boarders.
2. In the late nineteenth century, hypophosphites, minute particles of lime, iron, and other minerals, were given mixed with water as tonics in order to give strength

and vigor to the body, combating weakness, lassitude, and loss of appetite. Dr. Greene prescribed them for Willard as one part of her treatment regime.

3. Alice E. (Heckler) Peters (1845–1921), an Ohio temperance and woman suffrage speaker, was a close friend of Willard's.

4. Willard was probably receiving mild electric stimulation to various parts of her body, similar to the treatment her Evanston neighbor, Mrs. Huse, had given her nearly thirty years before, but slightly more sophisticated. Such treatment was still administered in the 1890s. Cupping was a process used to give relief from various forms of rheumatic pain and lumbago as well as from breathing difficulties due to asthma, bronchitis, and pleurisy. Glass cups were heated and applied to the patient's back in order to draw the skin up into the glass, causing sudden dilation of the blood vessels near the surface of the skin, bringing blood to the skin's surface. It is not clear what symptoms Willard had that were relieved by cupping, but she had had attacks of pleurisy in the past, so she may have evidenced breathing difficulties. Or cupping may simply have been a standard part of Dr. Greene's regime for restoring her patients' health. Various types of baths had been a prescribed treatment technique throughout most of the nineteenth century. Baths, combined with gymnastics and massage, were often prescribed in order to strengthen muscles.

29 December 1896

Nan has kept this for me since Marseilles. Some how I "gave out in me mind" as to this record. Here in Castile all days are alike—the same routine, diet, 10 hours in bed & so on. I have addressed myself to it as the thing to be done. Never did I feel more as though I had embarked in an enterprise of importance. Each day as I exercise, shaking my feet, twisting my trunk, bowing my shoulders, I say to myself "Your chickens have come home to roost—You didn't give your body its due when you were vigorous and now you must atone— make up arrears—do your first works over"—and then I put in my best licks and really I don't think that in *years* I've stood so firmly on my legs. Our genius of a "Dr. Cordelia" says this is the preliminary— organic force—and then the special disabilities of the "digestive tract" & most of all, tongue, mouth & throat will gradually yield—O may it be so for one hardly lives at this poor dying rate.

[Anna Gordon]   31 December 1896[1]

I am writing the balance of this journal on the last day of the year and am of course very sinful to have fallen behind in this lamentable fashion. But the exegencies of the writing and sending out over one hundred letters for Christmas and lots of requests for contributions to the *Union Signal* etc etc have been most engrossing. The character of the work varies with the correspondents with whom we communicate, but otherwise the days are alike as two peas.

Frances is faithfulness itself to her regime of diet deep breathing hypophosphites rest and exercise and although her tongue continues to be an unruly member,[2] Dr Greene says she is really *better.* Dr G comes over every morning and goes the round of the household. . . .

Dr G. is very original in her similes and in her vivid comparisons that reveal to the patients most clearly how they have been transgressing the laws of health. She says Frances has not been good to all the members of her family but has lived up in her head and let her stomach and extremities take care of themselves and they are paying back her slighting treatment.

At the close of the first month Dr G. is greatly pleased with the results. She says she believes F. is destined to live until she is 80 and she doesn't want her to go drooling through the period. . . .

1. Both Gordon and Willard wrote journal entries dated 31 December 1896.
2. Gordon paraphrased James 3:5, 8, "Even so the tongue is a little member" and "But the tongue can no man tame; it is an unruly evil. . . ."

31 December 1896

. . . And so the year is over. In it I have rejoiced & suffered more than any record shows save "the red tablets of the heart." And I have not been so good or patient as I wish I had. "Where is Mother?" That is the most frequent question. Why is there never word sign or token?—Why must Isabel & I be separated? Because we put our Work before our Love. . . . And now God bless everybody & goodbye.

[*Willard remained at Dr. Cordelia Greene's Castile, New York, sanatorium until early March 1897. Then her condition began to deteriorate and she and Anna Gordon went south to Atlantic City, New Jersey, hoping a few weeks in the ocean air would revivify her. From Atlantic City, she went on to Cambridge, Massachusetts, for several weeks, traveling north to New Hampshire in June. She spent the summer in northern New England, primarily resting but also planning for the fall conventions of the NWCTU and WWCTU. Late in August Willard embarked on a journey to revisit beloved places of her early life, stopping by her parents' ancestral homes in Vermont, as she and her father had done in 1863. She and her sister-in-law, Mary Bannister Willard, held a tender reunion, sharing hopes and plans for the future as they so often had done when they were young women with their entire lives before them.*

Willard worked on her annual addresses for the two conventions during September and early October, delivering them in Toronto (WWCTU) in late October and in Buffalo (NWCTU) in early November. She contin-

ued on her journey of remembrance, stopping at her birthplace, Churchville, New York, to see her Aunt Sarah; then to Oberlin, Ohio, where she had spent a portion of her childhood; and on to Chicago to stay with a cousin. From there she made trips to Evanston to renew longstanding friendships and see Rest Cottage once again. New Year's Day 1898 she was in Janesville, Wisconsin, where she revisited Forest Home, the scene of many pleasant childhood memories, and then went back east to New York City to try to raise funds for the Woman's Temple Building. She intended to sail for England after staying several weeks there.

Willard was looking forward with great longing to her reunion with her friend Isabel Somerset, but the reunion was never to take place. Instead she contracted influenza and, in her already weakened condition, had no strength left to stave off its effects. She became more and more ill and her family and friends were summoned to gather round her. Lillian M. N. Stevens, whom Willard had chosen to be her successor as president of the WCTU, other devoted temperance workers, her niece, Katherine (Willard) Baldwin, and Anna Gordon, her beloved personal secretary and companion, were at her bedside during the last week of her life. Finally, in a death-bed scene that echoed those of her sister Mary, her father, and her mother, Willard fondly took leave of each one in turn. Her last words, as Anna Gordon remembered them, were: "How beautiful it is to be with God." On 17 February 1898, Frances Willard died. She had, at last, gone home.]

Essay on the Source

The forty-nine volumes of Frances E. Willard's journal discovered in 1982 are deposited at the Frances E. Willard Memorial Library in the National Woman's Christian Temperance Union Headquarters (1730 Chicago Avenue, Evanston, IL 60201): forty-four volumes from the period 1855–70; brief notations in three volumes from 1881, 1883, and 1888; and two detailed volumes, one for 1893 and one for 1896. Although the journal had been missing for nearly half a century, it is, for the most part, in fairly good condition and readable. However, the ink is beginning to fade. Only small portions of a few volumes have suffered water damage, which may have occurred when the journal was sent to England in the first decade of the twentieth century for Rachel Strachey to use in writing her biography of Willard. Willard's handwriting is often quite difficult to decipher, but no more so than that of many other prominent figures whose papers have been transcribed.

Shortly after their discovery, the journal volumes were microfilmed as an *Addendum* (Series V) to the microfilm edition of *The Temperance and Prohibition Papers* (Randall C. Jimerson, Francis X. Blouin, and Charles S. Isetts, eds., *Guide to the Microfilm Edition of Temperance and Prohibition Papers* [Ann Arbor, Mich.: University of Michigan, 1977]). The forty-nine journal volumes comprise slightly over four rolls of Series V; the remaining three and one-half rolls consist of other WCTU material uncovered after the original microfilming project was completed. The published guide to the original microfilm edition of *The Temperance and Prohibition Papers* includes a detailed description of the WCTU material the edition contains, but the description of the *Addendum*, prepared by Gary Kwiatek, is very brief (four typescript pages). One short paragraph is devoted to the contents of the journal. It is followed by a list of the journal volumes on each roll with dates given for the entries that begin and end each volume; however, these dates are inaccurate in several instances. Many sections of the journal volumes are difficult to read on microfilm. There are no frame numbers or explanatory targets on the rolls and no index to the journal volume rolls, making access to the contents time-consuming and daunting.

In the process of preparing *Writing Out My Heart,* I made a complete transcription of the forty-nine-volume journal. A copy of the transcription (unproofed) has been deposited at the Willard Memorial Library for use by scholars. Transcriptions have also been prepared for two brief journal volumes found since the first forty-nine were microfilmed in 1982. One of these Willard titled "Melange" and dated 16 May 1859. (Some of the content of "Melange" is included in this edition.) The other contains several entries for 1875, including a brief description of a New Year's temperance pledge signing at the headquarters of the Chicago WCTU, notes on a surprise birthday party for Willard's mother hosted by Mary (Bannister) Willard, and a reunion of a small group of Willard's classmates from Milwaukee Female College held while Willard was on a speaking tour in that city; a short vignette from 1877 on her work with the evangelist Dwight L. Moody in Boston; and a few entries in early January 1889, when she had sequestered herself in a downtown Chicago hotel to organize her autobiography and was visited only by Anna Gordon, her publisher, and, each afternoon, a stenographer. Copies of these transcriptions have also been deposited at the Willard Memorial Library.

A transcription of a related item—a small page-a-day diary containing brief entries made by Anna Gordon on 17 February 1898, the day of Willard's death, and for a week thereafter—has been made and deposited with the transcriptions of Willard's journal volumes. Although these entries are brief, they convey the deep sense of loss Gordon felt at Willard's death. Gordon stayed with Willard's body during the embalming process and noted that she was "convinced that women embalmers should be employed for women."[1] The day after Willard's death, Gordon wrote out of her grief: "It is all an awful dream. She will come back."[2] She described the removal of the body from the Empire Hotel to Willard's niece's home, the arrangements for a memorial service at the Broadway Tabernacle, dressing Willard in a gown Isabel Somerset had sent her earlier as a gift, placing her body in a silver-gray casket, accompanying it back to Chicago where it was to lie in state at the Chicago headquarters of the NWCTU, and, then, arranging to move it to Rest Cottage in Evanston, where Willard once again lay in state, and where the sculptor Lorado

Taft made her death mask. On 24 February, after Willard had been buried, Gordon wrote poignantly: "I am alone now. Even her outward self is gone. It's in the cold dark vault tonight and I am alone forever more."

A third volume of Willard's journal was discovered after the microfilming was completed, a tiny volume dated 1852 that has suffered extensive damage, making much of it impossible to read. Thus no transcription has been made. On the back of the volume Willard wrote: "My First Journal." Entries begin on 31 March 1852 and continue erratically to 24 August 1852. She noted her father's trips to Janesville, Wisconsin, the town nearest to the Willard farm, her mother's visit to New York relatives, and her Aunt Sarah's stay with the Willards, but little else. On the inside back cover, in a notation dated three years later, 24 September 1855, she commented on her first journal: "Its full of faults as a nut is full of meat." In Willard's autobiography, *Glimpses of Fifty Years,* she wrote that she began to keep a journal when she was twelve years old,[3] and the volume described here is probably her first attempt at writing a journal. It may be that she wrote no more volumes between 24 August 1852 and 1 January 1855, the date when the microfilmed journal volumes begin.

There is evidence that two other journal volumes existed at one time but are now missing. The first volume, one of her "European Notebooks," contained entries from 18 February to 7 March 1870 (written in Egypt) and 11 July to 28 September 1870 (written in England, on board ship bound for the United States, and home in Evanston). Both Willard in her autobiography and Strachey in her biography include entries from September 1870. It is possible that the volume was lost when Strachey sent the journal back from England to Gordon in Evanston.

In her entry for 24 March 1875, Willard mentions a small diary given to her by her friend Louise Purington, a Chicago homeopathic physician, in which Willard detailed her temperance work during the first months of 1875. In her 8 January 1896 entry, she also refers to "a tiny red book—the journal of my first temperance work." According to Willard, the volume was in Purington's possession in 1896, but it has never been located.

Since I began to transcribe the journal in November 1986, the WCTU librarian and I, along with several others, have discovered more Willard and NWCTU material, none of which has been microfilmed. Several hundred letters written to Willard during the 1890s by Isabel Somerset, Hannah Whitall Smith, and other BWTA and WCTU leaders were found in summer 1987. In fall 1991, a large amount of material was collected from Rest Cottage, Willard's and Gordon's home. This included over one hundred more letters to Willard from Somerset, and to Gordon during her NWCTU presidency from many different early twentieth-century reformers, as well as much other miscellaneous material.

Four journal volumes written by Willard's sister, Mary, are in the WCTU collection. They cover the time period from 4 February 1860 to 7 April 1862, shortly before Mary's death. They are interesting not only in themselves, but because they were written during the time of Willard's friendship with Mary Bannister and her engagement to Charles Fowler, describing those relationships from a younger sister's perspective.

Researchers interested in Willard's journal will find much useful complementary material in sections of Series III (WCTU) of the microfilm edition of *The Temperance and Prohibition Papers.* Especially helpful would be roll 4, containing Annual Meeting *Minutes* for 1893 and 1896; roll 11, containing Willard family correspondence from 1858 to 1870; rolls 19 and 20, containing correspondence for 1893; rolls 23 and 24, containing correspondence for 1896; and rolls 30 and 40–45, containing scrapbooks kept by Willard, her mother, and, later, NWCTU staff members, which cover the years Willard kept a journal. Rolls 8–11 contain issues of the *Union Signal,* the weekly newspaper of the NWCTU, from 1893 to 1896. The material on these rolls provides a context for Willard's journal.

In the *Guide to the Microfilm Edition of the Temperance and Prohibition Papers,* one of the editors states that volumes 31–49 of the scrapbooks kept on Willard and the WCTU could not be located for microfilming and are probably nonexistent.[4] However, all of them, except for scrapbook 39, have been found. Most of them cover the years 1888–90. Some are arranged in chronological order and others are arranged topically. Many of them contain mostly newspaper clippings on events or book reviews of some of Willard's writings. Topics include: coverage of the national prohibition conference in 1888; biographical sketches of temperance leaders; coverage of the NWCTU convention held in New York City in 1888, especially clippings on the split over political partisanship by the NWCTU; reports on the Methodist General Conference of 1888, where Willard and four other women were denied seats as delegates; the 1890 failure of the Chicago bank owned by S. A. Kean, a friend of the Willard family and one-time partner of Josiah Willard; and a collection of temperance songs and poems.

In Mary Earhart's biography *Frances Willard: From Prayers to Politics,*

published in 1944, she developed the notion that Anna Gordon had
created a Willard legend depicting the WCTU leader as a one-dimen-
sional saint of the temperance movement, and making of her "an
idealized Frances—a woman not of flesh and blood but of mystical
character." Earhart charged that in pursuit of her aim Gordon
"burned basket after basket of letters and documents which fell into
her possession after Miss Willard died." Earhart noted that several
members of the executive staff of the NWCTU had told her the story of Gordon's destruction of Willard's papers.[5] Earhart had no reason not to believe what the executive staff told her, nor did later historians, who relied on Earhart's biography as authoritative for nearly
four decades.

The discovery of the journal brings the report of Gordon's destruction of Willard materials into question, however. As I was transcribing a volume of Willard's "European Notes," I came across an index
card stuck between its pages. The card was dated 12 April 1928 and
headed "DEAR FEW'S JOURNALS WHILE ABROAD." A brief note was typed
underneath the heading. It read: "She [Willard] has said that she
culled from these all she feels ought to be given to the public and
her quotations are in Glimpses of Fifty Years. I think at my demise
these should be burned." The note was signed by Anna Gordon. Similarly, when the first cache of several hundred letters written to Willard during the 1890s by Somerset, Smith, and other temperance
leaders was found in 1987, the letters were in three packets wrapped
with brown paper carrying instructions penciled on the wrappings
that they be destroyed. It is not clear who wrote the instructions (possibly Gordon), but, obviously, they were not followed. Instead, the
packets of letters were stored in a box in an obscure area of the Willard Memorial Library and forgotten.

Both Anna Gordon's note with the European journal volumes and
the instructions on the letter packets could have helped to fuel a
rumor that Gordon had destroyed many of Willard's personal papers.
By now it is probably impossible to determine whether or not Gordon actually destroyed any of Willard's papers. But it seems possible
that she did not do so. Based on what I have learned through reading Willard's journal about Gordon herself, and about her great loyalty, respect, and love for Willard, it is my guess that Gordon would
not have destroyed her leader's writings. Rather, she would have treasured and preserved them, unless she felt she was carrying out Willard's explicit orders by disposing of them. She apparently did think
exactly that when she suggested that the volumes Willard wrote while
abroad be burned. Even then Gordon's instructions were not carried

out when they involved destroying Willard's personal records, perhaps because no one could bear to burn them. In any case, Willard's journal was not destroyed. Instead, a rich, intriguing, and extensive source is now available for use by a new generation of historians interested in reinterpreting and reassessing the meaning and significance of Willard's life and the impact of that life on the history of the nineteenth century.

Notes

1. Diary of Anna Gordon, 18 February 1898.
2. Ibid.
3. Willard, *Glimpses of Fifty Years*, 49.
4. Randall C. Jimerson, in *Guide to the Microfilm Edition of the Temperance and Prohibition Papers*, ed. Jimerson, Blouin, and Isetts, 83, 87.
5. Earhart, *Frances Willard: From Prayers to Politics*, 4–5, and 389 n. 3. See also 55 and 391 n. 3, where Earhart specifically charged Gordon with destroying Willard's diary (by which Earhart meant Willard's journal).

Bibliography

Ahlstrom, Sidney E. *A Religious History of the American People.* New Haven: Yale University Press, 1972.

Alexander, Jon, O.P. *American Personal Religious Accounts, 1600–1980: Toward an Inner History of America's Faiths.* New York: Edwin Mellen, 1983.

Alger, William Rounseville. *Friendships of Women.* Boston: Roberts Brothers, 1868.

Alpern, Sara, et al., eds. *The Challenge of Feminist Biography: Writing the Lives of Modern American Women.* Urbana: University of Illinois Press, 1992.

Andreas, A. T. *History of Chicago from the Earliest Period to the Present Time.* 3 vols. Chicago: A. T. Andreas, 1885.

———. *History of Cook County Illinois: From the Earliest Period to the Present Time.* Chicago: A. T. Andreas, 1884.

Ascher, Carol, Louise De Salvo, and Sara Ruddick, eds. *Between Women: Biographers, Novelists, Critics, Teachers and Artists Write about Their Work on Women.* Boston: Beacon, 1984.

Auerbach, Nina. *Communities of Women: An Idea in Fiction.* Cambridge, Mass.: Harvard University Press, 1978.

Baker, Paula. "The Domestication of Politics: Women and American Political Society, 1780–1920." *American Historical Review* 89 (June 1984): 620–47.

Bateman, Newton, and Paul Selby. *Historical Encyclopedia of Illinois.* 2 vols. Chicago: Munsell Publishing, 1906.

Bateson, Mary Catherine. *Composing a Life.* New York: Plume, Penguin, 1989.

Bender, Thomas. *Toward an Urban Vision: Ideas and Institutions in Nineteenth-Century America.* Lexington: University Press of Kentucky, 1975.

Black, William. *Yolande: The Story of a Daughter.* New York: Harper and Brothers, 1893.

Blanchard, Paula. *Margaret Fuller: From Transcendentalism to Revolution.* Reading, Mass.: Addison-Wesley, 1987.

Bledstein, Burton J. *The Culture of Professionalism: The Middle Class and the Development of Higher Education in America.* New York: Norton, 1976.

Bliss, Edwin M. *Turkey and the Armenian Atrocities.* London: T. Fisher Unwin, 1896.

Blocker, Jack S., Jr. *"Give to the Winds Thy Fears": The Women's Temperance Crusade, 1873–74.* Westport, Conn.: Greenwood, 1985.

———. "The Politics of Reform: Populists, Prohibition, and Woman Suffrage, 1891–1892." *The Historian* 34, no. 4 (August 1972): 614–32.

Bordin, Ruth. *Frances Willard: A Biography.* Chapel Hill: University of North Carolina Press, 1986.

———. *Woman and Temperance: The Quest for Power and Liberty, 1873–1900.* Philadelphia: Temple University Press, 1981.

Boylan, Ann M. *Sunday School: The Formation of an American Institution, 1790–1880.* New Haven: Yale University Press, 1988.

Brodzki, Bella, and Celeste Schenck, eds. *Life/Lines: Theorizing Women's Autobiography.* Ithaca, N.Y.: Cornell University Press, 1988.

Brown, Irene Quenzler. "Death, Friendship, and Female Identity during New England's Second Great Awakening." *Journal of Family History* 12, no. 4 (1987): 367–87.

———. "Friendship in Jonathan Edwards' *Life of David Brainerd* (1749)." Unpublished manuscript, 1990.

———. "Friendship and Spiritual Time in the Didactic Enlightenment." In *Autre Temps, Autre Espace: Etudes sur l'Amerique Pre-Industrielle,* ed. Elise Marienstras and Barbara Karsky. Nancy, France: University Presses of Nancy, 1986.

Bruce, Dickson D., Jr. *And They All Sang Hallelujah: Plain-Folk Camp Meeting Religion, 1880–1845.* Knoxville, Tenn.: University of Tennessee Press, 1974.

Bucke, Emory Stevens, et al., eds. *The History of American Methodism.* Vols. 1 and 2. Nashville, Tenn.: Abingdon, 1964.

Buckley, Jerome Hamilton. *The Victorian Temper: A Study in Literary Culture.* Cambridge, Mass.: Harvard University Press, 1951.

Buhle, Mari Jo. *Women and American Socialism, 1870–1920.* Urbana: University of Illinois Press, 1981.

Bunkers, Suzanne L. "'Faithful Friend': Nineteenth-Century Midwestern American Women's Unpublished Diaries." *Women's Studies International Forum* 10, no. 1 (1987): 7–17.

Butler, Jon. *Awash in a Sea of Faith: Christianizing the American People.* Cambridge, Mass.: Harvard University Press, 1990.

Campbell, Karlyn Kohrs. *Man Cannot Speak for Her: A Critical Study of Early Feminist Rhetoric.* Vol. 1. New York: Praeger, 1989.

Carnes, Mark C. *Secret Ritual and Manhood in Victorian America.* New Haven: Yale University Press, 1989.

Carter, Paul A. *The Spiritual Crisis of the Gilded Age.* DeKalb: Northern Illinois University Press, 1971.

Chambers-Schiller, Lee Virginia. *Liberty, A Better Husband: Single Women in America: The Generations of 1780–1840.* New Haven: Yale University Press, 1984.

Chapin, Clara C., ed. *Thumb Nail Sketches of White Ribbon Women.* Chicago: Woman's Temperance Publishing Association, 1895.

Cherrington, Ernest Hurst, ed. *Standard Encyclopedia of the Alcohol Problem.* Westerville, Ohio: American Issue, 1925.

Clark, Elizabeth B. "The Politics of God and the Woman's Vote: Religion in the Suffrage Movement in America, 1848–1895." Ph.D. diss., Princeton University, 1989.

Cline, Cheryl. *Women's Diaries, Journals, and Letters: An Annotated Bibliography.* New York: Garland, 1989.

Cogan, Frances B. *All-American Girl: The Ideal of Real Womanhood in Mid-Nineteenth-Century America.* Athens, Ga.: University of Georgia Press, 1989.

Conway, Jill K. "Politics, Pedagogy, and Gender." In *Learning About Women: Gender, Politics, and Power,* ed. Jill K. Conway, Susan C. Bourque, and Joan W. Scott. Ann Arbor: University of Michigan Press, 1987.

Cott, Nancy F. *Bonds of Womanhood: "Woman's Sphere" in New England, 1780– 1835.* New Haven: Yale University Press, 1977.

———. "What's in a Name? The Limits of 'Social Feminism'; or, Expanding the Vocabulary of Women's History." *Journal of American History* 76 (December 1989): 809–29.

Craik, Dinah Mulock. *John Halifax, Gentleman.* London, 1856; New York: Harper and Brothers, 1859.

Cremin, Lawrence A. *American Education: The National Experience, 1783–1876.* New York: Harper and Row, 1980.

Curtis, Susan. *A Consuming Faith: The Social Gospel and Modern American Culture.* Baltimore: Johns Hopkins University Press, 1991.

De Witt, Annamary Horner. "The Many Faces of Love: A Study of Frances Willard." Master's thesis, Garrett-Evangelical Theological Seminary, 1987.

Dieter, Melvin Easterday. *The Holiness Revival of the Nineteenth Century.* Metuchen, N.J.: Scarecrow, 1980.

Dingle, A. E. *The Campaign for Prohibition in Victorian England: The United Kingdom Alliance 1872–1895.* London: Croom Helm, 1980.

Dobkin, Marjorie Housepian, ed. *The Making of a Feminist: Early Journals and Letters of M. Carey Thomas.* Kent, Ohio: Kent State University Press, 1979.

Dobschuetz, Barbara. "A Historical Study of the Religious Factors in Frances Willard's Development before 1874." Master's thesis, Trinity Evangelical Divinity School, 1992.

Dow, Bonnie J. "The Reformist Rhetoric of Frances E. Willard: The Romantic Appeal of Mother, God, and Home." Master's thesis, University of Kansas, 1987.

Earhart, Mary Dillon. *Frances Willard: From Prayers to Politics.* Chicago: University of Chicago Press, 1944.

———. "The Influence of Frances Willard on the Woman's Movement of the Nineteenth Century." Ph.D. diss., Northwestern University, 1939.

Epstein, Barbara Leslie. *The Politics of Domesticity: Women, Evangelism, and Temperance in Nineteenth-Century America.* Middletown, Conn.: Wesleyan University Press, 1981.

Faderman, Lillian. "Emily Dickinson's Letters to Sue Gilbert." *Massachusetts Review* 18, no. 2 (Summer 1977): 197–225.

———. *Odd Girls and Twilight Lovers: A History of Lesbian Life in Twentieth-Century America.* New York: Columbia University Press, 1991.

————. *Surpassing the Love of Men: Romantic Friendship and Love between Women from the Renaissance to the Present.* New York: Willam Morrow, 1981.

Finn, Barbara R. "Anna Howard Shaw and Women's Work." *Frontiers* 4, no. 3 (1979): 21–25.

Fitzpatrick, Kathleen. *Lady Henry Somerset.* Boston: Little, Brown, 1923.

Friedman, Lawrence J. *Gregarious Saints: Self and Community in American Abolitionism, 1830–1870.* Cambridge: Cambridge University Press, 1982.

Gaustad, Edwin Scott. *Historical Atlas of Religion in America.* New York: Harper and Row, 1962.

Ginzberg, Lori D. *Women and the Work of Benevolence: Morality, Politics, and Class in the 19th-Century United States.* New Haven: Yale University Press, 1990.

Goodsell, Willystine. *The Education of Women: Its Social Background and Its Problems.* New York: Macmillan, 1923.

Gordon, Anna A. *The Beautiful Life of Frances E. Willard.* Chicago: Woman's Temperance Publishing Association, 1898.

Gordon, Elizabeth Putnam. *The Life and Work of Cordelia A. Greene, M.D.* Castile, N.Y.: n.p., 1925.

————. *Women Torch-bearers: The Story of the Woman's Christian Temperance Union.* Evanston, Ill.: National Woman's Christian Temperance Publishing House, 1924.

Green, Harvey, with the assistance of Mary-Ellen Perry. *The Light of the Home: An Intimate View of the Lives of Women in Victorian America.* New York: Pantheon, 1983.

Greven, Philip. *The Protestant Temperament: Patterns of Child-Rearing, Religious Experience, and the Self in Early America.* New York: Knopf, 1977.

Gutman, Herbert G. "The Reality of the Rags-to-Riches 'Myth': The Case of the Paterson, New Jersey, Locomotive, Iron, and Machinery Manufacturers, 1830–1880." In *Nineteenth-Century Cities: Essays in the New Urban History,* ed. Stephan Thernstrom and Richard Sennett. New Haven: Yale University Press, 1969.

Hall, Albert. *River Forest: A Suburb of Chicago.* River Forest, Ill.: Forest Publishing, 1937.

Hall, David D. "The Victorian Connection." In *Victorian America,* ed. Daniel Walker Howe. Philadelphia: University of Pennsylvania Press, 1984.

Hall, Jacquelyn Dowd. "Living through Time: Second Thoughts on Jessie Daniel Ames." In *The Challenge of Feminist Biography: Writing the Lives of Modern American Women,* ed. Sara Alpern et al. Urbana: University of Illinois Press, 1992.

Hampsten, Elizabeth. *Read This Only to Yourself: The Private Writings of Midwestern Women, 1880–1910.* Bloomington: Indiana University Press, 1982.

A Handbook for North Germany. 20th ed. London: John Murray, 1886.

A Handbook of Rome and Its Environs. 9th ed. London: John Murray, 1869.

A Handbook for Travellers in Egypt. London: John Murray, 1867.

A Handbook for Travellers in France. 10th ed. London: John Murray, 1867.

A Handbook for Travellers in Switzerland, and the Alps of Savoy and Piedmont. 12th ed. London: John Murray, 1867.

A Handbook for Travellers in Syria and Palestine. London: John Murray, 1868.

A Handbook for Visitors to Paris. London: John Murray, 1890.

Harrison, Brian. *Drink and the Victorians: The Temperance Question in England 1815–1872.* Pittsburgh: University of Pittsburgh Press, 1971.

Hart, Elizabeth Phillips. *A History of the Pittsburgh Female College: 1854–1896.* Pittsburgh: Pittsburgh Female College Association, 1946.

Hausman, Harriet. *Reflections: A History of River Forest.* N.p., 1975.

Hewitt, Nancy A. "Beyond the Search for Sisterhood: American Women's History in the 1980s." In *Unequal Sisters: A Multicultural Reader in U.S. Women's History,* ed. Ellen Carol DuBois and Vicky L. Ruiz. New York: Routledge, 1990.

Heilbrun, Carolyn G. *Writing a Woman's Life.* New York: Norton, 1988.

Higham, John. *From Boundlessness to Consolidation: The Transformation of American Culture, 1848–1860.* Ann Arbor, Mich.: William L. Clements Library, 1969.

Horowitz, Helen Lefkowitz. "'Nous Autres': Reading, Passion, and the Creation of M. Carey Thomas." *Journal of American History* 79, no. 1 (June 1992): 68–95.

Houghton, Walter E. *The Victorian Frame of Mind.* New Haven: Yale University Press, 1957.

Howe, Daniel Walker. "Victorian Culture in America." In *Victorian America,* ed. Daniel Walker Howe. Philadelphia: University of Pennsylvania Press, 1984.

Hudson, Winthrop S. "The Methodist Age in America." *Methodist History* 12 (April 1974): 3–15.

Hurd, Harvey B., and Robert P. Sheppard, eds. "A History of Evanston." In *Historical Encyclopedia of Illinois,* ed. Bateman and Selby, vol. 2. Chicago: Munsell Publishing, 1906.

Hutchison, William R. "Cultural Strain and Liberal Protestantism." *American Historical Review* 76 (April 1971): 386–411.

Jelinek, Estelle C. *The Tradition of Women's Autobiography: From Antiquity to the Present.* Boston: Twayne, 1986.

———,ed. *Women's Autobiography: Essays in Criticism.* Bloomington: Indiana University Press, 1980.

Jones, Charles Edwin. *Perfectionist Persuasion: The Holiness Movement and American Methodism, 1867–1936.* Metuchen, N.J.: Scarecrow, 1974.

Karlsen, Carol F., and Laurie Krumpacker, eds. *The Journal of Esther Edward Burr, 1754–1757.* New Haven: Yale University Press, 1984.

Kett, Joseph F. *Rites of Passage: Adolescence in America, 1790 to the Present.* New York: Basic Books, 1977.

Lane, Ann J. *To Herland and Beyond: The Life and Work of Charlotte Perkins Gilman.* New York: Pantheon, 1990.

Larkin, Jack. *The Reshaping of Everyday Life, 1790–1840.* New York: Harper and Row, 1988.

Lasser, Carol. "'Let Us Be Sisters Forever': The Sororal Model of Nineteenth-Century Female Friendship." *Signs: Journal of Women in Culture and Society* 14, no. 1 (Autumn 1988): 158–81.

Lasser, Carol, and Marlene Deahl Merrill, eds. *Friends and Sisters: Letters between Lucy Stone and Antoinette Brown Blackwell, 1846–1893*. Urbana: University of Illinois Press, 1987.

Lee, Susan Dye. "Evangelical Domesticity: The Origins of the WCTU under Frances Willard." Ph.D. diss., Northwestern University, 1980.

Leeman, Richard W. *"Do Everything" Reform: The Oratory of Frances E. Willard*. New York: Greenwood, 1992.

Leete, Frederick De Lard. *Methodist Bishops: Personal Notes and Bibliography with Quotations from Unpublished Writings and Reminiscences*. Nashville, Tenn.: Parthenon, 1948.

Longfellow, Henry Wadsworth. *Kavanagh*. 1849. Boston: Houghton Mifflin, 1904.

Lystra, Karen. *Searching the Heart: Women, Men, and Romantic Love in Nineteenth-Century America*. New York: Oxford University Press, 1989.

McCarthy, Kathleen D. *Women's Culture: American Philanthropy and Art, 1830–1930*. Chicago: University of Chicago Press, 1991.

McFadden, Margaret. "The Ironies of Pentecost: Phoebe Palmer, World Evangelism, and Female Networks." *Methodist History* 31, no. 2 (January 1993): 63–75.

McKeever, Jane L. "The Woman's Temperance Publishing Association." *Library Quarterly* 55, no. 4 (October 1985): 365–97.

McLoughlin, William G. *The Meaning of Henry Ward Beecher: An Essay on the Shifting Values of Mid-Victorian America, 1840–1870*. New York: Knopf, 1970.

Marcus, Jan. "Invincible Mediocrity: The Private Selves of Public Women." In *The Private Self: Theory and Practice of Women's Autobiographical Writings*, ed. Shari Benstock. Chapel Hill: University of North Carolina Press, 1988.

Marilley, Suzanne M. "Frances Willard and the Feminism of Fear." *Feminist Studies* 19, no. 1 (Spring 1993): 123–46.

Merrill, Marlene Deahl, ed. *Growing Up in Boston's Gilded Age: The Journal of Alice Stone Blackwell, 1872–1874*. New Haven: Yale University Press, 1990.

Meyer, D. H. *The Instructed Conscience: The Shaping of an American National Ethic*. Philadelphia: University of Pennsylvania Press, 1971.

Meyerowitz, Joanne J. *Women Adrift: Independent Wage Earners in Chicago, 1880–1930*. Chicago: University of Chicago Press, 1988.

Motz, Marilyn Ferris. *True Sisterhood: Michigan Women and Their Kin, 1820–1920*. Albany, N.Y.: State University of New York Press, 1983.

Muncy, Robyn. *Creating a Female Dominion in American Reform, 1890–1935*. New York: Oxford University Press, 1991.

Myerson, Joel, Daniel Shealy, and Madeleine B. Stern, eds. *The Journals of Louisa May Alcott*. Boston: Little, Brown, 1989.

Niessen, Olwen C. "Temperance and the Women's Movement in Late Victorian and Edwardian Britain." Paper presented at the Canadian Historical Association Annual Meeting, Montreal, 1985.

Nord, Deborah Epstein. *The Apprenticeship of Beatrice Webb*. Ithaca, N.Y.: Cornell University Press, 1985.

———. "'Neither Pairs Nor Odd': Female Community in Late Nineteenth-

Century London." *Signs: Journal of Women in Culture and Society* 15, no. 4 (Summer 1990): 733–54.

Norwood, Frederick A. *From Dawn to Midday at Garrett*. Evanston, Ill.: Garrett-Evangelical Theological Seminary, 1978.

———. *The Story of American Methodism*. Nashville, Tenn.: Abingdon, 1974.

Outler, Albert C. *John Wesley*. New York: Oxford University Press, 1964.

Papashvily, Helen Waite. *All the Happy Endings*. New York: Harper and Brothers, 1956.

Parker, Robert Allerton. *A Family of Friends: The Story of the Transatlantic Smiths*. London: Museum, 1960.

Peabody, Emily Clough. *Corinna Shattuck: Missionary Heroine*. Chicago: Woman's Board of Missions of the Interior, 1913.

The Personal Narratives Group, eds. *Interpreting Women's Lives: Feminist Theory and Personal Narratives*. Bloomington: Indiana University Press, 1989.

Peterson, M. Jean. *Family, Love, and Work in the Lives of Victorian Gentlewomen*. Bloomington: Indiana University Press, 1989.

Phillips, George S. *Chicago and Her Churches*. E. B. Myers and Chandler, 1868.

Quilligan, Maureen. "Rewriting History: The Difference of Feminist Biography." *Yale Review* 77, no. 2 (Winter 1988): 259–86.

Reeling, Viola Crouch. *Evanston: Its Land and Its People*. Evanston, Ill.: Fort Dearborn Chapter, D.A.R., 1928.

Reynolds, David S. *Beneath the American Renaissance: The Subversive Imagination in the Age of Emerson and Melville*. New York: Knopf, 1988.

———. *Faith in Fiction: The Emergence of Religious Literature in America*. Cambridge, Mass.: Harvard University Press, 1981.

Richey, Russell E. *Early American Methodism*. Bloomington: Indiana University Press, 1991.

Roberts, George C. M. *Centenary Pictorial Album, Being the Contributions of the Early History of Methodism in the State of Maryland*. Baltimore: J. W. Woods, 1866.

Rosenblatt, Paul C. *Bitter, Bitter Tears: Nineteenth-Century Diarists and Twentieth-Century Grief Theories*. Minneapolis: University of Minnesota Press, 1983.

Rothman, Ellen K. *Hands and Hearts: A History of Courtship in America*. Cambridge, Mass.: Harvard University Press, 1987.

Rothman, Sheila M. *Woman's Proper Place: A History of Changing Ideals and Practices, 1870 to the Present*. New York: Basic Books, 1978.

Ruegamer, Lana. "'The Paradise of Exceptional Women': Chicago Women Reformers, 1863 to 1893." Ph.D. diss., Indiana University, 1982.

Rupp, Leila J. "'Imagine My Surprise': Women's Relationships in Historical Perspective." *Frontiers* 5, no. 3 (Fall 1980): 61–70.

Ryan, Mary. *Cradle of the Middle Class: The Family in Oneida County, New York, 1790–1865*. Cambridge: Cambridge University Press, 1981.

———. *Women in Public: Between Banners and Ballots, 1825–1880*. Baltimore: Johns Hopkins University Press, 1990.

Sahli, Nancy. "Smashing: Women's Relationships before the Fall." *Chrysalis* 17 (Summer 1979): 17–27.

Schlereth, Thomas J. *Victorian America: Transformations in Everyday Life.* New York: Harper Collins, Harper Perennial, 1992.

Schneider, A. Gregory. "The Ritual of Happy Dying among Early American Methodists." *Church History* 56 (September 1987): 348–63.

———. *The Way of the Cross Leads Home: The Domestication of American Methodism.* Bloomington: Indiana University Press, 1993.

Scott, Anne Firor Scott. *Making the Invisible Woman Visible.* Urbana: University of Illinois Press, 1984.

———. *Natural Allies: Women's Associations in American History.* Urbana: University of Illinois Press, 1991.

Scott, Leland S. "Methodist Theology in America in the Nineteenth Century." Ph.D. diss., Yale University, 1955.

Sears, John F. *Sacred Places: American Tourist Attractions in the Nineteenth Century.* New York: Oxford University Press, 1989.

Sicherman, Barbara. "Sense and Sensibility: A Case Study of Women's Reading in Late-Victorian America." In *Reading in America,* ed. Cathy N. Davidson. Baltimore: Johns Hopkins University Press, 1989.

Simpson, Matthew. *Cyclopedia of Methodism.* Philadelphia: Louis H. Everts, 1881.

Sizer, Sandra S. *Gospel Hymns and Social Religion: The Rhetoric of Nineteenth-Century Revivalism.* Philadelphia: Temple University Press, 1978.

Sklar, Kathryn Kish. *Catharine Beecher: A Study in American Domesticity.* New York: Norton, 1976.

———. "Religious and Moral Authority as Factors Shaping the Balance of Power for Women's Political Culture in the Twentieth Century." Paper presented at the 100th anniversary of the founding of Hull-House, Rockford, Illinois, October 1989.

Slagell, Amy R. "A Good Woman Speaking Well: The Oratory of Frances E. Willard." Ph.D. diss., University of Wisconsin–Madison, 1992.

Smith, Logan Pearsall. *A Religious Rebel: The Letters of "H.W.S."* London: Nisbet, 1949.

———. *Unforgotten Years.* Boston: Little, Brown, 1939.

Smith-Rosenberg, Carol. *Disorderly Conduct: Visions of Gender in Victorian America.* New York: Oxford University Press, 1985.

Solomon, Barbara Miller. *In the Company of Educated Women: A History of Women and Higher Education in America.* New Haven: Yale University Press, 1985.

Stevens, Abel. *The Women of Methodism: Its Three Foundresses . . .* New York: Carlton and Porter, 1866.

Stilgoe, John R. *Borderland: Origins of the American Suburb, 1820–1939.* New Haven: Yale University Press, 1988.

Stowe, Harriet Beecher. *The Minister's Wooing.* New York: Derby and Jackson; Boston: Brown, Taggard and Chase, 1859.

———. *The Pearl of Orr's Island: A Story of the Coast of Maine.* Boston: Ticknor and Fields, 1862.

———. *Sunny Memories of Foreign Lands.* 2 vols. Boston: Phillips Sampson, 1856.

Strachey, Barbara. *Remarkable Relations: The Story of the Pearsall Smith Family.* London: Victor Gollancz, 1980.

Strachey, Ray. *Frances Willard: Her Life and Work.* New York: Fleming H. Revell, 1913.

Sweet, Leonard I. "The Female Seminary Movement and Woman's Mission in Antebellum America." *Church History* 54 (March 1985): 41–55.

Taylor, William R., and Christopher Lasch. "Two 'Kindred Spirits': Sorority and Family in New England, 1839–1846." *New England Quarterly* 36 (March 1963): 23–41.

Theriot, Nancy M. *The Biosocial Construction of Femininity: Mothers and Daughters in Nineteenth-Century America.* New York: Greenwood, 1988.

Tillotson, Kathleen. *Novels of the Eighteen-Forties.* Oxford: Clarendon Press, 1954.

Tompkins, Jane. *Sensational Designs: The Cultural Work of American Fiction, 1790–1860.* New York: Oxford University Press, 1985.

Tyler, Helen E. *Where Prayer and Purpose Meet: The WCTU Story.* Evanston, Ill.: Signal Press, 1949.

Tyrrell, Ian. *Woman's World/Woman's Empire: The Woman's Christian Temperance Union in International Perspective, 1880–1930.* Chapel Hill: University of North Carolina Press, 1991.

Verbrugge, Martha H. *Able-bodied Womanhood: Personal Health and Social Change in Nineteenth-Century Boston.* New York: Oxford University Press, 1988.

Vicinus, Martha. "Distance and Desire: English Boarding-School Friendships." *Signs: Journal of Women in Culture and Society* 9, no. 41 (Summer 1984): 600–622.

———. *Independent Women: Work and Community for Single Women, 1850–1920.* Chicago: University of Chicago Press, 1985.

———. "'One Life to Stand Beside Me': Emotional Conflicts in First-Generation College Women in England." *Feminist Studies* 8, no. 3 (Fall 1982): 603–28.

Ward, Estelle Frances. *The Story of Northwestern University.* New York: Dodd, Mead, 1924.

Wayland, Francis. *The Elements of Moral Science.* Boston: Gould and Lincoln, 1834.

Welter, Barbara. *Dimity Convictions: The American Woman in the Nineteenth Century.* Athens, Ohio: Ohio University Press, 1976.

White, Charles Edward. *The Beauty of Holiness: Phoebe Palmer as Theologian, Revivalist, Feminist, and Humanitarian.* Grand Rapids, Mich.: Francis Asbury, 1986.

Wiebe, Robert H. *The Search for Order, 1877–1920.* New York: Hill and Wang, 1967.

Wilde, Arthur Herbert. *Northwestern University, 1855–1905: A History.* 4 vols. New York: University Publishing Society, 1905.

Willard, Frances E. *A Classic Town: The Story of Evanston.* Chicago: Woman's Temperance Publishing Association, 1891.

————. *Glimpses of Fifty Years: The Autobiography of an American Woman*. Boston: Geo. Smith for The Woman's Temperance Publishing Association, 1889.

————. *How I Learned to Ride the Bicycle: Reflections of an Influential Nineteenth Century Woman*. Sunnyvale, Calif.: Fair Oaks, 1991. Reprint of Willard, *A Wheel within a Wheel*, 1895.

————. *How to Win: A Book for Girls*. In *The Ideal of "The New Woman" According to the Woman's Christian Temperance Union*, ed. Carolyn De Swarte Gifford. New York: Garland, 1987.

————. *Nineteen Beautiful Years: or Sketches of a Girl's Life*. New York: Harper and Brothers, 1864.

————. *Woman and Temperance: or, the Work and Workers of the Woman's Christian Temperance Union*. Hartford, Conn.: Park, 1883.

Willard, Frances E., and Minerva Brace Norton. *A Great Mother: Sketches of Madam Willard*. Chicago: Woman's Temperance Publishing, 1894.

Willard, Frances E., and Mary A. Livermore, eds. *A Woman of the Century: Fourteen Hundred-Seventy Biographical Sketches Accompanied by Portraits of Leading American Women in All Walks of Life*. 2 vols. Buffalo: Charles Wells Moulton, 1893.

Winskill, P. T. *The Temperance Movement and Its Workers: A Record of Social, Moral, Religious, and Political Progress*. 4 vols. London: Blackie and Son, 1891.

Winslow, Donald J. *Lasell: A History of the First Junior College for Women*. Boston: Nimrod, 1987.

Yacovone, Donald. "Abolitionists and the 'Language of Fraternal Love.'" In *Meanings of Manhood: Constructions of Masculinity in Victorian America*, ed. Mark Carnes and Clyde Griffen. Chicago: University of Chicago Press, 1990.

Zunz, Olivier. *Making America Corporate, 1870–1920*. Chicago: University of Chicago Press, 1990.

Index

CAROLYN DE SWARTE GIFFORD is an associate editor of *The Historical Encyclopedia of Chicago Women.*

Books in the Series Women in American History

Women Doctors in Gilded-Age Washington: Race, Gender,
and Professionalization
Gloria Moldow

Friends and Sisters: Letters between Lucy Stone and
Antoinette Brown Blackwell, 1846–93
Edited by Carol Lasser and Marlene Deahl Merrill

Reform, Labor, and Feminism: Margaret Dreier Robins and
the Women's Trade Union League
Elizabeth Anne Payne

Private Matters: American Attitudes toward Childbearing
and Infant Nurture in the Urban North, 1800–1860
Sylvia D. Hoffert

Civil Wars: Women and the Crisis of Southern Nationalism
George C. Rable

I Came a Stranger: The Story of a Hull-House Girl
Hilda Satt Polacheck
Edited by Dena J. Polacheck Epstein

Labor's Flaming Youth: Telephone Operators and
Worker Militancy, 1878–1923
Stephen H. Norwood

Winter Friends: Women Growing Old in the New Republic,
1785–1835
Terri L. Premo

Better Than Second Best: Love and Work in the Life
of Helen Magill
Glenn C. Altschuler

Dishing It Out: Waitresses and Their Unions in the
Twentieth Century
Dorothy Sue Cobble

Natural Allies: Women's Associations in American History
Anne Firor Scott

Beyond the Typewriter: Gender, Class, and the Origins of
Modern American Office Work, 1900–1930
Sharon Hartman Strom

The Challenge of Feminist Biography: Writing the Lives of
Modern American Women
*Edited by Sara Alpern, Joyce Antler, Elisabeth Israels Perry,
and Ingrid Winther Scobie*